An Indian Social Democracy

VOLUME II

An Indian Social Democracy

Integrating Markets, Democracy and Social Justice

VOLUME II

Editors

Sunil Khilnani
Manmohan Malhoutra

ACADEMIC FOUNDATION
NEW DELHI

www.academicfoundation.com

First published in 2013
by

ACADEMIC FOUNDATION
4772-73 / 23 Bharat Ram Road, (23 Ansari Road),
Darya Ganj, New Delhi - 110 002 (India).
Phones : 23245001 / 02 / 03 / 04.
Fax : +91-11-23245005.
E-mail : books@academicfoundation.com
www.academicfoundation.com

Published in association with the
INDIRA GANDHI MEMORIAL TRUST
New Delhi

Cataloging in Publication Data--DK
Courtesy: D.K. Agencies (P) Ltd. <docinfo@dkagencies.com>

An Indian social democracy / editors, Sunil Khilnani, Manmohan Malhoutra.
2 v. cm.
ISBN 9788171889945
ISBN 8171889948

1. Socialism--India--Congresses. 2. Socialism--Economic aspects--India--Congresses. I. Khilnani, Sunil, 1960- II. Malhoutra, Manmohan. III. Indira Gandhi Memorial Trust.

DDC 335.00954 23

Typeset by Italics India, New Delhi.

Printed and bound by The Book Mint, New Delhi.
www.thebookmint.in

INDIRA GANDHI
(1917-1984)

CONTENTS

Volume II

(The present volume)

Section IV

The Social and Political Context of Social Democracy in India

Background Papers

Presentations and Discussions

CONTENTS

Volume I

(The companion volume)

Presentations and Discussions

Section II

Social Democracy in Global Perspective

Background Papers

Presentations and Discussions

Presentations and Discussions

Section III (b)

BACKGROUND PAPERS

- Pranab Bardhan
- Michael Walton

29

PRANAB BARDHAN

Inequality, Inefficiency, and the Challenges for Social Democracy in India's Economic Transition

The various inequities and deprivations

Different people mean different things by social democracy. Without going into that discussion let me start by briefly describing what I'd mean by social democracy in this paper and then go on to analysing the various challenges that the Indian economy faces in bringing it about.

Social democracy for this paper has three essential ingredients:

(1) Democracy primarily in the form of meaningful political competition, effective accountability mechanisms, and some basic human rights.

(2) A competitive and incentive-compatible economic system with individual property rights within reasonable bounds, and economic coordination mechanisms provided by markets, multi-tiered government as well as community organisations, with these mechanisms operating in different fields in mainly complementary ways.

(3) An effective and comprehensive system of social protection for the great masses of people from deprivation, destitution and vulnerabilities to individual and social risks of different kinds.

In this paper I shall keep (1) and (2) largely in the background, without a great deal of discussion, and look at problems of achieving (3) under the circumstances. Even though I am fully aware that we have miles to go on (1) and (2), India is at present particularly and atrociously deficient in (3). India is the world's largest country of illiterates and school dropouts, of child and maternal mortality, largest number of stunted and underweight children, and with the largest incidence of anaemia and TB, and the overwhelming majority of people lacking any of the social benefits that are considered as part of a minimum social safety net. More than 400 million people have less than what by Indian official standards will be considered the barest minimum poverty line. If one takes income inequality, or what is more important, inequality of economic opportunity, Indian inequality is one of the highest in the world, contrary to conventional wisdom. In a country like India inequality of opportunity largely depends on distribution of land, of education, and social identity—a child born in a rural landless *adivàsi* (indigenous) family with very little scope for education will be severely handicapped in her life chances for no fault of her own.

It may be well-known that land distribution in India is much more unequal than, say, in China (this is partly because India has a much larger landless population). But most people seem to be unaware that India's educational inequality is one of the worst in the world. If one measures this inequality, very crudely, just by looking at the years of schooling in the adult population, it is worse than that in almost all Latin American countries, and some African countries, not to speak of China—again, this is partly because of India's large illiterate and near-illiterate population. Taking a long view, what is more important than static inequality is inter-generational mobility. On this quantitative empirical work is rather scanty, but social mobility may be particularly low in India, partly no doubt because of the deadening legacy of the system of caste oppression and discrimination in India (though there is some evidence that social mobility is improving for some of the low castes).

Some people think that preoccupation with issues of inequality deflects attention from economic growth which is what mainly alleviates poverty, through creating new and better jobs and generating more public revenue for welfare programmes. But how much of growth trickles down to the poor itself depends on initial inequality (for example, it has been estimated that the same one per cent rise in growth reduces poverty by much less in India than in China partly because of the higher inequality in India) and the resultant distribution of economic and political power. Besides, inequality of opportunity itself can have serious adverse effects on economic growth. This is particularly important when there are barriers faced by the poor in land and capital markets and in skill acquisition and in coping with risks, which sharply reduce a society's potential for productive investment, innovation and human resource development. They often block the creation of socially more efficient property rights (for example, in land tenure) and investment in high-risk but high-return innovative projects on the part of small producers. Inequality that keeps the work force largely uneducated and unhealthy cannot be beneficial for private business either, apart from the law and order problems that inequality-generated conflicts may bring about. Moreover, institutional structures and opportunities for cooperative problem-solving are often foregone by societies that are highly polarised. Sociologists have noted how extremely hierarchical the work organisation within Indian factories is (often reflecting the social stratification outside), and this is not unrelated to the low productivity of Indian firms even in simple production processes compared to other countries, and the social distance and distrust between managers, supervisers and 'jobbers' on the one hand and the great majority of workers undermine the cooperation that is needed for day-to-day shopfloor innovations that characterise more productive workplaces. Equity and efficiency thus often go together, contrary to the opposite presumption of much of orthodox economics.

Apart from severe deprivations and high inequality of opportunity, another feature of the economy that raises special challenges for social democracy in India is that of all the major developing countries India has the largest informal sector, with 92 per cent of the labour force working informally, most of them daily facing the brutal insecurity of no retirement, disability, unemployment or health benefits. Even outside the agricultural sector more than 80 per cent of the labour force work informally. The tiny minority of formal sector workers (two-thirds of them government employees) cling on to their paltry privileges with nervous militancy, as they face the social vertigo of looking on the vast masses of the unprotected huddled down below. This great void, the absence of even a rudimentary framework of general social assistance, makes the implementation of social protection as difficult as it is urgent.

The process of economic growth in a world of global competition has made this worker anxiety and insecurity more acute. Even when market competition does not lead to net job loss, it usually causes a great deal of job churning and displacement. Even in rich countries with relatively weak safety nets (like the US, in contrast to the Nordic countries) this leads to stiff working class opposition to global competition. There is some evidence that increased global competition in the last two decades has wiped out some of the low-productivity tiny informal firms in Indian manufacturing, who may have then crowded the non-traded sectors. It is not surprising that in India where any safety net (outside the diminishing support of extended families and kinship groups) is absent for the overwhelming majority of people, most survey evidence suggests that market reforms are vastly unpopular. Yet these reforms are important for unclogging the channels of entrepreneurship and innovation.

The matter is made much worse by the fact that, unlike in China and Vietnam where the initial growth spurt has been in labour-intensive industries, in India the success stories so far have been largely in skill-intensive (software, business processing, pharmaceuticals) or capital-intensive (machine tools, petro-chemicals, vehicles and car parts) sectors, and as a result the high economic growth has not resulted in a large expansion of job prospects for poor unskilled workers. The public policy deficiencies in education and skill formation have also limited the employability of the poor workers in many of the new jobs.

A growth pattern that is skill- and capital-intensive obviously exacerbates the problem of inequality. In addition there is a peculiar bi-modality in the size distribution of manufacturing firms in India; most firms are bunched at the lower end with very low productivity, paying extremely low wages, whereas at the higher end (with a 'missing middle') of the firm size distribution wages paid are much higher. This large wage inequality in the same industry adds on to the inequality between capital and wage incomes.

On top of all this there are the usual processes of agglomeration economies of scale in the early stages of growth which lead to regional and sectoral concentration—resources and capital move to 'growth poles', the poorer areas fall behind. The large urban growth—driven by such agglomeration forces—that India is expecting in the next two decades, with the urban population expected to reach 600 million, will enhance this inequality, apart from straining the urban infrastructure to near breaking point and stoking the nativist forces in big cities in resistance to large-scale migration from the rest of the country. Yet the productivity gap between the rural and urban sectors or between agriculture and manufacturing and services is so large that such transition will be inexorable in the process of economic growth. In situations where economic growth involves extraction and processing of minerals from land currently belonging to the indigenous people of India who are uprooted in the process, or acquisition of land in general from the peasants for commercial and industrial development, a great distributive conflict is already shaping up, often turning into violence, ultimately turning on the question of the appropriate distribution of the large rental income from scarce appreciating resources, now accruing disproportionately to the corporate oligarchy, real estate tycoons, the mining mafia, and their political patrons and collaborators.

It is in this larger context of the mounting forces of inequality and displacement, the need for organising a viable system of social protection, already rather enormous, is all the more desperate. We'll desist from talking about larger goals of redistribution that many social democrats regard as part of their essential project, as they will remain distant objects of luxury for India which as yet lacks even the basic minimum of social protection for the masses of her citizens.

Approaches to social protection: A critical appraisal

In the Indian discussion there have been different approaches to the question of how to tackle social protection. A very popular approach these days is to couch it in terms of 'rights' (to food, education, information, jobs, etc.), and there is a great deal of commendable activism on this front, and already some achievements to show, particularly in the landmark legislations on the right to information and to work on public works projects (though their implementation in many states are as yet rather slow and feeble, and facing a great deal of resistance from bureaucrats, contractors, etc.). This approach can, at the minimum, serve to raise consciousness among the poor and vulnerable about their entitlements, a sense that they are not mere supplicants to the politicians or bureaucrats, that if the latter fail there is access to courts to enforce these rights, and public-interest litigation and court injunctions on these matters have attracted a great deal of attention.

But at the same time one should recognise some limits to this rights-based approach. If the delivery structure for implementing some of these rights remains as weak and corrupt as it is now, mere promulgation of rights will remain hollow and will, after a point, generate a great deal of cynicism. Indian public arena is already littered with hundreds of unenforced or spasmodically enforced court injunctions, and there is some danger of the proliferating judicial activism in stretching the interpretation of the constitutional 'right to life' ending up, for all its good intentions, in undermining the credibility and legitimacy of the judiciary itself.

For example, if the right to food is exerted with no consideration of the efficiency and cost-effectiveness of the ways of implementing it (like the current public distribution system (PDS)—which in many states is an enormous project of theft and wastage—a rough estimate is that less than a quarter of the subsidised food grains reaches the poor), it is an unwarranted and unfair burden on taxpayers who fund the galloping costs. In any case the programme as currently administered is weakest in the poorest regions that need it most. Food stamps that have been advocated from time to time will reduce some of the wastage and theft in the storage and distribution by public agencies, but will not eliminate the problems of: (a) fraud rampant in non-universal means-tested targeting like that to below poverty line (BPL) people, and (b) the development of secondary markets where merchants buy up the stamps in exchange of some (smaller) cash—in which case you might as well directly give people cash rather than stamps. The recent Right to Education Act does very little for the poor quality—and quantity—of education services actually provided in government schools (that drive children to private schools even though teachers there are by and large less qualified and less well-paid) or about the negligence with which the new poor students foisted on the private schools are likely to be treated without a proper quality evaluation of schools in place, or the remedial education that the poor-performing children (at private or government schools) and the school dropouts desperately need.

The current employment guarantee scheme, the largest of its kind anywhere in the world, for all its flaws (which would have been far less if a regular and institutionalised system of independent social audits were in place—only Andhra Pradesh government has institutionalised them), provides a possible fall back option for many able-bodied rural adults for working on mostly construction projects for a period of 100 days every year (though this limit of 100 days and timely payment of wages have so far been reached only in very few areas). This may have already exerted some positive indirect effects on the rural wage earned by the poorest people.

This is, of course, quite different from the right to job often demanded by organised workers in the formal sector. The right to job, if narrowly interpreted as the security on a given job, can considerably distort the labour market, if it freezes the ability of the employer (public or private) to adjust to changing conditions in technology or market, thus hurting the whole economy, and the job prospects of less privileged workers. It is very important to distinguish between economic security and job security. A worker should have the right to expect from society general economic security, but not security on a given job. My own empirical judgement, however, is that stringent labour laws that are aimed at ensuring job security in large industrial firms may not be the most important constraint on Indian industrial growth; other constraints like infrastructure, credit and marketing may be more important in many cases, but that they constitute a constraint cannot be denied. There is ultimately no alternative to a package deal between employers and organised workers: allowing more flexibility in hiring and firing has to be combined with a reasonable scheme of unemployment compensation or adjustment assistance, from an earmarked fund to which employers and employees should both contribute. No Indian politician has yet gathered the courage or imagination to come up with such a package deal.

The distinction between economic security and security of a particular job (usually in the formal sector) also brings to the foreground a particular conflict among workers which organised trade unions would rather slur over. It is well-known that social democracy in Western Europe came out of a historic compromise between capital and labour (the latter gets socially protected and a reasonable share of the economic pie, and in return gives up its democratic power of expropriating the former, so that it can carry on its innovations that expand the pie). In India where the informal sector is massive, social democracy may require an additional implicit compromise in the labour market, between formal and informal workers—since in many ways their interests may be in conflict (one example is stringent job protection of formal workers may be at the expense of the potential expansion of job possibilities for informal workers; another example is that the general strikes and *bandhs* frequently called by formal sector unions as part of their organisational muscle-flexing paralyse city life and rob the daily informal workers and street vendors of their subsistence). Besides, the strongest organised workers are those in the public sector services, and it is their corrupt and callous service non-delivery which the poor informal workers as potential recipients have to face every day.

In general one should not look at the social protection rights in abstraction from costs (direct and indirect), delivery mechanisms or even their political constituency. Well-designed, well-administered, cost-effective programmes of implementing some basic rights generate more political support even among those who are paying for them. One should, of course, mention here that one positive implication of the rights approach is that of universal principles and standards, which in some cases may help better administration. For example, it has been pointed out that the PDS for food generates less malfeasance when it is universal (as in Tamil Nadu and Chhattisgarh); as we have indicated before, when some people are excluded under a targeted system of delivery, it leads to dual markets and more incentives and opportunities for fraud, apart from eroding its larger political support base.

On universalistic principle of social protection one of the cleanest and least incentive-disruptive ideas, both ethically and economically compelling, is that of Universal Basic Income (UBI), under which everybody, rich or poor, gets an unconditional annual (or periodic) income supplement. This is an old idea, originally inspired by some European 'utopian socialists' in the 19th century, tried unsuccessfully in McGovern's Presidential campaign in the USA in the form of a proposed 'demogrant', currently supported by some Green Parties in Europe, and actually implemented in non-socialist resource-rich Alaska since 1999 (in the form of an annual Permanent Fund Dividend). In the West the discussion in opposition to the idea usually centres around the encouragement this may give to idleness and dependency and the 'unfairness' of a handout to the rich as well. I think we need to worry less about idleness in a country where the overwhelming majority of the people are extremely poor and overworked. Giving to the rich as well may be found administratively tolerable by many who know the formidable problems of monitoring and corruption in India in trying to target it only to the poor. The main question is: if we want it to be universal, can we afford it? Of course the answer depends on the amount to be given out, if this will be a replacement for the existing transfer programmes which have a lot of wastage and misappropriation, how the problem of misappropriation of the basic income supplement will be handled, etc. Let's make some back-of-the-envelope calculations.

Suppose in a country of 1.2 billion people we want to give out every year ₹ 5,000 to each family (assumed to have 5 members). This amounts to ₹ 120 thousand crore (not counting administrative costs, which need not be large, with electronic help). Let's assume, for the time being, that with the forthcoming installation of the electronic Unique Identification (UID) System the administrative costs of this unconditional transfer programme will be minimal. Let's now compare this sum of ₹ 120 thousand crore with some benchmark figures. The total estimates of how much is currently spent by the government on all the anti-poverty programmes together easily exceed this amount. What is even more important is that this amount is much less than the total subsidies the government gives out to the relatively rich every year. We do not have iron-clad estimates of the latter. The National Institute of Public Finance and Policy (NIPFP) has from time to time estimated the total amount of subsidies (implicit as well as explicit) given out by the central and the state governments. This comes to about 14 per cent of GDP every year. These subsidies are classified into 'merit' and 'non-merit' subsidies. Without going into the intricacies of the definitions, let us say, very roughly, that the non-merit subsidies mostly go to the relatively rich. Of the 14 per cent of GDP in total subsidies, roughly two-thirds have been estimated to be non-merit subsidies: that comes to about 9 per cent of GDP. Let us make a conservative estimate and bring this figure down to 6 per cent of GDP as going to the relatively rich. In 2009-10, the annual GDP of India was about ₹ 4500 thousand crores (at 2004-05 prices); 6 per cent of this comes to ₹ 270 thousand crore. So what the government pays out as subsidies every year to the relatively rich is more than double the amount it'll need to pay out a basic income supplement of ₹ 5,000 to each family, rich or poor. In other words, if one can somehow halve the existing subsidies to the relatively rich, that will be more than enough to cover the basic income supplement for everybody. And if this replaces some of the existing dysfunctional programmes (like PDS) or not very effective cash transfer programmes (like SGSY—Swarnajayanti Gram Swarojgar Yojana—or IAY—Indira Awas Yojana), the income supplement can be even larger (or the reduction in the subsidies to the rich may be smaller). All this is based on a very rough and ready calculation and one should not take the estimates too seriously, but it gives us some sense of proportion.

But are the possibilities of misappropriation that afflict most social protection programmes in India seriously lower with the basic income supplement idea fortified with UID? If the money is deposited in an account (at a nearby post office or bank) from which withdrawals require bio-metric identification, and no means-testing or rich-poor classification is necessary, many of the current problems of fraud and corruption and manipulation of BPL category are likely to diminish considerably. Yet one cannot rule out possibilities of clerks who'd issue the withdrawn money demanding bribes, or local musclemen regularly extorting some of the cash from the defenseless recipient (like robbers in many countries taking their victims to the ATM machines and forcing withdrawals). Of course, when PDS gives a poor man subsidised food that can also be robbed and sold in the market, but I suppose the lure of direct cash may be stronger for the criminals. Similarly, chances of alcoholics and drug addict recipients blowing the cash are a problem that worries many critics of such programmes. Of course there are two kinds of reaction to this. One kind is the libertarian one, saying that we should let people decide how they want to spend the money, bearing the consequences of their decision is part of the responsibility that every individual has to take, etc. The other is the soft-paternalistic kind, trying to minimise the problem by handing over the money to the usually more responsible female adult in the household, devising all kinds of good-specific vouchers, etc. In a country where women and children are among the most deprived in the usual way a household is run, and child and maternal mortality and malnutrition are among the worst in the world, concerns about how unequally the unconditional cash transfer is spent by the family are to be expected and the matter may not be left simply to the mercy of individual responsibility.

More importantly, just handing over more money to the poor resolves only part (the financial part) of the social protection they need. As petty producers they also need other kinds of assistance (knowledge, skills, marketing connections, etc.) or as patients they need information about doctor quality, health practices, nutrition and sanitation, and so on. In the urban slums where the rural kin group support structures are weaker, social protection has also to involve active social support structures against violence, drugs, family breakdowns, juvenile delinquency, etc.

In any case it is probably highly unrealistic to expect that the relatively rich in India will easily give up on much of the subsidies they enjoy or that the vested interests that have accumulated around long-standing wasteful programmes like PDS will allow anything more than moderate tinkering. So proposals like unconditional cash transfers or universal basic income supplements are unlikely to fly in the politics of the foreseeable future, as the question of 'can we afford such programmes?' will remain under those political constraints, even though, as we have seen, in principle it is resolvable. New programmes of social protection with a great deal of targeting (with lower costs but also more leakages) and some additional garnering of resources are more likely to be implemented. One class of such programmes is that of conditional cash transfers, with the added weapon of UID. In some sense the rural employment guarantee is one such programme, of cash conditional on work, with self-targeting saving some administrative costs and leakage as the non-poor will not usually want to work on such manual, often back-breaking, construction works. UID may reduce a great deal of current leakage in the form of false muster rolls of workers. In the delivery of social services, nothing on the scale of Oportunidades in Mexico or Bolsa Familia in Brazil has yet been attempted in India. Most of the conditional cash transfer programmes for these services in India have been relatively small and aimed at ensuring the survival of girl children (and their mothers at the time of birth), and their continued education in schools and in raising their age at marriage. We do not yet have enough rigorous evaluation of these programmes.

In general, the main presumption of conditional transfer programmes is somewhat paternalistic: left to themselves the poor do not exert enough effort in sending their children to school, health clinics, immunisation centers, etc. So transfer programmes try to induce them with contingent transfers. There is a large administrative cost in monitoring and enforcing the stipulated conditions. In any case, such demand-sided interventions (inducing the poor to demand the services) do not solve the supply side problems which are severe in India: not enough schools or health clinics, facilities, quality teachers or doctors, teacher and doctor absenteeism, etc. Of course, on the supply side, our bureaucracy is often not mindful of (or interested in) the fact that the government may be the financier but need not be the actual supplier and can work out all kinds of innovative solutions. For example, it can finance the education services but outsource some of them (as in the case of charter schools in the US); just as in the case of PDS, the Food Corporation of India (FCI) can outsource its warehousing to private companies, instead of letting its procured grains rot outside (about one quarter of the total in recent months) for lack of public warehousing space.

Governance issues in social protection

In the previous section we discussed the pros and cons of different approaches to social protection in the Indian context. In this section we discuss some generic governance issues that arise in any scheme of social protection and are particularly acute in India. First, let us take up the delivery mechanism itself. If the services are to be provided by the government, are there enough incentives on the part of the bureaucracy? In the Indian civil service (which has often been described as neither much service-oriented nor very 'civil') rewards are not in general performance-based, promotions are often mainly seniority-based. Frequent transfers, sometimes arbitrarily determined by the political bosses, discourage the development of any stake in any particular locality of service. Bad performance is very seldom punished; in any case the measurement of performance is 'noisy' particularly when the quality of service is necessarily multidimensional. This promotes a rampant culture of impunity. The school teachers and doctors and nurses are not punished for the dereliction of their duties, their salaries and promotions are decided from above, not by the local people who bear the brunt.

This obviously suggests the need for decentralisation and accountability downwards. In fact there is some evidence that in some cases (e.g., in Nagaland) where even a very small fraction of the teachers' salary was paid by the local *panchayat* or village council, it immediately led to a significant improvement in services. But in most parts of India, while local elections are now regularly held, effective decentralisation is missing, on account of a severe dearth of devolved funds or delegated power or appropriate professional personnel. Local elections are usually fought on supra-local issues, and more often than not the state-level politicians and bureaucrats hijack the process of mandated devolution. Such hijacking is made easier by the lack of inner-party democracy in almost all political parties, so that local political leaders are at the mercy of the higher-tier leadership. It has not been widely recognised in India how the lack of inner-party democracy, apart from making political parties structurally undemocratic, has the side-effect of corroding the vitals of local democracy in India.

The situation is particularly ironic in the cities, where the elected municipal governments, while presiding over areas where much of the booming wealth of India is created, have neither the autonomy nor the revenues to significantly improve the quality or quantity of municipal services. The electoral process also encourages political clientelism, politicians find it easier to lure voters with promises of private goods (say, color TV sets or loan waivers) than those of long-term improvement of public services (say, quality of schools). Both capture (by the local elite and the state-level parties) and clientelism have ensured that local democracy remains the weakest part of Indian democracy.

There are some extra incentive and structural issues in health services (qualitatively some similar issues arise also in education or nutrition programmes). At the moment health care in India is primarily private (and largely unregulated). Household survey data suggest that 85 per cent of all visits for health care in rural areas, even by the poorest people, are to private practitioners. While the poor quality of service in public clinics and hospitals (and absenteeism by nurses and doctors) often drive patients to private doctors (some of them quacks or crooks), in some cases even when the public services are available, the patients prefer going to private medical practitioners who more readily oblige them with unnecessary antibiotics and steroids.

The public health delivery system is afflicted by poor provider incentives, coupled with low accountability to the patients. The medical personnel are paid a fixed salary independent of the number of patients or of their visits, so they have no economic incentive to serve them in the public clinic (they have all the incentive to ask patients to come to their private chambers for paid service and send them for unnecessary diagnostic tests at labs in which they have a monetary interest). The poor have very little organised 'voice' in sanctioning the errant provider. They are assertive in elections, but even a local election is a blunt instrument of sanction for any particular service: electoral platforms are multidimensional where specific grievances about any particular public service provider get diluted, often by larger state-wide issues. In addition, compared to curative medical services, the Indian system is particularly deficient in systematic planning and delivery of preventive public health services or sustained programmes of large-scale disease control (the public health administration in Tamil Nadu, I understand, is a major exception). One of the cost-viability problems for any public health insurance service for the poor in India (like the as yet fledgling programme, RSBY—Rashtriya Swasthya Bima Yojana—that is supposed to cover up to ₹ 30,000 for only hospitalisation-related expenses for BPL families) is that the poor in most cases go for hospitalisation with illnesses (like diarrhoea or typhoid or malaria) which could be prevented by basic public health programmes like provision of clean drinking water, sanitation, spraying, etc. Thus, the deficiencies of public health administration in India in carrying out its primary duties make health care insurance so costly.

Outside of government or private provision of health services there can be other alternatives. Several NGO's in India, as part of their development programmes, have initiated community health insurance schemes for poor people, often linking up with an insurer (with a larger risk pool) and purchasing health care from an external provider. SEWA in Gujarat is an important example of organising community health insurance for its members and their families in this way. This and other similar models need to be studied and replicated in a much larger scale in worker associations and cooperatives in India, particularly in the informal sector. In the history of German social welfare programmes worker associations played a leading role. In India where the informal sector is much larger, small-scale associations need to be mobilised for social insurance, the NGO's can play a mediating role with insurers and help processing payments of premium (apart from identifying beneficiaries and giving them the requisite information), and the government can introduce some provider accreditation systems to help the choice of providers.

Livelihood protection as part of social protection?

When the informal sector is large and the majority of people are self-employed in tiny farms or firms, the boundary between a household and an enterprise is blurred, which means social protection programmes may have also to involve various kinds of protection of livelihoods. These include provision of credit, development of marketing networks, insurance against production risks (say, rainfall insurance in agriculture, renting out service for generators to cover power outages in small manufacturing firms or repair shops), roads, extension services, etc. For those who work in the casual wage labour market and for the unemployed, skill formation, vocational training and public facilities to connect them up after training with potential employers can all be part of a general social protection programme.

Of course all these programmes will cost a great deal of money (apart from organisational resources). To some extent and to the extent politically feasible, some restructuring of existing wasteful or ineffective programmes will save some money. But ultimately, as the European experience shows, social democracy is expensive on the public exchequer, it'll be more so in India where poverty and deprivation are so massive. India's tax to GDP ratio is at the lower end among major developing countries (much lower than in China). While keeping in mind that higher tax rates often encourage more tax evasion, there is a lot of scope for raising the tax to GDP ratio, particularly from capital gains, inheritance, and the burgeoning rental incomes of various kinds—in real estate (the corrupt property assessment system in our cities leaves out much of the enormous rise in value), in rural and semi-urban land around infrastructural projects, and in mines and other extractive industries. This will, of course, immediately raise loud screams from India's rich, but saner elements of the latter will realise that social protection for the poor will ultimately help them as well, particularly since the human capital chains are presently broken without which their business cannot thrive. As we have indicated before, there are many ways equity and efficiency can go together. Of course, the taxing government has to improve its credibility by minimising wasteful social programmes. At the local level if *panchayats* and municipalities can raise property taxes (assessed may be on area-based non-discretionary rates as is being currently tried in Mumbai, reducing the power of the assessor officials) and if the revenue is earmarked for spending on transparent and time-bound specific local benefit projects (which can be publicly discussed in *gram sabhas* and ward meetings), the tax-payers may be more willing to contribute.

If social protection has to involve livelihood protection, at some point one has to grapple with the controversial issue of how much of the traditional extremely low-productivity livelihood patterns have to be protected against the onslaught of markets and capitalist development. As the latter has often been identified with dispossession and dislocation of people from their land and despoliation of the local environment, there are now strong movements in India against acquisition of land from farmers and *adivasis* for the purpose of industrial and commercial development and mining. I do not have the space here to go into the details of this important controversy here, I shall only register here a plea for some balance between the need for economic development that creates productive jobs and enhances social surplus (which can potentially be redistributed) on the one hand, and on the other hand the need for minimising (and adequately compensating for) the dislocation by means of a process in which the local stakeholders can be full participants. Use of land and minerals by profit-seeking companies for non-traditional higher-productivity activities is indispensable if we want any change in the miserable way of life that the farmers and *adivasis* have endured for centuries—as the Marxist economist Emmanuel once wrote, the horrors of capitalism fade in comparison with the horrors of pre-capitalism, or as Joan Robinson famously remarked, what is worse than being exploited is not to be exploited at all. There is too much romanticising of the traditional life among some otherwise well-intentioned activists and too little interest in assessing the complex trade-offs involved. In fact there is a larger social-organisational issue here. Voluntary groups and NGO's more often than not being essentially single-interest advocacy lobbies lack the mechanism of transactional negotiations and give-and-take among diverse interest groups around those trade-offs that large party organisations representing and encompassing these diverse interests could facilitate. That the existing party organisations lacking in inner-party democracy do a bad job of it does not negate the general point. On the other hand, as we have mentioned before, in the current dispensation the surplus generated in the process of development in these areas is grossly inequitably distributed, much of it grabbed by the corporate oligarchy, real estate tycoons, the mining mafia, and their political patrons and collaborators. There is need for transparent and carefully-monitored auctioning of mining rights among competing companies, and for a substantial annuity paid to the local dispossessed people and for an environmental improvement fund out of the money thus raised and shares of the companies. We have to find a balanced, equitable, and sustainable way of dividing the surplus and minimising the loss (both private and social, including environmental). In this balancing NGO's can play an extremely valuable role in espousing the cause of the deprived, increasing their awareness and information, catalysing their organisations and acting as watchdogs against the abuses of state and corporate power.

Social protection and democratic mobilisation

Finally, the big puzzle in Indian democracy is this: the numerically large poor are so assertive at election time, and yet social protection for them continues to be weak, and election after election they select (or fail to punish) leaders who do so little for them in terms of social protection. There may be several factors at play here:

(i) It is possible that endemic poverty and lack of social protection are widely regarded among common people as a complex phenomenon with multiple causes, and they ascribe only limited responsibility to the government in this matter. The measures of government performance are in any case rather noisy, particularly so in a world of illiteracy and low levels of civic organisation and formal communication on public issues. A perceived slight in the speech or behaviour of a political leader felt by a particular ethnic group will usually cause much more of an uproar than if the same leader's policy neglect keeps thousands of children severely malnourished in the same ethnic group.

(ii) The latter suggests that what is more salient than social protection is dignity politics. Of course, in a larger sense social protection should include dignity issues. If electing a low-caste leader, however corrupt, reduces the chances of upper-caste thugs harassing or raping low-caste women or the police actually doing something about this, that surely should count as a gain in social protection.

(iii) Since the poor usually get mobilised on caste and ethnic lines, the modalities of such mobilisation are often multi-dimensional, and poverty alleviation or social protection is only one of the many issues that get articulated in the public domain. Also, the process of such ethnic mobilisation is often easy to be hijacked by the elite of these groups, who channel a lion's share of the benefits towards themselves. The intended poor beneficiaries are often unorganised and uninformed about their entitlements, and they also lack the ability to evaluate the quality of the particular education or health service provided.

(iv) It is possible that the observed preoccupation in North India with symbolic victories among the emerging lower-caste political groups maybe just a matter of time. The social and political changes have come to North India rather late; in South India, where such changes have taken place several decades back, it may not be a coincidence that there has been a lot more effective performance in the matter of public expenditures on social protection projects like food, health, education, housing and drinking water. This reflects the fact that in South India there has been a long history of social movement against exclusion of lower castes from the public sphere, against their educational deprivation, etc. in a way more sustained and broad-based than in North India. One may also note that the upper caste opposition to social transformation is somewhat stronger in North India, as demographically upper castes constitute in general a larger percentage of the population than has been the case in most parts of South India. So new political victories of lower castes in North India get celebrated in the form of defiant symbols of social redemption and recognition aimed at solidifying their as yet tentative victories, rather than in committed attempts at changing the economic structure of deprivation. There are now clear signs even in North India of an advance from symbolic to substantive issues.

One major difference between Indian democracy and the Western is that the emphasis here is more on group rights, less on individual rights (which are often crassly violated when there is even a remote chance of some group or other taking offence). One indicator of the emphasis on group rights is that 'reservations' are often the most popular tool of redistribution. Public sector job reservations for some historically disadvantaged groups, for example, fervently catch the public imagination, even though objectively the overwhelming majority of the people in these groups may have no chance of ever landing those jobs, as they and their children largely drop out of school by the fifth grade. Attention is thus directed at symbolic policies, and the patronage benefits are primarily enjoyed by the elite of these groups, deflecting public attention away from the more urgent and difficult challenges of improving the delivery structure of basic social services including education. Reservations often become a surrogate for effective action on the social protection front.

There is scope here for imaginative political leaders building on group solidarities of hitherto subordinate groups to focus political attention on basic social services they are denied, not just in lobbying with higher authorities but in mobilising group financial and organisational resources for this purpose (including revitalising the various traditional group-based charitable organisations). The emphasis has to be on group-based social movements that emphasise awareness of their public entitlements, of some judgement and advice on the quality of elementary health care and educational services they receive from village private providers of education and medical care, of the adverse effects of superstition, ignorance and faith-healing (somewhat on the lines of the historically successful peoples' science movement in Kerala), and of basic sanitation, drinking water purification, personal hygiene and environmental practices that improve their lives. As India becomes more urbanised, the difficulties and costs of such community organisations and social movements should decline compared to those in dispersed rural society. There are already many ward committees, residents' associations, cooperatives and self-help groups, which can try to integrate social insurance as a part of their general activities, at least in negotiating with the authorities, processing paper work, monitoring and social audits of government welfare programmes. In rural areas where livelihoods crucially depend on the management of local environmental resources (forests, fisheries, irrigation, grazing lands), historically community organisations (*pani panchayats*, water user associations, *van panchayats*, joint forest management committees, etc.) have been active. There are now many studies that have tried to understand the conditions under which they succeed and when they fail. One should derive the appropriate lessons from this experience. Above all, social protection has to involve the beneficiaries in active participation, away from the current framework of dole-giving from the top by an insensitive, unmotivated and corrupt bureaucracy.

In conclusion, while the discussion on social democracy in Western countries often puts the emphasis on its high costs (particularly in view of the austerities necessitated by intense global competition) and issues of incentives for work and enterprise, in India high inequality, massive poverty and a vast informal sector make the challenge of implementing social democracy extremely daunting as much as it is highly imperative. The particular governance issues in India, with inept, corrupt and unmotivated public officials in charge of the delivery system, make the mobilisation of social groups and community organisations and various participatory processes all the more important. But there is a more fundamental issue here that involves the interaction of the productive system and the political culture. As we have mentioned before, European social democracy is the outcome of a class compromise and a social pact: the workers who are electorally powerful enough to expropriate the capitalists and end the capitalist system have chosen not to do so, they have figured out that capitalism is the only viable way left for adequately expanding the pie, so they are prepared to bear some cost ('exploitation') and let the capitalists have a reasonable share of that pie which induces the latter to keep on their efforts at bringing about dynamic innovations. I am not sure if the Indian electorate has yet been confronted with this social pact, and if so confronted how they'll react.

After the demise of the short-lived Swatantra Party, India has not had a full-scale pro-business conservative party; even the right-wing parties are largely populist on many economic issues when they go to the electorate. In spite of the great flowering of entrepreneurial energies in recent years throughout the country, I believe there is a strong anti-capitalist (particularly anti-big-capital) streak in Indian political culture. This is not surprising in a country where small people (small and middle peasants, self-employed artisans and shopkeepers, *bazaar* merchants and petty middlemen, clerks, school teachers and service workers) constitute an overwhelming majority of the population, and their ranks are swelled by the inexorable demographic pressure and by the traditional inheritance practices involving subdivision of property. There is a deep suspicion of market competition whereby the larger economic interests, often utilising their advantages of economies of scale, deeper pockets and better political connections, can devour the small. Gandhiji had given sensitive and eloquent expression to this anti-market, anti-big-capital, small-is-beautiful populism and mobilised it in the freedom movement against the British. In recent decades those bearing the legacy of the Gandhian moral critique of market expansion and competition have joined forces with those espousing the left critique of capitalist exploitation of workers, peasants, and other small people and their rights over natural resources, in building active grassroots movements in parts of the country for the protection of the environment and of the traditional livelihood of the indigenous people, against the depredations of the capitalist oligarchy. Even though the private corporate sector is thriving in India and in some sense its 'hegemony' looks more pervasive today than before, it is involved in the work life of too few people (as it directly employs not more than 2 per cent of the Indian work force), and it is not clear that the electorate is still ready to accept the class compromise like the one behind the social democracy enterprise in the West.

On the other hand, the populist opposition, for all their strength in numbers, have not yet succeeded in pointing to any viable, incentive-compatible (i.e., not entirely dependent on revolutionary or moral zeal for sustenance), systemic economic alternative, outside the esoteric confines of their wishful thinking or utopian anarcho-communitarianism. The passionate intensity of their negative critique of capitalism is not matched by a convincing demonstration of a sustained positive alternative system on a scale large enough to generate the necessary surplus. Until this tension is resolved, the social democracy project in India will remain somewhat tentative. Under the circumstances the great danger for the social-democratic striving is that it may dissipate itself in various costly and in the long run harmful populist schemes, utilised by the political process for narrow patronage distribution goals.

30

MICHAEL WALTON

Can a Social Democratic Resolution Resolve Issues of Inequality and Growth for India?

Introduction

Social democracy has been most successful, politically, economically and socially, in Europe, and most of all in Scandinavia. These are relatively equal and, especially in the case of Scandinavia, homogeneous and conflict-free societies. Does it make sense to consider a social democratic resolution for India, that is much poorer, more unequal and more heterogeneous? And is social democracy consistent with sustaining rapid growth, especially as India is emerging into a globalised capitalism at a much later stage than the European countries? This paper examines these questions with respect to the desirability of social democracy, its design, and its feasibility for India.

This paper is organised around three ideas.

First, the point of departure for the paper is the exact opposite of the view that social democracy is only feasible in homogeneous, equal and conflict-free societies. I argue that a social democratic resolution should be thought of as a political response to deep inequalities and distributional fights, and not a harmonious product of a relatively equal social order. Indeed Scandinavian societies were unusually conflict-ridden prior to the major moves to social democracy (Moene and Wallerstein, 2008b). In similar fashion, some of the most interesting contemporary exemplars of moves toward social democracy are in highly unequal societies in Latin America—especially Brazil and Chile—in response to the long-run pressures from the democratisations of the 1980s (Cardoso and Foxley, 2009).

India's overall position is comparable: major inequalities alongside politically salient pressures for redistribution and broad-based social provisioning. A social democratic resolution is a desirable response for India, and, indeed, is arguably central to the management of future distributional conflicts and stability.

Second, however, issues of design are of first-order importance, 'both' for equity and for growth. It is obvious that design matters for the question of who is reached by programmes and whether they are effective. But the more interesting question for India is whether a social democratic resolution can be consistent with the sustained, rapid growth that is necessary both for the expansion of private income (and so reduction of income poverty) and to provide the tax base for government-intermediated parts of a social democratic system. I argue that there are growth-supporting designs, and that these depend crucially on three features: the form of finance; the incentives embedded in both provisioning and regulation; and the internal incentives for the state actors within the social democratic regulatory system. A social democratic resolution 'can' be supportive of dynamic and innovative capitalism—both via greater integration of smaller existing and new firms into formal institutional structures (of regulation and taxation) and via continued catch-up of large-scale and globalising firms toward the global technological frontier. But it is also really easy to get designs wrong, and to create a system that distorts micro-incentives for households, workers and firms, and becomes a source of growth-reducing sclerosis.

Third, a growth-supporting social democratic resolution is feasible in the abstract sense that India has the economic base and long-term organisational capabilities. But it is not at all clear that it is consistent with current trends. In particular, I suggest that an effective social democratic resolution depends on three factors: politically salient pressures for broad-based social provisioning; a state that is 'good-enough' at delivery of public goods (including of regulation); and a politically supportive capitalist class. India does have politically salient pressures for social provisioning. But the behaviour of the state is currently on a path of entrenching a patronage-corruption-political finance relation with society. And the position of large-scale capitalists, whose economic and political power will only rise in the coming years, is unclear. Furthermore, broad-based social provisioning is problematic at the 'margins' of state-society interaction: most clearly in areas of Naxalite conflict but also at the margins of legality in cities.

I conclude with three questions. Do rights-based approaches offer a way of building both a sound design and a political transition, or will they get captured and distorted by existing structures? Will major capitalists become a force for pressuring the state for a more efficient and universalistic system of social provisioning? And will major political parties support reforms that shift their support base from fundamentally patronage-based mechanisms to ones linked to effective state functioning? All three are deeply linked to the role of politics in the success of failure of the social democracy in India, and indeed the viability of India's long-run development path.

Inequalities, social democracy and long-term growth

The questions at stake concern the relationship between inequalities, the role of the state and growth dynamics. Inequalities matter in many dimensions: especially of citizenship, of security, of opportunity, as well as of income and wealth.

While a prism of income is limited, the issues can be motivated by the following stylised fact: there are no rich countries with very high levels of income inequality (Ferreira and Ravallion, 2008; see Figure 30.1). Above a level of GDP per capita (adjusted for purchasing power parity) of US$20,000, all Gini coefficients fall in the range of 0.25 to 0.45. (The Gini coefficient is a synthetic index of patterns of inequality between all individuals; it ranges from 0 for perfect inequality to 1 for complete inequality.) Sweden has an income Gini of 25; the USA of 41. By comparison, in 2008, Brazil had a GDP per capita of US$10,000 and an income Gini of 55, and Chile a GDP per capita of US$13,240 and an income Gini of 52. Both well-known cases of very high inequality. India's 2008 GDP per capita was much lower, at US$2900. India's level of inequality is controversial: according to the NSS 2004/05 survey—that is in consumption terms—the Gini was only 33—but the NCAER survey found an income Gini of 54, well into the high inequality and

Latin American range. Even more important, measures of income inequality are a proxy for the deep inequalities of opportunity, status and power that pervade Indian society.

Figure 30.1

Inequality and Income Per Capita Around the World

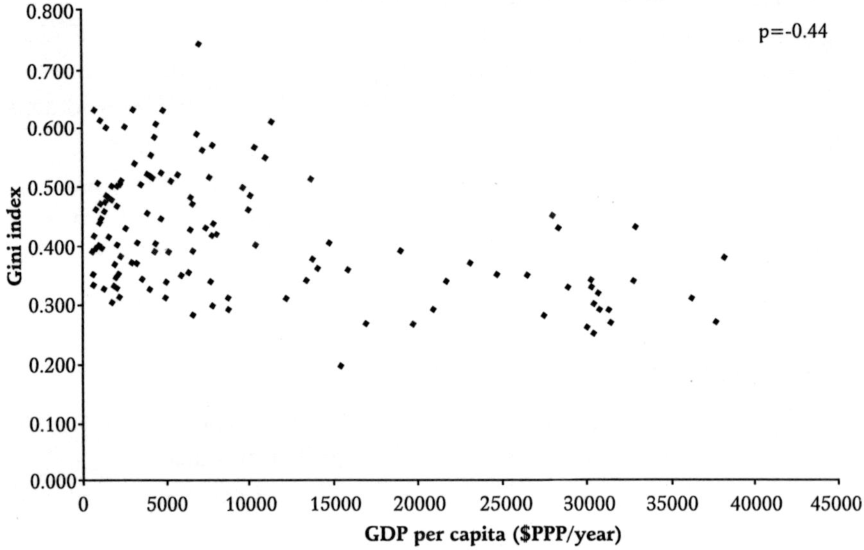

Source: Ferreira and Ravallion (2008).

High levels of current wealth reflect past long-run growth. So how should we think about this? Here are three alternative perspectives.

(1) Long-run growth leads, eventually, to the reduction of extreme inequalities. An example of this view is the Kuznets curve. Simon Kuznets hypothesised that long-term development involves along-term rise and fall in income inequality, as societies were transformed from predominantly low productivity to predominantly high productivity activities. Along the way some households move to high productivity, and so high income,activities, leaving others behind—working, for example, through access to jobs or education. The problem is that the evidence does not support the existence of such a curve (Banerjee and

Duflo, 2003). At one level this is bad news, since the Kuznets curve has a happy implication—inequality is benign for long-run growth.

(2) High inequality countries don't make it to high levels of prosperity, owing to the growth-sapping costs of inequality, manifest in specific economic inefficiencies (for example linked to the credit market), in the formation of institutions that further the interests of elites at the cost of long-term growth, and the accentuation of distributional fights. There is certainly evidence for this (see World Bank, 2005) though it is unclear if this is a permanent phenomenon, or if countervailing tendencies automatically emerge. This brings us to the third perspective.

(3) Now-rich countries experienced political and social changes that led to choices over policies and institutions that induced lower levels of inequality. A striking example of this is Denmark—now a paragon of Scandinavian egalitarianism—that had truly Latin American levels of inequality in the 19th century. The US is a less extreme example: with the important exception of black slaves, the US was historically more equal either than old Europe or Latin America (Engermann and Sokoloff, 2002). But it also went through important equalising policy choices, especially in the late 19th and 20th century, through curbing the power of the immense capitalist monopolies, known as trusts, the long-term expansion of access to education, and the big push on social provisioning in the New Deal in the 1930s and the Great Society of the 1960s.

This paper is organised around the third perspective. Social democratic transitions were political projects, that emerged in response to conditions of inequality and conflict. Even the seminal Scandinavian transitions occurred not in the context of harmonious and homogeneous societies but from societies that had experienced high levels of conflict. As Moene and Wallerstein (2008b) argue, Norway and Sweden had unusually high levels of industrial conflict in the 1920s. Social democracy was a response. Moreover, it was an explicit political project, that evolved from ideological and policy debates—not least within social democratic parties—and from a variety of class and party compromises (Berman, 2006).

Social democratic resolutions in rich countries have been neither complete, uncontested nor fully successful. Whether the criterion is inequality or growth there continues to be intense debate over both inequality and social democratic policy designs in rich countries. Income inequality has experienced a steep rise in the USA and the UK. At least some features of social democratic projects are hotly contested: think of recent debates over the affordability of established polices (e.g., fights over the pension age in France, the cutting back of universal child benefits in the UK), attempts to fill in of gaps in provisioning (health policy in the US) or concerns over incentive costs of current social policy designs (reflected in the re-election of a relatively right wing government in Sweden).

However, I'd suggest these debates are second-order to the issues at stake for India: that is whether an overall social democratic project is desirable for her stage of development, and whether it is a feasible political and institutional project, along the lines of social democratic resolutions in now-rich and middle income countries. It is here that the second perspective returns to relevance: even if a social democratic resolution is desirable—to support the reduction of inequalities in a design that supports long-term growth—the very structure and functioning of India's inequalities may effectively distort such a resolution

What does social democracy mean?

Before proceeding further, we need a statement of what is meant by social democracy. There are two ways into a characterisation of social democracy: a deep interpretation of the social and political origins and ideological features of social democracy; and description of its policy and institutional elements. This paper is not the place to make a contribution to the first, so I confine commentary on this to a few contextual points. My main interest is in the specifics of design choices and how these interact with economic incentives and political functioning.

In the big picture, social democracy can be thought of as emerging as a shift in strategies in the first half of the 20th century—within parts of the socialist political movement but also of non-socialist governing elites—toward pursuit of social and distributive goals within the context of capitalist and democratic systems. Thus for those socialist parties that chose a social democratic option, it involved a strategic choice to use democracy rather than revolution to pursue their aims (Przezworski, 1985). Amongst most (but not all) it also involved acceptance of capitalism, both as a pragmatic response to the economic and political resilience of the system, and in recognition that the game was not zero-sum. In other words, the question became one of how to harness capitalism for the benefits of workers and other subordinate groups. As a political project, social democracy typically involved the forming of cross-class alliances—between workers, farmers and middle groups—that were necessary to achieve electoral majorities (Berman, 2006). With different features this mix was true of Scandinavia, the UK, the continental European core, and post-democracy Spain. It was also true of the social democratic elements of the US, even though the term is rarely used there.

The strategic mix of working within democracy and in concert with capitalism has also been true of important parts of the Latin American left since the return to democracy of the 1980s. It is especially the case for Brazil and Chile, both of whom have had almost 20 years of centre-left coalitions in power under democratic auspices, pursuing an evolving project that blended support for capitalist growth with social provisioning. There is also a different tradition amongst Latin American left governments, that is more confrontational with aspects of capitalism—with partial nationalisations in Bolivia, Ecuador and Venezuela—but even these do not involve wholesale shifts to socialism.

In both Europe and Latin America, it is also striking that governments more clearly aligned with capitalists and economic elites have also maintained or furthered design features commonly associated with social democracy. For example, German's post-war social democracy was initially shaped by parties of the right. Mexico has actively pursued the expansion of social provisioning both under the long period of semi-authoritarian rule of the Partido Revolucionario Institucional (PRI), and under the notionally right wing governments since the full transition to democracy in 2000. In the UK, even Mrs Thatcher didn't seek to privatise the National Health Service.

There is room for debate as to whether social democracy is best conceived as a modification of a pro-market, liberal ideology—'embedded liberalism' in a classic formulation—or a distinct ideology as Berman (2006) argues. Since the fall of the Berlin Wall, and China's embrace of a form of capitalism, it is has rather lost its place as a 'third way', though a major recent collection edited by an ex-Brazilian president and Chilean minister, entitled half way there (*A medio camino*) has some of that spirit (Cardoso and Foxley, 2009). I leave this to debate to others.

So let's turn to the second issue: what are the key design elements of social democracy? This is what we want to assess for India. Here's a list, that can be treated both as a set of practical principles, and examined for the potential range of designs within each category.

(1) universal, state-guaranteed, provisioning to manage household risks—of health, old age, unemployment, disability.

(2) universal, state-guaranteed, access to quality education.

(3) a minimum level of material well-being.

(4) state regulation of capitalism, including in particular the legal underpinnings for labour organisation and capital-labour relations.

(5) institutions of citizen participation.

Poverty reduction, in all its dimensions, is part of this but social democracy goes way beyond poverty: including risk management, opportunity and societal concerns across all social groups. In addition, central to the Scandinavian social democratic design was a compressed, relatively egalitarian, wage distribution (see Moene and Wallerstein, 2008a in particular). But this has not been a feature elsewhere, and is not treated as an essential element here, in part because it is hard to see it as feasible for the Latin American and Indian cases.

Now, in each area there is room for a range of approaches to design, with actual choices driven by ideology, pragmatism and the workings of politics. This can matter a lot. Alternative designs can make a large difference to both access and incentives. I postpone discussion of that to the next section; here I rather note some issues on the 'range' of design choices.

'Universal, state-guaranteed' provisioning can be effected through a variety of means. One approach is to have universal, state-provided entitlements to all citizens, in the sense that the state raises taxes to provide the same entitlement (for example a child benefit, or pension) to all citizens. 'Universal' is sometimes used in this sense in European discussion on the welfare state. But this is not the only way of achieving universality. It is also consistent with a mixed system of public-private provision—of pensions, health services or education, for example—but with a combination of state regulation of private provision and state-guaranteed access to all, including via state provision (as in a basic government pension and government schools). This is the actual policy in most schooling systems around the world, including for Brazil, Chile, India, the US, the UK and Sweden. A mixed system raises questions of equity within the system but in practice so does a pure government system, given the variation in the quality of state schools in most countries.

A related issue concerns whether a society chooses to uses means testing: making access to social service or benefit conditional on an individual's material 'means', typically measured by their current income of wealth. This is relevant both to the minimum floor for material living, and to access to risk-related social benefits. It is a hotly contested issue in rich countries: the UK and the US make use of much more means testing than continental Europe. When a mild means test was proposed for child benefits in the UK in 2010 it was decried as an attack on the welfare state. In practice, most developing countries, including Brazil, Chile and India, make extensive use of means tests. Also common is the use of either categorical targeting (e.g., farmers pensions in Brazil) or self-targeting (as in workfare in India and Chile)

State regulation of capitalism can also extend to a range of distinct domains. I would highlight three:

(a) relations between capital and labour, in terms of the legal support for collective bargaining, and a variety of state-regulated labour rights, especially around health and safety, child labour and protection from abuse, sometimes around job security;

(b) other specific 'externalities' (the economic term for impacts of a firm's activities that affect others outside the marketised transaction), including effects of a firm's activities on local pollution, carbon emissions, or the social lives of citizens;

(c) the state direction of industrial choices, via ownership, subsidies or the provision of specific 'public goods' of infrastructure that benefit a limited set of firms. State support for innovation could fall in (b) or (c).

Finally, the participation of citizens via voting is an intrinsic to electoral democracy. But beyond the vote, most democracies (and indeed non-democracies) use a variety of mechanisms for making action of both the state and capitalists accountable to citizens, from rights to information, to complaint procedures, all the way to participatory budgeting. (See Avritzer (2009) for a discussion of the Brazilian experience.)

The point here is that there is room for policy debate within all these areas. I suggest the five areas of principle listed above are core features of social democracy. Then design choices can make a big difference to outcomes with respect to equity, poverty and growth incentives.

The centrality of design for equity and growth

Consider the following proposition. A social democratic resolution, in terms of policy choices and institutions, can be both effective at social provisioning and supportive of long-term, capitalist growth.

Yet what of impacts on incentives—won't work effort, investment and innovation be hurt? And don't the imperatives of globalisation render unaffordable the generosity of social provisioning that a social democracy entrails? Isn't a tradeoff between equity and efficiency a fundamental economic principle?

The answers to all these questions is: not necessarily. In particular, a social democratic resolution can be consistent with both: (a) a strong complementarity between greater equality of opportunity and a more efficient use of human resources; (b) a dynamic and innovative capitalism—both via greater integration of smaller existing and new firms into formal institutional structures (of regulation and taxation) and via continued catch-up of large-scale and globalising firms toward the global technological frontier.

However, such a growth-supporting, or 'incentive-compatible' social democratic resolution is contingent on design, and in particular on the choices within the design ranges outlined in the previous section. Key elements of an efficient design are as follows:

(i) *Social benefits*: Social provisioning can support human investment, effort, risk-taking and the mobility of workers and households. Many areas of intervention can actually compensate for efficiency-hurting market failures. Free or subsidised access to quality education can offset the absence of credit markets, that lead to premature school-leaving. A safety net, of unemployment insurance and social assistance, can encourage workers and households to move between jobs and locations. There are areas of tradeoffs, of course, for example in the high marginal tax rates implicit on making benefits conditional on means or being out of work but these can be reduced by design, as for example in the US and UK's earned income tax credit.

(ii) *Labour policy*: Labour policies and institutions are worth highlighting, since labour protection is frequently characterised as a natural enemy of dynamic capitalism—notably in Latin America and India. Yet, some forms of collective bargaining can lead to incentives for firms to increase productivity (an important argument in the case of Scandinavia, see Moene and Wallerstein, 2008a). More broadly, labour policies that provide protections for health and safety, or against abuse, are at least in part responses to market failures—they may add costs to firms but economic welfare is improved even in a narrow economic sense. And active labour polices that support re-training and re-insertion into work can also be efficiency-improving (even though evidence on actual effects is mixed).

(iii) *Risk and globalisation*: More broadly, an overall structure of risk management can provide the societal underpinning for political support for globalisation. Rodrik (1999) found that countries with more open economies have higher levels of social spending. He interprets this as a complementary relationship, with the greater exposure to the risks associated with open economies leading to greater political demands for social risk management.

(iv) *Regulation of firms*: A form of regulation of capitalism that is focused on the effective management of externalities and market failures is also intrinsically efficiency-improving—especially with respect to impacts on the environment, in inclusion of adverse external social impacts, in countervailing monopoly power, in providing the legal basis for protecting minority shareholders, in supporting innovation and in efficient risk-management (including reducing excessive risk-taking) in the financial system. A particular dimension of this concerns the mix of regulatory, tax and labour policies that provide incentives of firms to become formal entities.

The above list refers to the design of what state does, in terms of provisioning or regulation. Then there are two cross-cutting areas that are necessary supports for state action:

(v) *Finance*: Taxes are almost always distortionary but broad-based taxes (especially on consumption and wealth, also on income) are much less distortionary than systems that have narrower coverage with high tax rates, especially those that influence effort and investment.

(vi) *The behaviour of state actors*: All the areas of social provisioning and regulation involve an interface between actors in the state and households, workers or firms. Incentives for effective behaviour of actors in the state are necessary conditions for the implementation of an efficient social democracy.

Let's illustrate with the most extreme example—the high tax, high benefit countries of Scandinavia. Lindert (2004) in his major historical review of the long-term expansion of public spending in now-rich countries, devotes a chapter to the apparent Swedish puzzle. If taxes are as distortionary as economists argue (and the standard view is that distortions rise to a power of tax rates), then Sweden's tax effort should be a first order issue, inconsistent with the achievement of very high levels of productivity: Sweden's PPP per capita income was some US$39,000 in 2008. This is less than the US's US$48,000 but still extraordinarily high by historical or global standards. He argues that both the design of benefits and taxes pay actually much more attention to potential efficiency-reducing effects on effort than in the US, with lower effective marginal tax rates (in part driven by more use of universal benefits) at the bottom and top of the income distribution, major reliance on value-added taxes, and only moderate corporate tax rates.

A different, and complementary, argument comes from the important area of labour-capital interactions. Moene and Wallerstein (2008a; b) argue that a compressed wage schedule, supported by 'both' employer associations and an encompassing union movement, provided rewards to more productive firms, and incentives for less productive firms to increase productivity or close. The union movement was also a supporter of the value added tax in the post-war years, viewing this as a means to broad-based social provisioning—in stark contrast to the often vehement social protest to VATs in Latin America.

A more speculative issue is that the benefits and costs of social democracy may depend on where a country is with respect to the global technology frontier. It may be that the US is key to pushing out this global frontier, and this is related to the US being a more free-wheeling, innovative society, with intrinsically lower tax rates and the possibility of really high rewards to effort and innovation. In this case, European countries that have been growing through catching up, as one tradition of growth theory suggest (Aghion and Howitt, 2006), have been partly free-riding. It is not clear that the US's undoubted innovative, frontier-expanding role also requires her less well-developed social democracy but this is an issue worth exploring in the global context, and for countries that will be pushing the frontier in the future. However, it is not an issue for current emerging countries, such as Brazil, Chile and India, who are well within the global frontier—provided they have sufficient capacity to innovate to catch up, and push the frontier in specific areas.

Thus the message is not that social democracy is intrinsically pro-growth, it is that design matters. It is also easy to imagine design options that are bad for dynamism and efficiency across households and workers, and bad for the dynamism of small and large capitalist firms in both these areas. Latin America has suffered from its historical creation of a 'truncated welfare state', with Bismarckian type social provisioning for the minority of households connected to formal work (De Ferranti *et al.*, 2004). This was bad for both equity and for efficiency. Similarly, the renewed interest in industrial policy in the sense of state-direction of economic activities—notably in Brazil—is, at least according to some observers, potentially problematic

This section has been framed in terms of technical design issues. But they are a deeply a function of politics, and this is where inequality, institutions and histories comes back in. This brings us to the next question.

Is a growth-supporting social democratic resolution feasible for India?

So if the design is right, a country can move toward a social democratic resolution without sacrificing growth: indeed 'incentive-compatible' designs can actually be supportive of capitalist dynamics, including deeper integration into the global economy. But is this feasible for India? This gets deeply into the political and institutional system that shapes possibilities over design choices and sources of support and resistance. Here I first suggest some stylised lessons in the political and institutional arena from both the history of now-rich countries and contemporary Latin America, and then assess India's conditions in relation to these lessons.

Comparative lessons: Europe, the US and Latin America

This paper started with a comparative question. Surely India is not like Sweden, nor ever will be? I suggested, following authors such as Moene and Wallerstein, that at least along some dimensions this question is badly formulated. Sweden's famously egalitarian social democracy was not a product of a homogeneous, harmonious society but a response to a society in conflict.

In this section, I go further, and propose some general conditions that both make a transition to a social democracy feasible, and shape its design. In particular, I suggest that both the historical and contemporary Latin American experience suggests three aspects of relatively successful social democratic transitions: the political salience of reasonably encompassing coalitions of middle and poorer social groups; support from capitalists; and a reasonably effective, or 'good enough' state. These three aspects underpin the feasibility of a transition but are not enough to preclude distortionary designs, whether in terms of equity or growth-related incentives.

The political salience of an encompassing social coalition: This is perhaps the most obvious condition. It is sometimes framed in terms of the relative power of left-wing, worker-based parties, though we'll see that can be misleading. In Swedish, and more broadly European, histories, a central part of the political basis for social democracy was a combination of a coalitions going beyond the traditional industrial proletariat, to farmers and middle groups. This became particularly important in the reaction to the social costs of untrammeled market forces, in what Karl Polanyi characterised as a double movement (Polanyi, 2001/1944; see also Stewart, 2010). In some countries, this was reconciled in authoritarian, corporatist political structures, as in the rise of fascism in Germany, Italy and Spain in Europe, that had echoes in corporatist political structures in Latin America, notably in Mexico. But the most successful, and durable, resolution occurred under democratic auspices, creating the mix of social provisioning and capitalist production that is the essence of social democracy (Berman, 2006). In the US the major initial move toward social democracy occurred in the New Deal, itself a response to the deep economic crisis of the Great Depression.

Of particular interest to India are the parallels with the contemporary experience of Latin America—a region of high inequality, with heterogeneous populations, histories of conflict, and now politically salient pressures from poor and middle groups. The classic early path to industrialisation of the beginning in the first two-thirds of the 20th century involved importing a Bismarckian system of social security, with a range of social benefits, including pensions, health, and sometimes housing and childcare, that was linked to the labour contract in formal work, and often backed by job security and severance pay. This led to a highly inequitable, and distortionary, system of social provisioning—the 'truncated welfare state'. The reach was in almost cases to a minority of the workforce, creating protected, and vigorously defended rents, strong incentives for informality, with actual provisioning of services to these favoured groups typically inefficient to boot.

What really changed things was the return to democracy that swept through the continent in the 1980s, creating political pressures for broader social provisioning. This was particularly successful in Brazil and Chile, both of whom had developed a broad-coalition in the resistance to military dictatorship, encompassing a range of worker groups, social organisations of informal and urban neighbourhoods, and middle groups. (By contrast, Mexico's main union movement was more tightly embedded in rent-sharing arrangements and links to the dominant party.) Figure 30.2 illustrates for Brazil: the return to democracy was in 1985 and a new constitution with a range of social rights (including pensions and health) was finalised in 1988. This laid the basis for a substantial rise in both social security and social assistance, with the real takeoff under the centre-left administration of President Cardoso, extended under that of President Lula da Silva of the left-wing Workers Party. An important feature of the Brazilian process was the role of a variety of participatory institutions (including participatory budgeting and policy councils), that have played a

Figure 30.2

The Rise of Social Security and Social Assistance in Democratic Brazil

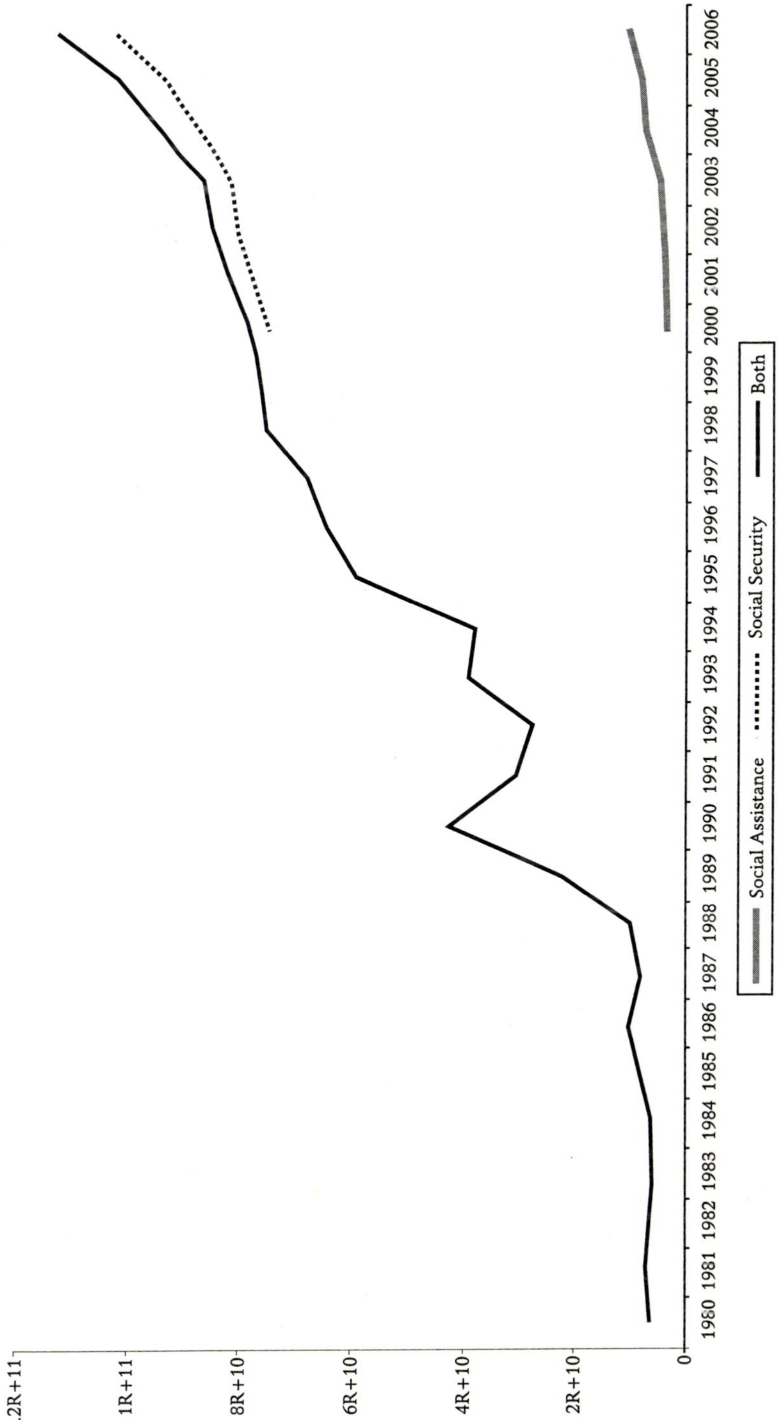

Source: Ferreira *et al.*, 2010.

significant role in opening access to disadvantaged actors to put pressure on the state, and creating space for distributional fights (Avritzer). It can be argued that Brazil is on a path to satisfying all five of the features of a social democracy listed above, albeit with distortionary effects of a continued dualistic system of social provisioning.

A similar story can be told on Chile. One additional comment is relevant: while a right wing government was elected for the first time in 20 years in 2010, there is little evidence of plans to roll back the extensions in social provisioning of the previous two decades. Indeed, in the wake of the dramatic rescue of trapped, mineworkers in October 2010, billionaire President Piñera promised a 'new deal' for Chile's workers, including in particular more effective safety regulations in mining.

More broadly, the expansion of social provisioning to "fill out" the truncated welfare state has become a phenomenon throughout Latin America, with considerable innovation in social instruments (Ribe *et al.*, 2010). However, the most common pattern (with the partial exception of Chile) has been the introduction of complementary social benefits for the households of workers outside formal work, as opposed to fundamental reform of the whole system. Santiago Levy has argued that this is consolidating distortions in the social system, leading to continued incentives for informality (Levy, 2008).

Support from capitalists: The second condition may be less obvious but of keen interest to India. In an in-depth historical analysis of formative episodes in social democratic policies in Sweden and the New Deal in US, Swenson (2002; 2004) argues that the support of capitalists was critical to the politics of the project. In other words, these transitions should not be interpreted exclusively as consequences of the relative rise in power of left, or middle-lower coalitions—of their triumph over capitalist interests. Rather major groups of capitalists had an interest in the expansion of state-mediated provisioning of social benefits. Reform would have probably not occurred in the absence of support from capitalists.

Two features of the historical experience are worth highlighting from Swenson's account. First, the US, typically considered a welfare state laggard, even ideologically against social democracy, was actually substantially ahead of Sweden in the New Deal reforms, especially in the creation of social security—and this despite the rise to political power of the Swedish Social Democrats. Second, while support of capitalist interests was central to both transitions, the form of interactions between capitalists, reformers and workers differed between the two countries, as did actual designs.

Sweden is famous for its 'solidaristic' approach: this included support from employers associations and an encompassing labour movement for centralised wage bargaining that led to an unusually compressed, egalitarian wage schedule. The beneficiaries of this were lower-wage workers, capitalist profits and especially more efficient firms in tradable goods sectors, inducing more rapid creative-destruction, with less efficient firms or activities forced to close (Moene and Wallerstein, 2008a). This was complemented by widespread state-mediated support for high employment, universal social benefits and active labour market policies. This specific form of social democracy passed as the capacity of worker organisations to sustain a compressed wage schedule declined and macroeconomic shocks led to open unemployment. Other features of social democracy remain, of course.

By contrast, the US never had national collective bargaining. Support for social democratic reforms was based in the interests of large-scale firms in key sectors, based in across-class alliance with unions: for these firms regulation of a high productivity, high wage and benefit was form of protection from competitors operating with lower overheads and benefits. State-mediated social security consolidated a level playing field. However, the legacy of firm-linked benefits has persisted, most importantly for company pensions and health insurance. The latter has been a source of the peculiar (by international standards) resistance to any form of national health insurance, despite the efficiency costs for firms of the link between social benefits and the labour contract (efficiency costs echoed in debates in developing countries—see Levy, 2008, on Mexico).

The lesson for India is not the particular form of social democratic resolutions and social democratic designs but rather that the interests and behaviour of capitalists can be critical to both support and design.

A 'good enough' state: The third condition concerns the capacity of the state. Social democracy involves extensive social provisioning and regulation. The question is whether state actors have both the organisational capacities to deliver on these functions, and, of equal importance, to do so in ways that support the universality and (in many areas), market-failure-compensating fashion that are key aspects of the achievement of both equity and growth-supporting, incentive compatibility.

Now no state is innocent of problems of incentives for effort, capture, or corruption. But there is a plausible case that the states of Scandinavia, of other successful European social democracies (from Germany to Spain), the US, Brazil and Chile, all had a combination of core competencies to manage the organisational requisites and autonomy to delivery on social democratic policies. Now this is not at all clear for other countries in Latin America—Boliva, Ecuador, Venezuela for example. Even Mexico is a mixed story, of effective management of some social programmes, but substantial capture by corporate interests, and effective resistance to the tax effort that even a basic social democracy would require (Levy and Walton, 2009).

So is social democracy feasible for India?

The historical and contemporary experience would suggest that a social democratic resolution could be feasible for India in the coming decade and beyond. High levels of inequality and heterogeneity strengthen the case for change. It is possible to imagine economic dynamics that would support the tax base for social provisioning. India already has relatively high organisational capacities for its level of development, including in the public sector—think of the impressive management of elections, or even the railways as an example of 'good enough' administration. And while European social democracy is traditionally associated with provisioning for formal sector workers and their households, the Latin American experience shows that social democratic principles can be pursued with programmes for informal and rural households. Finally, at an ideological and policy level, India already has a, sometimes uneasy, blend of support for both capitalism and social provisioning.

So far so good, but then comes the bad news. While a growth-supporting social democracy looks feasible in these abstract terms, it is not at all clear that current political-institutional structures and dynamics are supportive of India's transition in this direction. It is true that the long period of democracy—indeed with a much shorter authoritarian interlude than Brazil and Chile suffered—has led to salient political pressures from middle and poorer groups. But there are two big uncertainties. First, these social pressures get distorted in design, and even more so in implementation, by the nature of state-society interactions. And second, it is unclear whether the rising economic power of capitalists will translate into support for a social democratic resolution. A third uncertainty may or may not be of systemic importance but can certainly affect the distribution of social provisioning, concerns state-society interactions at what might be called the 'margins'—especially in Maoist areas but also in the cities.

Each of these three areas relate to structural features of inequality in India—in terms of the nature of state functioning, the effects of concentration of economic power in the corporate sector and the severe inequalities at the 'margins'. While deep inequalities, and associated conflicts, strengthen the case for a social democratic resolution, their particular form can lead to either resistance, or a half-baked resolution, that would be distortionary and inequitable. These issues matter for the Union Government, for both relatively dynamic and lagging states, and for major city governments.

These uncertainties over the practical feasibility of a successful transition apply to the broader conception of social democracy described above, involving comprehensive social provisioning and the 'efficient' regulation of capitalism. I do not even consider the possibility of a generating a compressed wage schedule, that was important in Scandinavia but is highly unlikely to be achievable in India, given the lack of encompassing organisations of workers and capitalists, and geographic diversity.

In the following paragraphs, I outline why each of the three areas is problematic for a successful social democratic resolution.

The patronage-corruption-political finance nexus: The problems of India's state are well-known. Large parts of state functioning are embedded in various forms of a patronage-corruption-political finance nexus. This flows from many sources. In many ways patronage, or clientelism, is a natural form of state behaviour, in which political loyalty (including, but not limited to, votes in an election) is provided in return for the delivery, or at least the promise of delivery, of specific goods, jobs or services to individuals or groups. It is pervasive throughout the developing world and in the historical experience of now-rich countries (including of city governments, as in the well-known US political machines). In the Indian case, it is amplified by divisions within lower and middle groups—the primary potential beneficiaries of social provisioning—of religion, especially between Hindus, and Muslims, of caste and of geography. This has biased the form of the compact between state actors and their various constituents/votebanks into fights over access to what economists would call static 'rents'—the distribution of jobs, subsidies, or specific services that divert resources from other groups, rather than supporting investment in people or capital, or efficiently managing resources. These distortions get biased further when the direction of state activities are further driven by the workings of corruption—where, for example, local contractors are also competing for the rents and bribing to get them.

Now this already antithetical to a genuine social democratic resolution, for which specific rights to risk-management instruments, decent education and minimum standard of living are intrinsic to an efficient resolution. This applies with or without means testing—since almost all provisioning in a social democracy is conditional on 'something'—on old age, on being unemployed and willing to work, being a child or being sick. The exact mix between means-testing and such categorical targeting is an issue of specific design, closely linked to the design of the tax system. A non-patronage and corruption-free state is only more important if a means test is part of the system.

The distortion is further compounded by the 'ineffectiveness' of state actors in many areas of social provisioning (not to mention state regulation of capitalism). Education is a vivid example. It is now well-documented that the quality of education in government schools is typically dismal and has shown very little progress in the past few years, not only in the North India status (PROBE, 1999) but also in many states considered to have relatively good governments, such as Gujarat and Tamil Nadu (ASER, various years). This is a product of a system of government education that provides little or no incentives for teachers to actually deliver quality teaching (Pritchett and Murgai, 2007), nor for local education administrators to support them. The Right to Education Bill has fine aspirations but is also problematic in being effectively silent on the quality of outcomes.

The health system is, if anything, worse, with evidence of extraordinarily low quality of service in rural areas (Banerjee *et al.*, 2008) and amongst urban government doctors (Das and Hammer, 2007). The unusually bad performance in child malnutrition is, at least in part, associated with government failures in the broader health-supporting system, and specifically in the early childhood, though here Tamil Nadu does much better owing to a longstanding tradition of provisioning of nutrition and other services for pre-school children in that state (FOCUS, 2006; Walton, 2009)

However, the real problem is that the nexus—or, to be more precise, varieties of nexuses—may well not be self-correcting. There are some positive pressures on making politicians more accountable through better information: the Right to Information Act is a potentially important instrument for this, better information can lead to changes in voter behaviour, e.g., toward less caste-base voting, and greater likelihood of punishing politicians with criminal records (Banerjee *et al.*, 2009). But this has to be set against the increasing monetisation of the political process, the murkiness of political finance (Mehta, 2009) and patterns of ownership of the media. Even if incentives for politicians improved, there capacity to deliver is in turn weakened by the ineffectiveness of the state, making a patronage-based resolution more attractive to them.

Thus the patronage-corruption-political finance nexus, and the associated weakness in state actors, makes less credible and less politically desirable, a resolution in favour of universal social provisioning, and more likely the continuance of inefficient, distorting and exclusionary resolutions—that at best may take the form of half-baked populist social provisioning, on the worst Latin American paths (that is not on the moderately distortionary Brazilian path). The big difference from Latin America is India's tradition of reasonable macroeconomic prudence—thus patronage and populist pressures manifest themselves in 'micro-populism' not macro-populism.

The position of capitalists: What of the growing economic power of capitalists, especially in the formal corporate sector? Can this group be both a general force for a more accountable state, and—as in the Swedish and US cases—for moves toward an effective social democracy? It is again highly uncertain, with current trends showing few signs of moves in this direction.

By way of context, the expansion of corporate incomes and associated private wealth has indeed been a marked feature of the post-liberalisation period. Two indicators illustrate. There has been a large rise in the share of profits in GDP of companies quoted on the Bombay Stock Exchange—typically the largest and most established firms—that rose from 2 per cent of GDP in 1989 to a peak of 7 per cent of GDP in 2008, before a (probably temporary) fall in the slowdown of 2009 (Figure 30.3). A large proportion of this is associated with often still family controlled conglomerates, as business houses in India. Even more dramatic has been the rise of private wealth: if we confine attention to the extremely wealthy, the ratio of billionaire wealth rose from less than 1 per cent of GDP in the mid-1990s to 23 per cent in 2008, and was still 14 per cent in early 2010, after a fall and partial recovery in tandem with movements in the BSE.

Figure 30.3

The Ratio of Profits to GDP for Firms on the Bombay Stock Exchange, 1989–2009

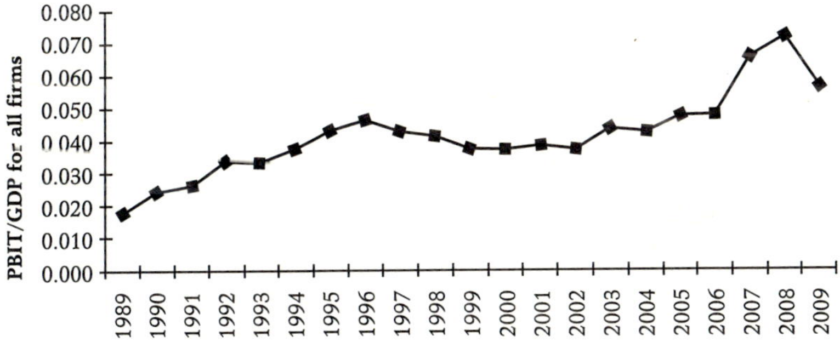

Source: CMIE, Central Statistical Organisation.

The corporate sector seems to present two faces. On the one hand there is the face of dynamic, creative capitalism, liberated from the license *raj*, that is not only rapidly expanding on a broad, diversified front but is increasingly represented by firms of global reach, investing in Australia, the UK and the US, as well as in Gujarat and Tamil Nadu. On the other, there are the frequent accounts of corruption, political finance and malfeasance in the sector, from the Satyam accounting scandal, to the Reddy brothers' political influence in Karnataka and widespread tales of influence and corruption in the infrastructure sector.

In fact, both faces of Indian capitalism appear to be true, and may often be true of the same firm. Here lies the question for this paper. Whichever face is relevant, it is not clear why large-scale capitalist firms should have an interest in social democratic reforms (and smaller-scale firms have insufficient influence, and probably even less interest). The current institutional resolution works reasonably well for the purposes of Indian capitalists. The suffocating features of the license *raj* have been lifted, and have been replaced by reasonably well-functioning market-supporting capitalist institutions (the stock exchange, finance, etc). These will undoubtedly be gradually improved over time. By contrast, where firms have to interact with the state, they have learnt to work in a privately effective, if socially inefficient, way, whether through corruption, political finance or other forms of political influence. Indeed, both corporate finance for politicians and the increased involvement of politicians in private firms are likely to consolidate and deepen the existing equilibrium. At the same time, globally efficient and ambitious firms can expand effectively on the international margin—further reducing their interest in domestic transformation.

The mix of engagement with an inefficient, rent-seeking state, and efficient global expansion has parallels elsewhere. Mexican capitalism is a vivid example: major family controlled-conglomerates use their market power and political influence to preserve rents at home (Levy and Walton, 2009). Yet firms such as the TELMEX in telecoms (a major source of billionaire Carlos Slim's wealth) and the cement giant SEMEX, are also globally efficient firms expanding internationally.

The one major area in which Indian capitalism does have an interest is in a more effective state is infrastructure. Great hopes are being placed on public-private partnerships as a means of solving problems. These may or may not reduce the infrastructure gap, and are highly likely to involve major new rents. But they have little to do with motivating support for social democracy.

State-society interactions on the 'margins': A final part of the political-institutional mix concerns the interaction between state and society in what might be termed the 'margins'. The obvious example concerns conflict in areas of Maoist presence. Maoist groups have not made the classic accommodation of social movements to work within democracy but are pursuing violent or extra-legal means against the state. However, this is also product of a resolution in which the Indian state is both failing and typically adopting violent means, both legal and illegal, to manage resistance. What is really troubling is that this looks like a bad equilibrium with self-sustaining properties, that is the direct opposite of a social democratic resolution. This often overlaps with questions of social identity, where the conflict and mobilisation is in *adivasi* ('tribal') areas. To quote Ramachandra Guha, "The first tragedy is that the state has treated its *adivasi* citizens with contempt and condescension. The second tragedy is that their presumed protectors, the Naxalites, offer no long-term solution either" (Guha 2007: 3305). And a further element concerns the interface with capitalist expansion, since there is frequently an overlap with some of the richest areas of mineral deposits. The combination of mining interests and institutionally 'weak' state governments is a recipe for corruption and exclusion.

While areas of Maoist conflict are mainly in remote rural areas, important areas of urban living are also enshrouded in illegality. Slum-dwellers systematically lack legal title—even if *de facto* rights vary substantially. There are ongoing disputes over the rights of hawkers to working spaces on streets. The homeless are often particularly vulnerable. Each of these areas are domains of worthy policy but with often conflicting legal judgments and ineffective implementation, a common pattern for India. In the meantime the consequence is that a significant group of urban dwellers suffer from a lower degree of citizenship, that translate into deep failures of public good provision. This is an issue of major importance, both now and in the future, since the coming decades will see a massive increase in urbanisation in India.

In both cases living at the 'margins' has resonance in terms of marginal citizenship but does not mean marginal interactions with the state. The problem is that the nature of the presence of the state is not as a provider of public goods but as an often rent-extracting or abusive presence. What does this imply for thinking about an Indian social democracy? At a minimum, failure to transform state functioning and state-society interactions in these 'marginal' domains would constitute a large gap in any social democratic resolution—for some of the most deprived in Indian society for which social democracy should be particularly precious. There maybe further pernicious systemic consequences, if these margins affect the broader functioning of the state.

Conclusion: Can there be internal sources of change?

In this paper, I have argued that a social democratic resolution is desirable for India and is potentially consistent with, and possibly necessary for, a long-term growth dynamic. India's deep inequalities of wealth, social status and citizenship make this more, not, less desirable. By social democracy I mean comprehensive provisioning for household risks, a floor on basic living standards, and efficient regulation of capitalism, including of capital-labour relations, backed by a full, and participatory, conception of citizenship for all. But I have also argued that design choices are fundamental to success, and that there are real questions of whether an equitable and growth-supporting social democracy can be formed. This is not because of India's overall stage of economic, organisational and social development but because of current political-institutional dynamics around the functioning of the state and the interests of Indian capitalism.

So what would be needed to shift current political-institutional dynamics? I conclude with questions in three areas, where there may be potential, and where the exercise of agency may make a difference.

Are rights-based approaches, complemented by citizen participation, a way of building both sound design and an institutionally supportive context, or will they get captured and distorted by existing structures? The combination of the rights invested in the 1988 Brazilian constitution was instrumental in subsequent social democratic moves. But the verdict is out for India: the courts give ambiguous support, the judicial system is itself desperately overloaded, and rights can be rendered meaningless in the absence of effective implementation.

What is the potential and likelihood of major groups of capitalists becoming a force for at least supporting, and potentially pressuring, the state (politicians and bureacracies) for a more efficient and universalistic system of social provisioning? Sound social democratic designs are almost certainly in Indian capitalism's long-term interest but this would involve a form of long-sightednes s and collective action that is not apparent now.

Will major Indian political parties—not least the Congress in this period—be able to undertake internal reforms to change the incentives for politicians toward the provisioning of public goods, as opposed to private interest and patronage? While societal pressure can play a role—from citizens or (potentially) firms—changing the behaviour of politicians, and parties, are a crucial complement, if social democratic designs are to be adopted and implemented. Here too the history of other countries suggest this will be a challenge: shifts from patronage-based to programmatic parties rarely occur within established parties in power.

These questions are deeply linked to the role of politics in the success or failure of social democracy in India, that is in turn of first order significance both for the well-being of all India's citizens and for the viability of the transition to prosperity.

References

Aghion, Philippe and Peter Howitt (2006). "Joseph Schumpeter Lecture. Appropriate Growth Policy: A Unifying Framework", *Journal of the European Economic Association* 4(2-3): 269-314.

Arellano, José Pablo (2004). *Políticas sociales para el crecimiento con equidad Chile, 1990–2002.* (Social policies for growth and equity.) Series Estudios Socio-Económicos. Santiago: Corporación de Estudios para Latinoamérica.

Austen-Smith, David, Jeffry Frieden, Miriam Golden, Karl Ove Moene and Adam Przeworski (eds.) (2008). *Selected Works of Michael Wallerstein—The Political Economy of Inequality, Unions and Social Democracy*. Cambridge and New York: Cambridge University Press.

Avritzer, Leonardo (2009). *Participatory Institutions in Democratic Brazil*. Washington DC and Baltimore: Woodrow Wilson Centre Press and Johns Hopkins University Press.

ASER (2008, 2009, 2010). *The Annual Status of Education Report*. New Delhi: The ASER Institute.

Banerjee, Abhijit and Esther Duflo (2003). "Inequality and Growth: What Can the Data Say?", *Journal of Economic Growth* 8(3): 267–99.

Banerjee, Abhijit, Esther Duflo and Rachel Glennerster (2008). "Putting a Band-Aid on a Corpse: Incentives for Nurses in the Indian Public Health Care System", *Journal of the European Economic Association* 6: (2): 487–500.

Banerjee, Abhijit, Donald Green, Jennifer Green and Rohini Pande (2009). "Can Voters be Primed to Choose Better Legislators? Evidence from Voter Campaigns in India", Processed.

Berg, Janine (2010). "Laws or Luck? Understanding Rising Formality in Brazil in the 2000s". Draftchapter.

Berman, Sheri (2006). *The Primacy of Politics: Social Democracy and the Making of Europe's Twentieth Century*. Cambridge and New York: Cambridge University Press.

Cardoso, Fernando Henrique and Alejandro Foxley (2009). *A Medio Camino Nuevos Desafíios de la Democracia y del Desarollo en América Latina* (Halfway: New Challenges for Democracy and Development in Latin America).

Das, Jishnu and Jeffrey Hammer (2007). "Money for Nothing? The Dire Straits of Medical Practice in Delhi, India", *Journal of Development Economics* 83(1): 1-36.

De Ferranti, David, Guillermo Perry, Francisco Ferreira and Michael Walton (2004). *Inequality in Latin America: Breaking with History?*. Washington, DC: World Bank.

Engerman, Stanley L., and Kenneth Sokoloff (2002). "Factor Endowments, Inequality, and Paths of Development among New World Economies", *Economia* 3(1): 41–88.

Ferreira, Francisco, Phillippe Leite and Martin Ravallion (2010). "Poverty Reduction without Economic Growth? Explaining Brazil's Poverty Dynamics, 1985-2004", *Journal of Development Economics* 93(1): 20-36.

Ferreira, Francisco and Martin Ravallion (2008). "Global Inequality: A Review of the Evidence", *Policy Research Working Paper #4623*. Washington DC: the World Bank.

Guha, Ramachandra (2007). "Adivasis, Naxalites and Indian Democracy", *Economic and Political Weekly*: 3305-12, August 11.

Levy, Santiago (2008). *Good Intentions, Bad Outcomes: Social Policy, Informality, and Economic Growth in Mexico*. Washington DC: Brookings Institution Press.

Levy, Santiago and Michael Walton (eds.) (2009). *No Growth without Equity? Inequality, Interests and Competition in Mexico*. New York: Palgrave-MacMillan.

Lindert, Peter (2004). *Growing Public: Social Spending and Economics Growth since the Eighteenth Century*. Cambridge, U.K: Cambridge University Press.

Mehta, Pratap Bhanu (2009). "Citizenship and Accountability: The Case of India", in Anis Dani and Ashutosh Varshney (eds.), *Citizenship, the State and Social Policy*. Washington DC: The World Bank.

Mody, Ashoka, Anusha Nath and Michael Walton (2010). "Sources of Corporate Profits in India: Business Dynamism or Advantages of Entrenchment?", Paper presented at the *India Policy Forum*, July.

Moene, Karl Ove and Michael Wallerstein (2008a). "How Social Democracy Worked: Labor Market Institutions", In Austen-Smith *et al.* (eds.).

———. (2008b). "Social Democracy as a Development Strategy", in Austen-Smith *et al.* (eds.).

Polanyi, Karl. 2001 (1944). *The Great Transformation*. Boston, MA: the Beacon Press.

Pritchett, Lant, and Rinku Murgai (2007). "Teacher Compensation: Can Decentralization to Local Bodies Take India from Perfect Storm Through Troubled Waters to Clear Sailing?" in Suman Bery, Barry P. Bosworth, and Arvind Panagariya (eds.), *India Policy Forum 2006–07.* Vol. 3. Washington, D.C.: Brookings Institution.

PROBE Team (1999). *The Public Report on Basic Education*. New Delhi: Oxford University Press.

Przeworski, Adam (1985). *Capitalism and Social Democracy*. Cambridge and New York: Cambridge University Press.

Ribe, Helena, David A. Robalino and Ian Walker (2010). *Achieving Effective Social Protection for All in Latin America and the Caribbean: From Right to Reality*. Washington DC: The World Bank.

Rodrik, Dani (1999). "Where Did All the Growth Go? External Shocks, Social Conflict, and Growth Collapses", *Journal of Economic Growth* 4(4): 385-412.

Swenson, Peter (2002). *Capitalists against Markets—The Making of Labor Markets and Welfare States in the United States and Sweden*. Oxford and New York: Oxford University Press.

———. (2004). "Varieties of Capitalist Interests: Power, Institutions, and the Regulatory Welfare State in the United States and Sweden", *Studies in American Political Development* 18 (Spring): 1–29.

Stewart, Frances (2010). "Power and Progress: The Swing of the Pendulum", Forthcoming in the *Journal of Human Development and Capabilities*.

Walton, Michael (2009). "The Political Economy of India's Malnutrition Puzzle", *IDS Bulletin* 40(4): 16-24. Institute of Development Studies at the University of Sussex.

World Bank (2005). *World Development Report 2006: Equity and Development*. New York: Oxford University Press.

This paper was prepared for the Tenth Indira Gandhi Conference, New Delhi 19-21 November 2010. Thanks to José Pablo Arellano, Francisco Ferreira, Luis Felipe López Calva, Roberto Pires, James Robinson and Ryan Sheely for discussions and comments.

Section III(b) *contd...*

The Political Economy of Social Democracy

PRESENTATIONS • DISCUSSIONS

This section presents the proceedings of the Third Session of the Tenth Indira Gandhi Conference, November 19-21, 2010, New Delhi.

Chair
- Rehman Sobhan

Presentations
- Pranab Bardhan
- Michael Walton

Discussants
- Abhijit Sen
- Aruna Roy
- Mirai Chatterjee
- Manish Sabharwal
- Anusha Rizvi
- Rohan Samarajiva
- Niraja Gopal Jayal
- Anu Aga
- Montek Singh Ahluwalia
- Rob Riemen
- Bina Agarwal
- Pranab Bardhan

31

REHMAN SOBHAN

Introductory Remarks

We move into the second part of the session on the political economy of social democracy. The focus of this particular panel is on the nature of delivering under the agenda of social democracy. That agenda should, and has essentially been, to bring the issue of justice and fairness into the agenda of democracy and development. This was sharply brought out in the address by Sonia Gandhi and has periodically entered the discussion. Injustice has been basically at the source of deprivation in our societies, and sources of injustice need to be addressed. The question is whether the discourse on social democracy is going to focus on the question of injustice and address its sources.

This is a very critical question. The presentations made have, to a great extent, concentrated on the broader issues of remedying injustice by interventions for provisioning. The presentations which will be made address the issue of comprehensive provisioning on flaws in basic living standards, which would be one way of reporting the problems. This then takes us into the issues of delivery quality and the political economy which really underlies the mechanisms for delivery that have been set up. The European agenda in fact did emphasise the broader issues of provisioning and a lot of the discussion has been inspired by some of the European experience. There was a strong emphasis on building a more just egalitarian society within the framework of European social democracy. The question is how quickly this element of justice and of creating a more egalitarian society is going to be essential to the project of social democracy in India.

Recently, I read in the papers that one of your presumably very successful businessmen has just invested a fairly large sum of money in buying a football club in England. Obviously, in any project on discussing justice and the architecture of social democracy, it might well be asked: is this a sensible way to use significant capital surpluses? In fact, if some of those huge investments were made in upgrading to world cup standards, the Indian football team itself would have been more efficient. These resources could have been used to create opportunities for improving football players across the villages of India. This is an element where a significant amount of wealth is in private hands. The method of its use may lead us to ask whether this would be of any concern to the project of social democracy. This has to be addressed.

I hope that the discussion can bring out whether we can move beyond dealing with compensating on the outcomes of a relatively unjust social order to really seeing what we can do to address the structural sources of the problem. Can we address the issue of enhancing the assets of the excluded so that they can actually participate actively in the economy in the way Chanda Kochhar pointed out? If 700 million people can be invested with resources and skills, the growth potential of that can be exponential. The mechanisms arising out of such investments would create permanent assets for them. The effort has to be to bring the most deprived groups, not just the income poor but even lower caste people and tribals, into the opportunity structures derived from access to assets. What can be done to bridge the huge divide which has emerged in our education system, where we have a privately-educated privileged elite, which is becoming or has already become self-perpetuating? There are large numbers of people who remain condemned at the base of society and are able to only marginally enhance their incomes. They have certainly not improved their positions in the opportunity structures. Of course, we also have to look at what could we do to make the lower income groups, whether in the non-formal sector, or farmers, participate in more competitive terms in the marketplace through instruments of collective action of the sort developed by SEWA. These strike me as some of the more substantive issues which should be part of any discussion of social democracy.

Finally comes the question of what we could do to make our democracy more democratic. Today, democracy has become a project where people with significant resources can buy their way into parliament and broad constituencies of people are voting only to be inadequately represented in our elective institutions. There is a certain injustice built into the democratic project itself which has to be addressed. I hope these thoughts will find their way into the discussion.

32

PRESENTATION BY PRANAB BARDHAN

Inequality, Inefficiency, and the Challenges for Social Democracy in India's Economic Transition

The chairman has talked about large structural issues, asset distribution issues. My paper is not about that. Its objective is much narrower. It is not even about the issues that have been discussed earlier, about redistribution in general, the promise of social justice etc. I have decided to confine myself to a very narrow set of issues. Forget about the larger issues, in India we do not have for most practical purposes, even the basic minimum social protection. I will therefore focus on basic minimum social protection.

In the first section of my paper, there is a discussion about inequality of opportunity. It is well known to most of you and is also in the paper. The one thing that I want to note in passing, and it is not well-known, is that inequality of opportunity in education however, crudely measured, is among the very worst in India of all countries. I find that among many of my friends in India and outside, this is not well recognised. In fact, crude measures of educational inequality are worse in India than supposedly highly unequal countries in Latin America. India's educational inequality is much worse than in Brazil, Mexico, Chile and Argentina. This is not well known. In fact, it is also worse than some sub-Saharan African countries. But I am not going to talk about inequality as such. As I said, I am going to focus on basic minimum social protection in a country where the vast masses of the poor, toiling Indians in the informal sector, where 92 per cent of our workers work, face brutal insecurity from all the various risks of life and livelihood, often without any minimum protection. The tiny minority of formal sector workers, two-thirds of them government employees, cling on to their paltry privileges with militancy as they face the social vertigo of looking on the vast masses of the unprotected huddled down below.

There are different approaches to social protection. In India, in recent times, probably one of the most popular approaches has been the rights-based approach. It has commendable activism on this front with some achievements already to show, particularly in the landmark legislations on the right to information and to work on public works projects, though the implementations in many states as yet are rather slow and feeble, and face a great deal of resistance. Since my friend Jean Dreze had an outburst against economists in the earlier section, let me mention I am one of the very few economists who supported NREGA at a time when many of the Delhi economists were opposed to it. But I also remind Jean that when Abhijit Banerjee and I wrote an op-ed piece supporting NREGA, it was still being discussed; it was not an Act. I think it was not even a Bill at that time. One of the things on which Abhijit and I had some difference was exactly on wage policy. If I remember right, some of the instances of wage policy we are worried about are exactly the problem you are facing today. Of course, it was an op-ed piece and we didn't have time to go into the details. I agree with Jean that this is an issue that has to be thrashed out. It should have been done before, but it is not too late to discuss wage policy, otherwise NREGA may be in serious trouble.

In general, I think there are many things to say in favour of the rights-based approach. At a minimum, it serves to raise consciousness among the poor and the vulnerable about their entitlements in the sense that they are not mere supplicants to the politicians or bureaucrats.

The other advantage is that a rights-based approach is usually universalistic in principle. I do not share the view of a rights-based fundamentalism because I do recognise some limits of the rights-based approach. If the delivery structure for implementing some of these rights remains as weak and corrupt as it is now, mere promulgation of rights, while it can serve some positive function, will ultimately remain hollow and will, after a point, generate a great deal of cynicism. The Indian public arena is already littered with hundreds of unenforced or spasmodically enforced court injunctions and there is some danger that the proliferating judicial activism, for all its good intentions, may undermine the credibility and legitimacy of the judiciary itself.

I also have some reservations about the right to education and also about the right to food security. I shall not go into the details. Let me say—I think it has already been said about the right to education—that the important issue of ensuring quality of education for the poor is not being addressed. India happens to be the world's largest country of school dropouts.

What school dropouts need is remedial education. Not enough attention is being given to remedial education. The poor students who need help and are failing in classes, don't receive help and very soon drop out. Remedial education is much more important than mere access to enrolment. On right to food security, and even the biometric identification, there are two problems. People have talked about enormous theft and wastage around the public distribution system. In fact, not entirely but to a large extent, the monopoly of public storage and distribution is a huge problem. In fact, I remember last year or the year before, in my state of West Bengal, the poor people in the villages started burning the fair price shops because when they go to the fair price shops, some people would be given some food and the shop would then be closed saying that not enough supplies had come. They could do this, apart from political accountability issues, because of monopoly. Of course, one way of solving this could be food stamps. Jean has already pointed out some problems of food stamps but I think that food stamps in principle are usable in public or private stores and are a step in that direction, but there are other problems. The food stamp will not solve, even in principle, the second problem with food security, if it is not universal. It is universal in some states like Tamil Nadu and Chhattisgarh etc. but not meant to be universal in many cases. It is not universal if it involves testing of APL and BPL. There will be scope for a large amount of fraud as has already been the case. These are problems that will not go away just by passing a Right to Food Security Act.

In general, as I said, one of the things that I like about the rights-based approach is its universality. In this connection, in my paper I discuss this quite a bit about a universal scheme of what I call basic income supplement, which everybody rich or poor has a right to get. This is not a new idea. It has been around in many countries for a long time, but not implemented. Sunil Khilnani referred to it and he may have given you the impression that I am an unequivocal supporter of it. I largely support it but I am equivocal about it. I am a card-carrying member of the profession of 200 economists on the one hand, on the other hand, there are economists who support this approach like Abhijit Banerjee, Arvind Subramanian, Devesh Kapur but I have some problems with it. One is of the first order and the other is of the second order. The first order problem would be: for example, to give every family ₹ 5000 in a year, given the gender and other social norms in a family, you know where it is going to be spent, not on the vulnerable or within the family.

Secondly, financial assistance is not the only thing that the poor need. Quite often they need information, skills, assistance in marketing, etc. That problem will still remain. Thirdly, in the urban slums, social protection also has to involve active social support structures against violence, drugs, family breakdowns, juvenile delinquency, etc. Financial assistance alone is not enough.

Second order problems have been briefly mentioned. For example, even if we give out cash or as Sunil Khilnani termed it, a 'citizens' growth dividend', it is the clerk who will hand it out even with all the biometric identification. That is a second order problem. Similarly, if word goes around that everyone is going to get some money in their remote post offices in remote villages there may be extortion by some people. These are what I regard as second order problems.

One of the main issues in India about all the social protection measures is that of delivery mechanisms. Here, the governance issues come in. As an economist, I think the main issue in governance is the incentive system: we don't reward good work and don't punish bad work. This is the fundamental problem in the civil service and government mechanisms. Unless that is changed, the present system will continue. Of course, one way to make people more accountable is decentralisation. In fact, there is some evidence that in some cases, for example in Nagaland, a very small fraction of teachers don't come to school. They didn't even come to school before. In Nagaland, they tried an experiment of leaving a small fraction of the salary to be decided, not by the government above, but by the local village council, that is the *panchayat*. That immediately brought about a big change. Even the slightest incentive reform can bring about big change but for various reasons, so far in most parts of India, decentralisation has not worked. In many cases, not only the local elite but the state level politicians and bureaucrats hijack the process on mandating devolution. This is called a capture problem.

Similarly, we can think of all kinds of schemes of private health insurance but we do not have a public health administration to speak of, except for Tamil Nadu. Most states do not have functioning public health sanitation, public hygiene administration. This jerks up the cost of private health and medical care insurance. For example, we have the Rashtriya Swasthya Bima Yojana, which is supposed to cover up to ₹ 30,000 for hospitalisation-related expenses for below poverty line families. But for the poor in many cases, even if it is available, for hospitalisation with illnesses like diarrhoea or malaria which could be prevented by basic public health programmes like provision of clean drinking water, sanitation, spraying etc, its access isn't easy. Thus, the deficiencies of public health administration in India and the deficiency in carrying out its primary duties make any medical insurance, private or public, so much more costly.

I have also elaborated on the issue of populism and oligarchy. I am afraid that we can clearly see in India today, reflected in much of the discussion as well, a lack of balance. There are trade-offs of various kinds but a one-sided approach is too narrow. We need a balance between the need for economic development that creates productive jobs and enhances social surplus which can fund large programmes of social protection on the one hand, and the need to minimise and adequately compensate for dislocation and dispossession, which is what development has become in many cases. The process has to involve the stakeholders and must bring down the excessive rent accruing now to the capitalist oligarchy and the real estate magnates, the mining mafia and their political patrons.

I think there is a big difference between the political compromise of social democracy in the West, particularly Europe, and in India. That is the fact that European social democracy is the outcome of a class compromise and a social pact. Workers who are electorally powerful enough to expropriate capitalists and end the capitalist system have chosen not to do so. They have figured out that capitalism is the only viable way left for adequately expanding the pie. So they are prepared to bear some cost and let the capitalists have a reasonable share of the pie, which induces the latter to continue their efforts in bringing about dynamic innovations. I am not sure if the Indian electorate has yet been confronted with this social pact and if so confronted, how it will react. In fact, it is very interesting that not a single party in India is a full-scale capitalist party since the demise of the short-lived Swatantra Party. India has not had a full scale pro-business conservative party.

Even the right wing parties in India are largely populist when it comes to economic issues when they approach the electorate. It is true that there has been a lot of flowering of entrepreneurial energies in recent years throughout the country. Still, in the popular culture, there is a strong anti-big capital streak. Whether we like it or not, it has implications on social surplus. In recent decades, those bearing the legacy of the Gandhian moral critique of market expansion and competition have joined forces with those espousing the Left critique of capitalist exploitation of workers, peasants and other small people and their rights over natural resources, in weaving active grassroots movements in much of the country for the protection of the environment and the traditional livelihood of the indigenous people against the depredations of capitalist oligarchy. Even though the private corporate sector is thriving in India and in some sense, its hegemony looks more assured today than before, it directly employs only a tiny percentage of the Indian workforce, unlike in Europe. It is not clear the electorate is still ready to accept the class compromise like the one that lies behind the social democracy enterprise in the West. On the other hand, the populist opposition—and I am sure what I am going to say is going to be controversial—for all their strength in numbers have not even succeeded in pointing to a viable incentive compatible alternative. By incentive compatible, I mean an alternative that is not entirely dependent on revolutionary or moral zeal for sustenance—viable system economic alternative outside the esoteric confines of their wishful thinking or Ethiopian anarcho-communitarianism. The passionate intensity of their negative critique of capitalism is not matched by a convincing demonstration of a sustained positive alternate system that can generate the necessary surplus. Until this tension is resolved, the social democracy project in India will remain somewhat tentative.

33

PRESENTATION BY MICHAEL WALTON

Can a Social Democratic Resolution Resolve Issues of Inequality and Growth for India?

I will seek to complement some of what Pranab has said. First, I would like to stretch the overall argument that well-designed social democracy for India is necessary for equity, equality of opportunity. I also believe it is good for growth. Second, the view that social democracy is only feasible in egalitarian and homogenous societies is, I believe, incorrect. The typical trajectory is that today social democracy emerges as a response to inequalities. They manifest themselves in conflicts and lead to response. But if one looks at experiences, the major issue is the nature of that response: it can either go down a route of an efficient, equitable social democracy and a well-regulated and dynamic capitalism, or down a route of social patronage and some combination of crony capitalism or unbridled capitalism. My concern is that if we look at India's current structural conditions, especially the nature of the state, inequalities of citizenship, state-capital relations, I think there is a substantial risk that India could go down the second route rather than the first route. I will try to expand on this argument.

First, I would like to state briefly why I believe worldwide social democracy is good for growth as well as for equity. I will leave the equity part aside because we have had a lot of discussion on that.

Why is it good for growth? I suggest that the international experience indicates that well-designed regulation of capitalism is necessary for solving the intrinsic market failures that are necessary to support innovative capitalism. I do not see the US model as an alternative model of the lowest order of a different, less complete social democracy. Joseph Stiglitz referred to this earlier that in absolute terms, the US is still defining the technological frontier. I see this as the product of features of the US around how it holds innovation, creative talents in universities, venture capital, which do not have anything to do with the actual incompleteness of America's social democracy. If anything, the direction of regulation in the US, especially after the crisis, has gone towards bad regulations that are a function of the excessive state capture by special interests. I do not see that as an alternative model.

The main thing I want to talk about is what I call the first-order question. What drives the countries, what are the choices to go to one path rather than the other? For that reason, I will talk less about specific designs for which you have many reason-specific designs. What makes the difference? Here I will say that there are three factors—politics, interests and institutions. I will relate this to two classic transitions in the Western countries. I see both in the case of Sweden and the US in the New Deal, where there was a combination of an encompassing coalition which leads to demands for social change. The capitalists were either supportive in the case of Sweden, or went along the progressive path with the New Deal in the US, and that was a good illustration. The most interesting case now for India is what is happening in Latin America. I take two cases—Brazil and Chile, two highly unequal societies that in the last 20 years have been systematically travelling in social democratic directions. What we see there is again an encompassing coalition, especially in the time of the transition back to democracy, which is a hugely important critical juncture in the 1980s and 1990s. Because of that juncture, any resistance from capitalist short-term interests was not sufficiently salient to stop the project. There is either a highly functional state in the case of Chile, or what one might call a good enough state in the case of Brazil. I would particularly like to expand on Brazil, which has already been mentioned a few times. It is particularly interesting for India because Brazil is certainly highly unequal, highly heterogeneous with major identity-based differences within its society. It is also known for clientelism and corruption.

What were the features of Brazil's transition that led it to make the significant moves? I think there are three in terms of the grand process. One was in 1988: the constitution that actually embedded a lot of rights to various social aspects of living for the society. It also embedded rights to participatory involvement of the society in their resilient implementation. Then, it was strongly criticised as a ragbag of rights with some saying that it would not be that effective. That was one element. Then there was almost 20 years of fairly continuous policy. I was delighted when Lula was awarded the Indira Gandhi Award but I would actually put more emphasis on the structural conditions and the continuity. In the gradual implementation of these rights, there was a combination of considerable experimentation, in particular the government designs linked to participatory institutions, which systematically put pressure on the government to perform better. Let me just give a couple of examples.

In the education sector, Brazil's record was shockingly bad. The inclusion in education was dismal in the 1980s. There was a huge commitment to the right to education with substantial financial equalisation but in addition, what I would emphasise here is that what the state had introduced was the actual testing of children in schools, which was unit-based as a management mechanism for the government and as a source of pressure on the schools. That is where, I think, India's Right to Education Act, for all its virtues, falls seriously short. That kind of public testing is not available. And we know that is a big problem these days in India's basic education. The quality of education in Brazil is still bad, but it is substantially better. We have seen significant improvement over the last 15 years at the primary and secondary levels. The second example is the Zero Hunger policy which had very similar aspirations to the right to food here. There are two aspects of that. First, it was designed over time with considerable experimentation as very much a comprehensive attack on the different drivers like food insecurity and malnutrition in Brazil. It happened in multiple sectors, some of it linked to agricultural production, health, nutrition surveillance, some linked to specific health interventions and to transfer programmes. The one that is most known is the one that has been referred to, Bolsa Familia, the mechanism that the Brazilians chose to get cash to poor families. What I wish to highlight about that is the fact that it actually involved a double conditionality, linked to poverty by a means test, and also linked to kids attending school. They do not have anything like the PDS, but do have things like community kitchens, especially in urban areas.

I am not at all sure or clear that both these familiar models are applicable to India, precisely at this stage. This is because of the significant problems over the BPL system, both in terms of its exclusion of poor people, and also because it can become an instrument of local patronage. A slightly different thinking on this is that the Brazilian principle is right, though the institutional application of it would be different in India's case.

Let me now turn to India's case. I would see it as stepping back in relation to the politics, interests and institutions. Of course, it is very clear and has been amply manifest in this conference that there is tremendous political support for doing something about injustice and the extraordinary social deprivation that exists. That much is clear. But my concern regarding India is that, what I might call the nexus between patronage, corruption and political finance, which shapes the way the state functions is a source of the low effort that is seen on the part of the state and the distortions within the state itself. These make it particularly difficult and could be a major bar to going the social democracy route, as opposed to the social patronage route.

It seems to me that the first order question is to have designs that seek the transformation of other state functions in practical implementation, as opposed to a new social programme. That is the first point. The second point I'd like to make is regarding a concern on the part of industry, about the business sector, of the capitalists in the country. I have done an analysis of this sector and am convinced that dynamic capitalism has been central to economic growth. If one were to look at the numbers, India's corporate sector behaves somewhat similarly to profit patterns in other countries.

But my concern is that if one looks at the sheer growing economic wealth, we have an enormous potential political economy issue. Let us take just one indicator, which is the tip of the iceberg. That is the relationship between Indian billionaires' wealth and the size of the economy. This is about two-and-a-half times the ratio in Brazil, itself a very unequal society. It is substantially higher than that prevalent in the US, comparable with that of Saudi Arabia and a little below that of Russia.

I'm sure that a substantial part of that wealth was a product of innovation and dynamic capitalism, though not all of it. But my concern is that this is not embedded in a state-capital relationship which will lead to the dynamic capitalism that is needed for India for the next 20 years. The short-run interests of capitalists may be distinct from their long-run interests.

The third issue that I'd like to raise as a worrying concern for India is what I call the relationship between state and society at the margins of Indian society. Some of these are obvious margins as in Maoist-infested areas, which has been discussed. But I'd also like to highlight the margins in the urban areas and what has been happening in many Indian cities. It is, in effect, the continuous creation of illegality, since many people coming in are not able to obtain sanction for legal residence in cities. That creation of illegality makes marginal slum-dwellers vulnerable to abuse from the police and to manipulation by politicians.

So, where might be the levers for change in this situation? I'd like to conclude with three questions. The first is: is a combination of a rights-based approach, which, as an economist, I used to be sceptical of, but now increasingly value as an effective mechanism for effective change, the answer? Structured participatory institutions and designs of governmental action are both based on an understanding of how the system works. That is why I found Jean and Kaushik actually agreeing in the last section. Moreover, one has to go beyond that to design systems that systematically put pressure on the state to change the way it behaves. Based on those criteria, if the first is not linked to current mechanisms, money is going to flow into old forms of patronage. If it doesn't put pressure on the state, we do not get the transformation required. That is my first question.

The second question is whether there is scope for progressive coalitions of the capitalists within the capitalists themselves, who will be campaigners, not just for an accountable state for themselves, but for an effective accountable state for social democracy. I believe that is in the long-term interests of those segments of capitalism that do have a long-term horizon. This is the strength of India in having an effectively functioning social democracy. Otherwise, conflict will break out in adverse ways.

The third question is whether the political parties can undertake the internal reforms of the political process that will lead to drivers of behaviour of politicians to be around the provision of public goods, as opposed to the perpetration of their power through patronage. In all of these three areas, I see that there is potential for change. But as an observer, at this point in time, I'm not sure in which direction that change will occur.

34

SECTION III(b)

Discussion

Abhijit Sen

The very excellent background given earlier by Sunil Khilnani, put out the problems, dilemmas and probably the definitions of social democracy. I am not a social historian or a political scientist and therefore accept the broad contours of what has been called social democracy so far.

I want to jump into our Prime Minister's speech that followed Mrs Sonia Gandhi's introductory speech. The Prime Minister said that our Constitution itself, and particularly the Directive Principles of State Policy, do amount to a charter for social democracy. He went further and said that in a sense, the Planning Commission, to which I at the moment happen to belong, was actually given the role of ensuring that the Directive Principles become a part of the way government policy pans out; Nehru did that. In fact, a lot of what one sees in terms of policies over the past have followed that direction.

What are these Directive Principles? Many things have been deleted and added to these principles by way of amendments. But the core of the principles and policies to be followed by the state are that citizens, men and women equally, have the right to adequate means of livelihood, that the ownership of the material resources of the community are so distributed as best to sub-serve the common good, that the operation of the economic system does not result in the concentration of wealth and means of production to the common detriment, that there is equal pay for equal work for both men and women, that the health and strength of workers, both men and women, and the tender age of children are not abused, and that citizens are not forced by economic necessity to enter avocations unsuited to their strength, that children are given opportunities and facilities to develop in a healthy manner and in conditions of freedom and dignity.

Now that is a charter for social democracy. I think at some stage, it also describes the house that Sunita Narain wanted to be defined right at the beginning. I think if that is done, we do have, like any charter, a basis to look into what we have done in the past and how to design whatever we want to, in the future. Of course, there are problems here, too. For example, when the Constitution was amended in 1976—the 42nd Amendment—which introduced the word 'socialism' into the Constitution, it also introduced into the Directive Principles, matters about environment for the first time. It also meant that from the other parts of the Constitution, the word "freedom of property" was shunned. The right to own property was restricted. That was the era of socialism, and the word is still present in the Constitution. There are signs of changes in policy, of things shifting back to the earlier era, things that we are often bothered about in this structure.

A lot of the time, we have played on those battles. But those are in a sense, past. If we accept that this is the house we are moving towards, we must also realise another thing, which is that like any charter, this is at best something for progressive realisation. The Directive Principles are non-justiciable. They are something that tell the state how it must act and are an agenda for progressive, not immediate realisation. It means that we have got to weigh what is possible now, what the trade-offs might be, in terms of both present choices as well as present benefits to future costs, if we go too far. That is the sort of matter we may be discussing about how we deal with it and how to do it for long. But I believe this to be important. Unlike any other social contract, we must look at what the Indian Constitution as a social contract was and what it wasn't.

As the Constitution of a country emerging out of a long national struggle against foreign rule, it was really a constitution that expressed a charter between the citizen at large and the state. It was the colonial state which was really at issue. What it was not, was the original social democratic contract, which was between capital and labour. In fact, the citizen is here, but the capitalist is not. I think, as many speakers earlier too have pointed out, that one of the big gaps in addressing social democracy today, is how to bring capital into either a contract, or enter into debate on what the roles and responsibilities of capital may well be.

I would like to step back for a second and ask if our Constitution can be read as a charter. Then obviously, there will be certain types of purely technical issues. Those issues will have to be sold to the people, though I also think that people understand those issues. Essentially, there is a trade-off with growth, between acting too much on reducing inequality or social risk today, and aborted means of growth. Those are the sort of issues which Vijay Kelkar talked about. Although one may have debate and dissonance about it, if the direction is right, I think people would be willing to wait. The real problem is that this social democratic charter has not even delivered on some things that are already universal, like civil rights, for example. One of the things we haven't talked about in this conference is the fact that equality before justice is one part of how to do it; it is part of the Directive Principles. We have not done that. Unless we do this, we shall continue to have all the problems of political capture. All of us, wherever we might come from and whatever we might do, agree that the delivery of justice, the most basic public service, has to be ensured. If this is not done, then other public civil services cannot be delivered properly. They will not be delivered properly simply because in a society like ours, people will be falling back on their social capital of caste and community and political parties will use this very social capital to actually deliver benefits to those who come first in the queue and decide for whom exceptions to rules can be made. Ultimately, that is the biggest source of political patronage and the way political systems entrench themselves. We have a lot of political rights, but civil rights are rather small. Social and economic rights come much later.

Nonetheless, I think we do need to emphasise two or three things here. The first, which I agree along with everybody, is that there cannot be a social democracy or a social democratic agenda without a universal construct. We cannot divide this into any community, but nor can we divide this into the poor and the rich, or the deserving and the undeserving. We must set out an architecture where the deserving get it first and get it most, but not by asking the question who is poor and who is not.

Let me conclude with an issue that is confronting us now. With the right to information in place, with the NREGA already there, we may possibly infer that the right to education also being there, and the right to food about to come, all the others, except the right to food, are universal rights. For various reasons, regarding the right to food, we have continued with a system that had a BPL and an APL; we might want to call it something different, but that is the way we are going. Surely, there is an architectural problem that we needed to counter, but didn't. This has been referred to by other speakers.

When the NREGA came, I remember some of us, including me, were of the opinion that if we had to bargain about something with those who were wary of the NREGA, we should be willing to bargain on the wage rate. Let there be a lower wage rate if the amount of money available from those who control finance is limited—this would mean fewer people coming in, which would make it more manageable—but let us not bargain on anything else. That would simply limit the amount of benefits to be given and the poorest sections would get it. But it was fairly clear that we should also bargain for certain other things. Pick the variable that we should bargain for and which we should, as economists, be willing to say would cause the least problems. In fact, too high a wage in NREGA is actually a bad thing, just as too low a price in the food security system is a bad thing, because these things distort the equation. Those are the things we should be bargaining for.

In the Food Security Bill, for example, though we in the Planning Commission obviously did not like it, we wanted a price that would be closer to the price we are paying the farmer, rather than a price that was much too low. This was simply because we felt that in this way, we could have the universal principle maintained. This can be done; a lot of people would drop out of food at that price. But there was more to it. Having put the NREGA in place, there is a whole set of people who can earn and are in a position to use that right. Provided that right generates the income to buy food, you do not need to be overly concerned for the able-bodied in terms of the price that is going to be charged for food in the PDS. We can fix that to some extent, but for the wage that you pay in the NREGA, an index linking would have to be done.

Similarly, there are large parts that are left out. These are people who are not able to work, like the old and the children. If we gave up the BPL for the older Antyodaya scheme, which simply defines requirements in physical terms, we would have something that we didn't need to target at all. In that case, we can even give it for free; it's a very small number. If we have come along the route that we have, back to the Directive Principles, we need to engage clearly on what is under the belt, where are we going, and what we can use from what we've already done for what we are going to do in the future. I think that is architecture that Montek was speaking about, though I don't think we have talked enough on that.

There are two other things I wish to say. The first is that service delivery is appalling. The main reason for it is our poor delivery of responsibility and incentives, a lot of which is related to the fact that long queues and exemptions from the rule of law are taken to be normal. The moment we acquiesce in such a situation, we create space for a lot of things to happen, which will create such poor incentives that public servants, at least, will not work. I think that is the single-most important factor. A lot of people and I think that India is rich. It has been rich before independence and has grown since independence through non-governmental organisations. Of course, there are a lot of NGOs that are offshoots of the main part of the system, but the great advantage in the delivery of public services is that most of them bring more expertise to the subject of delivery than many of us in government who are trying to design it, and many who are actually delivering themselves. One hole in our system is the way the government finances an NGO sector. Through the PPP mode, we have worked out some ways of how to finance the for-profit sector. But we have not been able to find out ways of financing the not-for profit sector, excepting in ways that were already there, like aided schools and things like that. I think this is a big challenge. But I think the most important challenge is the entry of expertise, which is very important for public services.

Most importantly, philanthropy has probably been less in post-independent India that it was in pre-independence India. This is one point, and a very important one, that any future contract between the state and capital, which I spoke of earlier, needs to be based on. At its base, we cannot have any beginning on this without talking about estate duties, the creation of incentives to form trusts to leave your bequest, so that what happens later is still in your name, but managed by foundations that have the expertise and can fund the NGOs themselves.

There are many other issues. It is to build up capital, which in a growing economy where the will to wealth is rising very quickly, to tax some of it away quickly, and to force others to actually be used in public purpose.

Aruna Roy

If we look at the entire debate, there has been a tendency to look at people who represent the poor, who come from the non-economic and non-academic background, people who are emotional and passionate but have no articulate thoughts, who have a vision but have no 'plumbing' or 'architecture' as probably mindless people who have a big heart and land up in rural areas and flounder along. That illusion must be set aside, if we suffer from it.

The Right to Information Act, in its essence, was designed by illiterate peasants and workers in central Rajasthan, suffering the non-payment of wages, struggling to get their ration delivered. Each time they tried, they were told that their records were fudged. When they demanded to be shown their correct records, they were bluntly told that these were "private and confidential documents" which the peasants could not see. They could not see a BPL list, a muster roll, the register of the ration food shops or the PDS. Therefore, the idea that things must come out and be made transparent was conveyed in a single sentence in Hindi by an illiterate Dalit couple, who said: "Jab tak wo kaagaz bahar nahin niklenge, hamein kuch nahin milega" (we won't get anything until we get hold of those papers). There was a clarion call to bring those documents out.

So we shall have to accept that the definition of change, in practicality, comes from many places. The architecture will sometimes depend on the materials and tools one has. One might want a palace, but if one has to build a house with mud or lime, one may have to do it; one may not have cement. I think we have to open our minds to what we plan to do. Talking about resources, India is very rich in resources, if we look at it in one way. The weaver I mentioned is an illiterate person. If we look at his literacy levels, he may be said to be a drain on the economy. But if we look at his skill at weaving a saree, it is simply fantastic. People like us cannot do it. It depends on how we look at people. I think there is something wrong in the way we do.

We have talked a lot about wages and I know that there are various views around this table on NREGA. A minimum wage is a minimum guarantee for the poor. They have nothing else. We may or may not give them a hundred days of work, depending on the levels of corruption in various states, or whether the applications are accepted or not. Thus, we are fighting corruption every single day. The minimum wage is a fundamental guarantee that Jawaharlal Nehru talked about in 1929 at the Lahore Congress. It was one of the first Acts passed in independent India to ensure that a wage worker would get at least a minimum wage. It's just a guarantee.

Before the NREGA came, the poor farmer/worker in rural India didn't get 20 days of work a year from the government. They made do with other things and still continue to do so. They are not dependent parasites on the government system. But nevertheless, the minimum wage is a guarantee. It moderates the wage in all other sectors. So the minimum wage cannot not be paid in the NREGA. What this scheme has done for the country is to have brought a wage rise in the extremely extortionist conditions in which people worked. Wage workers are still not employed 365 days a year, but have the capacity. Much of the agricultural angst against the NREGA is the anger that the minimum wage has now gone up, so they have to pay it. The marginal and poor farmer does not engage labour; he or she works on her own land. It is the richer farmer who employs labour. Thus, there has been a lot of distortion of all this.

I have just returned after a 47-day satyagraha in Jaipur in which more than 40,000 people from all over Rajasthan participated. They had understood the meaning of minimum wages much as we in this conference would have understood it. Their understanding is not less in terms of quality, but their expression is different. They know that the price of edible oil today is between ₹ 90 to ₹ 120 a kilo; *dal* has gone up to ₹ 60 to ₹ 90 a kilo. The most ordinary vegetable today is ₹ 30 a kilo. We say to them that we will not pay them a minimum wage of ₹ 135 or ₹ 112, and that is also linked to a task. They can't obtain the wage unless they produce the task, they have to fulfill certain norms set for production. I am saying this because most people here may not know the details but form opinions that matter to us. Therefore, the wage is important. Even if we say that the minimum wage is ₹ 135, most people will get ₹ 90, ₹ 100 or ₹ 85 or ₹ 112, depending on the quantum of work they turn out at the worksite. So when we talk about wages, we refer to what Mrs Gandhi said; that it is justice that the Constitution promises us. We have the right to a wage. If we tamper with that wage, we really tamper with many things. The NREGA, which gives us the right to 100 day work guarantee, cannot destroy another right, which is as fundamental, or even more so. Somewhere, we have to look at it from everyone's perspective and point of view.

I shall quickly go through other issues. We have not had enough time in this discussion. Apart from the panel speakers, none of us have been able to develop a single idea. We have come out with strong but extremely simplistic one-liners. I have not burnt the effigy of a computer ever and do believe in the biometric system. But then there's something like the UID, whose technology may be perfect, but whose political use one is not sure of, or the use of the particular technology. One can't diminish the argument by saying that people are always against technology. It is also true that no matter what the technology is, it can't deal with social injustice and corruption. Those ills need another set of tools. Technology must somehow go into this system and for that, a lot more dialogue is needed.

One of the sentences in the Act is reason for extreme worry. We need space to talk about these concerns. We want to know who will store the information. We are told that it will all be stored very carefully, but that is not enough for us. We want to know whether it will be an open or controlled system. There are so many questions we now have to ask, which we didn't know, say, a year ago. But now because of the UID, we've learnt and therefore need to know about this. I want to table this because it is being dismissed as either an anti- or pro-technology argument. I don't think most of us are anti-technology today. We cannot afford to be; we use ATM cards, travel in planes and use computers. But it is a question of how it is politically used. I wanted to say this because there has been a lot of argument and controversy about this issue.

The other thing that we have understood is the fine print. The British left us a legacy when they said that "the devil lies in the detail." Believe me, the right to information campaign has taught us that. Over and over again, we have accessed documents and have read the fine print. It is the fine print that really makes or mars things, as a bureaucrat knows very well. But people now have started understanding the fine print. So what we really need to develop is a discussion of the fine print. We also need to understand that we need platforms for discourse. The concept of a partial engagement, which is what we call it, is extremely important for the development of social democracy. We are not here to fight each other. We are struggling to find even ground. That struggle takes a lot of give and take and it is extremely worrying because we too have mandates. We have to go back to people and explain why things are like this. Someone may have a political party, someone else may have a government system; we all have different places to go back to.

One of the means of partial engagement has been the National Advisory Council. There was the National Common Minimum Programme. These are attempts to look at how there can be partial engagement. It is possible for one to agree on many things but disagree on many others. How do we settle disputes, disagreements and differences? If we do not have platforms to resolve these conflicts, we will never come together. No matter how good the economics is, or how good the political intentions are, we will have to develop these platforms. They have to be many more than the ones we have today. They may deal with political intent and political strategy, with economics, capital and labour, legalities and a number of other issues. Those platforms have to be provided in India for resolutions to be achieved. How we are going to do it is a challenge.

Mirai Chatterjee

I want to say something on social protection. I strongly endorse Prof Bardhan's view that social protection has to be part of our social democracy project, process or society. I want to give two examples from the social protection arena, but before that I want to say that social protection is not just insurance. Our experience of working with poor women in health care, child care, insurance or risk mitigation, pension, housing and basic services has also been alluded to. But I also want to talk a little about the architecture and design. Here, I want to give examples from our experience with two government programmes with quite different outcomes.

One is the National Rural Health Mission (NRHM), which I think is a work in progress as so much else is. We are now beginning to see results in many states. I would argue that one of the reasons for this is that there is a constant dialogue and discussion with civil society, particularly the community health movement. This movement has been very involved in the planning and tweaking of the programme, with sometimes quite radical changes. There has been a kind of bottom-up push, if I may say so. Some of the interesting things that have come out are what we have been talking about. For example, there is a lot more discussion about district-level health plans and going right down to village people developing health plans, village health and sanitation committees, Rogi Kalyan Samitis, primary health centres and the community hospital CHCs, which are ideas whose time has come. But these are ideas that were definitely not in any of our earlier plans. Of course, there is a lot of room for improvement, but what we are finding is that when poor people, particularly women and the *dais* (mid-wives) are sitting on these village health sanitation committees, and have ₹ 10,000 of untied funds for the first time to be used, they begin to ask the nurses where those ten thousand rupees have gone.

Why is that money being used for tables, chairs and curtains instead of for cleaning their village? An important process starts in this manner. Thus, there is some positive news from the NRHM. On the other hand, what has also been alluded to, the Rashtriya Swasthya Bima Yojana—health insurance, I am a bit embarrassed to say, has been partly designed based on the SEWA community. What came out finally was quite different. In the beginning, we were quite keen that the planning, implementation and handholding should be democratised, rather like the NRHM experience. But there were no monies and resources allocated for education of the poor on insurance, which is a new concept for most Indians. The same goes for handholding. In many states, one of the developments noticed was that in the first year, people simply didn't claim because they had no idea how to claim. They had no idea how to navigate the private and public hospitals. Frankly speaking, the net subsidy went to the insurance companies, who hardly needed subsidies.

From these experiences, we have learnt that when we are designing these kinds of programmes, we not only need to consult with as many groups as possible, we need to remain open to changing the architecture. The design should be such that it is as close as possible to the poor, particularly women, and the poorest of communities. It should be by the people and also of the people. They should feel a sense of ownership, as they begin to do in the village health and sanitation committees. Most importantly, they should promote collective action, because it is very difficult for the poor, especially women and indigenous tribal people, to withstand all the pushes and pulls, the forces they face every day. But if these programmes could also promote collective action, maybe they would have a chance.

I also want to make a quick point on urban development. I'd like to correct the impression some of our colleagues have created that growth has happened only because of a few sectors of the economy. Many economists have put a figure to it—about 60 per cent of India's GDP comes from the informal economy. The growth and the prosperity that we see have been because of the collective efforts of so many Indians, particularly the poorest in our country. In the urban areas, people like street vendors don't ask for anything more than to be left in peace and be provided earmarked markets. Yet they are kicked around, hounded, their baskets are overturned and they are beaten by the police. How long are we going to continue with this? We will have to have a law that will permit markets for them. Everyone else is acquiring markets, like Nano cars and low-price markets. Why can't this section of people also have their own markets?

The other issue is on basic services. Again, we need to pay a lot of attention to working examples. Gujarat may not be known as a good example in certain aspects of public life, but in one area in Ahmedabad city, we had a joint programme with the local municipal corporation. Costing ₹ 20,000 per family, seven basic services, including a toilet and tap in every home, have been provided in many slums, though not all. It is a joint effort with a community contribution, contributions from business and large contributions by the municipal corporation. I believe that these are the kinds of bottom-up and collaborative examples that we need to look at more when we design programmes, so that the process of social democracy is also furthered.

Manish Sabharwal

There are ideas to create infrastructure of opportunity other than paying minimum wages in NREGA and confiscating 25 per cent of school capacity. We can't give up in frustration that we can't execute what we say and therefore, we will try something else. If social democracy is about humanising markets then we must think about the labour market. We have to worry about the labour market because the most important decision that a child in India makes is choosing its parents wisely. We accept that but then there are three problems in the labour markets. There is a matching problem, which is connecting demand to supply; there is a mismatch problem, which is repairing supply for demand and there is a pipeline problem, which is preparing supply for demand. These rights, resources and outcomes and the role of the private sector are much related points. They are not mutually exclusive and the resources and the outcomes on which money is spent are the 3Es—education, employment and employability. In the last 10 years, money has not been the issue. It is the outcomes. It is the need for a different recipe. All the units of delivery, employment exchanges, ITIs and schools have all the money they need. But they don't have performance management; they don't have the fear of falling in the hope of rising.

Is money an issue? No. The focus on plumbing and execution is not a lack of ambition; it is actually higher ambition. We are saying we don't want to do this for 30 million people but for 400 million people and we want to do it for the rest of our lives. The difference between a baby and a dwarf is not more food or money. The difference between a dwarf and a baby is in the DNA and architectures. How do we construct these three Es to scale? Cost, quality and scale are dilemmas that India faces, which is pretty unique. We can lower cost, raise quality and improve scale.

From a labour market perspective, the execution of plumbing is very important. After Nandan has finished with his job, from my perspective, there are five revolutions which can happen in the labour market, purely in the private sector. We can develop a loan market; we can get 50 per cent of employees who are migrants to open bank accounts, along with backpack benefits. Fifty (50) per cent of provident accounts are dormant. It is not stupidity on the part of the people but lack of access that is the hindrance. Most importantly, we can verify education degrees and have a skill registry. Ten (10) per cent of the people who take exams are not the people who are supposed to give the exams in India. Twenty five (25)per cent of the education degrees we get very often are fudged. I think the plumbing is going to enable a sort of revolution.

Then there is the role of the private sector. One million people will join the labour force every month for the next 20 years, these people have to be educated, assessed, counselled, given apprenticeships and hired. It is unclear whether the delivery systems that are creaking currently will be able to do it. In India, more people have cell phones than toilets. There are two ways we can think about that. We can have the Right to the Toilet Act and confiscate 25 per cent of the toilet capacity or we could appreciate the wonderful partnership the government has had with the private sector in getting cell phones to everybody and replicate that. There might be a 'right to a toilet' which enables that partnership. But it is unclear to me that it is needed. I don't live in a village but 60 per cent of our children come from villages and are migrants. All they care about really is the three Es. They have ambitions and aspirations, and are contactable by SMS. I think that the very fundamental access they have is very important now, from a labour market perspective. If the execution is as important as the vision, then you can have contempt for plumbing but it does not scale or sustain. Note what the private sector has demonstrated. Chanda Kochhar spoke about ATM centres across the country, with cell phones being issued to customers every two minutes. Regarding execution capability, what educators need is exactly what they are looking for. These points of rights, private sector outcomes and resources are very closely related if we think through without the partition in our cerebral cortex which we sometimes approach them with.

Anusha Rizvi

I am a filmmaker from the broad base. I want to point out that the last two days have been a fascinating conference for me, something I have experienced for the first time. The references, the way we refer to our own community, to people, workers, weavers and the other small people have been quite eye-opening. When Mr Abhijit Sen spoke about people and mentioned community, that was the only time there was any sense of togetherness as far as I could make out. In that situation, when we talk about a moral duty to give to people, I am afraid I completely disagree with it, because it is not a moral duty at all. It is their right and we have not given them their right. Maybe, my understanding is not correct. To Nandan Nilekani, I want to say that I'm extremely worried. When we are talking about technology, we are not either anti- or pro-technology but we would like to know who owns that technology and who will be the one controlling it?

Rohan Samarajiva

I would talk on my idea of social democracy and how I would recognise it when I see it. I was given a clue by Mr Kelkar's presentation, when he spoke about the trust deficit. It seems to me that a society where there would be reciprocity, trust, and all good things would be a sort of social democracy. The fact that I don't have to be a slave somewhere in the 19th or 20th century is itself significant. We can move beyond the language to the essence of it. In this session we are focusing on the architecture, the plumbing, of how to do things. We must take into account that we have a trust deficit in our societies. We trust our immediate families and maybe the people from our villages but not other people in our country or even people in the next village or in the other community. We have to address that.

One of the things that Pratap Bhanu Mehta brought up is the importance of designing social instruments that do not exacerbate trust problems and do not cause us to separate ourselves too much. That is a very persuasive argument for universality but then we have to go to simplicity, it seems, going by Michael's argument. We have to go to much simpler systems where we don't really have to distinguish between different groups. If our overall objective is what we have been talking about, it is a sort of end-game. What we want to become, the house we want to live in, should be one that has greater trust. Whatever solutions we come out with should be such that lead to a reduction in the trust deficit, rather than those that seek to be precise. This comes to a certain extent from all the work we have done in infrastructure and our ideas of theoretical optimal solutions. But theoretical optimal solutions don't work in a number of countries because the conditions are not right for theoretical optimal infrastructure solutions. We can come up with very fancy regulatory agencies but when people don't have respect for contracts or when the regulatory agency does not have people who are honest or capable or competent in skills, they don't work.

Niraja Gopal Jayal

I just want to engage a little bit with Abhijit Sen, particularly his account of the Directive Principles of State Policy. In cloaking them in this mantle of virtue, I have a little bit of difficulty only because the Directive Principles were a product of a compromise. They are an extremely watered down version of what many leaders of the national movement, predominantly Nehru in 1929, Ambedkar in the Constituent Assembly, and a radical Bombay economist by the name of K.T. Shah who wanted to constitutionalise the right to work, strongly advocated. All of these are part of the records of the Constituent Assembly. It is just that the Directive Principles were the product of a political compromise. I think we need to keep that in mind. When we speak about the house which the Directive Principles represent, by the way, there was an interim stage when they considered it calling the 'fundamental principles of the governance' and finally settled for this phrase from the Irish Constitution. This house as Abhijit Sen terms it, these so-called rights which are not really rights but principles, were locked away in the basement and have only begun to come out 60 years later. You say that people can wait and are willing to wait but I really don't think so. I think it is unacceptable that we should expect people to wait for 60 years for things that should have been available to them but have begun to be available in only very recent times. Since Abhijit is another incarnation of my colleague in the Jawaharlal Nehru University, I should mention to him that every few years we get a letter from government, which asks: "what have you done to implement the Directive Principles of State Policy?" We never respond to it; after all, what can we do? I just hope that civil servants and politicians get such letters as well.

Anu Aga

I just want to add to what you have said. After over 60 years, in malnourishment we are the worst in the world. In education, though we have the Right to Education, the quality of education is so poor that poor children will be at a disadvantage for decades because of the kind of education they get. Against this background, what can we do? It has been said for years that out of every rupee the government spends, 85 paise is wasted on mismanagement and corruption. Is there something we can do; we the civil society, corporates and politicians here? If we have the will to do something, we can take up small areas—not the whole country which may be impossible—but small areas and demonstrate with the help of all these three, how at least 50-60 per cent can go to the poor. Then we are really talking of bridging the inequity gap. Otherwise, it is just theoretical talk here and everything will remain the same. Can we do something about this? I really feel that unless we address this issue, it will really be one more nice conference.

Montek Singh Ahluwalia

One is a point that I want to respond to and one is a commercial for the Planning Commission. The last one will be quite brief. The point which I want to respond to is something that Abhijit Sen raised. Mirai Chatterjee touched upon it. In the last four or five years, we have been doing PPPs with the big corporate sector. I think some of them are producing results and certainly producing some physical infrastructure.

The second issue is of why we are not using government money to energise the wonderful work being done by NGOs. To my knowledge, SEWA is the best example of this but there are many others that I am aware of. Why are we not using this money to support these activities? It is a very major question. All these things are actually delivered at the local level. The only thing that the central government can do is to facilitate state governments to use this money in support of local civil society PPPs.

Sometimes, the legal structure can create a problem. For example, in the Right to Information Act, the centre has to give money and we are doing so, of that you can be sure. Technically, nothing stops a state government from saying that every child must have an education, I believe these NGOs are doing an excellent job and I am going to give some of my money to them. They can do it but they don't actually do it. I think one of the reasons they don't do it is that money goes from a central government silo called education to a state government silo called education. There it is actually being used down the silo to multiply the public system. Many people have told me that there is even a danger of this sort of publicly supported money crowding out what is actually very good private activity on the ground. We do need to think hard about this.

Just let people know we are engaged with Mr Kapil Sibal in designing a PPP framework for the 2500 model schools which are going to be set up as part of our education strategy but those happen to be schools that the central government has decided to set up. Had we simply said that we are just going to give money to the states, then the states would be setting up these schools. The reason why we can do this PPP is because they are central government schools and I hope that they are set up. Then in two to three years, they would produce a lot of awareness that things are very good and good examples would replicate themselves. It helps what Abhay Bang and Rani Bang are doing in Gadchiroli. It is one of the remotest districts one can think of. They seem to have cut the infant mortality rate in half, whereas much more money being sent to various publicly funded outlets does not seem to be achieving the same result. Across the board, I think this is something that we want to do in the Twelfth Plan; we want to think of how the central government could facilitate efforts in each of these areas. If the state governments want to do it with civil society, we should simply let them do so. We could even incentivise. For example, the normal rule is that we share 75 per cent of the cost but we could do it through a PPP with the civil society organisation and share 85 per cent of the cost. That will cost us a little more money but will incentivise things. This has been a useful session for me because we do need to think about these things.

Lastly, I also want to respond to Aruna Roy. I share her view completely that we need many more platforms. Incidentally, for the record, we are great supporters of the Right to Information Act. I have not known a single person in government who has expressed reservations on the Right to Information Act. I think it has done tremendous good but the platform issue is important. Please go through the website of the Planning Commission and you will get, in the bottom right-hand corner, a little note saying "Approach to the Twelfth Plan" which we are now working on. If you click on that, you will go to a whole strategy matrix where things like governance, management of natural resources etc., are all shown under columns and the traditional sectors, agriculture, education, health etc., are shown under rows. In each of these cells, you can click and give us your ideas. We are going beyond just interaction with civil society, which is also happening. We are simply opening it up. So far, we have received about 15,000 hits on this, but the interesting thing is that 48 per cent are from the United States. I am pleased by the interest shown by the NRI population and academics. I have now put this advertisement everywhere and if the organisers give me the emails of all the participants, I would send you the details on emails. We really want to get ideas, particularly from the younger people. The truth is that all members of the Planning Commission and the Deputy Chairman set up committees of their generation and individuals who don't get a foot in for another 35 to 40 years probably have the brightest ideas.

Rob Riemen

I was puzzled by Pranab Bardhan's conclusion in what I thought was a supreme paper and talk, but it seems to me that your conclusion and its implications are in contradiction to the rest of what you said. You conclude your paper with a statement that the negative critique of capitalism that comes from the Left and from followers of Mahatma Gandhi is 'not matched' by a convincing alternative system that can generate the necessary surplus. I can quote Churchill's famous statement that democracy is a bad model but there is nothing better we have. I don't want to apply this to the idea and ideology of capitalism because what we see now, what we have seen before and what we will see again and again, is that capitalism is essentially a destructive force. The financial crisis is a crisis of capitalism and brings poverty, unemployment and exclusion. In fact, the environmental crisis is essentially a crisis of capitalism.

The incapacity of the Americans to create an affordable health care system is related to capitalism. Also, regarding the deep crisis of education—and with this, I want to include Harvard and Yale—we have to keep in mind the fact that if we make a list of people who are quintessentially responsible for the present financial crisis, they are all alumni of Harvard and Yale. They promote the myth in a big way that they are educating the leaders of the world. I sent a message and a mail to Harvard and Yale asking what went wrong with their form of education. I haven't got an answer yet and perhaps never will. There is something fundamentally wrong with capitalism and you can see it in America. Everybody who is there can face it, because it literally gets in your face through television, which wants you to believe that being rich is the most important thing in life. It has a tremendous effect on the identity of millions of kids not only in America, but also in that part of the world in which I live. They feel you are somebody only if you 'make it' and if you 'don't make it', you are a loser and a nobody. Who are the real heroes of American and European society? They are the rich, the billionaires, the bankers, etc. The big mistake social democracy made in the West is that at its very mould, it made the false promise that it can make everybody rich. It is a false promise because it cannot be realised. That is why people have lost a lot of faith in social democracy. To put the record straight, I'm in favour of free trade, private property, entrepreneurship and even more in favour of craftsmanship and the argument that people should pay for what they value. But the core mission of social democracy should always be that capitalism can never be the ruling world view. I read letters of a lot of people following Mahatma Gandhi that their criticism is this kind of criticism. It is essential to make sure that capitalism can never be the ruling world view, because if it is, as it is already in America and most of Europe, let us remember that these are the places from where all these crises come from.

Bina Agarwal

I want to go back to this whole thing about rights-based legislation which we agree has universal qualities. But I think it is useful to distinguish between two types of rights-based legislation. In 2005, the UPA government passed four significant pieces of rights-based legislation, bottom-up, RTI, NREGA, the Domestic Violence Act and an amendment to the Hindu Succession Act to give women equal rights as men to agricultural land. The first two are sort of policy-based rights. The passing of the acts itself requires and calls for implementation and so NGOs and government have proactively pushed the RTI and NREGA, but what about the others? I think these two are also very significant. If we take the Domestic Violence Act, it is a right to bodily integrity; you can pose it in terms of a capability approach. The Inheritance Act, in so far as it brings in rights to agricultural land, is absolutely critical for the right to livelihood. We do need different approaches and I am saying this both in terms of significant civil society actors and government where it requires individuals to be proactive to assert those rights. I hate the word plumbing but I prefer the word architecture and support systems for these other kinds of rights. Many rights, if you look at them, would be the second category of rights.

I also want to argue against what has become what I have called in my recent book, a lateral entry approach to policymaking. What do I mean by that? It is not merely setting up a committee, and inviting one's colleagues and so on, but a consultation with NGOs which has become common. In the next Five-Year Plan, we have these consultation committees. I feel that unless those who come feel that they have something important to say and do represent some branch of civil society, without processes in place whereby we can vet out what people want, things will not go very far.

I will give you two examples of something that I call dole and bowl. The discussion on this ₹ 5000 income supplement kicked off with Aruna Roy who said it is a dole, and Sunil Khilnani and perhaps Pranab Bardhan who said that it is a claim, it is a bowl. It seems to me the difference between the two was that it has not gone through a process.

Suppose villagers had said that they wanted the ₹ 5000 supplement and it came bottom-up, you might call it a claim but otherwise it becomes a dole. I feel this is important because this is what is happening when we are talking about minimum wages for NREGA and this sort of supplement. For instance, why aren't we talking about that ₹ 5000—Pranab Bardhan opted for ₹ 10000—buying a health insurance for all families if we agree that health is so significant, rather than giving out money for all the reasons that you yourself raise in your paper? We are giving out cash transfers to the man or the woman in the house; why not buy something that is useful and universal in that sense? I am not saying we should go down that route, but the point is we should not have lateral entry decisions which come in. On your website too, Montek, 48 per cent responses are from the United States with a lot of lateral entry going on there as well. I think this is a significant aspect of social democracy; we don't have enough answers but we do need to have deliberative spaces of decision-making and voices and need to think about institutions which go beyond local government.

Pranab Bardhan

Nobody is saying that capitalism does not have problems. In fact, I could add 20 more problems of capitalism to what you mentioned. My point was that I am quite used to seeing accounts of the problems of capitalism. I have also seen accounts of positive alternatives but to me, the positive alternatives that I often see make me worry sometimes as they are quite often too idealistic and too good. I would like to believe in them. But maybe it is my fault. As an economist, I would like to see an underlying inventive mechanism which will make it sustainable, which will generate a sustainable system of innovations, because that is what capitalism with all its imperfections, with all its injustices, to some extent has delivered.

Unfortunately, history has not yet given us enough of a large systemic alternative. In some cases, the non-capitalistic alternatives failed miserably. There are context-specific reasons for those. Essentially, I would like to see a viable alternative clearly specifying the mechanism which will make it sustainable. I can give you stories about small-level success but I am talking about large systemic alternatives. If anybody can provide some, I would be very willing to look at it, at least if not as an economist, because of a general interest in the socialist principles I believe in.

Bina, I don't disagree with you, but I do want to mention that you talked about the health programme *versus* giving a basic income supplement etc. I can give you plenty of other programmes; the problem is quite often that whenever you target it to a specific programme, in the implementation stage, there mainly arises what economists call an agency problem. You get somebody to do it but then this will be available to so and so, in implementing it, with conditionality. There will be problems of agency. The issue is therefore the basic supplement; if somebody wants to buy health insurance, nobody is stopping them. But as I mentioned earlier, merely giving them cash will not do. One needs other kinds of assistance and information, particularly in health, because most people make wrong choices even in health. That is why I said cash transfers by themselves are not enough.

Section IV

The Social and Political Context of Social Democracy in India

Given endemic blockages to state capacity, can the goals of social democracy be realised through more participatory, decentralised methods? Given cleavages and the electoral incentives towards polarisation, how can more universalist conceptions of social democratic provision be sustained? The political and social conditions in India present particular challenges for a social democratic project, and this section addresses some of these.

BACKGROUND PAPERS

- Niraja Gopal Jayal
- Sudipta Kaviraj
- Steven Wilkinson
- Yogendra Yadav

35

NIRAJA GOPAL JAYAL

Decentralisation and the Prospects of Social Democracy in India

We live in an age which is prone to celebrate democracy without prefixes or suffixes, without conditions or caveats. By common consensus, the only way in which democracy in this sense can better itself is by its deepening, and one of the important indicators of this deepening is more substantive participation –or "empowered participatory governance."[1] While participatory budgeting in Porto Allegre has become the emblematic exhibit of this phenomenon, participation in the institutions of local governance has become the template for the creation of empowered citizens. The local is now the premier site for the practice of citizenship. The implications of such a localisation of citizenship for welfare provisioning are at best uncertain, though the history of conceptual friendships and animosities could be read in a way that generates concern, especially in times when the idea of welfare itself has gone out of fashion.

The 21st century opened with a decisive rejection of the welfare-state models of the two previous centuries. Though the architect of the 20th century welfare-state was Beveridge, authorship of the first welfare-state of the 19th century is generally attributed to Bismarck.[2] The Beveridgian welfare-state in Britain represented an advance over the Bismarckian[3] model, as it was the first unified and universal system of social security providing, more generously

1. Fung and Wright (2003).
2. Bismarck's social legislation—health Insurance, accident insurance and old age and disability insurance—was ironically inspired by his desire to keep the socialists at bay.
3. The Bismarckian system of social insurance was financed through contributions and therefore provided assistance only to those who were employed. The Beveridgian system was universal and financed by taxation, and as such a redistributive model.

and therefore at a much higher cost, social protection for individual citizens. Today, as we approach the end of the first decade of this century, the illusion of its opening years, that welfare has crossed its sell-by date, increasingly lacks credence. The need to reinstate welfare and revisit social democracy is back on the intellectual agenda in Europe.[4] It has become apparent that providing social security, in a period of economic crisis, is not merely a social but also an economic, imperative.[5]

Curiously, the 21st century certitude that the very idea of welfare is an obsolete irrelevance was eagerly embraced by many countries of the global South. If the resuscitation of some form of welfare-state now seems warranted, it is also clear that welfare-states will have to be re-invented in context-specific ways. Among the countries of the global South, Brazil has already put in place an impressively wide-ranging programme of social insurance—most notably in employment, education, health and food security—in the implementation of which local governments are centrally involved.[6] In India, we are observing—arguably for the first time since Independence, even if somewhat puzzling given the current neo-liberal context—serious policy attention to social and economic rights.

These rights of social citizenship[7] lie at the core of social democracy, which therefore signals the ever-present but rarely remembered limits of an exclusively political understanding of democracy. It reminds us that a formally democratic polity in

---

4. Cf. The Policy Network's *Where Now For European Social Democracy?* arising out of a seminar of British, French and German social democrats.

5. In Michael Cichon's (2009) words, "In times of crisis, transfer incomes, notably social assistance and social security benefits paid to unemployed workers and other vulnerable recipients, act as social and economic stabilisers. Benefits not only prevent people from falling further into poverty but also limit the contraction of aggregate demand, thereby curtailing the potential depth of the recession."

6. Brazil has adopted a redistributive model, though it has had lower levels of economic growth than India. Ravallion (2009) argues that the Indian problem is not so much the lack of good policies for poverty reduction as the capture of policies by groups that are not poor, and weak state capability for delivering basic public services.

7. The idea of 'social citizenship' refers to T.H. Marshall's (1950: 11) definition of it as "the whole range from the right to a modicum of economic welfare and security to the right to share to the full in the social heritage and to live the life of a civilised being according to the standards prevailing in the society."

which citizens lack entitlements to a reasonable share of the social product—minimally, to provide the conditions of well-being that give them meaningful opportunities to realise their capabilities—is an incomplete and unsatisfactory form of democracy.

Can decentralised institutions of local governance be more effective guarantors of social citizenship than the centralised welfare-states conventionally associated with social democracy? This paper explores the possible place of decentralisation in an Indian social democratic project. It does so in three sections, the first of which asks the apparently provocative but simple question: are social democracy and decentralisation compatible? The paper argues that in contrast to recent western experience, in which decentralisation is associated with policies antithetical to social democracy, the Indian approach to decentralisation is designed to advance, rather than curtail, a broadly welfarist agenda. The second part of the paper evaluates the record and potential of the Indian project of decentralisation in the last two decades, specifically the conditions under which the recently created panchayati raj institutions[8] may be said to advance a social democratic agenda, admittedly through the promotion of inclusion and social justice, rather than in the ways conventionally associated with conceptions of social democracy. The third and final section of the paper identifies the potential of and the challenges to a realisation of the goals of social democracy through decentralisation.

I

Are decentralisation and social democracy compatible?

Across the world, in the last two decades, the rediscovery of decentralisation has been associated with a rejection of social democracy. India's recent experiment with decentralisation is a striking repudiation of that association. Neither did decentralisation come to India, as it did in many other countries of the global South, as a prescription from the Bretton Woods institutions. It is worth

8. Panchayati Raj Institutions (known as PRIs) are elected local bodies at three levels from the district to the village.

recalling when, why and how decentralisation and participation began to feature in the Indian policy and political imagination.

India does not have a history of social democracy in the way that many European countries do. Welfare in India was an integral part of the project of development. The founders of the Indian republic, circa 1950, had favoured a centralised model of development, in which the state alone could be entrusted with the task of advancing the welfare of the poor, and should therefore also be responsible for the creation of the social product through its assumption of a commanding role in the economy. The nearest approximation to social democracy in India therefore was in 'dirigiste' economic policies in the sphere of production. As far as the distributive dimension was concerned, unlike the west, where the rights of social citizenship were a core component of social democracy, the idea of welfare in India was not expressed in the language of rights, but of state paternalism. The state of independent India is thus more accurately described as an interventionist state with a developmentalist orientation than a welfare state. Even so, the creation of the social product and its distribution were conjoined, at least in aspiration.

This was of course entirely in consonance with the times, as social democracy in Europe was historically associated with top-down centralised welfare-states. In Britain, in particular, following T.H. Marshall's (1950) declaration that the citizenship whose history he was tracing was by definition national, the basis of the welfare-state was that 'need' rather than 'geography' should determine the distribution of welfare benefits, and therefore devolution negated the purposes of such a state. (Wincott, 2009: 40)

In the post-Cold War world, centralised governance became substantially discredited with the collapse of the erstwhile socialist states, on the one hand, and the whittling down of welfare state apparatuses, on the other. In Western Europe and North America, a reduction in the role of the state as well as its decentralisation was part of the institutional response to the fiscal crisis and the growing restlessness with large and ineffectual public sector bureaucracies, paralleling the ideological shift from state to market. As the legitimacy of the public sector as a service provider was called into question, decentralisation was presented as a component of the strategy to manage the economic crisis by allowing for greater local diversity in public service delivery, and as part of the search for the appropriate 'institutional mix' for an effective state-society synergy. In the enterprise of 'reinventing government' advocated by new public management, decentralisation was endorsed because it would further efficiency and economy. The contracting out of public service delivery to non-governmental and private agencies, or in partnership with these, had the same rationale.

The state, which had long been viewed as beneficent and kind, now suddenly appeared as a nasty overbearing beast, the hollowing out of which could be nicely compensated by markets as well as that new repository of social virtue and social capital, civil society. The acknowledgment of the market and civil society as actors in the new governance-speak signalled recognition of a horizontal displacement of national power. Simultaneously, vertical displacements—upwards and downwards—were also occurring, as a response to institutions of global governance, on the one hand, and to demands for devolution, on the other. Decentralisation thus became a part of the strategy of questioning and limiting centralised state power.

In this framework, the advocacy of decentralisation also purveyed a new model of citizenship. The critics of social democracy alleged that the highly interventionist welfare-state had created a community of selfish parasitical citizens, passive recipients of welfare, jealously guarding the entitlements guaranteed to them by the state, but completely unmindful of their own obligations and duties as citizens. Now, people were increasingly placed in charge of their own destinies. They were expected to be active republican citizens, preferably joining hands with other citizens—as Robert Putnam's (1993) book on the central role of social capital in the success of Italian democracy had urged—and the local was the obvious, because most proximate, site for their participation. Rights and entitlements however were not elements of this view of citizenship.

In India in the early 1990s, the shift away from state interventionism was also occasioned by economic (balance of payments) crisis; greater freedom for the market was justified as a remedy for governance failure; and there was a renewed appreciation of the virtues of civil society, and even the off-loading of some developmental burdens on to non-governmental organisations, with the expectation that these would be more effectively accomplished with people's participation.

The imperative for decentralisation was a deliberate way of addressing the democratic deficit in the polity and potentially enlarging the scope of citizens' entitlements.

> A wide chasm separated the largest body of the electorate from a small number of its elected representatives. This gap has been occupied by the power brokers, the middlemen and vested interests....With the passage of this Bill, the *panchayats* would emerge as a firm building block of administration and development....as an instrument in the consolidation of democracy at the grassroots (Prime Minister Rajiv Gandhi, 1989).

In 1992, the Indian Constitution was amended to give citizens greater voice in determining local developmental priorities and, through reservations for women, Dalits and *adivasis* (historically disadvantaged groups), to advance the project of social justice as well. By the 73rd and 74th Amendments to the Constitution, the *panchayats* and municipalities, in the rural and urban areas respectively, were entrusted with the task of formulating and implementing plans for economic development and social justice. These, it is worth noting, are the only clauses of the Indian Constitution where the phrase 'social justice' occurs.

There was, however, an important difference with the West, where the imperative of governance reforms, including decentralisation, was essentially administrative. In India, on the other hand, the imperative for decentralisation was political rather than administrative. Indeed, it could be argued that the administrative aspects have received rather less attention than they deserved, as this was in its intent an emphatically normative project of greater inclusion. As such, it had two central components: first, 'voice', as it sought to give people the power to determine their developmental priorities and participate in planning for economic development; and second, 'inclusion', as it sought to guarantee the representation of historically disadvantaged and marginalised groups—notably, the scheduled castes, scheduled tribes and women —ensuring their participation in the first process. Democratisation and decentralisation were thus indissolubly united.

The aspiration to provide opportunities for voice and participation to all citizens, but especially those belonging to disadvantaged groups, was therefore only tangentially a project of social citizenship. Though social and economic rights have been on the Indian political agenda since the Motilal Nehru Committee Report of 1928, the Indian Constitution placed these rights in the non-justiciable and non-enforceable chapter titled "Directive Principles of State Policy." State response to these rights has been at best ambivalent till recently, when, arguably for the first time since independence, there has been an attempt to not just legislate social rights, but also to support civil society action in empowering citizens to demand and monitor these. The new guarantees of social rights include the right to work—to be implemented through the *panchayats*—the right to education and even the (impending) right to food. On the one hand, high rates of economic growth make the prospects for financing social rights brighter than ever before. On the other hand, the same challenges of state capacity and the micro-politics of power as afflicted earlier initiatives threaten to bedevil their realisation. The next section comments on the performance of decentralised governance in India and analyses its potential for guaranteeing social citizenship.

II

Decentralisation and the possibilities of social citizenship in india

An appreciation of the specific purposes and design of the Indian project of democratic decentralisation is essential to evaluating its potential as an instrument of social democracy. Instead of a focus on the more technical aspects of social democracy, I essay an interpretation of social citizenship, howsoever limited, and the potential of decentralisation to help realise it. Given the overlap, in Indian society, between material deprivation and forms of cultural exclusion, policies aiming at the inclusion of members of disadvantaged groups may be viewed as plausible candidates for social citizenship. While it is true that rights of recognition do not strictly count as social rights, not least because such rights are usually attached to individuals rather than communities, they can be seen as forms of social rights because discrimination and exclusion based on social and cultural identity overlap with deprivation and even destitution. The role of *panchayats* therefore needs to be examined in terms of two aspects of social citizenship: first, material outcomes in terms of better targeting and delivery of public services; and second, symbolic goods. There are important obstacles to both, but equally some positive developments on both these dimensions.

The intellectual pedigree of the Indian idea of decentralisation can be traced back to John Stuart Mill who argued that local political institutions are "a school of political capacity", making citizens capable of genuine and informed participation. Implicit in this argument is the belief that the quality of political participation, and therefore of public life itself, will be substantively transformed only when people foregather to collectively debate and deliberate on issues of common concern, and are provided with decision-making powers to give effect to their shared consensus. This argument of enhancing the political competence of citizens informed the Indian embrace of decentralisation, as did the weaker and more instrumentalist view of decentralisation as a mode of decision-making that is informed by and responsive to local interests and local knowledge. The idea that centralised decision-making can only provide inappropriately uniform solutions to diverse local problems is self-evidently compelling in the context of large and heterogeneous societies like India.

Historically, India has had *panchayats* based on caste or territoriality (the village) and some of these have endured to the present day, usually in forms we would be reluctant to embrace. These were not traditionally democratic or elected bodies, much less participatory in nature. Where they have endured, they tend to be oppressively conservative, and not averse even to the use of brute force.[9] The Constitution of India 1950 placed *panchayats* in the non-justiciable Directive Principles of State Policy, treading a path of cautious neutrality between the romantic Gandhian view of India as a constellation of village republics, based on the principle of village self-sufficiency, on the one hand, and the rival vision of the Indian village described by Dr. Ambedkar as a "sink of localism, den of ignorance and narrow-mindedness", on the other. Ambedkar's opposition to decentralisation may seem puzzling given his simultaneous commitment to a social democratic position, and his legitimate conviction that political democracy in India would remain imperilled so long as social and economic equality were denied. The first could be explained by his personal experience of the oppression encountered by Dalits in rural India, and the second by the influence of the dominant idea of the times that welfare tasks are best accomplished by centralised states. Nevertheless, it is notable that Jawaharlal Nehru's commitment to the same principles of social democracy, and his pre-eminent role in shaping an interventionist welfare-state did not preclude a sympathetic approach to decentralisation.

There is now strong evidence to suggest that, despite his commitment to centralised state-led development, Nehru also recognised that effective rural development needed popular participation and frequently expressed his support for *panchayati raj* (Manor, 2010: 63). Not only was Nehru receptive to the ideas of the American architect Albert Mayer for initiating in 1948 a pilot project of the community development programme, he saw such projects, according to Alice Thorner, as "a school in which valuable lessons might be learned on how to mobilize the rural masses for developmental activities" (Thorner, 1981: 120). Unsurprisingly, bureaucratic resentment had much to do with its failure. Despite many subsequent state-level attempts at institutionalising *panchayats*, and a plethora of periodically commissioned official reports on the subject, *panchayats* remained a phenomenon confined

9. The evidence on these is rather mixed. In recent times, customary institutions like *khap panchayats* in the northern Indian state of Haryana that have levied extreme sanctions—from social ostracism to killing—on young people who defy social custom to marry a person of their choice. On the other hand, there is also some evidence of customary *panchayats* in Karnataka that engage in service delivery functions (AnanthPur, 2007).

to particular states at particular points in time, till the enactment of the 73rd and 74th Constitutional Amendments which decentralised power to rural and urban local bodies respectively.

The 73rd Amendment legislated the mandatory establishment of panchayati raj institutions (PRIs) at three levels from the village to the district. The purpose of the constitutional amendment was to enable the participation of citizens in the preparation of local-level plans for economic development and social and economic justice, as also in their implementation. The 73rd amendment was momentous for another reason as well: it provided for guaranteed representation of 33 per cent[10] for women at all levels of the *panchayat* institutions —the Gram (Village) Panchayat, the Panchayat Samiti (intermediate block level) and the Zilla Parishad (district level). The quotas applied not only to the members of these bodies, but also to the position of the *sarpanch/pradhan* (chairperson) of the *panchayat*. Similar guarantees were provided for members of the scheduled castes and tribes, in proportion to their percentage in the population.

The provision of quotas for women was particularly distinctive, as the disadvantaged castes and tribal groups have had constitutionally guaranteed quotas in the legislatures (federal and state) as also in public education and employment. Their significance lies in the multiple axes of inequality in Indian society, with overlapping and cross-cutting social cleavages, from language and caste to tribe and gender. Cleavages of a cultural or social nature also overlap substantially with inequalities of income and class. Thus, members of the scheduled castes (Dalits) and scheduled tribes (*adivasis*) are vulnerable not only on account of social discrimination, they also happen to be among the poorest and most economically marginalised and vulnerable groups. Women belonging to these groups obviously bear the additional burden of their gender identity, with all its implications for autonomy and voice, or the lack thereof.

At last count, the total number of elected representatives at all three levels of India's *panchayats* was 3,856,838 (only slightly less

---

10. Many states have increased this to 50 per cent, and there is also a nationwide initiative to make this uniform.

than the entire population of Lebanon and higher than the entire population of Uruguay), of which 1 million of 36.87 per cent are women, exceeding their quota of 33 per cent. Scheduled Castes (men and women) add up to 485825 (almost half a million), and Scheduled Tribes, men and women, to 304350 (a third of a million). A recent nationwide survey found that three-quarters of the elected women representatives (EWRs) belonged to the Scheduled Castes, the Scheduled Tribes and the OBCs and about half belonged to families below the poverty line. The reservations have helped women—as also men and women belonging to the scheduled castes and scheduled tribes—to gain access to elected bodies and the local public sphere, so that we now have the presence of a critical mass of representatives of variously disadvantaged social groups in these institutions. The evidence on whether access and presence provide guarantees of influence is rather mixed, as is the evidence on the effectiveness of *panchayats* as institutions of local self-governance.

There are primarily two types of obstacles in the way of realising the stated objective of the PRIs: institutional and social. Pre-eminent among the institutional or structural obstacles is the fact that the Constitution does not make it mandatory for the states to devolve specific powers to these institutions, leaving it to state legislatures to determine which of a range of 29 specified powers will be delegated to the local level. Most states have been rather miserly in devolving actual powers, and even more tight-fisted in channeling resources to the *panchayats*. The resources at the disposal of these bodies are also limited, coming as they mostly do from the central government, tied to centrally sponsored, centrally financed and centrally designed 'schemes' for employment, housing subsidies, widows' pensions and so on.

A centralised model of development administration has meant that state capacity at the local level has historically been notoriously weak. Into this scenario have entered elected institutions, with less than aware *panchayat* members often genuinely believing that their role is to make suggestions to the bureaucracy, or that they are accountable to the bureaucracy rather than to their electors. The local bureaucratic apparatus in turn is resistant to giving up powers to frequently unlettered representatives, tending to treat them as showpieces at best, and, at worst, inferior to the line departments of the government. This yields a complex scenario: with few substantive powers devolved to them, and even less financial resources, the *panchayats* remain functionally hamstrung. With little knowledge of the complexities of development schemes and technical requirements, they remain subordinate to the local state bureaucracy, their members often frustrated in asserting their status as democratically elected representatives. The functional competence of Gram (Village) Panchayats extends to the task of determining which individuals/households within its jurisdiction is eligible for particular welfare programmes, and distributing entitlements to these 'beneficiaries'. As such, they are more often than not mere channels for the local implementation of centrally designed and nationally resourced welfare schemes.

In its performance of these functions, the *panchayat* is accountable to the Gram Sabha or village assembly. Decentralisation in India sought to empower people and enable them to be citizens who would not only elect those that governed them, but were institutionally enabled to exact accountability from them. Arguably the greatest institutional innovation was the Gram Sabha or village assembly, comprising of all eligible voters. This is the forum which annually ratifies the accounts of the Gram Panchayat; that decides which of the officially designated poor among the body of rural citizens will be entitled to particular subsidies or welfare schemes; and that holds its local representatives accountable for developmental projects initiated and unsatisfactorily or incompletely accomplished. The Gram Sabha is designed as a forum of direct democracy, and one that has enormous potential as awareness about its role is enhanced. However, a deficit of political competence has prevented its potential from being even substantially, let alone fully, realised.

There are attempts to address these institutional constraints —for instance by entrusting the implementation of new welfare programmes such as the national rural employment guarantee scheme to the *panchayats*. However, the pouring in of large sums of money for these schemes also begets what Jean Dreze has memorably called "the decentralization of corruption." Recent *panchayat* elections in the state of Uttar Pradesh saw the stakes and therefore the expenditure in local elections rising considerably higher than before.

Notwithstanding these limitations, there is some evidence that the implementation of programmes through *panchayats* has yielded benefits in the delivery of public services. A study of the four south Indian states shows that, under specified conditions, *panchayats* have improved the targeting of public services delivery, getting public resources and welfare—housing, electricity and water supply —to the most needy of households and villages (Besley *et al.*, 2007).

The second type of obstacle is a product of social inequalities. Threatened by the quotas and the new opportunities to 'govern' being provided to the subaltern classes, upper-caste male notables evolved ways of controlling the *panchayats* whether through sponsoring (for reserved seats) candidates who would do their bidding, or else through a variety of strategies ranging from co-option and control to intimidation and violence. Dalits and *adivasis* are vulnerable in this respect, with Dalit or *adivasi* women being especially so. Elite capture of panchayats—on the basis of caste status or ownership of land—is common, especially in areas of high social inequality and poverty (Bardhan and Mookherjee, 2004).

However, despite the well-known resistance of local upper caste male society to women, Dalits and *adivasis* elected to *panchayats*, and notwithstanding the abuse of technicalities and procedures by dominant groups to subvert their functioning, the *panchayats* have often proved to be institutional spaces for the effective practice of citizenship. I will focus briefly, and in ethnographic mode, on the case of women's representation and participation in these institutions. One woman *sarpanch*[11] made an ingenious plan for the below poverty line (BPL) list to be rectified through a face-to-face interaction between well-off people whose names found mention on this list, and poor people whose names should have been on the list but were not. Having brought them face-to-face in the Gram

11. In Chhindwara district of Madhya Pradesh. Except for one, all the cases cited here are based on the author's fieldwork. The lone exception–the flag-hoisting case–is from a newspaper feature by P. Sainath (*The Hindu*, July 5 1998).

Sabha, she proceeded to ask the well-off who figured on the list to nominate which person/family in the other category (i.e., poor but not in the list) they would like to give their place on the list to, and succeeded in bringing about the desired balance. Women *sarpanches* have, in the face of intimidation and threats, asserted their constitutional right to chair—literally from a chair rather than a corner on the floor—Gram Panchayat meetings despite being told to make tea or go home. They have asserted their right to hoist the national flag on Independence Day, on occasion wresting it through a court decision. The public space afforded by the *panchayat* has been similarly empowering for Dalits,[12] as the *panchayat ghar* becomes an institutional public space in which discrimination cannot be practised as blatantly as elsewhere.

By guaranteeing the presence of historically disadvantaged groups in local representative institutions, the *panchayats* have thus provided an institutional framework within which they can and have secured incremental social gains. Through participation in these institutions, women have begun to recognise not merely political opportunities but also to perceive and eventually interrogate patriarchal norms that mandate their marginalisation in deliberative bodies to which they have been duly elected. Election to a *panchayat* brings self-confidence, and an awareness of new abilities—to contribute to family decisions on dowry or the age of marriage for children, or to privately discuss local politics with a spouse. Their inability to read agenda papers or minutes of *panchayat* meetings has created new aspirations for the education of their daughters.[13]

---

12. If a Dalit sarpanch attends a religious ceremony in a temple as part of her/his ceremonial duties, it becomes that much easier for Dalits in the village to obtain entry into the temple, from which their forbears have historically been excluded. Heerabhai, a member of the most oppressed Dalit caste of Valmikis and the chairman of the Social Justice Committee in a Gujarat village, had to make an important decision at the first meeting of the *panchayat* to which he was invited. He was offered tea, but in a chipped and old teacup brought out from under a cupboard. He had to make up his mind in an instant, and he did. He threw the cup out of the *panchayat* office because, as he says, had he accepted it, nothing would ever have changed. From that day on, he was given tea in the same cups as the others.
13. This recognition of illiteracy as a handicap is surely the first step towards combating it. From Dalit hamlets in Uttar Pradesh to tribal blocks in Gujarat, women *sarpanches* say they want to be like Indira Gandhi. Why, they ask, should our political careers be terminated at the Zilla Parishad (the highest level of *panchayat*)? Why can we not have quotas for the state legislatures and parliament, too?

The quotas may not have achieved dramatic change but have, in less than two decades, begun to chip away at patriarchal and caste hierarchies that have evolved and struck deep roots over centuries.

There is now plenty of evidence to suggest that, notwithstanding the many forms of marginalisation to which women are subject, the participation of elected women representatives has resulted in positive developmental outcomes. Women have generally attempted to address those developmental needs that appear to be more pressing from their gendered perspective. If male representatives notoriously prioritise infrastructural development (not least, the guess is cynically hazarded, because of the lucrative possibilities from the contracts), women have tended to work on schemes for bringing piped water into the village or for building a middle-school or high school in the village so that their daughters can study beyond primary school. They are also invariably more involved in monitoring the presence of teachers and medical staff in the school or the health worker, to inspect development works and nutrition centres under the Integrated Child Development Scheme (ICDS). Women have initiated efforts for smokeless stoves, crèches, community halls, and have taken the initiative in family and matrimonial matters, counselling abusive and/or alcoholic husbands. Women-headed *panchayats* have sometimes also experienced a substantial raise in their revenues, with a more proactive and community-oriented approach to the auction of village ponds, community forests and village markets.[14]

Overall, then, *panchayats* do play a small but often positive role in the implementation of welfare schemes, making programmes designed and resourced at the national level speak to the needs of the local. Simultaneously, the presence of women, Dalits and *adivasis* in these institutions opens up new opportunities for emancipation from traditional forms of exclusion. How might we think about the potential of these two dimensions of the *panchayat* experience for advancing a project of social democracy?

14. Jayal (2006).

III

The local and the national: Synergy for social democracy

Decentralisation, as we have observed, was an important element in the governance package that repudiated social democracy. In ideological terms, the ideal of decentralisation was ambivalent—the neo-liberal fascination with its potential for undermining the centralised powerful state was as real as the more decidedly left-wing view of its promise for alleviating rural poverty and giving voice to the marginalised. In general, scholarship on decentralisation has tended to emphasise its detrimental effects on welfare, as it is believed to produce lower levels of welfare spending (Huber *et al.*, 1993). Ravishankar's (2004) analysis of data on political and fiscal decentralisation and social transfers in 18 OECD countries from 1960-2000 argues the negative effect of decentralisation on welfare spending. Similarly, Klugman's (1997) study of the effects, on child welfare, of the decentralisation of education, concludes that both opportunities (process) and equity (outcomes) are adversely affected by the decentralisation of education. Fewer studies, such as that of the Nordic welfare states by Sellers and Lidstrom (2007), show that strong local government—with fiscal, political and administrative capacities—provides the necessary infrastructure for an effective welfare state, though it is seen to be less an outcome and more a prerequisite for it.

Today, despite a phenomenal surge in the production of wealth, the progressive policies needed for redistributionist taxation do not seem to be on any political agenda. What is nevertheless very much on the agenda is basic needs provision—insurance against unemployment and hunger, the implementation of the right to education and protection against the worst effects of poverty. In this sense, at least in Indian political vocabulary, social democracy acquires a rather more limited meaning which however has the potential to address some aspects of the rights of social citizenship. So while the Indian project of decentralisation may not bear a necessary predisposition to social democracy, much less a guarantee of it, it could nevertheless be said to contain a potential for social democracy in three distinctive but contingent ways.

Making voters into citizens

Firstly, the institutional design of the PRIs privileges democratisation over decentralisation. By bringing close to four million citizens into elected positions, this has created a new and unparalleled awareness of the possibilities of democratic citizenship. Even urban neighbourhoods that are technically illegal, and therefore devoid of representative mechanisms, have begun to institute electoral processes by which they select local leaders, endow them with legitimacy and even restrict them to fixed terms of functioning.[15] The idea of democracy as a political value —of representation, of accountability and even of solidarity—is assuredly more deeply entrenched now than when politics was a distant space, making itself apparent every five years. Just entering the political process as a candidate and as an elected member of a representative body, and participating in its deliberations, can be an empowering experience.

The primacy accorded to politics is, Sheri Berman (n.d.) has argued, central to the project of social democracy as originally conceived, as an ideology that seeks to use democracy to rein in the excesses of capitalism, and manage its negative social and political consequences. The contemporary social democratic imagination, she suggests, treads a middle path between the worship of the market and old-fashioned socialism, committing itself instead to "using democratically acquired power to direct economic forces in the service of the collective good" (Ibid: 23). It is arguable that institutions of decentralisation in India cannot play such a role, for the local is not—perhaps anywhere[16]—a convincingly hospitable site for either material production or redistribution. Neither of the two Indian states which had significant accomplishments in decentralisation before the Constitutional amendment came into force—West Bengal and Kerala—were high-growth states. Indeed, the success of the so-called Kerala model of development was soon undermined by a high level of economic and industrial stagnation.

15. Adam Auerbach, personal communication, 2010.
16. On the UK, see Greer (2009).

Regardless of whether the priority of democratisation over decentralisation in India's experience is a matter of design or default, it is not necessarily a bad thing. Supplying the deficits of decentralisation requires institutional initiatives—greater devolution of powers and finances—that are not impossible to legislate, and can be fairly swiftly accomplished if the political will to do so exists. 'Making voters into democratic citizens', on the other hand, is a more gradual process; one that, in the longer run, can empower citizens to claim greater voice, including to demand more decentralisation. This is surely a 'powerful political resource for future claim-making for the rights of social citizenship.'

Let me illustrate this with the help of an example from the sphere of education, the Education Guarantee Scheme of former Chief Minister Digvijay Singh in Madhya Pradesh, empowered *panchayats* that did not have primary schools to demand such schools and teachers. The programme drew upon those residents in these poor villages who had at least a secondary education and trained them so that they could be recruited and paid by the *panchayats*. In six years, more than 27,000 poor villages demanded and got basic primary schools, which gave the opportunity to receive a primary education to 1.2 million children (Manor, 2010: 77).

Channelling welfare and enforcing accountability

Secondly, as we have noted, under specific conditions,[17] *panchayats* have been found to be effective agents for channelling developmental goods and contributing to poverty reduction. (Bardhan and Mookerjee, 2004) Ensuring the implementation of welfare schemes is no mean accomplishment, one that is not easily achieved by administration at a remote level of governance.

Panchayats have also facilitated demands for accountability. The Gram Sabha (village assembly), the bedrock of the *panchayati raj* pyramid, was designed as a forum of direct democracy, calling representatives to account, and determining the selection of

17. In the context of West Bengal, Bardhan and Mookerjee identify these conditions as including variations in land distributions, levels of literacy, caste and political concentration.

beneficiaries for official development schemes. The additional innovation of mechanisms such as the social audit or the *jan sunwai* (public hearing) goes beyond this to negate the efforts of states which have officially sought to control both the calendar and the agenda of the Gram Sabha meetings.

The most successful and well-known accountability initiative has been the social audit of the implementation of Mahatma Gandhi National Rural Employment Guarantee Act. In Andhra Pradesh alone, the social audit mechanism found over 4000 officials guilty of irregularities amounting to ₹ 88 crores. Despite (or because of) the success of such accountability initiatives, social audits of the MNREGA have now been made illegal! (Chishti, 2010). When the Gram Sabha enforces accountability in the matter of the channelling of funds especially to beneficiaries from disadvantaged groups, it becomes an institutional guarantor of a redistributive benefit.

Social democracy has traditionally depended upon a material base of production that makes redistribution possible, within a framework of welfare capitalism. Decentralisation is self-evidently not a plausible site for the production of wealth that can then be redistributed. It can however be the site for containing the more unsavoury consequences of unrestrained capitalist activity. Possibly the most well-known case of this is the action of the Perumatty village *panchayat* in Plachimada, Kerala, which withdrew the license of a local Coca Cola factory that was over-exploiting the water resources of the area. In court, the *panchayat* argued that the factory had not only caused acute water scarcity, it was also generating huge amounts of cadmium-laden toxic sludge, which was given to the farmers as "free fertiliser" for their crops but produced severe health effects in the form of rashes and infections. These allegations were confirmed in the report of a high-powered committee of the state government, which has now instituted a dedicated legal agency to determine reasonable compensation (Krishnakumar, 2010).

The role of civil society

Thirdly, the original European practice of social democracy was frequently characterised by an organic link between social democratic parties and the working class movement. This link has now been decisively ruptured. There is however considerable scholarly evidence to suggest that the effectiveness of institutions of local governance often depends upon synergies with social movements and civil society organisations. This is true not only of India but of many other developing countries as well. In Brazil, for instance, the Bolsa Familia and Bolsa Escola (which enabled the universalisation of primary education) programmes showed that nationally guaranteed rights were more effectively implemented with the assistance of local-level NGOs, and the complementarity and synergy between these institutions made for more information, more accountability and transparency and therefore more robust outcomes in realising these social rights (Mendonca, 2004).

In the Indian experience too, the active support of civil society organisations has enabled the making of rights-claims on behalf of, if not always by, disadvantaged groups. The civil society campaigns leading to the National Rural Employment Guarantee Act and the constitutionalisation of the Fundamental Right to Education, as well as the ongoing Right to Food campaign, are all stellar examples of how popular mobilisation, along with political commitment to welfare, can translate into effective initiatives for social citizenship. Between them, these have (or shortly will) provide three critical rights of social citizenship—the right to work, the right to education and the right to food—and while it is true that these are not, in their origin, grassroots campaigns, they do have close links with the grassroots. The MNREGA is being implemented through the panchayati raj institutions; it is possible that food security will follow a similar route.

Enshrining a right in law is clearly not in itself a guarantee of its realisation but it definitely helps. Thus, research on the experience of an earlier right to work—the Maharashtra Employment Guarantee Scheme of the 1970s—has shown that a legal right of this kind provides powerful incentives for activist groups to mobilise people to claim the right, to contest its denial in courts and to monitor its implementation. (Joshi, 2010: 627) A study of the erstwhile National Employment Assurance Scheme in Bihar, on the other hand, showed poor outcomes, explained in terms of the absence of both functioning PRIs[18] and civil society activism, as well as the lack of statutory status for this scheme (Corbridge *et al.*, 2007: 2388).

Civil society organizations have frequently played a positive role in enabling elected representatives in *panchayats*—especially women, Dalits and *adivasis*—in discharging their functions more effectively. A nationwide survey on elected women representatives (EWRs) found that one of the most significant determinants of their effective performance was a prior history of participation in political parties, community organisations and self-help groups (MoPR, 2008: 35). Field-studies[19] support this finding. The non-governmental organisation Prakriti has worked in Maharashtra, Madhya Pradesh and Chhattisgarh, through a trained cadre of carefully recruited staff called Panchayat Sakhis (Friends of the Panchayat), rather like individual trainers who actively help women members of the *panchayat* by providing them with informational inputs on rules and procedures, news of government schemes, eligibility criteria for these, and the benefits/resources that can be tapped. They accompany the EWRs to meetings where they are available to guide and advise them if they require it. Former EWRs have now begun to volunteer as Gram Sakhis (Village Friend) self-fabricated clones of the Panchayat Sakhi, so that the source of knowledge is locally and constantly available. The ultimate testimony to the success of these programmes is that men, especially first-time representatives, have also begun to consult them.

In general, women who are active and effective as members of *panchayats* tend to be associated with organisations such as Mahila Mandals (women's groups) or credit societies and self-help groups (SHGs). Whatever the primary purpose of these organisations, they do seem to function also as talent pools and training-grounds for leadership. Sometimes, the Mahila Mandal may pick a candidate, support her (though seldom financially) and help her to win, even on an unreserved seat. These organisations also appear to play a role

18. Bihar was notoriously recalcitrant in adopting the Panchayati Raj Amendments, delaying both legislation and the holding of elections.

19. All the interviews cited here are from fieldwork conducted by the author in August-September 2005, in Karnataka, Gujarat and Madhya Pradesh.

in helping to dissolve caste prejudices. Self-help groups sometimes consciously support Dalit women, helping them to participate in the Gram Sabha, ask questions, raise issues of quorum, and learn to combat violence. Federations of women members have created networks which have gone beyond their original capacity-building goals to become recruitment pools for political parties, though sometimes the umbilical connection to NGOs can prove to be a deterrent to entering mainstream politics (Behar and Aiyar, 2003: 4936).

Overall, the persistent and obstructive micro-politics of local power hierarchies pose challenges to decentralisation, and impliedly to the realisation of social citizenship. While the legislation of social rights is vastly encouraging, the constant attempts at sabotaging them at the local level will require struggle. Often deeply enmeshed in local power structures, political parties have tended to abdicate their role in providing such leadership. Unless and until political parties with a serious commitment to social and economic rights mobilise their members at the local level to do so, it will be civil society organisations that will step into the breach. Already, such organisations have been effective in occupying some of this space, through successful grassroots initiatives in not merely delivering services but also in building capacities to claim and demand rights, and enforce accountability.

Is there reason to worry that decentralisation will result in a "territorialisation of social rights"?[20] In globalising times, this poses a disconcerting paradox. On the one hand, there is the irrefutable phenomenon of the deterritorialisation of citizenship—the delinking of citizenship from territory as a result of a range of phenomena from global governance to migration to world capitalism—and, on the other, decentralisation suggests a local re-territorialisation of citizenship. Where might social citizenship—the essence of a social democracy—be located? Does social citizenship entail the full restitution of the national state to its erstwhile position of

---

20. A study of social services in Italy, Spain and Portugal blames the risks of such territorialisation for the increasing dependence of "Mediterranean familialistic welfare regimes" on market provision (Saraceno, 2006).

pre-eminence? Or is it possible to think about the national and the local as situated in a relationship of mutual complementarity —or "welfare pluralism"[21]—in a contemporary project of social democracy?

There is clearly a need to contest the false dichotomy between the national state as concentrated evil and decentralised institutions as inherently virtuous. Ambedkar's worry about the village as the location of nasty practices of prejudice and discrimination has some validity even in the present day. The local can be the site for oppression, for women as much as for historically exploited and vulnerable social groups. At the same time, the national state remains vitally relevant to societies marked by acute poverty and deprivation, in order to counter the market, control rapacious capitalism, and guarantee the provision of basic needs. In such complex contexts, the national and the local can only exist in a relationship of complementarity rather than substitutability. The regulation of the social product—in terms of ensuring both the fairness of the processes by which it is created, of the terms of redistribution as well as the creation of a social consensus on it—remains the task of the national state. On the other hand, state capacity along with effective and empowered citizenship —expressed in informed decision-making about developmental priorities and local needs, and the ability to mobilise to make welfare-claims upon public resources—must remain the prerogative of the local. Both have their proper place in the making of a social democracy.

References

AnanthPur, Kripa (2007). "Rivalry or Synergy? Formal and Informal Local Governance in Rural India", *Development and Change* 38(3): 401-21.

Bardhan, Pranab and Dilip Mookherjee (2004). "Poverty Alleviation Efforts of Panchayats in West Bengal", *Economic and Political Weekly*: 965-74, February 28.

Behar, Amitabh and Yamini Aiyar (2003). "Networks of Panchayat Women: Civil Society Space for Political Action", *Economic and Political Weekly*: 4936-40, November 22.

21. I borrow the phrase "welfare pluralism" from Barbara Harriss-White (1995) though in her usage it draws attention to the necessity for the state, in addition to the market and civil society, to play a role in social provisioning. In this paper, the term is used to suggest a vertical rather than horizontal pluralism, such that the particular excellences of the national and the local may be harnessed and co-ordinated in the most socially useful manner.

Berman, Sheri (n.d.). "Understanding Social Democracy". *http://www8.georgetown.edu/centers/cdacs/bermanpaper.pdf*

Besley, Timothy, Rohini Pande, Vijayendra Rao (2007). "Political Economy of Panchayats in South India", *Economic and Political Weekly* 661-66, February 24.

Chishti, Seema (2010). "India's Social Audit of Schemes Draws World Attention", *The Indian Express*. November 2.

Cichon, Michael (2009). "Turning Crisis into an Opportunity: The Role of Social Security in Response and Recovery", in *World of Work: The ILO Magazine* No. 67. December.

Corbridge, Stuart *et al.* (2007). "Making Social Science Matter – I: How the Local State Works in Rural Bihar, Jharkhand and West Bengal", *Economic and Political Weekly:* 2377-89, June 14.

Fung, Archon and Erik Olin Wright (2003). *Deepening Democracy: Institutional Innovations in Empowered Participatory Governance*. London: Verso.

Greer, Scott L. (ed.) (2009). *Devolution and Social Citizenship in the UK*. Bristol: The Policy Press.

Harriss-White, Barbara (1995). "Economic Restructuring: State, Market, Collective and Household Action in India's Social Sector", *European Journal of Development Research* 7(1): 124-47.

Heller, Patrick (2001). "Moving the State: The Politics of Democratic Decentralization in Kerala, South Africa, and Porto Alegre", *Politics and Society* 29(1): 131-63.

Huber, Evelyn, Charles Ragin and John D. Stephens (1993). "Social Democracy, Christian Democracy, Constitutional Structure, and the Welfare State", *American Journal of Sociology* 99: 711-49.

Jayal, Niraja Gopal (2006). "Engendering Local Democracy: The Impact of Quotas for Women in India's Panchayats", in *Democratization* 13(1): 15-35.

Joshi, Anuradha (2010). "Do Rights Work? Law, Activism, and the Employment Guarantee Scheme", *World Development* 38(4): 620-30.

Klugman, Jeni (1997). "Decentralization: A Survey from a Child Welfare Perspective", Innocenti Occasional Papers, *Economic and Social Policy Series* No. 61. Florence, Italy: UNICEF International Child Development Centre.

Krishnakumar, R. (2010). "Plachimada's Claims" in *Frontline* 27(15). July 17-30. *http://www.flonnet.com/fl2715/stories/20100730271503300.htm*

Manor, James (2010). "Local Governance", in Niraja Gopal Jayal and Pratap Bhanu Mehta (eds.), *The Oxford Companion to Politics in India*. Delhi: Oxford University Press.

Marshall, T.H. (1950). *Citizenship and Social Class*. Cambridge: Cambridge University Press.

Mendonca, Patricia (2004). "Decentralization of Social Policies, State and Civil Society Relationships in Brazil: Towards Synergy?", Working Paper of the International Society for Third Sector Research Sixth International Conference on *Contesting Citizenship and Civil Society in a Developing World*. Toronto.

Ministry of Panchayati Raj (2008). *Study on Elected Women Representatives in Panchayati Raj Institutions*. New Delhi: Government of India.

Policy Network, The (2004). *Where Now for European Social Democracy?* London: The Policy Network.

Ravallion, Martin (2009). "A Comparative Perspective on Poverty Reduction in Brazil, China and India", *Policy Research Working Paper* 5080. Washington, D.C.: The World Bank Development Research Group.

Ravishankar, Nirmala (2004). "Decentralization and the Welfare State". *http://www.iq.harvard.edu/files/iqss/old/PEW/ravishankar.pdf*

Saraceno, Chiara (2006). "Social Assistance Policies and Decentralization in the Countries of Southern Europe", *Revue Francaise des Affaires Sociales* 5(5): 97-117.

Sellers, Jefferey M. and Lidstrom, Anders (2007). "Decentralization, Local Government, and the Welfare State", in *Governance: An International Journal of Policy, Administration, and Institutions* 20(4): 609-32.

Thorner, Alice (1981). "Nehru, Albert Mayer, and Origins of Community Projects", *Economic and Political Weekly:* 117-20, January 24.

Wincott, Daniel (2009). "Citizenship in Space and Time: Observations on T.H. Marshall's Citizenship and Social Class", in Scott L. Greer (ed.), *Devolution and Social Citizenship in the UK*. Bristol: The Policy Press.

36

STEVEN I. WILKINSON

Social Democracy and Ethnic Cleavages

Introduction[1]

There are two types of challenges that ethnic cleavages might pose for social democracy, defined as a polity that combines market incentives, democracy and social justice. The first type of challenge is the general difficulty that might be posed by greater ethnic heterogeneity—such as exists in India—for democracy and broad based development policies. There is now a very wide literature in the social sciences which argues that higher levels of ethnic diversity pose problems for democracy, for economic growth, for the provision of public goods such as water and roads, and for the quality of the institutions necessary for development. Can we then expect India's general levels of heterogeneity to limit its performance and development? The second type of challenge is a more specific social and political one: are Indians from poorer ethnic categories, especially SCs/STs, OBCs, MBCs and Muslims, benefitting equally or proportionally from state action and market liberalisation? And if not, what policies might help them to do so? Clearly if this issue is left unaddressed it can endanger the country's internal security—consider the Planning Commission's 2008 study on Development Challenges in Extremist Affected Areas, which highlights the poor condition of *Adivasis* and Dalits as a cause of Naxalite unrest—as well as the political coalition that has sustained the recent market reforms.[2]

---

1. I am very grateful for the research assistance of Cameron Ballard-Rosa for this paper.
2. This 2008 Planning Commission study recommends that "To reduce the anger of the people, it is necessary that they should feel that they are a part of the mainstream of Indian society and not an external element to be looked down upon by others," and recommends a variety of targeted social spending programs to address inequalities and reduce conflict (pp.70-71).

The first issue, the difficulties that ethnic cleavages in general pose for democracy and development has, I suggest, been overemphasised by scholars. Scholars have highlighted the negative effects of diversity for democracy, institutional quality and the provision of public goods, without acknowledging that the substantive effects they identify are often quite small, and that the measures of ethnic cleavages they employ in their regressions are often quite flawed. Moreover, India is not, in comparative terms, as politically dominated by ethnic cleavages as we often think, and those cleavages that do exist have not always had bad effects. India has arguably done much better than its similarly diverse neighbour Pakistan since 1947 in part because its political institutions and laws have promoted multiple ethnic cleavages, for instance those of caste and language. These 'cross-cutting cleavages,' which prevent any single group from dominating the centre or individual states, have sustained India's democracy and been highly effective at reducing communal conflicts and preventing the highly intense secessionist movements that have afflicted Pakistan.

The second challenge—the extent to which backward sections within Indian society are being excluded through state and market actions—is tougher to address empirically and from a policy perspective.[3] Most empirical evidence that we have on OBC, MBC, SC/ST and Muslim exclusion is on poverty, employment and educational 'outcomes', rather than on showing whether these outcomes are the result of unfair state and market exclusion. Perhaps the major failure of the Sachar Committee's 2006 report into the status of Muslims, for instance, was that it highlighted the various ways in which Muslims were doing worse than other communities, without showing whether this was because of state or market discrimination, or because of factors such as Muslims' lower levels of education and literacy.[4] From a policy perspective, of course, it would be enormously helpful to know whether it is

---

3. In this paper I consider largely access to the labour market, government programmes and formal employment, even though I recognise that for many rural people issues of land and forest access are critical, and there also needs to be discussion of those, especially in an environment where the state is often taking land for various development purposes.
4. Wilkinson (2010; 2007).

primarily imbalances in access to education, capital, housing and social services, or problems with the job market and things such as access to credit that are leading to worse overall outcomes.[5] In the past five years, however, there have been some pioneering experimental studies and deeper analysis of income and group data that attempt to get at this issue. These have found that employment outcomes for Muslims and Dalits in particular are often very poor, and these cannot be explained by most observable factors such as education, suggesting that market discrimination is at work. This seems to be confirmed by experimental studies and qualitative evidence showing that employment discrimination against Muslims and Dalits is pervasive in the Indian job market, even in the most modern segment that in theory ought to be least prone to discriminate.[6]

It would be a big leap, however, to conclude from this disheartening evidence of continuing discrimination that market and state action are not having any positive effect on lessening group imbalances. There are some surveys for instance, such as those by Kapur *et al.* (2010), which suggest that, on various social and economic dimensions, the lives of Dalits have in fact been getting better over the past two decades. And several studies find that discrimination against Muslims and Dalits in state employment is quite a bit lower than in the private sector. While no final word is possible here on the degree to which state action or market reforms are having a good or bad effect on backward communities, there are reasons to think that several policy responses would help to increase these communities' access to the fruits of both state action and market reforms, and I close this paper by adding my voice to those who suggest that a broad based EOC would be especially helpful in increasing fairness and monitoring the scale of imbalances.

5. Of course, discrimination might also be at the root of lower SC/ST or Muslim levels of 'pre-market' characteristics such as literacy or years of education. See Deshpande (2010).

6. The major studies are collected in two valuable edited volumes: Thorat and Newman (2010); Basant and Shariff (2010).

Is there a relationship between ethnic cleavages and bad outcomes?

The first aspect of ethnic cleavages that I want to examine is the allegedly negative relationship that scholars have found between higher levels of ethnic heterogeneity and a whole range of desirable social outcomes, such as democracy, growth, good institutions, and the supply of public goods such as roads and public schools.[7] Scholars and practitioners have long argued that ethnic cleavages make democracy more difficult. The strong (one might say extreme) version of this argument sees ethnic plurality as largely incompatible with democracy: the presence of different groups and their different goals makes the 'fellow feeling' necessary for national cohesion impossible, prevents agreement on policies, and in the worst cases allows authoritarian governments to use one ethnic group against another to stay in power (Mill, 1861). Thomas Jefferson (1903), writing in his autobiography, wrote that "two races, equally free, cannot live in the same government. Nature, habit, opinion, have drawn indelible lines of distinction between them." John Stuart Mill (1861: 72), writing in the mid-nineteenth century, wrote that (1972: 92) "Free institutions are next to impossible in a country made up of different nationalities. Among a people without fellow-feeling, especially if they read and speak different languages, the united public opinion, necessary to the working of representative government, cannot exist." More recently Alvin Rabushka and Kenneth Shepsle a have argued that ethnicity ultimately trumps all other goals and identities, and makes democratic negotiation and agreement impossible. They argue that, "Democracy, at least as it is known in the West, cannot be sustained under conditions of intense, salient preferences because....The plural society, constrained by the preferences of its citizens, does not provide fertile soil for democratic values or stability."

Many foreign observers in the 1940s and 1950s, when considering the prospects for democracy and peace in India, shared these negative views about the compatibility of democracy with ethnic cleavages. The tensions over 'sons of the soil' movements

7. A recent exception is Page (2007). Of course some of these outcomes may be related. Przeworski *et al.* (1996) argue that economic growth and higher GDP levels have a positive effect on democracy.

in Telugu-speaking areas and the northeast, over reservations in Madras, and conflicts over the national language and linguistic states all seemed to pose enormous challenges to national unity. Selig Harrison, most notably, thought that the regional, linguistic and caste tensions at the time threatened India's unity, its democracy, and its economic growth (Harrison, 1960: 322). His — very wrong—prediction was that, "Indian nationalism will most probably survive [only] at the price of a series of authoritarian political forms..."(Harrison, 1960: 4-5).

A weaker form of this argument, now probably the mainstream view, holds that ethnic diversity, while obviously not guaranteeing that a country will be undemocratic, certainly makes things a lot more difficult. For instance the two leading theorists of ethnic conflict and its moderation, Arend Lijphart (1977) and Donald L. Horowitz (1985: 681-84) both take as their starting point that ethnic plurality tends to pose real challenges for countries. Horowitz for instance says that "Democracy is exceptional in severely divided societies," and that "Unless precautions are taken, democratic arrangements tend to unravel fairly predictably in ethnically divided societies..." But both Horowitz and Lijphart ultimately take the view that such bad outcomes are not inevitable, and that the right set of conflict-moderating institutions—they differ on which ones—can prevent ethnic cleavages from leading to ethnic conflicts and the breakdown of democracy.

In addition to the many scholars who have looked at the connection between ethnic cleavages and the survival of democracy in general, there are also many studies linking ethnic cleavages to bad levels of particular desired outcomes such as growth or the provision of public goods. Easterly and Levine (1997) for example, in one of the most heavily cited studies, found that around 28 per cent of the growth gap between Africa and East Asia could be accounted for by the higher degrees of ethnic heterogeneity in Africa.[8] They conclude that "cross-country differences in ethnic diversity explain a substantial part of the cross country differences in public policies,

8. See also Masters and McMillan (1999).

political instability and other economic factors associated with long run growth."

In terms of social programmes and spending within countries, there is also a wide literature that highlights the difficulties that ethnic diversity poses. Easterly *et al.* (1999) look at local road and school bond initiatives in the USA, and find that there these initiatives get less voter support in more diverse communities, a result that may be due to different group preferences over these goods, but may also be due to a reluctance to support broad-based initiatives that may appear to benefit members of 'the other ethnic community more than one's own.' They find that the more diverse the local area in the USA, the more spending on roads, sewers and education goes down, and the less money is likely to be spent on welfare. Another recent study, looking at spending on public goods such as hospitals, lighting, schools and colleges, and drainage West Bengal, has broadly replicated for India this broader negative relationship between ethnic heterogeneity and public goods provision. The authors of this study (Sengupta and Sarkar, 2007), which looks at spending in 28 municipalities in West Bengal, find that higher degrees of caste diversity (SCs/STs and Others) are consistently associated with lower levels of public goods provision.

Why should there be a negative relationship between ethnic cleavages and outcomes such as growth and public goods provision? The literature highlights several causes: the difficulty of monitoring and disciplining people from different ethnic communities; different group preferences over the kinds of social spending that should be undertaken; and the need to wastefully duplicate spending initiatives or local government jurisdictions because each group wants its own separate school, water plant or council. Most fundamentally, scholars argue that ethnic groups start to see every decision in ethnic terms and simply do not trust members of other ethnic groups to act in their interests or spend money raised from their community fairly. Rabushka and Shepsle (1972) claim that "In plural societies, the extent of public goods consumption declines as ethnicity grows in salience. As ethnicity becomes increasingly salient, every political decision favors one community and hinders others. That is, the public goods which result from political decisions become the preserve of the advantaged ethnic community. Non-excludability, a defining characteristic of public goods, is violated. Ethnicity serves as a basis for exclusion. And the excluded communities clearly perceive such decisions as 'public bads.'"

Do ethnic cleavages lead to bad outcomes?

Do ethnic cleavages in general lead to bad outcomes, as the literature suggests? There are three reasons, I think, to doubt that they do.

1. Flawed data

First, the empirical cross-national literature which 'proves' the negative effects of social cleavages use measures of ethnic diversity that are flawed. The most often used measure, ELF, a measure of ethno-linguistic fractionalisation in the population, measures the underlying degree of ethnic diversity (usually defined in terms of language) in the population, which is often not a good measure of the number of actual groups competing over specific resources in a country (Chandra and Wilkinson, 2008; Posner, 2004).[9] For instance Posner points out that the ELF measure for Kenya suggests that around 20 ethnic groups are competing there, while in fact political competition in the country actually revolves around a struggle among 4-5 groups. To take another example, from the Sengupta and Sarkar (2007) study on public goods provision in West Bengal, these authors calculate the ELF measure of ethnic diversity using data for the only three groups that are available in census data for their required level of municipal aggregation: SCs, STs, and Others. But these three social categories are obviously inadequate to trace the real world competition in West Bengal that might actually explain these differences in public good provision. The CSDS for instance cross-tabulates voting across parties in West Bengal by five different groups: Upper caste, SC, SC, OBC, and Muslim.[10] And those CSDS categories are for state-level contests. Presumably the salience of particular castes would be much higher in smaller-scale municipal

---

9. ELF is calculated as $1- \sum si^2$ where si^2 is the share of each ethnic group in the population.

10. "West Bengal: Mandate for Change," National Election Study 2009, *Economic and Political Weekly*: 152-56, September 26.

contests than in the state as a whole, which might argue for an even larger number of categories being used if we really want to develop a good measure of ethnic cleavages at the municipal level. So there is a mismatch between the data and the process we want to trace.

Even if we were to have much finer-grained religious, ethnic and language data at the levels of aggregation we wanted, the data would still ultimately rely on census categories. And a large secondary literature shows that these categories are often highly biased and politicised, as well as frequently incomplete.[11] Sometimes countries aggregate multiple groups together—the Indian census aggregates 48 separate responses to the question 'which language do you speak?'—as Hindi, or multiple castes as part of a general Hindu category. Sometimes countries decide not to record some types of identities at all. For instance the French census does not ask about religion, and the Belgian census does not ask about religion; not because these identities are unimportant, but precisely because these identities are very important, and sensitive. Third, a country's ELF score is measuring many other things besides just the effect of ethnicity. For instance, Eugen Weber's book *Peasants into Frenchmen* shows how the linguistic diversity of France in 1815 was changed, through 130 years of often coercive state action and modernisation, to create a much more linguistically and nationally homogenous country by 1945. If we were to have calculated the ethno-linguistic fractionalisation measures for France at both 1815 and 1945, the ethnic diversity of the country would clearly have gone sharply down over this period. But would the association of such a lower measure with better growth rates in post-WW2 data have been an ethnic effect, or the effect of all the state-building, education, increased communications and modernisation that had taken place in the intervening period?

2. The bad effects of ethnic cleavages are often not large, and are balanced by good effects

Second, although ethnicity may have some significant negative effect on public goods expenditure or growth in regressions, the

11. See, e.g. the introduction and various country studies in Kertzer and Arel (2002).

substantive size of this effect is often not very big. For instance in the US study by Easterly *et al.* (1999), a move from complete ethnic homogeneity to complete ethnic heterogeneity would lower the level of average road spending in municipalities by only 9 per cent, which does not seem big for a social change of such magnitude. The recent study of West Bengal by Sengupta and Sarkar (2007) similarly finds quite small effects, which appear to amount to fractions of a rupee per capita per annum in expenditure as a result of higher levels of diversity.

And none of these studies, of course, counterbalances the allegedly negative effects of ethnic cleavages on the economy or spending with the positive effects of ethnicity in other areas. And such positive effects do exist. The system of linguistic states and caste reservations, far from entrenching ethnicity in a deeply harmful way as many argued they would, have in some ways been a very good thing for Indian politics, promoting cross-cutting cleavages that have helped to prevent the formation of even larger religious and regional blocs such as those that have caused so much conflict in Pakistan. This was hardly foreseeable in the late 1940s. Indeed, Nehru opposed most linguistic states (except Andhra) on the grounds that they weakened national unity as well as posed practical problems of implementation by creating new minorities: in 1947 he argued that "First things must come first and the first thing is the security and stability of India. Before we can undertake any major schemes we must have a strong state and a smoothly running governmental machinery."[12] Nehru was also opposed to most reservations, and wanted to move towards what we might term a caste—blind system. His ultimate goal, as he wrote to Charan Singh in 1954, was to end the caste system, which he saw as "the biggest weakening factor in our society."[13]

But strong southern opposition to the centre's policies on both linguistic states and reservations prompted a reversal. The fact that backward caste (BC) reservations had already been deeply entrenched in the south since the 1920s, and the strength of the

12. Constituent Assembly of India (Legislative) Debates 27th Nov. 1947, pp.791-3.

13. Gopal (1983).

BC movements there, especially in Madras, made Nehru and the national party change its mind on the issue. After large-scale riots over the issue of reservations in Madras in 1950 and 1951, in protest against the Madras High Court's overturning reservations on the grounds that they contravened the non-discrimination clauses in article 15 of the constitution, the centre passed amendment 15(4) in 1951, which clarified that, "Nothing in this article or in clause (2) of article 29 shall prevent the State from making any special provision for the advancement of any socially and educationally backward classes of citizens or for the Scheduled Castes and the Scheduled Tribes."[14] This clause, together with the reverse on linguistic states after riots in Andhra in 1952, and the subsequent appointment of the States Reorganisation Committee, paved the way for the creation of many new states and the proliferation of BC and MBC reservations that we see today.

Both these steps were opposed by many on the grounds that they posed a threat to national unity and social cohesion. Sardar Patel, for instance, opposed linguistic states before his death on the grounds that they would "unmistakably retard the process of consolidation of our gains, dislocate our administrative, economic and financial structure, let loose...forces of disruption and disintegration."[15] But both caste reservations and linguistic states have had, in retrospect, some major political benefits for India. The literature on ethnic conflict moderation is quite consistent that one of the best ways to defuse conflict is through the creation of more federal states and decentralisation, both to decentralise conflict, and so that groups that lose at one level can win real power at another.[16] The literature is also quite consistent that it is a good thing to provide incentives to break up solid majorities by encouraging cross-cutting cleavages within these groups, so that no one group is left as a permanent minority, excluded from a real share in political power.[17]

---

14. Radhakrishnan (1996).
15. Cited in Krishna (1995).
16. Horowitz (1991).
17. Horowitz (1985).

The creation of linguistic states and caste reservations have helped achieve both these goals, without substantially weakening attachment to the nation or to democracy among Indians, which remain strong in opinion polls.[18] The huge number of cross-cutting caste, religious language and regional cleavages in India has, paradoxically, helped to decrease the destabilising effects of ethnic cleavages on the system as a whole. The creation of linguistic states have defused the kind of Tamil-Telugu and Gujarati-Marathi conflicts that bedeviled large states such as Madras and Bombay before states reorganisation. And competition over caste reservations has broken up larger religious blocs both by solidifying and sharpening caste identities, as groups compete to be OBC, or MBC, for quotas within quotas, and over their relative shares of spending and jobs. Caste reservations have also aided party proliferation, as many of the OBC and Dalit parties have their origins in pro-reservation 'anti-Brahman' movements in the south, for instance, or in the case of the BSP the BAMCEF and DS4 public sector unions for Scheduled Caste employees (Chandra, 2004).

The fact that most states now have caste cleavages institutionalised through parties, unions and reservations may have had some bad effects, but as I have explored elsewhere, it has generally been a very good thing from the perspective of communal relations in India. This is because multiple cleavages among the majority community have led to a proliferating number of parties, which has tended to make minority and backward communities more politically pivotal. In return for their valuable votes, these minority communities can therefore demand both physical security and economic development policies. In 2002, as I explored in my book *Votes and Violence*, the 27 states with either high levels of party competition (a function of ethnic diversity) or in which the incumbent party won a significant (10% or more) of the Muslim

18. Interestingly, separate electorates, which were regarded by the Muslim League before 1947 as a vital necessity to preserve Muslim political influence, completely failed to play this function in Pakistan after partition, where Christian and Hindu representatives often argued that they would be better off being a pivotal group in general constituencies rather than being marginalised through these separate, powerless, seats. These minority objections led President Musharraf to abolish the electorates in 2002.

vote performed very well in preventing communal violence from spreading outside Gujarat. In these states, either because the incumbent parties relied on minority votes directly, or because politics was so competitive (in terms of the number of effective parties in the state) that they needed to form coalitions with parties that themselves had minority support, the parties imposed curfews, carried out preventive arrests, and quickly prevented violence from getting worse when it did break out.

3. Indians are not as heavily motivated by ethnicity as the literature sometimes suggests

Despite the fact that the ethnic politics literature tends to see ethnicity and ethnic cleavages as eventually crowding out all other political identities and issues, the empirical evidence on this is actually quite mixed. When Indian voters are asked what motivates their vote choice, they in fact seldom mention caste or religion as the only or even the prime factor.[19] Most Indians, like most people in other countries, rank the economy, inflation and crime as the most important factors they consider in their political choices. This is true even at times of quite serious religious or ethnic crises: for instance the Babri Masjid dispute was ranked only the 4th most important issue by Indian voters in a poll taken in December 1992-January 1993.[20] Second, national and state survey data shows consistently that no group gives its support completely to a particular party. Only 30 per cent of voters answered 'yes' to the question "Is it important for you to vote the way your caste/ community votes?" in 1996, down from 51 per cent in 1971.[21] Even the most cohesive groups of voters, such as Brahmins and Muslims in UP in the mid 1990s, supported particular parties at levels of

---

19. Academics frequently seem to regard such answers as dishonest, so sure are they that ethnic identities is the prime motivating factor behind voting.

20. See e.g. The Hindu-CPPS Poll, *The Hindu,* 25th January 1993. There were similar results in the Indian Institute of Public Opinion's poll of four Hindi heartland states carried out shortly afterwards. In that poll, issues such as rural development, rising princes, prevention of corruption and poverty alleviation were consistently seen as more important than minority or group-specific issues. IIPO Survey Vol. XXXVIII No.7 Dec. 1993-Jan. 1994, Table III-A p.XIX

21. The percentage was only slightly higher among Muslims, at 37 per cent. Source ICSSR-CSDS India Today Poll, 1996, *India Today*, August 31 1996, pp.28-43.

only 75-80 per cent, never giving total support.[22] And these levels of support can of course change quickly over time.

So while at an aggregate level it is certainly true that there is an association between the group that someone comes from and their vote, this may not be a case of ethnic particularism so much as members of the group responding to the fact that some parties are offering a bundle of policies and programmes that happen to fit well with their economic situation, and their policy preferences, as well as their ethnicity. African Americans in the USA for instance vote overwhelmingly for Democrats and Republicans rely overwhelmingly on white votes without observers usually characterising the system as a whole as 'ethnic.' As Kumar and MacMillan (2004) put it, in an insightful analysis of the 2004 elections, "while traditional alignment of caste groups matter in politics, most often the change in vote across two elections is decided by issues, opinions and voters' evaluation of government performance."

In fact in comparative terms, ethnic voting is actually less prevalent in India—at least at a national level—than in many other countries in the world. Political scientist John Huber (2010) at Columbia University has recently developed a measure of the degree to which ethnicity determines vote choice in different countries, especially those with different voting systems. His ethnic voting measure varies from 0 when the proportion of voters supporting each party is the same across groups to 1 when "each group is represented by one party, each group's party receives no support from outside the party, and all groups are of equal size." The general equation for calculating the Ethnic Voting score (EV) for a country is given by:

$$EV = \frac{1}{\sqrt{\frac{G-1}{2G}}} \sum_{g=1}^{G} (EV_g * S_g)$$

22. Ibid.

where for each country we know the number of political parties (p) and ethnic groups (g), as well as voting information for political parties broken down by ethnic group. We then calculate the squared difference between the total vote share for a particular party j and the vote share for that party within an ethnic group i.

Using over 70 opinion polls, Huber constructs estimates of the degree of ethnic voting in 45 countries. Countries like Uruguay and Germany have very low levels of ethnic voting on this measure, while Belgium and Nigeria have high levels of ethnic voting.

Table 36.1

Degree of Ethnic Voting (EV)

Country	*Survey*	*Year*	*EV*
Uruguary	WVS	1996	0.009
Germany	WVS	1999	0.011
Russia	CSES	2000	0.020
Finland	CSES	2003	0.147
India	NES	2009	0.167
United States	CSES	1996	0.168
Bulgaria	CSES	2001	0.190
South Africa	Afrobarometer	2002	0.348
India	WVS	1999	0.360
Kenya	Afrobarometer	2005	0.364
Nigeria	Afrobarometer	2005	0.370
Belgium	WVS	1999	0.418

In Huber's original attempt to measure ethnic voting in India (IND 1999) he used data on voting by language group. Because many Indians vote for regionally based parties such as the DMK or BJD, this measure came out as quite high, 0.360, close to South Africa and Kenya. This figure is of course inaccurately and deceptively high, because many Indians vote for regional parties in Lok Sabha elections knowing that these parties are part of a national coalition such as the UPA. If we were to control for this, or to look at other kinds of national ethnic cleavages, such as major caste groups and religious groups, India's measure of ethnic voting would be quite a bit lower. If we use 2009 NES data on Muslim, Sikh, Christian, Upper and Lower OBC, SC and ST voting patterns at the national

Figure 36.1

Ethnic Voting

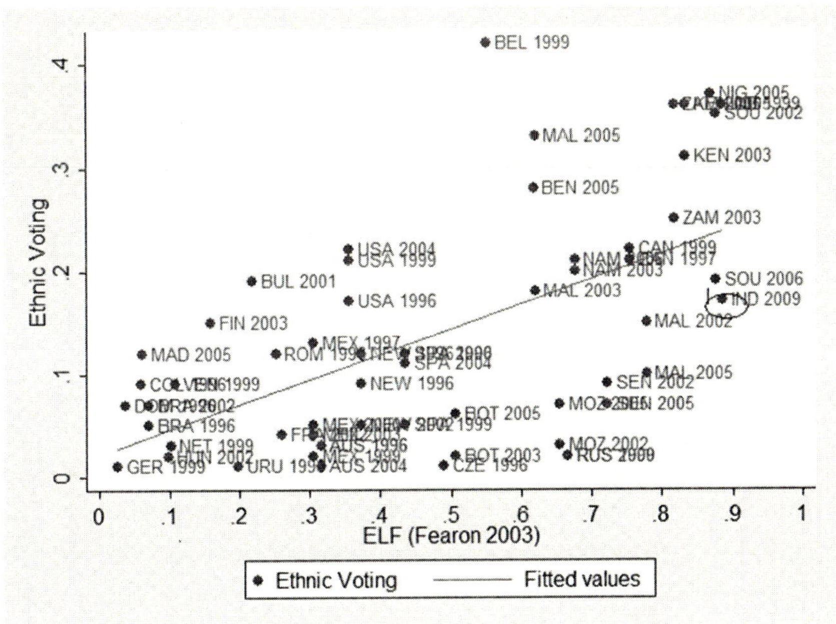

level, for instance, India's level of ethnic voting[23] ("IND 2009", in Figure 36.1, at the far right) would be only 0.167, quite a bit lower than the ethnic voting measure for USA, Bulgaria and South Africa. India's level of ethnic voting is, in other words, not as high as we often think and voting in India may be less than in countries such as the USA that we don't generally associate with ethnic voting.

Bad outcomes and ethnic cleavages in India?

The second broad issue I want to examine is the one of broader inclusion of backward sections of Indian society from both state programmes and market actions? How can both state and market be

23. Calculated from the vote shares given in Table 8: All India Vote for Major Political Formations by Caste-Community—LokSabha Election 2009, in Yadav and Palshikar (2009).

made to work better for people who may be excluded both in terms of their initial access to education, housing, health, etc., and then again by the processes of selection for employment and inclusion in government programmes? I consider here how under-represented groups are doing in terms of education and employment, though obviously the welfare of weaker communities is multi-faceted and also depends on such things as access to land and their degree of influence and representation within formal political institutions.

To assess the challenges India faces in providing OBCs, SCs, STs and religious minorities with a fairer share of jobs and access to government programmes obviously requires an empirical assessment of where things stand now, and whether these groups' access to employment or government programmes has got better or worse over the past few decades. And here we face significant data problems. First, we have very little data on how the OBCs and MBCs are doing, in large part because the census and NSS sample rounds, with a few exceptions (such as the National Family Health Survey), have not collected disaggregated information on these groups, and the few state studies that have done so have been carried out in a highly politicised and biased environment.[24] The Indian caste census in 2011 may help with this data problem, provided it can be matched to the finer grained socioeconomic data in other surveys, though it always has to be remembered that the OBC and MBC categorisations that the census will likely use are as much politically defined categories as they are sociological ones. So for the moment we are forced to rely on data on SCs and STs, and the major religious groups such as the Hindus, Muslims, Christians and Sikhs that are collected by government agencies and major private surveys such as the NCAER.

Until recently, most of the studies of employment and backwardness among these communities were not terribly helpful in understanding whether a group is doing badly because of its members' initial lack of education, wealth, training, literacy etc., or

24. In some cases political considerations have caused state surveys not be carried out. In Kerala, for instance, backward communities in the mid-1990s blocked a socioeconomic caste survey because of fears that it would have revealed that they were not as backward as some 'forward' communities. Vijayanunni, M. (2003). "Caste and the Census of India", Unpublished paper, pp.10-11.

because of exclusion once a group's members apply for particular jobs or programmes.[25] Instead, government reports typically look at the poor outcomes themselves—for instance collecting aggregate data that showed clearly that SCs and STs are doing worse than non-backward Hindus in private or government employment—as evidence of discrimination rather than analysing the available data to understand the causes of these bad outcomes. The Sachar Committee, for instance, presented an enormous amount of data—see Table 36.2—showing that Muslims are backward in terms of education, literacy, levels of capital, and employment. Sachar also showed that Muslims' recent progress in literacy and education has also not been as fast as other groups (SC literacy among the youngest school age children is now for the first time higher than among Muslims, though Muslims' overall literacy rate remains higher). But Sachar presented very little systematic data to show why this was the case, or address the question of whether recent state programmes or market reforms have improved Muslims' prospects or not, and how this ought to shape policy.[26]

Table 36.2

'Pre-Market' Social Disadvantage by SRC

	Literacy Levels (2001)	*Mean Years of Schooling of Children 7-16 (2001)*	*Proportion of Children 6-14 Enrolled (2004-05)*	*% Who Completed at Least Primary School in 10 Major States (2001)*	*% Coverage of Children for MDM (2004-05)*
All	64.8	3.95	85.3	--	26.8
Hindus	65.1		86.0 H-OBCs		
			94.9 H-GEN	--	
SCs/STs	52.2	3.35	79.7	61.4	34.7
Muslims	59.1	3.26	81.8	60.9	22.8
All Others	70.8	4.39	89.9	79.3	17.2

Source: Sachar Committee Report, p.182 (MDM coverage) and Appendices 4.1, 4.2, 4.3, 4.6, 5.8.

25. Of course, caste or religion may also be important in determining these characteristics, either by family and group choice, or because one's caste or religion lead to discrimination by others which affects education, health, literacy, etc.

26. For a much fuller discussion of these issues, see Wilkinson's two articles, cited above, and also Deshpande (2010).

Over the past five years, however, a number of excellent studies have been conducted that do help us understand whether—at least for Dalits and Muslims—a group is doing badly primarily because of factors such as the degree of education and health that its members bring to the market, or because of discrimination against a group's members once they apply for a government job or programme, or a position in a private firm. These studies also help us to work out whether things seem to be getting better or worse for members of these communities, compared with the beginning of the market-reform era in the early 1990s. On the whole, these studies suggest that there is a substantial amount of discrimination against Dalits and Muslims in both the acquisition of pre-market education and training, as well as once people apply for jobs and programmes, and a somewhat lesser degree of bias against them once they are in employment. The levels of bias against Muslims seem to be higher than those against SCs, and if anything the relative position of Muslims seems to have worsened over the past decade, something that has worrying implications for national integration.

Both Muslims and Dalits have less access to health, education, and training as children than members of OBC and forward caste Hindu populations. Some of this may be due to community preferences, e.g. against inoculations and for traditional forms of education but most of these differences seem to be because of lack of spending in their communities (at least spending that reaches the intended targets) and some element of discrimination against them in the provision of services. We know for instance from a 2003 survey that there are substantial patterns of caste-exclusion in the operation of Midday Meal Schemes (MMS) in some parts of Rajasthan, UP, Bihar, AP and TN, which presumably reflects wider patterns of caste exclusion in schools in some parts of these states. These exclusive practices involve at the extreme keeping Dalits away from the MMS entirely, but more often involve banning Dalit cooks (48% of villages) making Dalits sit separately (9.2% of villages) or giving them worse food (9.2% of villages).[27] A great deal of other qualitative and survey evidence suggests that there continues, for instance, to be discrimination against SCs and Muslims in the

27. Thorat and Lee (2005).

provision of government health and educational surveys, on top of the poor general quality of these services compared to the private alternatives available to many upper caste students.

It is clear that Muslims and Dalits are both doing much worse than other communities in terms of a number of outcome measures. As Table 36.3 shows, they are both more likely to be poorer (in terms of mean per capita expenditures) than other groups. Muslims are also much more likely to be self-employed, especially in occupations such as weaving, car and electric repairs and transportation that are increasingly vulnerable to both exports from other countries (e.g., the *sari* and carpet industries of eastern UP, which now have to compete with Chinese products) and to technological changes. Both communities also have a higher incidence of poverty than average, though the extent of this differs: Muslims have a much higher than average incidence of poverty in urban areas, while SCs have a much higher rate of rural poverty. And in terms of government employment, Muslims and Dalits are both doing badly except in the lowest categories: both groups were poorly represented in candidates called for interview by State Public Service Commissions in the five years prior to the Sachar Committee report.

But to what extent are Muslims and Dalits doing worse in job outcomes because of discrimination and to what extent because of worse 'pre market' qualifications such as educational endowments and poverty? One way to examine this is to look at what happens once the minority of Muslims and Dalits who do attain higher educational qualifications apply for jobs and government programmes? Thorat and Attewell (2007) recently replicated for India a pioneering study by Bertrand and Mullainathan (2004) on employment discrimination against African Americans in the USA. In this original study, fictitious but equally matched CVs from whites and African Americans were sent to employers, to determine if applicants with stereotypically African American names were called back as often as white applicants. Whites were called back 50 per cent more often than equally matched blacks, Bertrand and Mullainathan found. In the Indian study, Thorat and Attewell responded to all the 548 private sector non-specialised entry-level openings (requiring a BA) advertised in the major English language

Table 36.3

'Outcome' Disadvantage By SRC

	% Self-Employed Workers in Urban Areas (2004-05)	*State Mean Per-Capita Expenditures 2004-05*	*Urban Poverty Incidence 2004-05*	*Rural Poverty Incidence 2004-05*	*Proportion and under/ over-representation of SRC compared to population in candidates called to interview for higher positions in state PSCs (2001-06)*	*Proportion and under/ over-representation of SRC compared to population in candidates called to interview for lower positions in state PSCs (2001-06)*
All		712	22.8	22.7		
Hindus	44.0 UC					
	46.1% OBC	1023	20.4	22.6	87.2 (+6.2)	87.4 (+6.4)
SCs/STs	33.4	520	36.4	34.8	22.3 (-9)	40.1 (+8.8)
Muslims	57.4	635	38.4	26.9	7.3 (-6.1)	3.3 (-10.1)
All Others			12.2	14.3	5.5 (-1.5)	9.4 (+2.4)

Source: Sachar Committee p.153 (MPCE expenditures), pp.159-60 (Incidence of Poverty), 5.8, Table 9.8 p.175 (PSC interviews).

dailies (Times of India, Hindustan Times, The Hindu, Deccan Herald and Deccan Chronicle) for 66 months, beginning in October 2005. For each of these positions, they submitted strong applications, matched in all important educational and presentational respects, for fictitious Muslim, Dalit and high caste Hindu applicants. They found, strikingly, that the odds of an SC applicant with a BA degree being contacted for an initial interview or further information were only two thirds (0.67) of those of an upper caste Hindu applicant. And Muslims were worse off still: their odds of being contacted were only 0.33 of those of an applicant with a high caste name. Thorat and Attewell's (2007: 4144) conclusion was that "social exclusion is not just a residue of the past clinging to the margins of the Indian economy, nor is it limited to people of little education. On the contrary, it appears that caste favoritism and the social exclusion of Dalits and Muslims have infused private enterprises even in the most dynamic modern sector of the economy."

A second way to examine the reasons for poorer Dalit and Muslim outcomes is to examine a particular outcome such as labour market wages or education outcomes for each group, and to control for as many of the possible predictors of these outcomes as we can, such as poverty, to see if these alone are sufficient to explain the group's poor outcomes. Bhalotra and Zamora (2010) for instance, uses NFHS data to explore the reasons why it is that Muslims 6-14 years old might be losing ground in education compared to other groups in terms of education. They find, interestingly, that the poor results of most of the low caste Hindu children who are doing badly in terms of educational outcomes can be explained by observable characteristics such as having poorer diets. "In contrast," they find, "most of the disadvantages exhibited by Muslims are unexplained by a set of conventional covariates. In other words, Muslim children have more advantageous characteristics than low caste children but appear to suffer from less positive attitudes towards or less good opportunities for primary education"(p.192). We get a similar result in a paper by Vani Borooah in the same edited book as the Bhalotra and Zamora article, on group and employment risk. Borooah shows that even when we control for Muslims' low education and other observable characteristics, their disadvantage in terms of labour market access is still much greater than we would predict, and much worse than for Hindu OBCs and upper castes.

No one of these studies is conclusive but taken together they show that observable non-ethnic characteristics often do not explain backward groups' level of employment and educational success. Which group one is from matters a lot, much more than it should. Dalits and Muslims in particular face exclusion in a variety of ways, and for Muslims the degree of exclusion may actually be growing, given declines over the past decade in the returns to education for Muslims in the labour market, in contrast to other communities—as well as wider social concerns about extremism (Bhaumik and Chakrabarty, 2006).

Policy Options?

What might be good options to address the specific problems that communities such as Dalits and Muslims face in access to education and the market? The centre is of course trying to make sure that existing programmes such as JSS and MDM fully include towns and rural areas where SCs, STs and Muslims are concentrated. But beyond this, and given the scale of these communities' disadvantages, what else might be done?[28]

One argument that has been made—especially by politicians on the campaign trail in 2009—is that reservations for Muslims should be extended similar to those already existing for SCs and STs. Given the degree of anti-Muslim prejudice we find in the Attewell and Thorat employment study mentioned above, the appeal of such a policy is easy to understand. But given the terribly contentious history of religious reservations in British India, as well as the obvious problems of providing benefits for both the rich as well as the poor Muslims in such a policy, the likely negative communal consequences and the inefficiency of such reservations—leaving aside the constitutional prohibitions on religious discrimination—would I suggest make this an inappropriate policy response.

28. See e.g. Department/Ministry wise status of implementation on the follow-up action on the major recommendations of the Sachar Committee, www.*minorityaffairs.gov.in/newsite/sachar/Sachar_Annual_Report.pdf.*

Another proposal, put forward by the Sachar Committee in 2006, and considered in a very thorough June 2008 report, and now being considered by the center, is to introduce diversity indexes, which provide an incentive for government departments or private firms to have a higher level of diversity in general—i.e. including SCs, STs, Muslims, and MBCs, OBCs—without absolutely specifying, as reservations do, the specific group proportions or mix to be included.[29] One possible problem, however, as well as the formidable data and implementation issues the report acknowledges, is that such indices might benefit some groups much more than others, because employers—if the labour market discrimination studies are correct—might prefer to achieve the desired diversity level by focusing all their attention on hiring, say, under-represented Hindus rather than Muslims.[30] Weighting the index in such a way as to prevent this can certainly be done, as the expert committee proposes (Secs.4.5-4.7), but the result of such clear weightings may be to make diversity indexes just as inflexible as reservations, but with even more bureaucracy and data collection. Another issue is whether we calculate diversity within a firm or organisation in reference to the share of a group in the general population, with reference to the pool of educated or qualified people from the particular group in the local area, or with reference to the qualified share of the group over some wider area.

Another suggestion by Justice Sachar is to establish an Equal Opportunity Commission (EOC), at the national and regional or state levels, which would require more employers to collect data on who applies for jobs, their characteristics, and their success in the interview process.[31] An EOC would also be able, as the diversity committee in 2008 acknowledged, to generate the type of data that the diversity index would require to operate successfully, data that are often absent at the moment. The UPA committed to an EOC in

---

29. *Report of the expert group on diversity index* (Ministry of Minority Affairs, June 2008). *http://minorityaffairs.gov.in/newsite/reports/di_expgrp/di_expgrp.pdf.*

30. Although as the report says the index could be constructed so that the complete non-representation of some groups could be penalized.

31. This recommendation has been made by Attewell and Thorat, and in the concluding chapter of Sachar, pp.239-40.

President Patil's June 2009 speech and details are apparently being worked out now, on the basis of a very thoughtful 2008 report on the issue. This would surely not be popular among employers—though it would presumably be much less burdensome than private sector reservations promoted by some—but it would I think have two major benefits, assuming of course that: a) such a commission has jurisdiction over employment practices as they affect all groups, not just minorities;[32] and that b) companies and government departments are required to collect and report to the EOC basic selection, hiring and employment information as a matter of course, as they are in the USA, rather than responding only to particular enquiries, as seems to be envisaged in the 2008 report.[33] First, there is substantial evidence that the more bureaucratised selection processes used by the IIMs and by the UPSC, and that would be encouraged by the existence of the EOC, actually do quite a good job of ensuring employment and selection equity, and that they are widely regarded by Indians as fair. The Sachar committee was able to obtain data on the number of applicants, interviews, and rates of acceptance for all communities for admission to the IIMs and the civil services (the results of theUPSC competition). Sachar found that these procedures led Muslim candidates to have success rates similar to those of other SRCs in the case of the UPSC and actually slightly higher than average for the IIMs.[34] Second, an EOC data collection process without mandates would takes seriously the claims of those in private industry that markets can provide socially equitable outcomes, and provides a way of testing whether these

32. The 2008 report on the EOC, section 4.4 recommended that "The EOC should in principle be open to any person who feels disadvantaged, deprived or discriminated against on grounds of belonging to any social group." But there are recent claims that the EOC's mandate will be more restricted, which would surely undercut its effectiveness and legitimacy. See *Equal Opportunity Commission, What, Why and How?* (Ministry of Minority Affairs, Feb 2008), and Farah Naqvi, "An Unequal Opportunity Commission," *The Hindu*, Aug. 27, 2010.

33. The EOC commission report is a little unclear on this. At some points it seems to focus on creating a process that will largely run on complaints and its own targeted data gathering, while on p.52 it opens the possibility that "all notified employers and educational institutions could be asked to provide certain statistics on an annual basis to the EOC, which would monitor these and take necessary follow up action." The latter approach—collection of such data as a matter of course—would have benefits both in terms of alerting the EOC to obvious discrepancies, as well as encouraging a wider sensitivity towards fair hiring practices among the many employers that an investigative or complaint-based system might not reach.

34. Sachar Report, pp.68, 165-166.

claims are correct—using full information on applicants and their qualifications, instead of just looking at hiring outcomes—before considering more drastic interference with markets.

I would like to close by considering one last question: whether measures to alleviate discrimination such as job and educational reservations, necessary though they may be in the short term, might in the long term increase the importance of caste and religious divisions and increase conflict? Should we be worried about the long-term potential of caste reservations or EOCs, for instance, to 'freeze' caste identities and encourage casteism? I think that this is a real danger, though I recognise that such dangers are sometimes exaggerated by those who are opposed to greater caste equity. But I think there are several ways to make such an outcome less likely. First, and most importantly, the country should adopt policies that encourage broad-based and high economic growth, as well as a social safety net, because both of these will reduce the political and economic stakes in the conflict over reservations, which are largely over the small share of overall employment in the public sector and (potentially, if reservations and EOCs are extended) the organised sectors. As the pay-offs to 'caste' identities become less important than the skills and education necessary to take advantage of these wider opportunities, one can expect the salience of caste identities to decrease. Second, while continuing efforts must be made to increase employment opportunity for all in the private sector, through EOCs and diversity indices, for instance, these need to be designed to be flexible enough to incorporate non-caste identities and recognise different forms of diversity. Third, these measures' gradual success might be linked to their gradual relaxation, so that as markets are shown to be more equal and employment outcomes become fairer (and not until), the reservations measures might be relaxed and reduced. In this way we avoid entrenching identities permanently, without regard to the extent to which these measures are needed to rectify inequality.

References

Basant, Rakesh and Abusaleh Shariff (eds.) (2010). *Handbook of Muslims in India: Empirical and Policy Perspectives.* New Delhi: Oxford University Press.

Bertrand, Marianne and Sendhil Mullainathan (2004). "Are Emily and Greg more Employable than Lakisha and Jamal?A Field Experiment on Labor Market Discrimination", *American Economic Review* 94: 991-1048.

Bhalotra, Sonia and Bernarda Zamora (2010). "Social Divisions in Education in India," in Rakesh Basant and Abusaleh Shariff (eds.) *Handbook of Muslims in India: Empirical and Policy Perspectives.* Oxford. pp.165-98.

Bhaumik, Sumon Kumar and Manisha Chakrabarty (2006). "Earnings Inequality in India: Has the Rise of Caste and Religion Based Politics in India Had an Impact?", *IZA Discussion Paper* No 2008. March. Bonn: Institute for the Study of Labour. Available at *www.iza.org*

Chandra, Kanchan (2004). *Why Ethnic Parties Succeed: Patronage and Ethnic Head Counts in India.* Cambridge. pp.144-50.

Deshpande, Ashwini (2010). "When the Data Tell a Different Story", *Economic and Political Weekly* XLV(40): 33-35, October 2.

Easterly, William Alberto Alesina and Reza Baqir (1999). "Public Goods and Ethnic Divisions", *Quarterly Journal of Economics* 114(4): 1243, November.

Easterly, William and Ross Levine (1997). "Africa's Growth Tragedy: Policies and Ethnic Divisions", *Quarterly Journal of Economics* 112(4), November.

Gopal, Sarvepalli (1983). *Jawaharlal Nehru: An Anthology.* Delhi: Oxford University Press. pp.324-25.

Horowitz, D.L. (1985). *Ethnic Groups in Conflict.* Berkeley.

———. (1991). *A Democratic South Africa?*. Berkeley. pp.214-17.

Huber, John D. (2010). *Measuring Ethnic Voting?* MS, Columbia University. March. Available at *http://www.columbia.edu/~jdh39/Site/Research.html.*

Jefferson, T. (1903). "Autobiography", A. Lipscomb (ed.), *The Writings of Thomas Jefferson*. Vol.1: 72-73.

Kapur, Devesh, Chandra Bhan Prasad, Lant Pritchett and D. Shyam Babu (2010). "Rethinking Inequality: Dalits in Uttar Pradesh in the Market Reform Era", *Economic and Political Weekly* 45, August 28.

Kertzer, David I. and Dominique Arel (eds.) (2002). *Census and Identity: The Politics of Race, Ethnicity, and Language in National Censuses.* Cambridge.

Krishna, B. (1995). *Sardar Vallabhai Patel: India's Iron Man.* New Delhi: Indus. p.482.

Kumar, Sanjay and Alistair McMillan (2004). "Caste Matters, but so do a Whole Lot of Other Things," in *How India Voted Supplement, The Hindu.* Thursday May 20.

Mill, John Stuart (1861). *On Representative Government.* p.230.

Page, Scott (2007). *The Difference: How the Power of Diversity Creates Better Groups, Firms, Schools, and Societies*. Princeton University Press.

Przeworski, Adam, Michael Alvarez, José Antonio Cheibub and Fernando Limongi (1996). "What Makes Democracies Endure?", *Journal of Democracy* 7.1: 39-55.

Rabushka, Alvin and Kenneth Shepsle (1972). *Politics in Plural Societies.* Columbus, Ohio: Charles Merrill. p.85.

Radhakrishnan, P. (1996). "Backward Class Movements in Tamil Nadu", in M.N. Srinivas, *Caste: Its Twentieth Century Avatar*. New Delhi: Viking. pp.110-134, 120-22.

Sengupta, Jhumur and Debnarayan Sarkar (2007). "Discrimination in Ethnically Fragmented Localities: A Study on Public Good Provision in West Bengal", *Economic and Political Weekly*: 3313-21, August 11.

Thorat, Sukhdeo and Joel Lee (2005). "Caste Discrimination and Food Security Programmes", *Economic and Political Weekly* : 4198-201, September 24.

Thorat, Sukhdeo and Katherine Newman (eds.) (2010). *Blocked by Caste: Economic Discrimination and Social Exclusion in Modern India*. New Delhi: Oxford University Press.

Thorat, Sukhadeo and Paul Attewell (2007). "The Legacy of Social Exclusion: A Correspondence Study of Job Discrimination in India", *Economic and Political Weekly* : 4141-45.

Wilkinson, S.I. (2010). "Assessing Muslim Disadvantage", *Economic and Political Weekly* 45(35), August 28-September 03.

———. (2007). "A Comment on the Analysis in the Sachar Report", *Economic and Political Weekly* 42(10), March 10-March 16.

Yadav, Yogendra and Suhas Palshikar (2009). "Between Fortuna and Virtu: Explaining the Congress' Ambiguous Victory in 2009", *Economic and Political Weekly* : 33-46 (at p.41).

37

SUDIPTA KAVIRAJ

Indian Social Democracy and Questions of Culture

This subject is challenging because 'social democracy' is a European political ideal, and some of us have been arguing for a long time against purely imitative political construction. Let us address two objections to the basic proposal of Indian social democracy. The first is based on cultural-historical difference: that social democracy is a concept of the European social imagination, and imitation is never successful. Secondly, it could be said that trying to propose 'social democracy' in India in the 1950s or 1960s would have been understandable, because as a form of social institutions, these could be regarded as highly successful then. Since the 1980s both versions of the idea of socialism—Soviet-style communism and European-style social democracy have been seen as 'failures'. Why should we follow an ideal that its original adherents have abandoned? The first objection comes from 'indigenist' perspectives, and the second from currently influential neo-liberal ones. These objections are not frivolous, and should be answered first.

In my view, the political institutions of modern India have been relatively successful (though I disagree with some who apply what are in my view excessively stringent conditions of political success) precisely because these were innovative and peculiarly adapted to Indian conditions. I hope we have now moved beyond the common opinion, anchored in the prejudices of Western social science, that the Indian political system was essentially an inconsistent amalgam of segments selected from Western constitutions: and that to the extent Indians were successful, it was because of the intrinsic quality of those institutions, and the extent to which they failed was because they were simply not good enough in handling them, or using them as well as Western political elites. This view, anchored in a deep Westernist prejudice, has now been generally abandoned: and success in Indian political institutions is attributed not to the imitation but to the element of innovativeness and adaptation to the Indian context of history and culture. The lesson from this line of thinking is then that political institutions can be successful only when broad general principles, which are preferable on philosophical grounds, are inflected to answer the demands of a particular history. To every one of the institutional ideals of modern politics that India adopted—democracy, secularism, federalism—this rule applied. Constitution makers were attracted to a large principle, ethically adopted them but crafted an intricate system of rules and institutions which were, if seen closely, vastly different from their Western equivalents. It goes without saying that application of all these principles, as time went, became more particularised and indigenised through techniques of detailed political innovation. The lesson is that it is not imitation but adaptation and innovation that succeeds. Experiments in China also bear this out: there is a similar attempt at improvisation and adapting what were European socioeconomic principles to peculiar conditions in China. In strange ways, India and China might move in the same direction from opposite starting points. In India, a 'capitalist' economy with few social safeguards would change towards a social-democratic equilibrium; in China a wholly state-controlled economic system is already seeking to accommodate principles of private enterprise.

Why and how did social democracy arise in Europe?

Imitation is unproductive; but history is always useful. Let us look briefly at the conditions under which what we call social democracy emerged in Europe. The negative view of social democracy that old Marxists held was perversely correct in one respect: it is undeniable that the rise of social democracy helped capitalism survive as an economic system. To my mind, this also shows the undeniable truth of some of Marx's original analysis of a capitalist society. Contrary to general belief, I think that Marx's doctrine worked as a self-falsifying prophecy. He simply predicted that as a consequence of structural and cognitive changes in capitalism, the intensity of economic inequality and the rising cognitive powers of an increasingly skilled and unionised working class would make this system politically untenable. But the idea of a collapse of capitalism was based on the false belief that primary social classes like the entrepreneurs, the workers and the professionals will not work towards modifying this society but hurtle unheedingly towards a cataclysmic breakdown. What happened was a more complex course of events. If an engineer detects weaknesses in the structure of a boiler at particular points and predicts a breakdown, its users will patch precisely those weak points. As a consequence, the boiler might burst at other points but not on those where an explosion was correctly predicted. For our understanding of European history we need a reading which reconciles the views that Marx's prediction was correct and that it failed to come true. It did not come true because of a false deduction from a correct analysis. Both major classes in European society—for very different purposes and with different intentions—realised that this combination of high productivity and deep inequality was untenable as a social system. The power of democracy in particular gave the European proletariat an increasing self-awareness that by capturing governments through their political parties they could prise out of the classes which monopolised the benefits of capitalism's high productivity a share the augmentation of wealth: they could use electoral democracy as a veto against the excessive inequalities of early capitalist economies. They were able to do so because of three conditions. The first was the slow growth of elective procedures, so that even the poor, through universal franchise, came to have an at least formal capacity to affect high decision-making. Secondly, two processes of intellectual-cognitive change assisted this. As Marx noted, the growth of capitalist industries and their internal technical complexity, conferred on industrial workers a new kind of cognitive capacity. This was reinforced by the expansion of basic education for common people. Finally, concentration of capitalist industries themselves produced conditions for large organisations of the European proletariat. At the time of the rise of modern democracy, skeptics said this would give an opportunity to ordinary people to choose which section of their oppressors would oppress them for the next five years. Such prophecies proved false: the elective system worked to fundamentally modify the structures of extreme inequality. This produced a society which did not create an equal society but ended patterns of degrading inequality created by early capitalist development.

In thinking about India, we should examine whether we have similar conditions in our present history. I am struck by a paradoxical contrast between the histories of Western and Eastern Europe. In the early 20th century the two halves of Europe presented a contrast between two systems one of which was based on deep inequality and democratic politics; on the other hand, after the revolution, the Soviet Union created one of the most equal modern societies in history accompanied by a totalitarian political system. And what is historically remarkable is the contrast between the subsequent trajectories of these two political-economic systems which dominated the political imagination of the modern world. Western Europe moved towards a reduction of inequality, while communist Eastern Europe went towards a rapid increase in inequality through the use of differentials of political power. Capitalism, paradoxically, produced egalitarian results, while socialism produced grotesque levels of economic inequality, quite apart from monstrous iniquities of political power. For Marx, the levels of productivity—the extent to which social and political arrangements conduced to the production of wealth (as distinct from distribution)—would determine the existence and survival of economic systems. In this, his basic analysis has been confirmed: the communist system fell, among other reasons, because of its inability to sustain productive growth. Today, however, it would be shortsighted not to examine the collapse of the primitive form of capitalism that the Reagan-Thatcher economic reforms re-introduced in the 1980s. It is equally essential to observe the utterly irresponsible corporate economic processes through which American capitalism produced its own collapse, with a dark shadow of imminent poverty falling over the American middle class. It is true that the collapse of the ideal of primitive capitalism has been less comprehensive than that of the Soviet ideal; yet there is no doubt that it has survived for a considerably shorter time than the Keynesian welfare system which it triumphantly supplanted just 30 years back. To any observer of history, the achievements of social democracy—the idea that the market produces a buoyant economy, though its excesses require state control, and that this should be combined with a political system of democracy which is of irreducible integral value—are considerable, certainly much greater than its two competitors—soviet style communist dictatorships or primitive capitalism. Its more abiding value seems to lie in a more indistinct underlying idea—that it is impossible, if we seek a decent society of political freedom and social dignity, to rely exclusively on either of the two great engines/structures that modernity devised—the modern state and the modern market economy.

It is clear, in retrospect, that the economy over which Nehruvian economic reforms worked was not a capitalist economy in the full sense. The modern sector was small but dynamic, with a powerful impulse towards capitalist enterprise; but it was constrained by two factors. First, its overall proportional share over the economic life of ordinary people was limited: the agricultural segment of the economy was much larger. Secondly, large structures of state regulation imposed substantial restrictions on its effects over the society as a whole. So, although the modern Indian economy after independence underwent capitalist development—primarily through development of industries, and from the mid-1960s through the growth of capitalism in agriculture—it did not have the economic power to either transform the economy as a whole, or to create the vast inequalities that capitalist growth, unconstrained by state interference, produced in Europe. But the recent spurt of economic growth, under conditions in which state regulation has been steadily withdrawn, creates conditions that remind us of the grim European precedent. Rapid economic growth can create conditions like 19th century Europe very quickly in which a relatively small class of elites corner the results of spectacular growth in the economy—producing in them an arrogant and irresponsible sense of dominance, and equally intense resentment among those who have been bypassed by this prosperity.

Why social democracy now?

It appears to me as a layman that there is a striking difference between the role the governments played in the recent economic transformations of the Indian and the Chinese economies. The Chinese change was directed, managed and primarily driven by government policy, partly because of the prior nature of state-controlled Chinese economy. It was only the state which could reduce state control; and the state, even in its period of radical transformation, still micro-managed the economic process. In India, the process of change to high economic growth was established in a different way. Of course, the embattled Congress government, which introduced liberalising policies, takes a lot of credit for the immense change of policy; but this change was not deliberately planned and executed, but introduced under the compulsion of a an unrelenting economic crisis. But the present policymakers deserve credit for not doing what such a crisis-driven policy might do in usual circumstances. Once the immediate crisis was averted, they did not revert to older policies; they examined the overall economic scene deliberatively and continued with these policies, though there were pressures from inside the government party to revert to old practices. The most remarkable features of the Indian process of liberalisation were not merely what was done but also what was not done. The government refused to go into a precipitous transformation of all sectors of economic policy at the same time; instead, they disaggregated the package of liberalising reforms, reducing state control over selective sectors, preserving progressive legislation in others, and did not plunge headlong into an imitative policy, seeking to recreate conditions of African structural reforms or American corporate capitalism—both of which ran into deep troubles. Instead, Indian policymakers showed an admirable nerve, and recognised the need for deliberative consideration of our present state of affairs, the possibilities open to us, and for reasonable discussion of preferable courses of action. Indian policy making showed an entirely unusual capacity, shown once by Nehru in the 1950s in economic and foreign policy, not to assent under pressure to reigning ideological pieties. This is a proper moment again for historical reflection of the Nehruvian kind—because India appears to be on the cusp of historic changes. Precisely because we are not as gifted in one respect as we were then, it requires much more intense discussions of public policy. India was extraordinarily lucky at the time of independence in having a number of extraordinary political figures who were also the leading intellectuals of the nation. We cannot take such luck for granted: and it is particularly essential for people from various sectors of experience of the changefulness of modern life to come together and think about what should be the right course.

Features of Nehruvian political economy

The political economy that the Nehruvian elite designed has been severely criticised by some quarters for hobbling Indian economic growth. I find that opinion misguided: Nehruvian political economy was entirely justified for its time, for building the base of industrial growth, for defending political sovereignty from economic corrosion (as in S Korea, S Vietnam and the Philippines in the 1950s-1960s), though its ability to reduce poverty, precisely because the rate of growth was poor, was consequently dismal. The two serious failures of the Nehruvian elite were precisely the inability to reduce poverty and the unpardonable neglect of primary education—faults which still disfigure our society. It is hard to understand how elites, imbued with a spirit of nationalist idealism, could calmly see the depth of poverty around them, simply turn away, and not consider it a collective shame. However, the economic regime of the Nehru government exercised restraint on professional incomes, salaries and corporate profits. All these sociological-cultural parameters of Indian society have undergone a subtle but decisive change, though academic research is still ruled by radical orthodoxy and neglects engaging in a refined sociology of liberalising reforms. It appears that the culture which condemned business enterprise has changed decisively. This is also helped by a diversification of the business elites, drawn often from knowledge-based industries, which are viewed more positively by the government and the public.

Culture and inequality

The trouble with capitalism is that it stimulates productivity but it also produces a process of unrelenting dis-equalisation: that is, it tends to create new inequality, making people unequal who were equal before precisely through its process of productivity. Economists, particularly radical critics, often create a misleading picture of inequality in society by focusing excessively on its economic side. Economic inequality is certainly deeply disturbing, and undermines social cohesion; but in Indian society cultural inequality runs deep, and should deserve analytical attention. First, our society has a long tradition of linking productive with cultural inequality: the caste order systematically links productive positions in society with cultural inequality. On top of those traditional iniquities of culture, in the colonial period, our society added new kinds of cultural inequality linked to colonial power. Continuing the long tradition of secreting and restricting knowledge in the control of small class, through ritual prohibitions and uses of esoteric languages, colonial Indian society created a new class of elites who established their dominance over others not merely because they held strategic positions of political power, but they held crucial cultural capital; but it is also interesting to analyse what constituted this capital, and exactly how they held it. The emergence of modern culture during colonial times comprehensively disqualified pre-modern systems of knowledge, drawing the intellectual parts of Indian society to forms of modern knowledge. But, more subtly, this modern knowledge, which was the preserve of the intellectual classes, was further controlled by access to the esoteric language of English. What Sanskrit was to pre-modern knowledge, English was to modern. To call such languages a vehicle of communication is misleading: it allowed communicative relations amongst those who knew it; but its other functions, brutally evident to outsiders, was to shut others off, to deny access to ordinary Indians. Cultural inequality in India begins not with knowledge but with language, something more primitive than knowledge.

Elsewhere I have argued that Indian nationalism, to be successful, had to break through this restriction, the division between the narrow elites and the masses on whose support the success of their movement depended. It accomplished that by carefully constructed, intricate structures of bi-linguality. The internal structure of communication of Indian nationalism was bi-lingual. Political elites who led the movement to success communicated with the masses from their own regions in the regional vernaculars, and among themselves in English. Yet, after independence, this political elite mainly forgot about the problem of cultural inequality. Government policy towards language was driven primarily by considerations of 'national integration' rather than cultural inequality. Despite the undeniable achievements of the Nehru regime, it followed a policy of neglect towards cultural issues, particularly the question of everyday fundamental culture. By this I mean not the questions of art, literature, and 'high culture' to which the Nehru government devoted considerable, probably disproportional attention, but the culture that is carried in the everyday transactions of people—with nature, with society, with each other—their basic intellectual skills, their access of necessary languages, of knowledge about the world, and the consequent confidence with which they acted in the social world. Gandhi noted, I think quite rightly, a deep civility in the comportment of the Indian peasant, their economy of gestures, their tendency not to be theatrical and draw attention to themselves. While it made the political world more peaceable, this self-effacement also entrenched an inequality to attention by the state. Modern states are affected by noise, and concede advantages to those who are more clamorous. It is interesting to remark that in the bargaining in the political sphere—either in public debates, or in the more silent pressures exerted on the government by social interests—the peasantry as a group remained almost invisible. The primary discourse about development has also neglected the usually inexplicit spheres of culture. Yet cultural access is sometimes more significant than economic access, and often works as its silent precondition. If we really want to turn Indian democracy into a robust system it is essential to try seriously to rectify this state of cultural inequality between social classes. Let me sketch out in brief some of the effects of cultural inequality in our democratic system.

The public sphere and deliberative democracy

A strong democracy requires an unconstrained and vibrant public sphere—with not merely equality of access but also equality of competence. Habermas's account of the 'public sphere' was deeply flawed, as critics pointed out, because it did not acknowledge that social groups which have access to the public sphere can suffer from disadvantages. The public sphere might be 'open' but internally unequal, its plains sloped against some of the classes which have lesser skills of the kind that determines effectiveness in discussions. In the first two decades in the life of Indian democracy, the public sphere's is discussion about serious questions of public policy remained a debate among the upper class, English-educated intelligentsia, with others remaining mute in the shadowy penumbra surrounding this lighted circle. These circumstances began to change in the 70s, and by the 1980s, these inexplicit barriers were blown away by the growing power of democratic mobilisation. But any serious observer of Indian politics would have noted a paradoxical fact about this 'democratisation', though in my judgement the radical analysts defaulted in their responsibility and pursuing a line of political correctness, by not pointing out the increasing tendency of a group of political leaders who based themselves on identity mobilisation to claim immunity from other aspects of a democratic process. After all, the main purpose of democracy is to curb the power of political elites; and this is done by subjecting them to the procedural regimes contained in the constitution, the laws and enforced by the courts. Politicians often advanced an entirely one-sided picture of democracy to supporters who endorsed on the basis of common identity by equating it with just its elective side. In effect, they advocated a political system in which access to political office should be only through elections but after this election, the politicians should be immune to ordinary legality. This problem of a kind of electoral absolutism is linked, in my judgement, with the question of cultural inequality. It is because the sections of the electorate suffer from a sense of inequality not merely in economic terms but also in culture, that they become unwilling to subject these politicians to scrutiny. Deep inequalities of culture, rooted in different levels of education, differential access on the basis of language, prevent our democracy from developing a real deliberative culture. A true deliberative democracy requires an underlying equality of cultural voice, so that interests who argue their cases in the public arena are first of all able to argue in equal terms, and listened with equal respect. A large part of the electorate which cannot be reached by the deliberative process in the English-speaking media, are denied this access. In fact, in their case, the public sphere is not merely sloped but nearly closed off. And this inequality gets its revenge on the system by creating a different sphere of politics where such arguments do not reach. If we want to transcend the stage of political deliberation now, Indian democracy has to attend seriously to the question of cultural inequality.

Inequality of education

It is acknowledged widely that there is a particularly close relation between education and economic outcomes in peoples' lives. Usually, the market system is flawed, because the market does not affect or interfere with the initial conditions from which people compete; it tends in most cases to simply endorse, reflect or reinforce pre-existing inequalities. Social democracy, on the definition we suggested earlier, is a mechanism which does not stifle the productive power of the market system but mitigates the inequality it necessarily produces as a consequence. This leads to one of the greatest problems in the type of growth India has experienced. In European social democracy too, there was a connection established between economic growth and amelioration in the conditions of the working class and cultural inequality. Before the era of social democracy, European societies also had deep inequality in education and culture. Education and 'cultivation' was confined primarily to the aristocratic elites, but from the 18th century, bourgeois elites began to acquire similar levels of education by going to the universities and technical schools, reducing the differential between these two elite segments. Ordinary citizens, even when they acquired the right to vote went through a highly dissimilar education, though from the 18th century rates of literacy in most West European societies began to rise rapidly. In the two centuries during which social democracy emerged and became established in Western Europe, educational levels for ordinary people rose remarkably, until, in the 1950s, educationally, these societies enjoyed a fair degree of educational opportunity. To be sure, this change was a complex one—partly a condition and partly a consequence of the rise of social democracy itself. As ordinary working class people acquired more education, they perceived inequality more sharply, they were able to intellectually analyse its reasons and consequences, and they realised that extending opportunity of proper education was the real means of creating equality of opportunity. On the other hand, as these classes got more political power through social democratic change, they demanded and were able to implement policies which opened education to ever wider groups of the population. But it is also important to achieve a true understanding of the historicity of such Western achievements. European societies achieved a high degree of educational equality by the 1960s, the high point of Keynesian economic reforms. But subsequently, for a complex set of historical reasons, many of these societies have tended to retreat into an unequal system—with poor students from working class families, often trapped in the decrepit inner cities, or devastated de-industrialised regions, now tending to go to schools that are not randomly but systematically inferior to the schools of the middle class. This transformation in a retrograde direction also has a direct connection with social democracy: the Reagan-Thatcher policies of economic reforms, by dismantling earlier institutions of social democracy, have created these conditions of creeping return of cultural inequality. The resultant degeneration in the deliberative mechanisms of Western democracies are linked to the development of dangerous far Right strands of fanatical nationalism and neo-Nazism.

It is true that after independence literacy rates have slowly crept up. But I find it shameful that Indian political elites complacently celebrate the slow crawling movement towards universal literacy. It is shocking that our political elite finds this a fact to celebrate; but not surprising. Elites do not mind lower classes rising higher in the educational scale, as long as they can maintain their differential by rising even higher in terms of skills and educational opportunities.

Celebration of bare literacy is an act characteristic of this selfish middle class. As long as their children are protected from a real challenge from children of the lower class, they do not mind a little spread of literacy, which does not threaten their dominance. As a consequence, the spread of education in India, after independence, instead of helping real equality has been an inequality-generating process on a massive scale. When apologists for our flawed development point out the increase in the number of schools in a city, for instance, and deploy these statistics to claim that this has helped equality of opportunity, they make a seriously misleading case. To take a simple example, the secondary school system in India is vast but also marked by the grossest levels of inequality. A small sector of schools where middle classes and elites send their children deliver a level of education which is admirable, comparable in my view, with the best schooling available anywhere in the world. In the same cities, next to those schools, there are much larger numbers of inferior schools which cater to the lower middle classes, which are vastly outnumbered by municipal schools which offer a pitifully inferior substitute for education to children of the really poor people. It is a perversely elitist argument, which I come across frequently, to say this is an improvement in their condition, because in most cases these children's parents had no education at all. In fact, the irony lies elsewhere: because, often parents of poor children are themselves not educated, it is easy to cheat them into believing that their children are also getting an education, because they cannot judge the content of the education being delivered in these schools. Subsequently, when a child from that school system is not able to compete with children from upper class families in getting admission into prestigious educational institutions—like the good universities, or IITs—middle class parents can view this outcome as a pure function of intellectual merit; while, in fact, this a consequence of rigged and asymmetric system.

The case of IIT education illustrates another interesting problem. In the early years of their functioning, the IITs were linked fairly closely to the ordinary syllabi taught in public schools; at least it was common for gifted pupils from ordinary schools to pass the entrance exams and enter the IITs which of course gave them, on all accounts, an education of very high quality. Due to various complex pressures, by the 1970s, the IITs came to use an admission system which became hard to pass for students who were trained in common schools. Since that time a group of 'tutorial colleges' came up which trained candidates for the IIT and later also for medical college examinations. It was common knowledge that to have a serious chance of getting into these highly prized institutions of higher learning, students had to train themselves through these courses. But these courses charged high fees which could be afforded only by the middle class and the wealthy. Till very late, IITs and medical colleges in the public sector charged fees that were very reasonable. But this precisely created a perverse paradox. To get higher education at nominal fees, students had to go through a highly expensive preparatory course—which meant that these institutions became exclusive preserves of middle and upper classes in society. In purely formal terms, admission to these schools remained open to all, irrespective of their income; but, in actual fact, entry into them became effectively closed to the vast majority of students who went to India's ordinary public school systems for no fault except their parents' low income. This is just one example of a trend of informally excluding poorer people from what is officially an open system. These facts make a travesty of the formal rules of equality of opportunity.

The culture of reservation

From this angle, the system of reservation produces entirely counter-productive consequences. A curious aspect of the bitter debate about reservation is rarely observed. In most cases of this kind, beneficiaries of affirmative action policies are contented; those whose interests are harmed by affirmative action are sharply alienated and critical. The Indian case is marked by a peculiar disillusionment of both sides: both the beneficiaries and the others criticise reservation policies bitterly. The reason for this is not hard to find. In the Indian economy, only a small proportion of employment is in the organised sector, and state employment comprises a part of this sector. Reservation policies regarding employment apply only to this small sector of the economy.

Despite reservations in this sector of employment, naturally, the large majority of people who suffer from caste related poverty are not covered by these devices. These lower caste groups, as communities, not the individuals who benefit from them, can therefore legitimately criticise these policies as ineffectual, if not disingenuous; while other groups view these reservations as a proportion unfairly taken out of the general pool. Because of the scale mismatch—between what needs to be done and what it is possible to do through these reservations—our reservation policy has reached an impasse; and a new discussion needs to be started.

The policy of reservation has some significant achievements but the sheer persistence of the complaints from the side of the lower caste groups shows the limits of what it can accomplish. Particularly in education, which is the avenue for all later opportunities, the question of deep inequality needs to be addressed. With the growing incomes of the Indian middle classes, schools which cater to their children do not require government support. The middle classes earn enough now to support high quality education for their own children. In line with the basic principle of equalising opportunities, the government needs to invest much more heavily in educational preparation of children from poorer groups—provide them with a quality of education that is not inferior to those of others. This will address at least one of the major causes of grievance of the lower caste and poorer groups. This will also address the problem of the subtle inequality of access that exists, preventing real upward mobility from lower caste groups on a wide scale. If successful, this might also reduce the pressure for constant expansion of reservation.

Expansion of high quality education is required for two other reasons as well—related to the unprecedented processes of globalisation. One of the major changes of context which Nehruvian elites did not have to contend with is the process of globalisation—including globalisation of education and cultural structures. The decline of education in public schools in Western societies—much debated in the public sphere—is a primary result of the slow break up social democratic institutions. Neo-liberal reforms have dismantled some of the relatively egalitarian institutions of the

Keynesian period of the western societies, leaving them subject the deep disequalising effects of unregulated capitalist enterprise. Opportunities opening up through economic globalisation have already been used effectively by Indian and Chinese business groups; and in the Indian case, a major part of this growth has been based on the supply of highly trained personnel produced by institutions of higher education. Given the nature of our education, and its internal inequality, this is a small segment of the trained manpower that India can produce if high quality education does not remain a preserve of elites and middle classes but of ordinary people. This can give India an enormous competitive edge.

On the opposite side, with the rapid growth of elite and middle class income, a trend has started which runs opposite the purposes of Nehruvian policy. The objective of expansion of higher education in the 1950s and 1960s was the achievement of self-reliance, a reduction of dependence on the scientific and research capacities of the more technologically advanced economies. Now a substantial section of the Indian middle class elites possess the economic capacity to send their children abroad to acquire higher education. This can lead to a trend in which the best among the students go to Indian institutions only for the primary part of their education—the school system, and move outside for higher training. This will result in starving Indian institutions of their best products, precisely at the time when the society and its government has enough resources to support a wider structure of excellent higher education.

The primary reason for the attractiveness of social democracy is due to its capacity to balance the impulse of growth generated by capitalist enterprise with principles of social justice. Arrangements of social justice can be produced in a society not merely by the state, through its directive institutions but also by a variety of public institutions which in some cases, to perform their function well, ought to be outside the direct control of the state. In contemporary Indian society, it is essential to recognise first, that economic inequality carries cultural consequences, but also, that there are deep inequalities of culture which are specific to our history. To realise the ideals of social democracy in the Indian context is to address the problem of cultural inequality, not just the economic.

For redressing inequalities of culture, which disfigure our society despite its recent economic growth, we require a comprehensive debate about a serious and fundamental transformation of education. Pursuit of ideals of social equality in this historical juncture would be not merely ethically desirable; it might give India greater competitive advantage in an increasingly globalising world.

38

YOGENDRA YADAV

The Politics of Feasible Social Democracy

In this paper I wish to draw upon my engagements with political theory, political analysis and political activism to answer a question that lies at the heart of this conference: what would a feasible politics of social democracy look like in contemporary India? Specifically, I intend to build on an emerging perspective on democratic theory, some of the available and accumulating evidence on Indian elections and my own experience of working with non-party (or at least non-mainstream parties) political formations to address one of the most urgent and significant questions in contemporary India. Stated ambitiously, how can the political ideal of democracy be combined with the promise of social and economic well being? Or to state it minimally, how can democratic governance become much more responsive to the demands and needs of the vast majority of its citizens than is the case today?

Let me frame the question more carefully for analytical purposes: under what conditions can political competition lead to a political will on the part of the ruling party for using state power in order to carry out floor-securing social policies in India? Here 'political will' means more than just a wish or preference on the part of the rulers. Political will is an effective preference that overrides other competing preferences and overcomes routine systemic obstacles. I use 'floor-securing social policies' to refer to those policies which are aimed at securing minimum material conditions for dignified living for every citizen. Note that this stipulation is stronger than the requirement of social welfare as commonly understood, for welfare in this sense is compatible with a large proportion of population living below the basic level required for dignified life as long as they are provided with some relief. Also note that the point here is not just framing the policies (or just enacting laws) but carrying these out by providing resources and using state capacities. At the same time, this formulation is weaker than the demand for strict equality. A floor-securing social policy would of necessity lead to significant redistribution and reduction in inequalities, but in principle this requirement is compatible with a fair degree of inequality of outcomes.

This way of formulating the question assumes the existence and availability of intellectual design, material resources and institutional capacity for floor-securing social policies. But it does not presuppose a guarantee that such policies secure the floor for every citizen. It also assumes that such floor securing policies are not necessarily followed by democratically elected governments. Indeed, it implies that for democratically elected governments in post-independence India this is an exception rather than the rule. The crucial variable is the presence or absence of what is called here political will, which is assumed to be a function of political incentives and disincentives for the ruling party and is in turn related to the nature of political competition.

The question posed here lies at the heart of a project of feasible social democracy. Social democracy can mean three different kinds of arrangements. It could mean capitalism with 10 per cent discount (to steal a phrase from Roberto Unger), or may be 20. This version prevails in many western European democracies and is viewed with varying degrees of enthusiasm depending upon whether the discount is closer to 10 or to 20. Democratic this arrangement certainly is, at least in a minimalist sense, but the prefix 'social' makes excessive demands on charity. At any rate the West European experience of securing floor for a tiny slice of the poor is qualitatively different from the Indian challenge of lifting a majority of its citizens above a minimum threshold of access to goods and services. The second type, once called 'socialist democracy' sought to mix 'social' ownership of means of production with 10 per cent, or usually less, discount to democratic appearances. Socialist it was—if you were willing to equate state ownership of property with social ownership with socialism—but to call it democracy made excessive demands on credulity. Thankfully, Indian democracy is far too robust to attempt a repeat of the East European experiments with socialist democracy.

The third version takes seriously the challenge of combining 'demos' with 'social' without compromising on political self rule or social justice implicit in this ideal. This combination, like all attempts to combine two independent ideals, appears to make impossible demands on our imagination, for there are no ready-made models or precedents available for this. 'Democratic socialism' in its previous incarnation, this version has so far lacked energetic politics and intelligent economics. In this paper, I use the term social democracy in this third sense of the term. Not just because I prefer challenges to imagination over demands on charity or credulity but principally because to my mind this version presents us with an ethical ideal worth striving for. Besides, this ideal is very much embedded in the letter and the spirit of the Indian Constitution. This paper is about the political feasibility of this ideal. It searches for political means and social ends which are within the horizon of what can be realised within our life time or thereabout.

This search involves resolving a paradox of the co-existence of democracy with mass poverty in India since independence. Section I argues that there is something to be surprised about what happened in India. It does so by spelling out a model of why we should expect democratic politics in a poor country to attend to floor-securing social policies. The second section begins to suggest why this expectation was not realised in India by attending to the specificities of electoral politics in the Indian context. It identified three key and distinctive features of Indian elections that are relevant to understanding why operation of political competition did not generate political will for floor-securing social policies. The third section breaks down the chain of political causality and examines the operation of incentives and disincentives at each stage. The implications of this reasoning for politics of feasible social democracy are spelt out in section IV.

I

Paradox of electoral democracy in India

Let me begin by following the 'minimalist' tradition of defining democracy as a form of government in which those who rule are elected by the people in competitive elections and run the risk of losing power in regular elections. In this definition the election of rulers by the people is subject to some qualifications:

a. The election should be competitive in that there should be more than one serious contender.

b. The opposition should have a fair chance of winning, should they have popular support.

c. The electoral mandate cannot be revoked by the loser and the winner should get to exercise highest political power, and

d. The election should be held at regular interval irrespective of the wishes of the incumbent.

Looked closely, this definition is actually not so minimal, for these conditions cannot exist without there being a certain regime of freedom, rights and rule of law. But I do not wish to pursue that line of argument here. A minimalist definition of democracy is particularly suited to the task at hand, for it reminds us that democracy is only one of the things we value, and that it cannot be presumed (not by definitional fiat in any case) to usher in all other good things. We cannot assume that democracy has benign social consequences. Obversely, we must not insist that a regime that does not bring about social well-being cannot be called democracy. It reminds us that the conceptual trick of equating democracy with social democracy may have its rhetorical value but it comes with huge analytical costs.

Following this definition, it seems fair to categorise India since independence as 'democracy'. To be sure, there has been more than one instance where these minimum rules have been violated. The illegitimate, though strictly speaking not unconstitutional, extension of the term of the Lok Sabha during the Emergency period (June 1975 to March 1977) was one instance at the national level. There are several instances of gross violation of the minimum requirements of a democratic rule at the state level, where the overall verdict of the elections could not be described as a fair reflection of popular choice. I would put all elections in J&K except 1977, 2002 and 2008, all elections in Nagaland before 2003 and in Mizoram before 1987, the state assembly election in West Bengal in 1972, Assam in 1983 and Punjab in 1992 in that category. This is an embarrassing but a finite list of exceptions that otherwise serves to prove the rule that India since independence must be characterised as democracy.

The other side of the paradox is the continued existence of a vast population well below a floor of minimum goods and services required for dignified living. I do not wish to enter into a discussion on the very rich literature on competing approaches to defining poverty: absolute or relative measures, objective or subjective approaches, material or non-material dimensions. I am not competent to get into this dispute. For the purpose of the present argument it is necessary to reiterate what would be acceptable by nearly all the participants in the debate, namely that a substantial population in India is poor. The exact count does not quite matter to my argument here except in a minimal way: the poor are not a tiny fraction of the Indian population which may be explained away as a minor malfunctioning of the otherwise well-functioning system, nor are the numbers diminishing in a way as to make poverty a phenomenon of passing interest. Although the official count of the Government of India puts the proportion of persons 'below the poverty line' somewhere around a quarter of the country's population, all reasonable estimates point to a much higher figure. As has been pursuasively argued, the official 'poverty line' is really a 'starvation line'. Once floor level requirement of material needs other than food intake (clothing, housing, energy, medical care, education) are factored in, nearly two-thirds of our population lives below the floor of minimum goods and services required for dignified living.

Why are we surprised at the co-existence of democracy and mass poverty? Simply put, majority rules in democracies and we should be surprised if those who (can) rule do not use this power to improve their conditions of life. This is not to say that the desire or demands of every kind of majority is routinely fulfilled in any democracy (the strong desire of an overwhelming majority of the electorate in all the democracies to have clean, accountable and efficient government is routinely frustrated), but merely to suggest that its non-fulfillment calls for an explanation. There is nothing new in this expectation: democracy was always seen as the rule of the poor. Before the recent spread of democratic form all over the globe, democracy was the dread of the propertied classes and the hope of those who believed in radical redistribution.

The expectation is based on the following chain of argument: In conditions of mass poverty, it is reasonable to expect that those who live below the floor of dignified existence would desire to move out of it. It is also likely that the existence of mass poverty will generate a moral unease among a section of those who are not poor, unless this form of deprivation is culturally sanctified. Both of these, or at least the first one, will generate a reservoir of latent or revealed preferences for floor-securing social policies. Given a free media, it is reasonable to expect these preferences to be articulated in the public domain and translated into definite signals. This issue is expected to become at least one of the main issues of public life that is reflected in social and ideological divisions and is likely to attract the 'median voter' who is herself likely to be poor. In conditions of open and free competitive politics, the contending parties are expected to respond to these signals by changing their political agenda to reflect the priorities of the median voter. Since the issue has some salience in public life and the poor are a very large part of the electorate, the party that is seen as presenting a credible floor-securing social policy should stand a better chance of winning the elections. The prospect of winning elections and holding on to power in the next one is expected to provide the political will to design and carry out floor securing social policy.

This logic is summarised in Figure 38.1. The purpose of this simplified model is to spell out the logic behind an intuitive expectation and to identify the various stages where the real life experience of democracy can be compared with this expectation.

The model does not predict that its expectation shall be fulfilled. The point instead is to identify the mechanisms that account for the non-fulfillment of this expectation.

Figure 38.1

Why do we Expect Democratically Elected Government to Carry Out Floor Securing Social Policies

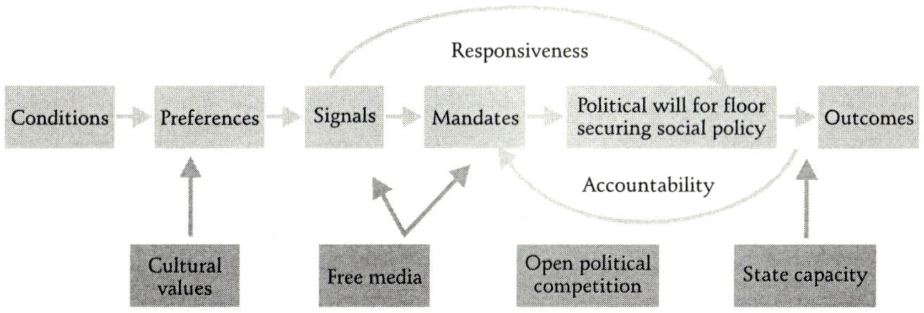

In fact, the paradox of the co-existence of democracy and mass poverty is deeper in India than in many other societies. Some of the common reasons why democracies do not care for their poor do not hold true for India. First of all, the institutional design of Indian democracy (parliamentary system, assymetrical federalism, flexible constitution amendment) is not 'demos-constraining' in that it does not put significant obstacles to the democratic popular will. There are not too many veto points which might account for the failure of floor securing social policies to be legislated and implemented. Secondly, the party system is intensely competitive with very high electoral volatility. The first-past-the-post system accentuates the effect of voters' volatility into dramatic change in seats and government formation. Though the level of volatility has come down in this decade compared to the previous one, a ruling party in an Indian state has just about 50 per cent chances of coming back to power. Parties cannot afford to be complacent and overlook issues that might concern a significant proportion of population. Thirdly, the poor have not opted out of democratic politics, at least not from the routine participation in electoral politics. The evidence put forward by the National Election Studies of the CSDS shows that the participation level and the sense of the efficacy and legitimacy of the system are still fairly impressive in the case of the poor. Table 38.1 summarised some of this evidence. Finally, the state capacity in India is higher than most of the comparable poor countries; it still commands the force to impose its will and is not crippled by absence of resources to meet some of its key projects. All this makes it even more intriguing that the ruling parties/coalitions should not (be able to) muster adequate political will to carry out floor-securing social policies.

II

Specificity of Indian elections

Before we ask why the system of open political competition does not lead to political will for floor-securing social policies, we need to understand the specificity of the Indian system of elections that structures political competition. "Modern politics in post-colonial societies involves strange objects masquerading under familiar names" (Kaviraj, 2009). Indian elections are a good case in point. As the system of competitive elections expands to most parts of the world, there is a tendency to interpret and evaluate electoral politics as if it is the same and familiar object all over the globe. This tendency often goes unnoticed, since the end-product of this game is recorded in a format that is universally recognised and lends itself to easy surface comparison. It's all about seats and votes, chemistry of popular mood or the arithmetic of alliances, advantage or otherwise for the incumbent government or representative and of course the charisma or otherwise of the political leadership. We do recognise the differences across countries in terms of the impact of the electoral system, the structure of political choices offered by the party system, the social basis of political preferences, agenda setting and public opinion formation, the invisible role of issues and ideologies, interests and identities. Yet we simply assume that elections perform the same role everywhere. The end result of this similarity is that the experience of electoral politics in societies like India is interpreted in the light of the narrow historical experience of Western Europe and North America.

One of the first things that strikes any observer of Indian elections is the centrality of elections in India's political life. Banners, posters and hoardings fill the streets; massive processions and rallies are a norm; the media is full of election news and every street corner is buzzing with political gossip. Though on a steady decline of late, this kind of visibility of Indian elections symbolises the pivotal role elections have come to occupy in Indian politics. If a tension between the pre-existing social form and the borrowed legal-political structure provides the basic frame for understanding Indian democracy, the story of Indian politics is a story of the attempt by millions of ordinary people to write their own political agenda in an alien script. An encounter such as this requires, if it is to lead to meaningful outcomes, bridges or hinges which connect the two different worlds. The institution of elections came to perform this crucial role in India. It became the hinge that connected the existing social dynamics to the new political structures of liberal democracy allowing for reciprocal influence. Election is often the site for a fusion of popular beliefs and political practices with high institutions of governance.

Thus election is an occasion for the transfer of energy and resources from the 'unorganised' to the 'organised' sector of democracy. This is the moment when the legal–constitutional order of liberal democracy makes a contact with the messy social and political reality of India. The 'formal' sector is highly visible, it leads a legal-constitutional existence, it involves 'civil society' groups and NGOs or a certain segment of political parties, it speaks a familiar modern language, mobilises secular identities and is easy to incorporate into a global register of democracy, even if it draws modest energy and participation. Every political actor is aware of another, 'informal' sector, often seen as a source of embarassment. Political organisations and movements that inhibit this sector speak home-spun hybrid langauge, fall back upon identity based mobilisation. Though political practices in this sector lead an invisible, often para-legal, existence below the radar, this sector remains the most happening political site in terms of popular mobilisation and energy. The chasm that separates the two worlds and the absence or non-functioning of the other possible bridges has resulted into the unusual salience of the institution of elections. This unique role is what accounts for the continued dynamism of the electoral process in India, while a number of other imported institutions and processes are floundering.

This hinge-like role has meant that Indian elections do simply too many things. All over the world elections perform the foundational function of legitimising the rulers in the eyes of the ruled and of ensuring transfer of power without violence. They are also expected to ensure responsive and accountable government. This in itself would have been complicated enough. Modern democracies, especially those with first-past-the-post electoral system as in India, expect their voters to use a singular instrument of vote to elect a representative, select a ruling party, choose from various policy packages and name a leader.

As if this was not enough, elections in India perform many more functions. For a post-colonial country like India, successful elections are still a symbol of a national political community, something of a festival of collective identity. For the poor and the marginalised, excluded from the normal functioning of state, elections are an affirmation of their citizenship and are seen as a sacred ritual of political equality. Notwithstanding a robust media that routinely uses public opinion polls, elections are still the principal site for dissemination of political ideas and information and also the only reliable method to gauge public opinion on the big issues facing the country. Elections force political parties to take into account ideas, interests, and entities that do not lend themselves to easy aggregation through instrumentalities of the 'organised' sector. Thus elections often appear as the only bridge between the people and power, as the only reality check in the political system.

Elections are also an occasion for settling, unsettling or resettling local equations of social dominance and the arena of struggles for social identity and dignity. Elections are a site for contestation for social dominance in a locality, leading to assertion by dominant social groups and protests by subaltern groups. Attempts by clever political entrepreneurs to manufacture a social majority often involve building of a local coalition of castes and communities. This often leads to invention of community boundaries and sometimes gerrymandering of the settled boundaries. In a micro as well as macro setting, elections are an occasion for distribution and redistribution of resources. This is the time for patronage distribution as well as the occasion for the ordinary citizens to collect their 'dues' from the political class.

All this accounts for the festival like character of the Indian elections and the fierceness with which elections are contested here. At the same time, this compression of multiple decisions into a single act also results in an under-emphasis on the representational functions of elections.

Two other structural features of Indian elections have accentuated this difficulty. One of these has to do with the problem of scale in politics. The design of representative democracy in India simply lifted a system meant for much smaller communities and applied it to a polity of continental scale. This resulted in a many-fold increase in the scale of representation and led to a qualitative difference in the nature of the relationship between the representative and the represented. An Indian member of Lok Sabha typically represents a population over 21 lakhs and an MLA in one of major states represents anything between 2 and 5 lakhs. A comparison with the scale in Britain (less than a lakh for each member in the House of Commons), which served as the model, brings out the sharp contrast. The mega-scale of the system of representation had many consequences for the nature of political representation. The minimum requirements of resources and information needed for this kind of election result in a very high entry barrier for a new entrant to the system. The impossibility of a face-to-face interaction between the representative and the represented has necessitated an army of rent-seeking intermediaries and is beginning to lead to mediatisation of constituency-level politics.

Finally, multiple levels of governments, with its corollary of multiple non-corresponding electoral cycles in a parliamentary system, have introduced a peculiar disjunction between different levels of government and elections. Over the years, state level politics has become the principal arena of political contestation.

But the design of Indian federalism allocates principal power and resources to the central government. And most of the principal or at least immediate problems faced by citizens require a solution at the level of local self government. In the absence of well functioning local bodies with matching resources or accountable local officials, elections to parliament and state assemblies also perform a routine municipal function of attending to local grievances and connecting the people to the administration. Parliamentary elections often reflect the verdict for or against state government. This conflation in levels has meant that the central government is simultaneously under-accountable and over-accountable. It is over-accountable, for every round of state-assembly elections is politically sensitive for the national government. At the same time the central government can be under-accountable, for its fate is largely determined by what some other governments do.

III

Working of competitive politics in India

Now that we have identified a paradox and some specifically Indian factors that can help explain it, let us look systematically at what goes wrong and where in the chain of causality that leads us to expect floor-securing social policies to emerge from democratic competition. Let us go back to Figure 38.1 and look at the various stages in that model in the light of the working of democratic politics in India. To recall, these stages and the relevant questions are:

Stage1—From condition to preference: Does the condition of mass poverty lead to preference for floor securing politics? To what extent and intensity do the people, poor and non-poor, see poverty as a problem and desire some steps to be taken for its removal? This is the domain of popular beliefs, attitudes and values.

Stage 2—From preference to signals: Once formed, are these preferences articulated in the public domain so as to constitute political signals? To what extent does this issue frame public discourse and becomes an effective demand? This stage involves the nature of the public sphere, especially modern mass media.

Stage 3—From signals to mandates. How do competing political parties receive these signals and incorporate these into their political platform so as to win a mandate? Does this promise of floor-securing social policies become a decisive issue? This stage involves the nature and structure of party competition.

Stage 4—From mandate to political will: How is the mandate decoded by political actors? What effective priority do the parties and politicians assign to floor securing social policies, once they are in power? This involves party-government interaction, policy formation and political judgement.

Stage 5—From policy to outcome: How are the floor-securing policies implemented? What sort of energy do governments and parties put into the implementation of the policies, once these are made? This is the domain of governance and public administration.

Let us take up these stages one by one to identify the specifically Indian mechanism for non-working of the expected logic of democratic politics.

Stage1—From condition to preference: The following reasons are usually put forward to explain why floor securing policies are not demanded by the worst-off groups in many democracies. One, the poor do not think they are poor, for they look at their poverty not in absolute terms but relative to their immediate reference group and to immediate past. Two, the disadvantaged tend to blame themselves for their own fate and do not expect the state to deliver. Three, the poor share the ideology of the well-off and therefore oppose any radical measure for redistribution even though it goes against them; what they want is direct and personal benefit, not structural change. Four, despite their unhappy present, the worst-off believe in the promise of future. Let us call all these mechanisms for ideological masking.

First impression might suggest that these ideological mechanisms work as strongly in India as elsewhere. Typically, the poor do not identify their problem as 'poverty'. There is no perfect match between the objective and the subjective measures of poverty as the poor compare themselves with their neighbours. Evidence shows that the poor do share in the optimism about economic conditions in future. There is of course widespread belief in *karma* theory which allows people to reconcile to their fate.

At the same time it would be premature, based on these impressions, to draw the conclusion that the structure of popular beliefs is a real problem in the democratic chain. Consider the following evidence from the recent surveys of the national representative samples carried out by the CSDS. There is a significant mismatch between people's 'objective' class measured by their income and assets and their self-perceived rank in society, but it works in favour of the politics of the poor. More than 90 per cent respondents thought that they belonged to the lower half in terms of the rich-poor hierarchy. Even among the 'rich' 80 per cent thought so. Two, while the poor in India tend to be more satisfied with their economic conditions compared to Latin America, but there is now a good fit between the externally measured economic status and the level of satisfaction with one's economic condition. Three, the poor report greater deterioration in their economic condition in the recent past compared to other groups and are a little less optimist than others. Four, virtually every opinion poll on the 'major problems' confronting the country has 'price rise' and 'unemployment' as the top problems irrespective of the level of inflation prevailing and the trends in employment. I would venture to suggest that in India 'price rise' has little to do with what the economists call inflation; it is a proxy for lack of purchasing power. Five, over the last four decades, the support for some egalitarian measures like land and wealth ceiling has not gone down substantially; among the poor the support for these measures is overwhelming.

In other words, there exists a fairly large reservoir of latent demand and support for floor-securing public policies. Ideological masking is not absent in India but that is not the real bottleneck.

Stage 2—From preference to signals: Given India's democratic system, the rapidly expanding and politically free media and the vibrant movement sector, it is natural that this latent desire is expressed in the public domain. But there are three factors that do not allow this articulation to become effective. One, greater 'professionalisation' of the media has resulted in exclusive attention of the media to its 'middle class' consumers. In the absence of professional instruments of public opinion, even opinion polls are encroached upon by the elite via internet and SMS polls. The worst off themselves do not take much part in the discussion on shaping of social policy, given the strong relationship between disadvantage and lack of education. Two, as and when poverty does get discussed, it is framed in such a way as to present it as episodic and accidental rather than chronic and systemic. The eclipse of left ideology has meant that the issue of poverty is not understood in a comprehensive manner. Regionalisation and localisation of the media in the last one decade has contributed to the fragmentation of poverty as an issue by creating largely exclusive zones of information. Three, there is of course blatant capture of media by vested interests, as revealed in the controversy about 'paid news'. Although much of the public discussion has remained confined to the phenomenon of news buying during elections, the malady is more widespread and extends to non-election time news. Especially pernicious is the practice of 'private treaty' through which economic interests purchase consistent and favourable news for their activities.

Thus, articulation is a crucial stage where 'slippage' takes place in the chain that potentially links democratic politics to social policies and thereby potentially strong popular preferences turn into weak signal. The real problem is not that there is a complete silence on poverty but that the issues and problems concerning a majority of the country's population is fragmented and dislocated. Perhaps it is better to see this not as a limitation of these agents but as a structural attribute of the public sphere in contemporary India.

Stage 3—From signals to mandates: Despite weak signals from the media, issues related to some of the social policies get fair amount of attention in the arena of party political competition. This is partly because the political actors are not fully constrained by the terms in which the media and opinion makers articulate this issue. As a rule, Indian politicians and political parties do not depend entirely on the media for information on matters that concern them directly and are better informed than the media on poverty related matters.

They have to be, for parties do compete with each other to be seen as pro-poor and in many cases the image of being anti-poor can deal a decisive blow to a ruling party. Political actors are quick to realise the value of the poor and the need to attract them. They seem to have an intutive sense of what the research in recent years has uncovered. Research has confirmed that the poor voters turn out to vote in no less proportion than the rest of the electorate; this adds to the sheer magnitude of their vote and confirms them as the key target for all parties. It is also clear that the poor cannot be targeted through the 'middle men' any more; they vote as much 'on their own' as anyone else and thus need to be wooed in their own terms. The poor fall behind the rest in taking active interest in politics and in taking active part in political mobilisation and agitation, yet their number makes them the largest group in this respect as well. The presence of the poor among the party decision makers and the winning candidates is very low and has shrunk rapidly, yet there is a critical mass of political workers within most parties who have seen or experienced poverty. This is more than what can be said of the media or bureaucracy.

All this ensures fair degree of general attention to the 'poor' as a category and 'poverty' as an issue. Yet it does not always translate into specific floor-securing social policies as key issues of electoral competition. Public political debates in India are notoriously devoid of specifics. Party manifestos manage to escape making specific promises and are not subjected to public critical scrutiny. Therefore, political parties succeed in taking a short-cut. As noted above, the incorporation of these issue in the party political agenda undergoes distortion of another kind due to structure of political competition and the nature of political incentives available to the participants. Scale of electoral competition (size of an assembly or parliamentary constituency, the population of a state which is the effective unit of competition) is too large for any of the 'local' poverty related issues or the movement of the poor to be viable; the smallest scale of political competition (an assembly constituency) is too big for an organisation of the poor to make a difference.

Similarly, the first-past-the-post system introduces a very high threshold of viability for a new entrant to electoral competition;

the established parties don't face effective challenge from pro-poor movements. The time horizon available to political actors to show results is very short and has shrunk further after the democratic upsurge of the 1990s; this pushes the political actors from a structural or institutional approach to poverty reduction in favour of the populist strategy of highly visible direct but ineffective doles. Finally, the regionalisation of polity in the last two decades has meant that the vote of the poor has got effectively fragmented across political blocs while the upper strata has been able to consolidate itself.

The cumulative effect of this structure of political competition is that when it is incorporated in political agenda, poverty becomes largely a symbolic issue tied to short term populist measures and the large scale participation of the poor is reduced to a marginal significance.

Stage 4—From mandate to political will: If there is one stage where the possibility of pro-poor public action is most severely curtailed, it is in the transition of mandate into political will for floor-securing social policies. The widespread public desire, its articulation and intensity of political competition ensures that even in the worst of cases, the party that wins elections is tied to a series of pro-poor policies or promises. What happens after the party wins the elections is a very different matter. The significance of this level ensures that pro-poor organisations and ideologues focus almost exclusively on this and much of the discussion takes the forms of tales of moral betrayal. Some of the limitations arise from direct instrumental control over needy and greedy political leaders by the rich. This takes various forms. In the absence of any mechanism for livelihood support for political workers, most political leaders who start as poor are forced to come under the patronage of and make peace with the local rich. The absence of transparent mechanism for party and campaign finance ties most parties to protecting the interest of the regional and national capital. Political corruption after coming to power takes various forms: political-political funds (collected for political purposes and managed by the party), political-personal funds (collected for future elections but controlled by the leader personally) and personal-personal funds (collected for personal and family wealth and managed personally).

But the strongest of these limitations arise from factors beyond instrumental control of politicians by the rich. Some of these structural factors are well known. There is a built-in drag in the system, for most of the crucial decisions affecting the economy are taken in the private sector driven by profit motive; this acquires a salience in India with the shrinking of state sector vis-à-vis the private sector. The emergence of independent centres of power (regulators, media, judiciary) have limited the scope of public action available to elected representatives. For the first time a fear of 'capital strike', 'capital flight' or inability to woo investors has become a political factor thus limiting the scope of governmental activity. Besides these factors well covered by the literature, we need to notice two more factors that play a crucial role at this stage. One, the weakness of institutions of accountability allows ruling parties more space to deviate from their promise than they would otherwise have had. Most of the regional media is closely tied to the interest of the ruling party. Formal institutions of scrutiny are either fragile or not quite independent of the ruling party. Civil society organisations are still very weak in their ability to name and shame the parties and leaders and hold them to their promises. Finally, there is a genuine cognitive paralysis of what really is the best policy or institution to bring about pro-poor outcome. One cannot blame the politician for being as confused as the economists.

Stage 5—From policy to outcome: This level is a continuation of the last one and shares most of the constrains mentioned above. Policies often do not achieve what they were meant to and very often the simple reason is the poor design of the policies. But pro-poor policies also do not succeed for they are poorly monitored and publicised. The absence of effective party organisation at the local level for most political parties has meant that the implementation of a policy is left to the governmental machine which is unable to disturb the local power equation.

IV

Political lessons for our times

The essay began by promising an understanding of politics of feasible social democracy in our lifetime. Much of the analysis offered above is about why there is no politics of feasible social democracy in contemporary India. It puts together various bits and pieces of the political mechanism which prevents successful politics from being social democratic or social democratic politics from being viable. It is time now to tie these threads together and offer a positive if synoptic account of what a feasible politics of social democracy could look like in contemporary India.

Let us go back to the question posed in the beginning: under what conditions can political competition lead to a political will on the part of the ruling party for using state power in order to carry out floor-securing social policies in India? The analysis offered above cautions against two simple minded answers. On the one hand, it offers reasons to question the idea that the needs, desires and demands of the overwhelming majority of the underprivileged would prevail in a free and open political competition in a democratic setting. This dominant and celebratory accounts of democracy turns out to be rather naïve understanding of how the logic of political competition works. As in open market, free competition with level playing field is an ideal that is rarely approximated in real life. On the other hand, the analysis offered above also resists the rather gloomy conclusion that this democracy is but a sham, that the final outcomes are predetermined to favour the interests of the economically and socially dominant classes. Open political competition in democratic setting does offer many openings, some of which can lead to radical social policies. The probability of enactment of social justice policies is higher when it depends on the survival instinct of the politician and their hunger for power than when it depends upon the goodwill of political guardians or the vanguard. At any rate, any rejection of the democratic system must be tempered by a realisation that this may be the only game in town, that the citizens, including the poor, may have invested more in this system than is often acknowledged.

A rejection of these two extremes opens the way for a tentative and contingent answer. Political competition can and does lead to political will on the part of the ruling party for using state power in order to carry out floor-securing social policies, but the prevalence of many factors ensures that it happens rarely. Some of these are structural and cannot be wished away. Gross economic and social inequalities, especially the system of private property and its skewed distribution, sets limits to how level playing the political field can be. In the absence of conscious efforts to neutralise the effect of private money on politics, the role of dominant economic classes has grown over the years and finds articulation in multiple ways, from control of political workers, leaders and parties to buying of media and setting limits of state policy. This is accentuated by some political institutions: the scale of political competition introduces remote control, multiple level of governance leads to conflation of choices and the pivotal role of elections as a hinge results in congestion of decisions while short political cycle reduces the time horizon of political actors. The institution of mass media introduces a specific distortion in the process of political agenda setting: it accentuates the pre-existing uneven access to information, foregrounds the voice of a privileged minority and masks the opinions, concerns and issues of the underprivileged majority. The systemic 'drag' introduced by these economic structures and political institutions puts the onus of correction on political organisations, political leadership and political practices. A rapid decline in party organisation across the political spectrum, atrophy of political judgement among the leaders and the non-political character of dynamic social movements has meant that the resistance to systemic drag has weakened, especially in the last two decades.

Does politics of social democracy stand a chance in this context? If it does, notwithstanding the structural, institutional and processual odds stacked against it, the driving force is the overwhelming number and proportion of those who need floor-securing social policies. An overwhelming majority of India's population still lives below the acceptable minimum level of access to goods, services and dignity. They use every available opportunity offered by universal adult franchise and open political competition to secure better conditions of life. Very often they don't succeed, for the political menu on offer is very narrow and hard to alter, especially at a time when mainstream political parties are more insular and party organisation is very fragile. Yet the sheer pressure from below has found many avenues for politics of social democracy. Two of these spaces deserve special attention.

In the 1990s, the rise of 'caste-based' and 'regional' political parties became an avenue for the politically excluded Indians to access political power and use it to shape policies of social justice. It led to reconfiguration in the party system, frequent change in power and a democratic upsurge in the electoral arena. Yet it did not change significantly the agenda of governance or the package of state policies. In that sense the 'second democratic upsurge' merely served to co-opt the vast proportion of hitherto under-included sections in the democratic system and alter the social composition of the political elite. In the last one decade, while the 'third space' in politics has consistently expanded with the inflow of newly incorporated communities and classes, the political formations representing the 'third front' have reached a plateau or have started declining. The political energy released by the second democratic upsurge awaits a political home.

The second space for politics of social democracy is inhabited by new social movements in the last quarter of a century. Peasant movements, movements for protection of *jal-jungle* and *jameen* (land, forest and water) from acquisition and encroachment, human rights movement, women's movement, Dalit movements and the movements for right to information, food and education have harnessed vast energy for politics of social democracy during this period. Yet this energy does not find itself adequately reflected in the agenda of mainstream parties or democratic governance. Unwilling to take the risky path of electoral politics, these movements have not been able to forge a political instrument of their own. Gradually, non engagement with politics and lack of exposure to hazards of governance has led these movements NGO-isation, one-issue fixation or an oppositionist frame of mind. Mainstream political parties have not managed to incorporate and internalise the issues and energy released by these movements.

Given this context, a roadmap for politics of social democracy has to have two parts. The first part has to be a package of political reform that reduces some of the institutional constrains that prevent the needs of the majority from being translated into political signals leading to political will for social policies. I have spelt it out elsewhere and can only provide here a checklist of the changes required. The basic idea is not to bring India in conformity with the global practices, for 'deviance' has been a strength of our system. Nor do we need to change our electoral system or decrowd the electoral arena of contestants. What we need is, first of all, decentralisation of political power by creation of smaller states, greater assured resources to state government, autonomous district level governments, greater funds, functions and functionaries to local bodies. Second, we need measures for strengthening of other mechanism of accountability and responsiveness by independent regulatory institutions, reforms of bureaucracy and police to bring it closer to people. Three, we need measures to reduce asymmetry of information such as a genuine public service broadcaster, regulation of cross-media ownership, checks against private treaties and stronger disclosure norms for public functionaries. Four, we need measures to reduce inequality of resources in politics such as public funding of elections by vote linked cash reimbursement on a non-discriminatory basis tax support for political contributions. These reforms are urgent, for their absence would hurt not just the prospects of social democracy but also the existence of democracy itself.

Constitutional and legal reforms may be a significant part, perhaps even a prerequisite, of improving the prospects of politics of social democracy but principally the challenge of creating a politics of social democracy is a political challenge. Specifically, the challenge is to create a firm and institutionalised bond between the constituency for social policies (which is large and expanding) and its political instrumentalities. It could mean forging a new political bloc that mobilises the energy released by social movements and identity politics and could take the space occupied by the Communists, the Socialists or the Congress-Left at different points in history. Or it could involve rehauling the existing political parties so as to forge a bond with the newly empowered sectors and their organisations. Both these routes involve reinvesting in party organisations and reviving some elementary organisational protocols of internal democracy. This is also an intellectual challenge that involves rescuing political judgement and marrying the moral ideal of social and economic equality with energetic politics and intelligent economics.

Table 38.1

Participation, Legitimacy and Efficacy of the Indian Electorate Compared to the Poor, 2004

Those who..	*Among All (%)*	*Among Poor(%)*
Reported (and double-checked) to have voted	58	59
Said they vote on their own rather than go by anyone's advise	60	58
Reported attending at least one election meeting	20	18
Reported to be the member of a political party	14	12
Said that their vote made a difference	80	76

Source: National Election Study, 2004, CSDS Data Unit.

Table 38.2

Widespread Support for Egalitarian Measures

Those who agree..	*All*	*Poor*	*Very Poor*
Ceiling on land and property	77	80	84
Poor not to be blamed for poverty	53	53	57

Source: NES 2004.

Table 38.3

Poverty Affects Perceptions

Those who say	*All*	*Poor*	*Very Poor*
Income meets needs	36	26	14
Satisfied with current economic situation	52	46	34
Economic condition worsened(last few yrs)	18	17	27
Optimist about future	69	61	58

Source: SDSA 2005

Table 38.4

Everyone Thinks He She is Poor

Self Placement	*All*	*Poor*	*Very Poor*
Top half (steps 6 to 10)	7	5	2
Lower middle (steps 4 or 5)	28	20	10
Lowest (steps 1 to 3)	65	75	88

Source: SDSA 2005.

Section IV contd...

The Social and Political Context of Social Democracy in India

PRESENTATIONS • DISCUSSIONS

This section presents the proceedings of the Fourth Session of the Tenth Indira Gandhi Conference, November 19-21, 2010, New Delhi.

Chair

- Bina Agarwal

Presentations

- Niraja Gopal Jayal
- Steven I. Wilkinson
- Yogendra Yadav

Discussants

- Bina Agarwal
- Niraja Gopal Jayal
- Steven I. Wilkinson
- Yogendra Yadav
- Sudhir Agarwal
- Aruna Roy
- Jonathan Cohn
- Sunita Narain
- Manish Sabharwal
- Joseph Stiglitz
- Rehman Sobhan
- Vijay Kelkar
- Wang Hui
- Montek Singh Ahluwalia
- Abhijit Sen
- Kumar Mangalam Birla
- Sudha Murty
- Chanda Kochhar
- Sunil Khilnani
- Pratap Bhanu Mehta
- Rob Riemen
- Sonia Gandhi

39

BINA AGARWAL

Introductory Remarks

I have decided not to talk about decentralised government and the other issues that the three paper writers have presented but rather peg my introductory remarks in a broader way. Although we have focused so far on the concept of social democracy with all its historical baggage, the concerns expressed have been broader. These are not just about social democracy but about social transformation. In that spirit, I suggest that the project of social democracy perhaps needs to have several other dimensions, some of which were touched upon in Section I, but I might take them further.

It seems to me that the project needs to be visionary and much more explicitly couched in terms of social transformation. I believe this is important because it could become a central idea for rejuvenating the task of nation-building. Perhaps it needs to be framed in that way to catch our imagination and build the sort of social consensus we need for moving towards a just society. It also, therefore, needs to be about values and hope. In the 1970s, many of us who were undergraduates in Cambridge returned home to India, Pakistan, Sri Lanka and so on because we felt we could contribute to nation-building. All around us, there were young, middle class, highly educated Indian men and women who left their comfortable homes in the cities and went into the villages out of a sense of commitment but also with the conviction that they could make a difference. Aruna Roy is a very classic example of that but also more generally, today's youngsters would say it was a 'cool thing' to be working for the common good. It was also considered in a different context, as I remember, to be a good life which was low on carbon footprint. I wear these bangles; I didn't wear them through all my teenage years because it was embarrassing to feel one had any wealth and a carbon footprint that was predatory on others or on nature.

But today we are amidst rampant consumerism, competition, corruption and might wonder how many of the younger middle class, this youth bulge, would be willing to do what people did in the 1970s and 1980s. Perhaps, not many would. But I think we are at a juncture in history where large numbers of the young need to believe that it is possible for citizens not only to get a better deal, which is what we have been discussing but also to make a difference.

Can we frame this project of Indian social democracy in a way that could achieve this and help turn what one might call a growing tide of individualism? Social justice and fairness are big ideas but they need to be widely shared, both to legitimise economic programmes of setting a social welfare system in place but also for citizens to feel that they would do their bit. This requires a change in values, of lifestyles and of social norms. We need values, not just schemes which are more universal. The question is: can social democracy be truly transformative?

Second, I feel that we need a social, political and legal framework of what I term social responsibility, not just from government but also from citizens. A project of social responsibility and social democracy requires that we make demands not only on the state but also from ourselves. The concept of a social contract which we have been talking about perhaps needs to be broadened to be a contract, not just between the state and the citizens but between citizens themselves. The reason is that corruption exists not just in government but in the public domain and in academia too. Look at the amount of plagiarism we see; we have software programmes to deal with that. There are other things that we do, which we should not be doing—we litter our streets, steal public goods, leave our accident victims to bleed to death on the roads. An evocative line from Harivansh Rai Bachchan's poem captures this:

Utre in aankhon ke aage woh haar chameli ne pehne
Veh cheen raha dekho maali sukumar lataon ke gehne

"The gardener himself is stealing the flowers and destroying the garden."

There is also a folk saying "what if the fence itself destroys the field" or "if the water itself ignites the fire." Although this is used in terms of how people hold governments accountable, I think we could also turn it to measure how we hold ourselves accountable. We need corporate social responsibility but also citizens' social responsibility.

Third, I feel we need a greater focus on what feminist economists have termed the 'care economy'. This includes both childcare and elder care. It has been sustained largely on the backs of women. Europe is beginning to recognise that care-giving is a major activity and in some countries, there is state support for caregivers. India too, although we have talked about the youth bulge, is actually facing a growing number of the elderly. The social contract over the elderly, which we seem to talk about with great pride, is actually breaking down. Recently, it was reported that four men killed their mothers because they couldn't afford to support them. If one goes to a village—and Aruna will bear me out—what does social support actually mean for families that have to support elders? There are families which share a roof, but a 70-year woman has a separate *chulha*, which means that she has to go out and fetch her firewood herself. The census will say that it is a joint family with care-giving but in fact, it is very minimal. More so, when we read cruel stories of the well-off middle class families who neither provide nor keep their social contract. Caring labour obviously needs more than monetary support. We know a lot about that, the pension schemes and so on. We can learn a lot about that globally, but care is also about social contracts, unpaid labour and social values. Can we build new mechanisms of socially responsible care giving that are gender equal, state-supported and also citizen-supported? For instance, how about every child resolving to take care of an unrelated elder person in its neighbourhood and also adding a tree in the neighbourhood?

Fourthly, I feel we need to speak more about community and collectivity; it should be an essential part of our vision. We have to see whether we can build on collectivities that are still intact and new ones where they have broken down or are absent. Mainstream economists have been very pessimistic about cooperation, emphasising self-interest as the primary driver of human motivation. But there is a very large body of work that some of you would be familiar with, both from experimental gains literature and from ground experience which indicates that trust and reciprocity can be built through frequent interaction. In fact, Paul Seabright has this lovely phrase, "cooperation is habit forming." But that habit forming is also because one builds trust and reciprocity.

We need to take these lessons forward in the schemes we design because cooperation has both intrinsic and instrumental worth. The examples of instrumental worth examples can be multiplied. There are many examples from SEWA, from self-help groups, from agricultural production collectivities but particularly from the field of environment—saving our forests, waters or soils has to be a collective approach. To deal with climate change, there is no other way than a much more collective approach and cooperation. As I said, we can be much more optimistic about human motivation from all the evidence that we have today.

Finally, I think we need to pay attention to spatial architecture and not just social architecture. For example, we are sitting in Hall 3, which is an auditorium in a circular shape, not Hall 4. A circle represents wholeness, like a *mandal*. We have heard of King Arthur's Round Table; the parliament building is round as well. The concept is that circles are about equality of participation; we can all see each other and speak to each other. This is an important idea but it is also about the architecture of how we interact. If we go to villages, we see everyone sitting in a circle precisely to recreate that. But then the question is: what are we doing in our cities and villages? Are there spaces left for democratic deliberations? Should Gurgaon be the example? My apologies to those who live in Gurgaon but should that be an example of a future city? Are there other ways in which we can visualise our physical architecture?

I just want to put these ideas and thoughts on the table which perhaps other paper writers could relate to. This discussion on democratic deliberation brings us right into the issue of decentralised governance.

40

PRESENTATION BY NIRAJA GOPAL JAYAL

Decentralisation and the Prospects of Social Democracy in India

I will basically make three sets of observations.

My first observation is about the specifics of an Indian social democracy, or an Indian caveat to the idea of social democracy. The second set of observations is about the Indian experience of decentralisation so far, and what it offers by way of potential for sustaining a social democracy. Finally, an institutional issue or two about what is the appropriate level of governance for particular public purposes.

Let me start first with the specifics of the Indian social democracy issue. Often times, we speak about social democracy equivalent to and no more than service delivery. I would like to submit that social democracy is much more than service delivery, even if it is well done. Since we cannot replicate institutional and organisational structures across the world from one place to another, and can't transplant them, I think the core of social democracy is the normative impulse that defines social democracy as a political ideal. For me, that impulse is what lies at the very heart of social democracy. It is the idea of social citizenship and I mean social citizenship not in the sense for instance that Sunil Khilnani used it earlier, which was to do with social solidarity that hopefully follows. I use it more in the classical T.H. Marshall sort of sense of economic welfare and security, unemployment insurance, public health, public education and those sorts of things. I think in India, the specificity comes from the fact that the kinds of inequalities that we contend with are considerably more complex than the inequalities that Western or European social democracies were contending with at the time they were constructed. The fact is that we have complex inequalities.

These are essentially overlapping inequalities. We have inequalities that are signified through material deprivation but also inequalities that are signified by the practices of discrimination, injustice, vulnerability and marginalisation of various kinds. We know, for instance, at the bottom rung of the Indian population, of Indian society, we have Dalits, *adivasis* and Muslims and all of these are groups that constitute the poorer sections of our society. That is what I mean by overlapping inequalities and complex inequalities. If we have complex inequalities, then obviously we need a complex set of rights of social citizenship to address them. Simply using the principles of the Beveridgian welfare state will not be sufficient. There is, I think, an obvious case in India for including in the rights of social citizenship what political theorists like to call the rights of recognition, in addition to the rights of redistribution.

The second caveat has to do with the trajectory of the relationship between social democracy and decentralisation. It sounds like an odd set of concepts to bear because in the European experience, welfare states, social democratic states have been centralised states. These have been centralised systems of governance. Historically as well as in scholarship, decentralisation and social democracy have been seen as antithetical and incompatible. After the end of the Cold War, under the influence of neo-liberal economic policies in Europe, there was a widespread discrediting of centralised governance and reducing the role of the state. Decentralising both of these was part of the institutional response to the fiscal crisis of that time and the growing restlessness with large and ineffectual public sector bureaucracies. Along with the attack on the big state came the attack on the right of social citizenship as defined in those contexts, possibly a case of throwing the baby out with the bath water. There was also privileging of the local and of civil society. Everyone wanted to come out, if not smelling of roses, certainly smelling good. Here was a new model of citizenship, a sort of do-it-yourself model which advocated not depending on the state for everything, raising local taxes, levying user fees and co-producing. The key words then became participation rather than rights and entitlements. Rights that were an integral part of the social democratic project were jettisoned at this point and decentralisation came to occupy an important place in governance arrangements in these countries. There is some convergence here between the Left and the Right; the Right favoured decentralisation for the reasons which, I have just discussed, as part of the neo-public management agenda and the Left did so because they saw it as a form of deepening of democracy. That is the story of social democracy and decentralisation, or if one may say so, a non-story of social democracy and decentralisation in the global north.

What about India? India is, I would submit, differently social democratic and differently decentralised, if it is social democratic at all. In the classical sense, I would hesitate to describe India as having ever been social democratic, let alone a full-blown welfare state. I would be more circumspect and say that it has been an interventionist state with a strong welfare orientation and it is only very recently that the idea of state provisioning through legislated social rights—really, in the last five years—that the idea of social rights as opposed to pure handouts have somewhat caught on. I disagree with Pratap Bhanu Mehta here as to accountability mechanisms, which have also now begun to emerge and which obviously depend upon citizens having the political competence to demand it. Some of these rights are claimed and enforced at the local level, often with civil society helping to mobilise claim-making and monitoring performance. In a sense, we are possibly coming to what one might describe as an inadvertent social democracy, if at all; one that has been constructed not by a blueprint, but bit by bit and the bits harmonising together, possibly to create a social democracy inadvertently. But we are also differently decentralised. Indian decentralisation has a very distinctive pedigree; it did not come as a part of the new public management by turning one's back on the state of the sort that happened in Western Europe. In Western Europe, decentralisation had a largely administrative rationale. In India, the imperative and the impetus was political in the best normative sense of the term. Decentralisation was a deliberate strategy to address the democratic deficit in the polity and to potentially enlarge the scope of citizens' entitlements through two basic mechanisms, voice and inclusion. The voice was to give people at the local level a say in determining their developmental priorities and local needs, and inclusion through bringing in historically disadvantaged groups, including women. For those who don't know, the one-third quota for women is now going up to 50 per cent in institutions of local governance.

Opinion on the performance of Indian decentralisation is divided, as we know. Prof Bardhan has said that in West Bengal, it has completely failed and he has been studying this for many years with very rigorous methodological tools. I have a slightly different experience but my experience is more ephemeral. I have wandered across several states and interviewed people. Therefore, it is a different kind of methodology, more ethnographic than the kind of thing Prof Bardhan uses. There are sceptics of *Panchayati Raj* and there are the evangelists too. The evangelists come on too strong and sceptics can also be too strong. I am closer to the evangelists, though not a full-blown evangelist of *Panchayati Raj*. I think it would be fair to say that across this country there has been a gradual but modest strengthening of both these aspects of voice and inclusion. There is no question about that, though much remains to be accomplished. But the achievements so far are not inconsiderable.

My second set of observations pertains to what the Indian experience of decentralisation offers us by way of potential for sustaining social democracy. I do not make a more ambitious claim than that. One may recall that democracy in the Western social democratic project, was supposed to be the peaceful means by which transition to a more egalitarian society could be mediated. Part of the problem with our panchayati raj institutions (PRIs) so far has been not inadequate democratisation, but inadequate decentralisation. When we complain bitterly about inadequate resources, inadequate powers and functions being devolved and all of those things by the states, we never complain about democratisation because democratisation is that aspect of our democratic decentralisation that has actually been successful. If it has not been as successful as it could have been, it is because decentralisation has actually lagged behind. I think precisely because democratisation has been privileged over decentralisation it has helped to what I might somewhat grandly and perhaps exaggeratedly call make voters into citizens by bringing close to 4 million citizens into elected positions. This is not a small number. It has created a new and unparalleled awareness of the possibilities of democratic citizenship; the idea of democracy as a political value, as representation, as accountability and even as solidarity. I can provide examples from field work in three different states for each of these values of representation, accountability and solidarity. I believe that these are certainly much more entrenched now than when politics was a distant space that people entered a couple of times in a decade or four times in a decade, if you take state assembly elections as well.

Supplying the deficit of decentralisation actually requires just more devolution of powers and finances. These are not things that are impossible to legislate if there is political will. Of course, we are within a federal framework, so that makes it slightly more difficult. But making voters into democratic citizens is certainly a more gradual process and I believe that it is a powerful political resource for claim-making, which enables claim-making for the rights of social citizenship. We may take a look at the 1997 education guarantee scheme in Madhya Pradesh during Digvijay Singh's tenure as Chief Minister when *panchayats* were actually empowered to demand primary education. The data of that period tells us that in six years, more than 27,000 poor villages demanded and got basic primary schools which gave the opportunity of primary education to more than one million children in just 27,000 villages in the state. That is one example, apart from political resources to make claims, of enabling claim-making for the rights of social citizenship.

The second channelling of welfare, which is what pretty much *panchayats* do, is basically to pass down the money and find the beneficiaries and hand it over to them. This is when they are not as robustly resourced and funded as they should be and enforce accountability under specific conditions. That would include some of Prof Bardhan's work with the villagers. Under specific conditions, *panchayats* have been found to be effective agents for channelling developmental goods and contributing to poverty reduction. They can also facilitate downward accountability. And when the gram sabha, which admittedly is a weak institution in most parts of the country, enforces accountability in the matter of channelling of funds, it becomes an institutional guarantor of a redistributive benefit. The gram sabha must be strengthened to play this role more affectively, but it is an institutional resource and one that can certainly be cultivated to play this role. It can play a role *vis-à-vis* the market but this can be debated later.

My last observation is about the appropriate level of governance to do particular things. There is a need to contest the false dichotomy between the nation-state as concentrated evil and decentralised institutions as pro-virtue. We may look at the question of social citizenship and ask whether this is the essence of social democracy, where it would be located on the scale of governance, which is a very complex scale now. Mr Pascal Lamy referred to it earlier; all the way from the local to the global, where the rights of social citizenship might be most effectively articulated, expressed, demanded and so on. At one end, decentralisation tends to localize citizenship. At the other global end, with migration, capital flows, globalisation and all the other processes that go with it, we are seeing the beginnings of a de-territorialisation of citizenship, a de-linking of territory and citizenship which occurs due to these global forces. I think the truth, as always, lies somewhere in between. Dr Ambedkar's animus against the village as the place where nasty practices, prejudices and discrimination played out, rather than a place of solidarity, is valid even today. Too much local is as bad as not enough local. The nation-state remains vitally relevant to societies marked by poverty and deprivation in order to control rapacious capitalism and guarantee the provisioning of basic needs.

The national and the local can only exist in a relationship of complementarity, not a relationship of substitutability as far as the social democratic project is concerned. The regulation of the social product, its creation in terms of ensuring the fairness of the processes by which it is created, of the terms of redistribution and the creation of a social consensus, which I think Bina was referring to, pretty much remain the task of the nation-state. On the other hand, effective and empowered citizenship, informed decision-making about local developmental needs, the ability to mobilise to make welfare claims upon public resources, must remain the prerogative of the local. Both, I think, have their proper place in the making of a social democracy. The 'social' in social democracy must come from above, at least for some time to come, and the 'democracy' must come from below. That's the way I see it.

41

PRESENTATION BY STEVEN I. WILKINSON

Social Democracy and Ethnic Cleavages

I shall discuss two broad questions that I think are raised by this particular topic. The first one that strikes me is a general question. To what extent, in general, have ethnic cleavages or as we might rephrase it, high levels of ethnic diversity such as those existing in India, been a problem for democracy? Have they caused problems for other factors such as growth, conflict, support for public programmes? This was discussed by Jonathan Cohn on the discussion on support for US health care. Although there is literature that says that bad outcomes are connected or associated with high levels of ethnic diversity, I think our literature is largely wrong. Diversity in India, especially at interstate level, has actually been a very good thing for the stability of Indian democracy and for the US. This is one general question.

The second question is an India-specific question. Given the steps that have been taken by India already since 1950 to address the ethnic inequalities and conflicts within the state, what additional steps might be taken now to deepen social democracy? I shall talk about some specific policies that are on the table at the moment, especially in the last few years. From a perspective of someone like me who works on the study of ethnic conflict, I think there is a danger of looking forward to institutionalising ethnicity too much in the policies we adopt, especially if markets or non-group specific policies are capable of solving them. I shall talk about the tensions I see in some of the policy options between, on the one hand, wanting to address the very real causes of some aspects of discrimination in India and elsewhere, and on the other hand, not wanting to institutionalise ethnicity too much, which I think carries dangers of instability for democracy more generally.

There are several reasons why people think that ethnic cleavages or high levels of diversity might be a problem for democracy in general, for things like public support, for expenditure on things like schools, roads, for economic growth, for conflict. Why are ethnic diversity and ethnic cleavages seen as a problem? There are some former models for these but for me very few people said it better than John Stuart Mill in the mid-19th century. He talked about what he called the lack of fellow-feeling in diverse societies necessary for the working of representative governments and the absence of trust. Some people have called it the absence of fellow-feeling amongst different groups. That creates problems when one is trying to cooperate on common goals. There is also an argument that says different groups have different preferences. If one group wants to load on a particular place, another group wants to load on another place, we value this model, you value that model, that kind of argument sells well in more multiethnic environments, where one has a lot more different preferences to aggregate.

I think one of the big reasons why there is so much political support for reservations in India, even though most people are not perhaps direct beneficiaries of reservations, is the simple lack of trust in the fairness of the state to deliver goods to one's group any other way. Most people don't trust the fairness of the state and therefore, it is better to have smaller awards through group-specific measures so as to be assured of benefit, rather than larger potentially but uncertain awards, which may or may not make it to you. This is why reservations have their great power.

Another argument that emerges is that if there are lots of different groups, there is unnecessary duplication of different regional governments, different local governments and different programmes, because each group wants its own. For example, as in Belgium, we have a duplicated state where they have two sets of everything in every part of the different aspects of the state. That is another argument and this is, in some sense, not very efficient. From that conflict, we see the argument that ethnic divides tend to crowd out virtually everything else. Over time, ethnicity becomes the macro identity cleavage around which everything else revolves. So every economic issue or other kind of issue is seen as an ethnic issue. There is no other space in politics; ethnicity just crowds out everything else and once it does that, you are headed for real government breakdown. We have seen this in places like Cyprus in the late 1950s and early 1960s, Lebanon in the 1960s and 1970s and Belgium today; there are various places we can think of where village or ethnic identities gradually crowd out other kinds of identities.

What is the source and empirical basis for these kinds of arguments? I am going to give some theoretical basis for them. Over the past decade, there have been a large number of studies; some using experimental methods and some looking at large-scale fiscal-based assets, which purported to prove that the general association between high levels of ethnicity and bad outcomes stuff is true. There was a cross-national soft data and reference in the case of growth which in one article found—depending on which date is used—a 28 to 40 per cent difference in growth between Africa and East Asia over a certain period, from 1960 to 1989. I think this is essentially due to the higher level of ethnic diversity in Africa as compared to East Asia and is responsible for these large aggregate differences. There are also lots of small-scale studies that look to individual support in the US for school-bound initiatives, for road initiatives in more diverse *versus* less diverse areas, which again find an association between lower levels of support for public goods and higher degrees of diversity. The assumption is that this has a lot to so with the feeling that other guys are going to get it and not our guys and so let us not support it. Those are some potential problems that might be out there, if one reads this literature.

The good news certainly is that, with respect to the cross-national literature on ethnicity and bad outcomes, this literature is, I think, wrong in part, because it relies on very flawed indicators of ethnic identity from country to country. Problematic measures are used, which is not to say on the other hand that ethnicity does not cause any problems. That is not the claim I am making. I am just saying that the general cross-national argument is wrong.

Why is it wrong? In most of these studies, the flimsy data that are used measure only language. For instance, in the main quantitative data set that measures ethnicity, it is assumed that Uganda and Burundi are ethnically homogenous countries because they speak the same language despite the obvious fact that other identities exist in these particular countries. The association that is drawn on the suggested basis does not really reflect the real ethnic identities. That is often true. There are various other problems with the data that I talk about in the paper. One is the idea that it is a sub-zero factor with ethnic identities whereas in fact, in the real world, people tend to exist quite nicely without going crazy whilst having multiple identities. I can be someone from the Bhojpuri region, in Bihar, and have other identities as well; it is not a zero-sum game for many people. They can add identities and so arguments that claim that there is one level of identity as the key for explaining all the kind of outcomes we are interested in, is simply not correct. One can have simultaneous loyalties.

Another issue is that the ethnic measures that I see aren't often measuring ethnicity so much as they are measuring state-building or education policies. One example that I like is a wonderful book called *Peasants into Frenchmen* where it said France had more diversity in 1815 compared with how it was in 1950, with respect to a century of nation-building, teaching people to speak French, teaching people they were French, welding the country together in the interim. So France appears less diverse in 1950. If you use that measure to explain how France was doing, would you really be tracking the inference of ethnicity or of 150 years of nation-building and state-building that had gone on in the interim? I think there is good evidence that you may be tracking the latter more than the former.

It is not ethnic diversity as such but specific ethnic imbalances and inequalities that drive conflict. I expect right institutions to moderate ethnic conflict as really important. In general, we want two or three things. We have to make sure that ethnically, inequalities are not cumulative where one group has all the goodies and the other group has nothing. That is very bad for political stability.

An important thing you have to do is to encourage inter-group accommodation, provide incentives to people to reach beyond their group and also encourage inter-group competition, so that no single large group like Hindus or Muslims votes only for their own people. We have to create multiple participants within each group so that they can feel across different group lines. India has, I think, done institution-building really well compared to Pakistan. They both started with the same level of ethnic diversity if one looks at quantitative indicators but India built the right institutions.

The reason is that India did not institutionalise religion in the constitution. That was a really good decision. It also did not impose things like Hindi on the south as that would have created a huge national cleavage between the north and south. In that sense I think Pandit Nehru and the party in his period deserve a lot of credit for being prepared to compromise, accommodate and not build the wrong kinds of institutions in that period. They also did a couple of other things which they regretted initially, but which turned out to be not so bad for India, which is institutionalising caste identities in 1950-51 when they went back on their original claim. The original policy did not have separate things for OBCs or allow certain things to be done for the SCs and STs with regard to reservations. The other feature is of linguistic states where Nehru and Patel, after the agonies of partition, were understandably not willing to immediately grant rights to different linguistic areas but they went back on this. These decisions have been relatively good in the long term. Why have they been relatively good? They have sustained what in political science we would call 'cross-cutting cleavages.' Multiple groups compete for power across lots of different areas, so there is no permanent winning coalition of just one group within each state. You can't win with the support of any one group; you have to win with the support of lots of other groups which were sustained by these caste reservations.

The level of ethnic voting, as I have shown in my paper, at the national level in India is actually somewhat lower than in Bulgaria, the US and South Africa. The national level uses the index of national voting because of these cross-cutting cleavages breaking up these national blocks. In a book I have written on Hindu-Muslim violence, I have also have shown that in states where you have many more caste Hindu parties competing for power, it has been a very good thing for minorities in terms of communal violence because the party in power either relies on Muslim votes directly or if it may need to form a coalition tomorrow with the party that does. The political incentive to protect the community is very strong and a very good thing.

I will now turn briefly to the second question. Given steps that have already been taken to spread resources among the groups, what additional measures might be taken to deepen social democracy? What is the situation today? We have got very high degrees of inequality with Muslims, Dalits, and Scheduled Tribes doing very badly on access to pre-market things like education as well as in the market when they get there. We also know that at least some of the bad performances in the market are due to the high degrees of discrimination. There has been a lovely replication of correspondent discrimination where equally matched applicants apply for positions in the English language. The most modern sectors of the economy have found that if the high caste person gets called back once, the scheduled caste person if equally qualified, gets called back two-thirds of the time and Muslims get called back one-third of the time. We know that discrimination is clearly an issue.

What might India do? One option is to rely on markets alone. It seems to me that this ignores the group basis of much of the discrimination that goes on. We know from studies like this that there is a clear group element. It also ignores the distrust issue. People aren't confident of getting fair treatment and it doesn't address in particular the declining position of Muslims in relation to the market. The returns for the educational goods they bring to the market have been declining in recent years. Their community, in particular, seems to be doing worse. Secondly, we could deepen the existing caste reservation system to new groups, or perhaps new areas of the economy. I know this is a very controversial issue. There are several issues one sees here; a couple of them were raised by Pratap Bhanu Mehta earlier.

The first is that institutions are sticky. If one builds them to solve a problem now, the history of institutions reveals that they solidify after a few years; they don't go away in a hurry. We're stuck with them for a very long time. The second is the issue of the tyranny of compulsory identity. Most of us have multiple identities. If we build institutions around one identity today, what do we do tomorrow, when identities change? Therefore, one has to build different kinds of institutions.

The experience of India before 1947 and that of other countries like Cyprus, Belgium and Lebanon who have ethnicity in every aspect of their societies has not really been a happy one. India is really fortunate today that very large proportions of its population don't seem to vote purely on the basis of ethnicity. The endeavour to build social democracy, it seems to me, does depend on the lessening of ethnicity over time, in the longer run.

So, what might be a few policy options? Firstly, you have to build institutions that address group inequalities of access and opportunity, but should also be flexible enough to be modified if those inequalities lessen. Don't impose more market distortions than necessary to address the problems and try not to institutionalise ethnicity in religion more than you absolutely need to do, to try and deal with problems. I know that this is a tall order.

What might be a good start for this? The first would be to better the processes of exclusion and access to equal opportunity that exist currently. I read the Sachar Report page to page, cover to cover. It is really quite bad at doing this, I think. It shows you the outcomes of inequality but doesn't show how people get there. It doesn't reveal whether they're doing worse because of the free market inequalities or market discriminations. All it shows is the outcome, i.e., how things are. So we don't really have an informed basis for policy. I think we need to collect data that address trends and not just overall aggregate levels. For instance, it is very interesting to know that Muslims, for the first time in India, in the lowest age groups, have a lower rate of literacy than Dalits. They have been a community that has been badly off but not quite so badly off as have been the Dalits. But this seems to be changing for the younger generation, *vis-à-vis* some other evidence that they are now worse off. That is an interesting thing to know, in respect of policy and the trends now.

I meet the business people present here who tell me that they don't make decisions based on the aggregate market share at the moment; they look ahead to see who is winning or losing and which kind of measure would be best tailored to a particular situation. I think there needs to be more of that rather than simply collecting data on how aggregate levels of a particular group are doing. Because if we know how things are going, with regard to employment or more recent employees, or different segments, we can work out whether the market is actually working to solve problems in particular age groups or not. It seems to me that this is vital information for policymaking. For example, are new businesses less prone to discrimination than older businesses? How are our different communities likely to be affected by technological change or the loss of leaving things as they are?

Another issue is the diversity index that was recommended by the Kundu Committee in 2008. It is an extremely good basis for moving forward because potentially, it can deal with multiple kinds of identities at the same time. Whatever the country collectively decides is important. It rates castes, sex and religion at the moment. Potentially, it could involve anything. It can broaden and deepen the version of diversity going forward, rather than link it particularly to ethnicity and different kinds of ethnic labels. I think that to enforce this you need to have an equal opportunity committee that collects data as a matter of course and not just as a response to particular kinds of complaints. That's vital. The US has found this to be a useful tool in working out the degree of under-representation in different segments of the economy. It is important that whatever is done in India now should not be just a response to complaints but actually have a broader base when you are collecting aggregate data. Employers now, at least in the organised sector, are going to be subject to shame if certain things don't happen. They can prove they are making progress with more recent recruits as opposed to older recruits.

Finally, both of these should look at the trends and the situation. Young, old and new industries must avoid taking too many harmful actions. You need to get a sense of whether it is appropriate in individual circumstances to use these group-specific things because group-specific things will not go away. Once you build them, you are more or less stuck with them. I can cite a large number of examples from across the world to show you that that is the case.

42

PRESENTATION BY YOGENDRA YADAV

The Politics of Feasible Social Democracy

I am almost tempted to join the debate with Steve on the equal opportunity commission possibility and the report in which I happen to be involved. That is the reason for my vested interest in it, which hasn't been apparently taken seriously by anyone so far, because that report actually recommends treatments precisely in the kind of measures that Steve suggested.

We have discussed the architecture of social democracy several times. By architecture, we have usually meant architecture of the policies of social justice; we have looked at decision-making, at resources, design and governance. The one question we need to address is the political architecture. Assuming that we have the best policy and that someone has designed it in the most perfect way, we can solve the problem cognitively. But why should anyone implement this policy? What are the incentives for the political player? Why should anyone take up a policy of this kind and then continue to implement it? It is a very serious question to which we normally don't pay attention. That is what I mean by the politics of feasible social democracy, which is the title of my paper, and is also a tribute to a forgotten book by Alec Nove called *Economics of Feasible Socialism*, which was published in the 1980s. Feasibility here is used in both senses, which is workability of the policies but more importantly, feasibility of working these policies for the actors who are meant to implement these things. It should be feasible for them, which is to say that it should give them incentives.

We have had much discussion about incentives, innovations and so on. I have absorbed the earlier discussion with a distinct sense of envy because I don't see such discussions happening in my discipline when it comes to political reforms. Incentives are one thing we are not interested in. Any discussion on political reform is deeply normative, moral and nothing else. What is its design? Why should anyone do it is really a concern. The real question and litmus test of architecture is whether it would routinely produce a political will. By political will, I just don't mean political preference, wish or political desire on the part of those who rule. Political will is what one gets to see, if I may say so, in the last seven days before the recently concluded Commonwealth Games, when the DMK government in Tamil Nadu wants to distribute colour television sets or when the CPM in West Bengal wanted to implement the tenancy reforms of the early 1980s. I am deliberately mixing things that I like and dislike simply to illustrate the fact that political will is that wish of the ruling class which they implement as if their existence depends on it. That is political will.

The question about the political feasibility of social democracy is this: under what circumstances will this political will be produced and under what circumstances will it be sustained? That, to me, is the question that we should be discussing in this session. In other words, why should a politician, a political party or a government regime carry out these policies? One reason can be altruism, ethical imperative, commitment or ideology. These things are not unimportant; on the contrary, they are very important things. They make a huge difference to history and I would be the last person to undermine these. But following what Prof Kaushik Basu said earlier, they are important but not enough, in a routine sustained way. To expect politics to deliver things purely based on these imperatives and drives is almost like expecting markets to survive on the goodwill of the shopkeepers to serve their customers. We know that markets actually don't survive on that, at least not on a day-to-day basis. In any case, benevolence of rulers is not something specific to democracy. All kinds of regimes have had benevolent rulers —monarchies, aristocracies and even dictatorships; all have had very benevolent rulers once in a while. What is distinctive about democracy is that it presumes a certain mechanism which does not depend on the sheer goodwill or benevolence of the rulers, but makes their existence conditional to approval by the people. It is this which makes the rulers do what needs to be done. This is what we call democracy. In other words, we are looking for a mechanism that would give a political actor good opportunities to build a political career, which is such a nice thing. A political party roots to come back to power and is anxious to retain power over a long time and implement its vision and policies. Is there such a mechanism?

Theoretically, yes; because that is what democracy is all about. What is that model? I have sketched that in my paper (and you might wish to take a look at it). There is nothing new about what I am saying here. I don't know enough about European democracies and what they did; the only democracy I have some familiarity with is India. Let me speak about India. The conditions where the poor or those who live under a certain minimum of access to goods and services are an overwhelming majority and are crucial to my argument. They are not the 26 per cent that could be above the poverty line which really is the hunger line. That's clearly about two-thirds of our society. In a country where the poor in this sense are an overwhelming majority, what are the mechanisms which would ensure that this majority's needs are actually taken care of by democratic decisions? Of course, the assumption is that democracies serve majorities. Don't we all know that? It does because in conditions where the poor are in a majority, we expect preferences to be formed according to them unless culture is a major obstacle, which it isn't in the Indian case. We expect those preferences to be turned into public signals in conditions of a free media. If the conditions are open, we expect those public signals to become an issue of competitive politics and to turn into political mandates. We expect those political mandates to translate into political will to implement these policies, because rational political actors would want to implement such policies so as to come back to power. Just in case they are less than rational, there is an election that follows to remind them. Thus there is an accountability mechanism though one also hopes that they would not wait for accountability to arise after five years. They should become responsive and start recognising the signals even before those five years. That is really what democratic theory tells us. In reality, we know this does not happen; this kind of a political will is rare, rather than something that happens routinely.

My paper is all about why it does not happen and why that particular democratic theory does not apply in our case, and probably does not apply in most cases. The history of most democracies is sometimes the history of rulers overlooking majorities. We have seen that example, not just in India but outside India as well; majorities are brutally overlooked. What we need really equates to what Jean Dreze said, about the discipline of political science. Sometimes, so little is written about this real life democracy. At least in the Indian case, the discipline of political science has so little to contribute to our understanding of how democracy routinely sidesteps majorities and still continues to be a democracy in the formal sense of the term. We need some discipline for that but I will skip it and simply talk about the consequences that we have now.

I want to discuss the consequences of the system that we have and then make some suggestions about what we can do to overcome them. The consequence is a system which is not a vicious cycle but a vicious system where there is a step-by-step narrowing of people who can enter politics. The potential pool, I must say, is fairly large in India thanks to the social movements and the vibrancy of the Indian national movement, which still has a shadow. The number of political actors available to the system is actually very large, larger than most countries in the world. These people come from social and political movements. Of course, there are two other kinds of actors; those who are from political families who routinely come there and those who have more money than they know what to do with. These three types of characters are available in the potential pool. But at the entry point, this is the guillotine point, the system actually systematically accesses the first category, i.e. those who are social and political actors. If one is a social and a political actor, or even a political actor and won't go into politics, what does one do? One can probably hope to contest a *panchayat* election; these days probably even that is also becoming too costly in terms of the resources being pooled in *panchayat* elections. It is still within the realm of possibility. But given the scale of a parliamentary constituency in this country, even the minimum entry barriers in terms of resources are simply too high. Entry barriers in terms of information are also so high that no MP can really afford to have anything like a face-to-face communication with his electorate. How can he possibly do it with more than a million electors in every case? The requirement of scale is such that it eliminates all the small movements. I very often say that most of the famous social movements in this country are smaller than the scale of one single parliamentary constituency and that is a problem. It eliminates social movements from elections right away. Party organisations are such that one needs resources and social networks. If I want to join a party tomorrow and want to seek a ticket, what do I do? There is no organisation to speak of. I can entertain myself with the notion that I am a member of a party, but the party does not know or recognise me. The smartest thing I can do, if I live in Tamil Nadu or Orissa, is to spend some money and spend a few months in the few square kilometers around the hall where we are sitting, go to *darbars*, try and put up huge hoardings saying "I love Soniaji", "Rahulji, desh ka neta"; that is the only way. Look at these gross and obscene things that happen in the capital every day. These people are not fools; they are small political entrepreneurs who are trying to get entry into the system somehow. The system allows them absolutely no way; in fact, the system encourages these things. There has to be some rationale as this kind of a thing cannot be done by fools. These are people who are trying to find some way into the system. At this entry point, therefore, all the social and political workers who have not chosen their parents or their patrons very carefully are eliminated.

Then comes the race. By the stage of entry, most important characters we wish to see playing any role are eliminated. In this race, the media plays an important role. I have had some of the longest discussions on the media; how the media systematically masks questions of poverty in this country; how it systematically overplays the concerns of a tiny minority and how, rather than making an even playing field, it actually creates a very uneven playing field. I am not even discussing the question of direct buying, which has started right now. For our foreign delegates who may not know it, some of the most respectable publications and newspapers in this country are into this game. There is a lot of good news but one piece of bad news is that some of the most respectable newspapers have straightaway offered their news spaces to be bought on a menu, on a catalogue. One can buy an interview for one's party, or can pay for the opposition to be blocked out. There are rates specified for everything. That happens in this country's media, which makes an already uneven playing field even more uneven. There is the question of resources in the election campaign and the end product is that by the time one reaches the end of the race and the election results are announced, those who could be winning the race are not winning. They may run faster than others but because there are so many exit points in this route, everyone else but the privileged have been thrown out. This is no comment on people present in this room, but we end up with a system where those who win this race are unrepresentative of the population. Sociologically, these candidates do not represent anything of the merit and energy in this country.

Finally, the political class of this country does not reflect the ideas, the energy and the dynamism that exist in this society. All that is blocked out by the time things reach the parliament. Naturally this small group in power is then hostage to vested interests. There is capture by the elite in ways that are so familiar and are played out all the time. There is systemic drag which our economist friends have talked about. The end product is actually not only evil but also a vacuum. In other words, the political party that has to win elections ends up with a political class which actually cannot even help it win the next elections. That is the irony. The political class has to supplement itself by bringing people from outside who do what politicians ought to be doing. Aruna Roy has been brought in to do things that an ordinary Congress politician ought to be doing. Actually, politicians ought to be saying these things. They must say that they have to win the next elections, and must demand an NREGA to improve wages. Why should Jean Dreze be saying these things? This is really the irony of the system, the final evidence why the system that we are dealing with is a system where even minimal democratic expectations are not being fulfilled.

The minimal democratic expectations are only of political animals wanting to come back again and again to power.

What do we do? What is the way out? I will quickly rattle off a few things which I hope most of our economist friends will endorse. Like the opening up of the economic market, can we have some opening of the political market as well? That is one big change waiting to take place in this country, which is the de-scaling of resource requirements. At the moment, the entry barriers in terms of money are simply too high. Something really big has to be done to make possible de-scaling of resources, which has to do with public funding based on the reimbursement principle on the basis of votes gained. I keep saying that the problem with politics is not that it has too much black money. The problem is that there is too little white money. In Indian lingo, white is legitimate money and black is illegitimate. The problem is there is too little white money in politics; we need to pour white money into politics even if half of it is misused. We need a de-scaling of polity, but not merely in terms of *panchayati raj*; we need a second state reorganisation commission to look at the question of smaller states. We need full-fledged government at the district level, with administrators almost at the chief minister's level. Every Indian district has about two million people, which is very decent. There are lots of countries of that size.

We need a de-scaling of the polity in order to ensure that effective decision-making takes place at a point where there is some responsibility and accountability possible. At the moment, accountability is to be enforced at levels which are simply inaccessible to citizens. We need better accountability mechanisms.

This is one thing we don't pay attention to. There is no way we can improve the quality of our politics by constitutional or legal reforms. Politics will be reformed by more and better politics. What do we mean by that? Pranab Bardhan spoke about internal democracy within parties. One of the major ways of opening political markets would be to institute something like the primaries within every political party, which would actually be a great step. We don't know what it would produce in the long run because all other elements of the systems are not under anyone's control, but it is a kind of step that can produce only good. This applies not only to the Congress party but to every political party. Open up and simply say that one can enroll as a member of a political party as long as one follows its principles and doesn't have certain disqualifications. Invite members to contest and become members. Ticket distribution will not take place from Delhi. If this principle is adhered to, things could begin to change.

We have to look at cementing party-movement relationships, because at the moment, the country's principal political energy is locked outside the main political parties. All the principal political energy is in social movements of the last 25 years. There has to be some way of connecting that energy to mainstream politics. This holds true not only for the Congress, but for all parties. Something has to be done about political judgement and thinking because I think these steps would institute something of a virtuous cycle. A virtuous cycle would mean new groups entering politics, new actors, new energies and ideas which continue to strengthen political will and ensure that there is a greater chance for some of these social policies being implemented. These social policies lead to better outcomes, which in turn, improve the possibility of political participation of these groups and their political leadership. This is the virtuous cycle that we need to institute.

Why should the existing ruling class commit suicide? Two good answers to that—one, ruling classes do face serious crises. People who have to distribute tickets are sometimes very lonely people who don't know what they are doing. They need systems to improve so that they can make sense of what they are doing with the power they enjoy.

We also have to look at where morality matters. Invoking morality for everyday politics is a useless business but for transformation of this kind which are things that are done once in 25-30 years morality, ideology and vision matter.

43

SECTION IV

Discussion

Bina Agarwal

Those were three marvellous presentations. There is a fourth paper by Sudipto Kaviraj. Since Kaviraj is absent, I will read out a few lines which I think present the kernel of his argument. The paper is titled "Indian Social Democracy and Questions of Culture" and I quote:

> Deep inequalities of culture rooted in different levels of education, differential access on the basis of language, prevent our democracy from developing a real deliberative culture. A true deliberative democratic culture requires an underlying equality of cultural voice so that interests who argue their case in the public sphere are first able to argue on equal terms and be listened to with equal respect. A large part of the electorate, which cannot be reached by the deliberative process in the English-speaking media, is denied this access. In fact, in their case, the public sphere is not merely sloped but clearly closed off. And this inequality gets its revenge on the system by creating a different sphere of politics where such arguments do not reach. If you want to transcend the stage of political deliberation now, Indian democracy has to attend seriously to the question of cultural inequality.

If there are questions on this, Sunil Khilnani and Pratap Bhanu Mehta may answer them.

Niraja Gopal Jayal

I find all the papers fascinating but am intrigued by the conundrum that arises out of what Yogendra Yadav said. He talked about election finance, including at the *panchayat* level. It seems to me that we always complain about under-resourced *panchayats*. There is not enough money or funding, which makes *panchayats* ineffective. In the recent *panchayat* elections in UP, for instance, we have seen over-resourced *panchayats* because there is a lot of development money flowing through agencies, especially NREGA. Over-resourced *panchayats* raise the stakes in *panchayat* elections and possibly carry other dangers. We need to think about that.

Steven I. Wilkinson

We have the accurate information for these discrimination studies. There are certain groups that are definitely being discriminated against in the market. One important piece of information we don't have is how it compares with other markets over the last decade. In other words, there may be a degree of improvement than in the past in which case one would be more confident of the ability of the market. Though these may solve some things for some groups, we just don't have that kind of information at the moment. That is why collecting good data over time is important because we can get some sense of the extent to which state or market action is needed at a particular time.

Bina Agarwal

That would hold for your conclusion about SC/ST and Muslims as well, because one could be doing better and the other stable rather than one doing badly and the other stable.

Steven I. Wilkinson

The evidences that I needed was the STs have relatively gained ground with respect to Muslims, because probably they have greater access to political power and reservations. This isn't to say that either group is well off but Muslims do seem to be losing some relative ground.

Yogendra Yadav

I request Steve to elaborate on the question of design of social policies. This has always bothered me. This country, whenever

Mandal 1, 2 or 3 comes up, is divided between those who believe in merit or suddenly remember merit two days ago and basically want any affirmative action to be dismantled and those who say affirmative action is equal to reservation, not an inch will be granted. We need some interventions here to think intelligently about possible designs. In some cases, it has to be by tweaking reservation and in many cases, adding on or supplementing the reservation. We need a whole range of affirmative action policies but this national debate reduces that merely to reservations and is one of the most regressive things that we have had in the country. Do you have some thoughts on that? I thought of bringing in the suggestion of an equal opportunity commission. While we have maybe eight to ten commissions, one to look after Dalits, one on *adivasis*, unfortunately most of these commissions, at best, become advocates for one particular group at the cost of everyone else. This is when they are working at their best. What we need is an integrative mechanism; more than integration, which does not overlap with any of these. We badly need simple mandatory information-gathering mechanisms about the social profile of the happening places in the economy and in education. We know more about the ethnic profile of US institutions than we know about this country's institutions. But for such a committee, for all its flaws, we would not have even known what we know today. Can we think of some mechanisms to strengthen that?

Sudhir Agarwal

I haven't spoken and so wanted to clarify Yogendra's question. It has been said that the media is going through a difficult patch in the country. I want to clarify that there have been some bad cases but it is not true of all the media.

Aruna Roy

Let me make a few responses on two or three issues. One is about decentralisation which is the most important thing that is politically relevant to the people of this country. But those institutions, I think, really need to be looked at extremely seriously. In Kerala, we have a *panchayat* system which is fully equipped to take care of development and look at issues because of the long history of the participatory process of planning. It took the planning process five years of looking at all kinds of issues, galvanising human resources and doing everything. It has worked very well though there is the problem of politicisation. In Kerala, if you say that you don't belong to any political party, they think you are an outsider. You have to belong somewhere politically otherwise you don't have any identity, which is very strange to me: you can have sympathies, but need not be a part of a political party. Nevertheless, the *panchayat* is very strong and is well equipped. But in the rest of the country, especially with NREGA becoming what it has and the amount of money coming into it, we need two or three very important things to happen. One is nowadays called 'capacity-building'. We all need to understand much more of the functioning of the *panchayat*. We have people on rotation because of reservation. One does not get the same old *sarpanch* who has been elected as the head of the village council for the last 30 years coming back again. It can be a woman with very little literacy. Capacity-building will have to be an extremely important issue. Financial management will have to be another because there is a lot of money coming in. In Rajasthan, a *panchayat* gets anything between 70 lakhs to more than a crore from NREGA alone. That is a lot of money to manage.

One also has to look at transparency and accountability issues because they don't want accountability. The vested interest system even in the tiny *panchayat* is so deep today that any questions about how the money has gone, where it has gone are difficult to raise. If there is an asset which you can identify, you know exactly where the money has not gone. You know the channel that has been booked three times and that the bridge would fall, but it is likely to fall more out of corruption than bad technology. Many bridges collapse in rural India not because of lack of technical knowledge but because there is corruption. At the *panchayat* level we need technical knowledge desperately but we also have to recognise that a stubborn belief in our own competence is not going to improve matters. We really need to take stock and when we do so, we need strong political will at the state level to implement what needs to be done.

Particularly in the case of NREGA, Andhra and Rajasthan are two examples. In Andhra, strong political will has made action possible. In Rajasthan, because of some tentative efforts being made and also because we started the transparency and accountability measures late, we have problems because the *sarpanch* isn't mobilised and organised. We had to have a massive mobilisation to show them that we could also mobilise. We are talking about political action and social democracy; people's mobilisation has been in many more thousands than the *sarpanches*. It has been conveyed to them that they also have a voice and can say what they want. These are the ways in which they have had to protest to establish the basic fact that money spent must be accounted for.

A lady who had passed only fourth class turned up and the authorities asked her why she had come there. She had come for the Right to Information. What did she know about it? She replied in Hindi that when she sends her son to the market with ₹ 10 and asks for her accounts, this government spends billions of rupees in her name. She was asking for her accounts, her money. That question today is generating a lot of reaction. Somewhere, we must educate our elected representatives at the grassroots to take this kind of a question. It will be very healthy and from there we will build, in my opinion, a much better political structure than only looking at the top.

We will have to look at *panchayats*. The fact that we inserted the word 'secular' into the constitution implied that groups of our own people on whom we committed atrocities for centuries would come up. But now when you suggest that people should be locally identified, it is a big issue. I am going to play the devil's advocate, but tell me, in any district that is Gurjar or Jat-dominated or with any one dominant caste, which candidate will be selected except from that particular caste? Of course, from other places too, the selection is the same because you look at which caste will vote and the candidate, from whichever party he/she may be, belongs to that particular community. How we are going to fight these other issues is something we will have to think about. One may belong to a minority community, not necessarily Muslims, it could be a caste-community, not necessarily Christians, it could be some other tribal community, but one may never get the ticket. In the same way, religion and parochialism disable many candidates. At the *panchayat* level, there is a tremendous amount of parochialism. We will have to deal with these contradictions somewhere in the political structure to see how we can improve them. Some things are wrong when they are too centralised. A comment earlier was that one has to have a kind of dialectics between the local and the rational. Politics also calls for the same kinds of things either through principles, controls or accountability systems.

Jonathan Cohn

This is on Yogendra's comment on election financing; I apologise for my ignorance about India. There is no public financing of national and other elections. Are there restrictions on private funding? In other words, how much can you donate to the campaign?

Yogendra Yadav

There are tax exemptions on donations to particular parties.

Jonathan Cohn

But there are no restrictions on how much people can get?

Yogendra Yadav

There are restrictions.

Jonathan Cohn

I am struck by your description of black money and white money. We also have a distinction: we call it clean money. It is very much the same concept and for a long time all of us have felt and still feel that the best thing we can do is public financing as the most effective strategy to drive out bad money. In fact, we can never keep dirty or bad money, or black money out totally, because corporations and very rich people will find a way to channel it in. The only two cautionary notes that I would add are that as media campaigns have gone really expensive, so candidates are beginning to operate under the public system, as it happened with us during the last couple of campaigns. But the restrictions on bad money actually do make a difference, which we saw in our recent elections. We had a Supreme Court decision about a year ago where the Supreme Court threw out a bunch of restrictions on what corporations could spend and tonnes of money flowed in during the last elections. I would actually come around on this a little bit in the sense that I just don't even worry about keeping bad money out. Let us simply get good money in. But now, I think you have to do both.

Sunita Narain

Picking up Niraja's issues, I guess I am more on the side of the evangelists. But when we look at decentralisation in India, it is incomplete. I hope in the coming years we will start looking at decentralisation not merely for decentralisation's sake but for development. There is a difference in that. It is not administrative. I am looking at it in terms of serious development, in terms of how we would reinvent development. If we really want to utilise those institutions for development, then we have to do a lot more than we have done till now. We have never given the *panchayats* and the communities the right to resources. What we have discussed is not new, but if we look at NREGA, part of it is an employment programme. For somebody like me, it is an ecological regeneration programme, it is a programme to create wealth and ecological assets for economic growth. But when we look at the ecological assets, they don't belong to anyone. The pond belongs to one department; the catchment belongs to another and the channel that brings water from the catchment of the pond belongs to yet another. We have not fixed those issues as yet. Forests are clearly another issue; there is a huge potential for using forest resources for livelihood development. Yet, as a nation, we haven't decided whether a bamboo is a tree or a weed. It is an important issue because if it is a tree and is timber, then it belongs to the forest department and if it is a weed, then people should have the right over it. I am on the side of the weed because I strongly believe that these are resources where trees are cut but are also planted. One has to create the conditions in which one could actually build an economic model out of trees and tree wealth.

The entire debate of using decentralisation for development is still incomplete and it is not an issue on which we have had sufficient debate, dialogue or work in this country. It is a tough one because again, as I said earlier, there are no models for us to follow. I have looked at the property regime of forests in other parts of the world. I have seen how tigers have been conserved in other parts of the world. But in other parts of the world, forests were not habitats of people; they were wilderness areas. There is a complete difference in the way economies and ecologies have been organised. In that sense, I do believe that in the coming years, we have to do the same if we want the *panchayat* not to deteriorate. We also sent our reporters to UP to look at the elections. I was appalled to see the kind of money going around and the kind of politics that is happening at the *panchayat* level. But there is a chance of getting it right. If we engage people in development rather than only in spending money, I think then we could achieve decentralisation for the purpose that it is required. That work is still an unfinished agenda. That is why we may have to hold back our opinion on whether *panchayats* have failed or worked because they have never really been given a chance as yet.

Manish Sabharwal

Good question. I cannot make out whether you feel that development could get a person elected. Whenever somebody like Chandrababu Naidu loses, we say it is because of the development factor. It is a simple correlation of causation and confusion. But at the base level, could somebody get elected talking about the three Es—education, employment and employability? We agree that people in villages and cities do care about these three things. But when I propose it to people in difficult parts of India, they say they know what to do about it but don't know how to get re-elected once they do it. Is there a problem in people understanding its importance or is there a problem in people saying that they have nothing to do with the three Es? One has to figure that out for oneself.

Joseph Stiglitz

I think the idea of viewing the political processes from the economic perspective of industrial organisation entry barriers is a very interesting way to approach it. On one side, TV is very important. The spectrum that TV uses in the cable rights is publicly owned. Originally, we tried to do one thing but didn't succeed because the networks make their money out of selling it. When we auction off the licenses, we put a restriction that a certain amount of time has to be given to the different parties for campaigns.

Second, when we think about this in relationship to what Vijay Kelkar said earlier, one of the reasons that people compete so fiercely is because they want special interest legislation and in particular tax expenditures, corporate welfare, each different from another. If one could somehow get an agreement that made it more difficult to get those kinds of special interest benefits, it would in some sense lower the entry and the race from those who are able to seize more value out of the political process.

I think the framework of the Freedom of Information Act is very important. We have a lot of stories and I mentioned one in my recent talk. The Federal Reserve did not want the people to know who got the money that it was giving out and Bloomberg took the Federal Reserve to court and said that it had to let them know what was going on. The court supported Bloomberg but the Federal Reserve still mentioned that they were not accountable, appealed and lost again. We found out why. The reason they did not want us to know was because the biggest recipient was Goldman Sachs. It was very clear that there were strong incentives not to reveal the information. I think this is an example of how important the Freedom of Information Act can be in the political process, but information alone is not enough. A lot of issues are very complex and information has to be processed. This is where independent bodies, think tanks and the US Congress budgetary office have done a pretty good job. In the UK, there is a more independent institute for fiscal analysis and it plays a very important role. For instance, when the budget was released in the UK, it was asked whose axe was being gored. It played a very vital role in the political discussion in the UK after that.

One of the reasons that the poor get disadvantaged is because information often does not reach out to them. One can set up public mechanisms for revelation of information.

I wish to make two other points. One is about the primary. I don't know how your discussion is about the primary in India but I want to make a comment. I think the US would want to have a discussion on the primary, and move from what they call smoke-filled rooms to the open primary. One of the consequences has been that it has increased polarity in the political process. The discussion on the Right is that one has to compete with democratic parties, who in turn think it is the parties on the extreme Right which benefit. Actually, it has not led to a politics that reflects the interest of the middle better.

The final point is on the issue of decentralisation. This is not a theoretical point; this is an observation from the US. The anti-poor polarising people favoured decentralisation because most of the vocal NGOs are at the national level. It is a collective action problem and they can get organised at the national level. It is much harder for them to get organised at the state level. Policies to move it down to the level of the state have, in fact, been designed by the Republicans to reduce redistribution and weaken social democracy. It is not an answer but at least it is something one has to be aware of.

Rehman Sobhan

I am particularly fascinated by Yogendra's presentation. He could explicitly answer some of the questions, though I am not sure how far these were answered in his paper. These relate to what one may call political market failure. That is why, in a system that has sustained democratic processes for 60 years, political parties do not adequately reflect the concerns of those who constitute the majority of voters. The reason is that voters in the end vote out incumbent parties. The last election was an exception to that and what constituted that exception seems to be of some relevance here. But on a general principle, we can see that pure political opportunism would demand that one takes into account the demands constantly being expressed by those who would be constituted as the 'aam aadmi' in the Indian political process. However, when we look at all the consultative mechanisms in here, it would be quite interesting to look at Montek's or Mr Pranab Mukherjee's calendar in terms of pre-budget consultations. Who would be the range of people with whom they would be constantly having discussions? What man-hours would be spent in having discussions with chambers of commerce and various business groups in the country who, in that sense, seem to get over-exposure? Admittedly, they play a very important role but if, in fact, there is a constituency that is producing 60 per cent of the GDP and that constituency has very low levels of productivity such that not only do we hear their constraints about how their productivity and thereby their incomes could be enhanced, it will then become a positively growth-inducing set of enquiries, which would be very much in the interest of any government that wants to promote growth.

What is there in the working of the democratic system in India that has led to this peculiar failure? Arising from this, I think it might be very interesting because Soniaji must presumably herself have had some sort of agenda in her mind. After all, you are not running a think tank. You are heading a powerful political party in India which constitutes the Government of India. Obviously, there must be some notion that there is a need for building the architecture of social democracy. How far does this need emanate from the political party that you represent? Is there an effective demand from the working politicians who are sitting in parliament and contesting elections for bringing about broad social changes, or do their minds work in completely different directions, which has very little to do with social change where one has to both induce and educate them to its advantages? This, I think, would be a very useful question to answer because I constantly face this problem in Bangladesh. I have been running the Centre for Policy Dialogue for the last 16 years in which we have held about 500 dialogues, which invariably bring in political leaders from the government and opposition to discuss their views on various policies. What is very interesting is the anthropology of this particular process. There is really no strong effective demand within the political community for realising significant social change. I call them because I have some access to them. They listen to me and politely participate in these discussions, but what economists call effective demand does not exist. No one comes to me saying they are seriously concerned about the fact that there is insufficiency of work in rural areas or the school system is crumbling or health services do not reach them. What sort of policy interventions can be made to resolve this problem? Do you face a similar problem in the way you obtain responses from within the party? It would be very interesting to know that. Is there, therefore, a significant constituency retained?

Vijay Kelkar

I started as a sceptic on decentralisation but over the last two years, my work at the Finance Commission almost appears to be evangelical. In the third year, as I mentioned in my remarks earlier, it is the unfinished revolution of Rajiv Gandhi that the country really needs. Aruna Roy raised an important issue about governance and the Finance Commission has given a large devolution to the third tier. We have put conditions precisely to improve governance. We have suggested that there should be CAG Audit, without which they are not going to get any disbursements.

We have also given training programmes in terms of capacity-building, because interesting work is being done in most countries, and in this country too. A very large amount of liquidity in public administration comes in two parts; some call it active leakage because of corruption and passive leakage because of incompetence. Apparently, the passive leakage is as bad or as much as the active leakage. We also give substantial resources for training, precisely for evolving solutions.

The third is the point with regard to reservation. To have a larger fiscal base, we are also giving devolution to the third tier, which really provides for a possible launching pad for the kind of things we want to have.

The point is still in the Finance Commission's report in terms of no architecture for budget-making. We are providing independent fiscal counsel precisely to do what you said, i.e., to give independent advice to the parliament. The budget is very complicated; we don't know how the expenditure is going to pan out. We have proposed setting up a fiscal council precisely for the reason you have mentioned.

Wang Hui

Though I know very little about India, I still feel excited about this kind of discussion. I want to contribute a little bit to these topics from the perspective of the Chinese experience. For example, decentralisation was one of the top issues in the entire reform era. Chinese reform, generally speaking, was the process of decentralisation, which was a real stimulus to economic growth, which was very important. But there were some by-products of that, not so much at the participation level, but at the government level. At the fag end of the 1990s, the quality of the educational programme, especially in the marginal areas and minority educational languages, had really diminished partly because the local governments usually focus on growth rather than these kinds of issues. At that time, the central government did not have enough money to pay for the investment of this basic infrastructure, schools and other measures. Only after the reforms in the 1990s, especially after the taxation reforms, did the central government become rich and could invest more on basic infrastructure and the education system. The second is the environmental issue, wherein the local governments usually seem to focus on growth no matter what the ecological consequences are. There was a counter-process after the end of the last century that made some movement in the system from horizontal to vertical. It means that for the Ministry of Environmental Conservation, the ecological conservation system was much more vertical because it could know through state supervision what happened. All large-scale dam construction or similar projects had to be approved through that process. That was a kind of dynamic propeller between the centre and local entities. On the one hand, in the market condition, a certain kind of decentralisation became absolutely necessary but on the other hand, there was a counter-process. Maybe that kept the balance between the centre and the local. In the Chinese case, that follows the whole process of regionalisation and localisation.

Another issue was regional differences which emerged again. The gap between regions, especially coastal and inland areas widened. Before that, in the common economy, through the direct tax, they could prove that it was a poor area but now the situation has changed. Recently, the Chinese government encouraged inter-regional aids of interaction. For example, in Tibet and Xinjiang, serious crises and conflicts have happened. There it is different in the sense that only the central government increased investments in these areas. Elsewhere, the Chinese government tried to establish a framework to encourage provinces such as Canton, Hunan and Jiangsu to establish a linkage through committee to committee, municipality to municipality, and city to city. There were different reasons to do that. The role of the central government became quite crucial because there was no manipulation, but mediation and regulation. The regional relations were intended for coastal areas, which made that region dependent on them but did not lose the sense of the meaning of real aid for those in these areas. This is a kind of interaction between the two, centralisation and decentralisation.

Another issue Yogendra talked about is the phenomenon of social movements. Their energy, from the Chinese perspective, is one of the most important features for us. A lot of Chinese intellectuals have really admired the development of social movements in India, which in the Chinese case was not as energetic as compared to India. Your suggestion is that a new interaction between social movements at the grassroots and political parties is necessary. But on the other hand, why does this not imply the reorganisation of social movements into party politics or something else? The weakening of party politics is a major political issue, not only in one country, but universally. Sometimes, the energy—whether or not created by social movements—can create autonomous space for local politics. I think the so-called local public space can be based on that, together with party politics. What kind of form and relationship between these social movements and party politics takes shape is the issue here.

Bina Agarwal

The need to distinguish between decentralised government and decentralised governance is important because there has been a move to decentralise governance in relation to forest resources in a serious way. The whole Joint Forest Management (JFM) programme was a form of decentralised governance, without it necessarily going to the government. Here, I disagree with Sunita Narain. Anil Agarwal played a very important role in moving towards decentralised governance for forest resources and all of us had this discussion in the 1980s. Whatever one might say of JFM, I do think it is a serious attempt to decentralise natural resources, at least as far as forests are concerned. The question really is whether handing it over to the *panchayats* is a good idea. My own view is it isn't a good idea because *panchayats* actually have nothing in their twenty-point programme. I have looked at all the state level Panchayats Acts and what has been given. There is virtually no green programme. In fact, virtually, no party has a green programme. I strongly urge that political parties should have statements on a green programme. But giving it to *panchayats* who are not interested and even when they have alternative technology, clean energy on their list as one of the twenty points, they have actually done very little on the ground. This is similar to your question about energy from social movements which will not always be supplementary to political parties. So local governance could supplement and sometimes interrogate local government, which is decentralised.

Montek Singh Ahluwalia

Many people have talked about capacity building. Aruna Roy made a very strong statement and I completely agree with that. The fact is that a very large portion of the central government's resources is now going to support schemes that can only be operated at the local level, where oversight by the local community and participation is absolutely crucial, otherwise they are just not going to work. We need to spend money on building capacity. We are proposing to do that in a more systematic way. The large amount of money that the central government spends on what are called 'centrally sponsored schemes' entails giving money, but it is in a sector that is normally the responsibility of the state and is implemented at the local level. It is very large, almost ₹ 170,000 crores, i.e., 40 billion dollars. Perhaps 3 per cent of that could be given for capacity-building. It does not make any sense to have such a huge amount of money being spent, governed, supervised, planned etc., at the local level and not provide them the resources to do so effectively. If we were to do that, you would be giving ₹ 5000 crores, over a billion dollars. Forty (40) billion dollars is a huge amount of money, much larger than any aid or international programme. We need to do that so that these people are able to hire whatever engineers or accountants they can, from nearby regional engineering or other colleges, to keep all these accounts.

The other point which Aruna talked about is that the people need to know where the money is going. Right now, even the central government does not know. When a ministry sends money to a state, as far as we are concerned, it is spent. But whether the state sends it down to the local body, which in turn actually gets a school room built, has to do with a process of reporting. One of the big things that is happening right now, is a pilot programme. We hope it will be done in a couple of years time where the central government will be able to say that it spent from the central government budget X and all this which went to the state, actually got spent. There will be a time lag but at the moment the last bit of information comes from a certificate. We have no idea; we just ask the state government and they say that it has been spent. This is another example where technology will make transparency possible. These two things basically imply putting money to build up capacity. Five or six years will make a huge difference; it won't make a difference immediately.

Abhijit Sen

The 13th Finance Commission did put in a lot of money into the *panchayat* sector. We had hoped that a fair amount of it would go to employing a *panchayat* staff, with accountants, engineers and things of that kind. None of the money is going there; it is actually going into doing things that the *panchayat* guys want to do. I think there is really a problem there. You have to guide the *panchayat* system and it has to have the equivalent of a minister having a secretary and a secretariat. That has to be there to some extent. That is really what we needed to build up but it is not there.

Niraja Gopal Jayal

These are very complex questions. I don't think we need to replicate the secretariat at the local level, at the gram panchayat level. Let me try and take all these together. What Dr Ahluwalia just said about the certificate reminds me of Anusha Rizvi's film where the certificate was the thing. I think what we have in place is something valuable. I don't want to use the word architecture; it has been overused today. Let us say infrastructure, the institutional infrastructure of *panchayats*: I would put my money on anything that is valuable, worth cherishing, nurturing and improving and strengthening. Now the question is what we need to strengthen. There are many ways in which we need to strengthen it and I fully agree with Aruna. On capacity-building, some NGOs in the country have done stellar work, including federations and so on. Financial literacy is not the only thing, though important. Strengthening the Gram Sabha is a big issue. I think broadly there are two sets of constraints and this is the way I have seen them: institutional constraints and social constraints. Social constraints range from patriarchy, tokenism, surrogate representation to caste intimidation, violence and elite capture—the most important one of them all. Institutional constraints are different. They have to do with devolution, finances, relationships between tiers and relationships between *panchayats* and local bureaucracy. Local government for me is a local state which is the *sarkari* or the line department. Local governance is a complex thing. It includes watershed management committees, joint forest management committees, things we otherwise call parallel bodies. I am no expert on this. All I know is that Scheduled Six areas do have control over forests. But when we use the word local governance, technically, we should also include civil society organisations which exist there. It is not only about elected bodies, but also about all these other local actors.

As far as development is concerned, the problem is basically what Dr Ahluwalia just said, which is that all the money going to panchayats, by and large goes—NREGA excluded—into centrally sponsored schemes, which is tied money. It is basically channelling it to beneficiaries who are to be identified.

Development and resources are a larger debate. The big problem, I think, is the planning institutions do with the *panchayats*, which have for the most part, not been put in place. Take our own cities, big cities, metros, and the 74th Amendment. Where are the metropolitan planning committees? They have not even come into existence yet. It is almost 20 years. The planning institutions and mechanisms, whether at district level or local level, have not actually come into existence, which is the sort of arbitrariness that Abhijit Sen refers to when he says that *sarpanches* choose to do as they please. There too, there are differences between not just one *panchayat* and another, but one *sarpanch* and another.

I absolutely agree with all of this and it is a very big problem. There are many dimensions to this problem and many things that need to be fixed. In principle, this is a valuable institutional infrastructure and we have to try and strengthen it rather than bash it.

Steve I. Wilkinson

I wish to respond to a couple of things. There have been remarks by Aruna Roy and also by some other people on the negative potential of the UID project. People link that to inflict violence on minorities or weaker castes. They have also linked it to greater use of caste in politics. From my perspective, both those things are already happening but the good things that could be happening through the unique ID are not. In the 2002 riots, US Municipal Corporation records were used to target individuals without any kind of unique ID system. Politicians I meet in India can tell the ethnic composition of their constituency. Many politicians have pressurised local census staff to actually generate independent estimates of this. All these bad things have happened without a unique ID. A lot of good things that could potentially happen, haven't happened. I think those fears, I would say, are overstated.

The second is Yogendra's point. It is obvious that a lot of discrimination is group-based: group-based targeted things to group-based processes of discrimination. Secondly, the political reality will be too costly for politicians and voters to consider doing away with whole bunches of the reservation system. This is why the temporary reservations that were introduced in 1950 have never been done away with.

What would I suggest? The Kundu Committee in 2008 and the Diversity Committee rightly recognise that disadvantages have multiple dimensions, both ethnic and non-ethnic. The simple caste reservations are a blunt way of dealing with those multiple dimensions. We could include multiple ethnic and non-ethnic things in the same kind of index. If you link the gradual success through these diversity indexes to their gradual demise, I think, is key. This was never done in the 1950s reservations. Instead, they were put there as a whole and nobody, of course, wants to dismantle the whole thing. Therefore, you gradually improve your level of representation in society based on caste lines, so that after chaotic reviews, not done by politicians but by some individual agency, reservations naturally expire rather than any individual politician having to make a decision to let them expire. We all know that is unlikely to happen in the political system. I think a fairer way is if you can come up with some kind of neutral basis for achieving a consensus that pure caste-based representation should go down slightly as things go up slightly. I think that is much more defensible than saying to any individual group, let's take everything away. You could weight it somewhat differently and weigh gender or poverty more and caste less.

Yogendra Yadav

Can development get someone elected? My answer is yes, it does, as long as there is clarity about what is being assessed. People not only reward good work, they reward even tiny bits of decent work which is what happened in Madhya Pradesh and Chhattisgarh, when Digvijay Singh won his second verdict. These were tiny bits of work and people are prepared to distinguish very slight shades of grey. There are times when we think someone who did good work has not been rewarded. That's largely because our gullible national media picks up images from the metropolis and portrays as if Andhra Pradesh was transformed by Chandrababu Naidu. It was never the case.

Political market failure is a large question, Prof Rehman. I actually feel that we really need some discipline to come up and the remarks I make are really very crude preliminary remarks about what appears to be the case initially. Our initial formulation is that the problem is not on the demand side at all. It is not that people fail to appreciate, are unwilling to reward or don't understand. The problem in this case is squarely in the supply side of politics; supply bottlenecks are the real issues here and that is why we have paid enormous attention about how political supply is being generated. My paper goes into some of these things but I admit this is a very preliminary way of thinking about it.

Movement in party dynamics and in which ways it needs to be changed, is a big question. In our country, for the first two or three decades, what were called movements were largely things that were spawned by political parties. So the party-movement relationship was very clear. From the 1980s onwards, we had independent social movements whose relationship between two parties is somewhat unclear. For instance, I actually believe that for the kind of political values that the Indian National Congress stands, those ideas and energies actually come from new social movements. The party does not have that cadre. In the case of the BJP, the other party, it is clear what their linkage to social organisations is but in the case of the largest party, the Congress, it is still unclear. And as yet, there is no formal mechanism through which that energy can be linked to the party. Innovative things have to come up, including rethinking our notion of what is a political party. Because in any case, what exists on the ground is a much caricatured version of the late 19th century in Europe. Since we have very different textbooks, we might as well formally reclassify these things.

There are some specific suggestions. I take your point on driving out bad money; we need to keep our eyes on restricting black money as well. In India, unfortunately, that is the only thing to which we have paid attention. All our legislations are to do with how to prevent black money from coming into politics, some of them ridiculous. There was a time when, if each Member of Parliament was to write one letter to his electors, his upper limit of permitted expenditure would have been exhausted. My essence, therefore, is that our principal energy should be directed at ensuring flow of white money into politics; white, accountable money, with least strings attached. There should bc ample freedom to spend that money over a five-year period, not just during elections.

Party campaign time on television used to exist. The real issue there is that it does not exist in relation to the private sector media. Everyone, including the Election Commission, wants every candidate to submit accounts of their expenditure every 48 hours. This is impossible. No candidate can actually run a campaign and do all these things. The same Election Commission is unwilling to go into such big issues as to how campaign finance is managed, whether private channels should be asked to give some time or how private channel time should be regulated. On the Indian media, I should clarify that it is indeed the case that there is enormous freedom of expression as must be evident to all our friends sitting in this room. We have a free media but this particular thing has hurt me personally so much. Many of us have been acting like ambassadors of the country about our democracy and what great things this democracy has done. It is only fair that we acknowledge this one black spot.

Lowering the stakes in elections would be a very good idea though the principal point is that there is no special interest legislation on taxation because our legislators actually do not legislate. It is only an old habit to somehow keep calling them legislators, whereas they have nothing to do with legislation. A party whip is issued and they have to vote accordingly. Some of them do attend parliamentary committees. Our members of parliament do enormously important work and I think they work five times more than any representative works in most parts of the world. But they do other things, not legislation. That is what needs to be brought about.

As for primaries, at the moment it is just a gesture towards the kind of thing that we need to do. I did not mean to say we should replicate the American system of primaries. Basically, the elementary idea that a party's candidate in the coming elections should be determined by the local workers in that constituency is an alien idea in India right now. It is decided not even in the state capital because that list is then referred to Delhi. Usually, it is a few thousand kilometres away from where the election is being contested that the decision about the ticket is taken. It is a gesture towards moving it in that direction. The form can be decided later.

Bina Agarwal

The remaining part of this session will be an open call on trying to pick up the threads of all the sessions and how we might take this project forward. I would also urge that we think a little about issues of building social consensus, questions of values, lifestyles, those sorts of concerns as well.

I request Pratap Bhanu Mehta and Sunil Khilnani to say a few words on where they see this project going forward and in what ways.

Kumar Mangalam Birla

Whilst we have had many discussions over the last two days, the fact remains that we have a lot of positives going for our country as well. I can reel off a whole list of them. Each one of us has an ideology and some of are more vocal than the others. But I think the real challenge is for us all to move a little away from ideologies, not from the point of view of compromising but collaborating and looking out of our silos. How can we work with each other to take the country to wherever we want to take it?

Sudha Murty

Normally, people don't like to part with money unless it is made compulsory. The government alone cannot do all the social activities in a country of a billion plus people as the issues are different. My suggestion is that whenever a corporate house makes a profit, then it should be made compulsory that they should adopt a village or particularly a school and a road. I think the main roads are taken care of by the Pradhan Mantri Sadak Yojana but the connecting roads are not. The government should make it compulsory that if one makes so much profit, then one has to adopt and run a school, not just give money, but build classrooms, hostels, water and road connections, etc. Unless we make it compulsory, people won't do it. If we make it compulsory, people will take it and over a period of time, we will assume that they will take it forward. The Tatas and the Birlas have done it and in a small way, Infosys also has done that. We are building 2,300 houses worth ₹ 30 crores without asking for even a penny from the government, whether state or central. We are doing it on our own. This is one of the suggestions where everybody can participate. The moment we have government and private partnership, lots of difficulties arise. The government cannot come back immediately and corporate houses cannot wait. It is like a mismatch. I feel responsibility should be given to us and our own contractors and staff to run these initiatives.

Chanda Kochhar

During the last two days of deliberations, while we have learnt and discussed a lot about what different countries have done and so on, I think we in India still have to find our own models for three reasons. Firstly, the scale of our country is very different from most others; secondly, the size of the opportunities that we have today, whether in the form of our demographics or our ability to roll out infrastructure or our need to roll out infrastructure etc., is really unprecedented which many countries may not have faced. So we have a huge opportunity. Lastly, the fact that we are looking at things at different stages in a way gives us the opportunity to leapfrog many of the legacies that other countries have had and create our own models. Let us use this opportunity to learn from everyone but create a model that will be very different in scale, size and shape. We have to realise that our model has to be very comprehensive as well as hugely collaborative. The public and the private sectors, the central government and the absolutely decentralised *panchayats* have to try and work together. The technology and the micro concerns of people have to be brought together. What we really need to do is find a model where everything collaborates and also an approach towards giving people the right to create an environment where they have the ability to participate, rather than just depending on subsidies. As we evolve, different roles may shift and at a certain point, some may play a larger role and some a smaller one but we first have to start collaborating. If we have understood this in this debate, I think we would have achieved a lot rather than living in silos.

Joseph Stiglitz

There has been some discussion about public-private partnerships. I wish to add a word of caution on how difficult it is to design them well. We have a lot of public-private partnerships in the US. The government absorbs the losses and the private sector takes the profits, and they don't work so well for social purposes. To give an example, the student loan programme was a public private partnership that went to a state-government run programme and over a 10-year period, they anticipated to save 80 billion dollars by the government directly rather than in a public-private partnership. That leads to the second observation, which is that a lot has to be done as part of the social democratic agenda. There needs to be an important role for the state at every level, not only at the local level but also at the state and national level. Walking away from government programmes and using public-private partnerships may not be the best way to build up a state. One of the ways to build up the state is by doing things gradually and carefully but it seems to me that a major part of the social democratic agenda will have to be with building a comprehensive set of partnerships with NGOs, with the private sector but also by having a strong state of its own.

Sunil Khilnani

Chanda Kochhar put the point very well of what seems to have come out in the discussions in the last two days. One thing that came through clearly is that despite the exceptionality of the Indian case, there is comparability as well. There are things one can pick up from other examples as we have heard about Brazil, Indonesia or the Scandinavian countries in very different ways. There seems to have been a general agreement that we are really at a turning point in the story of our country. The kinds of decisions that we make in the next five to ten years are really going to set us on a path that is going to be very important into this century really. In a sense, a lot depends on how we weigh up the choices we have and the decisions we make. This isn't just ordinary or routine politics in the next two years. This is really a very important historic moment in India's story. I think we are all in agreement about that. Going on from here, as governments start to become more accountable, there is going to be a need for very serious policies and policy choices that they can put forward to the electorate. This requires the development of those policies, thinking, formulation and judgement about what policies are right. Building up a broader repertoire of ideas which can feed into our policies and policy choices is another thing that we have to think seriously about.

Pratap Bhanu Mehta mentioned to me some of the other areas of agreement that have come through. Targeting still has an important role to play in dealing with the many inequalities and discriminations we still have in our society. But at the same time, we also have to realise the limitations of that approach and the difficulty of establishing the criteria, for example, of those who are above or below the poverty line, the transit from these categories and the importance of seeing them as not fixed and stable and similarly, when it comes to caste and other identities. Linked to that, the sense that came through was that we need to be moving away from those sorts of categories of targeted policies, towards a universal agenda and a more universalistic reach for the policies we want to see our governments provide.

Finally, the point that Manish, Chanda and others along with Pratap too made in his remarks is really one of the important things we will face in the next year. That is to move from the idea that redistribution is the primary activity of the state to creating the conditions for participation of the vast majority of our citizens in the possibilities that our market is opening up for all of them.

Pratap Bhanu Mehta

Two challenges that face us going ahead are that social democracies in a sense require a form of social self-knowledge, which is really about what their collective understanding is about the cause and processes that can make them go in one direction or the other. The interesting question is going to be how we are going to increase our knowledge about that. Part of what we see in even the emblematic representation in this room is partly a kind of contest over different principles of authority, of who can represent that—civil society, private sector, in fact, Marwaris were the only people we didn't mention. I am anti-Jacobin enough to still believe that representative government has to be the core of the idea of representation. In this sense, all of us together cannot substitute for that. That, I think, is going to be one sort of major challenge.

The second challenge, which is the historical challenge for all movements of social democracy, is what theories of social change are, as opposed to designs, objectives, visions. We have elements of that here in terms of good policy interventions. These can create virtuous cycles of change but one thing we should keep an eye out for is what John Donne calls the 'Cunning of Unreason'. It says the great opportunities come because of certain things happening elsewhere, because of exogenous change and I think intelligent politics requires attention to how we can actually leverage those much more intelligently. In fact, all the social democratic models that we discussed had that element—Brazil benefits from the growth of China and those kind of stories. How do we internalise those kinds of opportunities and in that process, what is our theory of change? I am very grateful that we have had this absolutely wonderful opportunity to discuss social democracy.

Rob Riemen

A lot of my life and work is organising public lectures and I am still proud that Sonia Gandhi was once a Nexus lecturer. I organise conferences and it has created in me the habit of thanking everyone at the end of the conference. I therefore thank the organising committee of this Indira Gandhi Conference.

First of all, thanks to Sunil and Pratap. It is not difficult for us to imagine how much intellectual effort you have put into this conference, to phrase the right questions into right topics, which are always a key thing to be done.

A special thanks to two gentlemen who have been silent and modest but who have proven their phenomenal organisational skills. I am absolutely certain that they have their own intellectual impact in this conference but I also want you to know how much I admire their patience with us.

Above all, I would like to thank the leading spirit of the Indira Gandhi Conference and that is Sonia Gandhi. I want to remind you of the expression of Thomas Mann, the German intellectual who felt inspired after meeting Nehru. He expressed his regret that he felt too old—he was 56 to follow Nehru's invitation to immigrate to India. The context in which he made the comment was that on the one hand, he was deeply disappointed by communism. He spoke about the infertile immorality of communism but also felt disappointed by the capitalist world, which he considered to be corrupt. So he saw in Nehru and his vision for India the true embodiment of social democracy as a symbolising political ideal, driven and inspired by a strong commitment. I think they were all aware of the paradox of history, which is the context in which our conference has taken place. Sonia Gandhi mentioned that in her opening address. In countries of the West where social democracy first took root, the spirit of social democracy is disappearing. Although the West is enormously wealthy, it is increasingly becoming a model of a society in crisis, whether financial, environmental, or civilisational. This fact should make all of us aware of two important things. First of all, social democracy will always be an ongoing effort for all of us, as in human nature, the laws of gravity want to bring us down and we have the tendency to indulge our low instincts. Social democracy always wants to appeal to our noble aspirations. Secondly, economic models and social projects are never enough to keep the spirit of social democracy alive. We will always need more. Here, this Indira Gandhi Conference is so essential. Sonia Gandhi and her co-organisers have managed to bring together a fascinating mix of top-level practitioners, activists and thinkers. Our common identity being here is that we all realise that Pascal Lamy was absolutely right when he urged us to realise that more than ever before, our world is in need of social democracy if it wants to remain a civilised world.

Long ago when I felt uncomfortable with my own conferences and was unsure as to whether it was a good conference, a family friend of mine gave me the perfect definition of a good conference. He said that if at the end of the conference and after the final day and a good night of sleep, one goes home and has at least one or more new ideas and if one has heard some things one never thought or heard about, if one also feels inspired and leaves with more energy than when one came to the conference, for sure, one has had a good conference. I think if I sense the mood among my fellow delegates, it is fair to say that we have had an excellent conference.

I have been organising conferences for the last 20 years. The quality of a conference and of our own contribution relates to a very important thing. First of all, we cannot do these things if there is no efficiency behind it. You have created a super-efficient organisation and next to this, maybe even more important, an overwhelming hospitality and kindness to strangers which makes my life a little bit more difficult, because Sonia Gandhi really set new standards for everybody who organises conferences.

Finally, to Sonia Gandhi, we all know that this Indira Gandhi Conference is your initiative and we are grateful to you for having invited us. I have to admit, and it might sound strange to you but I was deeply surprised to see you come here and stay for two days. I commented to Sunil Khilnani and asked him whether he could tell me of one person of the level of Sonia Gandhi who would spend a whole weekend with an intellectual gathering of people like us. I can assure you we thought over a long list. We came to the conclusion that there is nobody like her.

As a final remark, with this conference, you have given one more example of keeping something alive which has become a unique characteristic of the Nehru-Gandhi family, which is strong commitment to humanism. On behalf of all of us, I want you to know how enormously grateful we are for that.

Bina Agarwal

I formally thank the organisers and particularly Mrs Gandhi, for what I think is an extremely exciting idea and conference. I wish to use a line from a favourite poem of the Nehru family, "miles to go before we sleep", but I think the important thing is we have started on the journey.

Sonia Gandhi

It is left to me to thank you all for coming to the conference and for sharing your views and your experiences. The purpose of this conference is not really to arrive at an agreed position on the issues we take up; it is rather to stimulate the flow of thoughts and ideas. I think you will all agree that this has happened in full measure. As for myself, I have taken careful note of what has been said. I shall certainly continue to strive to take forward our work towards social democracy and maybe towards democracy in the party. I would like to thank you all for speaking out and sharing your knowledge. I am very grateful to those who presented their papers and the chairpersons who conducted the sessions. With this, I now bring the proceedings to a close.

Afterword

Afterword

JOSEPH E. STIGLITZ[1]

A Social Democratic Agenda for a More Dynamic Indian Economy

Creating an Innovative and Learning Society[2]

Jawaharlal Nehru has become a symbol of the fight for freedom, independence and democracy throughout the world. He had high aspirations for a resurgent India, aspirations that are today being fulfilled. But the struggle for dignity, equality and democracy, and for improving the living standards of all citizens within the country is a never-ending struggle. It is about this struggle, about the transformations of the economy, politics and society that are necessary to achieve victory in this struggle, that I wish to speak.

India has played a large role in shaping my views of development. I first visited India more than 43 years ago, and the transformation that has occurred in the almost half century since are hard to believe. I should also note the deep and long lasting connections between my university, Columbia and India's struggle for independence, freedom and human rights. B.R. Ambedkar, widely claimed as the architect of India's constitution and the champion for the rights of all—not just the untouchables, but also women's rights—spent some of his formative years at Columbia, receiving both an M.A. and Ph.D., as well as an honorary doctorate.

India, the world's largest democracy, should be proud of the successes that it has achieved over the past 25 years, and even more

1. The 2010 Jawaharlal Nehru Memorial Lecture, Delivered on November 18, 2010.
2. In this lecture, I bring together several strands of my work on development. I am particularly indebted to my co-authors Bruce Greenwald and Karla Hoff.

so of its growth in recent years. GDP per capita in 2009 was 2.3 times what it was in 1990, and, at least according to World Bank data,[3] poverty has been reduced from just short of 50 per cent of the population in 1994 to 42 per cent in 2005. Yet India cannot rest on these laurels. There are still more than 400 million in poverty and per capita income is still less than half of that of China in purchasing power parity (PPP).

The successes in development in Asia during the past quarter century were not only unprecedented, they were also unanticipated. Gunnar Myrdal described, just a few short years before these successes began, his pessimism about whether it would ever emerge from the poverty in which it had been mired for centuries.[4] Today, the questions have changed dramatically. Successful countries like India are asking how they can ensure that that growth will be sustained. And less successful countries, many of them in Africa, wish to know what the essential ingredients were that led to these successes. Can they be imitated? The successes and failures around the world provide a set of natural experiments, a laboratory in which we can make some inferences about what contributes to development, and what impedes it.

But even within the successful countries, there are questions, and not just about sustainability: Are economic policies leading to the well-being of citizens? Are the benefits of the growth being equitably shared?

Events of recent years have called into question long-standing presumptions, the conventional wisdom in much of the world about the right answers to these questions. The set of ideas known alternatively as the Washington Consensus, market fundamentalism, or neoliberalism has failed in the very country from which those ideas emanated. The institutions and policies that were put forth as examples for others to follow have failed: they failed to produce sustainable growth, and the fruits of what

3. World Bank (2010).

4. See Gunnar Myrdal's Nobel Prize Lecture, 1974 available at *http://nobelprize.org/nobel_prizes/economics/laureates/1974/myrdal-lecture.html* (accessed November 3, 2010); or his work Myrdal (1968).

growth occurred went to a few. Today, most Americans are worse off than they were in 1999, well before the previous recession.[5] Even before the crisis, trickle-down economics—the notion that so long as growth is ensured, all will benefit—was discredited. But American growth had not only been anti-poor; even the middle class has suffered. There is ample evidence of social distress that goes beyond these economic indicators—one of the highest murder rates in the world[6] and the highest rate of incarceration in the world.[7] Other factors contributing to individual well being—like social connectedness—also seem to not be faring well.[8]

In this paper, I want to put forward three hypotheses:

1. Successful and 'sustained' growth requires creating a learning society. And this is especially so in the 21st century as we move to a knowledge economy.
2. An open, democratic society is more conducive to the creation of a learning society.
3. Successful and sustained democratic growth must be inclusive.

Before turning to each of these propositions, I want to briefly review the history of development thinking over the past 50 years.

A brief history of development thought from projects to policies

In the years immediately after World War II, the view was that what separated developing from developed countries was a

---

5. Real median household income in 2009 is 5 per cent lower than that of 1999. See *Census Current Population Survey*, Table H-6, Regions—All Races by Median and Mean Income: 1975 to 2009, available at *http://www.census.gov/hhes/www/income/data/historical/household/index.html* (accessed November 3, 2010).

6. The United States was 16th in the world in 2002, with a homicide rate of 5.6 per 100,000 inhabitants, compared to, say, Sweden or Canada with rates of 2.45 and 1.67 respectively. See *The Eighth United Nations Survey on Crime Trends and the Operations of Criminal Justice Systems (2001-2002)*, accessible at *http://www.unodc.org/unodc/en/data-and-analysis/Eighth-United-Nations-Survey-on-Crime-Trends-and-the-Operations-of-Criminal-Justice-Systems.html* (accessed November 3, 2010).

7. A rate of 700.22 per 100,000 in 2002. Ibid.

8. See, e.g. Putnam (1995); and the discussion to which it gave rise, e.g. in Sander and Putnam (2010).

disparity in resources. Developing countries lacked capital. Global capital markets were imperfect.[9] Hence, what was required was the creation of a bank—the World Bank—to facilitate the flow of funds and help developing countries undertake projects that would raise income per capita.

It soon became apparent that providing money by itself would not lead to a developmental transformation. The focus then shifted to implementing the 'right policies', which usually meant the Washington Consensus, neoliberal, market fundamentalist policies.

The failure of the Washington Consensus policies

Even before the recent crisis provided the nail in the coffin of neoliberalism, these ideas had been thoroughly discredited: their intellectual premises had been undermined, and almost without exception, the most successful countries, the countries in East Asia, followed a markedly different course.

To a large extent, neoliberalism/Washington Consensus policies were the application of Reagan/Thatcher conservatism to developing countries. They were predicated on the notion that markets by themselves were efficient and stable, and that the benefits of growth would trickle down to all citizens. Even before developing countries were exposed to these new policy experiments, under the aegis of the international financial institutions, both theory and evidence had called into question these beliefs. My own work on the economics of information (with Bruce Greenwald) had shown that the reason that Adam Smith's invisible hand often seemed invisible was that it was, in fact, not there (Greenwald and Stiglitz, 1986). Markets with imperfect and asymmetric information and incomplete information were not efficient—and since all markets are characterised by imperfect and asymmetric information, this meant that markets were essentially never efficient. We should have learned from, the Great Depression that not only are markets not necessarily efficient but they are also not

9. At the time, there was little discussion over why capital markets were imperfect.

stable and self-correcting (at least, not in the relevant time frame). We have now learned these lessons again.

The experience with the Washington Consensus (WC) policies has now further undermined each of its central policy tenets. For instance, deregulation and liberalisation may not improve efficiency and stability. Indeed, the only period in which market economies have not been subject to financial crises was the three to four decades after the Great Depression when the US and other countries imposed strict banking and financial sector regulations. These decades happened also to be a period of rapid growth, with fruits widely shared.

Because under these well-designed regulatory structures, markets seemed to be so stable, some made the wrong inference that regulation was not needed. And the predictable results followed as regulations were stripped away, as governments refused to impose new regulations for the 'innovative' but dangerous financial products—derivatives—that were being invented, and as regulators were appointed who didn't believe in regulations. There were more than 120 crises around the world in the succeeding years, of which this crisis, wearing a made-in-USA label, is by far the largest.

While macro-stability is important, the notion that price stability was the only, or the most important, aspect of macrostability was wrong; the focus on price stability under the WC—the notion that low and stable inflation was necessary and almost sufficient for rapid growth—was misguided. This was an idea that didn't even work in the country from which the WC policies emanated, the US.

While WC policies promoted neither growth nor stability, what growth did occur didn't trickle down. Trickle-down economics never had much empirical support, but in recent years, it is an idea that has fared particularly badly. In the US, for instance, between 1999 and 2009, real median household income in the US fell by five per cent. Today, most Americans (and let me stress that: most Americans) are worse off than they were a decade ago. All of the benefits and more have gone to those at the top. We have had trickle-up growth, not trickle-down. Today, between a fifth and a quarter of all income goes to the upper one per cent.[10] Inequality in wealth is even worse.[11]

But from a developmental perspective, perhaps the greatest failing of the WC was just that: it was not concerned with development. It pretended that there was no difference between developed and developing countries, so that there was no developmental transformation. It was simply concerned with the efficient allocation of resources. It was almost as if the advocates of WC policies believed that this was all that was required. In a way, it followed from the belief in the simplistic neoclassical model, which had undergirded the first view: if resources were efficiently allocated, then the shortage of capital would be evidenced in a higher return to capital, and that would ensure the flow of capital from rich countries to poor. One didn't need to turn to an international institution to ensure the transfer of capital. This approach simply didn't recognise the existence of global capital market imperfections—other than those created by misguided governments. (There is an especial irony in this crisis: in the years prior to the crisis, money actually flowed 'uphill,' from poor countries to the US. The defenders of this anti-gravity phenomenon suggested that it was because the US was so much more efficient than developing countries that the return to capital was higher, even though capital was more abundant. This explanation seems less persuasive today; the US misallocated capital badly, so that the net return was probably much, much lower than it would have been had the capital been invested in, say, emerging markets.)

While I have stressed the ideology underlying the advocacy of WC policies, I would be remiss not to note that they did serve some special interests. Ideas and interests are intimately intertwined. Capital markets, and especially the big banks, made money as capital flowed into East Asia in the years before the East Asian crisis; they made money in the restructuring that followed, and IMF

10. If capital gains are included, the top 1 per cent of income earners in the US accounted for 20.95 per cent of income in 2008; in 2007 they accounted for 23.5 per cent. See Piketty and Saenz (2003).

11. Households in the top 1 per cent of the wealth distribution hold around 32.7 per cent of the wealth; the top 5 per cent hold 57.7 per cent. Source: Davies *et al.* (2009).

bailouts ensured that they were repaid their loans—no matter how bad their lending decisions.

Now, Americans are angry as they watch the big banks walking off with billions, and they confront the aftermath of the crisis: budgetary deficits forcing cutbacks in social programmes, millions facing extended unemployment and millions more struggling to make ends meet. But this is a familiar picture in many developing countries, one which I inveighed against in *Globalization and its Discontents* (Stiglitz, 2002).

So too privatisation served certain interests well. It is noteworthy that some of the most ardent advocates of privatisation—who claimed foreign ownership should not be a source of concern suddenly changed their tune as the sovereign wealth funds or Chinese companies tried to buy American assets.[12] A new set of arguments were put forward—private owners, whether foreign or domestic, could be trusted; it was only foreign governments that couldn't. The lack of alignment between social and private interests, so evident in the run-up to the global financial crisis, as American banks engaged in predatory lending and deceptive and dishonest practices on a massive scale, should lay to rest such contentions.

Needless to say, this approach of getting policies right was no more successful than the first approach, largely because what was conceived of as the 'right policies' were in fact the wrong policies. But even if the policies had been successful in ensuring the efficient allocation of resources, they would not have led to successful development. There is more to development than that.

In their defence, many in the international institutions used to say that the problem was not so much with the policies, as with the way that they were implemented. (Today, this refrain is heard less often, as it becomes increasingly clear that they were not the right policies.) But this defence is unpersuasive: good policies are policies that can be implemented by mortal individuals working within fallible institutions. If they fail repeatedly—as they did—then by definition, they are not well designed.

---

12. See, for example Summers (2007).

From policies to institutions

With the discrediting of the 'getting policies right' approach to development came a third approach, getting institutions right. But this approach too has had only mixed success, partly because we can't be sure what constitutes good institutions, and even if we did, we may not know how to create one.

Again, the crisis has brought out the problems. Before the crisis, many might have pointed to America's central bank, the Federal Reserve, as a model institution. But as the crisis has unfolded, confidence in the institution has eroded, and more fundamental defects have been exposed. It is clear that it was 'cognitively captured' by the financial sector that it was supposed to regulate; it came to reflect the ideology and interests of the banks. For instance, while it was given the powers to regulate the housing sector—and to prevent the kind of bubble and abuses that arose—it chose not to do so.

The bywords in good governance are transparency and accountability and the avoidance of conflicts of interest. With the head of the New York Federal Reserve Bank nominated by a committee that included the chairman of Goldman Sachs and AIG, institutions which received billions from the Fed, it is hard not to raise questions of good governance. When an American court ruled that the Fed, like other public institutions, was subject to the Freedom of Information Act (America's right-to-know law), the Fed fought to keep its secrecy. It fought to ensure that Americans would not know that the largest single beneficiary of the AIG bailout which it had helped engineer was Goldman Sachs. It fought to keep secret the terms under which the credit default swaps were settled, which were so disadvantageous to America's taxpayers. It never provided an explanation for the give-away that would pass muster.

These are matters of America's dirty laundry. I raise them here simply to emphasise that what might at one moment seem an exemplary institution, at another moment may seem full of blemishes. We should strive to create open, democratic, accountable institutions, but the task is not easy. India is lucky in having a Central Bank that has earned recognition for its integrity—it is one of the few central banks that were not effectively captured by the financial sector. It will be a struggle to ensure that that is the case in the future.

But these examples help bring to the fore several central issues concerning institutions. One of the important strands of modern research stresses the role of institutions in filling gaps left by markets. In this view, institutions help correct market failures. But a closer look at how institutions work in practice is that often their role is to enforce inequalities and preserve the interests of special interests.

The push for independent central banks, when taken too far, may do exactly that. To whom are such banks accountable? In many countries, the result has been a Central bank that has served the interests of the financial sector, not the broader interests of society.

Jim Crow was an institution in the US that enforced segregation, a system of discrimination against African-Americans that deprived them both of their rights and of economic opportunity. The caste system in India is an institution that has had similar adverse effects on large portions of the population in this country.

Institutions, like markets (which can be thought of as a particular kind of institution), are instruments. They can be used to promote development, or to impede it. Details matter. Everyone talks about the rule of law—and no one would defend a lawless society. But for almost a century after America's Civil War, the law was used as an instrument to deprive African-Americans of their rights and economic opportunities. In 2005, American banks used their money and political influence to change our bankruptcy laws, to institute what can only be called a system of partial indentured servitude, where a poor individual who is deceived by the banks to undertake debts that, say, equal his income, will have to turn over a quarter of his income for the rest of his life to the banks. There is no fresh start—rich corporations are treated, in effect, more favourably than poor individuals. Today, in America, the so-called rule of law is being used to take away homes from individuals who were never even indebted, and to transfer title to others who can't even prove their rights of ownership. The law is supposed to be the protector of the poor and powerless against the rich and powerful; but the rule of law can be used in just the opposite way.

Changing institutions is difficult, but that is what is required in the process of development. When there are institutions that preserve inequities and impede development they have to be stripped away. That has to be one of the central tasks of development; but neither of the first two strategies I described even recognised this as being at the core of successful development.

A balanced role between government and markets

The one positive aspect of the new institutional analysis is the recognition that government is important and that private firms (which are at the centre of markets) may also suffer from governance problems.

Indeed, one of the main lessons to emerge from the 'debacle' of the WC is that every successful economy requires a balance between government and the market (and civil society). That balance was lost in the WC policies. Government has a role in restraining markets (from the excesses exhibited, for instance, by financial markets), and in making markets work (ensuring, for instance, that they do not engage in anti-competitive practices, as is their wont). But, especially in developing countries, government has a catalytic role, in promoting entrepreneurship, ensuring access to capital, and promoting education, research and technology. (There are other roles too, most importantly in social protection.)

The modern theory of market failures has explained why government must fill these roles, why, for instance, markets, by themselves, will under-invest in R&D.

Once one recognises the importance of government, one has to ask two questions: how can we improve its performance (for example through better governance, better management practices)? And how can we best design how it interacts with markets and civil society? Among my most exciting responsibilities when I served as Chairman of the Council of Economic Advisers was my engagement in our efforts at 'reinventing government', which were directed at answering these questions.

Each of these strands—projects, policies and institutions—is part of the story of development. I have emphasised the complexity associated with each, and that we have been perhaps too facile in believing that we knew what good projects, policies and institutions were.

The comprehensive approach to development

One of the advances in development thinking that occurred while Jim Wolfensohn was President and I was Chief Economist of the World Bank was the recognition that any successful development strategy had to be comprehensive. It did little good to educate people, if there were no jobs; without entrepreneurs to create new enterprises and financial institutions to support them, trade liberalisation would destroy jobs faster than markets would create new jobs to replace them.

The failure of the series of approaches I have described lies, however, not so much in the pursuit of the 'magic bullet'—the single key to success—but more in not having a clearer understanding of what development entails. It is, as I have suggested, more than building dams and roads and ensuring that resources get efficiently allocated, or maintaining inflation at low and stable levels, or in having independent Central Banks committed to a monetary regime that ensures that inflation is low and stable. These may be necessary, essential parts, but they are clearly not sufficient.

I want now to turn to what I think of as the essential ingredients in successful development—creating what I call a 'learning society'. I want to explain why it is essential, and what has to be done to create and sustain it.

Creating a learning society[13]

In this section, I want to put forward three propositions:

1. The transformation to 'learning societies' which occurred around 1800 for Western economies, and more recently for

13. This part of the lecture represents joint work with Bruce Greenwald. These ideas are elaborated in our forthcoming book, *Creating a Learning Society: a New Paradigm for Development and Social Progress*, New York: Columbia University Press. A shortened version of these ideas is available as Greenwald and Stiglitz (2006).

those in Asia, appears to have had a far, far greater impact on human well-being than improvements in allocative efficiency or resource accumulation.[14]

2. Markets, on their own, are not efficient in promoting innovation
3. The policies that promote a transformation to a learning society are markedly different than those advocated by the WC. Indeed, from the perspective of creating a learning society, those policies may be counterproductive.

The importance of technological progress

From Roman times, when the first global data on per capita output are available, until 1800, average human standards of living increased only imperceptibly, if at all (Maddison, 2003). Consumption for the great majority of human beings consisted predominantly of food, and food was largely limited to staples—rice, wheat and other grains. Housing entailed barn-like living conditions with no privacy and climate control consisting only of necessary heat in winter. Clothing was utilitarian and rarely involved more than single outfits with the seasonal addition of over-clothes. Personal and medical care was almost nonexistent. Travel was rare, largely local, difficult and uncomfortable. Recreation was self-generated and primitive. Only a small aristocratic minority enjoyed what we would consider today an appropriate human standard of living—varieties of fresh food including meat, private well-warmed accommodations, multiple sets of clothing for varied occasions, rudimentary personal and medical care and opportunities for travel and sophisticated entertainment.

Beginning in 1800 and accelerating markedly after the mid-to-late 19th century, that privileged standard of living began to diffuse throughout Europe, North America and Australia. In the 20th century, elite standards of living became pervasive in these areas and in many parts of Asia, a trend which continues in much of Asia today.

14. The two are not fully separable, since investments in human and physical capital embody this learning.

The significance of these transformations can be seen in another way: until the beginning of the 19th century, most individuals spent most of their time meeting the basic necessities of life—food, shelter, clothing. Today, for most of those in the advanced industrial countries—and for an increasing number in the emerging markets—satisfying these basic necessities of life takes but a few hours of work a week. Individuals can choose whether to spend the 'extra' time available to work, to earn enough to consume more (higher quality 'necessities' or luxuries) or to enjoy more leisure.[15]

Although economists, such as Joseph Schumpeter (1943), had identified the source of these transformative developments as technological progress, it was not until Robert Solow (1957) that there was a way of quantifying the relative importance of capital accumulation *versus* technical progress. Changes in capital intensity could account for at most a third of changes in output per worker. The remainder, identified as the Solow residual, was attributable to various forms of technical progress.[16]

Kenneth Arrow (1962; 1962a) pioneered ideas in examining the economics of these 'learning processes'—the factors that promote or retard them, their likely response to normal market incentives and their relationship to the broader macro and microeconomic environment, notably in his papers on the economics of R&D and learning-by-doing (See also Solow, 1957a). He called attention to the fact that while some knowledge was produced as a result of the deliberate allocation of resources to research and development, much of technical progress was a byproduct of production or investment.

---

15. How they make those choices will, of course, have profound effects on *measured* growth, since increasing leisure does not show up in conventionally measured GDP. See Stiglitz *et al.* (2010). Keynes (1930) sparked a discussion of how those choices would be made. I speculated about why the U.S. and Europe seem to have gone in different directions in how they dealt with the 'productivity dividend' in Stiglitz (2008). (The original Keynes' article appeared in his 1931 book, *Essays in Persuasion*, London: Macmillan, pp.358 74.) See also the other chapters in the 2008 Stiglitz volume and the references cited there.

16. Subsequent literature suggested that the quantification was perhaps less robust than seemed initially the case. See, e.g. Griliches and Jorgenson (1966) which entailed a number of ways of calculating the value of capital that suggested a much smaller role for technical progress. Further problems were identified in the quantification of labour input, as economists attempted to assess the role of human capital in economic growth. See also, Klenow and Rodriguez-Clare (1997).

Markets, on their own, are inefficient in promoting innovation

Most importantly from the perspective taken in this paper, Arrow recognised that market failures in the production and dissemination of knowledge (whether as a result of the allocation of resources to R&D or as a result of learning) were pervasive.[17, 18] Analysing the nature of these inefficiencies—and their implications for public policy—requires the construction of a general equilibrium model in which R&D or learning is endogenous, which in turn requires hypotheses about knowledge spillovers and industrial structure (which is itself endogenous).[19]

While a full analysis is complicated, the basic ideas are simple: Knowledge is different from an ordinary commodity. The accumulation of knowledge is inherently associated with externalities—knowledge spillovers. Inevitably, many besides the inventor benefit from innovations like the computer, the laser, the transistor—and from the myriad of smaller innovations that mark the progress of society. Knowledge itself is a public good.[20] The use of knowledge by one person does not decrease what was available for others (non-rivalrousness), so that it is inefficient to exclude anyone from the benefits of knowledge, once acquired; and exclusion is often difficult, so that it is often difficult for innovators to appropriate more than a fraction of the value of what they contribute to society. Private and social returns can be markedly different.

---

17. In his earlier work on the efficiency of competitive equilibrium, he had taken the state of technology as given. But if technology is affected by human activity, then there was no presumption that the resulting market equilibrium was dynamically efficient. To the contrary, there was a presumption that it was not. Although Arrow did not frame the marke failure in this way, it was clear from his analysis that knowledge was a public good, in the sense that Samuelson (1954) had defined public goods a few years earlier; See e.g. Stiglitz (1987; 1999).
18. Kenneth and Debreu (1954).
19. Learning and R&D naturally give rise to increasing returns-to-scale effects, which mean that markets in which these effects are important are not likely to be well described by perfectly competitive model. At the same time, imperfections in competition in the presenc of imperfections of capital markets affect the level of profits available for investment i R&D. Thus, we typically need to describe the market structure and the level of R&I simultaneously. See, for instance, Dasgupta and Stiglitz (1980; 1980a).
20. Although Arrow did not frame the market failure in this way, it was clear from his analysis that knowledge was a public good, in the sense that Samuelson (1954) had defined public goods a few years earlier; see e.g., Stiglitz (1987a; 1999).

The failure of the Washington Consensus[21]

Once one recognises that there will be persistent differences between social and private returns, it is clear that the presumptions and premises underlying the WC/market fundamentalist policies are wrong. For the WC policies were based on the notion that markets allocate resources efficiently, enabling the structure to change as the (endogenous) endowments change.

As we have noted, classical economic development policy prescriptions were based on two ideas:

(1) Government should promote—and should certainly not interfere with—static allocative efficiency. (Indeed, in extreme versions of this perspective, governments need not even promote savings, because individuals are in the best position to make those intertemporal trade-offs on their own.)

(2) Growth in productivity arises chiefly from resource accumulation—physical, human and scientific capital. But these prescriptions do not apply in these dynamic learning environments.

As I have also noted, the standard market failures approach criticised these conclusions by focusing on a variety of market imperfections: for instance, there are pervasive externalities—not only environmental externalities but also those associated with systemic risk, so evidenced in the current crisis. Research over the past 20 years has explored the consequences of market failures like imperfect capital markets, traced these imperfections back to problems of imperfect and asymmetric information, and proposed a set of remedies, which in some countries, in some periods, have worked remarkably well. Imperfections in capital markets meant that finance was often not available to finance new enterprises required as part of this sectoral adjustment. Individuals on their own couldn't finance their education. Good financial regulations in countries like India protected them against the ravages of the global financial crisis.

21. This part of this lecture is adapted from Stiglitz (forthcoming).

But the perspective of a 'learning society' adds an important new dimension to the analysis.

Policies to promote learning

Policies to promote learning processes are especially important for developing countries. For more than a decade, economists have recognised that what separates developed from less developed countries is not just a gap in resources but a gap in knowledge. Thus, a central focus of development policy should be closing that gap—and that means enhancing learning.[22]

Traditional policy prescriptions not only don't focus on how to maximise learning, but are also often significantly at odds with those which are appropriate to enhance 'learning' performance.[23] As a result, though well-intentioned, they may actually lead to a reduction in societal well-being.

I want now to illustrate the contrasting implications between the static, neoliberal perspective and the dynamic one that I am advocating here by looking at one of the central questions in developmental policy—should government intervene in the market's sectoral allocation of production.

Static versus dynamic comparative advantage

Standard neoclassical theory emphasises that countries should focus on what constitutes their comparative advantage. The problem is that some of the most important elements of comparative advantage are endogenous. Switzerland's comparative advantage in watchmaking has little to do with its geography. What matters is dynamic comparative advantage, and government has an important role in shaping that.

Standard Heckscher-Ohlin theory (emphasising that trade in goods was a substitute for movement in factors) was formulated in

---

22. This perspective was reflected in the 1998-99 *World Development Report, Knowledge for Development*. See also Stiglitz (1998).

23. In that sense, our work is similar to that of Schumpeter *op. cit.* (See also Stiglitz, 2008). But while Schumpeter was correct in his critique of neoclassical economics, he never formulated a coherent 'analytic' nonnative or positive theory. For instance, his defence of monopoly was, as a result, not well-grounded.

a period before globalisation allowed the kinds of flows of capital that occur today. With fully mobile capital, outside of agriculture, resource endowments need not provide the basis for explaining patterns of production and specialisation.[24] In short, there is no reason that countries need limit themselves to patterns dictated by endowments, as conventionally defined. More important is the 'endowment' of knowledge and entrepreneurship. A major focus of policy should be how to enhance and shape those endowments.

Even if a government would like to avoid addressing these issues, it cannot, for what the government does (or does not do) has consequences, positive and negative, for the development of the 'learning society.' This is obviously so for investments in infrastructure, technology, and education; but also so for financial, trade, intellectual property rights and competition policies.

Industrial policies to create a learning society

Shifting the focus from short run comparative advantage to a country's long term or dynamic comparative advantage does not, however, fully capture the perspective I am advocating here.

At the centre of creating a learning society is identifying sectors more amenable to learning, with benefits not captured by firms themselves, so that there will be underinvestment in learning. Elsewhere, Greenwald and I have argued that an implication is the encouragement of the industrial sector, which typically has large spillovers to other sectors.[25]

This approach provides an interpretation of the success of Asia's export led growth.[26] Had Korea allowed market forces on their own to prevail, it would not have embarked on its amazing development successes. Static efficiency entailed Korea producing rice; Korea

---

24. Indeed the work of Krugman (2008) has emphasised that today most trade is not related in fact to differences in factor endowments.

25. I use the term industrial policy in this context to refer to any policy which seeks to shift the structure of production from that which would have arisen through market forces alone. Thus, a policy to encourage agro-business or telecommunications is, in this terminology, an industrial policy.

26. Successful import substitution policies have also had similar objectives. The import substitution policies were perhaps more successful than critics suggest: the lost decade of the 1980's owes more to macro-economic failures than to the failure of these micro-economic policies.

might today have been among the most efficient rice farmers—but it would still be a poor country. As Arrow pointed out, one learns by doing (and one learns how to learn by learning) (Stiglitz, 1987). Korea's success, though, is not just in the development of the particular sectors (like the chips industry) which its industrial policy encouraged. Its success arose in no small part from the spillovers that those sectors had to the entire economy.

This discussion highlights the fundamental difference with neoclassical approaches emphasising short-run efficiency. The fundamental trade-offs between static and dynamic efficiency should be familiar from the debate over patent laws. These laws not only restrict the flow of knowledge, but even may create monopolies, all justified because of the increased knowledge that (allegedly) results.

This discussion also highlights what's wrong with the standard criticism of industrial policies: the government is in no position to pick winners, and in particular to 'outsmart' markets. The objective of government is different: it is to identify externalities, and to encourage sectors with large positive spillovers.[27] Some governments actually have a very credible track record in doing so.

A major concern with industrial policies[28] concerns implementation—do developing countries have the requisite capacities? We need to put that question in context.

There is probably no country that has grown successfully without an important role—not just in restraining and creating markets, but also in promoting growth through industrial policies—from the countries of East Asia today to the advanced industrial countries, not just during their developmental stages, but even today.[29] The task is to adopt policies and practices, to create institutions, like an effective civil service, that enhance the quality of the public sector and its ability to carry out industrial policies

27. Such spillovers were an essential aspect of Hirschman's (1958) work, though he did not focus explicitly on learning spillovers.

28. We use the term broadly, to embrace any policy attempting to affect the direction of the economy.

29. Richard R. John (2010) presents a persuasive account of the large role of government in the development of the telecommunications sector in the 19th and 20th centuries.

effectively. The successful countries did so. Policies that either intentionally or unintentionally weaken the state (as critics suggest the WC policies did) are not likely to do so.

Economic policies have to reflect the capacity of the state to implement them. One of the arguments in favour of exchange rate policies that encourage export industries is that they are broad based: the government does not have to pick particular 'strategic' firms, or even products, to support. As always, there are trade-offs: efficiency might be enhanced if the sectors with the largest externalities could be targeted.

There are other broad-based policies, such as a development-oriented intellectual property regime and investment and financial policies that encourage transfer of technology and the promotion of local entrepreneurship, that can help promote a learning and innovation society (Emran and Stiglitz, 2009; Stiglitz, 2004; Hoff, 1997; Hausmann and Rodrik, 2003). Some forms of financial and capital market liberalisation may be counterproductive.

Interventions will never be perfect, nor need they be to effect an improvement in economic performance.[30] The choice is not between an imperfect government and a perfect market. It is between imperfect governments and imperfect markets, each of which has to serve as a check on the other; they need to be seen as complementary, and we need to seek a balance between the two—a balance which is not just a matter of assigning certain tasks to one, others to the other, but rather designing systems where they interact effectively.

Governments are sometimes criticised for their wasteful practices. When we talk about waste, we should remember that the full economic consequences of the dysfunctional American financial market—a cost in the trillions of dollars—entail waste on a scale probably beyond anything done by any democratic government (outside of war) in the history of the planet. We should remember too that as government has acted to address the recession, we often face unpleasant choices: a massive waste of resources as a result of

30. Indeed, if all projects were successful, it suggests that the government is undertaking too little risk.

the economy operating for an extended period below its potential, or a much smaller waste as a result of less than ideal government spending. So too for industrial policies: industrial policies may not be perfect, but the absence of industrial policies may be even worse.

Social transformation and the creation of a learning society[31]

While I have been discussing the economics of development, that subject cannot be separated from broader aspects of societal transformation,[32] as Hirschman (1958) emphasised in his writings. For instance, race and caste are social constructs that effectively inhibit the human development of large parts of the population in many parts of the world. The study of how these constructs get formed, and how they change is thus a central part of developmental studies. So far in this paper, I have emphasised the creation of a learning society. The economics of doing so entails policies that change sectoral composition. But at the root of success is changing mindsets. At the centre of that task is the education system, and how it inculcates attitudes towards change and skills of learning. Other policies (e.g., legal systems, gender based microcredit schemes, affirmative action programs) too can play an important role.

Myrdal (1968), in his studies of South Asia, focused on these issues. He argued, in effect, that certain social constructs affect behaviour and were part of what might be called a dysfunctional economic and social equilibrium that could persist. But he did not address the question of the mechanisms by which such social constructs are created, evolve or collapse. Nor did he ask how we might reconcile such constructions of the developmental process with the usual approaches taken by economists. In recent work with Karla Hoff, I have been attempting to construct a general approach to societal evolution that clarifies the critical—and unrealistic—assumptions about individual behaviour and cognition that underlie what has become the dominant developmental model within the economics literature. This work provides some insights

31. This part of my lecture draws heavily from Hoff and Stiglitz (2009; 2010).

32. See Stiglitz (1998).

into why Myrdal's predictions concerning Asia's prospects could have been so far off the mark.

In our work, we are concerned with what collective beliefs are an equilibrium, and how they change. There are three critical hypotheses:

1. Perceptions (beliefs) affect actions (choices) and are shaped by cognitive frames; the infinite set of potentially observable data and the infinite ways in which that data could be processed are limited by the finite set of socially constructed categories that are a part of what are called ideologies (or belief systems). Individual behaviour is based on beliefs that are more complex (or at least different) in their formation than is reflected in standard Bayesian theories about the determination of probabilities of the occurrence of different states of nature. Indeed, in our work, we employ well-documented results in psychology, where individuals recognise and process information that is consistent with their prior beliefs in a way that is different from the way they treat other information, to show that, in equilibrium these beliefs can be self-confirming even when, in a fundamental sense, they are wrong. That is why we refer to them as equilibrium fictions. As in Rational Expectations (RE) models, beliefs affect behaviour, which affect outcomes, which affect beliefs. But unlike a RE model, beliefs also affect what is perceived, the categories into which information is placed, and how information is absorbed and filtered. Biases—at every stage of the formation of beliefs—shape perceptions, widen the set of possible equilibria and make them history-dependent.[33]

2. The categories that shape cognition are social constructions. A second difference from the neoclassical perspective is that many beliefs, such as the categories into which information is placed, are social constructions. Individuals do not choose their 'software' in isolation but within a social context. A

33. On the other hand, the set of equilibria in our approach is much more constrained than the 'animal spirits' equilibrium, which presumes that virtually any set of beliefs could be sustained.

set of collective beliefs (ideologies) that serves a society—or some group in society—well under one set of economic circumstances may serve it less well under another.

3. Because belief systems affect the equilibrium, e.g., by shaping perceptions, elites have a strong incentive to influence people's beliefs. In contrast, in a RE equilibrium, this is not relevant—cognitive frames play no role. But the elites cannot simply 'choose' the cognitive frames that work best for themselves (nor can non-elites simply choose the beliefs that might work best for themselves). The task of 'choosing' for themselves and imposing on others cognitive frames is more complicated and is itself constrained by higher-order beliefs. Those in 'power' typically do not control all the determinants of the evolution of beliefs. Cultures are always contested.

4. The general beliefs about the world are a state variable that determine which beliefs are acceptable. Acceptance and legitimacy are a function, too, of collective beliefs. An institution[34] (like Jim Crow) may be accepted at one time, and not at another. It may be part of an equilibrium at one time, and not at another.[35] Redistributive institutions, too, function because they have 'legitimacy', because they are accepted. The acceptance and performance of institutions depend not only on economic variables, but also on the set of general beliefs about the world, which can at any moment be treated a state variable. Collective beliefs that emerge in one period shape the possible institutions in the next.

---

34. But it is not as if that group got together and figured out a set of beliefs that would accomplish what they sought. Our theory is thus incomplete. But we believe it is a step forward to break out of the mold of rational expectations, in which the variables described above play no role.

35. At one time, some economists suggested that institutions have a simple role in society–to fill in the 'holes' in markets, to remedy market failures (see North, 1971). Arnott and Stiglitz (1991) and Hoff and Sen (2006), as well as others, showed that non-market institutions purportedly resolving a market failure (like incomplete insurance markets) could, in this sense, be dysfunctional–they could lead to Pareto inferior outcomes. More recent literature has highlighted the role of institutions in preserving inequalities–in the context of repeated games, equilibria in which one group is exploited by others may be sustained. See, among others, Mookherjee and Ray (2003); Acemoglu and Robinson (2000).

Incorporating 'cognitive frames' (ideologies) as state variables provides part of a general theory of societal change that is markedly different from traditional theories, in which only capital and the distribution of power and wealth are state variables. If ideologies change, the equilibrium can change, with no change in the 'fundamentals'. At the same time, this perspective helps explain why institutional change can be so difficult and societies so rigid. A set of beliefs that may have been functional at one time, but is no longer so, can persist after the economics/technology that had led to the adoption of the beliefs has changed.

How such belief systems change—and how those (like governments) who seek to deliberately change belief systems—is thus a core part of developmental analysis, but regrettably, pursuing this question would take me beyond the confines of this paper.[36]

I want to turn now to one particular set of beliefs that have enormous importance in shaping societies in recent decades.

Democracy and the creation of a learning society

Ideas concerning human rights and democracy have been among the most important in shaping what is and is not acceptable. In the US and Europe, these ideas eventually led to the abolition of slavery, though there were large groups for whom the continuation of this institutional arrangement was advantageous, and those who opposed it reaped no economic gain from the abolition.

Democratic ideals question authority. When America's Declaration of Independence said, All men are created equal, it didn't mean that they were of equal physical or mental capacities, but of equal rights, including the right to put forth their ideas into a competitive market place of ideas. Democracy and an open society are intrinsically interlinked.

36. The complexity of the issues is illustrated by vicissitudes in attitudes towards government policies to re-stimulate the economy. In the aftermath of the collapse of Lehman Brothers, there was a moment in which all the world adhered to Keynesian ideas. But within two years, there was a shift towards 'Hooverite' fiscal austerity policies—even though the empirical (scientific) evidence that such policies would lead to slower growth with disappointing results on deficit reduction had actually mounted in the interim.

But it is exactly that same frame of mind which is so essential for creating a dynamic, learning economy and society.

A more open society generates more ideas, a flow of 'mutations,' which provides not only excitement, but the possibility of dynamic evolution, rather than stasis.

Unfortunately, even if in the long run, a more dynamic society benefits most members of society, in the short run, there can be (and normally will be) losers. And not surprisingly, those who might lose seek to prevent such changes through any means they can. The political process is one way that is often taken. Those who seek to maintain inequalities in wealth and power do so is not only through policies (economic, legal, etc.) which perpetuate existing bases of power and wealth, e.g., by creating entry barriers; but also through policies which attempt to maintain the legitimacy of these inequities of wealth and power. Media policies (control of the airwaves, right to know laws, and so forth) thus become important instruments for shaping public perceptions, and thus public policies. The political processes themselves evolve over time, shaped not just by history, but economics, especially in today's world. Firms long ago learned that they could partially shape individuals' preferences. Those with wealth have more recently learned how to use such tools to shape perceptions in ways that lead to outcomes in the political process that are more favourable to themselves. Sometimes, this entails creating a less open and transparent society—a more open society might lead to a questioning of the persistent inequities, a more transparent society might expose the nefarious ways by which inequities are maintained. When that happens, the long term success of the economy may be put into question.[37]

Inclusive growth

So far, I have emphasised the importance of creating a learning economy and society; that success requires not just an economic transformation but a social transformation; I have also argued

37. Earlier, we noted how, in the US, those wanting to insulate the Fed from scrutiny as it provided massive subsidies to certain banks opposed Fed transparency.

that, over the long run, democratic and open societies will be more dynamic. But, as I have noted, democratic processes can be shaped, and there are incentives on the part of some to maintain existing inequities. Democratic processes can then lead to the antithesis of an open and transparent society.

There is thus at least one more requirement for long-term success: inclusive growth. Earlier, I explained that trickle-down economics doesn't work. The critique of many of the WC policies though was not just that they were not pro-poor, that is, that the poor did not share in the benefits. Rather, it was that they were anti-poor. Policies that lead to greater volatility (which arguably capital and financial market liberalisation do) are anti-poor. It is the poor that bear the brunt of crises—nowhere evidenced more than in this crisis, where the bankers who caused the crisis are walking home with multi-million dollar bonuses. Policies that lead to higher levels of unemployment are anti-poor. Trade liberalisation destroys jobs, so that unless such liberalisation is accompanied by measures that lead to job and enterprise creation, it can be anti-poor. That is why it is so important that trade liberalisation be accompanied by appropriate financial sector and aid-to-trade measures to ensure that job creation occurs in tandem with job destruction. Markets, on their own, do not ensure this, even in seemingly well-functioning advanced industrial countries.

One of the big advances in development in recent years is that we understand not only that some policies can be anti- or non-pro-poor growth, but that we have instruments and policies (from broad policies, like micro-credit, to specific instruments, like more efficient cookstoves) to enhance the likelihood that the poor share in the growth that occurs.

My argument for why inclusive growth is so important goes beyond the standard one that it is a waste of a country's most valuable resource, its human talent, to fail to ensure that everyone lives up to his or her abilities.

The political economy of inclusiveness and openness

Rather, it is based on political economy, of an analysis of how inequality affects political processes in ways which are adverse to long term growth and inclusive democracy.[38]

Earlier I argued that government needs to play an important role in any economy, correcting pervasive market failures, but especially in the 'creative economy', e.g., financing basic research and providing high quality education. Moreover, innovation is always risky, and in societies with better systems of social protection, individuals are willing to take more risk. So too, societies (like Sweden) in which there are stronger social protections are more willing to expose themselves and their citizens to growth-enhancing risks, such as those associated with openness.

Consider, for a moment, a society in which there is very little inequality. The only role of the state then is to provide collective goods and correct market failures. A consensus can be developed on what that entails—since interests are aligned.

But this is not so in societies in which there are large inequalities. Then interests differ. Liberals may want to use the state to redistribute income. While ostensibly conservative high income individuals may claim that they are only trying to prevent such redistributions, a more careful look at the policies they advocate often entail redistributions toward themselves; and at the very least, they entail ensuring that the government does not curtail their activities exploiting the poor and extracting a disproportionate share of public assets. Distributive battles inevitably rage.

Often, the 'ideology' of the battle takes the form of an attempt to circumscribe government (an 'independent' central bank, in reality, a central bank accountable mainly to the financial sector, budget constraints that severely limit the scope of government activity, even when there are very high investment opportunities in the public sector).

---

38. I am deeply indebted to Tim Besley for discussions on the ideas in this section. See Besley and Persson (forthcoming); Besley *et al.* (forthcoming). In earlier work with Karla Hoff, I attempted to model the political economy of transition from communism to a market economy, employing analogous ideas. See Hoff and Stiglitz (2004; 2004a; 2007). See also Acemoglu and Robinson *op. cit.*, who have also have written about inequality and institutional change.

Many in the US are concerned that we have embarked on an adverse dynamic, moving us towards an equilibrium in which we will become a less dynamic and a less equal economy and society. As social protections erode and public investments weaken, including in education, inequality increases. The rich turn to private education, private parks, private health insurance, etc., even though public provision might be far more efficient. Rather than working to improve the efficiency of the public sector, those who seek to limit the scope of government work to tear down the public sector, to undermine its credibility, knowing that if they succeed, then there will be a broader consensus for limiting the role of government, and thus limiting the extent to which the government can engage in redistributive activities, even if in doing so, the government is limited in its ability to engage in collective wealth enhancement. As this happens, inequalities increase, confidence in public provision erodes, and the state takes on a less important role. It is problematic to gauge whether, in the end, even those at the top benefit; but what is not questionable is that the vast majority in the society lose out.

A casual look around the world suggests that different societies have taken different courses. The Scandinavian countries, by and large, have limited inequalities, have efficient and large public sectors, high standards of living for the vast majority of their citizens, and have succeeded in creating inclusive dynamic economies and societies. There are important differences among the political parties in these countries, but still, there is a broad consensus about most of the elements of the 'social contract'. America in more recent years has taken a different course. The image of a society with a high degree of social mobility is belied by the statistics, which suggest that such mobility is less than in many 'old' European countries. Social and economic mobility has decreased in the US, while it has increased in many of the European countries. In the beginning of this paper, I laid out some of the consequences for the US: decreasing standards of living for the majority of citizens combined with increasing social pathologies.

India, as a young democracy, has before it important decisions about which course it will take.

Concluding comments

I have attempted in this paper to cover a broad terrain. Economics, politics and society are interconnected. Too often, economists have lost touch with these broader dimensions—though I have argued that much of the conventional wisdom of economists even missed out on the most important economic elements in creating a dynamic and creative society.

In discussing the importance of creating an open, democratic and inclusive society as necessary conditions for the creation of a dynamic economy, I don't want to underestimate the importance of these as ends in themselves. Creativity, voice, security are all important ingredients to individual well-being and a sense of dignity. The central message of the International Commission on the Measurement of Economic Performance and Social Progress was that GDP was not a good measure of well-being, and policies which narrowly focused on increasing GDP were misguided (Fitoussi *et al.*, 2010).

India has had enormous success over the past 25 years in its increase in GDP, and it now seeks to ensure that the success continues and that the benefits of that success are shared by all of its citizens. The financial crisis has shown how misguided policies of financial market liberalisation and deregulation were. These were policies that the US and international institutions foisted on countries all over the world. These are policies that served special interests well, and the voices of these special interests are often heard more loudly than the voices of those that are hurt by these policies. Indeed, those in the financial sector touted the so-called financial innovations of recent years, suggesting that they brought on a new era of growth and prosperity, Paul Volcker was absolutely right in pointing out that there was not a single innovation (other than the creation of the ATM machine) that had been linked to improved economic performance. The innovations often enhanced the coffers of the banks and the bankers, but at the expense of the rest of society. And what we can say unequivocally is that the innovations introduced an unprecedented level of instability into the economy.

I have couched most of this talk in broad strokes. But the principles have strong implications for policy. I have hinted directly at the implications for financial and capital market liberalisation and the design of monetary policy and institutions. But the principles translate too into policies regarding intellectual property regimes, investment treaties, taxation, and expenditures on infrastructure, education and technology.

I hope that this paper has provided a new lense through which one can examine these and other policy choices facing India in the coming years. India might like to pretend that it could avoid matters of industrial policy—following the neoliberal doctrines that these are matters to be left to the market. But it cannot. For the choices it makes in each of these arenas will inevitably shape India's economy and society, for better or for worse, for decades to come.

References

Acemoglu, Daron and James Robinson (2000). "Why did the West Extend the Franchise? Democracy, Inequality and Growth in Historical Perspective", *Quarterly Journal of Economics* 115(4): 1167-99.

Arnott, R. and J.E. Stiglitz (1991). "Moral Hazard and Non-Market Institutions: Dysfunctional Crowding Out or Peer Monitoring", *American Economic Review*, 81(1): 179-90. March.

Arrow, Kenneth J. (1962). "The Economic Implications of Learning by Doing", *Review of Economic Studies* 29: 155-73.

———. (1962a). "Economic Welfare and the Allocation of Resources for Invention", in R. Nelson (ed.), *The Rate and Direction ofinventive Activity: Economic and Social Factors*. NBER, Princeton University Press.

Arrow, Kenneth and G. Debreu (1954). "The Existence of an Equilibrium for a Competitiv, Economy", *Econometrica* XXII: 265-90.

Besley, Tim and Torsten Persson (forthcoming). "The Origins of State Capacity: Property Rights, Taxation and Politics", *American Economic Review*.

———. (forthcoming). "State Capacity, Conflict and Development", *Econometrica*.

Besley, Tim, Torsten Persson and Daniel M. Sturm (forthcoming). "Political Competition, Policy and Growth: Theory and Evidence from the United States", *Review of Economic Studies*.

Dasgupta, Partha and J.E. Stiglitz (1980). "Industrial Structure and the Nature of Innovative Activity", *The Economic Journal* 90(358): 266-93, June.

———. (1980a). "Uncertainty, Market Structur and the Speed of R&D", *Bell Journal of Economics* 11(1): 1-28, Spring.

Davies, James, Susana Sandstrom, Anthony Shorrocks and Edward Wolff (2009). "The Global Pattern of Household Wealth", *Journal of International Development* 21(8): 1111-24. November.

Emran, Shahe and J.E. Stiglitz (2009). "Financial Liberalization, Financial Restraint, and Entrepreneurial Development", January, available at *http://papers.ssm.com/sol3/papers.cfm?abstract_id=1332399* (accessed November 3, 2010).

Fitoussi, J.P., A. Sen and J.E. Stiglitz (2010). *Misineasuring Our lives: Why GDP Doesn't Add Up.* New York: The New Press.

Greenwald, Bruce and J.E. Stiglitz (1986). "Externalities in Economies with Imperfect Information and Incomplete Markets", *The Quarterly Journal of Economics* 101(2): 229-64. May, MIT Press.

Greenwald, B. and J.E. Stiglitz (2006). "Helping Infant Economies Grow: Foundations of Trade Policies for Developing Countries", *American Economic Review: AEA Papers and Proceedings* 96(2): 141-46. May.

Griliches, Zvi and Dale W. Jorgenson (1966). "Sources of Measured Productivity Change: Capital Input", *The American Economic Review* 56(2): 50-61. May.

Hausmann, Ricardo and Dani Rodrik (2003). "Economic Development as Self-Discovery", *Journal of Development Economics* 72(2): 603-33.

Hirschman, A.O. (1958). *The Strategy of Economic Development.* New Haven, Conn.: Yale University Press.

Hirschman, Albert (1958). *The Strategy of Economic Development*, New Haven, Conn.: Yale University Press.

Hoff, K. (1997). "Bayesian Learning in an Infant Industry Model",*Journal of International Economics* 43: 409–36.

Hoff, K. and J.E. Stiglitz (2010). "Equilibrium Fictions: A Cognitive Approach to Societal Rigidity", *American Economic Review* 100(2): 141-46. May.

———. (2009). "Equilibrium Fictions: A Cognitive Approach to Institutions and Institutional Change, with an Application to Race", preliminary draft, December 28.

———. (2007). "Exiting a Lawless State", *Economic Journal*, 118(531): 1474-97.

———. (2004). "After the Big Bang? Obstacles to the Emergence of the Rule of Law in Post-Communist Societies", *American Economic Review* 94(3): 753-63. June.

———. (2004a). "The Transition Process in Post-Communist Societies: Towards a Political Economy of Property Rights", in B. Tungodden, N. Stern and I. Kolstad (eds.), *Toward Pro-Poor Policies: Aid, Institutions and Globalization.* World Bank/Oxford University Press, pp.231-45.

Hoff, Karla and Arijit Sen (2006). "The Kin System as a Poverty Trap?", in Samuel Bowles, Steven Durlauf and Karla Hoff (eds.), *Poverty Traps.* Princeton University Press, pp.95-115.

John, Richard R. (2010). *NetworkNation: Inventing American Telecommunications*. Harvard University Press.

Keynes, J.M. (1930). *"Economic Possibilities for Our Grandchildren",* reprinted in G. Piga and L. Pecchi (eds.), *Revisiting Keynes: Economic Possibilities for Our Grandchildren.* Cambridge: MIT Press, pp.17-26.

Klenow, Peter J. and Andres Rodriguez-Clare (1997). "The Neoclassical Revival in Growth Economic: Has it gone too far?", *NBER Macroeconomics Annual* 12: 73-103.

Krugman, Paul (2008). "The Increasing Returns Revolution in Trade and Geography", *Nobel Prize Lecture*. Available at *http://nobelprize.org/nobel_prizes/economics/laureates/2008/krugman-lecture.html* [accessed November 3, 2010].

Maddison, Angus (2003). *The World Economy: Historical Statistics*. Development Centre of the Organisation for Economic Co-operation and Development.

Mookherjee, Dilip and Debraj Ray (2003). "Persistent Inequality", *Review of Economic Studies* 70(2): 369-93.

Myrdal, Gunnar (1968). *Asian Drama: An Inquiry into the Poverty of Nations*. New York: Pantheon.

North, Douglass C. (1971). "Institutional Change and Economic Growth", *The Journal of Economic History* 31(01): 118-25, March. Cambridge University Press.

Piketty, Thomas and Emmanuel Saenz (2003). "Income Inequality in the United States, 1913-1998", *Quarterly Journal of Economics* 11 8(1): 1-39 (Longer updated version published in Atkinson, A.B. and T. Piketty (eds.) (2007), Oxford University Press); updated data for 2008 is available at *http://emlab.berkeley.edu/users/saez/* (accessed November 4, 2010).

Putnam, R. (1995). "Bowling Alone: America's Declining Social Capital",*Journal of Democracy* 6(1): 65-78.

Samuelson, P.A. (1954). "The Pure Theory of Public Expenditure", *Review of Economics and Statistics* 36: 387-89.

Sander T. and R. Putnam (2010). "Still Bowling Alone?: The Post-9/11 Split", *Journal of Democracy.*

Schumpeter, Joseph (1943). *Capitalism, Socialism and Democracy.* New York: Harper.

Summers, Larry (2007). "Funds that Shake Capitalist Logic", in *Financial Times*, July 27. Available at *http://wwwft.com/cms/s/2/bb8f50b8-3dcc-11dc-8f6a-0000779fd2ac.html* (accessed November 11, 2010).

Solow, Robert (1957). "Technical Change and the Aggregate Production Function", *Review of Economics and Statistics* 39(3): 312-20.

———. (1957a). *Learning from "Learning by Doing": Lessons for Economic Growth*, Stanford University Press

Stiglitz, J. E. (2008). "Introduction", in Joseph A. Schumpeter, *Capitalism, Socialism and Democracy.* London: Routledge pp.ix-xiv.

———. (2008a). "Toward a General Theory of Consumerism: Reflections on Keynes' *Economic Possibilities for Our Grandchildren",* in G. Piga and L. Pecchi (eds.), *Revisiting Keynes: Economic Possibilities for Our Grandchildren.* Cambridge: MIT Press, pp.41-87.

———. (2004). "Towards a Pro-Development and Balanced Intellectual Property Regime", Keynote address presented at the *Ministerial Conference on Intellectual Property for Least Developed Countries.* Seoul: World Intellectual Property Organization (WIPO), October 25. Available at *http://www.gsb.columbia.edu/ipd/pub/IPRjsl.pdf* (accessed November 3, 2010).

———. (2002). *Globalization and Its Discontents*. New York: W.W. Norton.

———. (1999). "Knowledge as a Global Public Good", in Inge Kaul, Grunberg, Marc A. Stern (eds.), *Global Public Goods: International Cooperation in the 21st Century.* United Nations Development Programme. New York: Oxford University Press. pp.308-25.

———. (1998). "Towards a New Paradigm for Development: Strategies, Policies and Processes", *9th Raul Prebisch Lecture* delivered at the Palais des Nations, Geneva, October 19, UNCTAD. Published as Chapter 2 in Ha-Joon Chang (ed.) (2001), *The Rebel Within.* London: Wimbledon Publishing Company, pp.57-93.

———. (1987). "Learning to Learn, Localized Learning and Technological Progress", in P. Dasgupta and Stoneman (eds.), *Economic Policy and Technological Performance*, Cambridge University Press, pp.125-53.

———. (1987a). "On the Microeconomics of Technica Progress", in Jorgi M. Katz (ed.), *Technology Generation in Latin American Manufacturing Industries.* Macmillan Press Ltd., pp.56-77 (presented to IDB-Cepal Meetings, Bueno: Aires, November 1978).

———. (forthcoming). "Rethinking Development Economics", *World Bank Research Observer.*

Stiglitz, J.E., J.P. Fitoussi and A. Sen (2010). *Mismeasuring Our Lives: Why GDP Doesn't Add Up*, New York: The New Press.

World Bank (2010). *World Development Indicators. http://data.worldbank.org/data-catalog/world-development-indicators* (accessed November 3, 2010).

Contributors / Discussants

Anu Aga, former chairperson and now a Director on the Board of Thermax Ltd., is a Member of Parliament (Rajya Sabha). She is closely involved with Akanksha, an NGO which supplements the educational needs of slum children. She is also the chairperson of the Board of Teach for India, an initiative that attempts to bridge the inequity gap in education, and a member of the National Advisory Council chaired by Mrs Sonia Gandhi.

Bina Agarwal is Director and Professor of Economics at the Institute of Economic Growth, Delhi University. She has written extensively on subjects such as land, livelihoods and property rights; environment and development; the political economy of gender; poverty and inequality; legal change; and agriculture and technological transformation.

Sudhir Agarwal is the Managing Director of the Dainik Bhaskar Group of Publications, India's largest newspaper group. He was ranked 19th among the 50 most influential personalities in India. Sudhir is an active member of the World Association of Newspapers, Paris.

Montek Singh Ahluwalia, Deputy Chairman, Planning Commission of India (since 2004), has been a key figure in India's economic reforms from the early 1980s onwards. He has contributed to a number of prominent Indian and international journals and books.

Pranab Bardhan is Professor of Economics at the University of California, Berkeley. He has been on the faculty of MIT, the Delhi School of Economics, and the Indian Statistical Institute, and visiting fellow at Trinity College, Cambridge and St. Catherine's College, Oxford. He is the author of 12 books and more than 150 journal articles, and the editor of 12 other books.

Kaushik Basu, formerly Chief Economic Advisor in India's Ministry of Finance, is Senior Vice-President and Chief Economist, World Bank. A Fellow of the Econometric Society, he has published widely in the areas of development economics, industrial organisation, game theory and welfare economics. Prof Basu has also contributed popular articles to magazines and newspapers, such as The New York Times, Scientific American, India Today and Business Standard.

Kumar Mangalam Birla is the Chairman of the Aditya Birla Group, a global conglomerate with operations spanning 27 countries. He serves on the Prime Minister of India's Advisory Council on Trade and Industry; is a director of the Central Board of Directors of the Reserve Bank of India, and Chairman of its Staff Sub-Committee. Recipient of many awards, he was named the Forbes India Leadership's "Entrepreneur of the Year 2012" and World Economic Forum's "Young Global Leader 2004".

Mirai Chatterjee is the Director of Social Security at the Self-Employed Women's Association (SEWA). She is responsible for SEWA's health care, child care and insurance programmes. She serves on the Boards of several organisations in India, including the Friends of Women's World Banking (FWWB), the Public Health Foundation of India (PHFI) and the Health Action Partnership International (HAPI). She is currently a member of the National Advisory Council (NAC).

Jonathan Cohn is an American journalist and author. He is a senior editor at the New Republic magazine, where he writes mainly about domestic policy and politics, and the author of "Sick", a 2007 book on the US healthcare system. He has been called "one of the best health care writers out there" by the New York Times and "one of America's leading experts on healthcare policy" by the Washington Post.

Nitin Desai is Chairman of Oxfam International. A former UN Under-Secretary-General for Economic and Social Affairs, he organised a series of global summits for the UN, from the Rio Earth Summit (1992) to the Johannesburg Sustainable Development Summit (2002). He has been involved in a variety of public policy activities nationally and internationally. He is Special Adviser on Internet Governance to the UN Secretary-General, a member of the National Security Advisory Board, the Prime Minister's Council on Climate Change and the National Broadcasting Standards Authority, as well as an Honorary Fellow of the LSE.

Jean Drèze was a Member of the National Advisory Council chaired by Mrs Sonia Gandhi. He has taught at the London School of Economics and the Delhi School of Economics, and is now Visiting Professor at Allahabad University. He has made wide-ranging contributions to development economics and public economics, with special reference to India. He is co-author of *Hunger and Public Action, India: Development and Participation, Public Report on Basic Education and Focus on Children under Six*, among other publications. He is also an active member of India's Right to Food campaign, and of the world-wide movement for peace and disarmament.

Sonia Gandhi is the President of the Indian National Congress (INC) Party. She is also the Chairperson of the Coordinating Committee of the ruling United Progressive Alliance (UPA); the National Advisory Council (NAC) and the Indira Gandhi Memorial Trust (IGMT).

Jamshyd N. Godrej is the Chairman of the Board of Godrej & Boyce Manufacturing Company Limited. He is the Chairman Emeritus of Aspen Institute India; Trustee and President Emeritus of World Wide Fund for Nature—India; Chairperson of the Board of Directors of Shakti Sustainable Energy Foundation; a Director of World Resources Institute, USA; and a Director of ClimateWorks Foundation, USA.

Wang Hui, intellectual historian, professor of literature and history, is the director of the Institute for Advanced Studies in Humanities and Social Sciences at Tsinghua University, Beijing. He was a fellow at the Chinese Academy of Social Sciences from 1988 to 2002 and executive editor of *Dushu*, the most influential intellectual journal in China from 1996-2007. He has served as fellow, senior fellow and visiting professor at Harvard University, University of Washington in Seattle, UCLA, Columbia University, University of Bologna, University of Heidelberg, Institute for Advanced Studies in Berlin, Stanford University, UC-Berkeley, NYU and Tokyo University, etc. His publications include *China's New Order* (2003), *The Rise of Modern Chinese Thought* (four volumes, 2004), *The End of the Revolution* (2009), etc.

Sri Mulyani Indrawati, former Finance Minister of Indonesia, is Managing Director, World Bank (June 2010). She is responsible for the Bank's operations in Latin America and the Caribbean, East Asia and the Pacific, and the Middle East and North Africa. She has received numerous honours and awards, including Euromoney Magazine's Global Finance Minister of the Year, and Emerging Markets Best

Finance Minister in Asia. She has also been regularly on Forbes List of the 100 Most Powerful Women.

Niraja Gopal Jayal is Professor at the Centre for the Study of Law and Governance at the Jawaharlal Nehru University, New Delhi. She is the author of *Representing India: Ethnic Diversity and the Governance of Public Institutions* (2006) and *Democracy and the State: Welfare, Secularism and Development in Contemporary India* (1999). She has edited, with Pratap Bhanu Mehta, *The Oxford Companion to Politics in India* (2010), and is also the editor/co-editor of, among others, *Democracy in India* (2nd ed. 2007), *Local Governance in India: Decentralisation and Beyond* (2005).

Sudipta Kaviraj, Professor, Indian Politics and Intellectual History, Middle Eastern, South Asian and African Studies, Columbia University, is a specialist in intellectual history and Indian politics. His other fields of interest and research include the historical sociology of the Indian state, and some aspects of western social theory. He is a member of the Subaltern Studies Collective. Prior to joining Columbia University, he was a professor in politics in the Department of Politics at the School of Oriental and African Studies, London. Kaviraj's books include: *The Imaginary Institution of India* (2010), *Civil Society: History and Possibilities* co-edited with Sunil Khilnani (2001), *Politics in India* (ed.) (1999), and *The Unhappy Consciousness: Bankimchandra Chattopadhyay and the Formation of Nationalist Discourse in India* (1995).

Sunil Khilnani is Avantha Professor and Director, India Institute at King's College, London. Earlier he was Starr Foundation Professor and Director, South Asia Studies at the Johns Hopkins University School of Advanced International Studies in Washington DC. His publications include: *The Idea of India*, translated into several languages, most recently Arabic and Tamil; and *Civil Society: History and Possibilities* (with Sudipta Kaviraj), as well as many essays and articles.

Vijay Kelkar is Chairman, Board of Trustees of the India Development Foundation (IDF), New Delhi as well as Chairman of the National Stock Exchange of India Limited, Mumbai. Dr Kelkar has been elected Chairman of the Board of the Forum of Federations, Ottawa, Canada, with effect from January 1, 2010. He recently completed his term as Chairman, Finance Commission, Government of India, in the rank of a Union Cabinet Minister. He has held several other key posts and chaired various committees.

Chanda Kochhar is the Managing Director and Chief Executive Officer of ICICI Bank Limited. She was conferred 'Banker of the Year' Award by Financial Express 2010; ranked 20th in the 2009 Forbes List of Most Powerful Women in the World; ranked 25th in the 2008 Fortune's List of Most Powerful Women in Business and featured in the list of 30 most powerful women leaders in Business Today for 7 consecutive years from 2002 to 2009. She is a member of the Prime Minister's Council on Trade & Industry, US-India CEO Forum, Executive Board of the Indian School of Business, Hyderabad, and the Board of Governors of Indian Council for Research on International Economic Relations (ICRIER).

Pascal Lamy is Director-General of the World Trade Organization (WTO) since September 2005. In Brussels (1985 to 1994), he was Chief of Staff for the President of the European Commission, Jacques Delors, and his representative as sherpa in the G7. In November 1994, he joined the team in charge of rescuing the French bank, Credit Lyonnais, and later became CEO of the bank until its privatisation in 1999. Between 1999 and 2004, Lamy was Commissioner for Trade at the European Commission under Romano Prodi.

Manmohan ('Moni') Malhoutra is a Trustee of the Indira Gandhi Memorial Trust and a member of other charitable organisations. A Rhodes scholar and a former member of the Indian Administrative Service (1961 to 1978), he worked with Prime Minister Indira Gandhi in her Secretariat from 1966-1973. He was Assistant Secretary-General of the Commonwealth Secretariat, London (1981-1993), where he played a prominent role in the dismantling of the apartheid regime in South Africa and the release of Nelson Mandela from jail; a member of the Board of the International Institute for Democracy and Electoral Assistance (IDEA), Stockholm (1996-2005), and Secretary-General of the Rajiv Gandhi Foundation (2001-2007).

Pratap Bhanu Mehta is President, Centre for Policy Research, New Delhi. He is also Global Visiting Professor at NYU Law School. His areas of research include: political theory, constitutional law, society and politics in India, governance and political economy and international affairs. Author of many books, Mehta has also published widely in leading journals in the fields of political theory, intellectual history, constitutional law, politics and society in India, and India's emerging role in world affairs. He has also done extensive public policy work and was Member-Convenor of the Prime Minister of India's National Knowledge Commission.

Sudha Murty is the Chairperson of the Infosys Foundation, established in 1996 to build a better future for the underprivileged. The Foundation's four key focus areas are: high quality health care, education, revival of dying art forms and provision of basic infrastructure. She has written 30 books in Kannada and English which have been translated into many Indian languages.

Kumi Naidoo became Greenpeace International's Executive Director in 2009. Born in South Africa, Kumi became involved in the country's liberation struggle at the age of 15. He was involved in neighbourhood organisation, youth work in his community and mass mobilisations against the apartheid regime. He became the founding executive director of the South African National NGO Coalition (SANGOCO), an umbrella agency for the South African NGO community. In 2003, Kumi was appointed by the UN Secretary-General to the Eminent Persons Panel on UN-Civil Society Relations.

Sunita Narain is the director of the Centre for Science and Environment (CSE) and the director of the Society for Environmental Communications. She is the publisher of the fortnightly magazine, *Down to Earth*. She is a writer and environmentalist who conducts research with rigour and passion, so that knowledge can lead to change. In 2005 and again in 2008 and 2009 she was included by the US journal *Foreign Policy* as one of the world's 100 public intellectuals. She is a member of the Prime Minister's Council for Climate Change, as well as of the National Ganga River Basin Authority, chaired by the Prime Minister, set up to implement strategies for cleaning the river.

Nandan Nilekani is the Chairman of the Unique Identification Authority of India (UIDAI) in the rank of Union Cabinet Minister, which aims to provide a unique identification number for all residents of India. He was most recently the Co-Chairman of the Board of Directors of Infosys Technologies Limited, which he co-founded in 1981. In 2006, he was named Businessman of the Year by Forbes Asia. Time magazine listed him as one of the 100 most influential people in the world in 2006 and 2009. He is the author of *Imagining India*, which was one of the finalists for the FT-Goldman Sachs Book Award for the year 2009.

Joakim Palme is Director of the Institute for Futures Studies in Stockholm since 2002 and Professor of Political Science, Department of Government, Uppsala University since 2009. He is also Honorary Professor at the University of Southern Denmark, Member of the

Royal Academy of Letters and Antiquities, and Vice-Chairman of the Olof Palme Memorial Foundation. He chaired the Swedish 'Welfare Commission' 1999-2001. His current research is focused on the future of the European social model and the financing of social protection.

Rob Riemen, an essayist and cultural philosopher, is the author of the bestseller *Nobility of Spirit: A Forgotten Ideal* (2008) which is translated into 14 languages. He is also the Founder and President of the Nexus Institute, an international centre devoted to the transmission of European humanism, intellectual reflection and to inspiring Western cultural and philosphical debate through the publication of its journal *Nexus,* and the organisation of lectures and conferences. Riemen is a leading public intellectual in The Netherlands and lectures all over the world.

Anusha Rizvi studied history at St. Stephen's College, and Human Rights at the Jamia Millia Islamia University, New Delhi. She has worked as a television producer for four years at New Delhi Television (NDTV). Over the last five years she has helped revive Dastangoi, the dead art form of storytelling in Urdu. Peepli Live is her first essay as a feature film writer and director.

Pierre Rosanvallon has held the Chair in Early Modern and Modern Political History at the College de France since 2001. He has also been *Directeur d'etudes* at the *Ecole des Hautes Etudes en Sciences Sociales* in Paris since 1989. He is President of the international intellectual workshop *La Republique des Idées* and the Director of the website *wwwlaviedesidees.fr* dedicated to books and ideas. His numerous works on history and democratic theory include a trilogy on the history of representative democracy: a history of universal suffrage in *Le Sacre du Citoyen: Histoire du Suffrage Universel en France* (1992); a history of representation in *Le Peuple introuvable: Histoire de la Representation Démocratique en France* (1998); and a history of popular sovereignty in *La Democratic inachevée: Histoire de la Souverainete du Peuple en France* (2000).

Aruna Roy, a social and political activist, is a member of the National Advisory Council chaired by Mrs Sonia Gandhi. Along with Shanker Singh, Nikhil Dey and others she helped to form the Mazdoor Kisan Shakti Sangathan (MKSS) which has pioneered village-based public hearings as a means of public audit and democratic participation. Aruna is one of the founders of the movement for Right to Information in India. In 2000, she was awarded the Ramon Magsaysay Award for

Community Leadership. She has also been a member of different public hearings, tribunals and peoples commissions including the "Concerned Citizens Tribunal", which investigated the organised violence and killings of innocent people in Gujarat in 2002.

Manish Sabharwal is the Chairman and co-founder of Teamlease Services, India's largest staffing and training firm. He is a member of the Prime Minister's Council on Skill Development and serves on various state and central government committees related to education, employment and employability.

Rohan Samarajiva is founding Chair and CEO of LIRNEasia, a policy and regulation think tank active across 12 emerging Asian economies, including India. He was Team Leader at the Sri Lanka Ministry for Economic Reform, Science and Technology responsible for infrastructure reforms (2002-2004), a founder director of the ICT Agency of Sri Lanka (2003-2005), Director General of Telecommunications in Sri Lanka (1998-99), Visiting Professor of Economics of Infrastructures at the Delft University of Technology in the Netherlands (2000-2003) and Associate Professor of Communication and Public Policy at the Ohio State University in the US (1987-2000).

Abhijit Sen is a member of the Planning Commission of the Government of India. He has held teaching posts in the UK at the Universities of Sussex, Cambridge, Oxford and Essex. He has served on the Senate or Executive Council of several academic institutions in India; has been involved with a number of official policymaking bodies over the years and has served as Adviser or Consultant to a number of international organisations.

Nemat (Minouche) Shafik is Deputy Managing Director of the IMF since April 2011. She was formerly Permanent Secretary of the UK's Department for International Development (DFID) and Vice-President of the World Bank. Nemat has authored, edited and co-authored a number of books and articles on the Middle East, international economics, development and the environment.

Manmohan Singh is the Prime Minister of India and a Trustee of the Indira Gandhi Memorial Trust.

Rehman Sobhan is a member of the Board of the South Asia Centre for Policy Studies (SACEPS) and Chairman of the Pratichi Trust (Bangladesh) set up by Nobel Laureate Amartya Sen. He has published a large number of books, research monographs and articles in professional journals, relating to the political economy of development, public enterprise and privatisation, foreign aid, petropolitics, agrarian reform, regional cooperation in South Asia, democracy and governance. His latest work is *Challenging the Injustice of Poverty: Agendas for Inclusive Development in South Asia*.

Erik Solheim was Norway's Minister of the Environment and International Development from 2007-2012, and was earlier Minister of International Development (2005-2007). He is currently chair of the OECD's Development Assistance Committee. He has long experience as a member of various parliamentary standing committees and delegations. He was an observer at the UN Conference on Environment and Development (1997); the UN Conference on Population and Development (1995); and the UN Conference on Environment and Development (1992)

Joseph E. Stiglitz, Nobel Laureate (2001), helped create a new branch of economics, "The Economics of Information", exploring the consequences of information asymmetries and pioneering such pivotal concepts as adverse selection and moral hazard, which have now become standard tools not only of theorists, but of policy analysts. He has made major contributions to macroeconomics and monetary theory, development economics and trade theory, public and corporate finance, to the theories of industrial organisation and rural organisation, and to the theories of welfare economics and of income and wealth distribution. Recognised around the world as a leading economic educator, he has written textbooks that have been translated into more than a dozen languages. He founded one of the leading economics journals, *The Journal of Economic Perspectives*. His book *Globalization and its Discontents* (2001) has been translated into 20 languages and is an international bestseller.

Michael Walton is Adjunct Lecturer in International Development at the Kennedy School of Government, Harvard University, and Senior Visiting Fellow at the Centre for Policy Research, Delhi. His recent publications include *Inequality in Latin America*, an edited volume on culture and public action, the *World Development Report 2006* on *Equity and Development* and an edited book on equity, political economy and growth in Mexico. Walton's current research is mainly on India and includes work on rural education, inequality, the political economy of cities and corporate behaviour.

Steven I. Wilkinson is the Nilekani Professor of India and South Asian Studies and Professor of Political Science and International Affairs at Yale University. His main research interests are in ethnic conflict, governance and democracy. Author of various books, his 2004 book, *Votes and Violence: Electoral Competition and Ethnic Riots in India*, was co-winner of the American Political Science Association's Woodrow Wilson prize for the best book published in government, politics and international affairs.

Yogendra Yadav is a Senior Fellow at the Centre for the Study of Developing Societies (CSDS), Delhi since 2004. His areas of interest include: democratic theory, election studies, survey research, political theory, modern Indian political thought and Indian socialism. He has been involved in designing and coordinating the National Election Studies, the most comprehensive series of academic surveys of the Indian electorate, from 1996 to 2009. A prolific writer, he has co-authored *State of Democracy in South-Asia* (2008), *Democracy in Multinational Societies* (2010), dozens of academic papers and over two hundred articles.

Organising Committee

Manmohan Malhoutra, Conference Secretary and Trustee, Indira Gandhi Memorial Trust, New Delhi.

Suman Dubey, Trustee and Secretary, Indira Gandhi Memorial Trust, New Delhi.

Sunil Khilnani, Avantha Professor and Director, India Institute at King's College, London.

Pratap Bhanu Mehta, President and Chief Executive Centre for Policy Research, New Delhi.

Jaideep Thakur, Administrative Officer, Indira Gandhi Memorial Trust, New Delhi.

Sunita Kohli

Rapporteurs

Rohit Chandra

Madhav Khosla

Index

K

L

M

N

O

P

R

S

T

U

W

Z

An Indian Social Democracy

Integrating Markets, Democracy and Social Justice

VOLUME I

Editors

Sunil Khilnani
Manmohan Malhoutra

ACADEMIC FOUNDATION
NEW DELHI

www.academicfoundation.com

First published in 2013
by

ACADEMIC FOUNDATION
4772-73 / 23 Bharat Ram Road, (23 Ansari Road),
Darya Ganj, New Delhi - 110 002 (India).
Phones : 23245001 / 02 / 03 / 04.
Fax : +91-11-23245005.
E-mail : books@academicfoundation.com
www.academicfoundation.com

Published in association with the
INDIRA GANDHI MEMORIAL TRUST
New Delhi

Cataloging in Publication Data--DK
Courtesy: D.K. Agencies (P) Ltd. <docinfo@dkagencies.com>

An Indian social democracy / editors, Sunil Khilnani, Manmohan Malhoutra.
2 v. cm.
ISBN 9788171889945
ISBN 8171889948

1. Socialism--India--Congresses. 2. Socialism--Economic aspects--India--Congresses. I. Khilnani, Sunil, 1960- II. Malhoutra, Manmohan. III. Indira Gandhi Memorial Trust.

DDC 335.00954 23

Typeset by Italics India, New Delhi.

Printed and bound by The Book Mint, New Delhi.
www.thebookmint.in

INDIRA GANDHI
(1917-1984)

CONTENTS

Volume I

(The present volume)

Presentations and Discussions

Section II

Social Democracy in Global Perspective

Background Papers

Presentations and Discussions

Section III

The Political Economy of Social Democracy

Section III (a)

Background Papers

Presentations and Discussions

CONTENTS

Volume II

(The companion volume)

Section III

The Political Economy of Social Democracy

Section III (b)

Background Papers

Presentations and Discussions

Section IV

The Social and Political Context of Social Democracy in India

Introduction

India's recent growth trajectory has at once rapidly expanded the range of opportunities for many Indians and has transformed the psychological horizon of expectations for almost all of them. Yet access to such opportunities has remained unequal, a reality that has sharpened an already inequitable distribution of social risks and insecurities.

The challenge that India faces today is to continue its growth path in a sustainable form. That means creating conditions that enable the majority of Indians to participate in the gains of growth. And that in turn will require the renewal of our social contract, based on a new bargain between the state, citizens and social actors, and the world of business and entrepreneurship. It would be a social contract that integrates and renovates India's foundational commitments to democracy and social justice with recognition of the necessity of open markets for economic growth.

Such a social contract is best described in social democratic terms—and indeed India has since its inception as a sovereign nation been engaged in creating its own variant of a social democratic model—an Indian social democracy.

Social democracy was a project to build cooperation between all sectors of the social order to create a model of economic growth based on principles of fairness. Invented in the poor lands of northern Europe towards the end of the 19th century, it was a philosophy and practical politics that maintained a commitment to democratic values and to open markets, and sought to integrate these commitments into workable policies that increased opportunities and reduced social risks for the citizenry.

The ideas and institutions of social democracy spread across many parts of the world over the 20th century, promising a more attractive alternative than those offered by communist or socialist ideologies, or those embodied in pure free-market liberalism. Today, however, the institutions of social democracy are in crisis in their original European homelands. While social provision still accounts for a considerable proportion of state spending in many parts of Europe, states are increasingly having to apportion their tax revenues to pay down debt accumulated by unsustainable past policies.

Yet, if social democracy is in crisis in the rich, low-growth economies of the North, in the high-growth but still relatively poor economies of India, China, Latin America and other parts of Asia, recent years have seen a fertile inventiveness in social policies and delivery mechanisms. Taken together, these policy experiments serve as a veritable reinvention and reinvigoration of social democratic values. Brazil has pioneered a number of remarkable anti-poverty programmes, including conditional cash transfers—which have succeeded in changing habits and attitudes among the very poor, and have dramatically reduced poverty levels in that country. India too has launched landmark initiatives—examples include the National Rural Employment Guarantee Act, as well as legislation encompassing food security and social security, and the creation of innovative delivery mechanisms employing new technological platforms, such as Aadhar.

The present collection brings together some of the world's leading policy thinkers and decision makers to debate—at a particularly vexed moment in the global economy and as social tensions have manifested themselves in many states—the possibilities and constraints on social democratic policies that can foster growth, mitigate social risks and promote fairness in access to opportunities.

The papers themselves were presented at the Tenth Indira Gandhi Conference, held to commemorate the memory of Prime Minister Indira Gandhi. The conference generated lively critical discussions, available in the transcripts included in this volume.

Through the course of these discussions several broad conclusions of particular relevance to India emerged. First, a sustainable social democracy for India must be based less on directly redistributive policies than on providing citizens with the capacities to participate in economic growth. Second, India will need to move away from the complex cats-cradle of anti-poverty schemes that have evolved over decades, each supposedly aimed at particular groups, and towards a more simplified set of universal schemes, delivered by more efficient and trustworthy mechanisms. Third, the state must be wary of assuming large-scale fiscal responsibilities, which in future it may be unable to fulfill. A more general conclusion that emerged was that an Indian social democracy would not simply seek to replicate a classical welfare state model of top-down state dispensed provisions: not least because India does not have the requisite levels of surplus wealth. Rather, it will need to be based on principles of mutuality, between state, citizen and enterprise. The individual citizen, as well as civil society and business, all will need to share with the state responsibilities for the risks and rewards that a growing economy produces.

Given those principled choices and prudential constraints, an Indian social democracy must give centrality to fairness, and to its social achievement. Because if we do not, the costs will be high. We know a great deal about the high economic and efficiency costs of inequality and unfairness. So too there are psychological costs on individual humans—and these ultimately can lead to high political costs for the legitimacy of the system, as people are either forced into extreme responses, or simply drop out of the system.

The capacity to create and deliver a social democratic model of sustainable growth poses the greatest challenge for Indian political leaders and policy makers. While the Constitution and subsequent legislation have promised our citizenry an array of rights, the administrative weaknesses and corruptions of the Indian state have chronically frustrated the delivery of such rights. These deficiencies of the state can no longer remain unaddressed, or addressed merely in piecemeal fashion: in a society where people's appreciation of their rights is rising, we require major and rapid reform of the leakages and blockages that pervade India's adminstrative structures.

The fairness principle is not merely idealism. There are also real practical imperatives behind the need to craft an Indian social democracy. Without a social democratic vision as an electoral option, the inevitable desire for redistribution will be pursued in other ways. Already in rural India, Maoist unrest marks a sharp rejection of electoral politics. In the industrial sector, labour activism is on the rise, often in violent confrontation with management. And there is the ever-present possibility of populist movements emerging, centred around identities of caste, region or religion—something we already see in the form of urban nativist parties that seek to disrupt the fabric of India's diversity.

Further, the inequities of our current growth path have even wider implications for our future. China's phenomenal economic surge over the past three decades traded on the build-up of massive global imbalances—its governing elites muzzled consumption by their own citizens, and commanded their factories to produce for America and the West. That Chinese strategy is unrepeatable for India: western electorates and their governments will make sure of that. India's economy will have to grow by different means. In essence, it's future growth will depend in very large part on domestic consumption; for that to increase, we will have to increase the purchasing power of most Indians, which involves spreading income and delivering entitlements. As part of that, social risk will have to be shared—we all have a stake in reducing it.

The social contract that the founders of the Indian republic like Ambedkar and Nehru hoped to establish was one based on social democracy—not on socialism. They were committed to the values of democracy and social justice—and viewed both markets as well as the state as instrumental means towards achieving those values. These founding impulses, however, came to be frustrated, in the form of reservations and in 'socialist' economic policies that prescribed punitive taxation and stifling regulation. Fortunately, many of those negative legacies are being dismantled, the result of economic reforms over the past two decades. The market is rightly being accorded its proper place. An Indian social democracy will have to give full scope to the country's entrepreneurial talents—not least to create much of the employment vital to our future.

The challenge remains of pruning the Indian social policy jungle and moving towards securing certain minimal universal provisions for all Indians—targeted where necessary, but targeted at universal categories, like the poor, and not at caste groups. Our current focus on pragmatism, with what 'works' narrowly construed, has obscured our larger vision. Spreading capitalism's risks more equitably across our society would protect our most vulnerable citizens. It would be good for social solidarity. And it would offer a political vision that many Indians might find attractive.

— Sunil Khilnani

1

SONIA GANDHI

The Ideology of Social Democracy

Indira Gandhi is celebrated for her unflinching courage, for her determined leadership and for her deep and genuine concern for the poor. Among Indira Gandhi's many personal qualities was her wide range of interests—her great curiosity about people, places and, most of all, about ideas. She kept abreast of new thinking in diverse fields and interacted with many individuals around the world who were exploring new ways of tackling contemporary issues. The Indira Gandhi Conferences honour this aspect of her personality. They also serve the broader purpose of shaping public opinion and contributing to public policy. These conferences are not just about developing a visionary agenda, they are also about ways of giving it political and economic momentum.

This year's theme of An Indian Social Democracy may not appear apt, at a time when social democracy is under stress in the very countries where it was born and where it flourished. Today those countries are all much wealthier than India, and sceptics might say that it is too soon for India to talk about social democracy. That misses the point. In country after country, where social democracy took root, it was once for them a dream for their tomorrow. It was built, brick by brick, over many generations, energised by economic growth. In turn, it stimulated and sustained economic growth—by opening up opportunities for human development, by building social cohesion and solidarity, and by providing the framework of an intellectual and political consensus. In those countries, social

---

Speech delivered at the Inaugural Session of the Tenth Indira Gandhi Conference, An Indian Social Democracy: Integrating Markets, Democracy and Social Justice, November 19, 2010.

democracy not only proved to be good politics, it also turned out to be good economics. It brought the state, business and labour onto a common platform in pursuit of a shared vision—the vision of a more equal, more caring society.

The issue of fairness is important in any democratic society. The broad mass of people must believe in the fairness of the system, if it is to survive. At the very least, it must offer equality of opportunity to all through universal and better education, health care and skills. This is not a matter of choice. It is a known fact that unequal societies cannot achieve their full potential or even sustain a high level of growth indefinitely. In other words, islands of prosperity in a sea of deprivation can only give rise to storms of conflict and instability. The story of India's contrasts is well known: ability, aspiration and achievement coexist with injustice, inequity and inequality. We have more millionaires than ever before, alongside millions who struggle for two square meals a day.

We are right to celebrate our high rate of economic growth. We must do all that we can to sustain it. However, let us not forget that growth is not an end in itself. Much more important to my mind is what kind of society we aspire to be, and the values on which it should be built. Our economy may increasingly be dynamic, but our moral universe seems to be shrinking. Prosperity has increased but so has social conflict. Intolerance of various kinds is growing. Graft and greed are on the rise. The principles on which independent India was founded, for which a generation of great leaders fought and sacrificed their all, are in danger of being negated.

A coherent social democratic agenda is therefore essential. It must be based on rights and entitlements, not charity. The Right to Information, the Right to Work, the Right to Education and the proposed Right to Food Security, represent a landmark shift in our approach to issues of welfare and human development. Under the leadership of our Prime Minister a new architecture of social provisioning is being put in place.

I am, of course, conscious of the gap between promise and delivery. The debate on social democracy in the West is often about 'big *versus* small government'. This is less relevant to India.

What we need is more effective and efficient government. The Indian state, at its many levels, needs to augment its financial and managerial capacity to deliver public goods and services better. We need greater probity, more transparency, an open attitude and a willingness to try out fresh ideas.

No social democracy is possible without a thriving and dynamic business sector generating wealth. There is a new spirit of entrepreneurship, a new awakening of enterprise in India. It needs to be encouraged. But surely, it is in the interest of business to be a major partner in promoting social objectives and caring for the environment. Some corporate leaders stand out for their dedicated engagement in purposeful and meaningful philanthropy. It is my hope that the swelling ranks of India's wealthy will be inspired to follow their example.

Civil society has been in the forefront of giving voice to the underprivileged, organising them collectively and mediating on their behalf. It is also able to provide models of service delivery that are, at times, more effective than those of the government. Partnerships with NGOs can only enrich our social democracy.

India has long presented the paradox of a democracy where the poor majority, despite its voting power, has not always commanded its due. The challenge before us is to transcend the divides in our society to ensure that this changes. Social democracy is not populism. It is not generosity. It is the justice that our Constitution promises. The backlog is huge. Without social democracy, Indian democracy could well be undermined.

Much of what I have said reflects Indira Gandhi's own vision of 'An Indian Social Democracy.' As I understand it, this had four essential pillars.

First, a belief that social democracy must not only be responsive and responsible, but also representative of the many diversities in society.

Second, a conviction that social democracy is unachievable unless economic growth empowers the disadvantaged, deprived, and discriminated against.

Third, a yearning for social democracy that pays the highest attention to the preservation of the environment and regeneration of natural resources.

And fourth, a passion for social democracy that provides for a nation-state as an instrument of change and protection of national sovereignty.

These issues are central to the welfare and future of any society. Drawing inspiration from this vision, we in India will continue to work towards a consensus for a social democracy that will truly ameliorate the lives of our people.

2

MANMOHAN SINGH

Indian Social Democracy

Growth with Social Justice

We are living through a momentous phase in the history of the social evolution of humankind. The past century has been witness to many intellectual debates on forms of social, political and economic organisation of human societies.

Some debates went out of control and ceased to be debates. They became battles. Blood was spilt in the name of ideology. Communism, fascism, monopoly capitalism, etatism and many other ideologies demanded such loyalty from their adherents that people have killed and died in their name.

More recent conflicts rooted in religious ideologies, and made worse by the cancer of terrorism, are no different from earlier ones rooted in political ideologies. Mahatma Gandhi mocked them all when he said "an eye for an eye leaves us all blind."

No battle of ideas has ever been won on a battlefield. It is, as Karl Marx said so profoundly, in the minds of men that the seeds of material change are sowed. A battle of ideas is won and lost in the minds of people. That is why freedom is so fundamentally important.

Our national movement began as a struggle for freedom but became a mighty fight for democracy. 'Swaraj is my birthright', said Lokmanya Tilak and sowed the idea of nationhood in a diverse people. But we did not seek freedom for freedom's sake.

Speech delivered at the Inaugural Session of the Tenth Indira Gandhi Conference, An Indian Social Democracy: Integrating Markets, Democracy and Social Justice, November 19, 2010.

We sought freedom to liberate ourselves from centuries of misrule, from the scourge of poverty, ignorance and disease, from tyranny and bigotry, from caste prejudice and communal divisions. Thus, the Constitution of India was a unique social charter—the boldest statement ever of social democracy.

When Panditji launched India's first five year plan this social democratic vision informed our plan strategy. The Resolution of the Government of India creating the Planning Commission, in March, 1950, stated:

> The Constitution of India has guaranteed certain Fundamental Rights to the citizens of India and enunciated certain Directive Principles of State Policy, in particular, that the State shall strive to promote the welfare of the people by securing and protecting as effectively as it may a social order in which justice, social, economic and political, shall inform all the institutions of the national life, and shall direct its policy towards securing, among other things:
>
> a. that the citizens, men and women equally, have the right to an adequate means of livelihood;
>
> b. that the ownership and control of the material resources of the community are so distributed as best to subserve the common good;
>
> c. that the operation of the economic system does not result in the concentration of wealth and means of production to the common detriment.

This was the vision that shaped our national policy. The First Five Year Plan (1951-56) opened with the lines:

> The central objective of planning in India at the present stage is to initiate a process of development which will raise living standards and open out to the people new opportunities for a richer and more varied life. ...But the economic condition of a country at any given time is a product of the broader social environment and economic planning has to be viewed as an integral part of a wider process aiming not merely at the development of resources in a narrow technical sense but at the development of human faculties and the building up of an

institutional framework adequate to the needs and aspirations of the people.

The entire saga of development in India in the second half of the 20th century has been a saga of converting this grand 'political vision into practical possibilities'.

New institutions of inclusive governance were created—panchayati raj institutions; training and extension centres and development administration; programmes for rural development and for the social and economic upliftment of weaker sections of society.

Some worked, others did not. Some regions benefitted others did not. Development was uneven, but its motivating force was our commitment to social justice and economic empowerment of all.

In the mid-1970s, when Indiraji took stock and gave a new thrust to pro-poor development, the Fifth Five Year Plan (1974-1979) observed:

> No Plan can ignore the deep-seated urges of our people for greater equality. The reduction of disparities of all kinds—social, economic and regional—must always remain one of the central objectives of our developmental planning. The direction of our planning is to solve over a period of time the problems of the poor of all communities, especially tribals, Harijans, backward communities and regions.

A new set of programmes and policies was crafted to more effectively translate our political vision into practical possibilities.

I submit to you that every generation must define its own vision and its own instruments to attain that vision. But, I also urge you to consider that the vision of 'inclusive growth' that we now talk about is in fact what has defined development planning in India from day one.

To realise that vision we created programmes and institutions. We have achievements to be proud of, and we have failures to learn from. Some programmes worked, others didn't. Some institutions played their assigned role, others failed or withered away.

We have made mistakes and sought to correct them, as we did, for example, in the early 1990s. But our journey has been nothing less than a unique struggle to realise the vision of a just and caring society, in the context of a backward and developing economy and in the framework of a free and democratic polity.

Indiraji's call for 'growth with social justice' defined the concept of social democracy for my generation. We understood that the two must go together—the search for growth and the search of social justice. That a developing economy like India needs resources and revenues to be able to distribute them equitably. This calls for both resurgent growth and prudent management of our public finances.

When growth was not forthcoming, we had to take steps to stimulate it. This among other things involved a relook at the role of the state and market forces in the development process, of incentives to promote risk taking and entrepreneurship and regulation of private enterprises. When distributional interventions seemed to fail, we had to create new instruments covering a mix of entitlement and empowerment approaches and new institutions to promote equity.

India has developed a range of institutions and programmes that have become the basis of social democratic policy in many countries. From the *panchayat raj* to the public distribution system, from public health programmes to mid-day meals programme, from educational interventions aimed to empower Scheduled Castes, Scheduled Tribes, Other Backward Classes, minorities, our women and the girl child, India has put in place a wide range of practical policies.

Our government has further strengthened the foundations of inclusive growth. The historic and revolutionary rural employment guarantee programme, that we owe to Soniaji's inspired vision, has been acknowledged around the world as a powerful instrument of social justice in a backword economy.

Our policies for health care, education and rural infrastructure are all aimed at making our growth processes more socially inclusive.

I have, therefore, two propositions for your consideration:

First, that there is an 'Indian' model of 'social democratic' development that is rooted in the ideas and ideals that defined our national movement, that define our Constitution as it has evolved. This Indian model has evolved with time, reflecting all the gains and limitations of our political, economic and social development.

Second, the reach and efficacy of this evolving model of social democracy is critically dependent both on its fiscal sustainability and institutional efficiency.

In addressing the challenge of fiscal sustainability, one cannot put the cart before the horse. The experience of other countries, especially in Europe, tells us that governmental over-reach and fiscal over commitment can sometimes lead to economic crises.

With higher growth has come the opportunity of generating more revenues that can be invested in human and social development. But, higher growth has also been associated with higher inequalities and simultaneously increased expectations of the people at large. There is a revolution of rising expectations underway in India which any government has to take note of.

Against this tide of rising expectations, we confront the challenge of revitalising institutions of development administration and getting rid of the cancer of corruption in our public life. We need institutions and mechanisms that can deliver effectively our promise of livelihood security, the Right to Education, to employment, to food and to shelter.

These institutions cannot be built top down. Development administration is the responsibility of State governments in our federal polity. Unless development administration is strengthened, is made more representative, more accountable and transparent, allocating more financial resources from New Delhi will only contribute to higher levels of corruption and leakage of funds.

We have seen from our experience with the employment guarantee programme that the effective realisation of a right we grant in New Delhi varies from state to state, from district to district. Local competence determines the outcome of national campaigns and this is the reality which has to be borne in mind.

The Indian Parliament has legislated the Right to Education. But the responsibility to educate lies mostly with the local bodies and district administrations. We are presently considering the legislation of a Right to Food, but this right can only be realised if we have an effective public distribution system in place in every neighbourhood. We can legislate a minimum wage from New Delhi, but its implementation is in the hands of local governments.

In short, we must appreciate that the vision of social democracy can only be translated into practical possibilities by institutions of governance at the level where the state interacts with the citizen. It is at that level that we need a state that is more sensitive, more responsible, more transparent, more efficient and more honest.

I urge social scientists studying the Indian reality, and committed to its change and improvement, to focus on governance at this level and show how it can be improved and modernised. Reality differs from state to state, from region to region, from sub-region to another. We have to bridge this gulf.

How can higher outlays be translated into better outcomes? How can a democracy of rights be transformed into a social democracy of rights and responsibilities—responsibilities of different levels of government, of elected representatives, of civil servants, of the corporate sector and of every citizen. Such is the challenge before us.

India's struggle for social and economic transformation of its 1.2 billion strong population in the framework of an open society and a democratic polity, committed to respect for fundamental human rights and the rule of law has no parallel in history. Our success in accomplishing this gigantic task could have great significance for the evolution of humankind in this 21st century of ours.

Section I

Social Democracy as a Political Value and Theory

Social democracy emerged in Europe as a response both to the demands of mass electoral democracy and of economic growth, unevenly distributed: it sought to use democratic means to mitigate the worst effects of capitalist economic growth and to channel its real benefits towards the ends of social justice. It defined itself against socialist and command economies, as well as paternalist welfarism: in contrast, it stressed active cooperation between parties representing social and economic interests, the corporate world, and the state. In India too, a similar outlook defined the immediate post-1947 project of state-building and economic development.

What are the core values of social democracy? How has it sought to balance utopian vision with practicability? How does social democracy view the relations between individuality and solidarity, rights and responsibilities? Can we recover an intellectual history of social democratic thinking within India? The first section sets out the theoretical background and problems to which social democracy emerged as a response, and the extent to which it remains relevant today.

BACKGROUND PAPERS

- Pierre Rosanvallon
- Pratap Bhanu Mehta
- Sunil Khilnani

3

PIERRE ROSANVALLON

What is a Democratic Society?

Democracy has two dimensions: it refers to a 'political regime' as well as to a 'social form'. As a political regime, it means universal suffrage, protection of individual rights, freedom of the press, and pluralism. As a social form, one word summarises it: equality. In the 20th century, social democracy[1] had been the modern translation of this ideal, with all that it implied in terms of social security, access for all to public goods and redistribution. Those institutions, with the values and the vision supporting them, have now been declared dead or dying. Even if that judgement must be softened, the fact remains. Hence the question: how can a democratic society be defined and institutionalised in a post-social-democratic age?

To come up with an answer, we must start with a historical detour in order to properly understand the deep meaning of the current crisis of the idea of equality in western countries.

At the origins of democratic equality

At the time of the American and French Revolutions, the two dimensions of democracy (regime and social form) were totally intertwined. Political and social equality were considered to be equivalent. But social equality had no 'egalitarian', i.e. arithmetic, redistributive, sense. It referred essentially to a quality of the social bonds among men. Today we have a different approach to equality. Our attention has come to be focused on arithmetic equality, the feeling that we must 'reduce inequalities', leading for example to a fixation on redistributive norms in relation to wealth or other

1. The word has to be understood in the broadest sense of the term, besides its initial historical definition.

matters. The debate on this category logically starts from two points: in the first place, the conditions of the distinction between a just division and an arithmetic division, and in the second place, the nature of the resources to be distributed. On the first point, there will be variables like those of merit, responsibility or fundamental duties, the role of which will be questioned; while on the second, it is the categorisation of the relevant resources that will be at issue. The works of John Rawls and Amartya Sen have recently touched on this subject (cf. Sen's lecture, "Equality of What?", which led him to formulate his theory of capabilities). To understand the spirit of equality in the American and French Revolutions, it is not to this redistributive kind of equality that we must look. Indeed it was much more in terms of what I have called an 'equality-relation', an equality-quality, that the egalitarian imperative was expressed at that time.

How should this idea be clarified? Understood as a relation, equality is primarily an active quality (while equality-measurement is passive and of a quantitative nature). Equality here means reciprocity, reversibility, equivalence. To be the equal of another is to be for him what he is for me; to revive on old but very speaking word, it is to be 'commensals', those who eat at the same table, in other words those who appreciably engage in society. This is a matter of the quality of exchange, of interaction between individuals. That defines a kind of relative position that obviously excludes dependence, contempt, differences of level, in short everything that tends to create separate worlds. More positively, it is to share an activity, to constitute a fully common world. The primary aim is to constitute a society of equals, not to measure individuals relatively. Building such a society of equals will therefore first be defined negatively in the rejection of everything that establishes divisions in the forms of fixed hierarchies or privileges, and in the criticism of individual or social situations that form obstacles to reciprocity. It is therefore always subject to discussion connected to the formation of publicly-elaborated criteria. Equality-arithmetic is not lost from view in this framework, but it comes to be appreciated only secondarily, when it constitutes a variable influencing the quality of a society of equals.

We can distinguish three features of this equality-relation: similarity, independence and co-citizenship. Similarity is in the nature of equality-equivalence; to be similar is to present the same essential properties, the remaining differences not marring the quality of the relation. Independence is an equality-autonomy; it is defined negatively as the absence of subordination and positively as a balance of exchange. Co-citizenship, for its part, is an equality-participation, it is the community of belonging that constitutes it. So equality-relation establishes itself in the forms of a world of similar people, a society of autonomous individuals and a community of citizens. It is these three dimensions that were validated during the American and French Revolutions.

The revolutionary insistence on qualitative equality has to be understood in the global economic context of the two sister revolutions, as well as in the context of the contemporary representations of the economic sphere. Economic differences were considered as secondary for two main reasons:

The approach to social problems was embedded in a precapitalist context. Especially in the USA, autonomy and equality are considered as two sides of the same coin. At the end of the 18th century, 90 per cent of the workforce was composed of independent farmers, shopkeepers and self-employed craftsmen. In such a context, economic differences do not distort the equal status of each individual. In the USA as well as in France, this precapitalist vision was sustained by an ethos of frugality. Nothing bears better witness to this vision of things than the writings of Benjamin Franklin, which constituted an almost perfect expression of what we could call the "American ideology" of the time. Thus, in his *Information to those who would Remove to America* (1782), he welcomed the fact that there prevailed in America "a general happy mediocrity", and that there was at that time neither the insolent fortunes nor the misery that were to be found in Europe. His words were thus those used for thinking about equality by Montesquieu and Rousseau, among others who could be cited here. In his *Poor Richard's Almanack*, of which every household possessed a modest copy, it is this same ideal that he appeals to his co-citizens to keep alive by the wisdom and moderation of their conduct. In that way, the history of America and the virtues of its inhabitants should permit it to have a form of society in which inequalities would have become secondary. The future of America was of the kind more readily conceived under the auspices of a "Christian Sparta" than those of a destructive capitalism.

Individual inequalities are not apprehended as social inequalities as long as differences in terms of situations are not assimilated to differences in terms of conditions. Against the immobility of privileges and castes, observers of the first stages of the modern economy opposed the advent of a new world founded on incessant movement in the circulation of persons and wealth. In contrast to stagnant economies founded on the exploitation of rents from land, an economy based on commerce, it was held, favours an incessant movement of goods, followed in its wake by that of men. The market economy is in this way understood as an engine of destruction of ordered societies. It undermines the very foundations of the old distinctions of rank. No one drew attention to this better than John Millar, one of the great figures of the Scottish Enlightenment. In his *Observations Concerning the Distinction of Ranks in Society* (1771), which on many points masterfully anticipated Adam Smith's *The Wealth of Nations* (1776), he underscored the social revolutionary effect of the new world of wealth acquisition. I have used the term 'utopian capitalism' *(capitalisme utopique)* to characterise the view of the market economy in this 18th century literature. But there is no doubt about the revolutionary character that this description then had, making it possible to understand (we shall come back to this) how money could for a time be seen—more in America, it is true, than in Europe—as 'the great leveller'. Before its accumulation led to a 'new feudalism', it did indeed have a powerful effect in disrupting former hierarchies. In the America of the first decades of the 19th century, becoming rich was not at all perceived as detracting from equality. The ordinary man saw in the *nouveau riche* a validating projection of his own possibilities, rather than an insult to the modesty of his situation. Besides, this *nouveau riche* did not generally connect his condition to any social claim to superiority. For the situations appeared above all to be very changeable, not yet having turned the rich into a caste or a class. Wealth characterised individual situations, it did not appear as a social condition. To illustrate this distinction, Mrs Trollope, in her classic work *Domestic Manners of the Americans* (1832), reports this statement by a prominent person: "If a man becomes rich, let us arrange that his grandson be poor, and in that way we shall maintain equality." The precariousness of fortunes at the time very prosaically translated into a large number of bankruptcies. Gustave de Beaumont thus recounts how he was struck by the fact that before introducing him to a group of his friends, an American had advised him that in talking with them he should not criticise bankrupts, for many of them had lived through that situation. Railing against the immobility of the upper classes in Europe, whose prosperity in his eyes rested on "monopolies of caste", Prince Murat, another observer of America *(Esquisse morale et politique des Etats-Unis [Moral and Political Sketch of the United States]*, 1832) praises in contrast the "universal pendulum" that regulates trans-Atlantic society and makes it "as permissible to ruin yourself as to make a fortune." He summarises in the following terms what he considers to be the heart of the spirit of equality:

> In every well-organized society there is an ascending current; it is formed by those who are bettering their social position.... There is also a descending current; it is composed of those who, being fortuitously placed above the rung on the social ladder that their industry and skills assign to them, do not know how to hold on, and they tumble down.... It is in the interest of society that these two currents have complete freedom of action. It is in this way that merit of every kind will find its place, and have the influence that should appertain to it. It must be as permissible to ruin yourself as to make a fortune.

This long quotation expresses very well the way in which Americans at this time connected equality of conditions with making economic distinctions secondary by their being changeable and attached to purely individual criteria. It is also in this perspective that we must understand the idea of this period that money was 'the great leveller' in America, some even calling it the 'great apostle of equality': its movement ensured that the immediate inequalities did not freeze into privileges, monopolies or perpetuities. The feeling of equality of conditions in America also appeared to be nurtured by the pride arising from leading an independent existence. Even though the number of those who found themselves in this situation had decreased in the 1830s, the idea of independence continued to reign in portrayals of self and society, in the form of a possibility or a promise when it was not embodied in facts. It was always a central element in the American democratic mind. Bearing witness to this is the truly cult status that Ralph Waldo Emerson's essay "Self-Reliance" has enjoyed since its publication. In this vibrant ode to individualism and autonomy, the writer displays the voice of an equality-singularity, making the non-conformity of each the condition of a true society of equals.

In these different ways and in these different aspects, one can say that the principle of equality-relation was not challenged by the existence of economic inequalities in this first revolutionary age. But in the middle of the 19th century, the rising power of industrial capitalism and the market revolution broke up this happy vision of equality, and created a gap between the progressive achievement of a democratic regime, and the increasingly remote perspective of a constitution of a democratic society.

Divided democracy and how to deal with it

In Europe in the 1840s, the development of large-scale manufacturing led to a sudden and radical break with the above idea of a society of equals, which has constituted the core of subsequent indignation and questioning. Indeed, along with the new proletariat re-emerged the spectre of a new fourth order, this time turned back at the gates of the city, excluded even from the commune of humankind. With the rapid development of the new kind of industry, society was radically divided. "At the moment of writing," notes Eugène Buret in his famous survey of 1840, *De la misère des classes laborieuses en France et en Angleterre (On the Misery of the Labouring Classes in France and England)*, "the disaffection and the separation of the two classes, the workers and the capitalists, extend to the highest point in England: it is truly a secession, and resembles a preparation for a civil war." This is the great leitmotif of his survey. The terms 'absolute separation', 'growing separation', and 'division into two opposed classes' never stop flowing from his pen. Although Buret first zeros in on England, for him the problem is quite general, and it brings a terrible contradiction. "At the moment when inequality is destroyed in the political and civil order," he sums up, "here it is back again, with an intensity that it never had before, reborn, both in fact and in right, in the industrial order." The coming of the proletariat thus shattered the hope for the development of a society of equals: it was as if European industrial societies had been divided into two hostile and foreign blocs. Referring to the moment this was coming to be recognised, Daniel Stern confirmed the sentiment of the time by noting in her *Histoire de la Révolution de* 1848 that a large portion of the working classes "had come to form a separate class, like a nation within a nation, so that they began to be designated with a new name: the industrial proletariat." A few years on, Benjamin Disraeli will be using nearly identical terms in his novel *Sybil,* or The Two Nations (1845). He will there speak also about the rich and the poor as forming two foreign nations, which shared nothing in common, as if they were "inhabitants of different planets."

The most famous political manifestos of the 19th century were written to denounce this gap and to demand equality. This is the case with Sylvain Maréchal's *Manifeste des égaux*, the publication of which in 1828 marked the birth of socialism. It is equally the case with *the People's Charter* in Great Britain (1838). The *Manifeste de la démocratie au XIXe siècle (Manifesto of 19th-Century Democracy)* by Victor Considerant (1847) and the *Manifest der Kommunistischen Partei (Communist Manifesto)* of Friedrich Engels and Karl Marx (1848) were also denunciations of the new divisions into classes of society. This was again the aim of the famous *Manifeste des soixante (Manifesto of the Sixty)*, of Proudhonian inspiration (1864). If the situation remained different in the United States, independent work remaining more common there than in Europe, the market revolution had nonetheless brought to that work effects of the same kind, with a strong development of the salariat (and, significantly, talk about the destructive effects of a new type of slave labour).

However, in Europe in the 1840s, the rupture between democratic regime and democratic society did not yet appear irremediable. Indeed it was then common to link property-based suffrage with economic inequalities, and therefore to think that reduction of the inequalities would necessarily come with the triumph of universal suffrage. In the United Kingdom, the Chartists had thus logically made extension of the right to vote the core of the manifesto they adopted in 1838. The battle for salaries, the issue of working conditions, getting rid of workhouses—everything woeful to workers was understood as the necessary result of property-based suffrage. If the rich are powerful, said the Chartists, it is because they participate in making laws; it is because they can legislate that they are rich. Bronterre O'Brien, the main theorist of Chartism, therefore made universal suffrage "the great panacea for all evils." George Harney, another leading figure in the movement, and a great friend of Engels, summed up things by saying: "We demand universal suffrage because we believe it will bring us bread, beef and beer. Universal suffrage will procure universal happiness." The same type of approach was to be found in France before 1848. "Representative government means governmental mechanism, by which the interests of the people will obtain satisfaction," stated a grand figure of the *Société des amis du peuple (Society of Friends of the People)*. At the time of the first battle for electoral reform, one of the most famous pamphleteers of the period, Claude Tillier, bluntly stated: "Political rights give bread to the people. If the people were sovereign, they would stop letting their toast be cut up as if they were children." "Those who make the law make it for themselves": such was in fact the *leitmotiv* of the time. When universal suffrage was proclaimed in 1848, the immense majority of the people thought that meant the beginning of a new economic and social era. Alexandre Ledru-Rollin, then Minister of the Interior, went so far as to say lyrically: "Dating from this law, there will be no more proletarians in France." The 'good representation' guaranteed by everyone having the vote was understood as before to lead to the establishment of 'good policy', necessarily benefitting most voters. These expectations and hopes were to be disappointed, but it was necessary to wait for the second half of the 19th century for the fact of immense inequalities to be seen as a specific and structural phenomenon, open to being treated as such.

But how could the inequalities be recognised and treated without adopting the radical position of all the prophets of the communitarian utopia who advocated abolishing even the principle of competition? Two paths were taken in the 19th century: attempting to legitimate these differences by relating them to factors purely 'natural' or 'moral', and reconstructing egalitarian consciousness around a sense of collective identity and very particularly of national unity.

If the 19th century in Europe and the United States was the century of universal suffrage, the conditions of its expansion varying in each country, it was also the century of the legitimation of economic inequalities. In the 1830s and 1840s it was thus the same social surveyors who attacked the havoc wreaked by big factories—which "produced at the same time cotton and poor people" in Marx's formulation—who also claimed that the vices of the working-class world were responsible for their woes. Their books were full of stigmatisations of the 'debauched and disorderly habits' that they said were the source of workers' bad conditions. But it was also by claiming to give an objective, natural basis to the inequalities that the increased distance between the dynamic of political democratisation and the constitution of a divided society was justified. In the 18th century, the appeal to follow the laws of nature had been at the heart of thinking about liberation. The natural science of Buffon, in emphasising that all men were alike and constituted one and the same species, had thus shaken aristocratic pretensions and contributed to the ascension of an egalitarian consciousness. In the 19th century it was conversely the sciences, or pseudo-sciences, claiming to demonstrate the physiological foundation for inequalities that would attract public attention. The American case particularly exemplified this point of view. For example, the fatherland of the equality of conditions had been from the middle of the 19th century the continent on which phrenology enjoyed an extraordinary public success. This was a way of smoothly reconciling the egalitarian moral imperative with the naturalisation of inequalities. At the end of the century, the craze for intelligence tests and the flourishing of racialist theories would allow justifying the same vision of the world.

Parallel development took place, in Europe as in America, of a whole ideology of collective identity which would serve to substitute for a truly social appreciation of equality. In Europe, the accent was placed on a new appreciation of the idea of the nation, connected with forms of xenophobia and protectionism. For example, the idea of national work was substituted for social justice. Thought about unity and identity, founded on the opposition of an interior assumed to be one, to an exterior judged to be threatening, took the place of the preceding questioning about the forms of social division internal to each country. (This explains the passage of extreme left-wing thinkers and activists in several countries to forms of ultra-nationalism.) In the United States it is in the perspective of such a rearrangement of the egalitarian mind that we must understand the veritable invention of racial segregation at the end of the 19th century. In one fell swoop all the divisions of the white world came to be seen as secondary because of the establishment of a radical separation from the black world.

We must take account of this background in order to understand the birth and the development of social-democratic ideas. Confronting the different perversions or derivations of the social-egalitarian ideal that we just touched on, social-democratic ideas have in fact tried to give back to that ideal a practical substance.

The birth and decline of the social-democratic ideal

Here we must understand the term social-democracy in its broadest sense of the redistributive state (thus, social-redistributive). This social-democracy has had different political expressions in each country: the Keynesian state of the new deal in the United States, reformist socialism in northern Europe, new liberalism in Great Britain, social republic in France. But it is everywhere characterised by the establishment of the same institutions:

- Adoption of a new taxation policy. Onto taxation considered simply as the counterpart of the use of public services, there has been superimposed a conception of taxation as an instrument for correcting inequalities and redistributing. It is the adoption of systems of progressive income tax that symbolises this rupture. Though it was everywhere put into place with very low rates (2% to 5%), it rapidly came to play a massive role. In 1936, the highest marginal rate of taxation of income was 79 per cent in the United States (it rose for a time to 94% in 1942!), and 60 per cent in France.

- Establishment of systems of social insurance covering workplace accidents, illness, disability and unemployment. All of these diverse ways of setting up forms of social security see the factors of poverty as risks and therefore treat them with insurance techniques.
- Development of institutions designed to structure the position of workers in order to improve it: procedures of collective bargaining, official recognition of unions, protective social legislation (minimum pay, firing procedures, and so on).

This was a real revolution, which was carried out in this way around the years 1900-1930, and was then consolidated with the cycle of reforms that followed the end of the Second World War. How was it possible? Three kinds of factors played essential roles.

First, political factors. On the right, the fear of revolutions played an essential role. When the socialist parties in Europe made a spectacular electoral breakthrough at the end of the 19th century (a breakthrough often connected with the broadening of suffrage rights), the conservative parties in fact saw in the adoption of reforms the means to exorcise the spectre of socialists coming into power (Bismarck had been the first to theorise this strategy in Germany in the 1880s). On the left, the social-democratic space took shape on the basis of a double rupture: first, with the communist utopia of an equality restrained by the absorption of the individual into a community; second, with the drifts of an equality-identity attuned to nationalism, xenophobia and protectionism.

At the end of the 19th century, European socialists thus denounced protectionism at the same time that they adopted a reform strategy that broke with the vision of a revolutionary millennium. In the traditional revolutionary perspective, we must remember, there was no place for any thinking about action to reduce inequalities. Rather, it was reckoned that in fact a radically different society would come one day. A certain convergence took place in this way between the right and the left.

To these political factors must be added a condition that one could say is sociological. Towards the end of the 19th century, the vision of a world composed of individual and self-sufficient sovereigns gave way to an approach founded on the idea of a primary interdependence. "The lone man does not exist", said Léon Bourgeois, the French author of *Solidarité*, the book that led a generation of republicans and radicals to restructure their political culture. In *Liberalism* (1911), which served in an equivalent capacity across the Channel, Leonard Hobhouse likewise considered that each individual is constituted by "the social atmosphere" that surrounds them. The Pastorian revolution dramatically validated this perception of the fundamentally social individual. "It is thanks to Pasteur," emphasised Bourgeois, "that the idea of a new humanity could appear and enter into people's minds. It is he who more precisely thought through the relations that exist among men; it is he who has definitively proved the profound interdependence that exists among all beings; it is he who, in decisively formulating the microbial theory, has shown how each of us depends on the intelligence and the morality of everyone else. It is he who has made us understand how each of our individual organisms by the countless army of infinitely small ones that it contains mounts an assault, so to speak, on all the organisms of the world; it is he who subsequently has taught us our mutual duty."

The ideas of right and of duty, of merit and of responsibility, of autonomy and of solidarity, were completely redefined in the new framework. Having become thinkable, the project of an equality-redistribution came into the field of the possible. We can in fact separate the introduction of progressive income tax, or the fiscal modifications of inheritance, from the diffusion of the more basic idea of a social debt such as the one that Bourgeois formulates in *Solidarité*. For him, every man is born a debtor to society. Each individual indeed owes something to the accumulated work of all mankind; he comes into the world loaded with obligations of all sorts towards society. This is true even for the most humble, as was emphasised by the philosopher Alfred Fouillée, an intellectual and moral model for all republicans, in an influential expression: "the person who invented the plough continues to work, invisible at the side of the labourer." But it is even more true for those who enjoy good positions. Hence arises the need for what Fouillée, in his pioneering work, "*La Science sociale contemporaine* (1880), called "repairing justice" (*justice réparative*). In the United States, Richard Ely, the great theorist and proponent of progressive income tax, justified redistribution by noting: "No such thing as strictly individual production of wealth exists in any modern community."

Thirdly, there is a historical factor that has played an essential role: the role of the two world wars in reinforcing the social contract. The deaths of millions on the European continent drove men to look differently on what united them. George Orwell summed it up: "If the war didn't happen to kill you, it was bound to start you thinking." The experience of the combatants had been the hardest, of course. In fact each of them was able to feel in the mud of the trenches that he shared with his companions in arms an identical insecurity, a same returning to a kind of state of nature. The troops had physically shared the same equality of conditions, in the shape of a limit experience, at the hazy border between humanity and animality: the experience of an absolutely naked life. "The consciousness of a community of nature instilled a very lively and comforting sentiment of equality," said one witness. This combat fraternity and the memory of the sacrifice of the lives taken from us are admittedly difficult to analyse. But they nonetheless prepared people's minds for more solidarity in civil life. The recognition of veterans' rights contributed to a broader reconsideration of the legitimacy of social rights and of the kinds of redistribution that they implied. The very idea of the nation was also redefined in this ordeal. Although war exacerbated the nation-identity idea, forged in the negation of the other, it also made more dominant the image of the nation-solidarity, which would allow greater legitimacy to be given to the imperative for greater equality. Thus we can see in the French case that the first important social insurance law, that of 1928, was presented by its proponents as being "born after the war, out of the solidarity that was asserted among the different social classes; out of the will to give to those who had defended the country in the trenches—to the working classes who had had to defend quite simply the common heritage—the help they needed in bad times; out of the memory of the efforts that they had brought to fruition; out of a great sense of national solidarity." Identical arguments were used throughout the European continent to justify the social reforms of the time. After 1945, the victory over Nazism, along with the shared lot of the ordeals experienced together that had preceded it, produced identical effects, the reinforcement of solidarity.

This historical reminder of what had made thinkable and possible the advent and the consolidation of the social-democratic order lets us understand its recent weakness:

- There is no longer fear of revolutions that push governments of the right to adopt social reforms.
- Contemporary societies are societies of individuals; they no longer understand themselves as organic wholes. The sense of solidarity in them is therefore dulled. Consequently, the idea of responsibility has also taken on greater importance in the assessment of the situation of individuals (whereas the development of social insurance had been based on the principle of the socialisation of responsibility, as the issue of workplace accidents had shown).
- In Europe as in the United States, citizens have finally no longer lived through ordeals equivalent to those of the two world wars.

The decline of the social-democratic ideal is often linked to the development of a triumphant neo-liberalism. The two phenomena are admittedly concomitant. But we cannot thereby infer a relation of causality of the second by the first. Neo-liberalism is in fact itself a product of the three things we have just referred to. It is one particular form of response to the problems posed by these current transformations that have induced a destabilisation of the representations of equality and solidarity that form the base of the old social-democratic order. Its emergence is thus linked to the contemporary crisis of equality (just as the resurgent reactions of xenophobia and protectionism are linked to that crisis).

But there are other possible responses to this crisis of equality. The current problem is to formulate them and not just to think about prolonging the old social-democratic order, as if it was just a matter of opposing forces of resistance to the forces of destabilisation. In any event, nothing that should be conserved from this order can be conserved unless it recovers its full moral and social legitimacy. So it is also a weakening of this legitimacy that translates into the crisis of equality.

The objective is thus to reformulate egalitarian ideals for the new world of individuals into which we have irreversibly entered.

The new age of equality

In the 1830s-1840s, the first western crisis of equality had led to the creation of a rhetoric justifying the new inegalitarian order, and at the same time a whole procession of perverse alternatives that replaced the preceding visions of social equality with the perspective of an equality-identity. In the second crisis of equality, we see a resurgence, with very similar expressions, of these same images of equality-identity. And it is also possible to consider neo-liberalism as the new form taken by the rhetoric justifying inequalities. But it is not only that. The conditions for the power of this ideology stem from the fact that it also incorporates into its underlying values some elements perceived as positive: the accent placed on merit, and especially on responsibility. Is it possible to separate the wheat from the chaff, and to detach from neo-liberalism the positive within it? It is in this perspective that some intellectuals and progressive personalities have tried to rethink equality by exploring the path of a radical version of equality of opportunity. To do this they have sought to dissociate individual responsibility from social determinisms, asking that we reduce, or even eliminate the latter. Whence the perspective of compensatory justice for social handicaps: the accent on education, forms of asset-based welfare, etc. That has been the central perspective around which the Labour Party in Great Britain constructed the Third Way.

In more theoretical terms, different thinkers, from Ronald Dworkin to Gerald Cohen, who have been put together under the label of luck egalitarianism, have clarified the terms of this ambition. But this approach runs up against three major difficulties:

- The practical difficulty of drawing a line separating individual responsibility from social determinisms. This however is the least fatal obstacle. For one can consider that the distinction is always socially established and that it is therefore public deliberation that makes drawing the line possible.
- This vision paradoxically leads to hyper-individualism. In this way it is underpinned by a very debatable anthropology.
- It also leads, in fine, to the construction of a universe in which spatial inequality will be accepted, even though there is little or no reason to assume that it reflects differences of individual aptitudes (let us note that this difficulty was at the heart of the argument of Michael Young's 1958 essay, "The Rise of Meritocracy").

Thus, even if such a perspective of distributive justice can supply the basis of certain social policies that reduce inequalities, it cannot on the other hand be part of a new philosophy of equality.

A new philosophy of equality is not the same thing as a new theory of justice. In the latter, in fact, it is always a matter of determining in fine a threshold of tolerability of inequalities. In place of this approach, which is structurally tied to a distributive or redistributive perspective, we must substitute a social, relational approach to the issue of equality. Here it is a matter of producing a society of equality and not only of reducing economic inequalities. Such a society could be organised around three principles:

- *Singularity*: Possibility for each individual to construct their own history and to be socially recognised. The key to this is a politics of dignity, of recognition and of development of capabilities.
- *Reciprocity*: Balance of rights and duties. Trustworthy society. Production of relational goods.

- *Community living*: Construction of forms of common life. Fight against social separatisms.

In this framework, admissible economic differences are determined by the fact that they do not hinder the implementation of these three aspects of the egalitarian relation.

4

PRATAP BHANU MEHTA

Citizenship and Solidarity in Social Democracy[1]

Introduction

Why are we debating social democracy in India at this historical juncture? There are three principal motivations and somewhat cross cutting motivations behind this debate. The first is this. Ever since independence, India has struggled with one central contradiction. Its constitution aspired to create a universally inclusive conception citizenship; and its social policies have aspired to fulfil those ends. Yet the reality is that the Indian experience has been massively egalitarian in distributing rights and privileges, often exacerbating social and economic differences rather than reducing them. Even the site where an inclusive conception of citizenship has been robustly practiced, namely electoral democracy, has produced new contradictions. While politics has, in some meaningful sense, become more deeply representative, it is not entirely clear that it has become more responsive. How does one explain these disjunctures?

The second motivation for the debate is understanding distinctiveness of the Indian path. Globally, there have been several different pathways through which different countries have developed. And there are still significant differences in the particular mix of participation, practices of citizenship, equality, liberty, occupational structures etc., that different countries have produced. Most of the story of development, has, contrary, to text book pictures, been a story of improvisation and adaptation,

1. I would like to thank Sunil Khilnani, Devesh Kapur, Arvind Subramanian, and most especially Partha Mukhopadhya for endless conversations on this subject.

rather than the neat unfolding of models. If there is a conception of change that has held up most robustly, it is probably what used to be called the 'sceptical whig' story, associated with the Scottish Enlightenment. On this view, development is a messy process, a strange amalgam of historical path dependence, luck, institutional improvisation, political economy and circumstantial conjunctures. It is also a process in which often good intentions lead to bad outcomes, and base motives, in retrospect, produce revolutionary changes. The focus here is not on theories, as much as it is on the mechanisms that produce change; it is an attempt to understand the full range of causal conditions that produce particular outcomes.

India has, through its own messy trajectory, embarked on a particular development path. It has made particular choices on state intervention, political democracy, macroeconomic tradeoffs, the balance between consumption and saving and so forth. It has its own combination of constraints and opportunities shaping the lives of its citizens. But there is beginning to be a sense that India is fashioning its own unique path to development, a path that is different from what has been dubbed the 'Washington' or the 'Beijing' consensus. What are the distinctive contours of this path? What are the possibilities and limitations of this path? Are there lessons in how India arrived at this distinct amalgam? While this path has emerged through a process of adaptive learning, can it be given a deeper theoretical articulation?

The third motivation is to push harder at the boundaries of what is possible. There is one indubitable fact about contemporary India. India is experiencing profound social and economic change. Different sections of Indian society experience this change differently. But there is very little doubt that a sense of possibility has percolated amongst all sections of Indian society. Indians are, in myriad ways, and often with an unprecedented sense of enterprise, shaking up the system, often through conflict. We don't know how all of this will work out. But we do know that amongst different groups in society (including the poor and historically marginalised) there is widespread energy, striving for improvement, the creation of new forms of reciprocity and innovative adaptation. Does this sense of possibility represent a historical force in its own right?

Can we capitalise on it to drive far reaching changes? There is a sense that India has a window of opportunity it has never had in its history. Can we make full use of this opportunity? But this sense of opportunity also represents a moment of anxiety. What if we let this opportunity slip? There is, rightly, a great sense of optimism in India, for India. For the first time in our history, real social and economic change seems possible, and the sheer unleashing of aspirations and energy across Indian society is staggering.

However, notwithstanding this newly buoyant and optimistic era, there are some concerns about the form the politics of justice will take. This is the theme of this paper. We first reflect on the limited set of instruments we have which can do full justice to the aspiration of social equality. This part discusses extensively the limitations of the current attempts to institutionalise social democracy, including the proposals to constitutionalise rights or provide universal cash entitlements. The second part reflects, somewhat more briefly, on why caste still remains such an entrenched category around which the politics of social justice is constructed and the consequences of this entrenchment. It tries to connect four different strands that have acquired salience over the last couple of years: new axis of social conflict; the rise of the new welfare state; the continuing power of caste; and the unanticipated consequences of the growth in state capacity. The aim of this paper is, to borrow Judith Shklar's phrase, to be more a tour of perplexities than a guide for the perplexed.

Distributive politics and social democracy

The present challenge of the politics of social justice must be seen against the backdrop of a general, perhaps more global and historical, pessimism about the relationship between democracy and equality. Democracies, in principle, derive their legitimacy from a certain form of political radicalism, promising new beginnings, a constantly challenged and renewed social order and an affirmation of equality. However, in practice, they have turned out to be remarkably conservative institutions. Perhaps a little historical perspective is in order. In the 18th and 19th centuries, many perceptive observers of 'democracy' saw its conservative potential. Adam Smith had very presciently predicted that a republic, the United States, would be the last to abolish slavery, much after many monarchies had done so. Alexis de Tocqueville, the most insightful observer of democracy, had commended it, in part, because democracies make revolutions rare. While democracies relentlessly abolish formal distinctions of social status, they are quite compatible with high levels of economic inequality. Contrary to those who feared democracy, Tocqueville argued that democracies promote stability in property relations. Though this is so for various reasons, one reason is quite subtle: in countries where inequality has been formally abolished, and a myth of formal equality becomes part of the self-understanding of the society, it becomes, paradoxically, harder to critique real inequality.

Why democracies have turned out to be so compatible with high levels of inequality is a wider, indeed a truly global, debate. In the United States, political scientists are puzzled by the fact that the democratic system has allowed inequality to grow immeasurably over the last two decades, with most of the gains of growth going to the top 10 per cent of the population and a decline in real wages for much of the middle class. There are several reasons advanced for this: from the role ideological mystification plays in democratic politics to the susceptibility of democracies to special interests. But in very different contexts—from the debate over democracy in China to the health of democracy in the United States—one question is being asked: is the inability to mitigate inequality a contingent feature of democracy? Or, are there deeper, far more structural, reasons for democracy's inability to mitigate inequality? On the contingent view, the inability of democracy to mitigate inequality can be explained by the way in which democracy is organised. The structure of election finance, forms of party organisation, the susceptibility of media control, voter apathy, lack of information—all contribute to making democracies less self-aware than they should be. On the other hand, some, like Adam Pzeworski (2010), argue that there may be deeper structural reasons for the difficulty in addressing the issue of inequality. One major reason has to do with what I call 'small liberty effects'. In a society which allows some basic freedoms, even small differences can over time accumulate and transform into great ones. This is most powerfully illustrated in a widely cited paper by Debraj Ray and Dilip Mookherjee (2003). Their reasoning goes something like this. Suppose productive assets were equalised, but there were very, very small differences in rates of return on these assets, due to a variety of reasons. Some get a return on 0.02 per cent while others suffer a small loss of minus 0.02 per cent. After 50 years, such minute differences of return will translate into one group having almost eight times the wealth of others. And this is with minor differences. These effects can be considerably magnified when differences in inherited endowments are slightly higher.

Democracy's inability to mitigate inequality may have other reasons too. It could be that the instruments of redistribution available to democracies have severe limitations. It might be worth considering, briefly, the set of instruments democracies have used for this purpose, and the politics around them in a country like India.

The most obvious instrument is redistribution through taxation. However, for several reasons, there is no serious politics structured around using this instrument. First, countries like India have recent and vivid memories of the distorting effects of high taxation in the context of low enforcement capacity. There is a generalised scepticism about the efficacy of high direct taxes. How far this scepticism is justified can be debated in economic terms. There is, additionally, an interesting ideological phenomenon also at work *vis-à-vis* taxation. The rich benefit from the fact that most people, at any level of society, do not like being taxed more; high taxes, even if only for the very rich, are often seen as a slippery slope for legitimising high taxes for all. So, while most democracies have some forms of progressive taxation, there are limits to how much they can tax. Second, in the context of globalisation and mobility of capital, there is scepticism about the efficacy of very high tax rates. Now it is possible to considerably increase total tax revenues and tax over GDP ratios without increasing tax rates. This is particularly true of countries like India which have historically low tax over GDP ratios. This increase in revenue collection often done through smart indirect taxes, provides great head room to the state to spend on welfare schemes. India is entering an exciting stage where it can expand welfare schemes by increasing tax over GDP ratios. But, as I shall argue, these schemes, while important are still too under ambitious to have really transformative effects. Third, and this is a point I will return to later, taxes provide redistribution through the instrumentality of the state. Often, there is scepticism about a state's capacity to use taxes wisely. The historical performance of states has certainly provided grist to the mill of those who are sceptical of more resources being poured into the state. Indeed, the case for lower taxes and an ideological delegitmisation of the 'public sector' as it were, go hand-in-hand. However, even when the state works, its welfare effects are likely to be higher than its equality effects. So, broadly speaking, there appear to be political limits to taxation as an instrument of redistribution.

The second major instrument of redistribution was collectivising productive assets, particularly industrial capital. This instrument has simply turned out to be an unviable historical option.

The third instrument of redistribution is one particular asset: land. On independence, land distribution was thought to be the major instrument of producing equality. But, and this is a global phenomenon, democracies have not been very successful at radical land reform. Most cases of successful land reform have been either through revolution or colonial powers destroying a landed aristocracy, as the Japanese did in Korea. Land reform in democracies has been, at best, ameliorative rather than radical. However, at the present conjuncture, in the context of India's uneven development, the politics of land is playing out very differently. First, the issue of land has become absolutely central to conflicts in our society: many major faultlines involve land, whether it is tribals desperately trying to secure use rights to their traditional lands, farmers contesting land acquisition, or conflicts over shaping urban zoning. Two, state regulation of land has also become central to the political economy of Indian democracy. There is a joke that, after liberalisation, the state controls only three things: land, liquor and learning. And these are three areas where the visible hand of rent-seeking is tremendously powerful.

Historically of course land reform has been associated with better economic outcomes: states with relatively more egalitarian distribution of land produced a more egalitarian politics. But, in a way, this fact only highlights one of the paradoxes of land politics: you already need a certain degree of asset equality to shape politics in a more egalitarian direction. The politics of land itself has turned out to be greatly path dependent. Politics itself seems a rather weak instrument for producing asset equality. But while land remains an issue of great social contention, it is, with some exceptions, not the locus of an egalitarian politics for several reasons.

As Partha Chaterjee and many others have pointed out, in much of rural India, the quest is now to get off the land. The fragmentation of landholdings (combined with large-scale shifts in life-style aspirations) are making working on land less desirable. While regularising the rights of tenants and share-croppers can have empowering effects, particularly in states like Bihar, the blunt truth is that access to small landholdings is not seen as considerably empowering. In rural India, the greatest fault lines are often between the interest of small farmers and landless labour; in some states, the greatest complaint about the NREGS (National Rural Employment Guarantee Scheme) raising wage rates has come from small and marginal farmers. In short, often the conflicts between 'adjacent' classes are more consequential and immediately severe than those between the top and the bottom, making politics less a matter of attacking privilege than holding onto small distinctions. Land politics in India is very complicated. But here I simply want to make one point: it is the axis of conflict, but no longer the main fulcrum of distributive politics. Parenthetically, one can make a stronger argument: that land assets are the means by which inequality is being reproduced and exacerbated rather than reduced.

Land acquisition has also become a mechanism for exacerbating inequality in India in three ways. First, property rights, which were weakened in India to facilitate land reform and help the poor, ironically ended up dispossessing them even more. Second, what farmers think of land acquisition depends, amongst other things, on two factors: location and their existing assets. Again, ironically, farmers in an area with a real estate boom or high circle rates (like

Haryana) are more likely to be willing to part with their land than farmers in poorer states. It is not an accident that land acquisition is harder in backward states like Orissa, West Bengal and parts of Uttar Pradesh (UP). The poor get a poorer deal in a poor state. High growth states like Gujarat have less of a challenge. As the recent conflict in UP has shown, large farmers also have a greater capacity to bargain, compared to small farmers, and are likely to get better deals. So, dispossession is also unequal in its effects. Finally, there is one aspect to inequality in the land discourse that is deeply insidious. While there is some focus on monetary compensation and promise of jobs, let us face two ugly truths. First, in most areas there has been insufficient investment in providing skills to the dispossessed to enable them to get meaningful jobs. Studies show that, particularly in backward areas, companies do not employ local labour: partly because of a skills deficit, partly because of fear that local labour will unionise easily. Second, there is the aspirational dimension. In Singur, it was startling to see the dispossessed being promised jobs as janitors by the government. Contrast this with what the mayor of a Chinese city is said to have told those displaced. He admitted that the adults would have to sacrifice, but with the promise that the children of those displaced would have the same opportunities as those of the most privileged. And the state would ensure that. Whether or not this is entirely implemented is not the point. The point is whether any Indian politician looks at the children of the dispossessed in the eye and promises them something genuinely aspirational: a first rate, instead of a third rate, school; a dream of a great job, instead of jobs low in the hierarchy. Land acquisition is often an occasion for reproducing social distance rather than closing the gap. It is important to be reminded of this because land conflicts are not just over compensation. Rather, the compensation issue has become a distillation of a complex set of issues: low trust in the state, resentment at inequalities which the land lottery can only exacerbate, and a politics that rests on the conviction that power is arbitrary, and access to it simply a means of making money. But, cumulatively, land politics is exacerbating inequality.

The fourth instrument for producing some kind of distributive justice is the state itself, primarily through the state provision of public goods, particularly health and education. At one level, this instrument is widely used. Welfare states have been the instrumentality through which lives of the poor have been improved. However, the welfare state has a very complicated relationship with the politics of equality, along several dimensions. First, and most obviously, the effectiveness of welfare states depends on a number of factors, including state capacity. In India, that state capacity is very unevenly developed across time and space. While state capacity is often a function of structural features like the ability to generate revenue, it is also a product of contingent political formations. The unevenness and distrust of state capacity has meant, at the very least, that support for public provisioning is still very limited in India. One striking illustration of this is the fact that our discourse on universal entitlements is so under-ambitious.

There was immense hope that India would universalise a set of economic rights. There was political reason for this optimism. There was a powerful narrative that United Progressive Alliance (UPA) wanted to project: that of universalising a set of basic entitlements from the right to education to employment. And there was the obvious fact that growth had made it possible to enhance governance revenues to the point where these schemes were at least a possibility. But 'scheme' and 'sanction' are two words associated with the state, which both mean themselves and their opposite. 'Sanction' can mean punishment or permission; scheme can mean either a project for public good or a contrivance to subvert it. While the intention behind greater attention to the social sector is genuine, the practice of the welfare state is less impressive. Rights are so tepidly defined even more haphazardly implemented. The brutal truth is that in India it is still a privilege to obtain what is by law a right. And most of the rights we have articulated in recent times are fighting yesterday's battles, not tomorrow's challenges. The Right to Education, for example, has been enacted just at the moment when formal enrolment in a school is no longer a major challenge. What is a major challenge is ensuring quality education for all. Yet, the focus of the legislation is largely on infrastructural inputs. While many of the bye-laws of this legislation have yet to be drafted, there is a real danger that this Act could hinder rather that support the pursuit of quality education. Similarly with food security: what is being proposed lags the practice in many states, including Tamil Nadu and Chhattisgarh. Tamil Nadu has universalised food security much more effectively than the centre is proposing to do. And on health insurance, we have taken the remarkably self-defeating view—we can run separate insurance schemes for the rich and the poor. It is self-defeating simply because insurance is one area where universal schemes are more likely to be sustainable than targeted ones. Hence, while welfare schemes are amelioratively helping people, their relationship to the politics of equality is much more tangential than should be the case.

The ways in which welfare rights are articulated do not produce either solidarity or momentum behind universalising entitlements. Rather it can exacerbate conflicts. This is so for a couple of structural reasons. In theory the different ways in which the government supports different classes of citizens should work in a similar direction. Take one example. NREGA should raise rural wages. This should not affect farmers because they are compensated through minimum support prices (MSP). Raising MSP should not have a detrimental effect on the poor because they can access subsidised food through the public distribution system (PDS). But if one link in this chain does not work (say PDS), these schemes begin to work at cross purposes. So you might raise rural wages, but also inflict food price inflation on the poor. Or you might raise rural wage rates without small farmers who hire labour believing that they have been compensated. The structure of difference creates a competitive politics of which scheme gets more government support, because these schemes are group specific. They are seen as zero sum games.

Second, it is not clear that the government understands fully the dynamics of consumption amongst the poor. Both health and education expenditures amongst the poor are extraordinarily high. As are fuel costs. The costs of these services are driven high by the fact that individuals, even poor individuals are accessing more and more private services, despite greater expansion of government outlays. One way of interpreting this is to say that while the government is able to compensate the poor through welfare schemes; it more than takes away what it gives by imposing costs on them in the form of poor governance.

There is another issue in the politics of welfare that needs some attention. Historically, the Indian state has been relatively bad at targeting. To take just one example, under-inclusion and over-inclusion in BPL (below poverty line) lists is often as high as 50 per cent. Just the history of targeting failures in India suggests that there is an administrative case to be made for universalisation.

For policy purposes, the poverty line is a disingenuous construct. Normatively speaking, this line is an exercise in bad faith because it arbitrarily separates those who can avail benefits from those who cannot. The difference between those immediately above and below the poverty line is miniscule, almost irrelevant from a practical point of view. Yet, that cut-off arbitrarily determines access to benefits. A poverty line, rather than being an expression of a commitment to equality, is a subtle exemplar of discrimination; the cut-off neither bears any relationship to the particular objectives of public policy, nor does it do much justice to the fact that the poor are unevenly deprived along different attributes. Any such list should be made with reference to objectives; the BPL construct is a classic case of state inversion that confuses ends and means.

Then, the process of creating BPL lists produces a strange intellectual contortion. At the outset, there is a survey that supposedly caps how many poor people there are. Then, criteria are evolved to identify which particular households fall within the set. This exercise is essentially a slight sleight of hand: the identifying criteria selected should be such that it does not yield a figure higher than the cap that has been predetermined. If you go by criteria, caps make no sense. If you are committed to the caps, the criteria look arbitrary. Another instance of the state engaging in circular reasoning unhinged to any objectives.

There is the practical difficulty of implementing any criteria for selection. Again, distinguished economists and planners have performed a heroic task of identifying easily implementable criteria that do not rely on complicated and dubious surveys. But objectively verifiable criteria that do not over-include or under-include are hard to design. That being so, the state then resorts to including whole groups, or sometimes districts, in a blunt way that again makes the list discriminatory. It is small wonder that the states are deeply dissatisfied with the centre setting the parameters of the criteria; the centre, in turn, is wary of allowing states to do their own thing fearing anarchy.

So why does the state continue to persist with so flimsy a construct, one that is normatively dubious and practically difficult? While in some schemes the state has made a departure, by making goods universal or by allowing self-targeting, the mystique of the poverty line remains strong. In one part, its hold may be attributed to state inertia—the state often continues along inherited ways of structuring the world even when circumstances have rendered those strategies futile. The other part is ideological: to show that something is being done for the poor, you first have to set the poor apart as a category, and make them a special object. How can we be seen for standing up for the poor if we are treating them as equal citizens rather than as special wards of the state? It is also a way of ensuring that schemes for the poor, by being exclusively for them, receive little attention from others. Ironically, all subsidies which the privileged enjoy, like petrol, are mostly couched in universalistic terms. Yet another part of it is a false fiscal scare: if you universalise rather than target, the costs may turn out to be prohibitive. But this assumption is mostly false: as states like Tamil Nadu which have universalised the PDS have demonstrated, self-targeting limits the fiscal burden. Finally, there is also political expediency. The Ministry of Agriculture and Food and state governments would rather let a catfight break out over who gets included or excluded than focus attention on the real issue at hand: how to design delivery systems with minimal leakage? The messiness of the BPL lists shifts the blame to civil society: if food is not reaching the poor, it can be blamed on the fact that people are gaming BPL lists. However, the real culprits are delivery mechanisms which include everything from the Food Corporation of India (FCI) to the ownership of food shops. Again, states that have done well with PDS focus less on futile controversies over lists and more on structures and technologies of delivery.

At this historical juncture it is clear that the BPL lists are serving very little purpose. They are unnecessary for most schemes that matter to the poor; these schemes can either be universalised or criteria can be evolved that bear some relation to the purpose of the scheme rather than rely on an antecedently given list that we have not got right in over five decades. It will also remove this great scramble in the states to make poverty the sole revenue generation industry. Government needs to make a distinction between two kinds of waste. One where the state incurs slightly higher costs, but the objective is fulfilled: universalisation of PDS will probably take this form. The other form of waste is one which neither saves the state any money, nor fulfills the objective of the scheme. The BPL abets this more insidious kind of waste, as our unconscionable nutrition outcomes show.

Great hope is being placed in the fact that Unique Identification (UID) will help overcome some of these problems. The UID is certainly a necessary instrument for an effective state; the state needs to identify its citizens, and poor citizens, in turn, need an identity. However, it is more likely that the UID scheme will be useful for universal rather than targeted schemes, as it remains uncertain if it will be able to overcome the challenge of targeting. Even as a matter of intellectual history, universal identification has gone hand-in-hand with the creation of universal rather than targeted welfare states. But this is a technical discussion.

For our purposes what is important is this. BPL lists have two consequences for the politics of justice. First, it is usually the case, as the saying goes, that schemes for poor people are poor schemes. As a matter of simple political economy, schemes in which the privileged do not have a stake are not subject to great accountability. Second, instead of producing widespread support for strengthening welfare schemes, it has produced more a politics of getting access to state resources by manipulating the categories of access, which again paradoxically ends up pitting the poor against the slightly less poor.

It is for these reasons that many have thought that a case for a new welfare architecture premised on two components: universalisation and cash transfers. Some of the elements that go into the reasoning behind universalisation have been outlined above. And the case for cash transfers is also often made on both normative and administrative grounds. On normative grounds cash transfers are seen as less paternalistic, they give individuals more control over the choices they exercise and allows them to nuance consumption baskets. On administrative grounds, the argument is that cash transfers reduce the need for the government to be a direct provider of services, and reduces corruption. There is something to both of these arguments. But I am not convinced that simply doing cash transfers will achieve social democratic ends.

The first is simple, a question of time horizon. Cash transfers will require putting in place all the technologies that make citizens 'legible' to the state, to use Jim Scott's phrase. We are probably at least 10 to 15 years away from even this administrative possibility; and to wait for this utopia to dawn will involve sacrificing a generation. But more seriously from a social democratic perspective there are two worries about doing universal cash transfers. The first is more administrative. There is an assumption that if individuals have cash, they can simply access services they need, since a market will develop to cater to those needs. Again, there is something to this assumption. But we also know that there are immense supply bottlenecks particularly in the kinds of services you want citizens to access—health, education, food and so forth. Access to education, to take a prosaic example, depends in part upon zoning laws that have a major impact on the price of schooling. Access to food will in part depend upon the price, which in turn is a product of several factors. And a lot of these will have to do with 'governance' in a broad sense. In the Indian debate direct cash transfers is being seen as a way to bypass governance failures. But it is not clear that the governance deficits that make current schemes weak will not, in turn, haunt the operation of cash transfers. Before cash transfers can work we need to fix supply side bottlenecks.

But normatively, the downside of direct cash transfers is this. There is a danger that it is seen as a substitute for governance, rather than an instrument of governance. It gives up on the state. It will give an ideological legitimation for the thought the state has simply done its job by providing cash transfers, which promote a competitive, private adaptation. There are risks in this that can be best captured by the metaphor of the market for security in India. Security services in India are substantially privatised (even for the poor who rely on local strongmen to provide protection). This privatisation may be producing security. This is a debatable matter. But it is also producing other effects less desirable from a social democratic perspective: sorting among citizens, the creation of enclaves, a reduced sense of allegiance to the idea of a shared public, and a corrosive withdrawal from the state. The social democratic promise is not simply that we have the means of private adaptation. It is also the promise that there is some collective deliberative control over the shared circumstances of our lives. This does not require that we completely agree. But it does involve the recognition that exercising deliberative control can be achieved only through social cooperation with whom we share social worlds.

The debate on where the Indian state needs to get out has been far more pronounced than the debate on where it needs to get in. The current debate over new modalities of service delivery has still no confronted the old truism: if you don't get the state right, you cannot get social democracy right, in whatever form.

There is a final point to be made about welfare states in relation to the politics of equality. Well-functioning welfare states can certainly contribute to an improvement in the lives of the poor. In that sense, they are necessary aspects for the politics of equality. However, welfare, in this sense, does not constitute the politics of equality for a couple of interesting reasons. In principle, access to health and education and other public goods that form a part of the welfare basket should enhance the capabilities of citizens to take advantage of opportunities. But these goods also enhance what one might call individuation. While they allow for a much wider pool of citizens who are capable of being upwardly mobile, they do not address the challenge of structural inequality.

One way of viewing this is by understanding how ideologies of education play out in relation to equality. At a normative level, there is no debate that all citizens must have access to quality education. However, the comparative history of the relationship between education and equality is a little sobering. First, access to equal opportunity in education is quite compatible with high levels of inequality. All equal opportunity does is widen the pool from which successful candidates are drawn; it does not, by itself, erase inequalities between different classes. Or, to be more precise, equality is as much a function of compensation patterns for different jobs than it is of education itself. In an openly competitive system, where the job market does not have the right kind of distribution across incomes classes, equality of educational opportunity is quite compatible with inequality. The more egalitarian an occupation structure, the less severe are the penalties for not coming out on top.

What is the relationship between education and that occupational structure? This subject merits more discussion than it has received. The conventional wisdom is that if educational levels are more equal, there is likely to be greater wage equality. Countries with historically lower levels of inequality achieved this result by equalising education. But there is reason to think that this may not be the entire story; structures of wage bargaining and employment opportunities may be as much part of this story. We have very little sense of what the emerging structure of employment opportunities will be.

Meritocracy also has two peculiar psychic consequences. One of its unintended consequences is that it inculcates the idea that those who are left behind are somehow less worthy, in turn creating a new form of inequality. There is also an argument to be made that, over the last 20 years or so, meritocracy has underpinned an ideology of great inequality. As some social observers have noted, people who rise through the system based on an idea of merit also have a greater sense of entitlement to all the fruits of their effort. What is interesting about income inequality in places ranging from the US to China is not the fact that it exists. Rather, it is that society in general, and particularly people at the top, believed that those at the top deserved what they had. They deserved it, in part, because they rose by the dint of their own talent. There is an odd sense in which privilege has to justify itself, but merit does not. It is perhaps easier to shame an aristocracy than a meritocracy, because the taint of undeserved wealth hovers over them. Since the idea of equality of opportunity in education is so aligned with the idea of meritocracy (or rather the two legitimise each other), education is often not seen as the locus of equality.

This little excursus on meritocracy is interesting in relation to the politics of justice for another reason. It is possible that within the upper classes, which have a sense that they have risen on the dint of merit, there is less support for an egalitarian politics. This is because a society which links achievement to educational attainment also gives the 'achievers' a sense of entitlement. It is perhaps easier to shame an aristocracy by claiming their wealth is undeserved; it is harder to induce guilt in those whose self-perception is that they have attained wealth by legitimate means. While an expanding professional middle class may support the expansion of education, this class may have less patience with any politics of redistribution because it is the very ideology of education that supports their sense of entitlement.

But there is just one more issue I want to flag before closing. Much of the discussion in this paper has focused on distributive aspects of social democracy in India. But the more serious questions of the future will be more on the dimensions of participation. By this I don't simply mean political participation. Rather it will depend upon people's ability to make occupational transitions and participate in wider economic changes. Several of the factors that facilitate this participation have been discussed: education, infrastructure, health, access to credit and so forth. But the big intangible is the form of urbanisation. Will our spatial and social patterns facilitate migration from the rural sector? The most important burden the poor face is often not resource deprivation. It is that the state actively prevents their participation in a wider economy. It does not let them set up businesses; it makes entry barriers to cities enormously high, under the pretext of regulating them, it excludes them. On the ground the simple truth is this: the license permit *raj* has been dismantled only for the privileged: the brunt of the state's licensing mentality is borne by small business, hawkers, small traders, artisans and even labour. The irony of our current emphasis on social democracy is that while it is focusing on the distributive side, it is actively preventing citizens from becoming productive citizens on their own accord. The next generation of conflicts will be less over distributive issues and more over tearing down barriers to participation. We have fragmented and dominated the rural poor through our welfare schemes; and we confine the urban poor to the margins of participation, by making their very presence, their very enterprise hover between legality and illegality. The next generation of conflict and (hope) will come precisely from these citizens, who are trying to wrest their rights of participation from a recalcitrant state.

There is something of a crisis in articulating an egalitarian politics of social justice. Though traditional Marxists believed that there is a subject or bearer of egalitarian politics, namely, the proletariat, there is no such natural subject, in part because all classes are now placed in very complex and contradictory relationships. And, as discussed above several of the instruments of equality have very limited reach. And, even when they are successful in delivering certain goods, they often enhance the ethic of individuation, mobility and competition rather than a politics of equality. It is therefore possible to articulate a discourse of improvement, but there is no locus of social justice.

Identity politics and social democracy

If this is the case, then a profound challenge confronts Indian democracy. When our republic was founded, Ambedkar very famously articulated the life of contradictions India was about to enter: a constitutional guarantee of political equality along side an actual social life marked by deep social and economic inequality. In some respects, this contradiction was not unique to Indian constitutionalism; it has been a feature of most democracies. In fact, the kind of political equality that modern constitutions introduce is often seen as Janus-faced: while these constitutions instantiate a normatively attractive conception of political equality, this feature is, in some respects, seen as threatening. So, while in the former construct, who one is should not matter to what political, or even legal, rights one has (the modern conception of citizenship is, in many ways, founded on this ideal), in terms of the latter, it is as much a doctrine of anonymity. To repeat: who one is, is irrelevant to what rights one has.

Why is this conception of equality a threat? The worry is that this anonymity, while it opens up certain formal avenues of access, can actually also throw a veil over inequality. Indeed, Tocqueville had argued that in societies governed by formal equality (or anonymity), it is harder to mobilise an egalitarian politics. So, as Ambedkar had rightly worried, constitutional anonymity can leave real structures of inequality intact. This is a general challenge faced by democracies. But, in a society marked by the particular form of inequality India had, this fear of constitutional anonymity was real and powerful. The challenge was to address this fear while, at the same time, retaining the attractive normative features of constitutional anonymity. It was in this context that the recognition of caste as an axis of equality became central to Indian politics. The idea was that whatever constitutional anonymity might do, it must not render this particular form of inequality invisible, particularly in the case of Dalits.

But I want to draw attention to two features of this politics and the impact it has had on the politics of social justice. The first I have discussed at some length in *The Burden of Democracy* (2003) but the gist of the argument bears repeating here because it explains some difficulties of egalitarian politics in India. Later in this section I will draw out some new implications of this argument to address one interesting analytical question about the salience of caste over class politics in India. I must, however, make full disclosure and state emphatically that I worry about the new forms in which caste is being entrenched in Indian political discourse. But here I try and analyse why caste defines the contours of what we think of as equality so insistently.

Democratic aspirations are in some senses tied to the idea of equality. The idea of equality is complex and immediately invites the question, 'Equality of what?' Income? Wealth? Political equality? Opportunity? But understanding the political trajectory of Indian democracy does not require beginning with an answer to this question. In any society, especially democratic ones, the meaning and scope of equality will be fiercely contested and will be the basis for ideological divisions. It is the psychological impulses that lie behind the demand for equality; the existential burdens that any demand for equality seeks to address that leave their imprint on politics. The variety of structures—caste, class, patriarchy—that maintain and reproduce inequality are all too familiar, and Indian society exemplifies many of these to an unconscionable degree. However, inequality is not simply a structural condition in which people find themselves; a condition measured by such objective indicators as Gini coefficients or development indices. Inequality is resented, and becomes salient for politics, because it is an experienced existential burden that inflicts complex psychic costs by diminishing a sense of self. Not all forms of inequality are unjust. And the ways in which the experience of inequality shapes the self is a complex subject. But, fundamentally, inequality imposes the profoundest existential burdens when it is seen as denying individuals the minimum regard due to them, or when it constantly puts them is situations that are experienced as humiliating.

It is now a commonplace observation, thanks largely due to Rousseau who most vividly wrote about the psychic burdens of inequality, that most human beings, unless they have been dehumanised to an unimaginable degree, place some value upon themselves. This does not mean that they are selfish; rather, they wish that the value they place upon themselves be somewhere affirmed. The institutions and practices of most inegalitarian societies deny individuals this basic form of recognition, the recognition that they are valuable in some sense, that they have some moral standing. In most such societies, this quest for having one's worth affirmed will take debased forms. The only way in which one can secure others' acknowledgement is either by seeking to dominate them, or by putting up a convincing show of attributes and accomplishments that are capable of winning the acknowledgment of others. This is because the only way one can get acknowledged is by having power over them, by being able to say, 'I know I am worth something, because I have power over you.' Those not in a position to dominate secure acknowledgement in other more self-debasing ways. They might say: 'Pay attention to me, because I can make your comparative sense of self-worth even more pronounced by debasing myself for you, by flattering you.' Inegalitarian societies where there is no public acknowledgment of individuals' self-worth will be characterised by both a fierce competition to dominate and, paradoxically, an exaggerated sense of servility. Both the desire to dominate and a kind of self-abasement, Rousseau suggested, would lead us to lead inauthentic lives: lives that were not governed by values or concerns that were properly our own. Such societies would also frequently give individuals reasons to consider their self-respect injured: inegalitarian societies will routinely humiliate it members.

The aspiration to democracy is, in part, an aspiration to have one's moral worth acknowledged. The charge that an arrangement or a set of procedures is 'undemocratic' carries moral resonance, not simply because it describes a faulty procedure, but because it is accompanied by the sentiment that, in being undemocratic, someone's moral standing has been slighted. Acknowledgment by others of one's moral worth is at least partly constitutive of one's sense of self-respect. A sense of self-respect is necessary to have a firm sense of one's own value, to have the conviction not only that life is worth living but worth living well. The absence of self-respect can be corrosive; it can make most pursuits meaningless.

In some senses, equal voting rights are a dramatic expression of an individual's moral worth. But, unless the collective arrangements of society give individuals the minimum bases for social self-respect, of which the equal right to vote is just one aspect, society is likely to be characterised by an odd combination of fierce competition for domination and abject servility; and, when neither succeeds, violence becomes a way of announcing ones moral standing. What institutions and objectives can satisfy the minimum requirements of acknowledging people's moral worth is a complex question? But, what is necessary is that, at the very least citizens are free from abject necessity. They are not subject to invidious and humiliating forms of discrimination. They need access to a set of goods that are minimal requirements for being a capable agent in the modern world? The great liberal hope, embodied in the Indian constitution, was that ameliorating serious material deprivation, and an effective equal standing in the eyes of the law would go some way towards mitigating the desire to have one's worth affirmed, either by dominating others, or by having one's own sense of self fashioned by what we think might get others attention. Indeed, arguably, if the basis for social self-respect is adequately protected, the existence of other inequalities might matter less, because they could not be used as a base from which to dominate, despise or negate others.

Conceptually speaking, there are many different ways in which equality of moral worth can be affirmed. One might say, for instance, that we are equal in the eyes of God. Within Indian history, religious traditions, and traditions of dissent, these modes have always been available. But they did not result in effective and enduring demands for ordering the texture of social relationships. It is not an impossibility to assert both that we are equal in the eyes of god and that a hierarchical social organisation such as caste is defensible; indeed, the theoretical radicalism of so many claims to equality in the past was compromised by their practical conservatism. It can be granted that Indian history provides at least some conceptual resources for affirming equality. But the introduction of democracy is radical. Democracy is a way of affirming human dignity by granting individuals civic standing. In a democracy, the desire for having one's moral worth affirmed and for emptying social space of humiliation is given open social legitimation and expression.

But, paradoxically, the struggle to affirm one's moral worth do not necessarily take the form of a demand for justice. Indeed, if Rousseau's diagnosis is plausible, the desire for having one's worth acknowledged can express itself in all kinds of debased forms—some which might require debasing others. Indeed, the paradox is that while individuals and groups can be acutely conscious of society's indifference towards them, they can, in turn, be acutely indifferent towards others. Indeed, you would almost experience this to the case in highly inegalitarian societies. The only meaning empowerment has in such a society is power over others, some claim of power or privilege or access that sets you apart, rather than a generally shared sense of empowerment as such. The paradox is that the more unequal the background institutions and practices of society, the more likely it is that politics will be a struggle to displace the holders of power rather than an ambition to bring about social transformation. The struggle to move ahead will not be a common struggle for justice (as little commonality exists) but a competitive quest for power. A society that is adept at humiliating its members is, as Rousseau convincingly argued, more likely to make them adept at humiliating others rather than teach them about justice. This perhaps explains one of the paradoxes at the heart of Indian politics. There are few other democracies where the universalist language of injustice, rights, even constitutionalism, is so profusely used and has become part of so many political mobilisations. But it is a stratagem for particular individuals or groups to gain access to power, not an acknowledgment of the due claims of all. Discourses of law, constitutionalism, rights, justice and obligations are the languages in which particular grievances are expressed or interests advanced without the least acknowledgment of reciprocal or parallel interests and grievances of others. A sense of justice towards someone presupposes a sense of reciprocity, it presupposes that you acknowledge others. The more the social distance, the less likely that such reciprocity obtains. It is quite possible for a democracy to experience great clamour for recognition by particular individuals and groups without these resulting in diffusion of norms of justice. This follows the general pattern of the ways in which Indian society has been democratised. Democracy in India has advanced through the competitive negotiations between groups, each competing for their interests, rather than the diffusion of democratic norms. It is, in some senses, a contingent outcome of social conflicts, not necessarily a deep-seated norm. The purpose of political mobilisation has not been to make the state more accountable but to get access to or share in its power.

This conception of politics was most dramatically manifest in the way in which citizens often thought of the state. Given the commanding presence of the state, underwritten by an ideology of state-led development, access to state power became, for good or for ill, the principal means of improving the life-chances of individuals. In an economy with slow and sluggish growth, averaging under three per cent, the state became a disproportionate provider of opportunity. Even access to opportunities and resources outside the state were mediated through state influence. Indeed, in one sense, politics, through access to state power, has become the swiftest route to social mobility, much more so than the market or education. Access to the state gave jobs and a likely class status that was better than anything available outside the state; the discretionary power the state conferred on all its officials was experienced by many as empowerment, or at least an escape from the subordination that resulted from being at the receiving end of that power. Access to state power was about the only way of ensuring that one counted for somebody. Big scams do not tell the real story of the connection between corruption and social mobility. It is the thousands of petty fortunes that are made through the state that seemed to most citizens a surer bet of improving their class status than the uncertainties of the market. One of the peculiar features of Indian society has been that political power became almost the sole means of social mobility. Is there any other sphere of activity that is less stratified and more representative of Indian society than politics?

However, the consequence of the growth of the state and its undoubted success in producing a kind of social mobility is attended by a paradox: that while the state is seen as a means for social mobility, it is not, for the most part, seen as the provider of public goods. The state exists primarily to satisfy the private interests of collusive interest groups. Although it is undoubtedly true that the dominant proprietary classes will have a disproportionate share of the state's resources, there is enormous fluidity in the nature of social groups that have at different times gained access to the state. The net result, however, was that almost never has that state been governed by a public philosophy; it is rather a high stakes competitive game in which individuals or groups seek advantages along particularistic lines. The *raison d'etre* of politics, the aims of public representation, are no longer to respond to fundamental issues impinging upon common life but to organise the state's power in such a manner that its resources can be channelled in the direction of particular groups or individuals to protect their exclusive interests. The cumulative impact has been a view of the state and constitutional fabric as institutions to be manipulated according to particularistic interests. One can appropriate Hegel's melodramatic phrase, "the state exists no longer." What Hegel meant in his context was that the state and constitution were being manipulated to serve particular interests, that the decisions that emanated from it did not carry the necessity of principle, but only the arbitrariness of expedience. To be sure, there are restraints internal to expedience, but how effective these restraints are will be a matter of some concern. It is extraordinary that the association of the state with the 'public' or the state with the 'common', the two sustaining associations of the state, are wearing so thin.

This politics continues because it has also acquired great normative depth. And it is this normative depth that I want to focus on in the remainder of this paper. The *de facto* competition of groups to gain access to state power is now being given constitutional depth in different ways. First, as Sudipta Kaviraj (2005) pointed out several years ago, India had a discourse of equality in which equality was not about transcending caste. It was rather about claiming equality on the basis of caste. The measure of equality becomes the share of caste power in institutions like the state. The most extreme version of equality on the basis of caste is the legitimacy of what you might call the mirror theory of representation. On this view, institutions are legitimate only in so far as the distribution of power within them mirrors, broadly speaking, the relevant social cleavages in society. To a certain extent, the attraction of this ideal is understandable. If groups are systematically excluded from structures of power, there is prima facie a case that a society is operating on mechanisms of exclusion. There was consensus that these mechanisms very visibly and oppressively operated in the case of Dalits. But, slowly, this narrative was expanded to include other 'backward castes'. And, one of the strange ironies of modern India is that the historical narrative of subjugation and marginalisation that was specific to Dalits has now been appropriated by other groups.

A society like India requires some form of affirmative action. What form that should take, who the state should target, why we should target them and how we should target them is an important subject that is best left for another occasion. Here I simply want to focus on some of the political and normative underpinnings of the kind of emphasis on reservation that we have institutionalised, and the implications of these assumptions for the politics of social justice. One way of bringing out the peculiarity of these assumptions is to ask: how will the demand for equality be expressed? How will society ensure that constitutional anonymity does not throw a veil over inequality. One other possible criterion for ensuring this, and one that has often been debated in the public sphere, is the use of economic criteria. At the time of independence, there was an understanding that this criterion would not cater to the specific form of injustice and discrimination Dalits faced. However, using this criterion could help address other forms of 'backwardness'.

But we have come to believe that using economic criteria or class as a basis for reservation or affirmative action does not express a politics of social justice. One oft-cited reason for this is administrative: caste is thought of as a more easily identifiable characteristic than income. Another reason was that the caste/class overlap was very strong particularly in the case of Dalits, even though this overlap is becoming much more complicated, particularly amongst non-Dalits, as the caste and occupation linkage is becoming weaker. But there is also a deeper reason at work. Reservations based on anything other than ascriptive criteria like caste are not seen as expressing a politics of equality for the following reasons. The first reason can be best highlighted by a little semantic experiment. Think of what the phrase 'equality of classes' might mean. As applied to distributive justice, it can mean only the abolition of classes; otherwise the phrase is a little bit of an oxymoron. And, for reasons mentioned in the first section of this paper, we do not have any instruments for the abolition of class. However, the phrase 'equality of caste' is not in this sense an oxymoron, as it does not require the abolition of caste. And the degree to which we have achieved equality of caste can be crudely measured by the share of different caste groups in structures of power.

Just continue this line of thinking for a second. What are the differences between how we represent caste mobility and class mobility? If a poor person becomes middle class, this may reflect a salutary fact that society has opened up avenues for opportunity. And, precisely by virtue of this mobility the person is able to change his class. A society with great class mobility is a desirable one; at the very least, it potently expresses the thought that one's birth does not determine the opportunities one might have. Class mobility is compatible with two things. First, it presupposes the continued existence of classes and inequality—all it suggests is that individuals can change their position. And the individuals who are so able to change their position no longer represent the class they came from.[2] A poor person becoming middle class is an instance of a poor person becoming middle class: there is a change in this person's position on the axis of deprivation being measured. Such a movement provides a measure of mobility; it is not seen as providing a measure of equality.

Caste operates somewhat differently. A Mala or Maddiga becoming rich may change their class status, but they remain a Mala or a Maddiga. They can still represent the caste from which they came in the calculus of power sharing. They may have become rich or powerful, but their position on the axis of deprivation being measured (in this instance, caste) does not change. In fact, one of the ethical dilemmas posed by reservation is the way in which it perpetuates a compulsory identity on citizens through officially-sanctioned categories: once a member of a particular caste, always a member of a particular caste. But this normatively disturbing feature of the way in which we want to perpetuate caste as a compulsory identity also makes it attractive as a locus of social justice. This is because caste now comes to be a measure of equality by virtue of an immutable characteristic. In a way, 'caste' answers the question "Equality with respect to what?" in a manner no other characteristic does, precisely because of its constructed immutability. Equality with respect to 'class' would require the abolition of class. Equality with respect to caste does not require

2. I do not mean that they cannot have views that are sympathetic to the poor, or that they cannot identify with the poor or act on their behalf. The reference to representation here is not a reference to substantive views in this sense. It is simply that on the dimension of class they have become someone else.

this abolition. This immutability can also be combined with a simple measure: simply count the 'representatives' of each caste in the share of power. This is impossible to do with class because the mere act of access to power transforms the individual's structural relation to class.

This institutionalisation of caste as the basis of equality has some interesting consequences. First, it is a form of legitimising class difference. Since we have limited instruments to achieve deep equality, class is now seen as an almost legitimate form of inequality. Caste has become the form in which the politics of social justice has come to be sublimated.

Second, in India there is no serious discourse on the relationship between justice and discrimination. This is, in part, due to the fact that the category of discrimination was specific to the Dalit experience. But the appropriation of the Dalit narrative by other communities has meant that power-sharing rather than discrimination has become the central normative category in our thinking on justice. And, in a way there is a tacit assumption by 'upper castes' as well that since a share to power has been reserved, discrimination is no longer a category one needs to think about.

Third, because equality can now be claimed only on the basis of an immutable identity, there is a growing clamour for the state to institutionalise these. Almost everyone knows that the politics of social equality depends on particular categories of identity being recognised and codified. The latest demand for a caste census is an inevitable outcome of this recognition. Social classifications recreate and solidify the realities rather than merely representing them. However, the focus of the politics of justice has shifted to identifying the appropriate identity categories that need to be so codified. This will, in coming years, take new forms. For instance, there will be greater political pressure to create new sub-divisions within broad categories like Dalit or other backward castes. The demand for these sub-divisions is inherent in the logic of equality on the basis of caste.

Fourth, identity politics and other forms of politics centred around welfare and justice are often posed as alternatives. Recent

Indian history has shown that identity politics is the form in which the politics of social justice is expressed. And there is no reason to believe that the force of this politics is going to diminish in the near future. Though its forms may change, the categories deployed will be contested and there will be a demand to expand this politics into new domains, including the private sector. The central axis of this politics will remain the demand for equality on the basis of an immutable characteristic.

The politics of social justice is at a deep impasse. The fear that constitutional anonymity must not draw a veil over inequality has led to the constitutionalisation of caste, as it were. It has provided a ready locus and measure of equality. But its price has been a move away from the ideals of Indian constitutionalism and the essence of democracy in two respects. It has reinforced the tyranny of compulsory identities and has reduced justice to crude and limited measures of power-sharing. Caste becomes the locus of a politics of equality in part because there is deep structural pessimism about addressing other forms of inequality. India is going through a profound change, and the gains in both growth and poverty reduction are very real and widespread. But these changes do not, by themselves, address the politics of social justice.

Concluding observations

India's growth has opened up new possibilities. It has certainly given the state more resources and potential for institutionalising welfare schemes. It is also producing new forms of improvement and mobility. However, it has also increased the potential for rent-seeking. Indian politics in recent times has been undergoing two subtle but pronounced shifts that may have larger lessons for the politics of democratic accountability. First, while identity politics—a politics structured around ascriptive identities—is still powerful in India, it will be complemented by another dynamic. Second, the rates of anti-incumbency—the likelihood of a sitting legislator or state government being re-elected—are coming down. Some argue that this is finally leading to a politics that is more focused on development than other issues.

What explains this changing trend? One hypothesis is that economic growth has allowed a phenomenal growth in the increase of government revenues, averaging more than 15 per cent over the five years prior to the financial crisis. The scale of government spending that is now possible is altering the incentives for politicians. Till the late 1990s, when the budgets of state governments experienced only incremental growth, the best-performing state government had difficulty in signalling that it made anything but a marginal impact on the lives of voters. The default position of both voters and politicians was that the marginal impact of the state was actually low. Hence, it made more sense to mobilise on identity than developmental coalitions. It also did not really make a difference who came and who went. Not surprisingly, India had amongst the highest anti-incumbency rates in the world.

Now the scale of spending has changed. To dramatically illustrate the issue, Bihar, India's poorest state, has given out contracts for the construction of more than 17,000 kilometres of roads this year, more than the previous two decades combined. A welfare scheme worth ₹ 1,000 crores used to be considered a big scheme; compare this to the National Rural Employment Guarantee Scheme which now costs more than ₹ 100,000 crores. This is leading some politicians to the conclusion that they have enough resources to send credible signals to large sections of the population; that is, in spending terms, their impact is no longer marginal. If they perform well, they will be rewarded by the voters. There is an argument in political science literature that, with the exception of India, you had to be a middle income country for serious democracy to take root. Political scientists often interpreted this to mean that you needed a middle class. An alternative interpretation would be that a politics of accountability kicks in only when the state is of a sufficient size.

For voters too the stakes of politics are becoming higher not lower with rising government spending, and it also pays to be more discriminating amongst alternative choices. Voters, particularly at the state level, are for the most part becoming more discriminating, and the vicious cycles of knee-jerk anti-incumbency are over. This will set in motion an healthier politics of accountability, and is making possible a shift away from the politics of identity to the politics of development. We have a long way to go, but this change has been made possible by growth. However, the hypothesis that bears investigation is this: Does the scale and rate of change of government spending induce a political demand for accountability?

The second interesting feature of enhanced state expenditures, it could be argued, is that they lead to more corruption: there is evidence that the rate of rents being collected from assorted instruments—telecom licenses, road contracts, mining leases, real estate regulation—is phenomenal. In this sense, growth and enhanced government revenues impede accountability. But there is another dynamic at work. While the quantum of corruption may be increasing, the structure of corruption may be changing in ways that are socially beneficial. As enough rent can now be collected from the kind of activities listed earlier, rent-seeking politicians may feel it unnecessary to extract rents from every single programme, particularly those that affect ordinary citizens. So, for instance, when hundreds of crores can be made in real estate deals, or licensing, is there really any need to extract money from the fodder programme, or the integrated child development scheme? Validating evidence on corruption is tricky, but there is some evidence that this is beginning to happen. Politicians are moving to create a virtuous cycle, where they can collect rents without extracting them hugely from social programmes. If this hypothesis is plausible, another prediction would follow. It is precisely in poor states, where there are fewer opportunities for rent collection from large infrastructure contracts, real state values and so forth, that you will still find more incentives to extract rents from social programmes on health and so forth.

The third mechanism by which enhanced state resources might produce accountability is that it allows the state to invest in instruments necessary for accountability. For example, one of the big reasons for the failure of so many anti-poverty programmes in India was that the state simply did not have instruments to identify and target beneficiaries. Part of the inefficiency of the state comes from the fact that it is not right sized. If increased state revenues can allow the state to invest in its own capacity, it could lead to a better functioning state.

It would be unwise to minimise the hurdles in the path of genuinely accountable governments in low income democracies. And, though social mobilisation and civil society monitoring helps, these instruments have their limitations. But there might be a deeper dynamic at work, that allows the cunning of unreason (to use John Dunn's phrase) to do its work in mitigating the ill-effects of unaccountable government.

Perhaps the best that we can hope for at the current conjuncture is 'small equality' effects that growth and welfare can produce. But how we will resolve the contradictions that Ambedkar talked of still remains an open question? Where will be the locus of a politics of justice? Will the historical logic that made caste the dominant paradigm in which we think of justice continue? And, will it crowd out the essential challenge we face? This challenge is best summed up in the striking formulation of the Chinese thinker Qin Hui: "What is excessive now is not liberalism or social democracy, but oligarchy and populism. It is therefore essential to critique both oligarchy from a liberal standpoint and populism from a social democratic standpoint." Reading these words I wonder if there can be any better formulation of the challenges for Indian democracy. And, I wonder how far we are from meeting these challenges.

References

Kaviraj, Sudipta (2005). "Democracy and Inequality in India", in Zoya Hasan and Francine Frankel (eds.), *Transforming India*. Oxford: Oxford University Press.

Mehta, Pratap Bhanu (2003). *The Burden of Democracy*. New Delhi: Penguin.

Mookherjee, Dilip and Debraj Ray (2003). "Persistant Inequalities", *Review of Economic Studies* 70(2): 369-93.

Pzeworski, Adam (2010). *Democracy and the Limits of Self Government*. Cambridge: Cambridge University Press.

5

SUNIL KHILNANI

The Idea of India as Social Democracy

> On the 26th of January 1950, we are going to enter into a life of contradictions. In politics we will have equality and in social and economic life we will have inequality. In politics we will be recognising the principle of one man one vote and one vote one value. In our social and economic life, we shall, by reason of our social and economic structure, continue to deny the principle of one man one value. How long shall we continue to live this life of contradictions? How long shall we continue to deny equality in our social and economic life? If we continue to deny it for long, we will do so only by putting our political democracy in peril.
>
> B.R. Ambedkar, speech in Constituent Assembly, 25 November 1949

> We want social security, but we have to recognise that social security comes only when a certain stage of development has been reached. Otherwise we shall have neither social security nor any development.
>
> J.L. Nehru, "The Basic Approach", 15 August 1958

I

The recognition that India would over time need to balance the political democracy inaugurated by the constitution's commitment to universal suffrage with some sort of social democracy and equality dates back to the very origins of our republic—and it serves at once as the anchor and the horizon of Indian politics. From Ambedkar's ominous warning that our political democracy would be 'blown up' if efforts to establish a sense of social citizenship were not pursued, to Nehru's efforts always to keep this dimension in mind in shaping India's policy choices, our most clear-headed political thinkers have sought to remind us of the need to bring closer together the dimensions of political and social citizenship. And yet, six decades on and more, we are very far from reducing this divide.

We are today at a moment when our democracy has deepened, and our economic growth, helped by the extension of the market and India's growing connection to the global economy, has accelerated. Yet, across our polity we see at the same time a greater resort to violence today than perhaps ever before. The failure of our efforts to build and sustain a sense of social citizenship are now putting in question the legitimacy of our democracy—and are causing many to secede from the political community, even as they feel excluded from the benefits of the market. After several decades of rising participation in electoral democracy, it may be that we are reaching a plateau (it was striking that in the 2009 elections, despite extensive efforts by various NGOs and groups to get people out to vote, this seemed to make little difference—especially in urban India).

It's not that we haven't, over the past six decades, tried to deal with the contradictions between political equality and social inequality. It was never, of course, part of the constitutional ambition to entirely erase the divide between political equality and social inequality—that ambition has often been licence for self-proclaimed egalitarian projects that are at best overbearingly paternalist, or worse, suppress political liberties. But even our present efforts to keep within humanly and politically tolerable limits, the degree of social and economic inequality in our society, appear inherently flawed. They oscillate, more in hope than conviction, between a belief that rapid growth will of itself spread its benefits across the social hierarchy and across an India that is definitely not Flat (a sort of waiting room theory of equality—your turn will, may, come)—what I would call an economistic vision; a quota view of redistribution, which sectionalises and divides society into social categories, castes groups, who are selected to receive benefits; and a rights-based legislative approach, which has lead to the creation of a multiplicity of social programmes that seek to deliver these rights to target groups. There are, by some estimates, around 150 or so major central government welfare schemes aimed at reaching the poor, as well as many more at the state level; there exist some dozen or so national commissions to deal with forms of injustice, inequality, and discrimination experienced by different minority communities; and there are, of course, a very large array of subsidies which are supposed to assist those groups who have been able to get their interests represented (all at a total cost calculated in 2007-08 to be ₹@180,000 crore: Kapur *et al.*, 2008).

What we have is a deeply fragmented reality when it comes to opportunities for economic and social advance, and to dealing with the risks of India's new economic identity. That fragmentation of the opportunity space available to citizens is at least four-fold, with rigid boundaries between the fragments. The split is between a) a dynamic private economic sector, which is delivering real goods to many, and raising the hopes of all; b) a fraught and bitterly contested politics of reservations, affirmative action, fought out between caste groups each seeking a larger allocation of resources to themselves, to maximise a calculus of quotas; c) a proliferating tangle of social welfare policies, dispensed at central and state level—with variable effects across the country (wherever locally effective—and some clearly have been—their overall effect, however, often serves only to accentuate disparities: a programme like NREGS appears to work least effectively where it is most needed, for example in UP, Bihar—the uptake in these states has lagged behind uptake in richer states), and with large wastage and misuse; and d) those altogether outside the pale of these enclaves, who have taken to violent efforts in desperate action for change.

If we could find a way to articulate it, an Indian social democracy could speak to some of these issues. Understood as basic provisions of a welfare state—food, education, health—it can claim to make the Indian economy more efficient through building essential human capital: and as such it provides compelling reasons for India's entrepreneurs to be prepared to invest in this task. It can also claim to advance the ideals of justice that are foundational to our republic: it can offer principles to seek remedies against discriminatory treatment of individuals on the basis of their socially-defined identities. But an Indian social democracy would go further, and in its own a distinctive direction.

The social democratic ideal in India has never been in thrall to the European experience of social democracy. For a start, it was always and unambiguously committed to democracy—as compared with European social democracy, which only gradually and often painfully came round to this commitment. As we take up our Constitutional promise and seek to extend its practical scope in India today, the task will be to give greater sustenance to the political right to democracy by implanting it in a more secure social world.

Indeed, the idea of India as a social democracy, as it was formulated by men like Ambedkar and Nehru, possessed a directly political dimension: and it's that that I particularly want to emphasise in my paper, since the philosophical dimensions have been raised and the economic aspects will receive discussion in other papers. For Ambedkar and Nehru were centrally concerned with building and sustaining a sense of the nation: of giving Indians, one by one—as individual citizens—reasons to believe in the idea of India.

Both men understood that moving India in the direction of social democracy would be a slow, gradual process—exactly because of that, they took a long view, seeing the building of social democracy against a distant future horizon. And, while each had intimate knowledge of European and Western examples and ideas, as Nehru wrote: "We have new problems for which there are no parallels or historical precedents elsewhere...We have thus to do our own thinking, profiting by the example of others, but essentially trying to find a path for ourselves suited to our own conditions." Both too did not seek to specify in advance the future society they might envisage: they were committed to constitutionalism and democracy not just as a means, but also as an intrinsically valuable process through which the very goals and ends of the society would come to be defined. Both men, therefore, rejected the options, at either end of the spectrum of Indian approaches to the problem of social inequality—represented by the revolutionary violence of the Communists and by Gandhi's constructive programme of social action—options that in fundamental ways denied the primacy of politics.

Most significant, and the point I want to emphasise here, was their conviction that to sustain an idea of the Indian nation one must appeal not to one among the many diverse identities that Indians possessed, but rather one had to persuade Indians, one by one—as individuals—that they were participants in a collective project of common development. Ambedkar spoke of the need for Indians to become a nation in 'social and psychological sense'—a task he saw as far more difficult than in the United States, because India's peoples were divided into thousands of castes—which Ambedkar saw as essentially 'anti-national'.

We are now approaching that horizon that Ambedkar and Nehru had projected somewhere in our future. As we speak, rightly, of India regaining its place in the world economy and recouping its share of global trade, so too we must recognise another momentous fact: we have it now in our capacity not just to end poverty in our country, but also to address some basic requirements of our citizen's welfare and of their exposure to the new risks that come with integration into the global economy.

In this instance, we must be mindful of the lessons of the west and elsewhere, as they have sought to build social welfare and justice into their fabric—but just as mindful that those lessons might be limited for country of India's scale, diversity, and with its huge informal economy. Take the rightfully acclaimed earned income tax credit in the US which offers incentives to the poor to seek work and provides a redistribution of income at tax-time. It's done a great deal in America to bring the underground, informal economy to the surface, and to materially benefit poor workers. However it is inapplicable as a widespread equalising instrument in a society that has India's rates of unemployment. The limits apply too to the incentives and disincentives of social policy. Thus, the concern—widespread in this new century—with welfare dependence, the break down of habits of work and personal effort, presupposes a state that actually provides a wide range of welfare:

for instance, housing and health care to its citizens as in the UK—something that Indians can only dream about.

Our situation demands its own thinking and experimentation. The measures of India's uneven growth are well-known: especially the wide disparities in the growth rates and trajectories of India's leading and laggard states; between India's booming cities, large and smaller, and the vast rural hinterland—leading more and more to move into the cities, yet bringing with them few relevant skills to benefit from opportunities that may be found there; the staggering social inequalities in a country that boasts growing numbers of billionaires (in proportion to GDP, only Russia has more billionaires) and hundreds of millions whose daily lives hover in poverty; the many social groups who remain subject to discrimination of various sorts.

These disparities, which are at once deepening old lines of conflict and opening up new ones too, are proliferating within a society that—to a degree different from the other new growth economies—is already distinctively diverse and vast in scale. In Brazil, for all its racial and religious diversity, they still all speak a single language; in China, the state remains in close control of cultural and social identities, and can impose its own national idea; South Africa's internal diversity does, in its depth, in some ways parallel India—but in scale it is no larger than an average-sized Indian state.

Seen purely from the point of view of sustaining a shared idea of the nation, of a sense of social citizenship, we should be troubled by the overall effects of our economic growth path. Especially troubled, if we factor into our disparate and fragmented economic reality the fact that we are a society whose composition will continue to become younger for some years to come. In the next five years, we are going to see the entry of more than 60 million young Indians enter the work force—with most of them at least likely to find such work as they can in the informal, unorganised sector. India's' young might temporarily place their faith in a kind of market nationalism: but that is not sustainable. An increasingly young nation, we are also diminishingly able to give the young reasons to believe in a positive idea of the Indian nation.

We will, therefore, need to invent ways to address the mounting strains on India's unity. When we speak today of two 'countries', Bharat and India, we are in fact invoking an old trope, that can be found in all democracies during periods of economic growth and social change (think of Disraeli's 'two nations'). And we know that one method, resorted to in European history, to try to reintegrate divided societies is to urge unity against an external, or sometimes also an internal, enemy—to foster a coercive, aggressive nationalism. Indeed, we have our own political leaders and parties who would have us pursue such methods. To avoid that destructive path, we'll need a positive definition of the nation—composed of citizens rather than opposed to enemies.

II

In recent times, partly as result of unease at the extent to which the search for social justice has come to rest on the politics of reservations, there have been two sorts of responses to the problem of social inequalities.

The first has urged a more wide-ranging and effective delivery to citizens of the rights promised them by the Constitution—by strengthening the Constitution's Directive Principles, that promissory list of social and economic provisions that the Indian state has long offered but never delivered to its citizens. The effort now is to make them justiciable in the courts: to turn ought into is. There is a good deal to be said for such initiatives—since it does help to spread a sense of rights among people. But such approaches do little to deliver these rights to those who need them most, and its not clear that they can actually lead to the state's greater accountability to citizens. There isn't all that much reason to be enthused by the Indian state spending more resources on building, ostensibly, schools and hospitals—proliferating unmanned structures, the domain of goats, pigeons, and the occasional determined children who wait in hopeless hope for their teacher to turn up. In fact, in India education and health are not domains that are likely to create shared forms of experience, a sense of community or citizenship: they are instead perpetrators of inequality, as the rich ever extend their secessionary domains. The constitutional rights—to education, to food—which are now being strengthened still have to be delivered by the state: the very same state which for so long has shown little interest in seeing these actually delivered, and whose incentives don't appear much changed.

A second approach has urged more precise targeting of policies towards those specific groups that are judged as subject to discrimination and deprivation. It reminds us of the multiple axes of disadvantage—and the need to hold these up to the light for public policy recognition. To accomplish this one requires much more detailed information than we currently have about specific social groups, including sub-groups within castes, in order to identify the differences in life chances that are internal to caste groups—hence the argument for a caste census. It relies on being able to devise a transparent 'calculus of compensation'—which could be acceptable to all, but which is always likely to appear discretionary and therefore subject to intense political contest and practical bending.

This approach is heavily paternalistic. It assumes that an expert elite possesses insight not just into people's needs but also how they should be provided for. More significantly, the targeted approach assumes the ideal conditions of an honest, effective, accountable state—and the possibility of rational evidence-based debate. I long for the day when this could happen.

In practice, current government policies designed to alleviate poverty by targeting or improving welfare have often strengthened networks of corruption, and diverted benefits to elites—or to those who enjoy their patronage. It's no wonder then that to many poor people, the market for all its harshness looks, in its judgements and calculations, more transparent than the capricious, self-serving state and its many, confusing programmes.

Most seriously from the point of view of a cohesive national idea, the current polices of targeting and reservations, with their politicised and discretionary qualifying criteria effectively serve to divide the poor—and often to set them against one another.

III

Perhaps it's time therefore to consider another line of approach: one that takes seriously the need for a universalist form of social provision, but which is less dependent in the short term on a functioning state. In the long term, however, this approach might well create more citizen demand for greater accountability from governments; and it could foster a sense of belonging to the political community. To some in government the prospect of mobilised citizen demand might seem a dangerous proposition—but it's crucial to the future of Indian government and a cohesive democracy.

When I speak of a universal (if, at this stage in our development, minimal) social provision, I hark back to Nehru and Ambedkar—for the starting point of an Indian social democracy has to be a reinvention of the basic ethos of our constitution: a commitment to constitutional universalism—to a conception of citizenship which sees Indians as members in a common project. That idea has been blurred and hazed by virtually every development in our history since the introduction of universal suffrage—from our system of civil law to our legislation for social and economic protections and advancement: all of which have been about the recognition of difference.

In what can be in part explained as a reaction to this, we've seen, in the conflicts that wracked us from the late 1980s to the early years of the last decade, the dangerous and destructive effects of claiming to unite Indians, to create a sense of the nation, by negative definitions—through evoking fear and hatred of the other. What's clear is the need, in a society that has the energy of youth and the frustrations of unequal life chances, for a positive definition of the nation.

And now we possess some of the means that might help articulate such a definition. The first steps will be limited—but they can help to set a process under way, which could see the creation of small, cumulative 'citizenship' effects.

Only by setting in place universalist forms of social provision and protection can we hope to bridge the widening gap between, on the one hand, the intense struggles over the discretionary distributions that are involved in reservations, the corruption and wastage of targeted programmes, and on the other, the resort to violent means in pursuit of some hoped-for more egalitarian distribution of resources.

Pranab Bardhan (2013) in his excellent paper speaks about the economics of his notion of a universal basic income, and the order of cost that some minimal provision is likely to involve. I want instead to focus my remarks on the political reasons for why a universalist approach, as against more particularising ones, has to be the one we now adopt.

So what could we do? Is there an idea that we might make our own?

As we think of a more universalist conception of social welfare, we could take and develop a lesson from what is at once at the base of the idea of India and also one of our historical success stories: Democracy, and the conduct of elections. This is one domain in which the Indian state has shown organisational competence in delivering a public good. The Election Commission is a model Indian institution: and it has used technology—the voter ID card—to enable Indians to vote. On the ground, enacted democracy is far from perfect, but rampant electoral corruption is today more the exception than the rule. This simple practice of voting has helped hundreds of millions of Indians identify themselves with a common project. After two decades and more of growth, its time to ask if there could be something in the social and economic realm that might provide a similar common field on which all Indians stand together?

The idea of unconditional cash payment or transfer (also often referred to as universal basic income) to every citizen has been in the air for some time, but has not much figured in Indian debates. Interestingly, one of the first people to raise this idea in modern times was Bertrand Russell, in a book, *Roads to Freedom* (1918), which sufficiently impressed the young Jawaharlal Nehru to move him to try and (fail) to write his first article. The idea returned to discussion in the economies of the industrial west in the late 1980s:

as precisely a way of addressing the problem of an emerging dual economy: divided not between capitalists and workers, but between those with formal, 'proper' jobs and those in informal work (Van Parijs, 1992).

To even raise it as a possibility—an apparent luxury of the prosperous west—in the Indian context might appear preposterous. But I don't think it is. For an economy like ours, that has the second highest growth rate in the world, and the largest poor citizenry in the world, in fact it seems precisely appropriate to think about how some of the benefits of that growth might be directed to reaching the wider populace—to give them a palpable sense of inclusion in the Indian nation. What I have in mind can be thought of as a dividend on our growth: and let's therefore call it, precisely, a 'citizen's growth dividend'. The overall amount set aside to fund this should be a specified percentage of India's GDP—thereby immediately establishing a connection between the size and growth of India's economy and some sharing of that with all Indian citizens. We might start, for instance, with a figure of three per cent of GDP set aside to fund payments of the citizen's growth dividend—an amount that the economist Pranab Bardhan has estimated would cover an annual payment of ₹ 5000 to every household.

My reasons to argue for this idea are above all political—and rely less on economic efficiency or philosophical justice arguments. But, since social policy in every nation thrives on over-promise, let's be clear, straightaway, what such a proposed citizen's growth dividend won't be able to do. It won't make our society equal, it won't make it just; it won't even make poor people grateful. Look at the streets of Paris (last month)—people get used to what they get. Nor can we think of this as a populist, Chavez-style buy out (anyone who thinks it might be quite mistakes the shrewdness of the Indian poor). Nor is it a Nixonian payment to an unruly underclass threatening to riot. Universal payment in the form of a citizen's growth dividend may help as an argument against Maoists, but it won't be a reliable inoculation against such frustration and anger. This idea is aimed at doing something else: something crucial for the future of Indian governance: in establishing, we are saying, in effect, that our state cannot yet give you what you really need—we cannot deliver the schools or hospitals, the functioning social infrastructure or the equal life chances—that we recognise that you as citizens should have. Rather it's a stop-gap offer—not a withdrawal of government, a turning away from its citizens: it's the first, not final step, in trying to build an Indian social democracy on a universal basis—which includes all in the Indian nation. "Please bear with us while we make improvements"—as the signs seem always to read in public spaces.

Unlike the divisive effects of current social welfare policies, the payment of a citizen's growth dividend would be a direct, simple and instantaneous transaction with all citizens. It would offer a basis on which to unite all citizens in relation to the state, and implant among all a sense that the state does owe us something as citizens—and that it can and will deliver this. This is likely to be an uncomfortable political proposition to the state. It would create something like a market of citizens, who possessed a certain minimal economic power—generating a demand for responsiveness from the state by creating expectations among people. As they unite to press these expectations, we can hope to see a kind of incremental citizen's learning effect—extending to demands for the functional schools and health care which the state currently professes to offer them.

I should stress the point that I see this as an initial step in building an Indian social democracy, not a final capstone. As citizens come to hold Indian governments and the state to account, it can help to swell a demand for accountability from below—rather than see accountability as a matter of institutional design to worked out by experts and then left to bureaucrats to enact. In short, it would give people across the country some sense that the state actually recognised them, their existence—just as the vote has done. It would add a sense of social and economic citizenship to the political citizenship embodied by the vote.

Whether we can afford it—and at what level—is a question that Pranab Bardhan will address, and I leave to him and to other economists to set out for us the options and possibilities. Just to anticipate his (admittedly rough) calculation, an annual payment of ₹ 5000 per household—which is far from being a windfall, and which is far from being enough to encourage anyone not to seek work—would be perfectly in the realm of affordability. It's just worth underlining that the amount India today spends on social programmes (related to education, health, poverty alleviation), around eight per cent of GDP, is a relatively low level of social spending (certainly by developed country standards); and as the economy grows, so this figure can be expected to grow.

There are certainly real economic benefits it can be expected to bring. It would incrementally boost economic demand especially in the countryside, and so direct producers towards meeting needs there. And, given how difficult politically it will be for an economy of India's scale to replicate the Chinese growth model, with its globally imbalancing effects, the need to generate internal demand becomes all the more imperative. (This is not to deny that there are serious questions about the fiscal commitments to which it would commit the state—as the unravelling of social security provisions in the US, UK, France make clear.)

If we can agree that, at some level of payment, it would be affordable, it is now also the case that we have within our grasp the technology that could deliver the citizen's growth dividend: in the form of the Unique Identification (UID) card, the Aadhar programme. There are, surrounding the programme, serious ethical issues that need discussions; but one thing the UID card can enable is a direct point of access between every Indian citizen and the state (just as the ballot box does). The UID number is envisaged as a platform for further social policy initiatives—and its uptake is essential for such policies to be developed. If it becomes linked to a universal payment, there would be a huge incentive for people to register for UID.

I think that it would be practicable; and it should also be possible to generate the political support for such a policy. We'll need to find ways in years ahead, to shift from a patronage state, based on subsidies for particular groups, to one based on universal basic provision for all citizens. This is a very difficult battle, and no political leaders have so far shown any willingness to engage it. But, one might feel more confident going into such a battle armed with a proposal for a universal payment of the citizen's growth dividend of the kind I'm suggesting—and it will be harder for those wishing to protect their subsidies to do so against a policy that will provide something to all Indians—and which is linked to India's foundational principles. In that sense, if crafted properly, the idea could provide a potentially winning electoral platform to a party.

But ultimately, I reiterate that I am interested in the political potentials of this idea for sustaining the cohesiveness of our nation. I can see that it is far from an ideal solution—but it would I think give people a sense of belonging to something larger; and it is do-able, unlike complex (for our state) policies for provisioning education or health. Just as elections do not render our governments benign, let alone accountable, a universal basic income payment in the form of a citizen's growth dividend would hardly yield a more equal society. Yet it would, in addition to potential economic benefits, signal to all Indians, in a time of profound transition, a time of unprecedented opportunities and risks, that they have an enduring stake in our nation, in its wealth—in fact, a claim on it. And it would remind governments that the idea of India is composed not of constituencies, but of citizens.

References

Bardhan, P. (2013). "Inequality, Inefficiency, and the Challenges for Social Democracy in India's Economic Transition", in Sunil Khilnani and Manmohan Malhoutra (eds.), *An Indian Social Democracy: Integrating Markets, Democracy and Social Justice*. New Delhi: Academic Foundation.

Kapur, D., P. Mukhopadhyay and A. Subramanian (2008). "The Case for Direct Cash Transfers to the Poor", *Economic and Political Weekly* 37-43, April 12.

Van Parijs, Phillipe (ed.) (1992). *Arguing for Basic Income*. London: Verso.

Section I contd...

Social Democracy as a Political Value and Theory

PRESENTATIONS • DISCUSSIONS

This section presents the proceedings of the First Session of the Tenth Indira Gandhi Conference, November 19-21, 2010, New Delhi.

Chair
- Sonia Gandhi
- Montek Singh Ahluwalia

Presentations
- Pierre Rosanvallon
- Pratap Bhanu Mehta
- Sunil Khilnani

Discussants
- Aruna Roy
- Rohan Samarajiva
- Manish Sabharwal
- Sunil Khilnani
- Chanda Kochhar
- Kumar Mangalam Birla
- Sunita Narain
- Pranab Bardhan
- Sri Mulyani Indrawati
- Rehman Sobhan
- Kumi Naidoo
- Wang Hui
- Michael Walton
- Niraja Gopal Jayal
- Eric Solheim
- Sudha Murty
- Montek Singh Ahluwalia
- Rob Riemen
- Jonathan Cohn
- Mirai Chatterjee
- Nitin Desai
- Bina Agarwal
- Joseph Stiglitz
- Pierre Rosanvallon
- Pratap Bhanu Mehta

Sonia Gandhi

I call the meeting to order and thank everyone for sparing their time to be part of this conference, especially those who have come from far away. I am grateful to those who have responded to our requests to write papers. Those papers will be the basis of our discussions over the next two days. I now hand over to Dr Montek Singh Ahluwalia and invite him to chair the first working session.

6

MONTEK SINGH AHLUWALIA

Introductory Remarks

There is a striking parallel between how concepts of social democracy evolved in the world and what has happened in India. Globally, I think in the middle of the last century, social democracy was found identical to democratic socialism. People who were not in favour of Bolshevik communism or Stalinism but at the same time generally shared a socialist ideal, viewed social democracy as a gradual evolution, or the transformation of capitalism into socialism in the belief that this could actually take place. We know that over time, this changed to a more realistic focus on transforming capitalism by making it more humane, which was a huge experiment in Europe after the second world war.

To my mind, there is a reason why traditional socialism, as it has been perceived, lost enthusiasm and intellectual support. At least, from an economic point of view, and obviously amongst democrats, there was the issue that one had to be democratic, whereas none of the socialist countries of the time were democratic. But more than that, there were two factors. One, there was some discrediting of the notion many socialist thinkers had, that the replacement of market decision-making by state decision-making would generally be better and that the state would be more rational. Over time, people realised otherwise. Of course, there are huge numbers of market failures and we know that even more so in the aftermath of the recent global economic crisis. But as a general rule, opinion shifted around to the view that markets are a very efficient way of organising many economic decisions and therefore, the notion that state-controlled, planned decision-making should ideally replace markets over a wider range of economic activity did not appeal to people. The second reason why traditional socialism lost appeal is that private entrepreneurship, being a highly decentralised kind of activity, brought a degree of energy to the economic system, which a state-controlled system could not actually do. State-controlled systems are very good for achieving very specific ends, but in economies that are constantly changing with the infusion of new information and new technology, we can achieve much more efficient results if we can have a much freer rein for private entrepreneurs and, of course, make issues of private property accepted. The notion of social ownership and social control over the means of production somewhat receded into the background. It was this that really led to socialists ultimately becoming transformers of capitalism.

Interestingly, in India, there has been a similar evolution of ideas. The commitment to democracy was never in doubt in India. It is the gift of the freedom movement and therefore, revolutionary socialism was simply not an issue, except maybe for some French groups. In the early years though, the Indian social democratic experiment was still being described as attempting a revolutionary path to socialism. Politically, the Avadi resolution of the Congress Party way back in 1955 talked about "creating a socialistic pattern of society." Later, the Constitution was amended and the word 'socialist' was inserted into it, describing the country as "a sovereign, socialist, secular republic." And of course, the public sector, its growth and placing it upon commanding heights in the economy was an important instrument of social transformation.

In practice, though, it is probably fair to say that what we were doing was actually running a mixed economy with an important public sector, but with also much importance given to the private sector. The underlying goal was to have high growth but also to make sure that this growth benefitted the mass of the population. This was very clearly stated right from the beginning. The country's first prime minister is quoted in the First Plan. When it actually comes to the commitment to growth, I would cite the earliest growth enthusiast, Jawaharlal Nehru, India's first Prime Minister, who before independence was made the Chairman of a Congress-appointed National Planning Committee in 1938. That committee never completed its work because the second world war interrupted everything. But we know from the papers of the committee that it had come to the conclusion that if everybody had to be brought up to a minimum standard of living in India, we needed to double or treble India's income, which actually translates into a growth rate of between 7 and 11 per cent. The imperative of achieving a high rate of growth was conceived quite early, but there was also the realisation that the growth would have to be spread.

In practice, after independence, growth targets were much more modest—around 5 per cent or so—as realism dawned on the system. Of course, we know in practice that even these proved difficult to achieve. I would like to go back to what Mrs Sonia Gandhi said recently. We have always recognised, both in government and outside, that growth was essential but not an end in itself. It is essential because without it, one can't bring about improvements in the standards of living of the majority of the population. Hence, the issue of the kind of growth to achieve that objective is very important. Obviously, there are two dimensions to it. One, we don't care about the pattern of growth; we just get the money which comes from the taxes and do some amelioration. That was not actually our approach; there is a very strong perception that the pattern can be effected to become more inclusive. Hence, the whole focus on small industries and agriculture. The general perception in India has been that we need a particular kind of growth, which is why governments have to intervene. We are not simply leaving things to the market. But even with the fullest efficiency in moderating the pattern of growth, a lot of people are going to be left out. That enjoins a role for the state and these two things were supposed to go together. It is reasonable to ask how we have performed, given that this was our broad conception.

Growth and inclusiveness are two distinct things. It is quite clear that we seem to have brought about a major change in the growth capacity of the Indian economy. In the 1950s, we grew at 4 per cent or so. In the 1960s and 1970s, it decelerated to 3.5 per cent. At that time, people were still focused on the fact that this was much better than growth during colonial times. Indian post-independence growth performance was better than colonial growth performance. But it clearly wasn't what Panditji had in mind when he talked about 7 per cent; it wasn't even what we had as targets. Southeast Asian and East Asian countries, other than China, were doing a lot better. Therefore, a lot of rethinking on policies became necessary. It would be fair to say that when Mrs Indira Gandhi came back to power in 1980, she initiated the first policy changes. Prime Minister Rajiv Gandhi, whom I had the honour of serving, accelerated those policy changes quite substantially in the second half of the 1980s. Then in 1991, we had a much broader and more systemic intensification of economic reforms. It is important to realise that this change was not imposed from outside. It is not as if the World Bank or the IMF told us to do certain things. It was really a homegrown effort, which is why it took much longer than in many other cases where changes were made in two or three years.

The results have actually been quite good. In the 1980s, a 3.5 per cent growth rate became 5.6 per cent and continued into the 1990s, till the East Asian crisis introduced a negative element and emphasis on agriculture began to go down. It is also important to bear in mind that there was some neglect of agriculture from the mid-1990s onwards. But looking at the decade from 2000 to 2010, the economy's growth rate is likely to be an average of 7 per cent. This is very good by global standards, but it is the lower side of what Pandit Nehru had targeted way back in 1938. By any standards, we can say that we are finally delivering on growth.

I am afraid we cannot say the same thing on the other very important side of the agenda, which is, social inclusion. Poverty has gone down and there is no doubt about that. While we keep recalibrating it, I think it is getting better. But it would be fair to say that it will not improve at the rate which the planners and the policymakers expected. As the Prime Minister said recently, we will need many programmes over the years to address this issue. Some have been successful while some have not. The bottom line is that there remains a gap in this respect, which is more sharply defined when we move away from a pure income or consumption-based poverty approach and focus on deprivation. We can have income but we don't have clean water, sanitation, access to good health care or education. In the last several years, there has been an important change in the government's perception. It realises that it needs to target not just income but also the delivery of the deliverables. How do we address these weaknesses? That is a very big issue and goes beyond the terms of this conference.

Roberto Unger a political leader of theorists and a leading member of the Critical Legal Studies School, probably the only very radical professor in Harvard Law School, was in India several years ago and in an interview he gave, he made a lot of points.

What has Unger said? First, we must find an alternative to the dominant project now called neo-liberalism. Actually, the fight against neo-liberalism has been one of Roberto's big priorities. Fortunately, he has almost won that fight because neo-liberalism is much less robust in the world; it was never robust in India, although the government has been frequently accused of following neo-liberal policies. What we have been doing is not neo-liberalism. What Unger said though, is really interesting. The starting point is the realisation that state control of the economy does not work. Neither however, are the neo-liberal attempts to surrender to the forces of the globalised markets and then moderate their social consequences through social assistance workable. This really is Unger's forte; he is an experimental revolutionary. Perhaps in Brazil, he may have a chance to try this out. Unger says that the most important thing is to democratise the market economy. He made five important points:

First, we must build up domestic economic strength by achieving a high level of domestic savings with a close connection of savings to production and a high tax structure. India has actually done quite well in this regard. On the tax front, we can do better and hopefully when the general services tax is finally introduced, we would be well on the way to doing it.

Second, social policy must give absolute priority to education not only at the beginning of life, but throughout life. This has been now inscribed on India's agenda, but delivering it is a big challenge and is going to take a lot of time.

Third we must democratise the market, not merely regulate it and compensate for its inequalities. This is the part that actually sounds very good, but I have to confess that I don't fully understand it. Danny Roddick, who is a Prof at Kennedy School, once said that he taught a course with Prof Unger and it was only three years later that he understood what Roberto had said. I think Unger's main concern, if we strip the political philosophy, was for the common man to actually benefit from the market, with a total revolution in the way credit systems and technologies are made available. This was an extremely crucial part of his whole thinking.

Fourth, we need to organise civil society at the grassroots level, across class and ethnic lines, to develop a form of local civil society outside of local government and parallel to it. One of the very positive developments in India is the development of a strong civil society.

Fifth, we need to create a high-energy democratic politics that encourages popular engagement with politics and rapidly resolves impasses among the different levels of government. Governments work in silos and virtually every silo wants to occupy every field. Getting governments to talk across the silos is really a big issue. The manner of achieving this, whether through a democratic process, enforcing accountability, or otherwise, is an issue that needs elaborate discussion.

As far as public perception is concerned, Mrs Gandhi emphasised the increasing disconnect between economic success and ethical issues. There is a perception of failure in the moral dimension, not just in India but around the world right now. There is a thin line between having a vibrant private entrepreneurial class and building a thriving set of crony capitalists. At the root of a lot of public concern is this issue. How the government responds to this will be very crucial.

7

PRESENTATION BY PIERRE ROSANVALLON

What is a Democratic Society ?

We face the question of how to deal with the idea of an Indian social democracy at the very moment when social democratic institutions, as they were invented and developed in Europe, are in a deep crisis. To answer this question positively presupposes a reinvention of social democracy itself. India and Europe are not alone in confronting this question. In a way, many pre- and post-social democratic countries are facing these very issues. Of course, there is also strong resilience in the former institutions of the welfare states in Europe. Schemes of public health insurance, unemployment benefits and basic incomes still represent between 15 to 20 per cent of the GNP in Europe. But such resilience in Europe is accompanied by a double crisis—a crisis of efficiency, a crisis of the goals of the welfare state. The conflict is between universalist measures, which were at the beginning the very definition of the welfare state, and a welfare state now turning increasingly into a fight against social exclusion that is being unleashed. Thus, it is no longer totally universalistic.

The result is a crisis of legitimacy. There is a crisis in Europe with regard to equality and solidarity. To measure such a crisis is very easy. There is a growing absence of state-administered taxation and also a growing acceptance of income and also capital inequalities. There is also an increase in urban segregation and old forms of social separatism. When social democracy, at the very beginning of the late 19th century, was based on schemes of insurance and income distribution, it led to the creation of tax savings, social contributions and progressive income tax. At the beginning of the 20th century, the progressive income tax rate varied between 2 and 5 per cent in Europe. Twenty-five years later, it stood between 45 and 70 per cent. Thus, the history of the welfare state is actually the history of progressive taxation and of social contributions.

The situation we now face can be called a counter-revolution of inequality in Europe. In order to understand this, we must return to the development of social democracy. Political factors and the Right's fear of revolution played a central role. When socialist parties in Europe made a spectacular electoral breakthrough at the end of the 19th century, the conservative parties saw in the adoption of reforms, the means to emphasise the spectre of socialists coming into power. It is worthwhile to recall the example of Bismarck. On the Left, the social democratic space saw a rupture with the communists. This break was on the basis of the propagation of a communist utopia, of an equality constrained by the absorption of the individual into a community. In the traditional revolutionary perspective, we must remember, there was no place for thinking about options to reduce inequalities. Rather, it was reckoned that a radically different society would emerge one day and suppress all inequalities. Thus, we have no consideration to reduction of inequalities in Marxist thought, for instance.

There is also a historical factor with a splintered central role for the development of democracy. The two world wars reinforced the social contract. The death of millions in the European continent drove men to look differently on what united them. If the war did not kill you, it was certainly bound to get you thinking. The experience of the combatants was very arduous. Each of them was able to feel the mud of the trenches. They shared with their companions-in-arms an identical insecurity, returning to a timeless state of nature. It was an experience of a kind of absolutely naked life and a consciousness of a community of nature which instilled a lively and comforting sentiment of equality.

The recognition of legitimate rights contributed towards a broader consideration of the legitimacy of social rights. It was a kind of redistribution that was implied. And the very idea of the nation was redefined in this ordeal. It also forged accessibility to the nation's identity in the negation of the ordeal, as well as making the image of the nation's solidarity more dominant, allowing greater legitimacy to be given to the imperative for greater equality. Developing social security schemes was presented as an aspect of solidarity that was asserted amongst different social classes arising out of the effort of the war.

Thirdly, to the political factor, must be added a condition that can be called sociological. Towards the end of the 19th century, the vision of the world composed of individual and self-sufficient sovereigns gave way to an approach founded on the idea of primary interdependence. "The lone man does not exist," said a famous French author of *Solidarity*. In liberalism, which served in an equivalent capacity across the Channel, people like Leonard Hobhouse considered that each individual is constituted by the social atmosphere that surrounds him. The Pasteurian Revolution at the end dramatically validated this perception of a humanity that was bound by the secret bonds of the microbes, the bonds of a new vision of solidarity. The ideas of rights and duties, of naiveté and responsibility, of autonomy and solidarity were completely redefined in the new framework. Having become more thinkable, the project of an equitable redistribution entered the field of the possible. We can't, in fact, separate the introduction of progressive income tax, a fiscal modification of immediate returns, from the vision of a more basic idea of social debt that a lot of people were thinking at the end of the 19th century. For social democrats as well as for social republicans and social reformers of every kind, every man was born a debtor to society. Each individual owed something to the accumulated world of the whole of mankind. He came into the world laden with obligations of all sorts towards society. "A person who invented the plough continues to work invisibly at the site as a labourer," it was said at that time. The notion of a repaying trustee was very strong at the end of the 19th century. Even in the United States, it was widely accepted—and is still alive as good theory—that progressive income tax justifies redistribution by emphasising that no such thing as strictly individual production of wealth exists in any modern community.

As a historical reminder of what had made the advent and the consolidation of the social democratic order thinkable or possible, let us also understand its recent weaknesses. There is no longer a free or fair evolution that pushes social reforms. In the US and Europe, citizens no longer went through ordeals equivalent to the two world wars. Moreover, contemporary societies are societies of individuals. They no longer consider themselves as an organic whole. There is, therefore, a dearth of the sense of solidarity. Consequently, the idea of responsibility has also taken on greater importance in the assessment of the situation of individuals whereas the concept of social insurance had been based on the contrary principle of socialisation of responsibility. The notion of socialisation of responsibility was established as the first law concerning the accident of the work place experience. The democratic decline of social democratic ideals is often linked to the development of a triumphant neo-liberalism. The two phenomena are admittedly concomitant, but we cannot thereby infer a relation of causality. Neo-liberalism is, in fact, itself a product of the three points we have just mentioned. It is one particular form of response to the problems posed by the current transformation that has induced distillisation as a representation of equality and solidarity that formed the base of the old social democratic order.

But there are also other possible responses to the crisis of equality. The current problem is to formulate those alternatives to this crisis and not just to think about prolonging the old social democratic order as if it was just a matter of opposing the forces of resistance through the forces of stabilisation. In any event, nothing that should be conserved from this order can be conserved unless it recovers its full moral and social legitimacy. It is also the weakening of its legitimacy that translates into a crisis of equality. The objective is first to reform those egalitarian ideals for the new world of individuals into which we have irreversibly entered. There are two directions to give an answer to the necessity for such a reformulation. The classical one deals with the theories of justice concerning the principles as well as the object of redistribution—in other words, equality. But theories of justice are mainly directed to aid the idea of reduction of economic equality. But let us imagine an alternative, by way of another approach. This is the theory of social equality—not only a reduction of economic equality but the necessity to develop a theory of social equality, enlarging the perspective.

Why? The Olshan perspective and its development has tried to rethink equality by exploring the path of a radical version of equality of opportunity. To achieve this, it has sought to disassociate individual responsibility from social determinism, asking that we reduce or even eliminate the latter. This entails the perspective of compensatory trustees *versus* social handicaps, accent on education, and forms of asset-based welfare and so on. That has been the central perspective in Britain around which the Labour Party constructed the 'Third Way'. In more concrete terms, different social and philosophical thinkers, like Durkheim, for instance, placed under the label of Left egalitarianism, have clarified the terms of such an ambition. But such an approach ran into three major difficulties. The first was the practical difficulty of drawing a line separating individual responsibility from social determinism. This, however, is the least stated obstacle, for one can consider that the distinction is always socially established and it is therefore, political liberation that makes drawing the line possible. This decision, paradoxically, leads to hyper-individualism because it is plain but with a very debatable anthropology. It also leads finally to construction of a universe into which 'good' social inequality could be finally accepted. It is a debate about meritocracy.

In the late 1950s, Michael Young in *The Rise of Meritocracy* described pure meritocracy as a real problem for future society. Thus, even if such a perspective of distributed trustees can supply the basis of social policies for reducing inequalities, it cannot, on the other hand, be part of a new philosophy of equality.

The alternative is a new philosophy of social equality, and not a mere theory of distributive justice. In some ways, it is a return to the origins of the French and the American Revolutions, in which equality was considered primarily in social, rather than economic terms. It meant similarity, independence, participation and citizenship. That was the very definition of equality.

The philosophy of social equality for today has, of course, to be different from its original definition. There are two pre-conditions for thinking about the welfare state and social democracy. The first is to think in a universalistic perspective. Social democracy is not only about a goal; it has to be a project for the whole of society. It has also to define what I would call a 'society of equals' along three principles.

The principle of commonality—making possible a society with more social interaction, a society with less separatism.

The principle of reciprocity—irrespective of whether humans are altruistic or egoistic—reciprocity should be the real base for a society of equals.

The third element for a society of equals is singularity. This is true of a society of individuals, in their role of performing for singularity, to become real individuals.

These three elements of commonality, reciprocity and singularity are sometimes conflicting. They have to be socially defined, but this could be the base for a new kind of social contract. Social democracy is not only about discussion of a part of the society, it has to be the definition of a global social contract.

8

PRESENTATION BY PRATAP BHANU MEHTA

Citizenship and Solidarity in Social Democracy

My task has been made more difficult by Montek Singh Ahluwalia who has argued convincingly that we are well on the path to social democracy. I believe Roberto Unger would ask: what is social democracy without perpetual critique? Let me present in a very schematic form, three or four challenges that arise from the current conjuncture we are at, both globally and in India.

Let us come to the reasons why we are discussing social democracy in India at this moment. One is simply because it provides a good normative frame in which to think about the gap between performance and aspiration in Indian democracy. What is it that we are lacking and in which direction should we head? More importantly, from a practical point of view, this is a time of immense historical opportunity in India for some of the reasons Mr Ahluwalia outlined. Growth has generated a new energy: there are new political configurations emerging pushing the boundaries of what is possible, and an immense new architecture of rights, of the state itself, of conceptions of welfare being put into place. The one thing we do know about these architectures through global experiences is that once put in place, they are very difficult to reform and change. Watch any debate in any country like China or the US to understand the kind of difficulties reorienting these structures entail. The stakes in getting right what we are doing right now are unprecedented and these will define the horizons of the possible, perhaps for the next century. From that perspective, we need to think harder about what we are doing.

The first challenge for social democracy has been outlined by Prof Rosanvallon very eloquently. In global terms, discussions about this subject are taking place at a time where there is a lot more renewed scepticism about the ability of democracies to generate the right kind of equality. Democracies have proved to be remarkably conservative institutions in the sense in which many 18th and 19th century thinkers like Adam Smith and de Tocqueville feared. They have allowed for certain forms of political liberty and for certain kinds of social distinctions but their capacity to put up with, and perhaps even generate, new forms of inequality have astounded many democrats. Much of the comparative literature tells us, as Prof Rosanvallon alluded, that the circumstances under which democracies had generated pressures towards greater reciprocity are actually very exceptional, arising out of particular historical experiences of war, external shocks or a real social catastrophe and crisis. This is a sobering thought that all democrats really need to confront very squarely, not just in India but globally.

The question we need to ask is: is there something, as it were, contingent about democracy's tolerance for inequality? Contingent in the sense of the kind of debate we often have in political science—if only we could get our media right, if we could only get a little bit of political reforms, if we could only get some campaign finance reforms, perhaps we would generate a different kind of politics.

Or is there something more structural about the instruments democracies have at their disposal for mitigating inequality? These have often proved ineffectual. My paper actually goes through some of the instruments that we have used historically in the past, like redistribution, collectivisation of productive assets, limits to taxation and so forth. And the sobering news is that there are no easy answers to those questions. It is important to put on the table the fact that democracy's compatibility with inequality has turned out to be remarkably high.

Coming to the Indian context, thanks to the efforts of the last few years, we are in the process of putting in place an exciting new architecture that describes itself somewhat in social democratic terms. There is an aspiration to equality, inclusive growth and citizenship built into it.

What are some of the challenges that this new architecture is going to face? The first thing to notice is that a lot of it is being legitimised in the language of rights. From a normative standpoint, that is a good thing, like the right to education, right to food, right to employment. There is a new cluster of rights emerging. But we also have to acknowledge that the content being given to these rights is still relatively tepid and haphazardly implemented. If we look at the range of these rights that we have institutionalised, whether it is the right to education, or perhaps what has now come, the right to food security, there is a sense that these rights are fighting battles that were relevant 10 years ago. They are less relevant to the challenges we are facing now. For example, ironically, the right to education comes at a moment when enrolment has crossed 100 per cent. The real issues are the quality of primary and secondary education, yet the structure of that right, as it is fleshed out, doesn't address the challenges of the next 15-20 years. The debate over food security may not even measure up to some of the radical things that individual states have done by way of universalising the right to food entitlements.

In this situation, when there is an explosion of the language of rights, we need to ask whether the content of these rights is much less ambitious than should be the case. Is the establishment basically rationalising a *de facto* reality or is it preparing us for the challenges of tomorrow? I think the debate around these rights takes a kind of circular form, which is that part of the government and public discourse that think these rights should not be scaled up because the state cannot implement them. The Prime Minister alluded to this by saying that one should not put more money into a leaky mug. The response to that is best captured in the Russian proverb that unless you scale them up right to begin with, you are not actually going to get any significant results. You cannot jump across a chasm in two leaps. This circular argument has been the central gridlock around which our understanding of these rights is stuck.

The second feature of this new architecture works somewhat at cross-purposes with the first, following what Gandhiji rightly said that the poor should have the first claims on our attention. There is a tendency to suppose that what follows from this claim is that the poor must have attention as a separate category. Partly, these are the incentives built up in terms of political signalling. But essentially, at the same time the Indian state is trying to universalise these rights. The entire structure of a lot of its schemes is built on the premise that the state can successfully target different groups through targets based on different criteria, whether below or above poverty line; there is a whole range of criteria used.

From the point of view of social democracy, there are three worries about this approach. First, most of the analytical categories we use to make these classifications make no sense from the point of view of poverty reduction or empowerment. I think the BPL is a classical example of that kind of confusion. It is more a bureaucratic classification than one that meets the objectives for which it has been ostensibly created. But secondly, distributing benefits along these group lines creates a strange politics where different groups look upon access to power as a non-zero-sum game. The very structure of official categories creates a different form of competition between groups for extracting more and more from the state, rather than thinking about architectural reciprocity in fairness. The politics of this competition is not between the privileged and the least privileged but actually between adjacent groups and classes who are engaged in this immense battle to gain access to the categories through which the state gives them benefits. This is also true globally. The most intense political competition actually is between adjacent classes, as Dr Ambedkar had said, and not between the top and the bottom. This is perhaps one of the reasons why you don't get pushes in a democracy for real equality. When this is inscribed into the way in which you think about welfare, you will actually have this outcome.

The worrying thing about this architecture is that most of what affects the poor in terms of their well-being will not come out of these schemes. It actually depends on what happens elsewhere in the economy. We could clear cash transfers and provide education, but in the end what we term as life chances is the ability to participate in the structures of the modern economy. If you are talking of food, it will address the food supply bottlenecks that have to do with your agricultural system and so forth.

My worry at this juncture is that there is a sense in which we are beginning to see welfare benefits in whichever architecture we imagine them. It is not a palliative or compensation for those left out of growth but a compensation for the fact that we cannot do other things that would allow individuals to participate. To give an example, one of the most significant determinants of people's well being is the ability to migrate and move around; jobs, cities, etc. The most insidious form of social exclusion emerging is people's ability to access cities, which has to do with the spatial structure of urbanisation and issues related to it. Those are precisely the kind of things which speak about people's ability to participate but are actually outside of this welfare box.

It is not that there is something both politically insidious and practically self-defeating about targeting. It actually makes the case for universalisation much stronger if schemes work well, if they are universalised and self-targeting. Certainly, with the investments the state is now making in UID, one could say that universalisation becomes a technological possibility. My own sense is that UID works better for universal schemes than it does for actually targeting. But there are things that we have to be careful about regarding this universalisation story. First of all, a lot of the success of any universal architecture that we create will depend on the success of the interventions we make in the rest of the economy, not merely on success in the schemes where we are transferring assets and wealth to the poor; what you do with your power sector, with roads and those kinds of things. The second worry about the universalisation story, as Prof Rosanvallon rightly pointed out, is that it is actually premised upon creating a new form of social solidarity. Universal schemes can promote new forms of social solidarity by allowing different groups to have a stake in the same kind of schemes rather than various exclusive schemes for the poor.

But I see three ideological difficulties in achieving that ideal. I am glad Prof Rosanvallon alluded to it. The reason why this ideology has gained ground is the idea that those who are wealthy, who have generated wealth—and we are rightly proud of them—are in some deep sense, entitled to it in a way that is a marker of their individual achievement. It is often said that it is easier to shame aristocracies than to shame bourgeoisies. They have a great sense of having made it on their own, with a great sense of entitlement. What is going to be the ideological basis among Indian leaders to make a push for this kind of equality? We know from the history of social democracy how the powerful legitimised their own places in society. This is at least as much of a driving force as a push from the bottom.

There is a second possible obstacle. India face an enormous challenge of social inequality which takes a very specific form namely, caste. In order to alleviate the extraordinary deprivations and humiliations that caste identity imposes, that identity has to be recognised in some form. There has to be some form of affirmative action. But the forms in which we are institutionalising the recognition of those identities is creating a citizenry where each individual will be classified under the tyranny of a compulsory identity which is deeply incompatible with social democratic projects. Social democratic projects have a basis; it matters where you are going more than where you came from. It is the freedom to transcend all identities rather than use identities as a basis for craving equality. Although historical reasons for that are understandable, we have to ask what is the kind of politics that classifying citizens is likely to produce.

Third, there is a real danger when we begin to look upon our welfare schemes not just as a substitute for the market but also as a substitute for governance. Our architectural choices are based on the premise that we know government can't fix it; therefore, we are opting to design an architecture that is outside the space of the government. In some cases, that is fine and makes perfect sense, but if a society's governing class gives up on governing, it does not matter what welfare schemes it produces, it will not be able to compensate for their lag.

Our historical mission is best captured in one of my favourite quotes from a Chinese thinker, Ching Hui who once said "what is excessive at this historical juncture is not liberalism or social democracy, but oligarchy and populism." It is essential to critique both oligarchy from a liberal standpoint and populism from a social democratic standpoint. We hope that soon, we will have some answers to these questions.

9

PRESENTATION BY SUNIL KHILNANI

The Idea of India as Social Democracy

We have two powerful diagnoses of the predicaments of the idea of equality and social justice in the West and in India. I want to build on the elements of that predicament that Pratap Mehta and Pierre Rosanvallon made but shift the angle of vision a little. I want to focus on the question of social cohesiveness, on the sense of membership in the community; it is a question that presses in on us. My remarks are going to be both sceptical and naive. I hope this can help generate some new thinking about possibilities and give some new ideas for discussion.

Modern India, to me, is the creation of men and women who embraced improbabilities; improbabilities about whether and how we could be a nation; about our being a democracy and about our maintaining independence of judgment in the world at large. I find this gave those improbabilities a sense of reality. It is for our generation to recover a sense of that improbableness which can be given reality and sustain India's own enduring improbability.

Today, we are at a moment where on the one hand, our democracy has deepened and on the other hand, our economic growth, helped by the extension of the market and connection to the external economy, has accelerated. Yet at the same time, we are seeing today, greater resort to violence in the polity than ever before. I think the failure of our efforts to build and sustain a sense of social citizenship is now beginning to put questions over the legitimacy of our democracy. Many are seceding from the political community as it were, in terms of participation or responsiveness, even as they feel excluded from the benefits of the market.

In 1958, Nehru wrote: "we want social security but we have to recognise that social security comes only when a certain stage of development has been reached. Otherwise, we will have neither any social security nor any development." Today, we are approaching that certain stage of social development that Nehru alluded to.

As we rightly speak of India regaining its place in the world economy, recouping its historic share of global trade, we still need to recognise another momentous fact, which is that we have it now in our capacity not only to end poverty in our country but also to tackle the new energy, new ideas and some basic requirements of our citizens' welfare and their exposure to new risks that come with integration into the global economy. Our present efforts to keep the inequalities we see around us within humanly and politically tolerable limits are inherently flawed. There are estimates of over 150 major welfare schemes aimed at reaching the poor. We have a dozen or so national commissions to deal with forms of injustice and, of course, there is a huge array of subsidies that are supposed to assist those groups which have been able to get their interests represented.

In the face of this scenario, Ambedkar and Nehru might have been bewildered. Both of them were concerned with building and sustaining the sense of a nation, of giving Indians, as individual citizens, reasons to believe in the idea of India. For all their disagreements with one another, what strikes me about Nehru and Ambedkar is their conviction that to sustain the idea of the Indian nation, one had to appeal not to only one among the many diversified identities that Indian possessed. Rather, one had to persuade Indians individually that they were participants in the collective project of common development. In the same text from 1958 that I earlier quoted, the basic approach narrowed their rights. We had to work out our own form of social democracy. We had to develop our own thinking essentially trying to find for ourselves the path suited to our own conditions. Until we do that, I think we certainly need to be mindful of the lessons of the West and elsewhere as they sought to build social welfare and justice into their fabric. We need to be just as mindful that those lessons might be limited for a country of India's scale, diversity and huge informal economy.

The measures of India's uneven growth are well known. It seems to me that these disparities are deepening all lines of conflicts and opening up new ones.

When we speak today of two countries, Bharat and India, we are in fact invoking an old trope that can be found in all democracies during periods of economic growth and social change. Perhaps it is time to consider other lines of approach. One takes us to the need for universalist form of social provision which is less dependent in the short-term on the assumption of a functioning welfare state. In the long-term, this universalist approach might well create a greater citizen demand for accountability from governments. It could foster a sense of belonging to the political community.

The idea of an unconditional annual cash payment or transfer, which is often also referred to as the universal basic income to every citizen, has been in the air for some time, but hasn't figured much in Indian debates.

To even raise this possibility in the Indian context might seem preposterous, but I don't think it is. For an economy like ours, which has the second-highest growth rate and also the largest poor citizenry in the world, it seems precisely appropriate to think about how the benefits of that growth might be directed to reaching the wider populace, above all, giving them a palpable sense of inclusion in the Indian nation.

What I have in mind can be thought of as a dividend on our growth. Therefore, let us precisely call it a "citizen's growth dividend". The overall amount set aside for this fund could be a specified percentage of India's GDP, thereby immediately establishing a connection between the size of the growth of India's economy and some sharing of it with all citizens. We might start for instance, with a figure of around 2.5 per cent of our GDP, which may be set aside to fund payments for the citizens' growth dividend, roughly what we spend on our defence budget. It is an amount Pranab Bardhan in his paper estimated would cover an annual payment of around ₹ 5000 to every household.

This idea is aimed at doing something crucial for the future of Indian governance. In establishing such a dividend we are in effect saying that our state cannot yet give people what they really need, cannot deliver the schools or hospitals, the functioning social infrastructure or the equal life chances that we recognise that citizens should have. Rather, it is a stop-gap offer. It is not a withdrawal of the government or a turning away from its citizens but it is the first step, not a final step, in trying to build an Indian social democracy on a universal basis.

It would give the people across the country some sense that the state actually recognises them and their existence just as the vote has done. It would add a sense of social and economic citizenship to the political citizenship embodied by the vote

The question of whether we can afford it or not, I leave to the economists. But I think it would be affordable and within our grasp, aided by the technology that could deliver the citizen's growth dividend in the form of the Unique Identification Card. Since that particularly is envisaged as a platform for further social policy initiatives, its uptake is essential for such policies to be developed. If it becomes linked to a universal payment, there would be a huge incentive for people to register for a unique identification card.

I think that it would be practicable; and it should also be possible to generate the political support for such a policy. In the years ahead, we will need to find ways to shift from a patronage state based on subsidies for particular groups, to one based on universal basic provision for all citizens. It is a very difficult battle but I think armed with this kind of idea of a citizen's growth dividend, it would be harder for those wishing to protect their subsidies to do so against a policy that will provide something for all Indians and which is linked to India's foundational principles.

Ultimately, my interest in this idea is for sustaining the cohesiveness of our nation.

10

SECTION I

Discussion

Aruna Roy

I come from a world where we look at policy from below. I have lived in a village for the last 36 years and work from there. I really talk from the bottom up. I read a small excerpt from Eduardo Galleano's address to a university somewhere in South America. He said the only thing that grows from top to bottom are holes; everything else grows from bottom to the top. My observations are based on perceptions of the people for whose sake these discussions are being held. I see democracy as the best gift for the poor in India, despite everything that goes wrong with much of its working. It is our only way of expressing our opinions and of making ourselves heard. Therefore, we want democracy.

However, what kind of democracy is a big issue. What we really want are policies that deliver and a say in the kind of policies we want. We are no longer as illiterate as we might have been 60 years ago, when we could be brushed aside. Today, we know what is happening; there is television everywhere, we listen to national policies being discussed and know the trends. So, what we say should be taken seriously by national policy makers. Indeed, some effort in this direction is being made by India in the last 10 years or so. I am going to raise one or two issues about equality and social justice. After all in the talk about social democracy, we should really not start thinking in terms of anything being absolute. The market for us is very exploitative. If one says that government is exploitative, the market is equally exploitative, as some of the speakers have affirmed.

How do we resolve this conflict? No one has asked us, but some of us should be asked and our views taken on board. One of the most important things to have happened in India is the right to information, which has not only impacted the way we access food from our ration shops, how we get *panchayats* and now NREGA to deliver, but has also made us interested in looking at what kind of policy options exist for us and how things are going to impact us. We really think that those doors must be open and a more consultative and a more democratic process of decision-making will have to be established in this country. Though I have regard for the Planning Commission and the institutions that exist in Delhi, I do think that the voices of people on major issues should be brought to the fore. For instance, look at corruption; it is a huge issue. Solutions to deal with corruption cannot come merely from institutions at the top. We have to look at processes from bottom up. The right to information has given us an extraordinary tool to make things transparent and, therefore, to know what is happening with our money. Our biggest slogan is "our money, our accounts" because we demand that accounts must be rendered to us as to how public money has been used. Nevertheless, the opposition to it is so strong today that it needs political solutions. We really have to apply our minds to ensure that accountability processes can be established. Unless we have accountability, no amount of talk about markets or anything else is going to work. We will have to look at controls and who controls what. I think policy and opinion-making are controlled to a large extent even today in India.

The NREGA is India's own programme. It is our way of dealing with employment issues for masses of unemployed people in rural India. Why don't we look at it as a big contribution India has made to social democracy? We have looked at policy and delivery systems. This one programme of enabling people to get jobs in rural India has made an enormous amount of employment generation possible from MIS to the use of computers to employing educated rural youth to do a number of jobs, thus bringing in a whole lot of people. What India really needs is development that deals with poverty, but which also helps others.

I am bothered that more people are now talking about cash transfer, of replacing NREGA with cash transfers, or about cash transfers independent of NREGA. These are different kinds of architecture. Cash transfers for instance, only increase dependency in the relationship with the government and is a dole; this is harking back to an old concept that is still in vogue in rural India, of an 'annadata' who will save our lives and will have to feed and look after us, whereas NREGA, through its process, strengthens all kinds of democratic participation. India really needs to see how such programmes which are rights-based, which also look at governance, democratic participation, the right to know and to demand accountability can be effectively implemented.

Ultimately, it is common sense that we need. Common sense has to be tapped if India has to really deliver on the issues being discussed. I want this voice to be heard amongst all the intellectuals and their knowledgeable discussions. We must understand that ultimately, states don't exist for the rich; they really exist for the poor and so does social democracy.

Rohan Samarajiva

In my view, the cardinal principle of public policy is doing no harm. When I listened to this proposal about a scientifically calculated amount that would be paid to all citizens, I can predict what the next election will be on, which is the amount. In Mongolia, by way of an example, the last election was fought out with political parties outbidding each other in promising freebies to the electorate. In Sri Lanka, where I come from, we had a wonderful programme which was intended to help the poor to become entrepreneurial and to create wealth. This programme was called Jana Saviya, under the late President Premadasa, a very interesting initiative. The problem with this model was just that when the next election came, it had to be perpetuated. The reason was that the scheme which had money, savings, assistance, coaching and mentoring could not be ended as originally envisaged because the opposition demanded its continuance. To me, that aspect of any public policy proposal is worth thinking about because then we get into a sort of Sri Lankan style auction of non-existent benefits. We don't actually have the benefits but we keep auctioning them on both sides of our political system.

For me, the real focus should be on the large numbers of young people coming into the market. That's the strength of South Asia, our challenge and also our danger. If we give them opportunities, we will have growth and if we don't, they will riot. The key point to me seems to be Pratap Bhanu Mehta's issue about participation. How do we create the conditions for them to participate in our economy rather than giving them a dole?

Manish Sabharwal

The state does owe us something; I think everybody accepts that. But can it and will it deliver? I am at the exit gate of employment in the labour market as we hire somebody every five minutes but we have had only two per cent of the kids coming to us because of delivery systems. The infrastructure of opportunities is not in the poetry, it is in the plumbing. The Right to Education Act or the NREGA, if it wants to run apprenticeship programmes or develop skills, is helping. The proposal to give minimum wages in NREGA should not be to make people stay on in NREGA. It has to reflect productivity. My limited point would be that this infrastructure of opportunity, if that is what the rights framework is evolving to be, is really all in the plumbing. It is really life in the fourth decimal place as opposed to the broader themes, which I don't think anybody in the private sector would oppose. We accept that the market does not work for half of India. The fact that we owe something is absolute, but whether we can and will deliver, is probably the bigger debate. We can't say that the plumbing does not matter and it will work itself out. Plumbing is all that matters. The next wave of public policy impact is all in the plumbing and not in poetry.

Sunil Khilnani

Judging from the responses, I wish to clarify a couple of things. The important point that I am suggesting is not the figures. It is the principle of something which is universal, not targeted to a particular group or the poor, but reaches all Indians and gives them a sense of belonging to something larger. Whether that takes a cash form or some other form is open for discussion. I am not committed to any particular form and certainly not to any particular amount. That is a technical question that economists and others can have views about. What I do want to emphasise is the principle of something that makes all Indians feel that they belong to this larger society that we have today. It is something which is designed to reach everyone.

Chanda Kochhar

We have discussed various aspects of social democracy and how to make growth more equitable. I want to add one more dimension to that, which is the role the private sector should be playing in this whole process. Is it not unfair to always expect the state to do everything without expecting the private sector to participate in it? I am saying this more in the context of what Pratap Bhanu Mehta said. We have to now look at moving away from simply compensating, to increasing people's ability to participate. If that is what we have to do, I think there is a bigger role the private sector can play. Sixty (60) million people will get added to the working age group in the next five years. We could feel very happy that literacy rates are going up substantially, close to 100 per cent, but on the other hand, if we look at the total working population in India, less than 5 per cent have gone through formal skill training. Is that the quality of the new working force that will be added to the working population? If we have to simply move from sheer literacy provision to skill training, then I guess there is a bigger role the private sector should play. My question is: what is the experience in other countries? Is there a tipping point where we should expect the private sector to play a bigger role? How does that really happen? Does it happen by a nudge and a push or because the economy evolves and moves in a manner that the private sector also finds economic value in participating in it, or does it have to be a combination? I think it is important for us to look at the role of the private sector as well.

Kumar Mangalam Birla

I endorse Chanda's point and wish to add to it. I shall talk about our example because that is the only example I really know well. We operated in 2,700 villages through self-help groups, water harvesting and so on and so forth. We spend about 50 million dollars a year, which sounds like a staggering amount. But interestingly the bulk of these funds come from government schemes like Sarva Shiksha Abhiyan, Rajiv Gandhi Water Mission. I think this spirit of partnership between the public and private sectors is something that can be taken to another level. The role the private sector has to play is much more onerous than perhaps we recognise. The fact that we are a democracy has been proven beyond doubt. We have had several rounds of change of guard both at the centre and in the states. We were the first and, I think, the only country to give universal adult franchise as soon as we became a republic. The more important point is that we are still a fairly young democracy, only 63 years old as compared to the US which is 150 years old and has only now got its first Afro-American president. The evolution of our democracy is at a very different stage as compared to Europe. Our social democracy has to be viewed in that context. When we talk about creating rights, NREGA or the right to education, it is perhaps a misconception to believe that this is creating a culture of dependency. I would urge all of us to consider that it is actually the first push towards social inclusion. The fact that we will simultaneously work on development programmes in education, or to create education facilities, or in agriculture is not something mutually exclusive. The two have to coexist. Given the state of our evolution as a social democracy, some of these initiatives are appropriate as long as we are clear that we will go on to become a full-blown meritocracy.

Sunita Narain

I wish to go back to what Aruna Roy talked about earlier. Do we need welfare or are we talking about how we can make people participate in the economy? The most important development of our times today is one that I think Europe needs to learn from because I don't see Europe having that kind of development. It is a fact that a rights-based approach is actually pushing India towards a possible change in the way we run our economy. One of the biggest issues that was not talked about this morning is that we do want the poor to participate more in the economy and we believe that's the way ahead, rather than welfare schemes. But we don't recognise the fact that the economy, or the structure of economic growth today, is inherently one which will create more disparities. Unless we can change the structure of the way we move ahead, the way we actually run our economies, we will not get more inclusion. What is happening in India about which people like me get very excited is the fact that we are beginning to see the rights-based approach actually pushing the country towards a changed approach in the way we go into the future. I can give you a few examples which I think are the possible answers. They are often very uncomfortable for people on the other side but they need to be understood. The potential of the change they offer is so enormous that we need to understand and celebrate these experiments in democracy.

We may look at the Forest Rights Act and the Environment Protection Act. I am an environmentalist and that is how my perspectives on life and development in India have been formed. The Forest Rights Act has given people the right to be prior-informed and their consent has to be sought legally over development projects. This really means any poor community can now decide whether they will allow a mining or a thermal project to come up. The Environment Protection Act allows communities through a public hearing process to also say whether the project is going to affect them or not. We require a deepening of these but nevertheless, these are the beginnings of communities actually asserting themselves to say these development projects are really going to impinge on their livelihoods. Modern development is development for some but it cannot replace livelihoods for all. Even if people are poor and are arguing, we need to understand them. They are arguing that though they are poor, modern development will make them poorer. There is an opportunity here because as we see, many of these projects are being cancelled. We have an opportunity to reinvent and rethink what we mean by development. If we cannot mine all our coal that is under our forests today, we will also have to think about how we can do better and different kinds of energy planning. We can also think about how we can plan better in terms of building livelihoods of poor communities out of forests, water systems and resources that we have discounted for so many years. There is an opportunity to reinvent economies and to reinvent growth without pollution, which the world has never even tried. This is because the planners and executors of projects have never had to face the pressure of entitlements from poor people who are desirous of saying and have the right to say that they want a different future. Just imagine, if we had that kind of global entitlement, the United States could not build another thermal power station. Then we would really have major issues of climate change. There are enormous opportunities and a huge space here for innovation in technology, the practice of development and reinventing economic growth, which to me is going to provide us the enormous growth dividends of tomorrow. It is not going to come out of welfare. It is a beginning but I think the rights-based approach will definitely provide us something that the rest of the world has not even begun to see.

Look at our cities. If only we gave everybody the right to mobility, we could actually change the way we designed our cities because we would then not design them for cars, but for walkers and buses. That would possibly mean that New York would have a completely different future in terms of its climate footprint. I think there is an enormous opportunity here. The opening of the rights and the opportunities that we have in some way will help reshape an economic future which will be very different.

Pranab Bardhan

A lot of people have already talked about the issue of participation, which is different from the approach of just providing welfare services. Since a few community organisers and their representatives are present, and have already raised that issue, let me emphasise another aspect of participation in local democracy, from which we had lots of hopes from, 1992-93 after the constitutional amendment and the decentralisation and participation of the local people in the governance process which it envisaged. For the last 15 years, I have been studying decentralisation intensively, going back to the same 90 villages again and again. I am afraid I have disappointing news. The participatory process is not working at the governmental level. Participation in terms of elections is very active, as a lot more money is spent now in local elections but participation in the governance process is very weak. Local democracy is the weakest part of Indian democracy. There are many reasons but one of the reasons why participatory democracy is so weak in India is the side-effect of the lack of inner-party democracy in all the major parties of India. As a result, political leaders whether at the state, district or the *panchayat* level, are quite often nominated from above. If you participate in the local elections, which I have, I find it is not local issues that dominate. It is the state level issues which dominate even the village elections even though the real problems of the villages are different. Lack of inner-party democracy makes all our parties basically undemocratic, infrastructurally undemocratic. More than that, it hobbles efforts in improving local democracy and the participatory process in local democracy.

Those who are thinking of a growth dividend are not thinking in terms of a particular dole, but of a particular claim. That claim will improve citizenship. Let me mention that this is not in replacement of existing anti-poverty programmes. In my paper, I present a calculation that the amount of implicit and explicit subsidies we give every year to the rich in India is at least 6 per cent of GDP, which is more than twice of what we will require if we give every family ₹ 5,000 every year. This is just to illustrate. I am not suggesting that we give ₹ 5,000. If we want to, we can give even ₹ 10,000. If we could halve but not eliminate the existing implicit and explicit subsidies to the rich and reduce some wasteful and often corrupt anti-poverty programmes—it would be feasible. Talking of rights, one of the basic rights on which I don't see a movement in India is the right to clean drinking water. Every year, hundred or thousands of our babies die of water-borne diseases; millions are incapacitated throughout their lives because of such diseases. This is something that the government can do. I don't see much of a movement about the right to clean drinking water. To me, it is much more important than even the Food Security Act. I have some issues with the Food Security Act, but we can discuss that later.

I want to endorse something that Pratap Bhanu Mehta mentioned, the issue of oligarchy, which we are all against. But we are also—at least some of us are, I am—against populism. If we really want to tackle the issue of social democracy, we have to come to terms with the issue of how we respond to the issues, particularly, of capitalist oligarchy. But on the other hand, populism to an economist like me is pitting the short run against the long run. We can always do many things in the short run; it is going to drain away the surplus which we could give to the poor or which could help build the lives of the poor. The populism issue, according to me, is not given enough attention in the debates on social democracy.

Sri Mulyani Indrawati

I would like to comment on the reality faced by many developing countries like Indonesia. Three things are very typical for policy makers: globalisation, democracy and decentralisation. These three complicate and sometimes reduce the ability to manoeuvre for many policy makers. Globalisation has been seen to provide a very strong energy for growth. Capital comes into the country but we also face the possibility of market failure and inequality. Then everybody calls for the state to intervene in the event of market failure. But many developing countries do not have the luxury like France or other developed countries have, who in the past had control over the process that could bring this about, especially when they combined democracy and decentralisation. To assume that the state can correct market failure is actually to assume that the state has the competence to do so. Basically, this is not there especially if one combines democracy with decentralisation. I will share a few Indonesian cases. We delegate authority to the local level but the competency is not there, and weak governance is making it even worse. Having this kind of institutional problem or failure, we are facing constant pressure because of globalisation which creates quite a dilemma for the policy makers about what policies can work in order to achieve the noble goal of creating social equality. The state then designs either subsidy intervention or any policy that is intended to reach the poor or the bottom poor in this case. We face a dilemma that good goals and intentions cannot immediately be translated into an effective policy because the capacity of the government to implement and execute is going to be very limited. This dilemma needs to be solved.

Policy levels can be easily compared or we can borrow other countries' or our own country's historical experience to see whether a policy works or does not work. For example, regarding subsidy or cash transfer, we can look at a lot of studies and lessons from many countries and then we can adapt from each specific country. But the most difficult part is actually to solve the problem of institutions. This is the reform that usually takes place after a longer period.

There has been talk of increasing tax revenue in order to allocate 3 per cent for the growth dividend. Growth does not come automatically but from a good policy and also an institutional framework which needs to be built. Building new institutions or reforming existing institutions will usually happen at its own pace. The problem with many developing countries is that they don't have the luxury of time and therefore constantly face market pressure, which demands good policies and institutions. But at the same time, we need time to make our bureaucracy competent and clean. Corruption is certainly the enemy of all—the government, the poor and for that matter, even globalisation.

How are we going to deal with this? Transparency and information is one thing. Access to transparency and information may open up the problem but may not effectively solve the problem. It can create more resentment when people know there is corruption and policy failure, but there is not the ability to correct that policy as well as those problems. That creates more problems.

The question of social equality in the shaping of a developing country with weak government capacity becomes even more formidable with corruption, combined with democracy and decentralisation, especially in a country as big as India. Indonesia may not be as big as India, but it is equally complicated in terms of what kind of policy design will work. For policy makers, it is certainly not enough only to identify or define the goals or have noble intentions. The most difficult part is to actually design a policy that will work within these limitations of institutional capacity. There is also macroeconomics which is slated for the next session.

Rehman Sobhan

Mrs Sonia Gandhi emphasised that all the growth still takes place in islands of prosperity, in a sea of deprivation which can only give rise to storms of conflict and instability. This is a very central element in the discourse on the whole agenda of social democracy. We have more millionaires today than before alongside millions who struggle for two square meals a day. Essentially, Mrs Gandhi projected the concept of social democracy as the need for addressing the issues of injustice, inequity and inequality and put the focus on fairness and the creation of opportunities. We should not, therefore, limit our discussion to addressing the problem purely in terms of social provisioning, whether it should be built around access to particular opportunities for target groups or opportunities which are universalised. These are only compensatory interventions for the fundamental structural injustices which, in fact, have created and perpetuated poverty and injustice in society.

What do we essentially need to put on the table in our discussions? I hope that all these eminent people around here would address the issue of what, in fact, constitutes fairness and what constitutes unfairness. It is basically about the hierarchies of opportunity and not just matters of income deprivation, because income deprivation derives from unequal opportunities. This essentially needs a focus on the problem of how to integrate the activities of the common people, who are in fact really operating at the base of the economy, into the processes of growth. So the relevant problem here is how to create, within a market economy, a socially just market and give people who participate in such markets an opportunity to do so on more equitable terms. Obviously, the critical issue which arises here is the issue of accessing assets. We talk about the right to food. Perhaps more paramount is the right to land, the right to water, the right, in fact, to own common property resources and to add value to them and the right to the products of the forests. These are issues which should be of concern to all of us. We should not just limit ourselves to land. We have mineral resources and assets which, in fact, are created in an urban economy. Here again, I hope that we can create opportunities for the deprived to access them.

I will give a few positive suggestions here to focus my ideas. We are all familiar with the rather sad Singur affair. It struck me that one of the ways we could have integrated the concerns of the people who were going to be deprived of their land with the dynamics of growth and investment by a globally recognised multinational such as Tatas, would have been to offer them an equity share in that company so that they would have been given access to a permanent income derived from a major asset which was being created by a world famous company. We have a number of eminent business leaders here like Mr Birla and Mr Nilekani. Are they willing to contemplate the possibility of opening up and creating opportunities for collectives of the poor to become shareholders in their companies? You are creating growth. If you could give half a million or a million people, collectively, equity stakes in all the growing enterprises which you have, that would connect the deprived with the growth processes. These would be long-term and durable ways of creating rights, which are not ephemeral, because they are not dependent on transfers of income by the state but are integrated with the very dynamics of the growth process. I leave some of these thoughts for you to address.

Kumi Naidoo

I wish to pick up on Prof Sobhan's last point. There is an emerging body of experience from South Africa, where collectives of women's organisations and other parts of civil society are actually gaining equity in the biggest corporate entities but it is related to a particular moment in our history which in today's parlance is called the black economic empowerment agenda. There is a body of knowledge, which is far from perfect, but is worth looking at. Listening to all the references to Mahatma Gandhi ever since I arrived here a couple of days ago, I thought as a South African I should remind you that you sent us a lawyer and we sent you back a Mahatma.

We should be careful to interrogate much more critically the quality of democracy as some of you have suggested. Right now, I think for many people in many parts of the world, democracy has actually become little more than an elite legitimising exercise. In fact, in many countries, we see the form of democracy without its substance. Some of the language that comes to describe the type of governance we have ranges from, on the more charitable end, a liberal oligarchy and on the more negative end, either a parasitic oligarchy or, as a cabinet minister in Mandela's government who after his first term wrote a book describing the new South African state as being a predatory elite. These words might sound a bit harsh and strong but that is the way ordinary public sentiment is, in many parts of the world. The gap between the rulers and the ruled is growing at an astronomical pace and threatens not only development and democracy but also peace and security in the long-term.

The democratic deficit also has a more interesting linkage. What struck me in our conversation so far is that we have been talking about social democracy, with a view that the dominant organising paradigm is still the nation state. We have not factored in the slogan that environmentalists used to raise in the 1980s: "Think globally, act locally." Today, if we think globally and act locally, it doesn't work for people, particularly in poor developing countries, if the real power is shifting from the national to the global levels. Today, we can have efficient, anti-corrupt, ethical leadership in small or not so small developing countries, but they have no power around trade, environmental issues, currency management and so on, because these are mediated at the global level.

Let me conclude by raising one elephant in the room and that is the question of how we discuss growth. Certainly, none of us are opposed to growth; what we want is quality of growth. But the elephant in the room which we are not willing to address and which tells us that we are stuck from an environmental perspective, is that if we are to deliver to the majority of the people, the material lifestyles that folks in developed countries and elites in developing countries are accustomed to, we will need between five to eight planets. We have to begin asking some really tough questions about the dominance of the current socioeconomic paradigm, particularly around a growth model which is growth without equity, jobless growth and also a growth pattern that is rooted in the idea of over-consumption, over-production and maldistribution.

Wang Hui

I have one question for the panel. You have spoken about the land issue and also about the necessity of a critique of oligarchy and populism. One of the bases was how to deal with this issue. It is this pattern in China that became a sort of base from which most of the oligarchy arose. There are more and more landless peasants, and the number has risen. But the situation is that property rights which were weakened in India to facilitate land reforms and help the poor, ironically, ended up dispossessing them even more. I would like to explain a little bit because I try to compare that situation with China. China in some sense has also seen the weakening of property rights; not of private property rights but of collective property rights, eventually at the expense of the peasants.

When we talk of social democracy, obviously one of the core concepts is of property rights, especially private property rights. Your question reminds me of the need to think afresh about the situation in China, not merely about property rights but collective property rights. When those collective property rights are weakened, the same result emerges. How do we deal with that?

Michael Walton

While I am sympathetic to Pierre Rosanvallon talking about the need for new thinking about social equality, we have a very long way to go on the concept of equality of opportunity. When there are such profound inequalities of opportunities, it takes us to the issues of dynamic change and life chances. I would like to highlight two corollaries. One is to reinforce the analysis offered by Pratap Bhanu Mehta that in thinking of achieving a more egalitarian society, the nature of the market is going to be fundamental. Tackling the profound dualisms in the market, thickening the market and tackling the problems of inequalities of infrastructure access to the city are as important to social democracy as are undoubtedly important social provisioning aspects.

The second dynamic issue was referred to by Sunil Khilnani. While I share the view that the problem of the state is fundamental, and is a sustained issue, the question is not a quick-fix but introducing measures that would put pressure on the state and its behaviour over time. This is where NREGA, I think, scores in design and is fantastic. Of course, there are problems but the system will change the way citizens relate to the state.

Similarly, getting more information on the quality of politicians changes the way people vote. This is actually empirical work. These things may have small impacts in the medium and short-run and big impacts in the long-term. I'm personally sceptical of the citizen's growth dividend actually having those dynamics. I think that is the right way to assess alternatives.

Kumar Mangalam Birla

I won't respond to Mr Sobhan's very relevant question about landowners losing their land and whether corporates would give them equity. I wouldn't jump in and say that we would give the equity because that is a double-edged sword. I am not sure landowners would actually value equity. But what I would really say is that there are lots of corporates who follow resettlement and rehabilitation policies for land-losers truly, both in spirit and letter. You should see the work that these corporates do in terms of the facilities they provide to the land losers, the kind of houses that they build for them, of a kind you would not see in tier one cities in India, as well as giving them jobs, providing them skills and development to make them productive at work. To paint all corporates with the same brush is not appropriate. There are many corporates who are doing their best to follow the spirit of rehabilitation. I think what happened at Singur was pretty much a local phenomenon. My last point is that I sincerely believe that the debate about having a two-party system in the country, two national political parties who have the interest of the country at heart, as opposed to having a proliferation of parties that create the kind of chaos they do, is a serious issue. A lot of people may shake their heads, but I think it is worth debating.

Niraja Gopal Jayal

I shall revert briefly to a concept that each of the panellists raised, which was reciprocity, aligned with solidarity and citizenship. Prof Rosanvallon raised it as a pre-condition for social democracy and so did Sunil Khilnani in the sense of a citizens' growth dividend being the instrument for creating solidarity. But one way or the other, all panellists seem to subscribe to the idea that some form of solidarity and reciprocity is a necessary underpinning for a social democracy, whether in Europe or in India. Both in Europe and India, we have also seen in the last 50-60 years great attention being paid to the question of diversity and difference and the importance of recognising difference. The Indian Constitution was arguably the first constitutional document to recognise that the equality deficit, in a certain sense, needed to be made up by making special provisions for historically disadvantaged groups such as the scheduled castes and scheduled tribes. That trajectory has continued.

In Europe, we have had a slew of multi-country policies, broadly speaking, mostly to cope with questions of immigration and race, if I may put it bluntly. It seems to me that there is an intractable issue here; the issue being to what extent does the construction of a social democracy or the revival of an old social democracy rest or hinge upon the erasure of these differences. These differences were recognised precisely to make up for an equality deficit and today, it is again in the name of social equality that we want to erase these differences. I am committed to universal citizenship in any case but I recognise the importance of differentiated citizenship and also recognise that the Indian constitutional commitment to differentiate its citizenship is a very important part of our social and political landscape.

The question really is how to recover a sense of solidarity and civic citizenship without shirking attention to that difference.

Eric Solheim

It will be very arrogant of me to go into the details of the Indian debate. Let me therefore give some perspectives from the European side, from what I consider to be a global debate. We argued that the idea of social democracy is in much better shape than has been stated here. Even conservative European leaders like French President Nicholas Sarkozy or Chancellor Angela Merkel can be considered social democrats. One can even argue that the Christian Democratic Party of Germany is the most successful social democratic party in the world. We may take a much broader perspective of the successful nations of the world, over the last decade. Among them, obviously, one would count Brazil, with its combination of a favourable investment climate with President Lula's Bolsa Familia scheme; China, with President Hu Jintao's "Harmonious Society" at its core; Ethiopia's success story; Turkey and the concept of Anatolian capitalism, which is also inclusive. Indonesia too is a success story. All of them are based on a compromise between capital and labour; on the idea that you need growth, otherwise there is nothing to share, but you also need inclusiveness. India fits into this under the leadership of the Congress Party. The Congress Party fits into this global scheme as I can see it. These to me are the central concepts of social democracy.

Coming to Europe, I will argue, though I don't want to feel too self-confident, that the Nordic model is by far the most successful model now within the developed world. We have rapid economic growth. I discount the fact that this is because Norway has oil, because all our Nordic neighbours are also in good shape even without oil. Norway has had a more rapid population increase in Europe because we have a successful policy of including women. What is at the core of the success story of Nordic European capitalism is the following.

We have been able to create a compromise between social security and capitalist dynamism. I think these are closely linked because the idea of equality, which is strong back home, makes capitalist dynamism much easier for a number of reasons. In the 1930s, the labour movement, to which I belong, gave up the idea of revolution and violence. The capitalist side of conservatism too understood that they had to include labour in their configurations. That was the basis of the class compromise.

We had a tripartite dialogue between labour, state and capitalists in all the aspects of society. The threat of strike is always there but with very few actual strikes because in the end, it has always been a consensus. With less conflict, we are more able to achieve a balance between social security and capitalist development.

This is also possible because Nordic people embrace new technology much more rapidly than anyone else. We have, by far, the deepest penetration of the internet or any new device. Whatever it may be, we embrace it. This is because people are less frightened of losing their jobs as the state will provide them some security. They are therefore more inclined to embrace new technologies, both at the workplace and back home.

Social security is thus a platform for dynamism, not a hindrance to it.

Let me mention another aspect which may look very different and very theoretical from the Indian perspective. We have very high pay for low qualified jobs while we have relatively low pay for high qualified jobs. It means that the tendency to eliminate low-paid jobs and move more into higher qualified jobs is very strong. That also, of course, imparts economic dynamism on the basis of social security.

Let me conclude by mentioning one factor which we may come back to, which is a huge revolution when it comes to inclusiveness in northern Europe of the last generation, which includes women. Labour was included to some extent before. But in one generation, our societies have been completely transformed when it comes to inclusiveness. Women have been included through many affirmative action programmes. Including 50 per cent of the workforce into the economy gives enormous impetus.

Sudha Murty

I stay in a village for 20 days in a month in Karnataka. I would like to talk about my experience with respect to Karnataka. I work in five states: Karnataka, Andhra, Maharashtra, Orissa and Tamil

Nadu. I found that in India if you travel 150 kms, the language, the food, the culture changes. India is not a country; it is a continent. When I started working with rural people, particularly in a village, they did not accept me immediately because I looked different from them. I dressed like them, ate with them and stayed in their house and thus became a part of their community. Then they opened up with me. They have certain issues that I want to discuss. This is my subjective experience.

In villages, they asked me five questions. Irrespective of whichever national or state party was ruling, people were really not bothered. That is my experience. They say, "let anybody rule, Kunti's children will never get the kingdom." The Pandavas never got their kingdom. They always say that. It does not matter to them who is in power; they want the following things.

They want to be involved in making policies. They complain that people in the Planning Commission sitting in Delhi will not understand what we really want. They make their decisions assuming that they know what we want, but we will not agree to that.

We all say that population is a big problem. People say they don't mind family planning. Once they have two children and after an operation, if their child falls sick, is there any good hospital which can treat them without much expense? They are worried about family planning because they are apprehensive whether their child will have good health.

They want drinking water which many people have spoken about earlier. That is their essential need.

The fourth point is one on which they are very keen. Karnataka has a policy prohibiting English education for the first five years or so. But people want English education. We respect Kannada as our mother tongue which is a 2,000-year old language; we want to retain it but we want English language as the medium of instruction so that our children can get jobs. For them, if their children get jobs, they can cross the line of poverty. Getting a job of ₹ 15,000 in a BPO, whatever the difficulties, is a big issue for them. It is big money for them and hence they want their children educated in

English, but don't have that provision. They insist that the decision regarding the medium of instruction should rest with parents, not with the government or its policies.

People want uninterrupted power. I work in the handloom sector, where without power, one cannot do any work. Often, they are unable to take orders.

Montek Singh Ahluwalia

Actually, all these things are in the Plans, except the issue of English education, which can only be done by state governments. But I hear you loud and clear.

Rob Riemen

I shall make a few quick comments on how the spirit of social democracy disappeared from my country, the Netherlands. In this respect, I totally agree with Pierre Rosanvallon and feel that Eric Solheim misses the point of what is actually going on in Europe at this moment. You can recognise that the spirit of social democracy is disappearing, in what used to be a paradise of social democracy, by the fact that the most powerful party in my country now can only be labelled as a fascist party. This is not name-calling and is also not funny; it is a disaster. The President of Indonesia understood it fairly well a couple of months back. At the last minute, he cancelled a state visit to the Netherlands, something unseen and unheard of in decades. The leading party in the Netherlands is a fascist party because the leader of the party is constantly exploiting the resentment and fear within people. It is extremely nationalistic, promoting the cause of violence all the time and has targeted all Muslim immigrants. If there is a problem, they do not send out any army. They are constantly using the politics of lies and because the hate object next to Muslims is the Left, especially social democrats, one of the biggest lies they constantly use all the time is that the "Hitler was a socialist". In the use of the term National Socialist, they constantly put "national" between brackets. Hitler, according to them, was a socialist and therefore, National Social Democrats are similar. Of course, they are profoundly anti-European. Our government has liberally chosen to make a coalition with those people, not with the Social Democrats, the Greens or the Labour conservatives but with this bunch of criminals. It is now being revealed that they have all been convicted for domestic violence, sexual harassment and so on.

How come that this party, whose history is well known, became the largest party in the polls and the Social Democrats are the fifth party at the moment? The reason is that social democracy committed suicide. It did so in two steps. First, since the 1980s, it totally embraced the spirit of materialism and was bothered only about material issues. It is the breeding ground for creating resentment because if it is only material terms, there is never going to be enough for all people. Secondly, they committed suicide by embracing the spirit of Polish modernism, which means a profound attack on translated values. As you know, for Polish modernists, there is no truth, no morality and no beauty because they are nothing more than social constructs. This means that social democracy became complacent in embracing the soft forms of nihilism and pragmatism, a soft form of market fundamentalism and education was reduced to only what is good for the economy.

This is how the social democratic paradise became a place for the return of fascism.

I have two final comments. I am not a social scientist, not a scientist at all. I am only a reader. I am a faithful reader of Thomas Mann who had an interesting meeting with me in 1949 and made some wonderful observations. The wisest statement was that had he been alive, "if I would have been a little bit younger, I would have moved to India." Probably, that is a good lesson for all of us. He was also closely related to Roosevelt and had a huge impact on all the lectures of Roosevelt.

I think it is important for this conference to recognise that the spirit of social democracy should always should be more than just an economic or a social project. It is essentially a humanistic project, to elevate people to lead a life with dignity, which of course means no poverty, no hunger, good health care, etc. But it also always means elevating people to a kind of culture that is more idealistic. Politics has to be always more than "the art of the possible" and should be rooted in truth. That is the only defence one has against populism. If you don't have that politics, you will get populism as a social movement.

The final point is by Thomas Mann. Education is essential but it should always include the arts, the classics, philosophy and the truly educational spirit, as well as protection of the spirit of free enquiry, which can confront the world of religion. In the humanistic project, people are also educated in the art of self-criticism. Undoubtedly, my main problem with the economic forces and even with economic scientists is that for too long, they have been pushing education to something that merely has to be useful for the state and also useful for the economy, which is a disaster. So, my friends, please don't take away from the plumber his poetry, because at the end of his life, poetry might be more important than his skills of plumbing.

Jonathan Cohn

I will start by jumping in on Rob's comments. Since I come from the United States, my basis for comparison is altogether different. I do think in all fairness that we should not minimise the threat posed by fascists, particularly those with criminal records but I think it does matter where you are starting on the spectrum. For a country with advanced social democracy like the Netherlands, I will be very shocked to see it backslide on social democracy to as far as where the United States is now. For those who are worried about the health of social democracy, I think the Nordic model does not get enough attention. It is only my country that is seen as an example of how a generous social democracy perfectly coexists with a thriving market democracy, though not everything works in it.

I apologize to ask a simple question, coming from someone who knows very little about Indian politics but instinctively thinks about what is possible in politics. The question is: what does equality mean in Indian politics? I was struck by Mrs Gandhi's address which was very moving. Its explicit talk about equality and the islands of prosperity in a sea of deprivation is something very foreign to any conversation one would have in the United States. We don't tend to talk explicitly about inequality per se. There isn't a moral dimension to the issue of distribution. It is the politics of vulnerability and security, but not the politics of distribution and inequality. I guess my question, for anyone who wants to answer at some point, is directed to the political culture of India and public opinion in India. To what extent do people who put a premium on equality for its own sake believe that there are resources in the society that everybody has a claim on? As society grows, everybody is partly responsible to see that all deserve to benefit from it. To what extent is it strictly about vast inequality that makes it hard to provide a minimum security for everybody? I guess one could say that it is moral *versus* practical, redistribution *versus* security, but I am curious about the political conversation here. Where does it come from and how does it affect the kinds of policies that one is able to enact?

Mirai Chatterjee

I want to talk a little bit about institutions and the need to create alternative institutions that provide voice and representation to the poor and particularly strengthen alternative organisations of the poor. Although I was not around at the time of independence, I do believe that the institutions that were created for nation-building, promoting democracy in our country, and providing broad-based opportunities could not pursue these goals. I belong to a union of women workers in the informal economy, SEWA. From our experience, we can say that these institutions have not been inclusive; they have been exclusive. We have been kept out. While we talked about islands of prosperity, we have top class islands of these institutions in my own city of Ahmedabad, but we don't get a look in. As a result, a lot of very vibrant and robust, growing, thriving organisations and alternatives have been developed by civil society. I know my own organisation SEWA and there are other membership-based organisations of the poor. These are organisations with a voice and most importantly led by women, which ties in with what Mr Solheim said.

I wish to cite a couple of examples. One of the first things that came up when we were organising poor women was that they needed banking and financial services. We knocked at the doors of banks. They took one look at us with torn sarees and babies at the hip, and said that we were not bankable. What was the alternative? The poor women did not give up; they gave ₹ 10 of their daily wage, set up ₹ 40,000 as share capital and built their own bank after a huge struggle, because the RBI refused to believe that this was possible. From ₹ 40,000 share capital, the net worth of SEWA Bank is now ₹ 1.5 billion, all from contributions of Rs. 5 or Rs. 10 from street vendors, *beedi* workers, *agarbatti* workers and others. But interestingly, many middle class women now in the cities of Ahmedabad, Baroda, Surat and other places are also investing in the bank. One can see the solidarity and the cohesion across caste and class, but it did not stop there. It was not just to be an urban project; we also began to organise small self-help groups in the villages and built federations. From these mini-banks and their federations at district level, I think it would be fair to say that the poor women of India along with their sisters in Bangladesh and other developing countries really invented microfinance. Of course, microfinance these days is a bit of a dark horse for other reasons but we have seen that with this kind of financial inclusion, women on their own have become engines of growth within the family, community, in districts and also across states. It also helped build the movement of women across caste, community, religions and ethnic divides.

The other experience we had was in promoting cooperatives, which I think are much maligned and not discussed much in India. We have built more than 200 cooperatives which are run, managed and owned by poor women themselves in dairying and artisanship. Many other landless women have got together and done productive work on land. We also have service cooperatives which are an alternative to what we call the leaking pipes of our delivery system in the country, running crèches, pharmacies and green livelihoods.

There is need to look at these kinds of alternatives as well, because not only are they engines of growth at the local level, but also democratic institutions. Women learn how to run their own organisations. They are on the board; they see a balance sheet for the first time. They have begun to understand profit and loss. If there is corruption, those sisters who are on the board are booted out.

It builds solidarity across caste and community lines. I would say that these are laboratories of social democracy, which we have not looked at. We are beginning to look at them because there are lots of lessons, particularly for the poor women of this country. We need to look at how to strengthen these organisations of the poor without taking away the spirit of self-help, enterprise and entrepreneurship. We welcome partnership but want to be in the driver's seat. If anybody wants to invest, we are not sure of accommodating them right now on the board, but we would welcome a line of credit and finance. It is our voice and representation at the policy table that will help us scale ourselves up and build our capacities.

Nitin Desai

I want to come back to what I think is the purpose of this first session. What should be the organising principle of social democracy? I was very taken by Rosanvallon's suggestion that started by emphasising the principle of social equality rather than distributive justice. The problem in taking social equality as a starting point for social democracy is that India is a deeply divided society. You talked of commensality but this is the home of homo hierarchicus; the one thing we don't do is to eat together. In India, if one believes in rebirth and reincarnation, then one is born with a credit balance or a debit balance, one comes on promotion or demotion; one is not born equal. There is a deep problem with the idea of equality in India. I am not sure social equality in itself will provide an answer.

I was more taken by the other suggestion, that of a radical approach to equality of opportunity. I think this is something which is very important, particularly given the vast numbers of young people that would be entering the fray. I would say we can conceptualise a lot of things that we do under this. I would put NREGA and microfinance under this, and in this way radicalise the approach. I would also put reservations, educational reforms under this. I would put new and friendlier forms of organisation under this. I would urge that we may well see this as a better way of organising a social democratic agenda in India though I am sure, we cannot ignore ideas of justice.

I want to make one final point which is that there were two dimensions of the ideology of social democracy which were mentioned but not elaborated. I hope we will do it later. One is the global dimension. One cannot have social democracy in isolation. The second is what Kumi Naidoo mentioned, which is fairness between generations. This is something I will touch on later.

Bina Agarwal

I wish to touch upon two points. Taking up from where Mirai left off, nation building which we have been talking about is really a collective project. But the way in which we conceptualise relationships between the state and citizens, schemes, cash transfers and so on is very much an individual-oriented approach. Even NREGA is a universal scheme, a self-targeted one that stipulates a minimum endowment for every household. Of course, it is very important that each citizen must feel that they have a right. But I think the way we conceptualise and deliver these ideas or schemes must have something more than just the individual. I want to really emphasise the importance of a much more collective approach for delivery by actually looking at the development schemes that have succeeded over the last many years, which even development economists have come to recognise, at least in theory. We can take self-help groups, SEWA and many other examples, which are collective approaches for delivery of a variety of things. We have numerous examples of forest rights groups, water harvesting systems where communities have gotten together and we see that these are working.

Yet, when we continue to talk about delivery, we don't bring this in as a central key element. We need to do that. We also have to extend that approach. Apart from service cooperatives, why don't we talk about land collectivity? There isn't enough land for every single household, but if we have a group, things could be different. We managed to include it in our Eleventh Five Year Plan, but are we going to implement it? The interesting thing is that many transition economies were de-collectivised—Nicaragua, Romania, East Germany. They had a choice to go for individual farming, but have chosen bottom-up collectivities. Three to fifteen families have gotten together and have become more productive. Recent research shows that they are much more productive than individual family farms, because they help them get over a variety of constraints. So here is a possible model for reviving agriculture, dealing with poverty and empowering the poor.

It seems to me that we tend to forget this. Andhra Pradesh needs to be looked at, where we have banks throwing money at individual women. This completely destroys the collective model. The same could possibly happen if money were to be given to individual households. What about communities, social norms and the ways of distributing gains?

Second, and very briefly, how did we arrive at a process of what will work for the poor? There are many examples like NREGA, the Right to Information Act, and other examples that are bottom-up, specifying what we want. But do we have systems in place by which we actually link government policy makers to what people are saying on the ground? Pranab Bardhan talked about how local government is not listening enough. But there have to be alternative institutional mechanisms through which we can link the collectivities of the poor. For instance, self-help groups and forest groups could be linked up in a strategic way. That will give voice to the poor. Why should we depend on local representatives? The RTI could make them accountable, but it is also necessary to link up different kinds of collectivities in different ways to make local government accountable. Finally, as an example, we already have an institutional framework for this. There are federations for self-help groups, but the most striking instance is of forestry groups in Nepal. Countrywide, they have what they call "forest user group federations". It has about 14,000 forest user groups covering almost everything. They also played a very significant role in the democracy movement in Nepal.

So there are links between these institutional forms, about which I believe we need to think in much more universalistic terms than we have been doing so far.

Joseph Stiglitz

We have had a very interesting and rich discussion. In this tribute to social democracy and its implications, let me begin with democracy. We have listened to statements that democracy has not been as effective, in some ways, as it should be in being inclusive. There is a very interesting contrast in the way economists think about what a lot of people thought would emerge with democracy. The standalone model that a lot of economic scientists used is called the median mode. It is supposed to mean that the person in the middle would be advocating redistribution. There was a real apprehension that there would be too much redistribution. That hasn't happened and it is an interesting discussion about why it hasn't happened.

Part of the reason has to do with the point that Pranab Bardhan made, that clearly the political institutions at all levels, but particularly at the local level, have not been that responsive. The consequence of this is that there is really a very negative dynamic and also a sense of disillusion with the state. This leads to poor participation and more active participation by special interests, which means that the state is less responsive. This is a dynamic that leads it to capture by special interests and more lack of participation.

Till the recent (mid-term) elections in the US, the unemployment rate among the youth is more than the voting rate. That really says something about what has been happening to American political processes. As India thinks about social democracy, it should try to avoid that kind of outcome.

The second point raised is something that wasn't emphasised enough as part of the social democratic agenda. I think that there is a social democratic agenda for the marketplace. This involves democratisation of the marketplace, which has come up in a lot of remarks about access to the market for poor individuals, barriers to entry, or access to finance. But there are a whole lot of other aspects. The whole variety of entry barriers and monopolies really should be viewed as antithetical to social democracy. I think anti-trust policies are a very important instrument of social democracy.

But corporate governance is also another important aspect that one sees in the United States and some other countries, which basically have corporations that are not accountable either to their shareholders or, in fact, to anybody. In the United States, we had a very intense debate about shareholders having a say in the pay of corporate officials. A general view on the conservative side says that they shouldn't have any say in pay. To me, social democracy necessitates that there should be broad participation. This takes us to some German and other models where there is more participation. But there are other aspects of a democratic workplace and industrial participation that ought to be on the social democratic agenda.

The third point is that in all the debates, there is a lot of behind-the-scenes differing conceptualisations of our society and how the economy works. These shape views of what the trade-offs are and what they are not and legitimise inequalities. For instance—this goes back to the 19th century—the Theory of Marginal Productivity was used to justify inequalities. The theory propagated the view that people who were more productive should be paid more. In a way, the recent economic crisis has really undermined that view, because what many Americans and people all over the world saw was that the bankers were getting compensated for record losses. You could relate the pain to productivity in an ailing way at the firm level or the suicidal level. It really undermined totally, I think, the justification that has existed for 150 years for income inequality. It is as if something else is going on.

Another conceptualisation that is very important is that government is inefficient. The fact is that this is not true. We may look around at examples of efficient governments and efficient government agencies. The social security administration which administers the old age pensions in United States is more efficient than any private insurance company and more responsive, a fact that is brought out through surveys. Miracure is a relatively efficient health care provider in the United States.

The third is the idea that there is a trade-off; the idea that growth will benefit all took a downturn. It is very strong in many countries. But it is not just that in many countries, growth has not been pro-poor. In some countries, it has been anti-poor.

I'd like to take a couple of minutes about where that leads us. First, the examples of Scandinavian countries and others show that this trade-off isn't necessarily there. In fact, I would argue both politically and economically, more inclusive growth can be more rapid growth and more politically sustainable.

Secondly, the statement that the government is inefficient, and being in the government means limited capacity, is really too often used as an excuse for the government not to do things. The example that Pranab Bardhan gave of distribution of water is something which would probably be within the capacity of the government. One may ask why doesn't the government provide this and make this a universal right within the country. The rules that are set, for instance, for the capital markets can expose the country to more volatility which can lead to more unemployment and poverty. Unless we accompany the capital market proposition with appropriate controls, circuit-breakers and things like that, we are possibly creating more inequality in society. The point I want to make is that it is not just the issue of particular actions, it is the whole policy framework that affects the outcomes. Even if the government has limited capacity to redistribute income, the policies should be designed to make sure that the income—before it is distributed—is more equal in society and a lot of instruments are available to effect that like intellectual property rights. Almost every legal framework has implications for this before tax distribution, not just of income, but well-being. The notion of how we measure growth, which was emphasised by the Commission I chaired on Measurement of Economic Performance and Social Progress, emphasises that. Even the way we measure growth only gives a warm view of how well we are doing.

Pierre Rosanvallon

The first point I can think of is that of inequalities. Inequalities are not only about addressing individual injustices. They are also about producing social dislocation. Social dislocation means diminishing of social trust. Social trust is a real condition for the productivity of our societies. If we want to rebuild trust, it is true that we need to have a policy of more cohesiveness; if we have less cohesiveness, we will have less social trust. A lot of social scientists today—I think of Putnam in the US—have discussed the relationship between homogeneity and trust. I don't think the term homogeneity is appropriate. It is between democracy and trust. We need more democracy, more knowledge of the people, more commonality and not homogeneity in the sense of belonging to the same group or same culture. It is more than democracy; it is a path to social trust and social trust is also a path to economic growth.

One part of the discussion was about the distinction between targeted policies and universal exit policies. That is a very important point. One thing not mentioned in the debate earlier is about urban politics. Cities are the centre of commonality. If we do not really have new politics for cities of the future, the very sense of commonality we desire won't be present.

The second point in the direction of universal exit policy is about free national rules. Some economists speak of free national rules. I think the production of free national rules that we respect, recognise, and fight against humiliation are very central for our societies. Of course, we have to provide a lot of access to a lot of goods. We have to provide economic resources but must never forget that free national rules are very central to democratic society. The quality of our cities is very central because democracy is not only a set of procedures; it is also about social quality. We have to think about the quality of our democracy and not just proceedings and procedures of our democracy.

Sunil Khilani

The central anxiety of the remarks I made earlier pertains to what is happening to this sense of solidarity in citizenship in our country in the phase of the current growth pattern and our policy responses to it. It seems to me that in both those dimensions, pressures are pushing against the creation of solidarity. The danger of economism, which Rob Riemen called materialism, and which I would refer to as market nationalism, is one potential danger we face.

The other stems from the proliferation of policies, whether based on rights-based claims or reservation-based claims, that did break up in differentiating the poor, often setting them against one another and separating them from others in society. I think that is weakening the pressure to make the state accountable to all citizens and not just to those who are receiving certain targeted policies. One danger Riemen pointed out in the European context is that there are right-wing responses to the question of solidarity, which are very dangerous and which we have to be aware of. That is one of the points that I really wanted to make; which is why the need to create a universal claim on the state from all citizens of India is imperative.

How do we create a situation where all feel that they have some stake in the state, in the kind of growth that we are experiencing? It is not about erasing differences but about trying to balance it with some common share and tangible stake in our growth. The question is: what can that be? Whether that takes the form of a certain amount of money or some other form is something we need to debate and discuss. But the problem, as I see it, is in those terms.

Pratap Bhanu Mehta

If we identify the gaps between the visionaries and the plumbers, where there is plumbing for innovation, I think there is one intellectual challenge we face. This, in a sense, is fixed to our politics where we often talk about the challenge of rent-seeking and accountability. That is one dimension of the challenge. The second dimension of the challenge is that we have a different kind of diversity in India as well, which is the diversity of ideological visions. It is not just ethnic diversity. The interesting question from the policy point of view is how society mediates that conversation. What form does that mediation take? One metaphor for that mediation is compromise. For instance, I give you two things, so you give me two things. The question is whether, from a social policy point of view, those forms of compromises are the worst of options that actually conceal something. One may be going down a path, let us say, of state delivery *versus* private vouchers. One has to make sure that at least within the logic of that architecture, one does everything right. My worry is that our architecture actually doesn't take that form. There is a nice sense of compromise where we include different voices. But in a causal sense, we can end up with a worse equilibrium by certain kinds of compromises. I think policy architecture is going to be our biggest intellectual challenge. Let us not get into the trap of a state list of pay-out vouchers. That's the worst of options than actually picking one and taking it through to its fullest logic.

Section II

Social Democracy in Global Perspective

Social democracy developed within the frame of the nation-state, and there is rich experience from Europe, Latin America, the US and China that India can learn from. Yet, in recent years, the globalisation of the world economy appears to have placed constraints on social democratic aspirations. What is the nature of these constraints? How were successful social democratic states and economies constructed, and what lessons can we draw? How were they resourced, and how did they command popular legitimacy? What sorts of difficulties have they run into—and how adaptable have they proved themselves to be?

BACKGROUND PAPERS

- Pascal Lamy
- Wang Hui
- Joakim Palme
- Jonathan Cohn

11

PASCAL LAMY[1]

Social Democracy and Globalisation

Social democracy is an ideology born out of a desire to reform capitalism and to align it with social justice. From its inception, social democracies have sought to combine the potential of market capitalism—the benefits of efficient markets—with their desire to promote freedom, equality and social justice, and solidarity. This belief inspired Indira Gandhi when she said: "If we want to be a modern nation, then we have to make a special effort to see that all those sections of the people, who have not had opportunities of development and progress, should be helped. Not by other people going and doing things but by helping them to do things for themselves."

The crisis and social democracy

With the recent crisis, market capitalism has just experienced an upheaval that is unprecedented in its globality if not in its magnitude. And yet, social democracy has remained muted, weakened, incapable of reacting to the excesses of the same capitalism that saw it emerge in the 19th century. What went wrong?

The explanations put forward thus far for this incongruous state of affairs rely on two analyses which in my view are both flawed and insufficient.

1. This contribution to the Tenth Indira Gandhi Conference is written in my personal capacity, as someone who has observed and practiced social democratic values throughout his life, and not in my institutional capacity as Director-General of the World Trade Organization.

According to the first of these analyses, social democracy has lost its relevance by allowing itself to be absorbed into a liberal economic ideology that it was too weak to resist—by lapsing into the comfort of day-to-day management, by engaging in backroom power-broking whenever the opportunity arose.

In my view, the facts belie this explanation: whenever social democrats had an electoral majority, the reformers pushed through major and progressive reforms. This is true of Chile and Spain, as it is of New Zealand and India. Still today, they remain the backbone of a politically viable alternative.

According to a second analysis, social democracy has been a victim of its own success. Its historical model is now exhausted. Its arguments, its positions and its solutions have now infiltrated the entire political spectrum, causing them to lose their originality and specificity.

But here again, reality suggests otherwise: the contradictions of market capitalism are still with us, and a significant portion of humanity continues to suffer its devastating effects. The 'social question' is as burning an issue at the beginning of the 21st century as it was in the middle of the 19th century.

A new global social democratic approach

I believe we must propose a different approach as a preamble to a new effort to restore social democracy's ability to uphold its values and act effectively not only to reform but to transform, market capitalism. We need to act on two fronts.

Revamping the social democratic critique of market capitalism

First, on the ideological front: we need to revamp the theoretical critique of market capitalism. The reformist Left of today offers only an incomplete and superficial critique of the prevailing system.

It is incomplete because it is still excessively influenced by the economics of social democracy's founding fathers. It rightly criticises the inherent dysfunctions and instabilities of the capitalist model, but it neglects three dimensions that should have brought about a change in the theoretical groundwork: globalisation, sustainability and anthropology.

Globalisation is more than just an expansion of the territory covered by capitalism. Technology, its essential driving force, is thoroughly altering the traditional domination of labour by capital. No longer is capital merely finance: it is also knowledge. No longer is labour merely force: it is also imagination. The social fallout can no longer be handled by welfare systems relying on communities with a strong identity (professions, nations, classes). We need to rethink these systems on a global scale.

The traditional capitalist model, as we know it today, is no longer merely socially unsustainable, or even economically unsustainable: it is now also environmentally unsustainable. This means that from a conceptual point of view we should be focusing our efforts on coming up with a different growth model, one that is less extravagant, less demanding of human and natural resources, a new version of 'prosperity'. Social democracy needs to embrace a green agenda. But in doing so, it must ensure this green agenda is compatible with a growth model which offers hope to the half of humanity for whom life is a daily struggle and for whom zero growth is a provocation.

As for the anthropological foundations of market capitalism, they are bound to be called into question with the advent on the national and international political scene of actors whose culture is not of Western origin. This long philosophical genetic sequence leading from the separation of body and spirit to the perpetual struggle between individuals with irrepressible appetites, ultimately resulting in the liberal economic theory of self regulation, has now produced another version of the invisible hand. Other human philosophies have emerged elsewhere, philosophies that do not rely on the capitalist anthropological code according to which man is wolf to man. There is an urgent need to revamp the critique of market capitalism from an anthropological point of view.

To accept these three limits to the current critique of capitalism clearly implies going beyond and engaging in some conceptual groundwork involving intellectuals, thinkers and civil society actors on a scale that far surpasses Western think-tanks and seminars. In other words, it involves creating a new social democratic platform to build an alternative model to today's market capitalism, not just to find ways to mitigate its effects.

Altering the scope of social democracy's action

Second, on the strategic front: we need to alter the scope of social democracy's action. Assuming that this ideological renovation exercise succeeds, we shall then have to introduce the same change of attitude at the political level, when it comes to defining priorities and building a new bargaining platform.

The priorities of social democracy must be shifted from the state level to the global level, and international regulation of market capitalism must be given the same importance as the introduction of the welfare state in the 19th century.

These regulations must be applied first and foremost to the sectors of international life that have already been identified: macroeconomics, social, trade, health, environment and human rights sectors, to name but a few. From there, global regulatory efforts must be extended to the financial activities' sector, where the 2008 crisis revealed a massive dearth of international regulations in what was undoubtedly the most globalised sector. Some of this is already underway as part of the reaction to the crisis. And finally, it must embrace the sectors where global regulations have not really being tested, such as taxation, energy and migrations.

The challenge facing us in all these areas is to create global public goods, capable of harnessing the effects of markets so that their efficiency can be enhanced, while making them subject to regulations designed to prevent excesses and, above all, to establish a collective framework of values that is currently lacking in the area of justice, fairness and profit sharing.

But we still need to reflect on how such regulations could be strengthened where they exist, or created where they are lacking. We need to invent and establish a balance of power in an international area that is essentially still governed by sovereign nation states, and in which the only way to ensure order by regulation is to negotiate. This is no small task given the enormous difference between the decision-making and legitimation processes at the global level and the processes to which national systems are accustomed. The only way to address this problem is to imagine, and then build, new alliances with the countries that are now at the negotiating table after having been excluded for a century by the western powers: India, China, Brazil, Indonesia, South Africa, Egypt, and many others.

Since we can reasonably assume that the position of these new players is, or will soon be, a product of their domestic political systems, we must seek to unite the progressive political forces in those countries which agree, in essence, on the analysis of the failings of capitalism, and then, through discussion and negotiation, adapt the critical work and the resulting progressive political response to this new environment.

I am not underestimating the challenge facing us, or the time required to address it. I am aware of the efforts involved in altering the outlook of the social democratic movement. It is a formidable challenge to put to work together members of the European Socialist Party, the US Democrats with the Congress Party in India, the Workers' Party in Brazil or the Communist Party in China.

I am also aware that this project will need to go hand-in-hand with changes to political practices at home. There will still be a need to dispel the view that social democrats are no longer present in the workplace and in people's lives to help those in distress; or that we more-or-less share the selfish and security-minded attitudes that serve merely to aggravate exclusion.

For there is need to act at the global level as well as at the local level. This is what I have tried to convey with the "Geneva consensus": a new basis for the opening up of trade that takes into account the resultant cost of adjustment. Trade opening is necessary, but it is not sufficient in itself. It also implies helping developing countries, and in particular the poorest among them, to build up their productive and logistical capacities; to increase their capacity to negotiate and to implement the commitments undertaken in the international trading system; and to deal with the imbalances created between winners and losers from trade opening. All this will require a blend of international actions—in the case of trade, a combination of a fairer multilateral trading system and development assistance in the form of Aid for Trade; together with local actions—improving health care, boosting education policies and ensuring fairer taxations systems, to name a few.

And yet, if we look at the forces that need to be united in order to build up an alternative, to carry out an in-depth transformation of the now globalised market capitalism, we must face the fact that the task exceeds the intellectual and geographical scope to which we in the West have become accustomed. Our task is to build a new political space in a world which will have to be exposed to the projects of other peoples, other civilizations, other sensibilities. And if it is to exist at all, that space must be open so that each one of the new forces to be mobilised has a role to play and feels that it is a stakeholder.

But as we build this global new platform, we must also ensure it translates into concrete political actions at home. Social democrats task is therefore to localise global issues. To translate global issues into proper local democratic debates.

Opposing and proposing globally while rooting these debates at home is the task of today's social democrats.

12

JOAKIM PALME

Social Democracy and the European Social Model

Reflections on the Past, Present and Future

One way of looking at *Social Democracy*, and its fate, is to see it as a response to two fundamental problems of capitalism; firstly, the unequal and unfair distribution of economic resources and, secondly, the destructive forces unleashed by free market competition on the national as well as international levels. With its emphasis on equality, social democracy has in value terms followed the heritage from the French revolution. With the break-through of democracy based on universal-suffrage, public policy opened up as an arena for pursuing these values and various instruments were invented. Gradually the prevalence and, equally important, the identification of various economic risks and social dilemmas has contributed to the development of modern welfare states. However, nothing has been changed without the political mobilisation of the interests of majorities in the electorates. This appears to be true for each and every step in the reform process but the ways in which social democratic parties have struggled with the Kautskian dilemma—the working class always appears to be in minority—have differed over time and among countries.

The concept of a European Social Model (ESM) could be understood in a similar context. The attention to the ESM is in part a response to a political crisis of the European integration. In 2005, after the 'no' in the French and Dutch referenda on the proposal for a new EU constitution, European politicians were reminded that the pursuit of a Single European Market and further political integration could only be successful only if the European populations supported it. This would only happen if there was trust in governments to handle the social consequences of production and service markets being exposed to competition. Even if the 'destructive' forces of market competition replace old inefficient structures with new more efficient and wealth creating ones, they also have to be met by 'constructive' social policies aimed at including potential losers. In a way, José Manuel Barrosso's (the President of the EU Commission) definition of the ESM in terms of "social inclusion and equality of opportunity" opened up for the pursuit of a social democratic agenda (even if there, so far, has not been much progress in this respect). To understand both opportunities and constraints, we need to broaden and deepen our analysis of the social dimension of the EU.

The purpose of the paper is to discuss the relationship between social democracy and the 'ESM' in order to cast some light on possible futures. The aim is moreover to go beyond this positive approach and discuss normative issues on what ought to be done.

The formation of national welfare state regimes

The concept of a 'social model' is however contributing to a more general confusion around the goals and means of public policy. Whereas the ESM clearly was formulated in goal terms, there seems to be a belief that there somehow is a European social policy model that delivers these desired outcomes, or at least a model that is different form the North American social model. Even if the differences between Europe and America often are exaggerated, there appears to be some truth in the claims about a broader middle class inclusion in the European systems of social protection, most notably when it comes to health insurance. However, the ways in which social protection has developed in different corners of Europe, expose a wide variety of strategies and pathways. If we are interested in the role of social democracy, it appears warranted to explore this variation a bit further (without any ambitious to fully exhaust the subject).

Here, the concept of 'welfare state regimes' will be applied to define the configurations of policy instruments in the form of a typology. The use of broad typologies for classifying countries is a useful tool for simplifying complex patterns of differences and similarities. The institutional structures of welfare states can be seen as a sort of intermediary variables, which can lend themselves to analytical purposes when it comes to causes and outcomes institutional differences, as well as for more precise descriptions of changes over time. In a society where potential cleavages such as socioeconomic stratification, status, ethnicity, religion, economy sector and region form a complex set of cross-cutting lines among citizens and provide competing bases for the formation of citizens' identities and interests, welfare state institutions can be used to emphasise some of these potential lines and bases and to suppress others. Citizens are put into categories varying in the degree of homogeneity in terms of resources and of risks. Socioeconomic stratification differentiates citizens in terms of economic resources. This stratification is also related to the distribution of some of the relevant risks, such as ageing, sickness and unemployment.

In today's European context, it is worth emphasising that the middle-class inclusion in the social protection makes the various European welfare regimes different from the targeted regime, where at least the more affluent parts of the population are excluded. The fact that a large majority of the population is not only contributing to but also benefitting from the system of social protection is likely to be important for the strong support among most Europeans to these systems. However, the ways in which the middle-class is included differ between the various models. The Beveridgean basic security regime only gives basic benefits and assumes a strong reliance on private programmes in order to provide for a decent income security of the middle class. The Bismarckian state corporatist regime includes the middle class but in segmented programmes. The Scandinavian encompassing regime is an attempt to organise the interests of the middle and lower classes within the same universal framework. The ways in which these programmes organise the interests of different social strata may have important effects on how policy makers respond to the current and future challenges of the systems. This is hence vital for understanding the political sustainability of different regimes.

European social policy history can here be interpreted as the emergence and development of social conservatism, social liberalism and social democracy as strategies of cooperation between capital and labour. Gösta Esping Andersen took the relationship between the ideological orientations and the institutional configurations serious and labelled the regimes as liberal, conservative and social democratic, respectively. This was not to deny that different political forces over time had been active in shaping each and every regime. It was rather to suggest that the relative strength of the different political parties would make certain imprints on the institutional designs of the social policy programmes. The social democrats would have a natural inclination to support egalitarian and universal programmes. Yet social democratic parties have of course found themselves constrained by the pre-existing structures, created by other political forces, and have resorted to 'more of the same' tactics rather than transformative strategies. However, during the early post-WW II years, there appears to have been a kind of momentum to push for more universal solutions, with some—albeit restricted—success.

The oil-crises along with the following mass-unemployment, the rise of neo-liberalism and the fall of the Iron curtain, all contributed to a shift in the old balance. And the previous ideological accords and cooperative strategies, were moreover challenged by neo-liberalism for more than two decades. Though, in the 21st century, that rhetoric appears to have lost steam. But when will employers view cooperation as a possible strategy again? The news is that there has been tilt of power in favour of 'capital' as a result of the exit options offered to capital in the wake of the deregulation of financial and credit markets over the past decades, and there appears to be no end in sight concerning this—despite the 2008 global financial crisis and its aftermath. The return on capital was elevated, possibly as a consequence of the exit option offered to capital. To the employers, this puts the question of cooperation in a different light. Are they still interested to instead foster cooperation as way of achieving positive sum solutions for conflicting interests?

The social dimension of EU

While the development of European welfare states to a very large extent has been national projects, there has also been a parallel development of a social dimension in the EU. Still, the Rome Treaty from 1957 set cogent goals for the economic integration in Europe, while the ambitions were, with one exception, modest in the areas that we associate with social policy. The main purpose of the treaty was to promote the 'four freedoms'—the free movement of goods, services, labour and capital. In practice, this meant that the social policy ambitions were limited to the free movement of labour. The point of departure of the four freedoms thereby meant that the primacy, sometimes labelled an asymmetry, of the' market' was established in the European cooperation.

The focus has thus been on the regulation that would guarantee that the migrating labour force in Europe retained their social rights was not only an exception, it has become a kind of cornerstone of EU's social dimension. The regulatory framework has gone through some changes over time. The goal was and is that the migrant labourers who work and pay social contributions in one country should be able to move to another EU-country without losing their earned social rights.

The first big legislative change came with the Single European Act (SEA) in 1987, which not the least meant a recouping of strength to get the inner market in place. By its strong emphasis on the internal market, the SEA also created an countermovement, which eventually was articulated in the Maastricht Treaty 1993. Here EU for the first time expressed clear social ambitions. In the so called social protocol, the Maastricht Treaty stated EU's goal for promoting employment, working conditions, social protection, and dialogue between the labour market actors. At the same time, the so called Maastricht criteria were asserted, which established the economic demands the member states were obliged to fulfil to eventually be able to transfer to a common currency. The criteria were criticised from some camps for diminishing the sociopolitical negotiating window, as well as the opportunities to maintain a countercyclical macroeconomic policy.

A growing number of countries had also been exposed to EU's different policy initiatives. From a social policy perspective, there were some differences between the six original Member States although the state-corporatist regime predominated. The differences within EU has increased rather than decreased since then. The countries joining since then, have as New Members States contributed to an enhanced variation when it comes to the social political architecture. No noticeable convergence towards the state-corporatist model can be traced to the original countries.

The European Court of Justice (ECJ) has over time played a particularly important role in the development of EU's social dimension. Already in the 1980s, the ECJ had been active advocates of gender equality in the member states. The ECJ also contributed to changing the view on regulation of social protection of migrant workers. According to the Court's ruling the social rights should not just include social insurance but also the right to health care, which is a logical consequence of how the social and health care insurance in the state corporatist regime functions. In the end of 1990s, the ECJ declared a number of important rulings, where the court asserts, emanating from the principle of free movement of services, that citizens in one country should be able to get health care in another country, even if they are not migrants and that the same rules apply to tax financed insurance and state corporatist insurance. The initiative that the European Commission has taken to continue the integration of health care has nevertheless met political resistance. During the fall of 2009, the Swedish presidency tried to set the agenda on emphasising enhanced patient rights without getting political support.

The Amsterdam Treaty 1999 contributed to put a social democratic profile issues on the political agenda, chiefly with the so called employment chapter, which developed a form of employment policy coordination on a European level given the maintained national competence within labour market policy. The new legislation thereby paved the way for the so called Lisbon Agenda from 2000, which was intended to make practical policy of the balance between the inner market and EU's social ambitions. The goals of the Lisbon Agenda were proudly expressed: that

Europe should become the most competitive economy and reach full employment by 2010 at the latest. The social part of the Lisbon Agenda aimed to modernise the European social model through investments in human capital and fight against social exclusion. Furthermore, the member states were encouraged to invest in education and to have an active employment policy to enable the transition to a knowledge-based economy.

Since these goals were aimed for political areas formally outside the EU competence, there was a particular cooperative method created, with the employment capital in the Amsterdam Treaty as a model, commonly known as the Open Method of Cooperation (OMC). Apart from traditional, binding EU legislation, this method is built on soft cooperative measures. An important part is social benchmarking, where the member states' degree of convergence to the common goals is measured and followed up through a number of indicators. Through naming and shaming there is an aim to create a political pressure to change where shortcomings are most obvious.

The OMC was first used for employment issues and was thereafter expanded to cooperation on pensions, social inclusion and health care. The onset for the method is that there is no competence for EU in these areas, that social policy, employment policy and taxes remains as a national competence. The OMC has come to entail a broad strategy to secure the common social opposition reached in a number of areas. Despite its Habermasian intentions, the OMC has remained unknown in the public debate. It might nevertheless have triggered processes, not least within governments, that will be of significance in the longer term.

The enlargement of EU to 27 Member States in 2004 and 2007 raised doubts on the social policy development in EU; with the articulation of fears for 'social dumping' (the member states reduce their social provisions aiming to lessen the employment costs to attract companies and capital from abroad). These concerns are related to the large differences in the ways that the labour markets of Member States are regulated. Research shows how the labour market is organised in the countries of the rich part of the world has led to an identification of different 'production regimes'. With that, the focus has moved from the welfare state models as the key to understanding how the most developed countries' societal institutions differentiate. However, it has become clear, through this research how the countries' labour market and welfare state institutions are mutually dependent on each other. A weakness in this literature is the great attention paid to the differentiation between uncoordinated labour markets in the Anglo-Saxon world and the coordinated labour markets in the rest of Europe, and the modest consideration of the difference between the Nordic countries and the countries on the European continent within the latter category.

European social democracy has of course tried to influence the development of the social dimension of EU. In the commission, the influence of Jaques Delors is of course critical. Then, in the middle of the 1990's there was also a political will to launch social political questions, in the wake of the political reactions on the SEA and the Maastricht Treaty. An additional example of a new approach in EU was a 'modernisation' communication that the commission presented 1997, which illuminated the need to modernise social policy in the member countries in the light of three types of structural changes: ageing of populations, a changed working life and a new gender balance. In the long run, the Lisbon Agenda could partly be interpreted as a result of the social democratic commitment, perhaps most pertinently expressed in the employment chapter of the Amsterdam Treaty.

The future challenges

The European Union encompasses half a billion people but will in relative terms decrease in significance in two fundamental ways: number of people and economically. It should be added to this scenario that in the coming decades, the populations of the member states will experience a 'new' phase in the demographic transition; that of ageing societies. There are good reasons to point to the common concerns generated by our common futures of ageing populations for the macroeconomic development. Weak growth of the European Single Market (ESM) has also repercussions for all countries. Given that a declining size of the labour force is problematic in a growth perspective, there are hence good reasons to suggest that a more balanced population development in Europe should be a common concern. There is very little to suggest that the OMC objectives can be reached without a stronger concern with human capital formation. This is in congruence with the work in the commission on modernising social protection but would also benefit from being operationalised within the OMC framework. Human capital formation ought to be an integral part of the thinking also around other common objectives of the member states.

The ageing of our European societies is putting increased pressures on redistribution, whether performed by the state, market or family. This warrants us to rethink our social and economic models. We should focus on how social policy interacts with education, fertility and other fundamental determinants of the future tax base. This strong policy recommendation is based on our observation a causal structure where education is the central driving variable for GDP increases in Europe. In order to design sustainable social policies for the future we hence need to put our children and youth first.

The reason is simply that without massive attention to the future tax base in terms of both the number of tax payers and their productivity, there will be little left worth labelling sustainable pensions and health care systems, not to speak about social inclusion. At the heart of this is the urgent need to find new ways to reconcile production and reproduction. This is what the new gender balance is about. Working life needs to be made more flexible also when it comes to the needs of families to balance the two spheres. The gap in the EU process needs to be filled; the situation of children, youth and their families should be a new domain. The social deficits of the member states need to be addressed as promptly as those in their public finances.

A fundamental question is if our welfare state regimes are adequate for the goals we have defined. Can social science make a contribution to the discussion? Here it is important to sort out the normative and positive arguments for and against various approaches. The study of how institutions affect the conditions and behaviour of individuals lies at the heart of social science research. This makes it highly relevant for examining both the intended and unintended consequences of welfare state institutions. Comparative institutional research can contribute by contrasting different policy interventions in order to assess the impact of different kinds of policy regimes. In the context of the OMC process, and its focus on micro outcomes, it also appears warranted to point to another strand of welfare research that has appeared in Amartya Sen's 'capability approach'. Like much of the OMC process this approach is multidimensional and resource-oriented. It also focuses on conditions that can be manipulated and thus is of clear policy relevance. The approach is also democratic, both in its recognition of agency and because it is open to differences in value judgements.

While the attention in this paper has been given to social insurance and transfers, and this is largely also true for the research and debate on social models. Social services are becoming increasingly important in many modern welfare states. It is also evident that they are interconnected with other policy domains of great importance in terms of their relevance for ageing societies. Three policy areas stand out as particularly important. One is the labour market which has been subject to a new discourse under the heading of 'varieties of capitalism', where researchers are primarily working with 'production regimes' referring to a set of policies. The second is the educational sector and what could be labelled as 'education regimes'. The ageing of populations and shrinking labour forces in many European countries is putting the focus on yet another policy area—'migration regimes'—that would benefit from being integrated with welfare state research in general. This implies that we not only have to develop a wider approach to what a social regime is all about, but also have to study production, education and migration regimes in addition to the welfare regimes that we usually associate with the concept of 'social regimes', and we have to study how these policy regimes interact.

There are a number of policy options that should be part of a future-oriented approach. To invest in human capital and to use migration as a way of increasing the labour force are good examples of policies for the future that will require substantial public intervention. Such policies boil down to increasing the number of future taxpayers and their productivity. What is required to succeed in this endeavour is a balanced approach: a synthesis involving a concern with the way that the welfare state supports different groups in society, on the one hand, and a realistic view of how society works, on the other hand. Such an approach could cast new light on an issue that is likely to be confused by zero-sum perceptions of social and economic development in ageing societies. Here, as in many other areas, theory is not enough. We need empirical data to understand what is going on in the real world. The case of family policy institutions provides an interesting case in point.

The case for the dual-earner model

'The modernisation of social protection' is an attempt to adapt the systems of social protection to change. One reason for change is that the system of social protection, designed decades ago, no longer is effective means to, for example, fight poverty. Another reason is that the system is overburdened financially, and cannot be fully financed, read; taxes cannot be raised without jeopardising competitiveness on the global market. Policies have to be seen as a productive factor, they have to be made employment friendly and they have to be financially stable when needs grow stronger as populations are ageing. The proposals for reforms concern both the benefits and how to finance them.

The welfare state channels support through a mix of cash benefits and social services between individuals at different positions in the lifecycle. The redistributive role of the welfare state over the lifecycle is also mediated by the structure of the tax system. The important role of income and consumption taxes within industrial nations implies that high-income middle-aged people contribute more public resources than other age groups. However, the redistributive effects of welfare states on the economic situation of different age groups are highly dependent on the exact design of taxes and benefits. This is why it is necessary to carry out precise institutional analysis of the fiscality of specific programmes and their interactions.

The most common type of family policy model, predominant not only in Continental European countries but also in new member states supports a male breadwinner family type, where paid and unpaid work is highly divided so that fathers have the main responsibilities for carrying out paid work on the labour market whereas mothers carries out the lion's share of reproductive care work in the home. Benefits in support of such a division of work include for example childcare leave benefits paid in low flat-rate amounts as well as various mainly flat-rate cash and tax benefits in support of children and the dependent spouse (wife). Earnings-related parental leave benefits to both parents hardly exist and childcare for the youngest children is less developed. In countries with male breadwinner models female labour force participation and fertility rates are generally at a comparatively low level. Poverty levels among children are typically at medium levels, possibly because male breadwinner support is generous enough to stimulate mothers to stay at home to care for the children at the same time as labour market participation and women's earnings are held at a lower level than what would have been possible otherwise.

The other main type of family policy is the dual earner model developed in the Scandinavian countries. This family policy model supports female labour force participation and to a large extent also male participation in care of children. The main characteristics of this model are parental leave benefits directed to both parents, which are generous both regarding duration and earnings replacement, and publicly subsidised childcare after the termination of parental leave. This model of family policy has enabled these countries to combine high levels of female labour force participation with relatively high levels of fertility. Countries with dual earner models of family policy also have the smallest gender differences in care work, which probably is partly due to family policy measures supporting male involvement in care of children. Due to the combination of generous earnings-related benefits, publicly subsidised services and high female labour force participation, poverty levels among households with children are kept at low levels in these welfare states.

Thus, whereas increased family policy generosity overall seems to decrease poverty and facilitate childbearing it appears to have a more ambiguous relationship to female labour force participation. High female labour force participation is in turn related to both higher fertility levels and lower child poverty. Comparative analysis evidence indicating first that child poverty has become associated with only one earner in the family. Thus, the traditional family model seems less and less able to provide for child welfare. This must raise concern about future human capital formation in several different dimensions.

Raising children in modern societies is linked to a social dilemma since children impose a costly economic burden on parents but are very valuable to society as a whole. Yet, the economic benefits of having children are small and if provided with efficient means of controlling their fertility, most parents will restrict their fertility in a way leading to population decline. Governments have an interest in supporting family formation. But then they have to recognise another dilemma; modern women want to be engaged in paid employment and not only carry unpaid reproductive work. The analysis of welfare state policies should hence acknowledge the potential effects of welfare state arrangements on issues of family formation. Welfare state programmes can hence be seen as attempts to solve different kinds of collective action problems, the increasing costs of raising children in modern societies being one obvious example. Another major dilemma concerns the issue of women's agency in terms of balancing participation in the productive and reproductive spheres.

The case for a social investment approach

What can be labelled as the emergence of a 'social investment strategy' with the Lisbon Agenda a decade ago can be seen as a response to a number of interrelated policy challenges: ageing populations but also a quest for sustainable social polices in the EU beyond the crisis. Need to establish a new gender balance and with flexible working life was seen as critical for sustaining the welfare states in the context of deregulated financial markets and mobile global capital. In the European Union, the need to promote social cohesion in countries with open economies has not diminished by the 'enlargement'. The setting has changed also in other ways as the global financial crisis has turned into a crisis of the 'real' economy, resulting in rapidly falling growth rates and increasing unemployment.

The EU expressed its aim of making Europe become "the most dynamic and competitive knowledge-based economy in the world, capable of sustainable growth with more and better jobs and greater social cohesion, and respect for the environment by 2010." The targets of the Lisbon strategy seemed difficult to achieve for many countries well before the global financial crisis of 2008, and it is now clear that these targets will not be met. The current economic crisis has accentuated the long-term challenges. Policies hence need to go beyond immediate responses to the current crisis. The social investment approach is best envisaged in a life-cycle perspective: the development of publicly funded child care and education programmes constitutes an essential dimension. Such services express the goals of this perspective in two ways: they invest in the human capital of mothers by helping them remain in paid work; and they invest in the human capital of children by providing them with quality educational stimulation at an early age.

Many of the policies currently being adopted for reconciling work and family life are inadequate. Strategies like long parental leaves or vouchers for the purchase of private services may offer some immediate support to parents but lack the long-term perspective that is central in terms of social investment. Human capital policies that promote participation in education throughout the life-course are crucial. Skill needs within advanced industrial societies have changed quite dramatically in the past decades. In particular, demand has increased for higher levels of skills as well as cognitive and social skills. Viewed from a historical perspective, investment in vocational education followed an economic logic whereby firms in European economies relied on specialised vocational skills. In the knowledge-based post-industrial economy, however, new skill needs outline an economic logic for the expansion of public education policies. Policy agendas aimed at advancing human capital policies as part of their social investment strategy need to address the growing economic benefits of investing in education.

There is also reason to think beyond the assumptions of the current era as a knowledge-based economy, which is the underlying rationale of the Lisbon strategy. A slightly different approach, here defined as 'the learning economy', focuses more on the rate of change and the consequential requirements of constantly renewing capabilities in firms and competences for workers. What the comparison of European economies shows is, firstly, that innovation tends to thrive in societies where workers are engaged in organisational learning and do creative work and, secondly, that creative work is most widely diffused in egalitarian societies with broad based and democratic education systems and with labour market institutions that combine flexibility with active labour market policies and income maintenance for the unemployed.

The social investment approach can be seen as a strategy that aims at simultaneously promoting competitiveness and growth, employment and quality of jobs. It is essentially about resolving the trade-off between efficiency and equality. Achieving this goal is dependant on how credible policies can be formulated and delivered. Different examples of best practices can be identified that help to simultaneously widen the tax-base, increase fertility, fight poverty and inequality, or improve the financial sustainability of certain key programmes such as pension schemes. Politics matter for what kinds of chances the social investment strategy will have in the future. Political courage is demanded for anyone who wants to bring in long-termism into policy making.

More analytical light is needed on the interplay between social, educational and labour market policies. European countries face the new requirements of the knowledge-based and learning economy. The current economic crisis and the common long-term challenges that Europe faces make such innovations urgent. The time is ripe to invent a new future. Here, the most brilliant moments of social democracy should not be reserved for the past.

* * *

We continue to witness fundamental transformations of economic systems around the world. With the instruments of globalisation in ICT-technologies, capitalist markets are with the industrialisation of Asian economies is a recent example. In great transformations there are always winners and losers. Schumpeter spoke about a constructive destruction but without public policy the losers are likely to be many irrespective of where on the globe this takes place. The relevance of the European experience in this context is not only dependent on how facts are evaluated but also on more specific value judgements.

Another observation is that the wealthier a nation the more risk averse the population will be. Eventually, India will also have to deal with an ageing of the population. It is the right to prepare for the challenges, and think more deeply about the responses now when there is time to invest.

The most obvious relevance of the European experience is that it should make it possible to avoid making the same mistakes and repeat policy failures. Another relevant aspect is that it provides alternative development paths and invites the observers to evaluate the advantages and problems with different courses of action beyond mere thought experiments. When it comes to the more successful parts of public policy and social development another set of problems arises. The notion of best practise is problematic in many ways. Simply to copy specific programme might prove misleading insofar as policy success is dependent on good interaction between different policy fields.

In the end, if European social democracy wants to be relevant in a future that will be increasingly influenced by the Asian continent, it is critically importance to extend the dialogue on economic, social and democratic developments in the world, and learn from the Indian discourse.

13

WANG HUI

The Dialectics of Self-Reliance and Opening

China's Experience and Challenges

How can we interpret China's growth along with its political situation? There are three ways. The first and the most influential is to attribute the success to the open door policy after the Cultural Revolution. The second, almost as influential as the first, is to paradoxically link the economic achievement with the authoritarian nature of the political regime. The third, by highlighting the heavy price of social inequality, environmental crisis and new conflicts in the society; many left intellectuals maintain a critical view toward growth itself. Prof Hui Pokeung and I co-edited an anthology entitled *Fazhan de Huanxiang (Illusions of Development)* in 1999, which was just such a critique of the rising trends of neo-liberalism and developmentalism. But even critical intellectuals must confront the question of China's unprecedented economic growth. Only by presenting an analysis of growth that differs from the neoliberal analysis can their critiques be truly persuasive. In the discussions surrounding the 30th anniversary of China's reform and the 60th anniversary of the founding of the People's Republic, the universal issue of concern among Chinese intellectuals was how to view the road China has taken over the past 30 or 60 years. Given the continuing urgency of this question, I wish to briefly highlight several of these views below for a comprehensive interpretation of the Chinese experience and its political implications.

Self-reliance (*duli zizhu*) and its political connotations

In discussing the Chinese mode, many scholars are in the habit of comparing China's development to the disintegration of the Soviet and Eastern European system, emphasising China's stability while forgetting conveniently that the general crisis that broke out in 1989 began in China. Its traces can still be found in different spheres in China today. Like the recent financial crisis, the 1989 crisis was part of a larger global crisis, but although it also occurred in the context of an economic crisis it appeared to be political in form. Why did China not collapse along with the other communist party-led socialist countries in the Soviet Union and Eastern Europe? What factors helped to maintain China's stability and created the conditions for rapid growth? Having undergone 30 years of reform, how have these conditions now been transformed? This is the first question to which we must respond.

The collapse of the Soviet and Eastern European system involved many deep and complex historical factors, including the opposition between the bureaucratic system and the people, Cold War political absolutism and the mass poverty brought on by shortage economies. By comparison, a more widespread consciousness of self-renewal existed within the Chinese system. The cultural revolution was a tragedy, but some legacy was left to later period. As a matter of fact, the mutual permeation between state and society in China, or the integration and adapbility of the admistration, was not only the result of 1960s, but also of the whole long Chinese revolution. However, after 1949, after the first five-years plan, the framework of bureaucracy had developed rapidly and became rather rigid by the 1960s. Under the cultural revolution, middle- and senior-level bureaucrats in the Party and state were sent by Mao Zedong to work and live in factories, farms and within other basic units of society. When they returned to positions of authority in the late 1970s, an unexpected consequence was that the state was better able to respond to the needs of the lower strata of society, which was a significant difference from the rigid bureaucratic systems of the Soviet and Eastern European countries. Space limitations do not permit me to elaborate on these issues and the stories surrounding them in greater detail, only to concentrate on the distinguishing characteristic that sets the Chinese system apart from the Soviet system—namely, its independent search for its own path of social development, the unique sovereign status it achieved as a result and the relative flexibility of state policy in integrating demands from different social estates.

In his memoirs, the last General Secretary of Eastern Germany's former communist party, Egon Krenz, explained the reasons for the collapse of his entire country after 1989. He mentioned many aspects, but the most important of these was the transition that had occurred in the Soviet Union and the transformations this produced within the Soviet–Eastern European bloc. During the Cold War, Western politicians often referred to the Brezhnev Doctrine as a way of ridiculing the Eastern European countries for their condition of 'incomplete sovereignty'. Under the Warsaw Pact system, Eastern European countries were not completely sovereign and were limited by Soviet control, so that once problems began to appear in the Soviet Union, the entire Soviet–Eastern European system collapsed as a result. After World War II, the system of sovereign nation-states was established formally, but from a global scope, very few countries actually achieved real independence and autonomy (*duli zizhu*). Which countries in the Soviet Union and Eastern Europe, or even among the Western European allies, were truly independent? In Asia, the positioning of Japan, South Korea and Taiwan within the Cold War structure meant that their sovereignty was limited by US global strategy, and as a result they were incompletely sovereign countries as well. Within the Cold War structure, both camps were systems of allied nations, so that transitions and policy changes in the hegemonic countries of each side profoundly affected all the other countries.

In the early years of its founding, China was part of the socialist camp within this polar Cold War system, and during the war to resist US aggression and to aid Korea in the early 1950s, China entered into armed conflict with the US and its allies. In this era—particularly during the first Five-Year Plan—China's industrial development, post-war recovery and international standing were greatly aided by the efforts of the Soviet Union, making it dependent upon the Soviet Union in some ways and to some degree. But China began supporting non-aligned movements in the mid-1950s together with India and other third countries and later engaged in open debates with the Soviet Communist Party, gradually shedding its 'suzerain' relationship with the Soviet Union in the spheres of politics, economics and the military, and establishing its own socialist system and achieving independent status on the international scene. Although the Taiwan Strait still represents a line of division, the Chinese state is now sovereign and self-reliant in its political character. The national economic and industrial systems that were constructed under this political climate are also highly self-reliant as a result. Absent this condition of self-reliance, it would be very difficult to picture how China's path of reform and opening-up would have looked, and it would be very difficult to imagine what China's fate might have been after 1989. When the period of reform and opening up began, China already had a self-reliant national economic system, which laid out the conditions for reform. China's reform was self-directed and had an internal logic—it was an active and not a passive process. It also differed from the dependent economies of Latin America and their related crises, as well as the dependent development of Japan, Korea and Taiwan under the Cold War Structure in the first years of the post-war era (i.e., their dependence upon the US-led regional political structure and war economies (Korean and Vietnam Wars) were the critical junctures in their early development). In this way, mainland China's development has followed an entirely different path.

China's relatively independent sovereignty was achieved through Party practices, which was one of its most prominent characteristic in the 20th century. Regardless of how many mistakes the Chinese Communist Party (CCP) committed in either theory or practice, its anti-imperialism and, later, its disputes with the Soviet Union provided important historical foundations for Chinese sovereignty and independence. Its open debates with the Soviet Communist Party helped the CCP to break its suzerain relation with its Soviet counterpart, and only once this occurred could the Chinese state extract itself from its corresponding suzerain relation with the Soviet Union, producing a new model of independence.

In other words, the roots of China's sovereignty are political, and this political independence that developed through party relations came to be manifested in the state and economic spheres. In effect, China's sustained critique and struggle with the Cold War polar structure was connected to its gradual disintegration. In the economic, political and cultural spheres, China's explorations and attempts at reforming the socialist path produced various deviations, problems and even tragic results, but in the fifties, sixties and seventies, the policies of the Chinese state and Party were continuously being adjusted. These modifications were in essence self-modifications, carried out in response to the demands and problems of reality, rather than having been driven by external force or guidance. Because the Communist Party lacked democratic mechanisms, line struggles often turned into violent power struggles, but these factors should not conceal the historical importance of those factional and theoretical debates. From this perspective, it is necessary to rethink our conventional wisdom on reform, for instance that there are no ready-made models of reform or policies, making the notion of "crossing the river by feeling for the stones" correct. But the fact is that the lack of ready-made models has been a characteristic of the Chinese revolution as a whole. Without any basic value orientations, who knows where "crossing the river by feeling for the stones" will lead us to? The theoretical origins of reform and the concept of a socialist commodity economy emerged through theoretical discussions on commodities, commodity economies, the law of value and bourgeois rights; they were also constituted through socialist practice. Discussions surrounding the problem of the law of value originated in China in the 1950s against the background of the Sino-Soviet split and Mao Zedong's analysis of contradictions in Chinese society. This problem became the central topic of inter-party debate once more in the mid-1970s. Absent such a theoretical debate, it would be extremely difficult to imagine how subsequent Chinese reform would follow a developmental logic from the law of value, the division of labour and a socialist commodity economy up to the present socialist market economy. From this perspective, the economic reforms which begun in the late 1970s contained an intrinsic theoretical vein.

The role of the peasantry and its transformations

The Chinese revolution occurred within a traditional agricultural society in which the peasantry became the revolutionary subject. Whether in the early stages of revolution or war, or during the era of social reconstruction and reform, the sacrifices and contributions of the agricultural class were always significant, and their expressions of active spirit and creativity left a profound impression on people's minds. Through the entire 20th century, the mobilisation of China's rural society and the transformations of rural social organisations could be described as earth-shattering and wholly unprecedented. The agricultural class achieved a strong sense of political consciousness through the agrarian revolution and a transition in the rural social order; in the Eastern European countries and even the Soviet Union, such prolonged armed struggle and agrarian revolutions were rarely seen. Absent such a background, it would've been impossible for the transformation of land relations to become the central aspect of a prolonged rural mobilisation.

This is also a premise for understanding radical politics in China in the first half of the 20th century. The CCP was established as a result of the international communist movement, but the central task of China's socialist party was to mobilise peasants and to construct a new politics and society through a rural movement. Through 30 years of armed revolt and social struggle, the Party finally became the foundational core of the social movement and was a party of the rural and worker's movements in particular. Its grassroots nature and capacity for organisation and mobilisation set it far apart from the parties of the socialist Eastern European countries. China's observers tend overwhelmingly to attribute the successes and failures of the Chinese revolution to individual leading figures without discussing this process itself to its full extent. In the reflections on the Chinese revolution, the focus on its violence has also resulted in the neglect and even the denial of the new social subjectivities created through this process. In a socialist revolution carried out in a society where peasants are the primary subjects, the subjective initiatives and wills of the leaders are certainly important, yet they alone are not the key to understanding its history.

The new land relations created through the Chinese revolution and their subsequent reconstruction created the conditions for China's reform, which was something Lenin had already recognised in his appraisal of Sun Yatsen. After the revolution in 1911, Lenin pointed out in his commentary on Sun Yatsen's Jianguo Dawang (Programme for Construction of the Republic) that the agrarian program of the Chinese revolution and socialist-leaning national plan provided the preconditions for the development of agricultural capitalism. It's difficult to imagine how traditional farmers and their village organisations would have displayed such enthusiastic spirit of initiative if these social transformations had not occurred. On this point, we need only to look at the situation of peasants in other farming societies and market conditions, including those in Asia—and particularly South Asia—or Latin America, to see clearly how profound this was in China: these other societies have yet to initiate any significant land reforms, so that farmers remain largely bound in landlord or plantation economies and are unable to develop a strong consciousness of their own autonomy. The process of land reform has been closely connected to the popularisation of village education, the rise in literacy, the capacity for self-organisation and an increase in technical abilities. Under conditions of market reform, these early inheritances became the preconditions for a more mature labour market in China.

Compared with many socialist and post-socialist countries, the value of equality may have taken root to a greater degree in Chinese popular consciousness than in other societies. But under conditions of marketisation and globalisation, discussions concerning the equal standing of peasants and migrant workers today will nonetheless differ drastically in content from discussions concerning how the standing of farmers changed in the early 20th century. At the end of the last century, the questions of agriculture, peasants and rural community (*sannong*) and of migrant workers became key topics in contemporary China once more, surrounded by the issues of how to resolve urban-rural relations under market conditions and how to resolve the land issue in China. The strong dependence of the rural economy upon the urban economy and the impacts it has felt as a result of urbanisation have led peasants to migrate on mass scales, transforming them into a new urban working class. These peasants, who have experienced the process of rural land reform, are now being transformed into a cheap labour force in the coastal and urban industries. Following urbanisation, the marketisation of land has emerged as a critical issue. It is roughly estimated that there are about 50-60 million peasants who have lost their land completely and 60 per cent protests arose because of controversies over the expropriation of land. This process is closely related to the contemporary rural crisis. Most importantly, peasants as political subjects are currently undergoing a transformation into a free labour force, thanks to the definitions and categories of property rights. When an urban middle class is struggling for private property rights, a high percentage of rural population dislikes the idea of the privatisation of land. The implication of this issue is this: what kind of public policy or public administration could integrate demands of different social groups?

The position of the state

Another key element to understanding China's period of reform is the explanation of the nature and evolution of the Chinese state. In *Adam Smith in Beijing*, Giovanni Arrighi (2008) writes: "National markets are no more a Western invention than national states and interstate systems...through the eighteenth century by far the largest national market was to be found not in Europe but in China." He even goes one step further to analyse the factors behind the development of the contemporary Chinese economy, looking in particular at its attraction for foreign investors. He writes: "Contrary to widespread belief, the main attraction of the PRC for foreign capital has not been its huge and low-priced reserves of labor as such...The main attraction, we shall argue, has been the high quality of those reserves—in terms of health, education, and capacity for self-management—in combination with the rapid expansion of the supply and demand conditions" (Ibid.: 351). Peking University economist Yao Yang also offers a similar perspective in his overview of the conditions for China's economic development, identifying a neutral government or neutral state as the condition for the success of Chinese reform.

The question of national resources in reform is an important one. I have two supplementary points to make regarding Arrighi and Yao Yang's discussions. Arrighi, for one, establishes his narrative of the Chinese and Asian national markets within a long national tradition, but without the Chinese revolution or its reorganisation of social relations, it would be difficult to imagine how the traditional 'national market' would transform into a new national market on its own. Through national efforts during the late Qing to construct a military and commercial system, as well as the agrarian revolution that continued after the Xinhai Revolution (1911), a new form of internal-external relations were created that differed from those under the traditional national market. In discussing the state character of modern China, it is impossible to leave aside the transformations in land relations and rural identities that occurred as a result of the Chinese revolution. For instance, critiques are often carried out of the people's commune experiments, but very rarely do these also discuss the fact that this experiment resulted from the continuous transformations in land relations in modern China. On the one hand, the small-scale peasant economy that takes the family–household as its basic unit no longer exists, but on the other hand, household, family and geographical relations have been restructured under conditions of reform and through other means to fit within the new social configurations. Rural reform was a reform of the commune system, yet at the same time it was also built upon social relations that were transformed through these experiments. The initial period of rural reform was driven by the state and was a reform movement that had at its core the management and adjustment of agricultural prices through different methods. The grand development from the rural industries of the 1960s through to the rural enterprises of the 1990s has brought with it a vastly different context of political and economic management, but this sequence obviously cannot be explained using the logic of neoliberalism.

As for Yao Yang's perspective, the political preconditions behind the initiation of modern revolutions and socialist histories by neutral states were not neutral. Chinese socialism in practice strove to establish a state that would represent the masses and the universal interests of the overwhelming majority, and this led to a break between the state or government and special interests. At the level of theory, the state practice of socialism was a revision of early-Marxist class theory, with Mao Zedong's works, including *On the Ten Major Relationships* and *On the Correct Handling of Contradictions among the People* providing the foundations for this new state theory. Because the main objective of the socialist state is to represent the interests of the overwhelming majority, under market conditions its connection to special interest groups is looser than under other state forms. But only in this way can we describe it as a 'neutral' state. The success of the early years of reform can largely be attributed to this, and it was a source of legitimacy for reform, without which it would've been very difficult for members of the different social strata to believe that the state-led reforms represented their own interests. But the real meaning of 'neutralisation' is often concealed in the use of the term, which is that the universality of interests represented by the state was established upon Chinese revolution values and socialist practices. At least in the early years, the legitimacy of the reforms derived from the universality of interests represented by the socialist state.

But it is very difficult to determine China's state character if we only look at one of its standard point of origins, for the state itself contains different traditions. In the reform process, people often use the concepts of 'reform' and 'counter-reform', 'progress' and 'conservation' to describe the contradictions and struggles between these traditions, but from a dynamic historical perspective, the ways these traditions come into harmony with one another, check and balance one another, and contradict one another are also useful in significant ways. In the socialist era, we saw how the strength of the two or many social forces fluctuated in concert with one another, and how the 'far left' and 'far right' were overcome; but as marketisation reforms become the predominant trend, the absence of a check and balance by socialist forces between the inner workings of the state, the inner workings of the Party and the entire social sphere will quickly shorten the distance between the state and special interest groups. The social resources accumulated during the socialist era have been transformed under these relations to become limitations on socialist policy. The state's 'neutrality' was achieved through non-neutral forces and the reciprocal relationship between the two.

Chinese reform has yielded many experiences worth overviewing, for instance the implementation of a talent strategy, education reform and other economic policies, but I think that the few elements listed above are the most fundamental and also the most frequently neglected. These points also represents some of 20th century China's most unique experiences.

Shifts in the sovereignty structure

Under the new conditions of globalisation, localisation and marketisation, the conditions mentioned above are being significantly challenged: the foundations of social relations, economic life and political subjectivities are undergoing change. If we are unable to grasp these new historical conditions and the direction of their change, it will be very difficult to construct structurally new and effective mechanisms and policies. To understand these transformations, I wish to point out some of the new tendencies in the contemporary world

First, the traditional form of sovereignty is undergoing significant transformation under globalisation. The current process of globalisation appears to be manifesting primarily in two directions. The first is the transnational movement of capital and thereby transnational production, consumption and circulation; large-scale immigration and a market dependence that has arisen through trade and investment; and the globalisation of various risks as well. The second is the creation of international regulatory mechanisms to manage and respond to this transnational movement of capital and to control risk. These include the WTO and the European Union, alongside other international and regional organisations. The former is something like an anarchical force, while the latter is a mechanism for harmonising and controlling it. These two forces simultaneously came into effect.

The shape of national sovereignty will also inevitably change alongside these other important transformations. With the first trend just mentioned, and particularly after the late 1980s had passed, China gradually began to take on the form of an export-led economy. The transnationalisation of production made China into the 'industrial workshop of the world,' and this configuration differed completely from the forms of labour force and resource deployment of the past, forging a new relationship between the coastal and inland areas, and between urban and rural regions as well. With the gradual liberalisation of the financial system, China's foreign exchange reserves shot up to become the largest in the world, and its economic development became highly dependent upon international markets, and especially the American market. The concept of 'Chimerica' that describes the symbiotic relationship between the Chinese and American economies is perhaps a little exaggerated, but in light of the transformations of these relatively independent national economies into dependent economies of varying degrees, this concept also has very strong implications.

As for the second trend, China has joined the WTO and other international treaties and agreements and actively participates in other regional organisations, such that it is now difficult to describe China's structure of sovereignty in the traditional sense. The current financial crisis has shown that crises arise precisely from shifts in the autonomy of societies, so that a crisis elsewhere can quickly become China's own crisis, and these crises cannot be overcome simply by reasserting old ideals of sovereignty. International cooperation cannot be avoided. Thus, under conditions of globalisation and the open global networks involved, the question of how to achieve new forms of autonomy must be asked with reference to history alongside new explorations on the situation.

Next, the role of the state is undergoing transformation not only within the realm of global relations but in domestic relations as well. Simple descriptions of the role of the Chinese state as 'totalitarian' often confuse the positive with the negative aspects of the role of the state. China did not undergo 'shock therapy' in its period of reform, as did Russia, but was significantly more skilled at economic regulation than the latter country. That the Chinese financial system has shown itself to be relatively stable is due to the fact that China has not fully begun down the neoliberal path, and this is the product of conscious policy planning and not from limitations imposed by social movements, social contradictions and the socialist tradition. Land has not been privatised in China (although it can be exchanged relatively freely to adapt to the demands of market conditions), which has not only been essential for China's low-cost rural social security system but also enables the state to utilise land resources for organisation and development, and for increasing the possibility of undertaking land profit-sharing reforms. The large tax revenues from China's state-owned enterprises have also provided essential resources for the government's regulative capacity under crisis conditions. These aspects are certainly connected to state capacity and will. But the Chinese state should also step up on those spheres it is responsible for, such as resolving the rural crisis in a positive way, reconstructing the social security system, ecological and environmental protection, increasing investment in education and initiating educational reform. The Chinese government will be correspondingly be required to shift from a development-oriented government to a social services-oriented one, which will also transform the Chinese economy from being reliant on exports to being led by domestic needs. The real issue is that this is not a question of will but of social forces and the games they play.

Whether these positive social policies can be implemented is not purely dependent on state will. After 30 years of reform, in which it has acted as the driving force behind marketisation reforms, state apparatuses are now deeply embedded in market activities. The various state departments within the current state cannot appropriately be described using the concept of neutral states. The state is not isolated but rather interwoven within the social structure and relations of social interest. The present issue of corruption not only involves individual corrupted officials but also the question of the relationship between social policy, economic policy and special interests. The development of the hydrocarbon industry and energy projects, for instance, are often impeded or led by individual special interest groups. The influence of these special interest groups in the area of public policy have primarily limited public discussion, social protection movements and the different traditions emanating from the state and within the Party. In the recent past, the large-scale discussions in the late 1990s on the *san nong* question resulted in the modification of state rural policy;

the debates on the medical insurance system that were initiated in 2003 by the SARS crisis facilitated a change in the direction of health reform; the large-scale labour movement and the debates on the restructuring of state enterprises that began in 2005 led to the appearance of related policies; and calls from the people to do something about corruption and for strict party discipline provided internal strength for China's anti-corruption movement. But domestic and international special interest relations have now seeped into state mechanisms and even the process of legislation to an unprecedented degree. Under these conditions, the question of how the state can represent the so-called 'universal interest' has already become extremely tenuous.

The paradox of the statification of the Party

Discussions on the state are directly related to questions about the formation of democratic mechanisms. There is one basic paradox one must face, which is that on the one hand, China's ability to govern effectively has been widely acknowledged in comparison with the governments of many other countries, from its disaster relief mobilisation after the May 12 Wenchuan earthquake to its rapid response in initiating a bailout plan after the financial meltdown, and from its successful management of the Olympic Games to the efficacy of its various local governments in organisational development and controlling the crisis. But on the other hand, contradictions have appeared between officials and the people in certain areas, and have become sharp at certain times, with the administrative abilities and levels of honesty of different levels of government having come into question. The key issue is that such contradictions are often blown up into large-scale and widely-debated legitimacy crises. By observing the situation in other countries, we can see that an institutional political crisis may not result even if the capacity of the state declines, the government accomplishes nothing, the economy is in recession and social policies remain unimplemented. This issue is closely connected with democracy as the source of political legitimacy.

In the 1980s, the democratic question was fairly simple. The wave of democratisation had been building over 20 years, and on the one hand, democracy remained the most important source of political legitimacy. But on the other hand, the method of simply imitating Western democracy had lost the attraction it had possessed in Asia in the 1980s. In the wake of the crises in the emerging democracies and the fading of the 'color revolutions' after 1989, the tendency toward democratisation began to decline in Eastern Europe, Central Asia and other regions. At the same time, the vacuousness of democracy in the democratic nations of Western society and in the some of third world countries is creating a universal democratic crisis, one closely connected to the neo-liberal conditions of marketisation and globalisation. For one, the dominant form of the postwar political democracies were multiparty or two-party parliamentary systems, but under market conditions, political parties in some countries are becoming less representative each day than they were in the early days of democracy. In the drive to increase votes, the political values of the parties are gradually becoming obscured, so that the representative system of democracy exists now in name only. Second, the connection between democracy and states is also being threatened under the condition of globalisation: as economic relations gradually exceed the traditional categorisations of national economies, and as its related activities become difficult to balance within the confines of a single country, the political plans of any country are forced to adjust to the international system. Third, in some countries, the shift toward oligarchical forms and the consolidation of special interests in political parties has resulted in the gradual disconnection of democracy as a political structure from the basic units of society. The interests and needs of the lower strata find no expression within the political sphere. As a result, they resort to a self-defensive anarchy (i.e., the rise of Maoism in India). Fourth, the reliance of the election process on large amounts of money and financial resources has resulted in the existence of both legal and illegal forms of election fraud in many democratic countries, thus destroying public confidence in the election process. This is not to say that democratic values are dead. The real question is what kind of democracy do we need and what form should it take? How do we make democracy something more than an empty form, into something with substantive meaning?

The Chinese political system has also undergone significant transformations, including a change in the role of the Party. In the 1980s, the primary goal of political reform was the separation of the Party from the state, but after the 1990s, this grew out of favour as a popular slogan, so that the government and Party intersected more frequently in concrete practice and institutional arrangements. I interpret this phenomenon to be part of the shift toward Party statification, and it is worth analysing why this tendency arose. According to traditional political theories, the Party represents the will of the people—through parliamentary struggles and debates, or through procedural democracy—to become state and public will, and even the expression of sovereignty. In China, the multiparty cooperation system, under which eight other democratic parties are led by the ruling Communist Party and are also involved in state affairs, is built upon multiparty representation. But under market society conditions, state apparatuses are directly involved in economic activity, and the various branches of the state become entangled with special interests. This infiltration of the state by the Party is not a new phenomenon—the primary issue faced during Mao Zedong's time was not simply the bureaucratisation of the state but also the bureaucratisation of the party—but its intense permeation of the state under market society conditions of is new. What was called the 'neutral state' in the early years of reform is now undergoing a transformation. Because the Party remains relatively disconnected from economic activity, it is able to express the will of society with relative independence and 'neutrality.' The weeding out of corruption, for instance, is largely reliant upon effective implementation by party mechanisms. After the 1990s, the will of the state was presented primarily through the goals and slogans of the Party, including the "Three Represents," the "Harmonious Society" and the "Scientific Outlook on Development,"[1] but these were no longer direct and special expressions of the Party but instead directly invoked the interests

1. "Three Represents" signifies the threefold representation of the developmental needs of China's advanced production capacity, the progressive direction of China's advanced culture, and the fundamental interests of the broad majority. The "Harmonious Society" was a socioeconomic vision forged under Hu Jintao that advocated a shift in focus from economic growth to social balance and harmony. The "Scientific Outlook on Development" is a socioeconomic ideology that is prioritises the interests of the people and aims for sustainable modes of development.

of the entire people. In this sense, the Party has become the core of public sovereignty.

However, the statification of the Party also involves a dual challenge. For one, if the division between the Party and the state vanishes entirely, then what forces or mechanisms can prevent the Party from becoming trapped within the relations of interest of market society, as the state has? Second, the universal representation of the traditional party (and the 'neutrality' of the early socialist state) was built on its clear political values. The statification of the party will mean a weakening and transformation of the Party's political values, so that if the achievement of a 'neutral state' is closely connected to the political values of the Party, then what apparatuses can enable China to maintain its broad representation of interests under these new conditions? What force can the Party rely upon for self renewal, and how might the voices of the common people find expression in the public sphere? What is required to initiate change in the basic lines and policies of the state and Party, through true freedom of speech, venues of negotiation and continuous interaction between officials and the people? How can we attract and consolidate international and domestic forces on a wide scale to achieve the most widespread democracy? These questions cannot be avoided in discussing the self-renewal of the Party and the formation of a new public space.

These are also questions we need to consider in thinking about China's political transformation, alongside the question of China's democratic road. Specifically, I think there are at least three aspects we need to consider. First, China experienced a long and profound revolution in the 20th century, so that Chinese society retains an acute sensitivity towards the demands of fairness and social equality. How should these historical and political traditions be translated into democratic demands under contemporary conditions? In other words, what is the mass line or the popular democracy of this new era? Second, the Chinese Communist Party is massive and has experienced significant changes, becoming more entangled with state apparatuses with each day. How can this party system become more democratic, and how can the state's ability to represent the universal interest be preserved while the role of the Party is being transformed? Third, how can a new political form be constructed upon the social base, granting greater political capacity to mass society and thereby overcoming the condition of 'depoliticisation' created through neoliberalism's marketisation? These questions have bred important theoretical questions, including: under conditions of globalisation of marketisation, in what political direction will the PRC move towards? How can a dialectic of increased self-reliance and increased opening up be forged in Chinese society? This 'self-reliance' does not refer to nationalistic or ethnocentric tendencies but rather the reestablishment of values and politics along different lines—if anything, it is a new internationalism and a new social democracy which will be able to overcome the gaps or ruptures among Chinese population. The global significance of this exploration should be obvious given the universal crisis of democracy and market.

The necessary change of the mode of development

China's economic reform since the 1980s has brought about tremendous achievements, but it has also led to social re-differentiation. During all these years, Chinese intellectuals have been debating how to explain such contradictory phenomena. After the middle of the 1970s, the discourse of developmentalism centred on neoclassical economics gradually started to dominate in many countries. With ideas such as private property, free market and formal democracy, this discourse criticises state interference and the tradition of welfare state, opposing popular democracy and any socialist legacy; it changed the social system in post-war West Europe with the political power of Reagan-Thatcherism. In the latter half of the 1980s, this trend of thought reverberated powerfully in socialist countries. The ideas of private property, free market, and formal democracy became the most powerful weapon against the socialist state system centred on planned economy and its socialist ideology. In the historical process when the Cold War collapsed and the socialist system disintegrated, 'neo-liberalism' became one of the most important methodology to explain the reform process in China. After the world-wide events in 1989, almost all historical interpretations of various social movements and of the progress of reform in China were subordinated to the main-stream discourse of 'neo-liberalism'. This mainstream discourse, however, can not adequately explain the drastic differentiation in classes, stratums and regions that are taking place in China and worldwide. Nor can it provide any alternative plan to the developmental model mainly in the form of market expansion, which has caused environmental crisis and social disintegration. Therefore, the market economy of 'neo-liberalism' incurred forceful resistance from various directions.

The mainstream discourse of 'neo-liberalism' is established on the polar opposition between free market and state intervention, capitalism and socialism, globalisation and anti-globalisation, private property and state ownership. It applies this framework of dualism to interpret the reform process in contemporary China. However, if we situate in a concrete historical process contemporary Chinese intellectuals' debates on free market and state intervention, capitalism and socialism, globalisation and anti-globalisation, and private property and state ownership, such a discourse of dualism itself will manifest different connotations.

First of all, the formation of China's market system includes two basic directions: internally, through transferring rights and profits from the centre to the local, nurturing decision-making power of enterprises, reforming the finance system, and privatisation, the state allowed market mechanism to permeate into all fields of social life; internationally, through reforms in foreign trade and in the finance system, the state gradually brought China into the global market relationships that are dominated by the WTO and the IMF.

This process was related to profound transformations in social structure, and also ignited profound social crisis. In the second half of 1988, because of social instability caused by inflation, price reform had to be terminated. The year 1989 is therefore often regarded as a brief interval in China's urban reform. But this interval happened to overlap the time when the state adjusted its policy as it confronted the first cycle of crisis. This period became the period of preparation for further market expansion. In September 1989, the price reform that had been aborted twice started to be implemented again. At that time, major adjustments focused on price, exchange rate and interest rate. The event of 1989 and the changes that took place after 1989 demonstrate the paradoxical relationship between market expansion and the state. On the one hand, the nurture and development of market is almost unthinkable without the state's policy adjustment, legal system and political support. On the other hand, the dependence of the market on the state is at the same time the premise of the dealings between power and market. From this perspective, we discover the internal historical relationship between the reforms of the 1980s and the post-1989 period, and see a peculiar interaction between traditional socialist system and market creation—the expansion of market relied on an 'anti-market' power, namely, state intervention, and the state overcame the crisis of legitimacy exactly through market expansion. In this sense, the dualism of market/state cannot explain the process of market expansion in China. The 'neo-liberalist' idea of state retreat cannot explain the great achievements accomplished since the reform because of effective state policies in regard to price and industries. Nor can it explain the outrageous exchange of power with profit and the severe social stratification that took place in the process of large-scale privatisation of state-owner properties.

Secondly, since the end of the 1980s, the social conditions in which the state system functioned have changed so drastically that the system itself and the social interest relations that it represents have been thoroughly reformed. During China's high-speed economic development, the income gap between various social strata, groups and regions expanded extensively, and the destitute population increased rapidly. This historical transformation rendered the state's old ideology (namely, the socialist ideology based on equality) and the state's practice extremely contradictory, and therefore the state could not perform its ideology function. It is in this situation that 'neo-liberalism' became a new dominant ideology. Therefore, the traditional socialism/capitalism duality basically cannot be used as a framework for historical analysis. It is only in this process of ideological transformation that we could understand the following phenomena in the field of thoughts: new trends of social criticism was resisted and denounced as old ideology, the simple socialist elements in the social movements that took place in the end of the 1980s and their internal relationship to appeals for democracy were covered up with the pattern of reform and anti-reform, and etc.

Thirdly, the social movements in the end of the 1980s tried to accomplish the organic interaction between society and state through popular participation. But after 1989, the interaction mechanism between market and state replaced the interaction between society and state. In the discourse of 'neo-liberalism', the concept of society is gradually replaced by the concept of market, and the basic driving force that precipitated the reform in the state system and the transformation in the legal system is no longer 'the society' or 'the people' but domestic and international markets. Therefore the connotation of 'politics' itself underwent a significant transformation: the state becomes the major executive to maintain the market system and to reconstruct the legal system according to WTO regulations. From such a historical perspective, the relationship between social movement, crisis of reform and the role of the state need to be reconsidered. The trend of social thought that was developed in the 1990s with the slogan 'reflecting on radicalism' replaced the view of democracy as based on popular participation with the view of democracy as step-by-step and formalistic. As a result, the real momentum of democratic practice is theoretically invalidated, and social protection movements of different social levels since the 1990s are excluded from the category of democracy.

Fourthly, when privatisation becomes a trend, and private property becomes a key point in the constitution reform, it is necessary to historically differentiate two forms of 'privatisation.' The first kind is private economy developed from local social relations and small markets (for instance, market relations based on regional and blood relationships in the Wenzhou area, and market expansion propelled by the production of small goods and low-profit production)—this economic form showed its strong vitality after the finance storm of 1997. The second kind is the large-scale privatisation that took place under the supervision of the state, in which process large amount of state-owned property was misplaced or transferred illegally. Corruption, large-scale unemployment, social injustice and the disintegration of social security in contemporary

China took place largely in the second kind of 'privatisation'. It is a process of reform dominated by the state, but in the form of 'state withdrawal'.

According to the above observations, we must make three basic differentiations.

Firstly, we must differentiate between the idea of market that competes freely or adjusts itself and the historical process in which modern market economy came into existence and functioned. According to the first differentiation, market society and its rules are formed and function in the interrelationship between state intervention, institution innovation, monopolisation, social customs and historical events. Free competition only constitutes part of its conditions. Therefore the criticism of market society and its crisis in reality does not equal the negation of market system.

Secondly, we must differentiate between neo-liberalist market ideology (often characterised by the demand for complete state withdrawal) and neo-liberalist market order and economic policies (often characterised by reliance on state policy and enforcement). According to this differentiation, neo-liberalist ideology requests the state to adopt a non-intervening policy, namely for the state to give up its duty of social welfare and social security, to give up its economic methods to adjust market activities, and furthermore, to cut off the link between politics and economy. But the giving up of duty is itself the result of arrangements through institution and policy. The crisis of China's state-owned enterprises and agriculture is the very result of active institutional and policy arrangement. Therefore the slogan of anti-state intervention happens to be the premise of state policies, the essence of which is another form of active 'intervention'.

Thirdly, we must differentiate between the category of market and the category of society. That is market rules and regulations do not equal social rules and regulations, and social democratic system does not equal market operating system, so the orientation of the state toward democracy does not equal the transformation of the state into political organs to set up a market system. The crisis of 1989 demonstrates that market expansion under the supervision of the state created social crisis, while social crisis became an opportunity for the state to control the society (not only the market) in all aspects, and that the market system was established when the society (not the state) completely withdrew from the field of 'politics'.

I will outline some orientations here based on the above analysis.

First, economic inequality caused by market expansion is always closely related with inequalities in other fields such as politics, economics and culture. So struggles for freedom (including labour contract freedom, freedom to exchange, political freedom and etc.) must at the same time be struggles for social equality. The discourse that completely opposes appeals for equality with appeals for freedom must be rejected.

Secondly, resistance against monopolisation and domineering market tyranny cannot be simply equalled with the struggle 'against' the market, because such social resistance itself includes the efforts striving for fair competition in the market and for economic democracy.

Thirdly, the resistance against economic hegemony and multinational monopoly does not mean closing the country to the outside world, and a certain degree of trade protection does not equal 'anti-market'. Social movements in relation to the WTO and the struggle between rich countries and poor countries in WTO negotiations show a new form of struggle, that is, not to oppose international organisations and international adjustments as a whole, but to promote the democratisation of international institutions including the WTO and of international regulations through participatory social movements, and furthermore, to connect domestic economic justice with international economic justice.

Fourthly, the movement of economy is always embedded in politics, culture and other social conditions, so to strive for the conditions of fair market, competition does not equal getting rid of state political system, social customs and any regulating mechanism. On the contrary, the perfection of market conditions aims to reform, limit and expand these systems in order to create social conditions for fair interaction. In this sense, the struggle for social justice and fair market competition cannot be equalled with the opposition to state intervention. It rather requires social democracy, namely, to prevent the state from becoming the protector of domestic monopoly and multinational monopoly through the society's democratic control of the state. Here participatory and popular democracy is still the real momentum for contemporary democracy. The method that opposes popular democracy with formal democracy must be rejected. On any scale, namely, no matter on the scale of a nation-state or on the scale of world market, the struggle for freedom will necessarily manifest itself as the struggle for democracy and freedom.

I summarise these orientations as a kind of thinking in relation to the democratic system of market, a kind of thinking in regard to the development of society and not just the development of economy. Only in this framework, can the struggle for economic justice be connected with the struggle for social justice and political democracy and with the exploration of different development models.

The 1990s era is over. This post-1989 process has shown signs in the past few years that it has already reached its end, but the year 2008 has provided the clearest signs of all. Globally, neoliberalism's economic path has been hit by a massive crisis, while in China this became evident through a series of events: from the March 14 Tibet Incident to the Wenchuan earthquake, from the Beijing Olympics to the financial crisis, Chinese society has come to understand its own global position in a different way. In Western societies, discussions regarding China's rise have been occurring for quite some time, but amidst the crisis, people suddenly realised that China was an economy to be reckoned with, second only to the US economy. Its rise has occurred more quickly than had been predicted, expressed in a corresponding level of self-confidence. This change was dramatic and some of its elements were coincidental, though not accidental. The issue may be that China is still scrambling to adjust to its new international identity. The contradictions that have accumulated in Chinese society during the process of marketisation and the dangers it now faces as a result of globalisation are both unprecedented. Whether we are talking about the so-called 'end of the 90s' or analysing the 'end of the revolution,' the real goal is to clarify the situation we face, and to question and to formulate a new politics, a new path in a new direction. This 'end' is not an end in the Hegelian sense but rather the will to break with the past and the desire to construct a new politics. It is from here that we must look back upon the revolutionary inheritance of the 20th century.

References

Arrighi, Giovanni (2008). *Adam Smith in Beijing*. New York: Verso Books. p.321.

14

JONATHAN COHN

The Strange Life of American Welfare

It was just before 11 pm on Sunday, March 21, 2010. Inside the chamber of the US House of Representatives, history was about to unfold. In the gallery above, officials, reporters and a few lucky tourists filled every seat and every spare inch of the aisles in between. Below, on the House floor, more than 500 members of Congress representing every district in the country took turns inserting their cards into electronic voting machines. Under the chamber rules, members have 15 minutes to vote and, typically, the members stand around chatting as the clock ticks down, seemingly oblivious to what is happening around them. Not this time.

The vote was on the Patient Protection and Affordable Care Act—or, as it's since become known, as the 'Affordable Care Act.' It was the Obama Administration's signature legislative effort—a controversial measure that would seek to make health insurance a right of citizenship, as it is in most of the developed world. All but one member of the Republican Party planned to vote against the bill. Several members of the Democratic Party planned to join them, even though it meant defying party leaders. But, thanks to extended negotiations that had ended just hours before, the outcome was no longer in doubt. The Democratic majority was large enough to withstand a few defections. It would take 218 votes to pass the bill. And as the electronic scoreboard showed the 'Yes' tally moving pass 210, the room fell quiet—until it reached 217. At that point, Democrats huddled towards their side of the chamber began chanting, "One more vote, one more vote..." And then, when number 218 was cast, the chorus changed to the slogan of Obama's 2008 presidential campaign 'Yes We Can.'

Back at the White House, the staff cheered as Obama embraced his closest advisers. Two days later, at a White House signing ceremony, the president spoke of the moment's historical significance. Guaranteeing access to high care and financial protection from medical bills had been a project of the American left for nearly a century. Virtually every one of his Democratic Party predecessors, going back to Franklin Roosevelt, had seriously contemplated trying to pass a law 'universal health care.' Two former Democratic presidents, Harry Truman and Bill Clinton, had made the effort—and failed miserably.

But the celebration would prove short-lived. The legislation was the product of a 14-month debate full of acrimony, dishonesty and shady legislative deals. By the time that debate was over, polls showed that popular support for universal health care had fallen. The vast majority of Americans remained confused about what was actually in the law and more people seemed opposed to it than were in favour. Some eight months after Obama's signing ceremony, his party suffered a devastating rebuke in the midterm elections, as the Republicans picked up more than 60 seats in the House, their largest gain since the 1930s and more than enough to take over as the majority party. Political scientists agreed that America's weak economy was the main reason Democrats took such a beating. But even if pursuing universal health care had not hurt the Democrats, it certainly didn't seem to be helping, much to this disappointment of its champions.

Partly as a result of that election, the Affordable Care Act's fate remains somewhat uncertain today. Right-wing activists and media figured have called for repealing the law and, during the campaign, Republican leaders pledged to do just that. They are unlikely to get enough votes in the Senate, the upper legislative chamber in which Democrats maintain a slim majority. Even if the Senate did agree to repeal, Obama would almost certainly veto it. But Republicans say they will press the cause in the 2012 elections, when they will have a chance to both wrest control of the Senate and to put one of their own in the White House. They have also announced their intent to undermine the law by denying funding for its implementation. Meanwhile, right-wing political organisations and several Republican state officials have filed lawsuits in the judicial system, claiming that a key element of the Affordable Care Act—the requirement that all individuals carry health insurance—violates the American constitution. If the case makes its way to the US Supreme Court, as seems likely, it's uncertain how the judges, a majority of whom are Republican appointees, will vote.

As a well-known advocate of universal coverage and supporter of the Affordable Care Act, I believe these legislative and judicial efforts to repeal the law will ultimately fail—and that, 10 years from now, Americans will look back on the passage of Obama's health care bill as a great milestone in social progress. But I also understand why so many people, not just on the political right but also on the political left, find the legislation wanting.

It is in many ways a flawed statue, starting with the fact that it's a universal health care bill that isn't actually 'universal.' The best available projections suggest that, once fully implemented, in 2014, between 2 and 5 per cent of legal residents will still not have health insurance. That's far less than the 16 per cent who lack coverage now. But it's more than the proportion of uninsured people one finds in the countries of Europe and the Pacific Rim, as well as Canada—all places in which only a tiny fraction of people go without coverage. Another main goal of the Affordable Care Act is to slow the explosive growth of health care spending in America, which is draining resources from government, businesses and individuals. But projections show that it will slow cost growth only incrementally.

One reason the Affordable Care Act will neither cover as many people as it could nor slow costs as much as it could is that it leaves the existing health insurance system, which is primarily private insurance for working-age people, largely intact. Had the Affordable Care Act instituted a single-payer, government run system—or even introduced a public insurance option, as many on the left were urging—the Affordable Care Act likely would have accomplished more.

This mish-mash isn't surprising. It is altogether typical of the American welfare state and its evolution. Going all the way back to the burst of left-wing economic reforms at the beginning of the 20th century, in what is known as the 'progressive era,' the US has been slow to develop its welfare state. And when it has moved along the path to social democracy, whether in the form of regulation or programmes that distribute resources, it has done so tentatively—passing minimal laws, full of flaws, that succeeding generations would be forced to improve. The US record on some forms of public investment, particularly public universities, is exemplary. But, overall, most experts would agree that social democracy in the US is smaller, and has developed more slowly, than social democracy in the rest of the developed world.

The reasons for this pattern have been the subject of debate among academics for generations. Some emphasise American political culture, with its strong emphasis on individualism. Others cite the fractured structure of American political institutions, which make sweeping policy action of any kind difficult. Some believe the answer lies in the relative weakness of more left-leaning political organisations, particularly labour unions. Others find an explanation in the racial and ethnic diversity of the American population—which, although in many ways a strength of American society, can also reduce enthusiasm for social democracy.

As a close observer of the health care debate, I would argue that all of these factors were instrumental in shaping the debate. And while I am not particularly familiar with the politics of India, I believe the advocates of social democracy in any country can learn by understanding the obstacles to social democracy in the US—and the ways in which reformers have been able, however imperfectly, to overcome them.

America's weak welfare state—and four explanations for it

Both within the US and in other countries, experts consider the American welfare state to be weaker than its counterparts in other economically advanced nations. And the simplest way to demonstrate this is by comparing what different countries spend on programmes that provide either direct government services or social insurance. In the US, government spending represents a lower proportion of gross domestic product (GDP), relative not just to

Scandinavia (where the figure reaches 50%) but most of Europe and the Pacific Rim (where the figure approaches 40%). Because the US devotes a larger share of its federal spending to the military, the comparative expenditures on its welfare state—everything from child care to pensions—is even lower.

The private sector makes up for some of this gap; the US spends more for private pensions and health insurance, for example, than most of its peer nations. Employers, in particular, have traditionally supplied for many employees the kinds of benefits that, in other countries, governments provide directly. But the private provision of social programmes tends to be more unequal, as it tends to leave out the unemployed, part-time workers, and those who lose jobs even for relatively short durations of time. It also can be more insecure: private pensions depend not just on the generosity of an employer to provide the seed money but also the performance of the stock market to keep the pensions flush with money.

The US government frequently provides assistance exclusively in the form of 'means-tested' programmes—i.e., programmes available only to those who are poor. The US does not have universal early childhood education, for example but it does have 'Head Start' and an assortment of other programmes that offer schooling and day care, for very young children. The US does not provide long-term care insurance to everybody, but Medicaid, a health insurance programme for the poor and disabled, will finance nursing home care for elderly people too poor to pay it on their own. These programmes serve a vital function, keeping many individuals and families out of abject poverty. But precisely because these programmes serve the poor, who lack political clout, they suffer from chronic under-funding and managerial neglect. They may provide not enough help, serve too few people, or some combination of the two.

Why is this? Scholars have traditionally focused on four general theories, starting with the idea of 'American exceptionalism'. The essence of this theory, expounded famously by the late political scientist Seymor Martin Lipset and typically based in part on the 19th century writings of Alexis de Tocqueville, is that Americans hold a unique set of political beliefs that evolved naturally from its geography and history. Among other things, Americans are highly individualistic: they have great faith in the idea of the 'self-made man.' They also have no feudal tradition. They put an unusually high premium on personal liberty and have since the time of the American Revolution, when they first rebelled against intrusions of their colonial overlords in Britain. Under this theory, these ideas cause Americans to be wary of strong, interventionist government and to disdain assistance for people who have not, as the saying goes, helped themselves.

Another theory posits that America's weak welfare state is the inevitable product of its weak political institutions. This explanation, put forth by (among others) the political scientist and sociologist Theda Skocpol, focuses on America's fragmentation of political power—fragmentation that occurs in two, cross-cutting ways.

There is, first, the separation of power between the federal government, based in Washington, and the 50 state governments. (The state governments, in turn, share authority with local authorities.) The rivalry between state and federal authorities has been a constant theme in American history and was at the root of the Civil War, during the 1860s. Although that war settled the question of whether the federal government was sovereign, states have continued to challenge and fight federal authority through non-violent means—and sometimes they have won. State power doesn't make passing welfare legislation more difficult but it does complicate implementation.

And then there is the separation of power within the federal government, among the executive, legislative and judicial branches of government. Each branch effectively wields enough power to prevent an idea from becoming law: Congress can choose not to pass a bill, the president can choose not to sign it and the courts, given an opportunity, can choose not to certify it as constitutional. And that's not to mention the way power is fragmented within the branches. This is most obvious in the legislative branch, in which each house of Congress must approve bills to pass them, but it's also true in the executive and judicial branches, since the executive branch's bureaucracy can be at odds with the president and lower courts in the judiciary can fight among each other, at least until the Supreme Court rules on a matter.

The third popular theory for the slow evolution of America's welfare state is the 'diversity of its population'—a source of national strength, in many ways but also a possible hindrance to passing social legislation. Among the best-known proponents of this argument are political scientists Alberto Alesina, Edward Glaeser and Bruce Sacerdote. A simple, if slightly simplified, summary of this view is that, all else being equal, people are more likely to support government programmes when they feel a sense of solidarity with their fellow citizens. But that sense of solidarity is stronger in countries where most people share a common heritage. The racial and ethnic divides in the US tend to undermine that sense of solidarity. Caucasian Americans, who constitute the majority and hold the most political power, have eyed social spending proposals warily, for fear they would take money out of their pockets and give that money to somebody else.

The other well-known explanation for America's languishing welfare state is 'its lack of strong left-wing institutions', particularly labour unions. Even at the peak of organised labour, during the middle of the 20th century, unions never represented as many people in the US as they did in other economically advanced countries. And particularly in the last 30 to 40 years, membership in private sector unions has declined precipitously, falling below the density necessary for unions to maintain bargaining leverage and exert broader influence over the economy as a whole.

Only the growth of unions representing public sector workers has kept unions from falling into complete irrelevance but, even with that boost, they remain what they always have been in this country: a relatively weak counter-weight to the power of the business community, whose self-interest (in low taxes and regulation) has generally led them to oppose social democratic legislation. A related factor, often discussed as part of this same theory, is the lack of proportional representation in legislative elections—a feature of many parliamentary systems and one that tends to enhance the influence of more left-wing political voices.

These are not the only obstacles to enacting social welfare legislation in the US Nor are they insurmountable. During the 1930s, Franklin Roosevelt and his Democratic allies in Congress enacted the New Deal, which created, among other things, the Social Security Act—for the first time providing the elderly with a guaranteed public pension. In the 1960s, Lyndon Johnson and his allies created the Great Society, which strengthened social security, introduced medical programmes for the elderly and poor, and started a series of targeted initiatives to help feed, educate and house the poor. But it took some combination of extraordinary political majorities (Johnson's 1964 re-election, shortly after the assassination of President John F. Kennedy, ushered in the largest Democratic majorities in a generation) and extraordinary national crisis (the New Deal was Roosevelt's answer to the Great Depression).

In both cases, the moments for vast social democratic change turned out to be fleeting. And, in both cases, the products of reform were something less than comprehensive. Social security originally left out agricultural workers and was, for the first few decades of its existence, so meager that it still left vast numbers of elderly in poverty. To this day, Head Start—a crown jewel of the Great Society—serves only a tiny portion of the population of poor people in need of education for their very young children.

The case of universal health insurance

The story of universal health care in the US illustrates the way these forces have conspired to retard and, eventually, to shape the development of the welfare state. And it's a story that goes all the way back to the early 20th century—to the dawn of what is now considered the modern era of medicine. Prior to that time, medicine was more art than science. Doctors didn't have much power to cure. Hospitals existed largely so people had places to get pain relief and, eventually, to die in the presence of clerics who could deliver last religious rites. But that changed with innovations like the development of anesthesia and the sanitary technique, which made surgery possible. Suddenly doctors could perform tonsillectomies, appendectomies, and all other manners of–'ectomies'. Soon hospitals were full of people who expected not just to survive but also to get better.

These developments came at a steep price—literally—as medical care became far more expensive. Previously, the chief financial risk of illness was that people who were sick had to leave work and miss their paychecks. Now they had to worry about paying the doctor and hospital. In the late 1920s, a group of foundations convened a commission called the Committee on the Costs of Medical Care. Its survey of medical care, completed in 1932, demonstrated that medical bills were imposing severe hardship on people, few of whom had sufficient savings to pay those bills on their own. The solution, according to the Committee, was to create health insurance—to use small contributions from populations of mostly healthy people to pay the high medical costs for that small minority of individuals with severe health problems.

The question was how to organise insurance. Roosevelt thought about adding health insurance to the Social Security Act. Had he done so, the US would have embarked on the same path that some countries (like Germany) had already started and that others would soon join: the path of universal health insurance. But groups representing businesses and individuals that provided medical care—chief among them, state societies representing physicians—were opposed to the idea, because they feared government interference and reductions in income. Already they were denouncing the idea as foreign and un-American, suggesting the idea had come from Germany, which was already seen as a menace. They claimed it was an infringement on personal liberty and that it would destroy the doctor-patient relationship. Fearing that these groups could have defeated the Social Security Act, Roosevelt dropped the idea.

Instead, insurance came to the US through the private sector—as hospitals, facing their own financial crisis, began offering not-for-profit 'pre-payment plans' to groups of employees. The emerging network of plans, which eventually became known as the 'Blue

Cross system,' would form the basis of American health insurance. It was affordable to most of the middle class. It was available to all people who could afford it, even those buying on their own rather than through employers. It had the support of business groups, who preferred it to government-run insurance—or, as they liked to call it, 'socialised medicine.' And, as the years went on, it was covering more and more of the population. When Truman, in 1948, proposed the government take over health insurance and simply give it to every American, opponents cited the success of the Blue Cross plans as proof that national health insurance was unnecessary.

But the system began to falter once commercial insurance entered the field. Insurers sensed an opportunity to make a profit by insuring only the healthier and wealthier parts of the population. Soon, people with existing illnesses found it more difficult to get insurance. So did the elderly, who had no employers through which to buy coverage and whose age made them likely candidates to become sick. The poor, meanwhile, had always struggled to pay for coverage, since they couldn't pay the premiums.

The creation of Medicare (for the elderly) and Medicaid (for the poor) as part of the Great Society, in the 1960s, helped ameliorate the access problem. But they did so only partially, since Medicaid covered only certain classes of poor people (mainly, unmarried women with children) and left out 'working poor', people who had jobs but made too little money to pay insurance premiums. And neither programme was able to arrest the rising cost of medical care, which was making employers reluctant to provide employees with coverage. (If anything, the creation of Medicare exacerbated the cost problem.) The number of people without insurance and the number of people with insurance too inadequate to cover their bills began to rise.

In 1992, Bill Clinton ran for president promising to deal with this situation. And he deliberately embraced a proposal that might fit within the narrow political space that America's welfare state had traditionally resided. In deference to the skepticism of government, private insurers would offer most coverage. Government would regulate and subsidise the product, but businesses would be the ones providing it. The programme would cost a lot of money but the government would pay for all of it, through a combination of new revenues and savings from existing programmes. In deference to the disdain for public assistance, his programme would emphasise personal responsibility, by requiring that everybody with adequate means pay for their coverage and that everybody obtain insurance in one way or another.

Clinton's plan failed to pass and, for a few years, the buoyant economy obscured the deterioration in health coverage. But by 2008, the problem had become acute again—and Obama, like Clinton before him, decided to pursue universal coverage. But Obama and his allies, many of whom had worked for Clinton or were in Congress during the previous health care fight, were determined to avoid the same mistakes. Not only did they propose to rely heavily on private insurance; they crafted a system under which most people who already had private health insurance would get to keep the policies they already had. This programme, like Clinton's, would pay for itself. But it would also involve much fewer outlays. In particular, the architects of the Obama plan decided that the entire initiative could not involve new spending of more than $1 trilliion over 10 years (10 years is the standard budget window) because the public would see anything bigger than $1 trillion as too expensive.

These concessions had a tremendous impact on the shape of legislation. Most conspicuously, the decision to keep spending under $1 trillion limited what the plan could do. The architects reduced the guarantee of coverage: instead of promising that all Americans could have the same level of insurance as members of Congress—a motto Obama, among others, had used frequently—the plan would permit insurance plans that would leave individuals with high out-of-pocket spending. (This would be a particular hardship on people with serious medical problems, since they are the ones most likely to run up high bills.) And even after thinning the benefits, the architects of the plan realised that $1 trillion still wasn't enough to finance universal insurance for 10 years. So they delayed implementation, until 2014, and reduced the financial assistance so that several million people, at least, would still find insurance out of reach financially. (These people would not be subject to the requirement to buy insurance.)

But the architects of the Obama health care plan had to make other concessions, too. Even though Obama's party, the Democrats, controlled both houses of Congress, they knew they would struggle to pass legislation through the Senate. Some of this was because of its constitutional arrangement: every state, no matter what its population, gets two seats. And in present-day America, the states with the smallest populations are mostly rural and Western states that are to the right politically, tend to elect Republicans. Obama had Democratic majority, in other words, but not a left-leaning one.

To make matters worse, norms of behaviour in the Senate had changed just in the last 10 to 20 years. Opposition parties had started making routine use of the 'filibuster'—the right of any senator or senators to object to legislation and stop a debate from proceeding, until 60 of the Senate's 100 members vote to continue. Prior to the 1980s, senators used filibusters sparingly. But after that they began using it more often and, by the time Obama came to office, they had made the maneuver so routine that it effectively took 60 votes to pass any meaningful piece of legislation. Mathematically, given the disproportionate representation of small states, it had become possible for senators representing just a fifth of the nation's population to block legislation.

With such little margin for political error, Obama and his allies felt they could not afford to fight the business groups that traditionally opposed reform—at least, not all of them—no matter how much backing they had from more left-leaning groups that, however large their numbers, just didn't have the same financial resources or lobbying clout. Instead, Obama and his allies sought and eventually forged alliances with several key groups, including the drug and hospital industries. The primary goal of these industries was to avoid regulation or any other legislative changes that might negatively affect their incomes. Of course, reducing their incomes was one of the ways health care reform was supposed to reduce cost increases in health care and make it more affordable for everybody.

These deals weakened the political opposition; the drug industry, alone, almost certainly had the power to kill health care legislation if it so chose. But it also weakened the legislation itself. To win the drug industry's support, Obama and his allies promised not to reduce the companies' incomes by more than a token amount—and signalled a willingness to keep government from negotiating prices directly with pharmaceutical manufacturers, the way most other countries' governments do. Those agreements made it even harder to deliver benefits in a timely, generous manner—and limited legislation's ability to slow down the rising cost of health care. By the time the Affordable Care Act had come through the legislative process, the Congressional Budget Office, the government's 'scorekeeper,' was predicting that spending on medical care would be rising only slightly less quickly once the plan was fully implemented.

As word of these deals leaked out into the press during the summer of 2009, the public, sensing corruption, became disenchanted with the legislation. Meanwhile, the opponents of reform began to hit upon an argument that resonated with misgivings many middle class voters already had. In the early stages of the debate, reform was popular in part because it seemed merely to guarantee security for all without threatening the financial resources and access to care, that insured people already had. But opponents of reform started arguing that, in order to finance the expansion of insurance to people who already had it, Obama and his allies intended to take away money or coverage from the insured. They warned that universal health care would mean 'rationing care' to the elderly, even as government financed insurance for undocumented immigrants. They said the idea was 'un-American' and told stories of government denying life-saving care to elderly people in England or Canada. They said that the programme would cost more than it took in, forcing taxpayers to pay the government even more, and that the overall cost of medical care would go up, resulting in higher premiums for everybody.

At one point, a disreputable right-wing activist wrote in the Wall Street Journal that the health care bill would create government 'death panels' with power to decide which people would still be allowed to get life-saving care. It was the most egregious, but far from the only, lie that the opponents of universal coverage told. But the idea resonated with preconceptions about government and the welfare state. And it was spread by well-funded organisations of the right and their allies in the media, while the left and the non-partisan media were unable to persuade people otherwise. To this day, polls show that large pluralities of Americans believe the Affordable Care Act includes 'death panels.'

The future of the US welfare state

That Obama and his allies could manage to pass a universal health care law, or a nearly universal health care law, despite these obstacles is perhaps testimony to their political skills, the depths of the crisis they sought to address or some combination thereof. But it remains an unfinished story, at least as long as the opposition has power and the will to repeal it. And it remains a frustrating story, insofar as the programme is neither as generous nor efficient as it could be. European and Pacific Rim countries will continue to cover more of their populations, at lower costs and with (arguably) more convenience, than the US—even after the Affordable Care Act takes full effect in 2014.

But history suggests that the story of the Affordable Care Act is also one that will result in a happy ending. The social welfare programmes that came before it, most notably Medicare and Social Security, improved over time. Opposition parties reconciled to them, while business groups adapted to them. The groups that depended on them, meanwhile, began demanding improvements—and the politicians answered. In fact, when Johnson and his allies enacted Medicare, they were essentially finishing the work of protecting the elderly that Roosevelt and his allies had begun in the 1930s.

As the Affordable Care Act neared passage in early 2010, Tom Harkin, a senator who had helped shepherd the bill through his chamber, described the measure as a small 'starter home,' rather than a mansion. But it was a house with a strong foundation, he explained, and a sturdy roof above. Plus there was room for expansion. His message was pretty clear: The Affordable Care Act wasn't perfect, perhaps. But it was a good start—and it was bound to get better. That's always been the story of the American welfare state. And perhaps it always will be.

Section II contd...

Social Democracy in Global Perspective

PRESENTATIONS • DISCUSSIONS

This section presents the proceedings of the Second Session of the Tenth Indira Gandhi Conference, November 19-21, 2010, New Delhi.

Chair
- Joseph E. Stiglitz

Presentations
- Pascal Lamy
- Joakim Palme
- Wang Hui
- Jonathan Cohn

Discussants
- Joseph E. Stiglitz
- Rehman Sobhan
- Pranab Bardhan
- Kaushik Basu
- Eric Solheim
- Nemat Shafik
- Kumi Naidoo
- Aruna Roy
- Kumar Mangalam Birla
- Sri Mulyani Indrawati
- Sunita Narain
- Rohan Samarajiva
- Jonathan Cohn
- Joakim Palme
- Wang Hui
- Pascal Lamy

15

JOSEPH E. STIGLITZ

Introductory Remarks

A few facts describe what has been going on in most countries around the world. There are growing inequalities even in developed countries like the US. It is not just growth in inequality. Those at the bottom and even in the middle are actually worse off in absolute terms than they were a decade ago. It is not just inequality; it is actually growth of poverty and stagnation, or worse, in the middle class.

In the discussions earlier, one of the defining characteristics of social democracy is opportunity. In some countries like the US, there is actually a decrease in social mobility. Things in that sense are getting worse. Even some of the singularly committed social democratic countries like Chile have got no kudos for instituting social democratic policies. Their only actual success has been mainly in preventing things from getting worse.

There are many factors that have contributed to this and a diagnosis of them is obviously important in thinking about the solution. Globalisation is one of the factors and I hope we talk about why globalisation has had that impact. How can we shape globalisation to reduce that impact? Most importantly, how can India manage globalisation in a way that mitigates these adverse effects? There are several ways in which globalisation can contribute to this growing inequality. The first is that there is an asymmetrical relation between capital and labour. This has two very large impacts. One of them is it changes the bargaining power. Capital says we will leave, if you tax us. We will leave if you insist on environmental regulations, on Merkel conditions. Workers, particularly young skilled workers, cannot leave and asymmetry affects outcomes inevitably.

Secondly, it affects the scope of taxation so that around the world, countries face the threat that capital and skilled labour will move away if you impose progressive taxation, so that too reduces the scope for response.

Thirdly, resources are available to countries, but the problem is worse where the resources available have diminished. Many aspects of globalisation increase volatility; in particular, financial market inequity and deregulation. We saw that most vividly in the recent crisis where America's toxic mortgages were exported around the world and the recession that began in the US then became a global phenomenon. There are many other instances like this.

The fourth relates to part of the earlier discussion which is that globalisation involves not only economic globalisation, but also the spread of ideas. Good ideas have spread around the world, like ideas of democracy, but so have some bad ideas, including a set of ideas that are used against the welfare state; a whole set of views about how economies ought to be organised. Some of these views have become less persuasive in the wake of the economic crisis. That particular model is not in vogue. It was there before the crisis, but clearly there has been the spread of ideology. It is interesting, particularly in the light of Eric Solheim's remarks earlier, that the success of the Scandinavian and Nordic countries doesn't get the attention that it deserves. Eric put it very clearly. This is not the view of much of the world and this matter was not talked about. When they did, people said Scandinavia is different. Without exploring why it is different, it is to tell you they are peculiar up there in the north and that is why somehow there is some difference. Others said that the Scandinavians have other characteristics, that we couldn't do what they do. I think that is wrong.

These ideas have a particular effect on inequality. For instance, when it comes to issues like privatisation of education, which can, in many countries, lead to perpetuation of inequality. This, I think, is one of the forces that have led to decreasing opportunity and the change in social mobility that I referred to earlier.

I want to make a few remarks about how to counter these arguments and then suggest some policies to mitigate the adverse effects. Some arguments were put forward this morning. The first was that social protection actually allows for more risk-taking. People are more able and want to take more risks if there is a fallback that is better.

Secondly, greater utilisation of all the resources makes the economy more competitive. This has really been the part of the framework under which many Scandinavian countries are bringing women into the labour force. But it is also necessary to bring in the poor to the labour force in a more productive way by giving them education.

Thirdly, social protection increases political support for openness. Openness is viewed by many people as risk and this is a way of mitigating that risk.

Finally, we come to greater social protection and greater equality in general support for wealth-increasing government programmes. There are many aspects of economic activity that are better conducted or framed collectively, like public goods, R&D, infrastructure, education and I would also say, health. There are a whole set of activities that are more efficiently done; if they can't be done by inefficient governments, there are many cases of doing and financing them through the market. We have problems of adverse selection and a whole set of other problems. There is considerable evidence that in societies where there is more inequality, there is more concern on the part of those at the top that there will be redistributive politics and an attempt to decelerate the state. Therefore, redistributive politics undermines the ability to do wealth-enhancing public activities. Over the long run, I think that this is one of the reasons why the US is weakening; failures in education, infrastructure will, in the long run, be bad for long-term economic growth. I think it is a vicious cycle.

I shall quickly mention the policies to promote and deal more effectively with the consequences of globalisation. The first social equality-propounding social protection initiative is full employment. That is why I think employment schemes are so important but in general, creating an economy that gets the economy towards full employment is the most important item in the social agenda. Unemployment is probably the greatest source of poverty and inequality.

Beyond that, there are two other things that I think are critical. One is realising that some policies expose countries to more volatility and more risk and that macroeconomic risks are inevitably hard to manage and adversely affect the poor. I have long been a critic of unviable capital market and financial market liberalisation for that reason. One wants to open up economies to foreign direct investment thinking that it will create more jobs. But one ought to be very sceptical of short-term money. We cannot create new employment from money that comes in and goes out overnight. Financial market and capital market liberalisation, I think the evidence is pretty clear, does not lead to faster growth but does lead to more instability.

Finally, a modern economy requires adaptability. That is where education becomes absolutely critical because one of the attributes of good education is the ability to adapt to changing circumstances.

As I said earlier, there are two aspects of social democracy; one is the social and economic agenda that we have been talking about, and the other is democracy. Other complex issues are associated with how globalisation interacts with democracy. I want to highlight one, which is that countries that are open capital markets and get themselves into debt are at the risk of economic, social and other policies dictated from abroad. This was very clear in the case of Brazil where on two occasions, Lula lost elections. On the third occasion, he succeeded but the capital markets even then had some tremors though it was managed. In a global world, the more money is dependent on the bond market, the more subject one is to these international judgements which tend to be very short-tagged; their interest would not coincide with the long-run interest of the growth of India. It is like saying that it is good to have an outside referee to pass a judgement about whether you are doing the right thing. But in fact, the bond market interests are short-term and not coincident with India's long-term growth interest and particularly, the long-term interest of social democracy. Subjecting yourself to that kind of discipline, erratic as it is, is actually, I think, a fundamental mistake. I am really concerned with how you integrate yourself into the global economy.

16

PRESENTATION BY PASCAL LAMY

Social Democracy and Globalisation

Let me start from where you and Kumi Naidoo left it. Kumi had observed that until now, most reflections on social democracy have remained within the classical traditional parameter of the nation state which for reasons we already had occasions to discuss together is, I believe, now wrong. I think the time has come to adopt a more global perspective on these issues while, of course, recognising that politics remains and will remain mostly local.

The fundamental reason why we have to go global in any serious reflection on today's and tomorrow's social democracy, its values and their implementation, is simply because market capitalism has gone global. If we understand globalisation as one construct where transformation in market capitalism is driven by important technological changes, what's distinctive in the present phase is not that it was triggered by major technological changes, which was the case in the past. This time, it has gone really global-global; not just global between Europe and Latin America or Europe and Asia but global-global. In doing so, the forces of global economy connect social systems much more than before, which raises new issues because of the discrepancies between the social systems about which nobody had really cared for a long time. These cannot now be ignored because social systems have been pushed into competition by economic globalisation. Hence, this sort of debate reminds us of what happened in the 19th century between those who were well off and those who weren't, especially when it came to the Industrial Revolution. Let us remove social systems, regulations and conditions that impede our competitiveness is an argument that is put forward. There is a sort of race-to-the-bottom syndrome and many say that this isn't the way out. The result is to progressively construct some sort of international abasement for social systems.

We have plenty of evidence of that, lately, with the US-China currency friction. What the US and China have in common is a big fear of unemployment. They both know, in each of their own specific political systems, that rising unemployment is a political bomb. That is why the US has created an extremely active monetary policy with inevitably some impact on the exchange rate. That is also the reason China does not want to revalue its renminbi, and not just because the wages in China are increasing, which already exerts pressure on employment. The fundamental reason of this divide is the fact that both the US and China have very poor social security systems. That is the reason unemployment is a political bomb in both countries; because unemployment benefits are still a big problem. Apart from this example, one could cite many others in the field of environment, in the field of social inequalities which Joe Stiglitz just mentioned, tax issues, immigration, limitations to mobility and all other issues which we now have to look at globally, that have a strong component of different social systems. The question remains whether the social systems are going in a positive direction or a negative one.

My first point is that the forces of market capitalism are global. The power of market capitalism is global and we cannot remain with scattered, local social democratic forces. Social democracy has in a way, to be bit of a global power as well.

Given this basic diagnosis, how can this be accomplished? I think it first calls for some sort of global social democratic platform. It is good that India looks at its problem, Sweden looks at its, Chile and New Zealand look at theirs but in my view, this is not the most promising avenue. The most promising avenue is to try and come together in some sort of a global social democratic platform.

Let me just mention a few suggestions of how to get there. It is a long haul navigation. In my view, there should be an intellectual component, odyssey component, toolbox component, actors component and scope-scale component.

Starting with the intellectual component, what we need is a new revamped, reshaped, actualised critique of market capitalism in the name of social democracy, which is fundamentally justice.

What are the inherent contradictions in market capitalism that create so many injustices and inequalities naturally in the system? We have to go back to this fundamental question. It is a question about market capitalism, about markets and also about capitalism. There is no singularity, philosophically or economically, between markets and capitalism. It just happens that the system we live in is a system with market capitalism. Digging into the real roots of the capacity of the system to create and doctrinise injustice and inequalities, in my view, remains to be done and it just cannot be done by economists. It has to be done by social scientists and anthropologists. Going back, let me mention what the martial science says about this and what are the basic roots, not only philanthropic but anthropological too, of market capitalism. Undoubtedly, this ideology was born in the Western world and has no equivalent in other cultures or continents. Basically, man is a wolf to other men and we need to organise the economy in such a way that man's wolfishness to man works collectively. This, in my view, is a fundamental issue which we need to revisit as well. We probably will have to revisit the limits of merchandisation. There must be in a market system limits to what one can buy and sell. I am not saying that it is easy to determine this limit; this is something which we need to do together. I think this sort of approach is also necessary policy-wise. The issues of education, health, immigration, energy, culture have to be taken in a more holistic global view, the fundamental purpose probably being how to define a new growth model, something that would be less extravagant and less demanding on human and natural resources. It will be a new definition of prosperity and also a concept of sustainable prosperity.

I don't insist on the toolbox component. A lot of that already appeared in the earlier discussion, which spoke of the classical social democratic toolbox—regulation, redistribution, collectivisation, cooperative methods, new elements like participation and empowerment. I think the debate within India is extremely telling for many of us who have identified this problem of what the right toolbox should be. It is interesting to see in a country as large as India how this debate is shaping up. This probably should lead to a sort of innovative approach of what we can and should do globally. Globally, the biggest instrument that we have at our disposal is regulation. Redistribution is not the right tool unless understood in the sense of creating a global public good. The level of redistribution worldwide is 0.3 per cent. The Europeans who have created the brand new supranational system painfully accept 1 per cent of their GNP for redistribution, which is three times bigger than the global level, but which is roughly 20 times smaller than what we have at the national level.

I think the actors' component should also be part of this platform, with the diversity between public systems, civil society, trade unions, entrepreneurs, with each of them having their own input. There is a lot to be said about the diversity of these actors in their contribution to enhancing justice or using social inequalities. India is a very good case. Brazil, South Africa, Indonesia and even the German experience probably say a lot about some solutions that can be found.

Finally, we touch upon the component for scale-scope around the question of what the relevant level of solidarity is. My personal assumption is that solidarity stands for a feeling which is connected to a feeling of belonging and togetherness. If you believe you belong to a community then the reflex solidarity will be there. If that is not the case, it is very difficult to impose it on people. This is where I disagree with Joseph Stiglitz when he said that the Nordic model was not specific. I believe and have been thinking about this for a quite a bit of time, that the Nordic model is specific. I don't have to enter into why; maybe we can do that in the discussion.

This is the central point of this platform. I am aware that I am making a political statement more than an academic one, which is that this social democratic platform is not just about mitigating the adverse effects of market capitalism. This platform must be geared with a view of an alternative to market capitalism. If we do not try to give an alternative to market capitalism, then the moment we are confronted in a political battle, we have the wrong battle-lines.

We need strong battle-lines for political action, to be then able to bargain for a compromise.

Assuming all this is true, it will only materialise if it is translated into concrete political action. And on this, we have to recognise that the traditional actors, which are the political parties, are very weak in their own capacity to translate this into their own action and platform. NGOs have done a better job in this regard. NGOs are intellectually and ideologically much more globalised than political parties. There is one element in between, which are the trade unions. They have cleverly understood that they need a single international trade union movement but the truth is that within this single trade union movement, the level of discussion and debate on social democracy is weak for one reason, which is that Indians, Brazilians, Chinese, Indonesians, Egyptians and South Africans are basically not there. I have personally participated in many of these debates and have found that they remain very exclusivist. This is an issue and at the risk of appearing a bit traditional, I do not think any debate on social democracy can do without trade unions and their international components.

A word about trade, which is a very good example of a global issue. The benefits of open trade connect with domestic systems, which is more social security. I agree hundred per cent with Joe when he says that social protection increases the support for openness. We know fully well there is no big policy debate about trade. We know fully well that openness in trade works better than the rest and we also know that it works through the cost of winners and losers, plusses and minuses. One can say that overall there are more plusses than minuses, the problem being that many of these minuses appear in domestic systems which is where legitimacy runs. That is a very good example of how a close link between policy and politics should be done. This may lead to one point about global governance, which has been a sort of preoccupation of social democracy for the last 20 years. I have spent 10 to 20 years thinking and reflecting on this and as a provisional conclusion, I think social democracy, social democratic and progressive forces have a big job to do, not in globalising local issues but in localizing global issues. The way to global governance, in my view, does not lie in complex, sophisticated international architectures and institutions. There is a bit of that, but the fundamental political problem remains where the political legitimacy is created. I think that is the horizon which I would give to such a social democratic global platform, to translate global issues on which all have to now cooperate, into proper domestic democratic legitimate debates. This is not very different from going back to the intuition of the fathers of social democracy in Europe that internationalism is an inbuilt dimension of any progressive movement.

17

PRESENTATION BY JOAKIM PALME

European Social Models

I am grateful for this opportunity to say something about the European experience. I would like to say something on a personal level first. I particularly wanted to speak at the Indira Gandhi Trust as my father had strong personal links with Indira and Rajiv Gandhi and I was truly inspired by Sonia's eloquent speech. After a long time, I heard such passionate argument for rational social democratic politics. It is a bit odd when you hear these connections of the social democratic model with the Nordic countries and have to travel to New Delhi to get fresh inspiration. I was also reminded by Sunil Khilnani of another family link I have with India, with another relative from another generation. The sister of my great-grandfather had a son by an Indian doctor she met in London. This son, Rajani Palme Dutt, had a major role in the creation of the Communist Party of India but he also had connections with Nehru and the formation of the Indian state. At the outset, I must apologise for not really contributing anything new. I have listened to the earlier discussions and the important issues raised. Perhaps, I may be able to add some dialectic dimensions.

My starting point is what Pascal Lamy also stated. Social democracy has to be the critique of capitalism or address its fundamental problems, its large inequalities and unfair distribution of economic resources and also the fact that competitive capitalism is destructive in the sense that it destroys old structures and potentially leaves large numbers of losers on the way. On the European level, we can see social democracy as a response, using universal suffrage and democratic institutions, for mobilising redistribution, inventing instruments to compensate for these two basic problems of capitalism. But it also struggles with the fact that the working class has always been in a minority and has been critical in the policy development to find broader coalitions beyond the industrial working class.

The concept of the European social models should be seen in this context. It was sort of invented in 2005 when the French and the Dutch populations rejected the new constitution and European politicians interpreted that as a protest against further economic and political integration on the European level. The protests were based on the fact that this political integration was not complemented by robust social policies that would take care of the losers or the victims of the intensified competition.

Its formulation by the present amalgamation in terms of social inclusion and equality of opportunity in a way opens up a social democratic agenda on the European level, an agenda that perhaps has not resulted in a great policy advantage, but I think we can still utilise this opportunity.

The concept of the social model is a bit confusing in the sense that it has been formulated with the idea that there exists a European social model different from the American model. There is some truth in that, especially in the health care sector, but often we have a misguided view of the American state by not seeing the big programmes, such as social security and medical care. But there is an even more problematic assumption. This is that a social model exists which actually delivers the objectives of social inclusion and equality of opportunity whereas in reality, we are very far from fulfilling these goals and also have institutions that are not well designed.

This brings me to the discussion of actually looking at institutions, not in terms of goals, but of how policy instruments are designed. It is useful to talk about welfare state regimes as a way of introducing an analytical approach both in terms of simplifying complex patterns of similarities and differences within countries, but also to be able to examine whether the existing institutions actually deliver the goals and use the cross-national variation across European countries, as a way of testing the advantages of certain designs compared to others. I also think it is important to see that the way we create institutions and political economies sort of tie both the interests and identities of citizens to the design of institutions. Particularly important here is the middle class. We often connect with the American model, the targeted model, and those social policies are targeted towards the poor. This excludes the big middle class from being recipients of provisions. But they are still paying the taxes for these programmes. The Beveridge model, the basic security model on the other hand, was a way of including the middle class in the systems of social protection not only as contributors, but also as recipients of flat-rate benefits. This leaves a lot of room for market solutions to top up these basic provisions.

The Bismarckian model is another way of including the middle class but organising protection systems separately for different corporations. It includes the middle class, but not in the same systems.

One could then see the Scandinavian encompassing model as a way of combining the basic benefits of the Beveridge model with the earnings-related benefits of the Bismarckian model within the same framework and the same risk groups in the social insurances. The key here is that the different ways of including the middle class has meant that the European systems have been more politically sustainable than the more targeted ones.

Anyway, the Danish, American and now the Spanish sociologist Gosta Esping-Anderson have put labels on these different welfare state regimes calling them the liberal, the conservative and the social democratic welfare state regimes and saying that even if historically different forces are influencing the ones existing, the emphasis on the universal in the Scandinavian model has clear links to the ideological notions that are strong in social democracy. But one should then understand that many other social democratic movements in other European countries have been caught up in other kinds of structures. Only at times of war have there been real attempts at transforming such structures into more universal programmes.

On the European level then, the social dimension, I would say, is underdeveloped. The European Union is based on market making;

the four fragments are the constitution of the European Union. The regulations are linked to the free movements of labour and not to citizenship or universal rights. I think that was then reinforced by the Single European Act in 1987 but since then we have seen various kinds of responses in terms of introducing clearer social objectives in the European Union. In a way, Europe has become a sort of test-bed for this tension between markets and politics. One can see that in the different steps taken with the Maastricht Treaty and the Amsterdam Treaty. The formulation of the Riksbank agenda has in different ways strengthened the social ambitions but with soft means. It is not that countries that don't perform according to the common needs and goals are sanctioned or punished by the European Union. It is a name and shame operation, more about benchmarking and about very hard goals.

Of course, the enlargement of the European Union to 27 member states has created a situation where more countries are farther from the agreed goals and are diverse in terms of instruments which have increased rather than the opposite.

When we now look at the future challenges of the European social model, we must see it in the light of not only globalisation, but also the ageing population. This is a double challenge both in terms of eroded tax bases and demands of increased redistribution from ageing population.

I would try to make a case for two policies. The first would be to speak of a policy instrument or regime that I would label as a learner model. In the light of the increased need for distribution, the need to mitigate the goals of production and reproduction, there is an option for public policy to actually provide instruments that make it possible for women to divide paid work in the market with caring responsibility. This will put some of the caring responsibilities on men as well, which might be the downside of the equation, but it is true. This has been the Scandinavian success in combining reforms of economic incentives with investment not only in education but also in human services. However, policy changes have not worked, unless there have been macroeconomics incentives. This is a way of illustrating what was earlier said about the necessity to be successful, not only in social policies but in macroeconomic policies as well.

The second example is what we try to label as social investment strategy. We look at social policy and inequality beyond the economic measures that we usually use with the timeframe of only one year, poverty rates and generic coefficients and also look at how public policy is investing in the basic resources of the population. We look at it from the point of designing policies, from the cradle to the grave or at least till retirement. At every step, it can be linked with good policies that are making this vision of lifelong learning and flexicurity more realistic than what we are currently seeing in Europe. We see good examples but we don't see a coherent policy paradigm.

What does this have to do with India? I have been struck by the similarities of the kinds of discussions we have in Europe and in India. India, of course, has the advantage of drawing from the lessons of European development and avoiding repeating the mistakes, possibly learning some new ideas. Hopefully, India won't just blindly emulate Europe's best practices, but look at specific combinations of policies. I think the greatest lesson is that perhaps you can do things in a different way than the American model. Milton Friedman was right; we are free to choose between different models. But maybe, there is another lesson that we have to learn from these discussions. Europe is going to be less important population-wise and in terms of economy. The kinds of decisions that you make here will be of fundamental importance for the kinds of decisions that we are able to make in future.

18

PRESENTATION BY WANG HUI

The Dialectics of Self-Reliance and Opening

China's Experience and Challenges

I have been thinking about social democracy and the Chinese experience. Obviously, it is a very difficult task for me to talk about social democracy in the Chinese context because generally speaking, nobody believes that China has social democracy. It has a tradition of being a socialist country. But on the other hand, it is really interesting in these discussions, to find a lot of similarities with differences of course, in different contexts. The way we may think about this is to reflect on the commonality through the singularity, and through commonality, try to understand the singularity for each country. I am not an economist; I deal with intellectual history. I will try to give some historical analysis of the Chinese experience.

It started with some kind of discussion about change in 1989. We know that the events of 1989 began from Tiananmen Square but following that, in the subsequent years, the Soviet Union and the Eastern European system collapsed. After that, we realised that China still remained as the only political system, working in the new conditions of globalisation and marketisation. What was going on there? Most discussions in China were mainly about comparing China with Western countries or with America. Chinese intellectuals too did that. But one of the great differences, I think, is that in China and the former socialist countries, including Russia and the Eastern European countries, divergence continued to develop, although each side was closer to Western models. This could be the reason why China after 1989, didn't collapse along with the other former socialist countries. Several issues made China quite singular amongst those socialist camps.

The speciality of that sovereign state is that after 1949, with the establishment of the Peoples' Republic of China (PRC), China fought a war in the Korean peninsula with America. Then in the mid-1950s, China, together with India, supported the Non-Aligned Movement (NAM) and later tried to appease the Soviet Union. Then a series of political developments happened that gave China a sovereign status. At that time, China was not a legal member of the UN but it opted for more self-reliance and independence. The first Chinese economic plans, first five year plans were supported by the Soviet Union but after the 1950s, the situation changed greatly. Those developments explain why after 1989, the Soviet Union, together with some other former socialist systems collapsed, but China survived. Although it was a socialist country, its sovereign status was different from the others. Also, its national industrial economic system was much more self-reliant given its historical condition.

Secondly, it is the political nature of the political culture in the system. We know that sovereign status was at that time achieved through party politics. The trapeze between the Soviet Union and China originated in the manner two parties trapeze. There was very strong political involvement on the issues of sovereignty in order to make China more independent. The first step was to make the Communist Party more independent from the others, especially the Soviet Union. At that time, many historians looked closely at the trapeze between China and the Soviet Union and the cultural revolution, when China went through a very tragic period. However, some unexpected consequences arose from that period. History is full of paradoxes. On the one hand, China had huge problems during the cultural revolution but as a result of the cultural revolution, high-ranking officers from different ranks, from the top to the middle and lower levels, were sent to the countryside. They got to know the people and their needs, and when they went back to their positions, they were able to be more responsive to the demands from the lower social strata. That was the beginning of Chinese reforms. It was a kind of interaction between the political cultures. It helped them to reduce the stiffness of bureaucracy, which was very much a feature of the Soviet Union and former socialist countries. It made the Chinese state structure much more flexible for doing things. That, I think, is a very important issue.

Thirdly, when we talk about Chinese political reforms, the role of the party is a big issue. The kind of language to describe the role of the party is a big issue. To talk about the Chinese Communist Party without having a background of the agrarian revolution is not possible because that was a long period of revolution almost from the 1911 revolution down to the cultural revolution, which is the longest revolution in the twentieth century. This happened in China. When I travelled to different provinces, I could realise how deeply social mobilisation had reached the lower social strata. The political organisations and the party system had also penetrated into the roots of the peasantry and workers at different levels. The Communist Party is the biggest party with 70 million members. We don't know any other kind of political organisation of such a scale. But that came from that long process that had the capacity to mobilise the people to do things and also transformed the social subjectivity of peasants. During the early phase of the cultural revolution and rural reforms post the cultural revolution, peasants played a great role. Land reforms came with enormous human sacrifice but eventually, these reforms were fulfilled through the Chinese revolution. That was the given pre-condition for China's reforms; redistribution of land equally to the families of peasants. Also, the principle of equality in those rural reforms was quite crucial. This was one of the basic pre-conditions together with many other policies—economic policies, market policy, prices, education and so on and so forth. But generally speaking, historical conditions were important.

Now the situation has changed a lot. The role of the state is in transformation. Prof Yao Yang, an economist from Beijing University argued that one of the achievements of Chinese reforms can be attributed to the neutrality of the state. That means that the state has no special interest and can be neutral to special interests in the process of growth. That made people believe that any policy issued by the central government was beneficial to the whole population. That is why even when things are being settled, weaker people are reached first. People still believe that everybody would become richer later. But now that belief has gone. Why did the neutrality of the state change following that? There are two aspects to that. Ironically, it was the political values of the Communist Party for equality and proletarian guarantees that led the state to not align with special interest groups. Now the party itself comprises interest groups. The party never talks about working hours and similar issues. They now talk about the harmonious society and general interest of the national population. At the same time, the state and the party also played a crucial role in launching the economic reforms which meant that different levels of government penetrated into economic injustice. That is the base of some kind of corruption. The neutrality of the state itself is in an ambiguous position now; I am not saying everything has succumbed but some people criticise it.

The second is that there was a very important change in the rural-urban relationship because especially after the 1990s, China underwent a radical urbanisation. We now have huge number of agro-migrants who emerged as the new working class in the coastal areas with very low salaries providing cheap labour. That created problems because a sudden kind of rupture happened. Sociologists have described this new society as a society with ruptures. This means, for example, that the new middle class in urban areas argued for political reforms based on arguments for private property rights, the legal system, and so on and so forth, but most of the agrarian population, especially in the inland areas, did not argue for that. One reason was that the collective ownership of land was the basic guarantee of their social welfare if they lost their jobs. From coastal areas and urban areas, they could go back to their hometowns for cultivation and continued to do that. That is the cheapest basic social guarantee not only in agriculture but the basic social guarantee for their daily life, if there are lay-offs or loss of jobs. It is a challenge for national policy to integrate different interests through a more participatory political process and a more democratic orientation.

This is the situation at present. At the same time, another challenge is in regard to people, talking about our alliance in the 1950s, 1960s and 1970s and so on and so forth. But that kind of old concept of national sovereignty shifted because of globalisation and China's entry into the WTO and international organisations and its working together with some other countries. If we had remained fixed on the old idea of sovereignty, it would have become impossible. On the other hand, self-reliance or a certain kind of independence for the government, for special interest groups not only from within but internationally too, was important. Making the whole system of policymaking more transparent became the big challenge. Also, a lot of people talked about political reforms. Recently, Premier Wen Jiabao also spoke several times about political reforms. We still don't know whether reforms remain an empty slogan, partly because a lot of other people have been talking about political reforms within the party. But I don't think they can be really effective without social change. In the last two decades, I think some change has happened because the policymaking process has become much more open than before. For example, the rural crisis issue was raised not within the regime but at intellectual debates in the beginning and then spread to the mass media. Eventually, the government publicly recognised that their agrarian policy was wrong at the end of the 1990s. In the beginning of the 21st century, we had long debates emanating from intellectual circles which spread over to public debate in the media about the medical system. In the 1990s, they pursued the idea of privatisation of the whole medical system and we criticised that. In 2003, after the outbreak of SARS, the government was worried about its spread to the countryside because the whole countryside had no medical system at all. That was very dangerous. At that time, public discussion and intellectual debates as an intervention were eventually effective. The Minister of Medical System Public Care recognised that the whole plan for the privatisation of medical system was wrong and new plans needed to be made. We had seven schemes for research into different medical systems but the basic orientation was more social democratic.

Generally speaking, China is not the kind of typical social democracy in a political regime. But a lot of issues have been shared together in different countries in different political contexts.

19

PRESENTATION BY JONATHAN COHN

The Strange Life of American Welfare

I'd like to begin by asking how many of you have followed the debate over health care in the US over the last year and a half, and how many of you would say that when the process was over, you were enthusiastic about the product. Judging by the responses denoted by the number of raised hands I see, I must say that you guys are even tougher on the President than the American voters are. That is impressive. I understand that feeling. I don't know how many of you know anything about me. I have come to this conference not just as a close observer of this debate over the last year but also as a long time, well-known advocate for universal health care. First and foremost, as a moral priority. I simply believe that in a civilised society, every human being deserves the right to medical care and shouldn't have to go bankrupt paying for it. I think that is a very simple proposition. I am also a student of health care systems, both in the US and abroad. Today, health care for me is not just about extending benefits, but also finding a way to make the entire health care system sustainable because it places such a huge financial burden on our society as a whole and individually. I also recognise that health care is a quintessential case of market failure for reasons like adverse selection. Many of you are familiar with the fact that health insurance does not work as a private market without government intervention. In fact, from what I have seen, the countries that do the best job on health care tend to be the ones that have the government acting the most aggressively, which is not exactly what we tend to do in the US.

By those standards, there is a lot of reason to be disappointed with the Affordable Care Act, which is the formal name of the law. Instead of wrecking the system and starting over, which is what I would have done if I had my way, it leaves the system in place and dotes on it. It is supposed to control the cost of health care but projections suggest a slowing of the growing cost of health care incrementally by a very small amount and even that is uncertain. Finally, this is the strangest universal health care law in the world because it is not actually universal. Even when it is fully implemented in 2014, the projections suggest that 15 million people will still not have health insurance. By those criteria, I would agree that this is a flawed and disappointing law. I want to spend the rest of my allotted time in telling you why the law turned out the way it did, but also telling you why despite these disappointments, I am actually surprisingly hopeful about the future, not just for the US but everyone around the world who are trying to move social democracy forward.

The story of America not having a welfare state equivalent to what the Europeans have is an old story, one that has been debated endlessly by political scientists and generally tends to cluster around five explanations. One is the history of American exceptionalism. There is something in the political DNA of Americans that just makes us listen to Glenn Beck or Ruslin Bob, but it's not that part of the DNA I'm referring to here. The reference is to that part of the DNA that makes us very individualistic, very resistant to authority, very distrustful of government. It has taken extraordinary circumstances, historically, for social democracy to dawn in our country. It has taken the crisis like the Great Depression. It has not come easily to us.

Another theory is the fragmentation of our political institutions. This is a strategy that everybody thinks they know but unless you happen to be inside this beast or write about it as I do, I don't think you can quite appreciate the extent of fragmentation. It is not just that we have the federal government and the state government; the executive, legislature and judiciary but even within these branches of government, there is fragmentation. Take the legislature; we have the House, the Senate and a Congressional budget office which is the creature of these two that make the economic projections, which everybody is supposed to listen to. It goes on and on and every single one of these can be thought of as a veto point. Every one of these has the power to stop progress. That makes it very difficult to pass any sweeping legislation.

Another factor that people talk about is the diversity of the American population. In many ways, I think this is the great strength of America. We have a better history, at least relative to a lot of other developed countries, of absorbing and being enriched by immigrants to our country. But at the same time, the flip side to this—and there is a lot of theoretical work on this—observing that when we have a very diverse country, people are sometimes less enthusiastic about sharing resources in their country. To put it in crude political logic, American politics is often very hard put to convince middle class tax payers to support programmes when probably the beneficiaries are going to be people who are poor and have a different skin colour than them. That is the hard reality of American politics.

Another factor often cited is the lack of strong Left-leaning institutions. We have very weak labour movements in the US. We also have powerful corporations and don't have public financing of elections. The political power in our country is very much tilted against progressive forces.

One final factor is what political scientists call 'path dependence', which is a fancy way of saying that if we made a mistake seven years ago, we spend a long time paying for it. Decisions made at the very beginning, when we are starting a debate, tend to have repercussions that will shape the way we are able to make policies many years later. In fact, health care actually turns out to be a classic example of that. The debates that have helped turn our country are about a 100 years old, and trace back to the early 20th century, the time when medicine first entered the modern era. It is the first time when the financial risk of the onus isn't just that you are going to miss your job for two weeks; you have got to figure out how to replace your income. For the first time, you have to think how you are going to pay the doctor and the hospital. Of course, we know the economics of health care; it is an old story. We call it the 80/20 rule, which is that 80 per cent of the cost in the health care system is borne by 20 per cent of the people and at any one time, it is the small number of people with very high expenses. The challenge is how to get a larger group of people to contribute equal amounts of money to pay for those, and to create an insurance system.

All this happened in the early and late 1920s and the early 1930s, which also happened to be the time of the Great Depression. Franklin Roosevelt was elected and put forth the New Deal. There was very serious debate, during the crafting of the Social Security Act, of adding medical insurance to it. To this day, that was the moment. If Roosevelt had decided to include medical insurance in the Social Security Act, I am convinced we would have had a system like that in much of Europe today. But Roosevelt did not make that decision because he was a pretty smart politician. Already, during that time, there was talk that the state medical societies, the physicians, people who had already invested in the system as it was, saw this as an intrusion by the government. The generous interpretation is they didn't want somebody interfering in their medical practice. The less generous interpretation is they didn't want someone cutting their pay cheque. But they were worried that their position would basically kill the Social Security Act. They did not do that and instead it was left to the private sector to invent a system for medical financing. It was the hospitals who came up with the system in the end, because they needed to stabilise their finances. They needed to have beds for the patients who could pay and not for patients who could not pay their bills. They traded these private plans built around the workplace and that was the way American health insurance started and grew. It was fairly popular and worked for a lot of people. The plans were operated as non-profits originally and they were willing to take anybody, because health care wasn't that expensive then. It was a good way to expand the base of people who could pay their hospital bills.

Unfortunately, over time, this system started to deteriorate. There were two big changes. One was the entry of the commercial insurance industry whose goals weren't just to fill hospital beds with the insurance. They wanted to make profits. They couldn't do that and saw very quickly that the way to make profits was to figure out who in the population wasn't going to get sick, and insure those people. That has really worked well for insurance companies.

Unfortunately, it did not work well for the people who got sick. In addition to that, the system that was built around employment obviously left out people who did not have jobs—the poor and the elderly. In 1965, in the second great phase of social democratic energy in the United States, Lyndon Johnson as President finally pushed through medical care and the Medicare Act. This insured all senior citizens and some, but not all of the poor. That was a great step forward. Until this day, a lot of us think of Medicare as one of the great achievements in our country's history. However, it did not address the lingering cost problems. Even the hospitals back in the 1930s said insurance would pay whatever the hospitals wanted to be paid. The government has now hedged the system. Suddenly everyone from doctors, hospitals, drug companies, device companies are writing really big cheques, which is costing a tonne of money and therefore, this system is doomed to fall apart.

That's where we are basically today. This debate actually began in the 1990s when Bill Clinton became the President. It was he, also a very good politician, who understood that this is the US and we are not going to impose a single fair system, particularly not with this history. He wanted to try to marry a market solution to this and make a system where everyone gets a private insurance but, with careful regulation, regressive cost control. That's how universal health care came. I say this as one of the only three living people who actually think that Clinton health care plan was a good one. The problem was that the political system could not handle it. It offended too many special interests and especially the middle class people, who already had insurance and did not want to give it up.

Fast forward 15 years. Now Barack Obama is the President and he is a pretty good politician too, determined to avoid the mistakes of the Clinton administration. Number one was the caution not to touch anybody's insurance. People who have insurance would be left alone to just build around this system. They were going to do private insurance but Americans don't want to spend a lot of money and don't like government spending. So we are going to make sure that this plan does not have more than one trained hour in outlays over 10 years. By the way, we are going to be very careful with this thing; we are not going to offend all the special interests. We are going to play a game of musical chairs. Let me tell every special interest and health people that there are three chairs here. You guys decide who is in there but if you feel you can join us, we will make an alliance with you and we will go forward that way. They made deals with the pharmaceutical and hospital industry and the American Medical Association, which is the medical industry. This is how they went forward. These bargains had a lot of costs. It meant that by capping the outlays we couldn't start until 2014. It meant that even when it does start, it won't be as generous as a lot of other systems are. These deals with the pharmaceuticals, the hospitals and the doctors are the reason the plan does not control costs as much. It is the reason we don't have a public insurance option which would have been a way to introduce more government bargaining into the health care system. All these are imposed costs. On top of that, it turned out that the political situation was even worse than they imagined. Not only did we have the House and the Senate but now the situation was that in the Senate, the first law has disproportionate representation. So North Dakota, whose population is roughly the number of people in this room, has the same number of Senators as the state of California which would be something like the 20th most populous country in the world. That is some measure of the political influence in the US Senate and over the conservative side, it happens to be the small states in the US that right now are conservative.

On top of that, the US Senate functions through the filibuster, which once upon a time was used in extraordinary circumstances through this very dramatic stance where the Senate gets up and talks for three days, reads the phone book and they make a movie about it and it is all very exciting. But now, it is routine. You need 60 votes in an unrepresentative chamber of a legislature to pass anything. So with all that, they had to backtrack and make more compromises. That is how she got the law she got. Even then—and this is the most depressing part—they passed this law, but come November, you may have noticed that they didn't do too well in the US mid-term polls. It's very much a matter of debate whether health care was or wasn't a factor in last year's polls. But there's no question that the general public feels very ambivalent about this law. They're quite confused about it and don't understand what to do. Even to the extent they do understand, they're quite apprehensive that it is going to take something away from them and give it to somebody else, who theoretically and perceptibly, doesn't look like them.

All this is quite depressing. Furthermore, the people who are elected want to repeal the law and by the way, they're following lawsuits in the Supreme Court. People who study American law tell me that there is no way in the world the US Supreme Court would overturn this law. But then, these were the same people who told me in 2000 that there was no way in the world that the Supreme Court would get involved in a Presidential election. So there is reason to be a little apprehensive.

Having said all this, I did say that I was hopeful and continue to remain so. There are two reasons for this. First, the history of such programmes in the US is very clear. Once you get them passed, they improve. Tom Harkin, who is currently the Chairman of the Health Committee in the Senate, I thought, had a wonderful analogy when he said that this bill is "a star home, not a palace or a mansion." It's got a really solid foundation, a sturdy roof and room for expansion. We have got this bill, and over time, we will improve this law because once it is implemented, people will start demanding. This is what happened with social security and medicare and will happen with this bill too, over time.

The other reason I'm optimistic is that even if this seems like only a partial victory, I have some appreciation for what it took to get here. People have been working towards this for 20 years. They have been meeting at places like this, holding endless conferences about how to structure and decide upon this issue. I have personally sat through a 100 such conferences, where issues have been discussed threadbare. These ideas resonate, get around and get people thinking about them. It does take time and is difficult. But these things do happen and progress really does take effect. It may take a while for the voters to appreciate it, but at the end of the day, this kind of work pays off and that is how, I think, progress happens.

20

SECTION II

Discussion

Joseph E. Stiglitz

We have had a very good introduction, both of the experience in a couple of countries as well as of the global aspects of trying to create a social democratic agenda.

Rehman Sobhan

I want to comment on the global social democratic platform which Pascal Lamy outlined. In terms of his five things I suppose you could say that the intellectual content of policies is reasonably well defined now, particularly in the work of people like Joe Stiglitz and others. The policy content is also probably getting better defined because of UN conferences, trade negotiations and so on. My concerns are with the other three. In some ways, what I hear is language which tries to transpose the European social democratic agenda to the global level. The big difference is that the political structure at the global level is different. And it is not necessary, if we do not have the same political base at the global level as you have at the national level. This is why the issues of scope arise. I do not think the global social democratic agenda can be entirely in the economic space or the environmental space. It will have to cover politics. The legitimate desire for engagement, participation, influence and power, which new players want, is a dimension which is in some ways different from the social democratic agenda. The second is in terms of the actors. We have to emphasise the actors; we know the power of transnational corporations, and the importance of global NGO networks in shaping ideas. But the system of multilateral negotiations that we have, particularly in trade and finance, leaves very little room for their engagement. It remains an inter-governmental negotiating system. We do not have a process for getting to action in terms of a global social democratic agenda and tools. As you correctly said, tools like redistribution or collectivisation are not available at the global level. Maybe regulation is there in certain areas like environment but frankly, we have not made much progress beyond the classical agenda of trade-and-aid in terms of how we actually translate these into goals and policies as one comes into real action at the ground level. I just wanted to see your reaction because you skimmed over the tool factors and scope dimension. To me, those are the real challenges; that is certainly my experience from my years in the UN.

Pranab Bardhan

I want to make a couple of points. One about China, which Wang Hui talked about, and the other about the Nordic social democracy experience, from the Indian point of view. I think it is worth emphasising something that Wang Hui emphasised. I have emphasised in my recent book on China and India that one of the big ways in which Chinese economic reforms succeeded, at least part of the underlying foundation was created by a highly egalitarian land distribution, which made the wrenching adjustments of market reforms much easier to bear. One of the reasons India has problems in adjustments, at least in terms of popularity of reforms among working class and peasants is that, in contrast to China, we have extremely unequal land distribution. In fact, in China, almost every family, at least up to very recently, had an equal amount of land. We have almost 40 per cent of rural households landless or near landless. In that situation, when you don't have something to fall back upon, you are worried about changes brought about by reforms.

But I wanted to ask Wang Hui one thing. He said in a delighted way that China, until very recently, did not have oligarchic interest group formation. Of course, China did not have the special interests until very recently, i.e., the special interests of the usual kind. But I remember the first time I went to China in the 1980s, people were already talking about princelings. I have cited data in my

China-India book that of the multimillionaires within China, the overwhelming majority are relatives of high-ranking party officials. That, to me, is an oligarchy, not the usual special interest oligarchy that we know in capitalist countries but an oligarchy. In fact, one of China's most senior economists, Wu Jingliang of Chiang University described this as crony capitalism. To me, this was formation of an oligarchic group, but of a different kind.

I will now come to the Nordic case, which is found to be fascinating all over the world. I remember that even as a young college student in Kolkata, I used to be a great admirer of social democracy. I am so today too. But at that time, in my youthful idealism, I used to think it is applicable to India. I am less sure about it now. It may not be feasible but I am not sure even about the desirability, particularly feasibility. One day, I remember as an undergraduate student in Kolkata, it suddenly dawned on me that Norway is smaller than South Calcutta, forget about the rest of Calcutta. That is flippant but for a long time, I have been writing on and thinking about what the political scientists call 'the theory of collective action' or more plainly, why it is difficult. I think it is a big problem in India. Even when we all know what is to be done, we cannot get our act together. That, in more fancy terms, is the collective action problem. Why so? Things that are difficult to do at a Calcutta level, may probably be easy to do at the South Calcutta level. In that sense, more than size, that is where the diversity, heterogeneity, conflicts of interests come in and it is difficult to get our act together.

The other thing is that over time, it has dawned on me how fragmented our labour movement is. One of the big secrets of the success of Nordic social democracy is the centralisation and confederation of labour organisations. India is at the other end of the spectrum. In India, by the 1926 Trade Union Act, any seven people can form a trade union. You can imagine how many trade unions you have. We don't have secret ballots and it is difficult to recognise majority unions. Even in a single industry, the whole labour movement is fragmented and it is difficult to get our act together. Just imagine, in Nordic countries, they are doing that at the whole country level. As someone said, capital, labour and state get together. India is completely at the other end of the spectrum. However desirable that is, it is a huge issue which we cannot even begin to think about.

Going back to China again, I recently saw some data, wherein Wang Hui talked about the party. The Communist Party of China since a long time has no longer been a workers' and peasants' party. Of the 70 million members of the Communist Party that Hui talked about, I saw a study of the composition of the membership. The actual number of workers and peasants in the year 2005 was only 29 per cent; 71 per cent were not workers or peasants. They were composed of businessmen, professionals and college students. The CPC is now a majority professional and business party and not a workers' or peasants' party, and has been so for a very long time. The data is now emerging. That, I think, is an important implication of the special interests, which you are interested in.

Kaushik Basu

I wanted to pick up a bit on Joe's introductory remarks and also what Pascal Lamy has said and to what Nitin was getting to. There is a connection between globalisation and democracy, which really has to go beyond redistribution of goods. A redistribution of voice is really needed. One way of looking at it is that democracy is being able to choose people who can influence our lives. It is entirely arguable, and is not an exaggeration at all, that for someone in Afghanistan, more important than who is chosen as the leader of Afghanistan is who is chosen as the leader of the US. As globalisation takes place and one country can influence the well-being of the people of another country, unless we have better systems of people in one country having some sort of a say in what is happening in the more powerful country, there will be a deficit in global democracy, which is a steady process. Now, of course, one can't be idealistic and think in terms of that happening immediately, but at least international organisations can be a forum providing a much greater voice for countries. This is beginning to happen, but it is still centred on the economic criterion. India and China are beginning to claw in and acquire some more say, but the African countries have very little say in these bodies. The standard reaction used to be that one is putting in more money and so one must have more say. A remark like that, to me, just shows how rudimentary our notions of global democracy are. Suppose, within a country, if someone said that Bill Gates should have more votes because he puts more money, we would say that it is a misunderstanding of the very meaning of democracy, whereas in the global forum we keep using that argument. I feel this is something that ought to be brought into the global space more energetically.

Eric Solheim

Let me first make a comment about how particular we are in North Europe. I think we are very particular, very special like everyone else, like the people of Kolkata or Beijing or whatever group you want to name. There are particularities everywhere and we are not more particular than anyone else. Some Nordic countries are old and some are not. Some have a very violent history, while some have a very peaceful one. Some have been historically very homogeneous, some very heterogeneous. The business mix is completely different. There is one feature that is similar for everyone, which is that all Nordic nations are small. That is the one and perhaps only issue similar to all Nordic nations; otherwise, we are very diverse.

I think what we have achieved comes back to the issue of solidarity, created by men. At some point, solidarity was not any more defined as some kind of act of the Mother Teresa type. It was seen as enlightened self-interest. You help someone else because you expect to get something back when you need it. You pay taxes because you get something back from the state. You help your fellow labourers because you will then get assistance when you are in need. In some matters, we have achievements and in others, we don't. But let me state one matter the experience of which can provide some inspiration. This is something that happened among the women of my generation. When I was a child, my mother was the only mother in my street with full-time employment. Everyone else was a housewife. There was one female minister, the Minister of Family. There were no businesswomen. No one had even heard of women business leaders. There was no kindergarten or maternity leave. One generation later, we had every child having guaranteed rights to kindergarten from age one. There is one-year maternity or paternity leave prior to that. The government has 50 per cent women representation in parliament. By the way, India is making similar quotas; maybe not in parliament, but what you have done at the local level is very courageous from an international perspective.

We have just passed a law stipulating that there must be 50 per cent women on the board of any company. The business community protested when it happened, but now there is no protest. Everyone has accepted it and the reason is that we must tap into the talent of the people and women are 50 per cent of the talent pool in the nation. Whatever 50 per cent one keeps out, whether 50 per cent of purists, lower castes, women, or people from a particular region, one loses talent and meritocracy which take every nation forward. So, on these matters, I think we may be able to inspire others.

Then there are many other areas where we should be inspired by others. The very weak point of European social democracy, at the moment, which was hinted to by my Dutch colleague too, is our inability to handle the matter of immigration and the issue of religion. In these matters, I think we have a lot to learn from India and not vice-versa because the Left in Europe has not really been able to handle these issues. We believed that religion would disappear with science. It did not happen, religion in fact bounced back and we were not prepared for it. We have not been prepared how to adapt a welfare state into a situation wherein there are many Indians or Pakistanis or other ethnic groups. The Right has been able to tap into this. To this extent, the shift to the Right in Europe is basically because the Right has unfortunately been able to tap into the burning issue of immigration and the resultant strains amongst the people.

I shall touch upon one final point. I very much appreciate everything that was said. That was a very good presentation about Obama's health law. What was said about the neutrality of the Chinese state was also very interesting. Pascal Lamy advocated some kind of global social democracy. If that is to happen, it must be on a completely new footing. It cannot be a kind of extension of the European social democracy. It must step into the Chinese idea of a harmonious society, to what is happening here in India with inclusive growth, to what Lula has done in Brazil. It is very impressive. Maybe, Brazil is the best example of a functioning social democracy in the last decade. The growth is a little lower than India but Brazil's states have a very business-friendly investment climate. Adding to that, one of the most, maybe the most successful social policy scheme in the world, the so-called Bolsa Familia, gives every poor man in Brazil money but they have to send their children to school. It also has the most successful environmental policy of any nation. The level of deforestation in Brazil has gone down by 70 per cent in seven years. No one would have contemplated this was possible seven years back. We don't have the figures for this year but we know that they are likely to decrease this year. By far, this is the biggest measure taken by any individual nation to combat climate change as well as to protect biodiversity. Environmental, social and business success go hand in hand. Lula got his candidate re-elected by a wide margin last week and it's a success story of social democracy. My point is that we have to widen the concept because we are now embarking upon a multi-polar world. That is why we have challenges with trade and climate change but it's a much more fascinating and favourable confirmation than any previous one. We should shed all this pessimism and introduce a new and fascinating multi-polar world with confidence. Social democracy must be redefined in this global sense.

Nemat Shafik

I have a question for the panel. There is a view that Pascal Lamy put forward. Globalisation will force convergence of a pro-justice social democracy around the world. But I think, based on Jonathan's presentation, and the Nordics agreeing even on an appropriate level of taxation and redistribution by the state and a common view about how much the state should provide public services, it feels a long time away. My question is: should we be thinking about convergence of a pro-justice social democracy? Or should we be thinking about tolerating different approaches? The US will always opt for lower taxes, less redistribution and less provision of services and the Nordics will always be at the other end of the spectrum. Most countries will be somewhere in between and tolerate divergence in approach, turning on national politics and history, but agree globally that there is a minimum standard below which no one should go. They will develop international transfer mechanisms to protect people at the very bottom. For example, during the financial crisis in 2008, there were the beginnings of that approach when it was realised that many poor people would be hit hardest as a result of the financial crisis and its impact on growth. In countries that had cash transfer schemes in place, one has the mechanisms, such as the Bolsa Familia. The Mexicans but also many African countries and a few Asian ones also had the mechanisms in place. It was possible for richer countries to pump more money into those cash transfer schemes so that poor people would get an extra cushion when the crisis hit. That was the beginning of a sort of opening for the world. The idea was that people in rich countries would transfer cash to people in poor countries going through tough times, to protect them from falling into absolute poverty. I wonder whether that is the microcosm of thinking about a global safety net that doesn't require the convergence of social democracy but really a collective minimum standard that everyone could support.

Kumi Naidoo

I hope in everything I am about to say, I am completely wrong, because it is a sort of doomsday scenario. I actually believe that we are sleepwalking into a crisis. I think that if we genuinely believe the signs about climate change alone, just to take one issue, by 2015 the emissions must peak and start coming down, otherwise, we have catastrophic runaway climate change. We know that the political realities that we face at the moment do not actually give us any optimism that that is going to happen. The reason I say this is because I think the moment of history that we are living in right now has to be understood as being quite unique. For the last three years we have seen a convergence of a range of crises in a very short concentrated time span which can be called a perfect storm or a boiling point. Essentially, we have a fuel price crisis which produces a knock-on effect in the form of the food price crisis. We have an ongoing poverty crisis and we should remind ourselves that it's the loss of close to fifty thousand men, women and children every single day, from preventable causes. The climate crisis is not a crisis of the future. Already, we know that in 2008, according to Kofi Annan's Foundation, three hundred thousand people lost their lives from climatic impact and it is going to get worse. It was only when the financial crisis hit that those with power acknowledged that we were in a crisis.

But our response to the crisis has largely been a business-as-usual approach. It has been to ignore what Albert Einstein once said. If we are trying to address the big problem, we can't use the same thinking logic and frameworks that got us in the problem in the first place. But, largely that has been our response. So, when we think about the future of social democracy right now, we have to contextualise it in this current moment and be rigorous about how actually serious things are. For example, people say that climate change will give us resource wars in the future. My reading from the reality in Africa is that resource wars have started. If we look at the genocide in Darfur, we can see how it is some ethnic conflict, but water and land scarcity are the biggest rivals. Lake Chad was one of the largest inland seas in the world. It has virtually shrunk to 25 per cent of its size. Lake Chad is right next to Darfur. This context is important and we have to rethink on how to give voice and influence to people who have been marginalised and recognise that governance has shifted so much in the last two decades. Today, we have to ask where the citizens can exercise the energy, voice and participation where they can get the social outcomes that they need. For some things, it is best done at local levels and for other things, it is best done at the national level. But increasingly, there are some global issues like trade and environment where one can fight and win only at the global level. There is also another dimension of governance that has become much more important in the last decade, in particular during the last 15 years, which we haven't spoken about. That is the importance of regional governance. By this, I mean regional inter-governmental organisations. We talked about the European Union but if we look at what is happening in Africa and in South Asia and so on, it's still a bit nascent. We are seeing the importance of regional inter-governmental organisations increase. One mistake we sometimes make is that when we have global discussions, we always use the examples of India, China, Brazil and sometimes Indonesia. We should bear in mind that those four countries are different in one crucial aspect, scale and size, which is very important too. I have jokingly been saying ever since the euro came into effect, if Europe can have the euro, I don't see why Africa can't have an afro. I am not talking about the 'A' style but Africa doesn't stand a chance without serious political and economic integration.

In all of this mix there have been positive references to the role of civil society. Pascal Lamy, I think, made a really important point about the role of the trade union movement in trying to get this compact, notwithstanding the fact that it is different in different countries. There is a lot of lip service to the importance of the role of civil society, which means NGOs, trade unions, faith groups and so on, but if we actually look at the impact that the war on terrorism has had on the shrinking of civil liberties and of political space, I am sad to say that some of the culprits in driving that shrinking of the space have been parties that profess to be leaders of social democracy. Look at the British Labour Party and the kinds of things it attempted. Thankfully they lost, and weren't able to introduce new laws for detentions without trial, racial and religious profiling and so on. I want to remind us of the challenge that we should not take social democracy as a given thing. Social democracy is the best that it can be at this point, but in fact, it has lost its way in practice in many places. If we have this chance to actually recover, then there has to be a serious opening up of the space and the creation of a serious enabling environment for the full spectrum of civil society to be able to make a positive contribution.

Aruna Roy

I bring back to you some of the issues we raised at the World Social Forum, which is very much part of India and of the world. There are issues that concern us. For instance, when we speak of land today, what comes to my mind are large multinational corporations which take over chunks of India, people being displaced, forming protest groups who are then attacked because they are seen as anti-national or violent groups. A whole chain of action begin from there. Actually much of this is really social democratic protest. All they are saying is you are taking away our land and our natural resources and we want to be heard. But in a social democratic framework, unless the world addresses displacement, disposition and listens to peoples' voices, there will be a number of problems.

The kind of role we assign to debate, dissent and protest in a social democratic system and political system determines the nature of the political and social democratic structure we have. If we don't listen to protest and don't give it space, we are doomed. In India, we still have a lot of space to protest but it is shrinking and we are worried because if the space shrinks then what we fear is violence. As long as we can protest and be heard, violence doesn't happen. But the moment that there is no hearing or understanding of our protest, things happen. In fact, I think that the major campaigns that have got these right-based laws were a fantastic example of a dialogue between people, political parties and governance. We had a lot of debates and many disagreements, but finally laws were made. Though they did not satisfy each one of the groups, they led to some addressing of the issues that concerned people in a fundamental way. Platforms for dialogue are therefore very important.

Jonathan Cohn raised an issue which interested me because he said people were not convinced enough about the need for health security. One thing we have achieved in India is the ability to dialogue with varied groups. We say that these are very intellectual issues and people don't understand them, but they do. They often understand it better than we do because we have developed an idiom of exchange. These are things that can contribute to public policy reflecting the needs of people and therefore, a much more viable social democratic framework.

I'd like to add a note of caution. We have had a lot of differences over the UID, which Nandan Nilekani knows about and we have had debates in all kinds of fora. The problem is that there is nothing that is good or bad. But quick technology solutions are frightening. Technology is a kind of a beast that, once let loose, takes its own shape. No one doubts Nandan's intent. But the point is once the technology comes out, it becomes universal in your language, but compulsory in mine. What it will do to an India which is divided across communities, languages, castes, ideological groups, is quite frightening. Today we have a political party in power which is fair, tomorrow there is no guarantee. In Gujarat we have elected somebody whom we don't want to elect to power, over and over again, who has a stated fundamentalist position. Supposing, God forbid, if there is such a point in time in history when India gets ruled by a fundamentalist party with information at a push of a button, they can profile every community, every ideology in India. It would be frightening and Nandan knows this. We have talked to him about it. Unless there is a political statement about the limitations of that technology and its use of that technology it can be horrific for the people on the other side.

The other word of caution is that with a technology like this which is useful—nobody says we shouldn't have biometrics, or that we shouldn't have UID—there should be a lot more public debate and interaction so that people who are now awakening to what might happen to themselves, including minority groups, can express their opinion, find out what will happen to them and then of course, we can use the UID. We have a proposition. Regarding civil society, the right to information campaign, we have met some of those who have been working in this field and know them well; people like Shekhar Singh for instance. Many of us now feel that we need to have a transparent pre-legislative process from the time of policy to the time of lawmaking so that people know what laws are going into Parliament. Very often, even MPs do not know what laws are going into Parliament. Many of my friends who are members of Parliament do not know what is coming to them because so many laws get introduced into Parliament. They do not have time to read many of them. They want time to deliberate. A country which plans to be a social democracy and wants to take people along with it will also have to have a transparent pre-legislative process.

Kumar Mangalam Birla

I want to make a few quick points. We have two issues at a global level which are looming very large over us. One is the issue about currency wars and how that translates into the issue of social democracy by actually impacting the competitiveness of different countries. The other is the issue of protectionism, which is a direct fallout of globalisation and how our policymakers can together work around these issues and who are as sensitive to social democracy as they are to the process of globalisation.

I agree with Joe that financial liberalisation doesn't create jobs. In the Indian context, the biggest creator of jobs is going to be the manufacturing sector because we have a track record in manufacturing. We have natural resources, cheap labour and because we have the largest number of young people in the world, the manufacturing sector has the biggest ripple effect in terms of economic growth and creating jobs. Creating an enabling environment in the country encourages the setting up of manufacturing activities in a way that India becomes a manufacturing hub for the world just as we now recognise it as an intellectual hub for the world.

We spoke about education. Education in India is going to be perhaps the greatest leveller across society. Whilst there has been a lot of focus on primary education, it is as important to focus on secondary and higher education and by way of deregulating education. We have a huge need for engineers, scientists and so on. We are going to have many first-generation educated people in India, more now than ever before. Deregulation of education is therefore important, so that there is a process of globalisation even in education. For example, foreign universities that want to come and set up campus in India are as important to the progress of India and to the fact that we want to keep up the pace of growing at the rate of 8 to 9 per cent as an economy.

Sri Mulyani Indrawati

I want to add to the discussion by bringing the Indonesian case because this is very important while looking at globalisation and democratisation combined with decentralisation as I said earlier. When we were under Suharto's rule, there was much appreciation of the achievement of reducing poverty, introducing family planning that created a social safety net at the lower level, and improving equality. But it was an authoritarian government which was corrupt, centralised and closed. The agenda of the global infiltrated to countries through many channels. NGOs which came to Indonesia and maybe to some extent multinational corporations, although enjoying the benefit of a favourable government, felt that this was not going to be sustainable enough in the long run. Therefore, Indonesia changed to become democratic, decentralised and open through this kind of mechanism which localised the global agenda. At elections, whether presidential or parliamentary, local government and so on, issues of sustainability, climate change or social protection become a public debate. It is a healthy public debate which gives quite a lot of hope. The problem of the past 10 years with this democracy, openness and decentralisation, is that it does not always guarantee the delivery or certainty of results, especially if you have to contend with oligarchy or power cartels. Some of those who have power can have their own media, political party and become governors or even parliamentary members. They can really hijack this democracy and create obstacles for the agenda of social democracy or even sustainability, because they derive legitimacy through the formal political process. Decisions can be diverted, which will benefit only this interest group. This is the kind of dilemma Indonesia faces under the current circumstances. Global power exercised through multilateral development banks or the IMF, World Bank, is no longer as important. If we talk about the World Bank now, the ability to use its lending to influence public policy is decreasing because the government budget is becoming very big and banks are becoming very small players. Even if one combines ADB with the other regional banks, it is not going to be as significant as it was earlier.

Therefore, it is going to be a situation in which one can engage in political debate, discuss social democracy, concerns about the environment and so on but the institutional mechanisms will not provide certainty about the solutions which are needed by society and the country in the long run, as well as the delivery.

Although much of Indonesia still believes in democracy and openness, there is a growing concern about its effectiveness especially if you try to connect with the many new problems like climate change which need a consistency of policy in the right direction.

These are issues that we should think about when looking at how to combine globalisation, democracy or even decentralisation in a country as big as India, and how to develop mechanisms to provide a solution in the form of social democracy or on other issues of concern like the environment. This is a real problem for Indonesia. In this situation, I'm trying to be quite optimistic that checks and balances and openness can have certain mechanisms to prevent bad policy from being implemented. But in the short run, a populist and a bad policy could actually happen under this kind of situation and the cost is going to be very huge for the country.

Sunita Narain

I want to take forward Kaushik Basu's point. It is very clear that we have economic globalisation. We also know that the fallout of economic globalisation, in some sense, is ecological globalisation. The world is finding that it is very interdependent; what happens in one country can impact another country. We are getting a whole set of new rules being developed globally through many treaties and agreements, whether in bio-diversity or desertification. There is a whole set of two kinds of treaties that are being worked on. What we really see and what many of the panelists also talked about, equally frustrating from our point of view, is that we are not seeing enough political globalisation. When I talk about political globalisation, I really mean the principles that should drive the globalisation process. We heard about this very strongly, whether it comes from the US, China, India or Brazil, I think each country within its own circumstances is debating and discussing the best forms of political principles and keeps working on it. But at the global level we still haven't arrived at those principles which would actually make for good governance. At the end of the day, we all realise that we need principles at the national levels which will drive towards equity, justice and inclusion. But we do not have these at the global level. That is a big issue for us that we need to talk about. Jonathan will forgive me, but the big elephant in the room is the US. It is in some sense the global discourse which we must take on board. When we look at climate change, at all the work that we have been doing for the last 25 to 30 years, I have seen the enormous power of one nation in making sure global rules are not made. We need to be innovative in this, similar to what we are talking about being innovative within Brazil and India. It is difficult, but we need to find innovative mechanisms that can actually bring compliance from the richest and the most powerful. We never talk about this at a global level. We talk about compliance at a national level saying that we need to make the rich comply and the weak have to be protected. But at the international level, we haven't been able to come up with mechanisms that can make the rich obey rules and strong compliance mechanisms. The only two mechanisms that exist globally are trade, and in some senses, aid or money, but those are not mechanisms that we can use against the powerful; we can use them only against the weak. The world has to start discussing today those mechanisms that can actually enable the poor to assert rules against the rich. Even if they don't work in our part of the world, at least we have a semblance of them. But we don't have that globally. That is really where the debate on globalisation must move now, putting good politics into it and finding ways in which we can hold the rich accountable.

Rehman Sobhan

I want to touch upon the dimension of globalisation which has indirectly entered the discussion now. Globalisation has, in fact, been working quite well and a lot of countries have become export-competitive and have benefitted from this. Bangladesh has now raised its exports from half a billion dollars to 20 billion dollars, mostly through exports of garments. Export competitiveness derives largely from low cost of labour. This has given us a significant market niche. Now the relevant question is how to pass on the benefits of globalisation to the people who have made us export competitive, which are, in fact, the workers. The people who have derived the benefit are 2,000 garment owners who have become enormously rich and now have apartments in London and New York and educate their children in the US and Britain and go for health care to Singapore and also to India. But the workers continue to get an average wage of 30 dollars a month. They walk two hours to work and back. They are mostly village women. As a consequence of this relationship, no single day now goes by in Dhaka where there is not some rioting going on in the streets, or where the workers of one or the other factory are not protesting the unfair way in which they are actually being treated. This is becoming increasingly violent.

How does a social democratic agenda take cognizance of this peculiar outcome of the globalisation process? We have to really apply our minds to this. Why do we not move towards minimum wage legislation? A huge battle has been going on over raising the minimum wage from 25 to 30 dollars or beyond 30 dollars. They say that if we do that then the investors and the markets will move away and our buyers will move from Bangladesh to Southern Africa or Cambodia. So this is presented as an unchallengeable argument. Our suggestion would be that in the social democratic context, one way to address this problem is to bridge the capital-labour conflict by giving workers the opportunity to become partners in the equity of their company and share in the value addition of their labour and the profits being generated by it. This should be recognised not only as an instrument of social democratic policy in our respective countries but also receive global recognition. For instance, the European Union has very generously given Bangladesh duty-free access because we are an LDC. You have done it on the ostensible grounds that we are a very poor country and therefore, somehow or the other, poverty will be alleviated. Well, part of this would be to give us this privilege with the conditionality that you demonstrate that the companies bringing in their products into the European Union, duty-free, can demonstrate that 25 per cent of their equity is owned by their workers. This would be a direct transmission of the benefits which you give any particular company to the people most in need of it and this would then have a significant poverty alleviating effect. I put this before you as an important proposition.

I noticed that in India there has recently been legislation, if it has not been actually passed, wherein you are now going in for mineral development, and are going to give a 25 per cent share to the local people over there. Is this now legislated? Not yet. Hopefully we will get to see it. Is this being resisted? Not yet. We found this a very inspirational piece of legislation as similar discussions were going on in Bangladesh where we were going for a big coal mining development with a multinational and there was huge resistance from the people who were going to be affected. Now, at the national level and perhaps even at the global level, where people are going to face an environmental crisis or displacement, their collective interest should be recognised by making them stakeholders in the value addition which would come from the investment by these particular mineral investment companies. So, this again would be a proposition of universalised relevance.

Coming to the last point about Scandinavian or Nordic interventions, the relevant and most interesting parts of the Nordic or one may even say, the European model, was the democratisation of education, where the sons and daughters of coal miners and factory workers and bus drivers would in fact get the same level of education being offered to the sons of school professors or big businessmen. This was the singular achievement of postwar social democracy in Europe. It is a relevant lesson that unless we can democratise education and not just universalise it by having 100 per cent enrolment in crumbling primary schools all over the country, we are going to miss the lesson of the human development intervention. Human development has played a big role. The Millennium Development Goals (MDGs) were important, but somehow they have been passed on and we are missing the central lesson that educational opportunities have to be given at a uniform level. Today, the greatest dividing line is being created by disparities in educational opportunity. To expect the sons and daughters of people coming out of village primary schools to compete with those from Doon School or St. Xavier's is an unacceptable notion and we are never really going to bring social justice to the market place unless we democratise educational opportunity. This should be the central challenge that we should recognise.

Rohan Samarajiva

I pose a question to the panel. We started this as a session in which the experience of social democracy in other countries can be compared to what we may be thinking about. I think we have ended up with a much richer agenda. Can we actually think in terms of social democracy for the world as a whole? That is quite a different question. Pascal Lamy made a statement to that effect, though my question is very simple. Can globalisation, the uncertainties of climate change and all of these make social democracy stronger or weaker in each national country? I think they are two separate questions.

Jonathan Cohn

I have to say that many ideas of global social democracy sound wonderful but are completely far-fetched and outside the context of American power politics right now. Something I gave a lot of thought to is a question to answer a question, which is about the role of labour unions in social democracy. I have theories on why we don't have more general social democracy in America. The weak labour movement was a part of that but I think in the context of globalisation, if we can imagine a solution to this problem where the workers of every country, including advanced countries like the US can benefit from globalisation, organising more workers is a big part of that. I am still curious about how to do that since we have all these fundamental dilemmas. Every country gets to the point where they advance with lower costs of labour. I don't know how we will solve that problem.

Joakim Palme

To start with this question about worldwide social democracy. Maybe we need to have some global democracy to achieve that. I don't think that we should stop thinking about it. It's taken about a 100 years to establish democracy on a national level. It may take another 100 years to establish global democracy, but I think we really have to consider how we could get there.

Can we learn from the Nordic model? Why not? We cannot import a fixed model but why shouldn't we learn from programmes that actually work? We need to unpack the welfare states in terms of different components and combination of programmes. I also believe that we should think not only in poverty terms but also in developmental terms. The critical thing is to plan for the coming generation. We had a discussion earlier on what was happening 10 years ago. We should move our time horizon forward and try to fix the agenda in terms of the kinds of issues that we will have to deal with in 20 years. In that perspective, education is the key factor to work with and is an area where social democracy could play the important role of promoting good public policy.

Wang Hui

Pranab is right that since the late 1980s there was a kind of so-called crony capitalism we talk about. The students' movements raised the slogan and our political party sprung up because of that. But generally speaking, now it is not only in economic affairs but also in political and cultural affairs that the elites of the second or the third generation were in opposition but compared to Russia or some other countries, the oligarchy structure was not that bad. Basically, the staid old enterprises were reformed and fully privatised. In that process, a lot of corruption took place and people got rich at a local level. But at a bigger national level, they still remained the old state companies. Some of them became leaders, not necessarily as a private oligarchy. That way, this also relates to the issue of democratisation. Ibu Indrawati mentioned the danger of this in Indonesia's case because the oligarchy can use that process to legitimise its illegal possession of property. That's why people complain. Also, if you compare popular opinion in say, China and Russia, it was found that in China, ordinary people had extremely strong views against corruption. But in Russia, they broadly accepted that their situation now is more 'legitimised' in this way. So, these social movements in China sometimes resort to the oldest slogans to play with the role of balancing in terms of an equal process. Thus, the checking process became the confining power. The second issue is about the party. Not only in the party system but also in the People's Congress and consulting committees, the percentage from the working class has become much lower than before. There is now a lot of criticism about this, which has changed a little bit. But generally speaking, this is still the case. Not only that, I think that when we talk about social democracy and also the contradictions and crisis, there has been some similar phenomena between China and other countries in relation to party politics. There has been what I call the 'de-politicisation of the political party'. Generally speaking, even multiparty and two-party systems are centralised. They try to address the general population for getting the votes right. This cost them relevance and political value, which is a problem for political democracy. In the Chinese case, this was a long process, which I call the stratification of the political party. This means that the political party integrated into the framework of the state itself, and played the role of the state rather than a political party. That's the kind of transition from the party state to the state party. That should have made it simple to end the corruption campaign but without the party's discipline, it became very difficult. So, on the one hand, one argues for the rule of law, the legal system, and its independence, but on the other hand, the system was not effective as it depends on the party handing over cases to the legal system. These kind of things happen there, which means that the political party has been playing a role of the state organ in that sense. That kind of de-politicisation of the political party was not really good for the guarantee of social equality because when the party integrated into the state and its different parts, it also penetrated into the socioeconomic network. How can you be convinced that the political party has neutrality, as these are no longer political values?

This is a new phenomenon for the Chinese situation and its political system. How to reform the process of political reform itself, especially when we say that we need to take consideration of these new phenomena, like marketisation or globalisation? It is not possible that such things can happen on the basis of the old agenda of political reform. Together, we need to think about the new agenda for political reform.

Pascal Lamy

I am not at all suggesting transferring a European social democratic agenda to the global level. On the contrary, what I am seeking is something which is global, which is much more inspired by where social democracy has worked in recent times, which is elsewhere than in Europe.

I disagree with Nitin's point that we should not overbank on NGOs. I'm not talking specifically about the American solution, but when we look at the results that worked and what organised movements have produced at the global level for the last 15 years, NGOs have done better than trade unions and trade unions in turn have done better than political parties. I know that you believe in your project, but I am giving you the answer of a practitioner. If you look at environment, global health issues, climate change, ocean depletion and development issues, NGOs have had a much better agenda and applied more pressure than political parties. It is not because they have succeeded in transforming themselves into multinationals. Certainly, all important influential NGOs today are organised on the model of corporate multinationals. They have globalised themselves. But the way they really operate efficiently remains at the domestic level. Where is OXFAM most influential? Not in the WTO; the place where OXFAM is most influential is in the UK. The evidence of the influence of OXFAM is that today a British Conservative, fiscally tight government says it is not going to touch development assistance. Why is it so? That is the political reality. It is not the Labour Party, it is not the Conservative Party and it is not the liberal state. There may be more like OXFAM to come if we really agree, and that is the way to go.

In the observation about global democracy, I know well that it is a desirable thing, but also know that it may not happen during my life, probably not in my children's or grandchildren's lifetimes. One simple reason is that the nation-state remains the basic molecule of the international system and legitimisation happens within the nation-state. We can fiddle a bit with this, because we have some beliefs and can try and open a bit of this space, but that won't create a global democracy in today's international system based on the Westphalian principle of national sovereignty. The only global democracy is the democracy of 190 nations, which is not that great a democracy when we look at the shape it is in, which is why we have to go back to the national level, back to where legitimacy is expiated. It remains an inter-national, inter-governmental system. The right and priority focus for political action must remain with governments. This has nothing against doing anything at global levels in terms of engaging, but if it is a question of priority, priority has to remain local.

On protectionism, we could have a long discussion. In my view, a perfect example of how attractive an idea can be in the populist way, and how totally inefficient and destructive it is in reality, is in today's world. A very good example of something that can seem right and that is just shooting your own foot. In today's conditions, bringing more of these to the size of equations is something which public discourses need to do. The idea of social conditionality for trade preferences for developing countries has until now, and I suspect for some time, been categorically opposed by developing countries.

A short point on the observation by Jonathan Cohn on the labour movement. You are right; in the US the labour movement has weakened, but I think that's not the main problem. The main problem is that the labour movement in the US has not been identified as important. Whereas in some European countries, notably Germany, they identified their strategic problem 15 years ago in order to remain competitive in the world economy. Therefore, they invested a lot in services. There is a trade union in Germany only for the services sector which has become pretty powerful. The AFLCIO people have never really succeeded in recruiting elsewhere than truckers, which is a big service industry plus steel machinery and the car industry. Of course, this economy has in turn been eroded by international division of labour, which is why they exhibit a rational behaviour, which is to be protectionist. That's perfectly rational; if I am the boss of the AFLCIO I cannot knock the protectionists because I do not recruit in Silicon Valley. So, there are intrinsic contradictions there.

Finally, I haven't heard the contrary during the discussion. I say that trying to acquire such a platform is worth a try. Not that we should harmonise the whole vision, the whole tool box, I 100 per cent agree that there will be a big subsidarity, a big level of local and national difference. But nevertheless, I think we have to try something that is more holistic, architectural, which is not piecemeal, with a detailed debate about the minimum wage, whether it is the right to food, to housing or urban policy. We need something more holistic which then serves as a right. We need what Sunita Narain suggested; a set of principles, which will take time to put together, because we come from different cultures and political horizons. But what I heard in the discussion is more encouraging, though I would have expected a bit of provocation.

Has globalisation been good or bad for social democracy? The reality is that globalisation has been bad for social democracy in rich countries and it has been good for social democracy in poor countries. When I look at the proportion, I think the sense and the direction is pretty clear.

Joseph E. Stiglitz

Let me present a couple of comments on the discussion. Nemat's observation was that during the crisis, there was a very strong response in the G20 in the form of providing funds to developing countries, probably out of self-interest but also probably, I think, out of a movement of global social solidarity. There is an interesting proposal that the World Bank ought to set aside funds if countries create adequate social safety nets, a kind of social protection framework that would be able to be used, should there be an economic, global or regional, downturn. There ought to be money that would be automatically put in for contingency funding. I think that is an interesting idea that ought to be discussed.

The second comment is that the currency conflict illustrates very strongly that in the current climate, we are going to see two years after we have answered the crisis that various countries are pursuing their own national interests. They are each asking the question very clearly—what is the policy of maximising my jobs, regardless of the consequences for other countries? This is not a surprise, but there is no sense of global solidarity as they approach this question.

This, I think, is an example of why, although we won't get to a global democracy, there is a need for more global governance. This would entail a high degree of global solidarity, not at the local levels but more solidarity than we have today. Part of the reason for the problem existing today is that much of international negotiations in the past have occurred in what I call the smooth tax structure, where in trade we have trade ministers and in each of the other areas, we have the finance ministers of the central banks. In some cases, I can strongly say from the perspective of the US that the US trade ministry has probably been among the two or three areas most dominated by special interests. I think it wins the contest of among the most, I won't say corrupt, but anybody looking at us might describe it that way. Obviously, if there are various kinds of ministries negotiating, we are not going to get an outcome that reflects the general interest of the US, let alone the global general interest. That is why, in a way, the recent G20 is an important step which elevates it from the level of ministries to the level of Presidents, Prime Ministers where at least in principle, we have somebody who is looking at this from a more holistic perspective. But the G20 faces two problems. There are 172 countries that are not in the G20. Secondly, it doesn't have what one might call legitimacy. But I hope that these reforms that a number of people in the G20 have talked about, trying to bring it in one way or the other within the UN framework and to expand it, to gain the legitimacy and at the same time remain a small group of 20 countries, could somehow evolve into a more representative, constituency basis than some other way of combining smallness with legitimacy and representativeness.

Section III

The Political Economy of Social Democracy

The prerequisite for any social democratic project is economic growth and investment. Are there distinctive social democratic growth strategies, and ways of balancing efficiency and equity? How can incentives to growth and entrepreneurship be combined with provision of social protections? What are the most effective delivery mechanisms for basic education and health, work safety, pensions entitlements? What role can foundations, partnerships with private capital and civil society, play in furthering social purposes and public goods? How should tax regimes be structured to encourage this? What do environmental constraints on growth mean for social democratic ambitions? What are the specific challenges facing efforts to build social democracy in a largely agrarian society, and how can it address the uneven development of countryside and city?

The Section is broken into two parts, as follows:

Section III(a)

Section III(b)

Section III (a)

BACKGROUND PAPERS

- Vijay Kelkar
- Ajay Shah
- Kaushik Basu
- Nitin Desai

21

VIJAY KELKAR and AJAY SHAH*

Indian Social Democracy

The Resource Perspective

Executive summary

This paper examines the strategy for obtaining adequate resources for the Indian state, where the goals of the state comprise the provision of public goods (which, by definition, benefit everyone) and income transfers to those below the poverty line.

Living beyond our means is infeasible in the long run. A government has to fundamentally spend only tax revenues. The failure to live within our means yields the risk of crisis, it reduces the headroom available for policy makers to respond to catastrophic events, and it reduces the average GDP growth rate. The key parameter that requires focus is the ratio of government debt to the output of one year (i.e., GDP). This is analogous to the ratio of the indebtedness of a person divided by annual income. The two key rules which India must attain are: (a) this ratio must not cross 60 per cent and (b) in most years, this ratio must decline. It must be emphasised that this discussion of the debt/GDP ratio pertains to the aggregate consolidated debt of centre, states and local governments, and not just the debt of the central government.

Unlike some Asian countries who have a long history of fiscal prudence, India has a long history of fiscal stress. Hence, these concerns have to be taken seriously. At present, the debt/GDP ratio is well above 60 per cent and an immediate reduction of over 20 percentage points is required. Happily, the international experience

* We are grateful to Joseph Stiglitz, Arbind Modi and Josh Felman for useful conversations and suggestions.

shows that it is not difficult for a country to get sharp reductions in the debt/GDP ratio over a few years. The fiscal consolidation plan presented in the report of the 13th Finance Commission envisages a reduction of the debt/GDP ratio (of the centre alone) from 80.7 per cent to 68 per cent over five years.

Once spending by borrowing is ruled out, resourcing the state is primarily about tax revenues. The most powerful determinant of tax revenues in India, in coming decades, is going to to be sheer GDP. The international evidence shows that a country of India's level of per capita GDP finds it very hard to achieve a tax/GDP ratio of above 20 per cent. The experience of other countries including emerging markets suggests that it is only when per capita GDP crosses $9,206 that the tax/GDP ratio is able to get beyond 20 per cent. Hence, for the forseeable future, the scenario that we have to envisage is one where the tax/GDP ratio works out to 20 per cent. It must be emphasised that this prospect, of a tax/GDP ratio of 20 per cent, pertains to the aggregate total tax revenues of the Indian state, summing across centre, states and municipalities.

While keeping this goal of a tax/GDP ratio in mind, there are seven immediate areas where tax policy can yield immediate increases in GDP. These are worth undertaking because even though the tax/GDP ratio will not go beyond 20 per cent or so, the overall tax revenues will go up owing to larger GDP.

1. When a series of distortionary taxes is replaced by the Goods and Services Tax (GST), Indian GDP will go up significantly, reaping the benefits of a dynamic 'common market'. The GST will help spur labour-intensive manufacturing, including export-oriented manufacturing, in poor regions of India.
2. The second is a gradual evolution of the personal income tax to a point where a full one-third of the households of India pay income tax, albeit at a low rate. This will encourage a better engagement of the citizenry in public goods: A citizen that pays income tax is likely to be more demanding about the performance of government agencies. In addition, a broad tax base enables reduced rates, which strengthens GDP growth by reducing tax-induced distortions and reducing the size of the black economy.

3. We are now ready for the end-game of customs reforms, which involves eliminating customs duties on manufacturing.
4. New thinking needs to be brought into the question of taxation of capital. Conceptually, Indian GDP growth critically requires immense 'capital deepening' where trillions of rupees need to be devoted into building up the capital stock of the economy, which is the path to high output and high wages. The key idea proposed here is a scaling up of the exempt-exempt-tax (EET) system of taxation to cover a much broader array of investments by individuals, through which individuals will be incentivised to save and invest (thus helping the growth of the country), but will be taxed when they liquidate their investments for the purpose of consumption.
5. Fundamental rethinking of the taxation of corporations is called for. Corporations, associations, clubs, partnerships, etc., are all mere mechanisms through which individuals obtain income. As long as the comprehensive income of individuals is taxed, once, the purpose of tax policy is met, and this implies elimination of the income tax on corporations. It is more efficient for India if we tax the individuals who own corporations, instead of getting into the complications of taxing corporations while trying to have a dividend distribution tax in order to counter-balance the double-taxation.
6. As with all maturing middle-income countries, India needs to graduate to the 'residence-based taxation' approach for dealing with cross-border capital flows. At present, this is the *de facto* reality given the Mauritius route. Efficiency gains are available by making it the *de jure* route for capital coming in from all major countries, e.g. the members of OECD.
7. There is a case for an estate duty, through which the intensification of wealth concentration across generations can be counteracted. At the same time, the size of this estate duty needs to be modest, so as to avoid distorting the incentives for hard work in each generation.

All these seven areas for reform will foster higher GDP, and interacting with relatively small changes in the tax/GDP ratio, will yield bigger resources for the exchequer. Alongside this, a fresh approach to the portfolio of assets of the state is required. It is far better for the government to own 2000 km. of highways or 'greener' environmental capital, instead of owning ₹ 10,000 crore of shares of Air India.

There are two areas where ownership of companies or shares by the government is clearly inappropriate. The first is the goods and services of ordinary competitive markets (e.g. hotels or steel). These things are best done by competing private firms. The second is in regulated industries. The ownership by government of companies in a regulated industry—e.g. telecom—reduces the confidence of the private sector in the extent to which policy and regulation will be unbiased, and thus deters investment into these areas.

A fresh effort on rethinking the portfolio of government, shifting away from public ownership either in competitive markets or in regulated industries, will generate massive resources for the exchequer, and also spur GDP growth. Since the proceeds from the sale of assets will not be a continuous flow of resources coming into the state for the long term, spending this money on consumption expenditure of the government (e.g., for paying salaries of policemen or for running welfare programmes) is not appropriate. The best use of these resources would be to unburden the government of debt, thus bringing down the flow of annual interest payments which presently stands at 3.6 per cent of GDP for the centre alone.

We turn to the challenge of envisioning a European-style social democracy in India. Evidence is offered showing low levels of 'trust capital' in India. As is well known to political scientists, welfare states are unlikely to be successful or flourish in countries with high heterogeneity and low levels of trust capital. Hence, we argue that India is not fertile ground for the creation of a European-style welfare state, for the coming 10 to 20 years.

A more fruitful line of enquiry concerns a rethinking of government programmes in an incentive-compatible way. Three key ideas need to be emphasised. The first is the 'Aadhar' programme, which can ideally culminate with every household under the poverty line having a number, a bank account, and being known in a master table of the poor households of India held with the Ministry of Finance. Once this is in place, the comprehensive elimination of poverty in India is feasible through the direct transfer of ₹ 2,292 per month into each household directly from North Block into the bank account of this list of the households below the poverty line. The cost of such a programme would be 2 per cent of GDP, which is well within the goal of spending no more than 20 per cent of GDP.

The second theme that deserves emphasis is decentralisation. Local governments are of particular importance in cities. We need to pursue the 'unfinished revolution' launched by Rajiv Gandhi through the 73rd and 74th Constitutional Amendments by achieving genuine local government, atleast in cities. The GST reform can be accompanied by a mechanism through which a part of the GST collections of a city are paid as tax revenues of that very city, thus closing the loop from public goods to higher GDP to greater resources within each city of India. The third theme that deserves emphasis is the decoupling of public expenditure from public provision. In many areas, it is more efficient for government to contract-out the actual production of public goods, while continuing to fund their creation. While this can work well in some areas (such as education or health) it is not useful for core public goods which are defence, police and judiciary.

European-style social democracy is seen as a safety net where individuals are protected from an array of risks. Social programmes which interact with individuals are transaction-intensive and hard to implement, particularly in the contemporary Indian governance environment. However, a substantial part of the problem that these programmes seek to address can be addressed by macroeconomic policy frameworks which reduce the fluctuations of the market economy. As an example, in the downturn of 2008, many workers in India were thrown out of job. While a system of unemployment insurance is one way to address their concerns, it is also important to undertake the fiscal, financial and monetary institution building through which business cycle stabilisation is achieved. This is a key area where the new issues that India faces, as a middle income economy, necessitate substantial reforms when compared with the institutional apparatus presently in place.

Two scenarios for the next few decades are presented in the paper. In the first scenario, India pushes ahead to a tax/GDP ratio of 24 per cent, with an early expansion of welfare programmes, weak institutional reforms in the areas of fiscal, financial and monetary policy, and a low pace of integration into the world economy. This scenario is projected to yield a trend GDP growth of 6 per cent. In the alternative scenario, India accepts a tax/GDP ratio of 20 per cent, and holds back on expenditure programmes which will go beyond this level of resources. This is a scenario which goes along with strong reforms of fiscal, financial and monetary policy, and a high pace of integration into the world economy. This scenario is projected to yield a trend GDP growth of 8 per cent, thus capturing the 'once in a lifetime' demographic opportunity that is available to India today.

Even though the tax/GDP ratio in the second scenario is lower by 4 percentage points, over the next 10 or 20 years, the tax revenues of the state prove to be significantly higher. In addition, of course, citizens would prefer the latter scenario given that personal incomes would be much higher over the next 10 or 20 years by going down that route.

In summary, this paper emphasises the primary tool through which the state can obtain resources is higher GDP growth. A tax/GDP ratio of 20 per cent, with expenditure that is just slightly above 20 per cent, is the reasonable scenario which can be envisaged for the coming 30 years. Mobilising greater resources for the state is thus synonymous with undertaking reforms which yield higher GDP growth. Alongside this, a good part of the concerns which lead to a desire for European-style social democracy can be addressed by undertaking fiscal, financial and monetary policy reforms through which business cycle fluctuations are diminished and governance vastly improved. In addition, fresh thinking about mechanisms of expenditure can yield greater bang for the buck thus freeing up resources while improving social justice and welfare outcomes.

***

The role of the state in the new India

A large fraction of the Indian people lead a difficult life. A better functioning State is of critical importance in improving the lives of the people, both through its impact on everyday life through public goods, and through its positive impact on GDP growth and growth in employment.

In terms of the central tasks of government, there is a broad consensus about eight elements:

1. Effective legal protection and the justice system,
2. Defence and internal security,
3. Elementary education,
4. Public goods that enable better health outcomes,
5. Policy frameworks which reduce transactions costs,
6. Protection of the environment,
7. Macroeconomic risk reduction, and
8. Income transfers to people below the poverty line.

One of the key tasks that is faced in Indian economic reform is that of fostering a State apparatus which can deliver these eight functions efficiently, with requisite resources being obtained in a non-distortionary manner.

Many in India aspire to additionally embark on two more functions: providing risk insurance to the population at large and undertaking population-wide redistribution. It is argued that some advanced countries, such as Sweden, perform these 'social democracy' or 'welfare state' functions relatively effectively, and that Indian voters desire such an expansive State. In countries like Sweden, the tax revenues of the government exceed half of GDP. This agenda involves much more ambitious social engineering, where massive tax revenues would have to be obtained, and politically directed towards certain households through suitable government programmes. In this paper, a resource perspective is brought to bear upon these two distinct sets of objectives.

Living within our means

In recent months, television screens worldwide have highlighted the contrast between Greece and Sweden. Both countries aspired towards constructing a similar social democracy. While Sweden has been able to achieve stability, Greece was living beyond its means. Political compulsions can often lead to the enactment of ambitious social programmes. However, as economists emphasise, there is no free lunch, and when there is a gap between the resources commanded by the state and the expenditure profile which has been adopted, this can have devastating consequences.

The divergence between resources and expenditure-aspirations are met by borrowing from citizens or from foreigners through financial markets, resulting into growing indebtedness of the state. Financial markets often accept such slow increases in sovereign indebtedness upto a point. But at some point, financial markets can abruptly get extremely uncomfortable about solvency of the government. Disruptive mistrust of solvency on the part of the financial markets often, unfortunately, coincides with political or economic crises, thus exacerbating the difficulties.

This 'nonlinear' behaviour of financial markets suggests that the present relatively calm conditions should not induce complacency in Indian policy thinking. It is important to be clearly in safe territory, amidst the ranks of the fiscally healthy countries of the world, so as to rule out the scenario of a sudden financial crisis. In addition, the extent to which the country is far removed from fiscal distress represents the headroom that is available for fiscal expansion in the catastrophic situations that seem to arise in the global economy once or twice a century.

Identifying the danger zone

The most important parameter which describes fiscal distress is the ratio of government debt to GDP. Fiscal prudence involves ensuring that (a) this ratio is not increasing and (b) this ratio stays at reasonable levels.

It is useful to have a sense of what is the danger zone for the debt/GDP ratio. While some OECD countries (e.g. Japan) have very high debt/GDP ratios, the practical reality of being a developing country is that debt tolerance is lower. Government debt was below 60 per cent of GDP in most episodes of default by governments in emerging economies in recent years (Reinhart *et al.*, 2003).

India has some advantages on the outlook for debt owing to the hope of attaining and sustaining high GDP growth. Yet, until India becomes a high-income country, it is prudent to assume that financial markets will be wary about fiscal, financial and monetary policy institutions in India, and will become uncomfortable about owning Indian government bonds at high levels of the debt/GDP ratio. The Indian rules about the debt/GDP ratio should hence be calibrated based on emerging market experiences with default, and not the experiences of countries like Japan which have sustained very high levels of the debt/GDP ratio in recent years.

Impact of reducing the debt/GDP ratio upon growth

While large values for the debt/GDP ratio go along with enhanced crisis vulnerability, 'reductions' in the debt/GDP ratio directly impinge upon growth. A recent paper (Kumar and Woo, 2010) measures the direct contribution of a reduction in the debt/GDP ratio upon growth, after controlling for a diverse range of extraneous factors. They find that on average, a 10 percentage points of GDP reduction in the debt/GDP ratio, by itself, adds 0.2 percentage points per year to GDP growth. The mechanism through which this works is increased investment and increased productivity growth.

From an Indian perspective, this suggests that when the debt/GDP ratio is brought down from the region of 90 per cent of GDP to the desirable target of 60 per cent of GDP, this (by itself) would yield a rough acceleration in growth of 0.6 per cent. In addition, the risk of a fiscal or financial crisis would be reduced, which is a prerequisite for a sustainable social democracy. Fiscal prudence is thus good for growth in addition to being good for stability (Feldstein, 2004).

Debt capacity as a reserve for extreme conditions

When a country has healthy values for debt and deficits under ordinary times, this creates the space through which the rare use of discretionary fiscal policy can help the economy in rare and extreme events. The deeper consequence of this fiscal space is that the private sector feels more confident in the outlook for the country, knowing that the state has the capability to marshall remarkable responses when extreme situations arise once or twice a century. This confidence induces bigger investments in financial and human capital and into long-term projects.

As an example, Table 21.1 looks at the experience with the consolidated deficit of the UK. From 1998 till 2007, the average value for the deficit was 1.43 per cent of GDP. From 1999 till 2001, the fiscal balance was in surplus. In 2007, the deficit was at 2.6 per cent of GDP.

Table 21.1

Deficits in the UK

Year	*Consolidated Deficit*
1998	0.1
1999	-0.9
2000	-1.3
2001	-0.6
2002	1.9
2003	3.3
2004	3.3
2005	3.3
2006	2.6
2007	2.6
2008	5.4
2009	9.8
2010	10.9

In 2008, when the UK was hit by a once-in-a-century financial crisis, this healthy starting position gave the government the ability to undertake emergency actions, which more than doubled the deficit to 5.4 per cent of GDP in 2008, which went further to 9.8 per cent of GDP in 2009 and is estimated to be 10.9 per cent of GDP in 2010. If the UK had not engaged in fiscal prudence from 1998 till 2007, with an average deficit of 1.43 per cent of GDP in this period, it would not have been possible to enlarge the deficit in this fashion in response to the once-in-a-century crisis.

A longer historical perspective on the UK, going back to the late 18th century, shows a long-standing pattern where large deficits were run and debt was enlarged to deal with catastrophic events like wars. In normal times, for decades on end, fiscal surpluses were obtained and used to pay off debt, thus rebuilding the position for a next catastrophic event which might necessitate borrowing. Such a framework gives fiscal policy the opportunity to respond in extraordinary ways to the extraordinary events which take place once every few decades.

This suggests that sound fiscal institutions should yield an equilibrium where, in the typical year, the debt/GDP ratio goes down. This would create the space for government to enlarge debt substantially once or twice a century through discretionary fiscal policy, when catastrophic events come about.

At the same time, when these rare catastrophic events materialise, and governments desire a substantial enlargement of the debt/GDP ratio, the bond market is concerned about the possibility of insufficient repayment through inflation. The willingness of the bond market to fund public debt in these episodes is critically related to the extent to which such a scenario is ruled out. An inflation targeting central bank, which reassures the bond market that unexpected inflation will not arise, is an important component of the institutional architecture that makes discretionary fiscal expansion possible without driving up interest rates.[1]

Feasibility of reduction of the debt/GDP ratio

If India starts out with a daunting value for the debt/GDP ratio, how difficult is it to bring this down to the sub-60 zone of comfort?

1. See *http://tinyurl. com/inflationfears* on the web.

There is a somewhat unexpected relationship between deficits and debt. When deficits are held down to modest levels, and when GDP grows, the debt/GDP ratio comes down quite dramatically.

As an example, the UK debt/GDP ratio dropped dramatically from 65 per cent to 40 per cent from 1996-97 to 2001-02. In other words, in a five year period with only modest surpluses, the debt/GDP ratio declined by 15 percentage points.[2] In similar fashion, the Canadian strategy of 'budget balance or better' resulted in a decline of the debt/GDP ratio from 70 per cent in 1996 to 40 per cent in 2004. These examples show the feasibility of obtaining large reductions of the debt/GDP ratio in relatively short periods of time, through a combination of the prudent policy of running surpluses in normal times, alongside GDP growth which increases the denominator.

Reductions of the debt/GDP ratio critically rely on the primary surplus (the budgetary surplus calculated after excluding interest payments) and on the GDP growth rate. When GDP growth is high, and when there are primary surpluses, rapid reductions in the debt/GDP ratio are feasible (Mundle *et al.*, 2010). The former has been repeatedly achieved in India, but the latter has not.

Table 21.2 shows some examples of developing countries which obtained strong gains in the debt/GDP ratio in recent years. The average starting point of these examples—a debt/GDP ratio of 80.7 per cent—is coincidentally similar to India's present starting point. Over an average five-year period, in these examples, the debt/GDP ratio was reduced by an impressive 26.1 percentage points. Of this, 10.6 percentage points came from the primary balance ('PB'), 8.1 percentage points came from the gap between GDP growth and the nominal interest rate, and 3 percentage points came from currency appreciation. This gives us a rough sense of the contours of the composition and scale of a strong fiscal correction, judged by the standards of developing countries.

---

2. Source: *Debt and Reserves Management Report, 2008-09* of the UK Debt Management Office.

Table 21.2

Emerging Markets which Achieved Strong Reductions in the Debt/GDP Ratio

Episode	Initial Debt	Reduction	Contribution		
			PB	r − g	Curr. apprec
Poland ('93-'98)	84.3	47.7	3.3	22.6	9.6
Chile ('90-'98)	45.9	33.0	30.0	11.5	3.9
Ecuador ('88-'90)	113.5	32.1	4.1	11.4	-11.8
Pakistan ('01-'07)	84.8	29.7	6.4	17.1	5.1
Egypt ('03-'07)	114.9	27.7	-11.0	29.9	1.9
Jamaica ('02-'07)	122.0	27.4	50.8	-30.3	3.8
Brazil ('02-'05)	85.0	20.8	12.4	1.7	4.6
Colombia ('02-'07)	49.8	16.4	14.4	1.0	4.6
Malaysia ('03-'07)	44.4	14.5	-4.3	8.3	2.4
Tunisia ('01-'07)	62.7	11.8	-0.7	8.1	6.4
Average	80.7	26.1	10.6	8.1	3.0

Source: Table 6.3 from "Fiscal implications of the global economic and financial crisis", *IMF Staff Position Note*, 9 June 2009, SPN 09/13.

A modest literature has now sprung up on understanding the enabling conditions (on an international scale) for large debt reductions, of the kind that are now needed in India. A recent contribution to this field is Nickel *et al.*, 2010). They find that over 1985-2009, many events of total debt reduction averaging 37 percentage points of GDP can be identified, across the world. This encourages us about the feasibility of the quest for large debt reduction in India. Under what conditions do such large debt reductions materialise? They identify two key factors. The first is an environment of high GDP growth. India satisfies this requirement. The second requirement, in their words, is:

> decisive and lasting (rather than timid and short-lived) fiscal consolidation efforts focused on reducing government expenditure, in particular, cuts in social benefits and public wages.

This suggests the area of focus for policy today.

Summary

India has a long history of fiscal indiscipline (Buiter and Patel, 1992). Hence, the fiscal problem requires particular focus. Any plans for expenditure by the state must stay within the budget constraints of taxation. This, in turn, translates into one tangible goal and one intermediate test.

The tangible goal is that the government's debt (fully measured) must not be increasing through time and must not cross 60 per cent of GDP.

Table 21.3

Central Government's Fiscal Stance

	(Per cent to GDP)						
	2005	*2006*	*2007*	*2008*	*2009*	*2010*	*2011*
Receipts	15.6	14.2	13.5	15.0	15.1	16.5	15.9
Expenditure (ex. interest)	11.5	10.1	10.1	11.0	12.4	12.9	12.3
Interest payment	3.9	3.6	3.5	3.5	3.5	3.5	3.6
Expenditure	15.4	13.7	13.6	14.5	15.9	16.4	15.9
Primary surplus	0.0	-0.4	0.2	0.9	-2.6	-3.1	-1.9
Stock of debt	61.6	61.0	59.3	57.3	56.7	56.4	56.5

The intermediate test is that every year, India must run primary surpluses. That is, there must be a fiscal surplus once interest payments are excluded. In good years, there should be strong fiscal surpluses, and in bad years, the fiscal surplus can dwindle away to zero. Once this intermediate test is satisfied, under ordinary circumstances, the Indian debt/GDP ratio would decline from year to year. This would create the space for enlargement of the debt/GDP ratio when faced with exceptional situations. However, Table 21.3 shows these key calculations for the central government in recent years, which shows that we are far from this required configuration. These years had India's greatest ever business cycle expansion.

The recently submitted Finance Commission report has outlined a feasible path of fiscal consolidation which will reverse this trend. The Finance Commission has shown that under the proposed Fiscal

Responsibility and Budget Management (FRBM) Act framework, the consolidated debt/GDP ratio would decline from 80.7 per cent to 68 per cent in next 5 years. Such a reduction in debt/GDP ratio should be considered as a minimum achievable target, since these calculations have assumed a rather modest growth path for the economy. With energetic implementation of tax and expenditure reforms, the growth performance of the economy can be even better and consequently the reduction in debt/GDP ratio can improve upon these projections.

How can resources be obtained?

Once a sound set of rules are in place governing borrowing, the expenses of a government are largely circumscribed by its revenues. Modifications in tax policy can yield greater tax revenues. In addition, there are also some important opportunities for obtaining resources from non-tax channels.

Architecture of the tax system

The simple channel—higher tax rates—involves two problems. The first is that of tax evasion. Higher tax rates inspire greater efforts at evasion. This matters directly insofar as an increase in the tax rate fails to yield the hoped-for tax revenues. More importantly, high tax rates induce citizens and firms to undertake far-reaching re-organisation of business and personal life so as to evade taxes. This sets the stage for deeper problems for law enforcement and for the political system. It is, hence, important to avoid high tax rates.

The second problem is that of economic distortions. High tax rates distort behaviour and the organisation of production. Economic analysis shows that the distortion associated with a tax rate goes up with the square of the rate. Higher tax rates produce much larger distortions. These distortions adversely affect the foundations of economic growth. Since economic growth is the only robust foundation of poverty alleviation, and given that the very resource base of the state is linked to GDP, these distortions are worth avoiding.

In thinking about tax policy, the ideal channel is one where reforms of tax policy are undertaken which yield higher tax revenues by increasing efficiency and thus GDP, and by building mechanisms for obtaining tax revenues which are very hard to evade. Our strategic thinking about the tax system should be grounded on three big ideas:

- *Fiscal rules:* As emphasised above, government must live within its means. Tax revenues must define expenditure aspirations.
- *The criticality of growth:* Once we have a commitment to live within our means, growth in expenditure can, then, only be achieved through growth in GDP. The tax system is an important part of the determinants of GDP growth. A well designed tax system is one which would be compatible with high incentives to save and invest, to organise production efficiently and achieve high growth. This is the path to achieving large values for the absolute size of resources of the exchequer.

Table 21.4

The Opportunity for Tax Revenues

Range of Per Capita GDP	*Tax Revenue (Per cent to GDP)*
Below $745	14.1
$745–$2975	16.7
$2976 – $9205	20.2
All developing	17.6
Above $9206	25.0

Source: Gordon and Li (2009).

- *A sense of the possible:* Using modern computer technology, tax revenues can and should improve. Systems such as the 'Tax Information Network' can have a major impact upon tax collections. But India cannot aspire to Western European style tax/GDP ratios. The cross-country evidence shows that until $10,000 of per capita GDP, there is only a modest rise in the tax/GDP ratio. Table 21.4, shows the striking empirical regularities on this subject. This suggests that till India achieves per capita income of $9,206, tax revenues of all levels of government put together, are unlikely to go much beyond 18-20 per cent of GDP. The task is, then, one of using these revenues effectively to get beyond $9,206 of per capita GDP, after which bigger opportunities would become visible.

Elements of Indian reform of tax policy

Within this strategic perspective, seven big ideas should now shape our thinking about tax policy.

1. *GST:* Ten (10) years ago, our fiscal experts felt that a well structured GST in India was infeasible. Gradually, this pessimism has eased. The automation of income tax showed that India can build IT systems; the State VAT effort showed that coordination between states could happen (Rao, 2005; Kelkar, 2004).

   Done right, the GST will be accompanied by removing almost all other existing taxes, leaving only three taxes: the income tax, the GST and the property tax. This will reduce compliance costs, economic distortions and harassment. Many of the taxes that would be removed are 'bad taxes' on turnover such as the stamp duty or octroi. This policy package has been termed the 'Model GST': single rate GST that covers all goods and services, which replaces all indirect taxes of the centre and states, with a a harmonised exemption list, and a common IT platform.

   The GST will enable the next phase of customs or import tariff reform. The sound architecture is one where imported goods are charged GST at entry, and exports are refunded the full GST. By this arrangement, local firms face fair competition in both the domestic market and the global market.

   The GST would unleash India as a common market. Even though India is a giant economy with a GDP of $1.25 trillion, Indian firms often operate within one state. Nationwide optimisation of production, storage and logistics is not taking place. The GST would make possible productivity gain, GDP growth and lower prices.

When market forces govern behaviour, firms gravitate towards low-cost production centres. A firm that sells in Gujarat might setup a factory in Madhya Pradesh. But this evolution—which tends to reduce inter-state disparities—is blocked by barriers to movement of goods. The GST would promote growth of lagging regions; in particular, poor states adjoining rich states will obtain sharply increased investment.

Global manufacturing now involves a large number of processes, spread across many firms in many countries. India has not been able to achieve Chinese-style employment-generation in manufacturing partly because of the burden of cascading taxes. GST will make India a competitor in Chinese-style manufacturing and employment, and set the stage for a great boom in employment-intensive and FDI-intensive manufacturing exports.

One of the major impacts of GST will be on the construction sector. Bringing real estate into the GST will have many beneficial effects. It will reduce housing costs, improve the working of the land market and greatly reduce the 'black economy' alongside yielding improvements in governance in the urban and semi-urban areas (through visibility of real estate prices and thus the establishment of a tax base for the property tax).

Many economists have argued that achieving the 'Model GST' is the most important single reform in Indian economic policy. A recent NCAER study has estimated the impact of the GST upon GDP. They find that the economic value of the 'Model GST' reform will exceed $0.5 trillion (Chadha, 2010).

There are four stepping stones to a functioning GST:

1. The first task concerns IT systems. The Tax Information Network (TIN) system is the right foundation for implementing the GST. TDS in an employer/employee context is exactly the same as GST in a supplier/purchaser context. Since TIN does TDS, it is ideally placed to also do the GST. TIN already reaches 700,000 establishments.

IT development work needs to be initiated at NSDL, for enlarging the TIN to do GST for the identical 700,000 establishments.

2. The first test case for the new IT system should be a merger between CENVAT, the service tax and VAT on imports (i.e., CVD) into a single tax called the 'central GST.'

3. The next task is that of arriving at a 'grand bargain' with states. The most fair formulation involves placing the entire GST collection into the hands of the Finance Commission for sharing with States. As all commentators have emphasised, a piecemeal allocation of certain services for taxation by States will derail the possibility of such an agreement. The fair deal that States should be offered is one where they tax all services, in return for cooperation in the administration of the GST, and removal of distortionary taxes.

4. The last task is that of coordinating tax administration with the states. Each firm should face only one tax man, and all firms should face the same IT system. One possibility is that of using the centre as tax collector for big firms and the state as tax collector for small firms.

2. *A third of India paying personal income tax:* The fundamental feature of the social contract between citizens and State is one where citizens pay tax and the state delivers public goods. On both fronts—the extent to which citizens are law-abiding and pay taxes, and the extent to which the state actually delivers public goods—there are severe collective action and principal/agent problems.

   A tax system where a large fraction of households pay income tax, albeit at a low rate, is one in which a large number of citizens would be more demanding about public service delivery. A tax payer is likely to demand public services as a matter of right, and is less likely to be a supplicant.

   The overall performance of the economy is enhanced when the tax rate is low and tax payments are dispersed across a large number of households. High tax rates generate heightened efforts on evasion and large economic distortions.

In the coming decade, a reasonable outcome would be one where 33 per cent of India's households pay income tax. CMIE household survey data (December 2009) shows that this is a cutoff of ₹ 45,000 of household income. A simplified flat tax of 10 per cent can be employed for household incomes from ₹ 50,000 till ₹ 100,000 per year. Higher tax rates, and a more complex tax code, can kick in from incomes of above ₹ 100,000 per year.

Through the years, as this cutoff of ₹ 50,000 is held intact, a bigger fraction of the population would fall into the income tax system through bracket creep, thus generating a larger participation by the people into a government that should work for the people.

3. *Import Tariff Regime:* India has benefitted enormously from the opening up to the international trade. The average import tariff or customs collection are now at single digit levels and it is now time to move forward towards elimination of import tariff or customs duties altogether, for manufacturing. Such a policy will also enable India to pursue a 'Zero for Zero' option at WTO trade negotiations and, thus, strengthen the multilateral trading system in which India, as a rising trading nation, has great stakes. The tariff policy governing agriculture sector will require a separate and more nuanced treatment. This zero import tariff will be accompanied by the full force of GST on imports. This will give a level playing field to our industry.

4. *Taxation of capital:* Taxation of capital income has long been seen as something that stands symmetrically alongside taxation of labour income. It is often felt that the capital gains tax should be similar to the income tax on wage income. However, both need to be seen in a unified perspective: one of fostering high GDP growth in the long run.

A central source of high GDP growth in the long run in a poor country like India is growth of capital stock. A poor country has to save and invest, to build up the capital stock. This 'deepening of capital' increases the productivity of labour and underpins the expansion of labour income.

Fairly modest changes in the annual savings rate translate into an elevated trajectory of per capita income over long periods of time. Conversely, if five years elapse at a lower investment rate (e.g., owing to a period where tax policy incentivised consumption), then this permanently depresses the future trajectory of capital and thus per capita GDP.

The question that should be posed of tax policy is: How can the tax code be structured to foster a high rate of savings and investment? Once seen in this perspective, taxation of capital income is shown in poor light. Many projects which have a positive net present value (NPV) in a world without taxation are tipped into the zone of negative NPV once some cashflows are paid to the government (at future dates) as taxation of capital income. Hence, the introduction of taxation of capital income into an undistorted world leads to fewer projects being undertaken. It reduces the pace of capital deepening in the economy, and reduces the long-term growth of the country.

As an example, a prominent recent review, which summarises the lessons obtained from 50 years of research in optimal taxation policy (Mankiw *et al.*, 2009) identifies Lesson 7: *Capital Income Ought to be Untaxed, at least in Expectation*. As they say:

> ...the logic for low capital taxes is powerful: the supply of capital is highly elastic, capital taxes yield large distortions to intertemporal consumption plans and discourage saving, and capital accumulation is central to the aggregate output of the economy.

Going beyond the individual perspective, the behaviour of corporations also changes when there is a capital gains tax. Without a capital gains tax, corporations are neutral between paying dividends or reinvesting post-tax profits. The rule that is prescribed to companies is that when a firm has internal projects that will yield a return on equity that is higher than investing in the market index, then the dividend payout ratio should be zero, otherwise it should be 100 per cent.

When capital gains are taxed, firms have a tax-related incentive to payout more dividends. This reduces the savings of corporations and hinders their capital deepening.

A unified and symmetric solution to the treatment of labour and capital income is the Exempt-Exempt-Tax (EET) system of taxation. Under this, the income of a person (from any source) that is used for investment is deductible. Further, reinvestment is exempt from taxation. It is only upon exit, where money is taken out of investments for the purpose of consumption, that these withdrawals are treated as ordinary income, and taxed as ordinary income.

The key insight here is to encourage and support saving and reinvestment. So when a person takes labour or capital income and puts it into investments, this part should be tax-exempt. Further, when securities are sold and reinvested, the capital income should also be tax-exempt. This gives strong incentives for capital deepening in the economy. It is when the person liquidates assets and brings money into consumption that two taxes should come into play: the long-term capital gains tax that is paid on money that comes out of an EET system, and the GST that is paid on consumption goods purchased.

This approach requires scaling up the EET system to go from the present vision, of a few lakh rupees per person in the context of long-term savings, to cover all financial activities of citizens. Systems like the NSDL's Tax Information Network (TIN) can be designed to track a comprehensive portfolio of each individual, whereby sale of assets and reinvestment is tax exempt, but exit from the EET track is subject to the long-term capital gains tax.

5. *Fundamental rethink of taxing corporations:* In any country, production can be organised through clubs, associations, partnerships, limited liability corporations, etc. All these structures are a means to an end: they result in personal income for individuals involved in the production process. That personal income would be taxed in a well designed income tax system. As a consequence, the taxation of any organisational form constitutes double taxation.

   The taxation of corporations induces two kinds of effects. First, there is a distortionary bias in favour of tax-efficient organisational structures such as proprieterships or partnerships. If a certain kind of production is best organised as a limited liability corporation, then the productivity of the country is reduced when tax considerations bias entrepreneurs in favour of an alternative organisational structure.

   The second problem is that of locating production outside the country. In the European Union, the average value for the corporate tax in 2009 was 23.5 per cent: a reduction of 11.8 percentage points from the level of 35.3 per cent in 1995. This portrays the average: many countries have a corporate tax rate of below 23.5 per cent. Many developing countries, of course, have lower rates than those seen in the EU. India stands out as a high tax location, with an effective marginal rate of 33.99 per cent for domestic companies and 41.2 per cent for foreign companies. To the extent that India is a high corporate tax region, there is a greater bias in the favour of both Indian and foreign companies to avoid investment in India.

   There is a broad consensus that the Indian marginal tax rate on corporations should not exceed that prevalent with other developing countries, which suggests a value such as 20 per cent. But there is a strong case for going further, and eliminating the corporation tax altogether.[3]

3. A paper-length treatment of this proposal is presently under development.

This would yield three direct benefits. First, it would eliminate the compliance costs at both corporations and government in the administration of corporation tax. Second, it would bring India to prominence in the investment planning of Indian and global firms. Third, it would remove the tax-induced bias in favour of debt financing for firms, thus reducing the extent of leveraging and thus risk taking. By reducing the demands for debt by large firms, greater space would be freed up in for bank borrowing by small and medium enterprises (SME).

When corporate income flows through to shareholders, it would be taxed as ordinary income. The increased resources of corporations would also generate increased employment, at which point increased flows of income tax would be obtained. Through this, the income of corporations would be fully taxed once—in the hands of the individuals associated with the corporation (shareholders and workers).

The residual problem with this strategy is the possibility that corporations might choose to not pay out dividends for extended periods of time. This can be avoided by having rules about a minimum dividend payout every year. At the polar case, it is possible to envisage a world where the entire profit is required to be paid out as dividends. This would flow through to shareholders and be taxed as ordinary income in their hands. Investment activities of the firm would take place through rights issues and external finance (both debt and public issues). This would have the additional advantage of improving corporate governance, by requiring that managers justify all investment plans to shareholders.

One of the profound implications of removing the tax paid by corporations on their profit is that it will vastly reduce the lobbying or rent seeking behaviour by the corporate sector as there will be no tax benefits to obtain! This will help preserve a healthy distance between business and politics. Corporate lobbying has been one of the contributors to the creeping 'crony capitalism' and consequent difficulties of governance in India. Improvements in governance are of essence for India in the coming generation, and the elimination of the corporation tax will be one element assisting that governance transformation.

An important objection to this proposal is that no other country has a 'zero corporate' tax rate. But then, there is no country in the world other than India which has a possibility to register double-digit growth rate in coming two to three decades. We must radically rethink our policies so as to exploit this opportunity, so as to decisively break with the curse of poverty. The rapid removal of poverty requires miracle growth rates, as was done in China. This would crucially depend on increased investments and improved governance. The policy of zero corporate tax with full taxability of dividends and capital gains in the hands of recipients will greatly facilitate achieving such a growth turnpike.

6. *Residence based taxation of finance:* A core principle guiding discussions on tax policy and globalisation is that taxation should not generate distortions which influence the economic decisions of individuals or firms. Taxation should be neutral and neither generate a bias in favour of doing business at home nor a bias in favour of doing business abroad.

   Tax neutrality as regards trade in goods and services has been achieved by focusing taxation purely upon the point of consumption through the destination principle. Under the VAT system, a British consumer of an Australian shirt only pays VAT in Britain. The global market for shirts is fully competitive: all high seas prices are free of taxation. The VAT system actively participates in the process of achieving neutrality, by refunding the entire burden of domestic taxation that was faced by the exporter. Critics of the VAT have sometimes termed this 'subsidising foreign customers at the expense of domestic customers', which is of course an erroneous characterisation. This approach of focusing taxation upon residents has delivered high levels of current account integration in the world economy without tax-induced distortions of behaviour.

Similar issues arise in the treatment of capital account integration. In order to achieve tax neutrality, the strategy which has been adopted worldwide is to have "residence based taxation" (Sinha, 2010). A country taxes the global financial income of residents but exempts all income of non-residents. Critics of residence-based taxation in finance have sometimes termed this "subsidising foreign financial players at the expense of domestic ones," which is of course an erroneous characteristaion. Under a residence-based tax system, the global market for financial services is undistorted by tax considerations to the extent that the investor does not have to take into account the tax regime of the source country. The British buyer of an Australian financial product only pays income tax in the UK. This delivers the end result of global competition and freedom of choice. The UK tax authorities tax the global financial services income of UK residents and the Australian tax authorities tax the global financial services income of Australian residents.

India has a *de facto* residence based taxation system through the Mauritius route. Foreign investors route their capital flows to India through Mauritius, and are thus immunised from domestic taxation, while local tax authorities tax the global income of residents. The construction of a rational tax framework requires shifting this from *de facto* to *de jure*, by giving all non-residents the Mauritius treatment.

There are concerns about entering into tax treaties with residence-based taxation when dealing with capital inflows from tax havens. In the long run, relatively complex tax policy needs to be crafted in order to deal with the issues associated with tax havens. In the short run, it is immediately feasible for India to enter into reciprocal residence-based tax treaties with all countries who are members of the OECD, none of which are tax havens, and all of which have high quality governance.

7. *Estate duty*: Alongside this framework, there is a case for a modest level of estate duty on wealth holders beyond inheritances of ₹ 50 crore. This would generate certain fiscal

revenues without inducing significant distortions. Such an estate duty will also play an important role to improve inter-generational equity and to promote philanthropy, while preserving incentive-compatibility on the core business of savings and investment through the working life of each person.

To sum up, over the next few years, we need to head towards a tax regime with zero import tariffs, zero tax on corporations (with rules about paying out profits to shareholders so that income tax is applied there), a 'Model GST' which is essentially a consumption tax, and a small estate duty.

These seven directions of policy will yield a tax system which is compatible with high GDP growth by encouraging integration with the world economy, by encouraging savings and investment, by generating low distortions in the economy, and by encouraging efficient organisation of production. It is not difficult to show that with our proposed tax reforms, the Indian tax system will become more equitable than the current one. All this would yield high and sustained GDP growth, which is the only long-term foundation of resources for the state. The ideal scenario which we should aspire for is one where Indian inflation is at 4 per cent and GDP growth is at 8 per cent, where an unchanged tax/GDP ratio yield a 12 per cent nominal growth in tax revenues year after year. Under these conditions, tax revenues would double every 9 years in real terms through sheer GDP growth.

In this scenario, the tax base of local bodies will essentially consist of tax on properties and a share in GST. As introduction of the model GST implies elimination of distorting taxes such as entry tax, octroi, etc., the local bodies will require a commensurate share in the GST tax collection.

All seven areas involve questions of transition. In the short term, deficits may rise. These reforms have many implications for the fairness of resource sharing with the states. Technical studies need to be undertaken on estimating the magnitudes of these effects, and finding transition mechanisms to smooth the short-run effects.

Non-tax sources of resources

The Indian state possesses a large stock of assets, particularly in the form of shares of PSUs and land. There is a need for a strategic perspective on the portfolio composition of these assets.[4]

Budget constraints are a harsh reality of life. Ultimately, there is a budget constraint in terms of the overall assets of the state. When the state chooses to own ₹ 1 of something, this comes at the cost of owning ₹ 1 of something else.

The interesting and important question that we should all be asking ourselves is: What should the portfolio composition of the government be? What assets should be held by the state?

The portfolio composition of the state is not something that should remain static at all times. A few decades ago, India was in a very different setting. After independence, the Bombay Plan was drafted by the business community. It envisaged government investment in capital-intensive and technologically-complex problems of the time, such as production of steel or electricity. In the 1970s, the argument was made that if the government did not run an airline, then the private sector could not. By 2010, conditions have changed considerably.

Most of us would agree that the airline industry works quite well as a purely private affair. All over the world, governments have got out of airlines. The decades of losses and poor performance of Alitalia is commonly held up as an example of what goes wrong when a firm is brought under public ownership. At the opposite end, most of us would agree that rural roads have to be on the balance sheet of the state. These roads typically do not have adequate traffic, and tolling would not generate adequate revenues. If the government did not own rural roads, these roads would not exist. Similarly, a significant fraction of the stock of capital involved in public health in our cities will need to be owned by the government. Equally, the preservation and improvement of forest cover will have to be a new priority for the public sector assets.

4. This treatment draws upon Kelkar (2010).

So there is a spectrum of assets, ranging from airlines to rural roads, where government ownership is inadvisable for airlines but required for rural roads or public health infrastructure. How should we think about where each problem falls? There are two broad categories with considerable clarity:

- *Goods and services in ordinary competitive markets:* The first area where we have a good understanding is goods and services on ordinary competitive markets. An example is steel. Now that India has near-zero tariffs on steel, it is a globally competitive market. Many private companies produce steel. The old argument—about capital and technology required for steel companies being out of reach for the private sector—is no longer convincing. We are now seeing Indian firms exporting steel into the global market—which demonstrates that there is no gap in technology. And, we are also seeing Indian companies turning into multinationals and buying up global steel companies—which demonstrates that there is no gap in capital availability for Indian companies.

  Under these conditions, private ownership works best. This should be seen at different levels. First, under ordinary circumstances, private ownership generates the best incentives for cost-minimisation, innovation and dynamic adjustment of corporate strategy. This is not an ideological position. An extensive research literature has examined privatisation experiences from all across the world, and the findings suggest big gains in productivity from private ownership.

  The second aspect of public *versus* private ownership concerns the issues that arise when a company approaches bankruptcy. In the private sector, bankruptcy is taken seriously. The fear of bankruptcy generates drastic responses in terms of selling off parts of the company, modifying business strategy, etc. These are healthy responses from the viewpoint of the economy. When an unhealthy company sells off a factory to a strong company, the control of assets of the economy moves into the best hands.

Output and employment are optimised through these adjustments. In contrast, in the public sector, managers have a tendency to be relatively relaxed about the prospect of bankruptcy. Drastic adjustments when faced with extinction do not take place, because the managers know that there is no real danger of extinction. Public sector companies are always able to draw on the taxpayer to pay for losses. So there are two problems. Adjustments do not take place because of the lack of fear of extinction, and the taxpayer suffers from periodic claims on resources every time the company gets into trouble. There is also a deeper problem here. If in the market place, one of the participants like a PSU is operating under a 'soft budget constraint' and that too with deep pockets, then it can adversely affect the performance and fortunes of even efficient private sector companies operating in that sector and such a market structure will systematically misallocate resources.

- *In regulated industries:* The second area where private ownership is clearly desirable is in regulated industries. In India, we are now seeing numerous regulated industries, ranging from finance to infrastructure, where a government agency performs the function of regulation and multiple competing firms are located in the private sector. Here, the simple and clean solution—government as the umpire and the private sector as the players—is what works best. This configuration is used in every advanced country, and we in India also face the challenge of setting up this architecture of government as regulator with massive investment coming in from the private sector which builds multiple competing firms.

  In many of these industries, we have a legacy of government ownership either directly by government departments or in the form of PSUs. The problems described above are very much there: productivity tends to be lower in public sector companies, the fear of bankruptcy is absent, and the risk of asking for money from the taxpayer is ever present. There is an additional issue. This is the conflict of interest between government as an owner and government as the regulator. For instance, the formulation and implementation of competition policy will be more vigorous and fair if government companies are not in the picture. One example is the recent measures taken by the government to support Air India: many of these can be construed as anti-competitive as these vitiate the playing field for our private airlines.

India's future lies in building a new institutional architecture with government as regulator and with the private sector doing investment. There is a problem when the government is conflicted. If the private sector feels that the regulator will not be an unbiased umpire in the competitive process, because a ward of the government is one of the players, then this makes the private sector feel uncomfortable. In the eyes of the private sector, this is a political risk. To pay for higher risk, the private sector demands a higher return. Fewer projects are implemented: the magnitude of investment goes down. With a higher rate of return on capital demanded by the private sector, user charges go up.

If we think of the next 25 years, a very substantial portion of the investment in all regulated industries in India is going to come from the private sector. It would be myopic for the government to have a regulator who is conflicted, which reduces the quantum of investment and drive up user charges. It makes more sense for the government to reorganise itself, shifting into the role of the umpire and away from the role of the player. We must move towards a clean solution: government as an umpire and the private sector as players.

There are other areas where there are shades of grey or complexities. For instance, natural resource based industries such as upstream hydrocarbons sector are a complex question. Here, there is a strategic issue as well as the issue of optimal appropriation of the underlying vast resource rent. Similarly, the role of government *vis-à-vis* universities is also complex. Barring a few such grey areas, we can confidently set about reformulating the activities of the state in the following two key areas. Firstly, the state should not be producing things which can be produced in competitive markets: this covers areas like steel or aluminium or cars. And secondly, the state should not be a player in regulated industries: this covers areas like airlines, running railway trains, shipping, telecom, banking or insurance.

A useful way to visualise this is essentially as a balance sheet adjustment. Suppose the government undertakes a portfolio adjustment, where ₹ 10,000 crore of shares of Air India is sold and used to build 2000 km. of highways. Let us trace through the full implications of this. Even if ₹ 10,000 crore of shares of Air India constitute a minority sale (i.e., 'disinvestment' in the Indian jargon), then certain efficiency gains are obtained. We now have our own Indian empirical evidence which shows that the mere act of listing induces improved productivity. Four channels seem to be at work: listing induces increased transparency, the stock market brings pressure on senior managers by doing daily performance evaluation, corporate governance is typically improved after listing, and to the extent that employees are given some shares, they become more aligned towards the growth and success of the organisation.

If ₹ 10,000 crore of shares of Air India constitutes a majority sale (i.e., 'privatisation') then even bigger efficiency gains are obtained. Extensive international evidence shows that productivity goes up strongly after privatisation. The increase in India's GDP because of a better run Air India is the first gain from the proposed portfolio adjustment. The second gain from the proposed portfolio adjustment lies in obtaining an additional 2000 km. of highway. The benefits for India of this public asset are simply enormous. The 2000 km. of highway that we do not have is the opportunity cost that we suffer every year owing to an investment of ₹ 10,000 crore in Air India.

It would make a lot of sense for India to undertake this portfolio adjustment of public sector assets to switch from owning Air India to owning highways or public health infrastructure or augmenting 'environmental capital'. The full picture should be seen. The motivation for disinvestment or privatisation should not be narrowly seen as being only about maximising the proceeds from the sale of assets. The real big gains come from the full picture.

We gain when the private sector obtains higher productivity (and this happens even with mere disinvestment, but it happens much more strongly with privatisation). We gain when the private sector becomes more comfortable bringing capital into investing in India in regulated industries. And, we gain when the government is able to build highways and canals, metro systems and railroad, which are crucial for India's growth and legitimately belong on the government's balance sheet.

Over the years, the size of the public sector has increased in our economy and currently, there are 473 central PSUs including banks and insurance companies. Of these, 104 are listed and 369 are unlisted. At the state level, there are 1160 state PSUs. It is estimated by informed financial analysts that the valuation of central PSUs (on a P/E basis for the listed companies and P/B basis for unlisted companies) can work out to roughly 500-600 billion dollars or 40-45 per cent of GDP. These are very substantial resources which would become available to the government to unburden itself of debt thus freeing up fiscal space, and to pursue its own legitimate expenditure goals.

One area of concern about privatisation lies in its political consequences. If PSUs are auctioned off, many of them would be purchased by the top 100 business houses of the country today. This would lead to a further increase in their economic and political influence in the country. In addition, in many regulated industries, there are concerns about the possibility of corruption when profit-maximising firms interact with weak governance. The strategy which addresses these concerns is one in which the shares of PSUs are dispersed across the wide investor community, and the firm is run by professional managers. Such firms, examples of which include L&T or HDFC, are controlled by no family or business house.

Intelligent design of government programmes

There is widespread discomfort with the inefficiency of government expenditure programmes in India. A recent paper (Bandiera *et al.*, 2009) proposes a useful distinction between 'active' and 'passive' waste by government. Active waste generates private benefits for politicians and bureacrats while passive waste does not. In India, there is a strong focus on the former. As an example, a recent article[5] estimates that a government of the size of the state government of Karnataka yields ₹ 3,000 crore of bribes per year. Scaled up to the level of India as a whole, this suggests a very large scale of flows of money through corruption.

Corruption represents an immense roadblock to the prospect of achieving an effective government. Controlling corruption is a moral imperative. However, Bandiera *et al.* (2009) harness a fascinating dataset and estimate that of the total waste in government programmes, 83 per cent is passive waste. That is, in an OECD country, the elimination of corruption would only eliminate 17 per cent of the overall waste. Further, corruption control might often require overheads which further increase passive waste.

The challenge, then, in obtaining an effective government is that of finding mechanisms of public administration through which both passive waste and active waste are controlled. This is a truly daunting challenge in India. In addition to the 'active waste' which is prominent in policy thinking in India, where there is a strong attention upon corruption, there is also a big problem of 'passive waste' that needs to be confronted. Until far-reaching new ideas are implemented on these questions, spending more money on public programmes is often futile.

Envisioning European-style social democracy in the Indian setting

European-style social democracy involves the establishment of large-scale population-wide programmes which directly address risks faced by individuals and which undertake redistribution. But building a large state, beyond the minimalist functions of a 'watchman' state, involves solving complex problems of collective action. Social norms are required that prevent a small number of citizens from exploiting the welfare state, which would result in exploding public expenditures. Political scientists have long emphasised the greater feasibility of of establishing a welfare state when a country has low heterogeneity and high social capital.

5. Kulkarni (2010).

When a country is homogeneous, voters believe that social programmes benefit people like them. India has very high levels of heterogeneity by ethnicity, religion, language and class. The analysis of size of government across developing countries and across time by Shonchoy (2010) shows that on average, a one standard deviation increase in linguistic fractionalisation is associated with a decrease of expenditure to GDP by 1.07 percentage points. India has one of the most extreme levels of linguistic fractionalisation, which would tend go along with a smaller state.

A related issue is that of trust capital, or the extent to which individuals in a country agree with the statement 'Most people can be trusted.'

Cross-country data from the *World Values Survey for 2006/07* is shown in Table 21.5. Among major countries, China stands out as a country with high trust capital: 52.3 per cent of the overall population believes that most people can be trusted. India has much less trust capital, with only 23.3 per cent of the population feeling similarly trusting.

Table 21.5

Trust Capital: A Cross-country Perspective

Rank	*Country*	*Agree that most people can be trusted*	
		Overall	*University grads*
1	China	52.3	70.1
2	United States	39.3	43.2
3	Japan	39.1	46.9
4	Germany	36.8	48.8
5	UK	30.5	42.0
6	South Korea	28.2	38.0
7	Russia	26.2	29.7
8	India	23.3	21.4
9	South Africa	18.8	23.5
10	Brazil	9.4	18.8
11	Turkey	4.9	4.5

Source: *World Values Survey, 2006/07.*

It is useful to focus upon attitudes among university graduates since this gives a sense about how things might evolve in the future with the spread of university education. University graduates are generally more trusting: in China's case the proportion of the trusting goes up to 70.1 per cent when considering university graduates only. In India's case, only 21.4 per cent of university graduates believe that most people can be trusted. Only Brazil and Turkey have less trust capital amongst university graduates than India.

In recent work, Bergh and Bjornskov (2010) offer empirical evidence which emphasises a causal connection between trust capital and the welfare state. They conjecture three mechanisms through which high trust levels increase the feasibility of social democracy:

1. Social programmes are, by definition, available to all. With low trust capital, individuals are more likely to free ride on the system to the maximal extent, leading to exploding costs.
2. A key dimension of trust is trust in the bureaucracy. When trust capital is low, bureacrats cannot be trusted with discretionary power, which makes it more difficult to build and implement universal welfare policies. European-style social democracy involves case workers interacting with poor families, making discretionary decisions. This requires building and running large transaction-intensive discretionary programmes, which present the hardest problems in public administration (Pritchett and Woolcock, 2004).
3. Finally, large welfare programmes require a high tax/GDP ratio. In high trust societies, tax compliance would not deteriorate and a large underground economy would not develop.

Trust capital evolves only slowly over the decades. Hence, for the coming few decades, we have to work within the existing environment, where India is a highly diverse society, where voters are likely to think that the people benefitting from a welfare programme are unlike themselves, where trust is low, and where civil servants cannot be trusted with discretion in the operation of welfare programmes.

From a resource perspective, trust capital matters in thinking about welfare programmes in two respects. First, with low trust capital, citizens are likely to engage in strategic behaviour and maximally exploit the provisions of welfare programmes, thus exacerbating their cost. In addition, with low trust capital, a high tax/GDP ratio is likely to be elusive.

Sophisticated thinking with incentive-compatible programmes

Given a budget of the tax revenues of the state, high efficiency in provision of public goods and in operations of poverty programmes is supremely important. A key dimension which needs to be brought into the process of design and refinement of government expenditure is the power of incentives. The behaviour of individuals and firms is remarkably malleable: once 'rules of the game' are established by the government, behavioural changes are undertaken by the private sector aiming to maximise self-interest. This often leads to unanticipated effects.

Hence, the task of public administration in India has to be rooted in sophisticated and incentive-compatible government programmes which deliver a high bang for the buck—where resources are used frugally and yet a great deal is done in terms of delivering consumption and risk-reduction to the bottom quartile.

As an example, consider the public distribution system (PDS). At first blush, the objective of giving food to poor people is a noble one. However, the PDS distorts market signals, promotes black market activity and smuggling, is poorly targeted. As Rajiv Gandhi observed, the bulk of the money spent on PDS fails to reach the poor.

Even when PDS money 'does' reach the poor, there are subtle consequences which need to be taken into account. By lowering the cost of wheat or rice, PDS free up resources that can be spent in other ways. Households may shift resoures towards expensive foods (such as meat) or towards non-food items. The overall impact of the

PDS money that reaches the poor, for nutrition of the poor, is not obvious.

The academic literature offers many warnings about these effects. Kochar (2005) finds that the PDS has only a limited impact on calorific intake (suggesting switching by households towards non-food consumption). Tarozzi (2005) finds that PDS had a limited impact upon the weight of children. Jensen and Miller (2010) undertake randomised experiments in China, and find no evidence that subsidies improved nutrition.

This example illustrates the basic point: While it may appear that subsidised rice and wheat for poor people is a desirable activity of the government, the overall impact is far from clear, both in terms of the leakages in administration (which were visible in Rajiv Gandhi's time) and in the overall impacts upon households (which are now visible in the academic literature).

The subsidy on petroleum products, which became deeply entrenched in India and has taken considerable effort to remove, needs to be seen in a historical perspective.[6] From 1970 to 1973, the world price of oil went up from $1.2 to $3.65 per barrel. This tripling of prices was fully passed on to the Indian consumer. In 1973-74, the world price went up further to $10 a barrel. This next tripling was also 'fully' passed on to the Indian consumer. Finally, a third tripling took place in 1980, when crude oil tripled to $30 a barrel. Once again, Indira Gandhi passed on the entire price rise to the consumer. Policy makers in India need to go back towards this ability to abjure from administered prices under conditions of dramatic fluctuations of the free market price.

From this cautious perspective, three big ideas can be identified that are quite likely to be useful.

The first is the Aadhar programme. If each household has a unique number and a bank account attached to the number, and if cash can flow directly from North Block to this account without any intermediaries, then the only impediment faced in poverty alleviation is a master table containing the names and numbers of

6. We are grateful to Swaminathan Anklesara Aiyar for these ideas.

all poor households in India. With this table in hand, the Ministry of Finance could directly eliminate mass poverty in India. A rough calculation is highly revealing: If 2 per cent of GDP or ₹ 110,000 crore are devoted to cash transfers into the poorest 20 crore people, this constitutes a transfer or ₹ 27,500 per year (i.e. ₹ 2292 per month) for a household of five. With such a capability in hand, a broad array of existing government programmes and interventions, aimed at addressing the problem of poverty, can be dismantled, thus yielding enormous improvements in India through the elimination of corruption, downsizing of government, reduction in expenditure, and removal of economic distortions thus enabling higher GDP growth. This scale of expenditure—2 per cent of GDP for the comprehensive elimination of poverty in India—is consistent with the broad goal of living within a tax/GDP ratio of 18-20 per cent of GDP.

The second grand theme is that of decentralisation. The 73rd and 74th amendments represent an 'unfinished revolution' that was begun by Rajiv Gandhi. The implementation of the Model GST, and transfer of a fraction of GST revenues to the local government, will create a new resource flow into local government. The creation of such a fiscal base is also incentive-compatible as it aligns the interests of citizens with the interests of elected officials of local bodies. As an example, the GST collections of Bhopal will partly go back into the municipality of Bhopal, thus closing the loop from local public goods to local GDP to local tax collections to local expenditure on local public goods. By improving accountability, the outcomes in critical local public goods would be improved, which would yield strong increases in the welfare of citizens.

The third grand theme is that of public provision coupled with private production. As an example, the Rashtriya Bima Swasthya Yojana (RBSY) combines public resources with access to privately run health facilities. Participating households are empowered to become customers, to choose from multiple competing private health service providers. Payments are only made to a private health service provider when a household patronises this provider: thus poor people are empowered as customers, and there are strong incentives for producers to serve the citizen. This is in contrast with public sector health facilities, where salaries and budgetary allocations are insensitive to the views of citizens. There are enormous efficiency gains which can be obtained by separating public sector provision from public sector production and by empowering citizens as customers through public funding.[7]

Diminishing economic risk

European-style social democracy involves two grand themes: redistribution from the rich to the poor, and of risk management at the 'individual' level by the state. The risk faced by individuals on account of unemployment, health, disability, etc., is sought to be addressed by government programmes.

When the government interacts with the individual 'citizen' in understanding events such as illness, unemployment or disability, onerous challenges of public administration are faced in running transaction-intensive systems where civil servants have discretion. There is, however, an alternative path to risk reduction which works at the level of the 'economy' and not the individual. This involves reducing macroeconomic risk.

The poorest of countries lack macroeconomic policy frameworks through which fiscal and monetary policy stabilise the business cycle. This yields substantial fluctuations of output, and generates political pressures from individuals faced with negative economic shocks. The volatility of GDP growth in India is between two to three times larger than that seen in OECD countries. A crucial part of the evolution into middle income is the creation of these policy frameworks through which macroeconomic uncertainty is lowered.

Macroeconomic crises have direct and adverse effects upon the poor. As an example, Bozzoli and Quintana-Domeque (2010) document the impact of Argentina's crisis of 2002 upon birth weight. The deterioration of birth weight in the crisis works out to one-sixth of the distance in birth weight between a rich country (the US) and a poor country (Pakistan). Reduced birth weight

7. The Centre for Civil Society has produced a series of research papers on the subject of rethinking education on these lines.

is associated with sustained difficulties through life on issues of health, learning and labour market outcomes.

The poor bear the brunt of business cycle volatility. Guillaumont and Korachais (2008) find that in addition to the negative impact of macroeconomic instability upon 'growth', macroeconomic instability reduces the amount of poverty reduction that is obtained per unit of growth. Those with tenured jobs and nominal wage rigidity do not experience the ups and downs of macroeconomic fluctuations. The industrial worker in the fringes of Surat is the one who lost his job in the global crisis of 2008. Once the poor fall into poverty traps in a downturn, they find it difficult to break free of the cycle of indebtedness, ill health and loss of human capital.

Stabilisation policy is important in that it would reduce the shocks that these households suffer. In recent years, considerable work has been done in India on designing the policy frameworks for reducing business cycle fluctuations (Rajan, 2008; Shah, 2008; Shah and Patnaik, 2010), and a good deal of international experience is available. The three key elements of this include:

1. Recasting RBI so that it has independence, and is held accountable for achieving an inflation target. This would involve divesting RBI of numerous other roles.
2. Achieving a high level of fiscal soundness, so that the debt/GDP ratio stays below 60 per cent of GDP at all times. This involves achieving surpluses in good times and deficits in bad times.
3. Allowing automatic stabilisers to vary the deficit through the business cycle. In a downturn, the spending on NREGA would be higher and tax collections on personal income tax would be lower, thus yielding an enlargement of the deficit. Conversely, in good times, surpluses should ensue automatically.

Macroeconomic stabilisation thus requires relatively simple institutional structures such as fiscal, financial and monetary policy. From the viewpoint of public administration, this is an easier path to take because it involves policy frameworks at the level of the economy and not transaction-intensive programmes which interact with individual citizens. In this sense, prevention is better than cure.

Policy directions in middle income

In the last 30 years, India has expanded GDP by six times, by achieving an average growth rate of 6.17 per cent per year. This has abolished the level of deprivation which was manifestly visible circa 1979. This growth acceleration is the first time in millenia that India has substantially enlarged the pie within a generation. This expansion of output has changed the opportunity set of policy makers. In 1979, it was not possible for India to build highways in India, given the price tag of $1 million per km.; today it is.

The main goal of economic policy today should be to achieve a minimum of 8 per cent GDP growth over the next 30 years, so that GDP will grow by more than 10 times. This would take aggregate GDP from the existing value of $1.2 trillion to a level of over $12 trillion. If this is achieved, then the resources available to the state would be completely transformed once again, as they have been through the last 30 years of growth. When GDP is $12 trillion, if 2 per cent of GDP is earmarked for cash transfers, this would represent a sum of $240 billion.

While this is a highly desirable destination, we should not take it for granted. Over the last 200 years, we have seen numerous examples of countries which failed to achieve sustained high growth. The task for a middle income country is to build state capacity on the core functions of the state, so that the engine of growth is able to continue to work for a few decades more, so as to avoid the 'middle income trap' where many countries have failed to produce sustained growth over long periods of time.

Empirical guidance on the two key questions

The empirical literature guides us on the constraints faced by policy makers in two respects:

- How large can the tax/GDP ratio become, in a low income country?

Gordon and Li (2009) analyses the tax/GDP ratio for developing countries from 1996 to 2001. The tax/GDP ratio for all developing countries, consolidating across all levels of government, averages to 17.6 per cent. For countries in India's range of GDP the average is 16.7 per cent: this is not significantly different from that seen in India today. It is only beyond a per capita GDP of $9,206 that a tax/GDP ratio of 25 per cent is achieved. This suggests that for a few decades, it would be wise to live within our means with an aggregate expenditure of all three levels of government to below 18-20 per cent of GDP.

- Table 21.6 envisages the consequences of a direct pursuit for a high tax/GDP ratio through higher tax rates, with weak fiscal discipline leading to threats of a fiscal crisis, with poor fiscal/financial/monetary institution building that induces high GDP fluctuations with the consequent adverse implications for investment and immediate political pressure for welfare programmes. This is also a scenario where a weak and unconfident India engages in reduced international economic integration out of fear of international crisis.
- The two key parameters which characterise this scenario are: average GDP growth over the coming 20 years of 6 per cent per annum, and a high tax/GDP ratio of 24 per cent. An average population growth of 1 per cent is assumed. All calculations are in real terms, at 2009-10 prices. Hence, rupee values are directly interpretable as relating to the 2009-10 value of the rupee.

Table 21.6

Resourcing the Indian State: The Inefficient Scenario

Year	*GDP (Trn. Rs.)*	*Population (Bln.)*	*GDP (per capita)*	*Tax revenues (Trn. Rs.)*	*Tax revenues (per capita)*
2009-10	58.6	1.10	53,272	12.9	12,785
2019-20	104.9	1.22	86,367	25.2	20,728
2029-30	187.9	1.34	140,021	45.1	33,605

- When can a country achieve significant redistribution? Ravallion (2009) analyses data for 90 developing countries, aiming to measure the 'capacity for redistribution'. This is measured by the marginal tax rate on those who are not poor—by rich-country standards—that is needed to cover the poverty gap or to provide a poverty-level of basic income, judged by developing-country standards.

  He finds that for low income countries such as India, the required tax burdens are found to be prohibitive: often calling for marginal tax rates of 100 per cent or more. The opportunity for doing such redistribution is found later in the development process: after per capita consumption exceeds $4000 per year.

These arguments suggest that the opportunities visible to policy makers differ dramatically between two groups of countries: the rich and the poor. In the present phase of India's growth, it seems appropriate to have modest aspirations for the tax/GDP ratio and for redistribution.

An illustrative calculation

These alternatives on resourcing the Indian state are illustrated by comparing two scenarios. In both scenarios, population growth of 1 per cent per year is projected for the next 20 years.

The first inefficient scenario is one which envisages the consequences of a growth-friendly environment, with a pursuit of a reduced tax/GDP ratio through lower tax rates, with high fiscal discipline, with high fiscal/financial/monetary institution building that induces low GDP fluctuations with the consequent positive implications for investment and reduced political pressure for welfare programs. This is also a scenario where a strong and confident India engages in high international economic integration without concerns about international crises.

The two key parameters which characterise this scenario are: average GDP growth over the coming 20 years of 8 per cent per annum, and a tax/GDP ratio of 20 per cent. An average population growth of 1 per cent is assumed. All calculations are in real terms, at 2009-10 prices. Hence, rupee values are directly interpretable as relating to the 2009-10 value of the rupee.

1. A direct pursuit for a high tax/GDP ratio through higher tax rates.
2. Weak fiscal discipline leading to threats of a fiscal crisis.
3. Incentives for distortionary policies including financial repression and monetary policy distortions in an attempt to respond to the fiscal problem.
4. Poor fiscal/financial/monetary institution building that induces high GDP fluctuations, with the consequent adverse implications for investment and continual political pressure for welfare programmes from citizens exposed to high economic risk.
5. A weak and unconfident India engages in reduced international economic integration out of fear of international crises.

In this scenario, a higher tax/GDP ratio of 24 per cent is obtained. However, this combination of features is projected to yield an inferior growth rate of 6 per cent per annum.

The calculations about this scenario are shown in Table 21.6. Per capita GDP expands strongly from ₹ 53,272 per person today to ₹ 140,021 over the coming 20 years. Through this, tax revenues per capita—the resource base of the state—are projected to expand from ₹ 12,785 per capita to ₹ 33,605 per capita. This enhanced resource base will be available for the state for the purpose of either producing public goods or undertaking poverty alleviation for the poorest 20 per cent of the population.

Table 21.7

Resourcing the Indian State: The Efficient Scenario

Year	*GDP (Trn. Rs.)*	*Population (Bln.)*	*GDP (per capita)*	*Tax revenues (Trn. Rs.)*	*Tax revenues (per capita)*
2009-10	58.6	1.10	53,272	11.7	10,654
2019-20	126.5	1.22	104,119	25.3	20,823
2029-30	273.1	1.34	203,494	54.6	40,699

The alternative efficient scenario is one where:

1. The state aspires for a reduced tax/GDP ratio, with lower tax rates.
2. High fiscal discipline leading to the elimination of fiscal stress.
3. Strong fiscal/financial/monetary institution building generates reduced GDP fluctuations. This bolsters investment, and also reduces the immediate political pressure for welfare programmes.
4. A strong and confident India engages in high international economic integration without fear of international crises.

In this scenario, a reduced tax/GDP ratio of 20 per cent is obtained. However, this combination of features is projected to yield a higher growth rate of 8 per cent per annum. These are modest and reasonable differences: A difference in projected GDP growth of 2 percentage points, and a difference in the tax/GDP ratio of 4 percentage points, across the two policy packages. Even in the pessimistic scenario, India is projected to be safely away from the 'Hindu growth rate' of 3.5 per cent: the projected value of 6 per cent optimistically replicates the average growth of 6.17 per cent obtained in the last 30 years.

The calculations about the efficient scenario are shown in Table 21.7. Per capita GDP expands strongly from ₹ 53,272 per person today to ₹ 203,494 over the coming 20 years. Through this, tax revenues per capita—the resource base of the state—are projected to expand from ₹ 10,655 per capita to ₹ 40,699 per capita. This enhanced resource base will be available for the state for the purpose of either producing public goods or undertaking poverty alleviation for the poorest 20 per cent of the population.

The comparison between these two scenarios is striking. Table 21.6 assumes a higher tax/GDP ratio of 24 per cent: it assumes that the state will set forth in a quest for a high tax/GDP ratio and actually attain it. In contrast, Table 21.7 assumes a reduced tax/GDP ratio of 20 per cent. Yet, under the scenario shown in Table

21.7, the power of compounding with a higher GDP growth rate is so powerful that the per capita resources available to the state endup being 21 per cent higher—₹ 40,699 per person as opposed to ₹ 33,605 per person. This emphasises the idea that the indirect route—of strengthening GDP—is a superior path to resourcing the state when compared with the direct path—of higher tax rates and a high tax/GDP ratio.

More importantly, the scenario of Table 21.6 yields inferior personal incomes because the GDP per capita is projected to grow to ₹ 140,000 per person, while the alternative scenario yields a superior value of ₹ 203,494 per person: a difference of 45 per cent. From the viewpoint of the individual, the scenario of Table 21.7 is thus superior because personal income is higher and because there is a greater provision of public goods by the state. If the citizen of India was presented with a choice between these two scenarios, there is no question about which one is superior.

These calculations are, of course, only illustrative. The results are entirely driven by two numbers: GDP growth of 6 per cent *versus* 8 per cent, and a tax/GDP ratio of 20 per cent *versus* 24 per cent. There is room for legitimate disagreement about how alternative policy packages can yield different numerical values for these two parameters. Yet, this calculation illustrates the key point: about the dominant role for GDP growth in generating substantial resources for the state.

Both scenarios err on the side of conservatism. The policy package sketched as the 'inefficient' scenario could easily yield outcomes worse than those projected, for the GDP growth projected envisages that India will replicate the performance of the last 30 years of economic reform. Global economic history encourages us to be cautious about trend extrapolation in economic growth: most countries which got high growth for 30 years failed to replicate that high growth in the next 30 years (Pritchett, 2000). Numerous countries got out of the ranks of the poorest, but floundered in the 'middle income trap'. Conversely, there is also a good chance that the 'efficient' policy package described above could unleash growth of above 8 per cent; a few countries like Korea and Taiwan have managed to achieve long-term trend growth of above 8 per cent thus proving that it can be done.

Conclusion

The broad picture emphasised in this paper is one where in the next three doublings of per capita GDP—from $1100 per capita to $8800 per capita—the gains of the poor will come primarily from growth and from superior supply of public goods. In this period, there is limited scope for redistribution, and the focus of public policy should be on a government that delivers genuine public goods, which benefit all. This includes the establishment of frameworks for macroeconomic stabilisation, since reduced fluctuations are a public good which benefit all.

The primary tool through which the state can obtain resources is higher GDP growth. A tax/GDP ratio of 20 per cent, with expenditure that is just slightly above 20 per cent, is the reasonable scenario which can be envisaged for the coming 30 years. Mobilising greater resources for the state is thus synonymous with undertaking reforms which yield higher GDP growth. Alongside this, a good part of the concerns about economic uncertainty, which lead to a desire for European-style social democracy, can be addressed by undertaking fiscal, financial and monetary policy reforms through which business cycle fluctuations are diminished. In addition, fresh thinking about mechanisms of expenditure can yield greater bang for the buck thus freeing up resources.

GDP growth is thus the most important element of all three points of view: the elimination of mass poverty, the increase in welfare of the entire population, and the resourcing of the state.

Very few countries of the world have sustained growth for many decades. The economic reforms of the early 1990s decisively broke with India's dirigiste past. This gave an escape from the Hindu growth rate which afflicted India in the 1970s. But it is important to avoid the complacent assumption that India will replicate this 'miracle' over the coming 30 years, or do better.[8] While

8. Episodes of high growth sustained over many decades are so rare in development economics, that Nobel Laureate Robert E. Lucas, Jr. termed them as 'miracles' (Lucas, 1993).

the possibility is real, it would be incorrect to assume that our fond hopes are our destiny. Many countries have made policy mistakes through which the fundamental microeconomic foundations of high GDP growth have been damaged, through which an episode of growth petered out.

Considerable caution needs to be exercised in Indian policy thinking today. The gains of the last 20 years were rooted in the economic reforms of this period. If the pace of reforms slackens, then growth will decline. At the same time, India has an enormous opportunity over the next 30 years—rooted in sound demographics—to move GDP growth up, if fundamental change is achieved in the functioning of the state. If growth accelerates, then per capita GDP growth of 7 per cent is attainable. This would yield one doubling of per capita growth in each decade, through which per capita GDP would reach $8800 over 3 decades.

If this happy scenario comes together, it will put India into the zone of per capita GDP of $9,206 in 2040. Once this phase is completed, the state capacity would be at a different level. The tax/GDP ratio would be higher and GDP would be higher, thus bringing bigger resources into the coffers of the state.

Administrative capacity would be higher. The burning problems of weak public goods on fundamental issues such as the police and judiciary would be absent, thus allowing a focus of top leadership upon other issues. At this point, it will become possible to evaluate a more ambitious expenditure plan for government since the tax/GDP ratio can then potentially rise above 20 per cent.

A premature escalation of expenditure plans has the possibility of contaminating the foundations of GDP growth, through three channels of influence. First, welfare programmes undermine the incentives for work. As an example, to the extent that NREGA has reduced the incentives in favour of migration, this runs against the strategic picture of Indian growth being associated with rural to urban migration. Second, a large state requires high tax rates. The economic distortions associated with taxation goes up as the square of the tax rate; thus high tax rates undermine GDP growth. Third, expansive expenditure plans are often associated with an array of problems such as fiscal crises, financial repression, capital controls, and underdeveloped institutions on fiscal, financial and monetary policy. The slowly unfolding demographic transition, which led to a gradual crumbling of the European welfare state by reducing the number of workers in the economy, is an even greater problem for India given the projected rapidity with which the demographic transition will come about in India. All these three channels imply that there is a conflict between the core goal of high GDP growth and the prospect of undertaking a large expenditure programme in the short run.

This thinking takes place at a time when India faces a unique and historic opportunity for high GDP growth, from 2010 to 2035, owing to the 'demographic dividend'. If this opportunity is not utilised properly, it will never recur again in the future. India will then face the bleak problems of a combination of mass poverty with an ageing population.

The most important responsibility of our generation is that of correctly executing the economic policy decisions today, so that this happy scenario does arise: one with 8 per cent average growth over the coming 30 years. If this correctly comes about, then the frontier of possibilities for policy that will be faced by the next generation will be enlarged. That generation will be able to choose whether it is beneficial to go beyond a tax/GDP ratio of 20 per cent.

References

Bandiera, O., A. Prat and T. Valletti (2009). "Active and Passive Waste in Government Spending: Evidence from a Policy Experiment", *American Economic Review* 99(4): 1278–308.

Bergh, A. and C. Bjornskov (2010). *Historical Trust Levels Predict Current Welfare State Design*. Discussion paper. Lund University.

Bozzoli, C. and C. Quintana Domoque (2010). "The Weight of the Crisis: Evidence from Newborns in Argentina", *Discussion Papers of DIW Berlin* 1054. DIW Berlin. German Institute for Economic Research.

Buiter, W.H. and U.R. Patel (1992). "Debt, Deficits and Inflation: An Application to the Public Finances of India", *Journal of Public Economics* 47: 172–205.

Chadha, R. (2010). "Moving to Goods and Service Tax in India: Impact on India's Growth and International Trade", *Discussion Paper* 103. New Delhi: NCAER.

Feldstein, M. (2004). "Budget Deficits and National Debt", *L.K. Jha Memorial Lecture*.

Gordon, R. and W. Li (2009). "Tax Structures in Developing Countries: Many Puzzles and a Possible Explanation", *Journal of Public Economics* 93(7-8): 855–66.

Guillaumont, P. and C. Korachais (2008). "When Unstable, Growth is Less Pro Poor", *Working Papers* 200827. CERDI.

Jensen, R.T. and N.H. Miller (2010). "Do Consumer Price Subsidies Really Improve Nutrition?", *Working Paper* 16102. National Bureau of Economic Research.

Kelkar, V. (2004). *FRBM Implementation Task Force Report*. Committtee report. Ministry of Finance, Government of India.

———. (2010). "On Strategies for Disinvestment and Privatisation", *Sir Purshotamdas Thakurdas Memorial Lecture.*

Kochar, A. (2005). "Can Targeted Food Programs Improve Nutrition? An Empirical Analysis of India's Public Distribution System", *Economic Development and Cultural Change* 54(1): 203–35.

Kulkarni, Vivek (2010). "Government, a Lucrative Business", in *Hindu Business Line*, October 28.

Kumar, M.S. and J. Woo (2010): "Public Debt and Growth", *Discussion Paper* WP/10/174. IMF.

Lucas, R.E. (1993). "Making a Miracle", *Econometrica* 61(2): 251–72.

Mankiw, N.G., M. Weinzierl and D. Yagan (2009). "Optimal Taxation in Theory and Practice", *Journal of Economic Perspectives* 23(4): 147–74.

Mundle, S., N. Bhanumurthy and S. Das (2010). "Fiscal Consolidation with High Growth: A Policy Simulation Model for India", *Working Papers* 10/73. National Institute of Public Finance and Policy.

Nickel, C., P. Rother and L. Zimmermann (2010). "Major Public Debt Reductions: Lessons from the Past, Lessons for the Future", *Working Paper Series* 1241. European Central Bank.

Pritchett, L. (2000). "Understanding Patterns of Economic Growth: Searching for Hills among Plateaus, Mountains, and Plains", *The World Bank Economic Review* 14(2): 221–50.

Pritchett, L. and M. Woolcock (2004). "Solutions when the Solution is the Problem: Arraying the Disarray in Development", *World Development* 32(2): 191–212.

Rajan, R. (2008). *Committee for Financial Sector Reforms*. Committee report. Planning Commission, Government of India.

Rao, M.G. (2005). "Tax System Reform in India: Achievements and Challenges Ahead", *Journal of Asian Economics* 16(6): 993–1011.

Ravallion, M. (2009). "Do Poorer Countries have less Capacity for Redistribution?", *Discussion Paper* WPS5046. World Bank.

Reinhart, C.M., K.S. Rogoff and M.A. Savastano (2003). "Addicted to Dollars", *Working Paper* 10015. National Bureau of Economic Research.

Shah, A. (2008). "New Issues in Macroeconomic Policy", in T.N. Ninan (ed.), *Business Standard India,* Chap. 2, pp.26–54. Business Standard Books.

Shah, A., and I. Patnaik (2010). "Stabilising the Indian Business Cycle", in S. Kochhar (ed.), *India on the Growth Turnpike: Essays in Honour of Vijay L. Kelkar*. Chap. 6, pp.137–54. New Delhi: Academic Foundation.

Shonchoy, A. (2010). "What is Happening with the Government Expenditure of Developing Countries: A Panel Data Study", *Discussion Paper* 2. University of New South Wales.

Sinha, U.K. (2010). *Working Group on Foreign Investment*. Committee report. Department of Economic Affairs, Ministry of Finance.

Tarozzi, A. (2005). "The Indian Public Distribution System as a Provider of Food Security: Evidence from Child Nutrition in Andhra Pradesh", *European Economic Review* 49: 1305–330.

22

KAUSHIK BASU

Social Democracy, Capital and Growth

Preamble

I never met Indira Gandhi. My closest interaction with her was one step removed. When I began teaching at the Delhi School of Economics one of the persons I enjoyed talking to most was Sukhamoy Chakravarty. Chakravarty was then senior Professor at the Delhi School, the pre-eminent economist of his time, a scholar of unbelievable breadth, and a key adviser to Mrs Indira Gandhi. She clearly respected his formidable intellect and he, in turn, stuck it out with Indira Gandhi through her good times and bad. This was a case of genuine respect since, as a friend of Sukhamoy's had observed, it was impossible to corrupt Sukhamoy. The catch was that his needs were so frugal that there was nothing that could be used to corrupt him with. One day, while talking to him about Adam Smith and David Hume, I quietly slipped in the mundane question as to what it was that drew him to Indira Gandhi. The promptness of the answer caught me by surprise; he needed no time to think. Two things, he said. Her sympathy for the poor and the marginalised was instinctive—there was nothing put on about it. And her secularism—the ability to treat human beings as human beings, with no concern for the person's religion or caste or regional origins—was beyond question.

These are remarkable qualities. As we set out to discuss social democracy, let me add that it is important to remember that secularism must, ultimately, transcend even national boundaries. The suffering of a person in Africa or Latin America must not be discounted on grounds of the person's passport. This international humanism is evident in numerous speeches of Indira Gandhi, and, before that, in writings and speeches of India's founding intellectuals, such as Jawaharlal Nehru and Rabindranath Tagore and even some of our early mystical thinkers. Let me quote Nehru:[1]

> Ultimately even nationalism will prove a narrowing creed, and we shall all be citizens of the world with a truly international vision. For the present, this may be beyond most people and most countries. For us in India, we have to build a true nationalism, integrating the various parts and creeds and religions of our country before we can launch out into real internationalism. Without the basis of a true nationalism, internationalism may be vague and amorphous, without any real meaning. But the nationalism that we build in India should have its doors and windows open to internationalism.

There is a time and place for ideas; and, as Nehru suggested, internationalism may have to bide its time. While we must not lose sight of it and avant-garde thinkers will, luckily, continue to write about it (see Nussbaum, 2008), we have to, for now, develop our ideas concerning political economy, social development and growth, in the context of the nation state, since that is the primary domain of policymaking in today's world. That is the spirit in which I will develop my ideas in this paper. Most of the analysis will be confined to matters of policy for the Indian nation state.

Remembering Nawadih

In the late 1980s and early 1990s, I undertook a series of field studies with groups of students and some professors from the Delhi School of Economics to a village in Jharkhand (then Bihar) in Giridih district, called Nawadih. We conducted a census of the village and collected data on what were the fashionable ideas and arguments among economists of those times—interlinkage in agrarian relations and the causes of share tenancy, for instance.[2] I spent large amounts of time talking to a cross-section of village people and kept notes. I wished that all the data and the notes would someday result in a classic book, maybe like M.N. Srinivas's *The Remembered Village*.

1. From "A Secular State," foreword to Dharam Nirpeksh Raj by Raghunath Singh (1961). See p. 195 of Gopal and Iyengar (2003).
2. Two of this conference's participants, Pranab Bardhan and Joseph Stiglitz, made seminal theoretical contributions to that literature.

Srinivas wrote the book from memory, after his anthropological field notes were destroyed in a fire at Stanford University. Shorn of the weight of scholarly notes and copious field data, he wrote a book that was at once lucid and profound.

Unfortunately, nothing came of the planned book of mine. Even the strategy of holding my field notes close to open flames in the hope that they would catch fire and I would be able to repeat Srinivas's feat did not work.

Even though I never wrote the book, the experience did influence my thinking deeply. First, it was evident that for people living in abject poverty in remote villages the question of helping them through mechanisms of the market does not arise, because they live outside the reach of the market system, and in ways more profound than we may realise at first glance. This can be because they are priced out of the system (Atkinson, 1995), or because the social norms that are ingrained in them and the institutions that they have imbued from childhood make them think in categories not conducive to participation in modern capitalistic markets. It is arguable that the Native Americans lost their lands to the Settlers from the old world because of their inability to comprehend the market-based contracts they were getting into. The categories in which their thoughts were framed proved a handicap for the system that the Settlers brought to them.

Likewise, the marginalised people of India are at times 'outside the system' in a deep cultural, political-economy sense. Before we can reach them through the standard market-based policy interventions, we have to think of ways of drawing them into the mainstream of our economy and polity.

Second, the state of the people of Nawadih was to me a reminder that, while free market forces may have the ability to deliver on efficiency—Pareto efficiency, in the strict parlance of economists—and even growth, they have no natural propensity to reach out to the poor. This must, therefore, be a moral commitment of the government and civil society. I stress the word 'moral' because it is often pointed out how, if we do not manage to curb widespread poverty, this can destabilise the entire economy and come to haunt us. This appeal to the self-interest of the well-off people may be a good strategic ploy to have action on this front, but we must remember that ultimately this ought to be an end in itself and of innate moral worth. The poor must not be left in poverty, the marginalised must not be left in the margins, irrespective of whether this is good or bad for the rest of us. Further, because of our inheritance laws, there are people who are born poor and those who are 'born' rich. To so totally tilt the scales at the start of one's life is clearly a moral injustice (see Basu, 2011, for discussion).

This moral precept may sound radical, but similar sentiments have been expressed by moral philosophers through the ages. Thomas Aquinas, the 13th century philosopher and theologian, who was also a priest in the Catholic church, went so far as to argue in his classic, *Summa Theologica*, that, when a person's deprivation is sufficient, then other people's property is no longer sacrosanct—the deprived comes to acquire a moral right to other people's property:

> In cases of need, all things are common property, so that there would seem to be no sin in taking another's property, for need has made it common...(I)f the need be so manifest and urgent that it is evident that the present need must be remedied by whatever means be at hand, then it is lawful for a man to succor his own need by means of another's property, by taking it either openly or secretly... [Aquinas ([1265-74] 1911, II-II:66.7)]

This did not endear Aquinas to the rich and powerful. Though he would later be canonised, he was in his lifetime condemned by the church for using reason and the logic of Aristotle to override the dictates of God.

Intention and design

While these moral reminders have to be kept firmly in mind, there is also a converse word of caution that one must not lose sight of. Moral commitment and the passion for change are essential ingredients for a better society and a better economy, but they are by no means sufficient. There is need to have objective, professional input that assesses what is feasible in the real world and what is not before designing an actual policy. It is like building a bridge over a turbulent river. One needs passion and commitment to want to build such a bridge. But one also needs the dispassionate analysis of an engineer or a professional architect to make sure that the bridge that is built can withstand traffic and pedestrian usage. Indeed, in the absence of such professional design, the well-intentioned bridge could well turn into a disaster.

Likewise, with economic policy. The laws of the market and structures of incentives need to be analysed and understood in designing good policy. One may not like the relentlessness of the laws of the market but one must not make the mistake of denying these laws. As John Stuart Mill had argued in his inaugural address delivered at the University of Saint Andrews in 1867, a sailor may not like the winds and the waves but, if for this reason, the sailor pretends that these forces of nature do not exist, he is likely to come to grief. The right approach is to understand the laws of the winds and the waves and then to use them in one's best interest.

History has been known to be harsh to those who misread its laws. Contrary to some recent conservative writers' claim, China's Great Leap Forward of 1959 was not a malevolent move on the part of Mao Zedong. He genuinely wanted to take China's agriculture forward in leaps and bounds for the benefit of the ordinary people of his nation. And he did not lack determination and passion. However, he mis-analysed the laws of the market and did not understand the forces he had helped unleash. The forced collectivisation played havoc with the peasants' incentive to produce and the consequence was one of the worst famines in human history; it killed anywhere between 15 to 30 million people (Basu, 2009).

To emphasise the importance of dispassionate professional analysis, let me remind the reader that the Russian revolution of 1917 and the policies that followed were not meant to be exploitative of the larger population or to stall growth. If Russia became a society of crony capitalism, this was because of design flaws in what the well-meaning early revolutionaries attempted to do.

The incentives of individuals and groups were misunderstood and, as a result, what began with the intention of an equitable socialist society became an inequitable crony capitalistic system.

Both these matters, moral commitments and dispassionate analysis, contradictory though they may seem, have to be treated as precepts, as we set out to build an economy that not only grows rapidly and is efficient but also functions as a social democracy with the benefits of progress reaching far and wide, and with empowerment reaching all segments of society across barriers of caste, religion and genre.

After joining government, as I did in December 2009, I often found myself amidst a motley crowd trying to explain some fine point of economic analysis. Every time, after such a discourse, when someone said, "That is very good economics," I knew the next word would be "but". It would then be pointed out how "but the world does not work that way." It is true that many an economic theorist brings to popular discourse arguments which lack applicability or are lacking in commonsense. But, if something is really 'good economics,' it is also relevant for real-world decision-making. The cliché, "Good in theory and bad in practice", is a self-contradictory observation. The need is to marry commitment with good economics. That is not always easy, but that is what we must strive towards.

Social democracy

In addressing concerns of social democracy and equitable growth, it is important to emphasise that social democracy goes beyond the precept of one-person-one-vote to the principle of equitable distribution and the empowerment of ordinary individuals. Moreover, government has to show restraint in dealing with the fissures and strains that appear in any society. Too heavy handed a response to civil protest can easily undermine democracy (see Nilekani, 2008: 161-4). This paper is predicated on the recognition of these multiple precepts of democracy.

The principle of one-person-one-vote is however arguably the most critical requirement of a social democracy. It is important that an individual, no matter how small, should have the right to register his or her preference in the choice of a leader who can have an influence on the voter's life.

It is worth pointing out that even this basic principle is not satisfied in many domains of life. Here I am not just speaking of individual nations that are under military rule or some kind of totalitarian system but, in a curious way, for the world as a whole. Let me explain.

As globalisation has proceeded, the ability of one country to affect the well being of people in another nation has increased in tandem. By cutting off trade or the flow of international capital into Cuba, the US can affect the lives of ordinary people in Cuba. Likewise China can, through individual policies, have deep and lasting effect on the well being of the people of Taiwan. No doubt something similar is true of India and its smaller neighbours. The fact of the matter is that in today's world it is entirely possible that, for a person living in Iraq or Afghanistan who gets elected as leader of the US is more important than who gets elected as the leader of Iraq or Afghanistan. However, as things stand today, despite economic globalisation we have very little political globalisation. There is no way that a citizen of Iraq or Afghanistan can express a preference for who gets elected President of the US. Nor does a person in Nepal have a say as to who gets to form the government in India.

This means that, as economic globalisation has progressed, global democracy has been eroded. People cannot express franchise over the election of leaders who can affect their lives. This is, however, a matter that I will push aside here in the present paper, for my focus here is not on globalised or international economic well being but social democracy and economic growth confined to the nation states.

The first and foremost requirement of social democracy is that people ought to have a sense of belonging *vis-à-vis* society, a sense of citizenship, a sense of empowerment. The fact that these are often lacking in our society came out very sharply in some experiments that were run in Uttar Pradesh by Hoff and Pandey (2006). In a remote, caste-ridden village they made groups of school children take some tests in puzzle-solving which would give an indication of the intelligence of the children. In one set of experiments the names of all the children were read out in a roll call and they were then made to take these tests. The children of lower caste did as well as the children of upper castes. In another round of experiments the names of the children were read out along with the name of the caste to which the children belonged. In these tests, the children of lower castes, performed significantly worse than the children of upper castes. Clearly the mere public announcement of a child's caste along with the centuries of stigma and the societal believes that the lower castes were also less intellectually endowed made the children of lower castes perform worse than what they were capable of. They were almost living out the role that society had scripted for them. Similar tests have been found to reach similar conclusions with statistical significance in many other domains (see, for instance, Field and Nolen, 2005).

Some years ago I studied the results of general knowledge and intelligence tests that had been administered to students in a school called Anandan in Kolkata. Anandan was founded and is run by my sisters and its aim is to provide education to slum children who go to municipal corporation schools for their formal education but clearly needed remedial education. It turned out that how these students performed in these tests depended not so much on their gender, wealth or even age, as much as on whether the children lived with the parents, and whether the parents talked to each other and to them. A person's social circumstance clearly has a large impact on a person's capacity to learn and perform.

To reject someone from the high table of society evidently has a demoralising effect on the individual which hampers his or her participation in society. It is clear that we need to strive in India to draw more people into the mainstream; and here I am not talking about economics—I will come to that in a moment—but about social and political inclusion. Though in India we do have adult franchise, we still have a great distance to go in making all segments of the population feel a part and parcel of society. This has to be as much of a social project as an economic project. Given my own specialisation, I shall here focus on the latter.

Economic inclusion

To create a vibrant democracy it is essential to give all adults, irrespective of colour, creed, religion, and other identities, a vote. But, as was argued in the above section, this is not sufficient. Individuals need to feel socially and politically included. However, even that is not sufficient. A person who is excluded from the market and has no stake in the nation's economy cannot be expected to feel a part of the nation. This is what gives rise to the important idea of 'economic inclusion' (see Ahluwalia, 2010; Rangarajan Committee, 2008).

Economic inclusion is important in itself, for it gives a person a sense of belonging to society, which contributes to the happiness that all human beings deserve. But even beyond that, economic inclusion is important as a vital constituent of social democracy.

Economic inclusion is not the same as having an income above a certain cut-off level (see Ahluwalia, 2010). The rich man who lives a life that is self-sufficient but one of isolation on an island can be rightly described as economically excluded. We may not have much concern for him because for him this is, presumably, a matter of choice but we can, nevertheless, not describe him as a part of the economic system of the nation.

Extreme poverty, on the other hand, will on most occasions imply economic exclusion. But for those who are poor but not in extreme poverty, whether or not they will count as economically excluded will depend on how they earn their livelihood, whether they trade their wares on the market and whether they keep their savings in a bank or under the pillow. However, this immediately means that a policy of economic inclusion must entail (a) the eradication of extreme poverty and (b) the integration of people into the nation's system of trade, banking and finance. The latter, namely, (b), is often referred to as 'financial inclusion.' In India, currently, both poverty eradication and financial inclusion are part of the national policy agenda. What is being argued here is that such policy, effectively implemented, is not only good for the people but can also nurture social democracy in the nation.

But how does one achieve (a) and (b) above? The ultimate path to the eradication of poverty is to think of transformations in the very way in which economic life is organised. Prominent thinkers from the mid-nineteenth century and even earlier have toyed with various radical agendas. However, their failure to find a solution has often led their ideas to be dismissed as pipedreams. I argue in Basu (2011) that such utopian plans must not be banished out of hand, that the inequality that we see in the world and even within India is unacceptably large, no matter how we choose to measure inequality (Sen, 1973) and that, in principle, it is possible to conceive of viable societal arrangements that are more equitable and fair than the system we have at present. However, we do not yet have a blueprint for how to get to such a society. As a consequence, for now, we are forced to practice what may be described as 'normal economics,' that is, policymaking within the present system.

As far as normal economics goes, the best way to mitigate poverty is to do approximately what India is currently trying to do, that is, to subsidise the poor and deliver some basic services to them. The qualifier 'approximately' is important because there are flaws in what we are doing. One important flaw in what we often do is to try to benefit the poor by lowering the prices of essential goods. This can be done in two ways. One is to lower the price of the good for all citizens, such as selling LPG gas at below market price to all; the other is to lower the price for the target population, such as when we sell subsidised kerosene to households certified to be below a certain level of income or to be particularly vulnerable in some sense.

Both are undesirable, but the former especially so, since lowering the price for all citizens in order to benefit the poor is too wasteful. The subsidy that is given to the rich in the process has little justification. Further, this could imply pressures on the government's fiscal expenditure that an emerging economy can ill afford.[3] One reason why arguments against such generalised

3. A well-reasoned case for universalisation of food subsidy is made by Himanshu and Sen (2011). However, it has to be kept in mind that if one nation adopts a universal subsidy scheme but its neighbouring nations do not, the subsidised food is likely to go over the national boundaries. So if we do go for universalisation we have to think of this being done at the level of a cluster of nations. This is technically feasible but may not be organisationally implementable at this point of time outside of the Euro zone nations.

subsidies find so little support is precisely because the well-off have vested interests in this.

Lowering the price specifically for the poor and vulnerable households is a better strategy but still not good enough. If government was run by perfectly moral agents or by robots that mechanically did what they were supposed to do, this would be fine. In reality, we have to keep in mind that the hundreds of thousands of officials who carry out the directives of the government are ordinary human beings with their own personal interests and motivations. We have to take realistic account of the proclivity of these people in designing our subsidy schemes. In the language of economics, our schemes must meet the test of incentive compatibility of the agents involved in implementing them.

The way in which the lowering of price for the vulnerable population works is as follows. Let us take the example of providing subsidised wheat. What is currently done is a good example of this. The wheat is procured by the government and handed over to the roughly five hundred thousand public distribution system (PDS) stores all over the country. The store-owners are instructed to sell this wheat to designated below poverty line (BPL) households at a price that is deliberately kept well below the market price.

Now think of the incentives facing the PDS store owner. If he can divert some of this wheat and sell it on the open market, he can fetch a much higher price for it. So he will have a tendency to sell a part of this wheat he has received at low price from the government on the open market and to either send away the poor on the ground that the supplies have not arrived or adulterate the wheat that is handed over to the poor. There is evidence that both these happen in large measure in India. In fact, for wheat, the diversion can be as much as 67 per cent of what is meant for the poor (Jha and Ramaswamy, 2011; Khera, 2011).

Fortunately, there is a way of correcting this, which can ensure that the poor get as much benefit as intended and there is much less wastage in the process of delivery. This entails giving the subsidy directly to the poor households. This can be done by giving them coupons or smart cards that have some designated value. Prices are left to be determined by the forces of demand and supply. The poor go and buy the food from the market at the market price but they use the coupons or the smart card (along with some of their own money) to pay for it. Stores have no incentive to drive away the poor because they pay as much as any other customer. The incentive to adulterate food is also down since the poor can then simply take their smart card to another store.

It is true that some areas of India are so remote that private traders may not set up shop there and so the state-run PDS stores will still have a role to play. It is just that in this system the PDS stores will be charging the market price and, also, people will in principle be free to buy from any store.

One by-product of this, which is also good for nation building, is that people will gain greater mobility. Under the current system people are tied to particular PDS stores for their food and kerosene rations. This puts a break on people's freedom to migrate, since they then lose out on the rations, at least till they once again do the paperwork for their new location. With the smart card, especially when one can establish one's identity using the Aadhaar system, a person will be more free to move within the nation. Such labour mobility can do a lot to stem secessionist tendencies in some parts of the country.

As for financial inclusion, India has a great distance to go but, fortunately, there are initiatives afoot that are exactly right. The recent scheme of Swabhimaan, which will try to create a system of 'barefoot ATM machines' so that ordinary people who do not have bank branches near their homes can nevertheless have bank accounts, is one such example. The idea is to have ordinary people such as the local merchant be 'business correspondents.' They can enable people to open accounts by identifying them from their fingerprints and maybe retina readings. Once a person has an account, if the person needs money, she can go to the local business correspondent, have herself electronically identified and get the money from the business correspondent who later has the money transferred from the customer's account to his. This is what I meant by barefoot ATM machines. If India manages to run this effectively, this can be a model for a host of poor or emerging economies.

It is important to recognise that the use of bio-markers to identify people is not without risks. Government can build up a lot of information on individual citizens and this can be potentially misused to harass individuals or groups. However, the benefits of this system are so great, especially for the poor, that it is a system worth bringing on. We simply have to ensure that we have proper legislation in place to protect the basic rights, including privacy rights, of human beings.

This section discussed at some length how natural market forces can be harnessed by government to design better systems of subsidy delivery. It should be emphasised that the line being taken here is very different from the market fundamentalist one of treating whatever dessert is meted out to people by natural market forces with no government intervention as just dessert. It is worth reiterating that the fact of so much poverty and such wide inequality as exists in our nation is morally unacceptable. In keeping with Aquinas' observation cited earlier in the paper, I take the view that poverty and malnutrition in a society that is growing and has its share of the rich is unacceptable, as is inequality at the level that prevails in India and the world. The poor and malnourished must have unconditional rights that enable them to get out of such a state. Their condition must not be tolerated simply on the ground that it is the outcome of the natural market forces. When such poverty and inequality exist it is incumbent on the government to devise policies to cure these ills. However, and this was the point being made in this chapter, to cure these ills we must not pretend that the market forces do not exist but device policy interventions that utilise these forces to achieve our targets as best as possible.

Mores, morals and development

The argument in the above section may have given the impression that I was making the assumption, common in economics, that all human beings are self-seeking and we have to design our policies keeping this in mind. That was, however, not my argument. The position I take, elaborated at great length in my recent book (Basu, 2011) is somewhat more complicated than that.

On the assumption of human selfishness, I would like to break tradition with mainstream economics. While human beings are self-seeking in many ways, they are also (1) naturally hardwired with altruism and (2) creatures of habit and norms. I shall not comment on (1) here. (The interested reader may consult Basu, 2011.)

The latter, that is, (2), is extremely important and by ignoring it mainstream economics is that much poorer. To understand the design of policy and to think of ways in which we may create a better society, it is essential to appreciate the importance of social norms. Let me illustrate this with a real-life example. In my mother's household in Kolkata, she had an aide called Rakhal (name changed). Send him out to do the shopping, and you would believe that inflation had taken a new leap upwards. He would systematically inflate prices and pocket the balance. However, you could leave valuables scattered all over the home and leave him alone in charge of the home. Not an item would be touched. Rakhal was one of my mother's most trusted helpers. My mother put him fully in charge of the household and not in charge of shopping. She designed the household incentive mechanism right.

It is important to realise that human beings, like Rakhal, are invariably endowed with norms. There are things they will not do even if there is a personal gain to be made there. Moreover, these norms are often societally conditioned. An American shopkeeper will not jump a queue even if he feels he can do so easily and save a lot of his own time. But, on the other hand, he will raise the price of the apples he sells if he feels that he will make money that way.

What is not appreciated by mainstream economics is that some of these self-restraining social norms are critical ingredients of a successful market-based social democracy. Just as we need animal spirits and the entrepreneur's zest for profit for society to grow, we also need norms of self-restraint and other-regarding preferences for an economy to be efficient and for growth to flourish. Qualities like trustworthiness and personal integrity are not just important moral qualities in themselves, the presence of these qualities in a population is important for a democratic society to function effectively.

Economists concerned with the task of promoting economic growth—be it sustainable, inclusive or of any other hue—will tell you how it is essential to get our economic policies right—how we have to get our fiscal house in order, we have to get our monetary policy on target; key economic variables, like the repo, the reverse repo, the CRR and the SLR, have to be handled with judiciousness; and projects have to be undertaken using the best principles of cost-benefit analysis, calculating present values as accurately as possible.

At first sight this seems natural enough. Economic growth must surely depend on economic policy. All the policy measures mentioned in the above paragraph are unquestionably important. But in our concern with these economic variables, it is easy to forget what sounds paradoxical but is true, that economic development does not depend on economic policy alone. There is a close connection between economic growth and social and political variables such as the nation's stock of social capital, the extent and nature of social democracy and even the culture prevalent in the nation. What is not often recognised but is true is that appropriate social norms and capital, and culture are essential pre-requisites for economic development. Markets cannot function properly unless we have the relevant social and political structures and institutions in place. Getting the monetary policy right cannot promote growth if these social preconditions are not in place.

When economists talk in terms of human qualities, such as honesty, altruism and trustworthiness, they treat them as good values to have but of little consequence to economic development and growth. Recent research shows that that is not the case. These moral qualities are not just important in themselves, they are critical for the smooth functioning of an economy and for development. Altruism in a society is not just good in itself but good for development. From cross-country studies to game-theoretic experiments conducted in laboratories, we know that the level of trustworthiness can differ across groups, and groups that have a higher level of trust and trustworthiness do better economically.

That capital is critical to growth has long been appreciated and this has been given a central place in seminal works in economics, such as those by Roy Harrod, Evsey Domar, Robert Solow and Trevor Swan. However, recent research by political scientists, political philosophers and some economists, has drawn our attention to the fact that, while capital is certainly critical for growth, the concept of capital needs to be understood in broader terms than the narrow definition used in conventional economics. In particular, there is the notion of 'social capital', which some societies have in large measure and which they can leverage to create more economic growth.

Thanks to the fact that the academic literature has ignored the importance of these moral qualities, we have not done enough research on how some societies come to acquire these qualities. There is great need to study this, so that, alongside getting our fiscal and monetary policies right, we can build up qualities of altruism, trustworthiness and honesty in society.

What the two previous sections warned us was that to the extent that these qualities are absent in a society, to design policies under the pretence of their presence is to court failure. On the other hand, while designing mechanisms on realistic assumptions concerning the proclivities of the society in question, we must simultaneously work towards building a better society and polity. In brief, what we have ahead of us is not just a policy agenda that comprises economics, society and institutions but also a research agenda that is truly multi-disciplinary.

References

Ahluwalia, Montek Singh (2010). "India's Prospects in the Post-Crisis World", *The 2010 K.R. Narayanan Oration*. Canberra: Australian National University.

Aquinas, Thomas [1265-74] (1911). *Summa Theologica*. Allen, TX: Christian Classics.

Atkinson, Anthony (1995). "Capabilities, Exclusion and the Supply of Goods", in K., Basu, P. Pattanaik and K. Suzumura (eds.), *Choice, Welfare and Development: Essays in Honour of Amartya Sen*. Oxford: Clarendon Press.

Basu, Kaushik (2009). "Famines", in *Encyclopedia Britannica*.

———. (2011). *Beyond the Invisible Hand: Groundwork for a New Economics*. Princeton, N.J.: Princeton University Press and India: Penguin.

Field, Erica and Patrick Nolen (2005). "Race and Performance in Post-Apartheid South Africa", *mimeo*. Cornell University.

Gopal, Sarvapalli and Iyengar (2003). *The Essential Writings of Jawaharlal Nehru*, Volume 1. New Delhi: Oxford University Press.

Himanshu and Abhijit Sen (2011). "Why Not a Universal Food Security Legislation", *mimeo*. New Delhi: Planning Commission.

Hoff, Karla and Priyanka Pandey (2006). "Persistent Effects of Discrimination and the Role of Social Identity", *American Economic Review* 96.

Jha, Shikha and Bharat Ramaswamy (2011). "How Can Food Subsidies Work Better? Answers from India and the Philippines", *Asian Development Bank Working Paper* 221.1

Khera, Reetika (2011). "India's Public Distribution System: Utilization and Impact", *Journal of Development Studies*, forthcoming.

Nilekani, Nandan (2008). *Imagining India: Ideas for a New Century*. London: Penguin.

Nussbaum, Martha (2008). "Toward a Globally Sensitive Patriotism", *Daedalus* 137 (Summer).

Rangarajan Committee (2008). *Report of the Committee on Financial Inclusion*. New Delhi: PMEAC.

Sen, Amartya (1973). *On Economic Inequality*. Oxford: Clarendon Press.

Srinivas, M.N. (1976). *The Remembered Village*. Oxford: Oxford University Press.

Acknowledgements. The paper was presented at the Indira Gandhi Conference in New Delhi, 19-21 November, 2010. It was a remarkably vibrant conference. As a consequence, by the time my turn came to speak, what I presented was different from what I had intended to present and had been written up in a long abstract. Subsequently, when writing this up as a paper, I made numerous further changes. These were in response to the discussion and debate that occurred over the two-and-a-half days. I hope this is a better paper as a consequence and I am grateful to the participants of the conference for their many comments and suggestions. For research assistance I am grateful to Supriyo De.

23

NITIN DESAI

Social Democracy and Environmental Protection

Nearly 40 years ago, at the Stockholm Conference Mrs Indira Gandhi posed the question "are not poverty and need the greatest polluters?" She went on to argue that "the inherent conflict is not between conservation and development" but "between environment and the reckless exploitation of man and earth in the name of efficiency".[1] At that time, nearly 40 years ago, she was the only head of government, other than Olaf Palme, the prime minister of the host country Sweden, to attend the Conference. Her participation demonstrated her commitment to environmental protection. The question she posed reflected her faith in social democracy. This paper argues that the two goals are entirely compatible and, in fact, reinforce one another.

Conceptual connections

Environmental problems arise precisely when there is some injustice. An industrial plant spews out noxious pollutants into the atmosphere or water because it does not have to bear the costs of ill health borne by those who have to breath the foul air, drink the polluted water and live with the toxic hazards. The run-offs from fields on which chemical fertilisers and pesticides have been used are also a similar type of injustice. Those who are upstream in a production or consumption process that uses a natural resource can pass on costs and consequences to those who are downstream. In a metaphorical sense the same upstream/downstream relationship

1. Gandhi (1984).

holds when one generation passes on costs to those who are not yet born in the form of long term wastes, resource depletion and endangered ecosystems.

Social democracy is an idea that is also rooted in the idea of justice and fairness. But the concern with social justice in social democracy is not just about deprivation, low living standards and income poverty. It is also about vulnerability when a natural disaster or a severe illness can throw a family that was just about coping into the ranks of the poor. It is about discrimination on the basis of some accident of birth, be it caste, religion or ethnicity. It is about marginalisation in the political process. Environmental stress connects with every one of these elements of the poverty syndrome.

Deprivation, low productivity and income poverty are more likely in ecologically fragile regions if subsistence agriculture remains the main source of livelihood. Drought-prone and desert areas, coastal areas affected by salinity, hilly regions, are typical examples. This may not show up in the statistics like consumption surveys, because the coping strategies of the poor may well include seasonal or long term out migration. The resulting remittances may allow a higher standard of living at the cost of the social anomie of separated families.

Vulnerability is even more directly connected with environmental stresses. The poor who live in ecologically fragile regions are in any case more exposed to the usual variations in weather that lead to storm surges and saline intrusions in coastal areas, droughts in dry areas, landslides caused by heavy rains in hill areas and so on. Environmental changes like deforestation and climate change increase these risks of instability of livelihoods, vulnerability of habitats and may even threaten survival. The issue of whether these changes are man-made or natural in their origin is of little interest to the people affected. If land in the coastal areas of the Sunderbans is being lost to the sea, those who live on that land have to cope regardless of whether the cause is climate change induced sea-level rise or the normal processes of delta subsidence.

Vulnerability also connects with poverty because in villages and towns the poor are forced to live in flood-plains of rivers, marshy coastal lands exposed to frequent water logging, congested urban slums with inadequate drainage and water supply and shanty towns on the fringes of rail lines.

Discrimination is an important aspect of the forces that push the poor into vulnerable situations. Thus communities who have been at the receiving end of caste discrimination because of the nature of their traditional occupation, for instance scavengers and leather workers, are pushed into areas at the fringe of the village, often far from the better drained central core. This not-in-my backyard attitude also drives them to environmentally stressed areas like Dharavi (in Mumbai). The essential point is that these communities are driven into vulnerable areas not just because they are poor but also because they are discriminated against in the social system.

The poor are at the receiving end of environmental stress because they wield little influence in the political process at local, provincial or national level. If they were less marginal in the political process and more organised to voice their interests they would be able to secure greater equity in how the burden of environmental stress is distributed. A social democratic political movement that seeks to alleviate their poverty and vulnerability and fight against discrimination is in fact a plus point for environmental ends.

The belief that the two goals of social democracy and environmental protection could come into conflict rests on the way the two connect with the idea of economic growth. The social democratic agenda needs economic growth, because only that can generate the resources needed to provide a good life for the multitudes deprived of it today. Growth also reduces the need for drastic redistribution which is not possible without the type of revolutionary violence that social democracy seeks to avoid because such violence would inevitably threaten democratic freedoms.

Economic growth necessarily involves the exploitation of natural resources and the emission of pollutants that threaten the integrity of the environment. The environmental movement has had a strand of thought that questions the merits of growth and argues for limits to growth. This is based more on the situation in the richer countries where the ecological footprint of consumption is well above the global average, which, now, in turn, is above the earth's bio-capacity. [2]

The situation in India and other developing countries is radically different. A large proportion of the population lacks access to the basic minimum of goods and services needed for human dignity. The per capita ecological footprint is well below the global average.[3] It is also clear, that leaving people in a state of poverty and deprivation will not protect the environment. Hence, in a poor society, growth and development are necessary even for environmental protection, a link that is captured in the concept of sustainable development.

There is a certain parallelism between the concept of social democracy and that of sustainable development. Justice is at the core of both concepts with the first focusing on justice here and now and the second on inter-generational equity. In fact one can capture this connection with a pair of matching definitions:

- Sustainable Development: Meeting the needs of the present generation without compromising the ability of future generations to meet their needs.[4]
- Social Democracy: Meeting the needs of the deprived without compromising the freedoms of all.

The formulation of the definitions implies that the first term in each definition, meeting needs of the present generation/meeting the needs of the deprived, is the objective and the subsequent term is the constraint on how the objective should be met. Clearly the objectives of social democracy and sustainable development are compatible. The difference of emphasis is in the constraint, with

---

2. This is based on the calculations of ecological footprint published in Worldwide Fund for Nature, *The Living Planet Report 2010*, Gland, Switzerland, 2010. The calculations work out the hectares required to meet the consumption demand for cropland, grazing land, forest land, built-up land and an equivalent for fishing grounds and for carbon absorption. The result is expressed in hectares per capita per year. The calculations for 2007 presented in the 2010 Report indicate that the global average footprint is 2.7 hectares as against the available bio capacity of 1.8 hectares, a deficit of 0.9 hectares per capita. The per capita footprint of the high income countries is 6.1 hectares, of the middle income countries, 2.0 hectares, of the low income countries 1.2 hectares. India's per capita ecological footprint was 0.9 hectares.
3. See footnote 2 above.
4. This is the definition in the World Commission on Environment and Development, *Our Common Future*, Oxford University Press, 1987 (The Brundtland Report).

one recognising the needs of future generations and the other on the preservation of democratic freedoms.

The two concepts have something else in common. They are an attempt to build a bridge between epistemic communities that are separated by a river of distrust. Thus, social democracy seeks to connect those who wish to use the power of the state to correct injustices with those whose primary concern is the protection of democratic freedoms. Sustainable development tries to connect ecologists and environmentalists who wish to protect eco-system integrity with development theorists and practitioners interested in accelerating economic growth and human welfare. Both concepts provide a language which allows a dialogue between these communities of practice. The difficulty sometimes is that, like many bridges, the communities on both shores, treat it as the other shore's attempt to encroach on its territory!

The political dimension

The dialogue between the partisans of social democracy and of environmental activism has to take place in the plane of politics as both are essentially movements for the mobilisation of people for change, Environmental activism comes in many political flavours. When the agenda is about conservation, with a focus on sanctuaries to protect species (pandas, tigers, rare butterflies, orchids, etc.), the political flavour is of the right, with many supporters from the ranks of the old aristocracy. This is an agenda that is now largely obsolete and many who started at this end have moved on to a much wider set of concerns.

A broader agenda that attracts support from both sides of the political spectrum is one that seeks to restrain the mining of nature for short term profit. The support from the right often comes from conservationists and from the left from those who are concerned about the impact that such resource mining has on people's livelihood and health. This agenda acquires a more leftist political flavour when it starts talking about people's rights to resources, to good health, to a voice in corporate and governmental decisions.

All of these flavours are present in India. But from the point of view of making common cause with the partisans for social democracy, the most relevant environmentalists are those whose agenda focuses on the impact of environmental stress on livelihoods and health, on the resource rights of poor and marginalised people and the importance of people's participation in resource management.

The anti-poverty and environment agendas can be brought together quite readily on a broad social democratic platform as long as the focus is on national action on immediate problems, on the here and now, so to speak. But this imposes limitations of geography and time frame that have to be addressed.

Social democracy is a political movement and its geography is the geography of political action, which is essentially national and local. But ecosystems do not respect political boundaries. Disease carrying parasites do not need passports. The wind and the flowing waters that carry pollutants do not stop at border check points. Hence, the geography of environmental action has to look beyond national and local political boundaries.

The time frame of social democracy will necessarily be defined by the time frame of democratic politics which is often very short term. Many environmental issues require a long view stretching decades ahead. They involve protecting the interests of those who are not yet born and whose voice or vote cannot be heard in today's decision-making processes.

The conflict between the compulsions of the here and now and the longer term can be seen in stark relief in the issue of climate change. The threat of climate change is very real; but the most adverse effects will be seen many decades into the future. The costs of mitigating the risk however have to be borne now. Waiting till the harmful consequences are more imminent will raise enormously the costs of adjustment. In effect, the present generation is being called upon to bear certain costs to reduce the risks of a future generation having to bear very much higher costs. A further complication is the global nature of the process so that politically complex questions about historical liability and current responsibility have to be resolved.

It could be argued that the costs of immediate mitigation measures like promoting high cost solar power and in, the medium term, the costs of adaptation to climate change for instance in protecting coastal zones, will eat into resources required for social programmes with more immediate benefits. To place this argument in context Figure 23.1 presents an estimate of the costs of carbon mitigation in India prepared by McKinsey & Co. This estimate shows that the initial round of abatement would actually have a negative cost, that is, it would deliver benefits in the form of cost savings that would justify the expenditure even if there were no carbon benefit. Beyond that several of the positive cost measures like afforestation have collateral benefits beyond carbon sequestration that are desirable.

The challenge for social democracy is how to factor in a global and intergenerational dimension including climate change into its current dynamic. The global or transnational dimension requires a measure of social democracy in global politics. This can come from some extension of the principles of a welfare state to the international level, an idea whose elaboration is beyond the scope of this paper. The longer-term view that environmental activism demands can become a part of social democracy's political platform if it can be integrated into the development agenda which constitutes the core of this platform.

The development dimension

The prospects for the integration of the social democratic and environmental agendas can start at either end. The goals and concerns that provide the starting point for programme design for anti-poverty and for environmental programmes do differ as is illustrated in the matrix below:

	Anti-poverty Programmes	*Environmental Protection*
Water/Energy	Access	Ecosystem balance
Mineral Resources	Displacement	Depletion
Forests/Land	Rights of the poor	Conservation/Rehabilitation

Figure 23.1

India's Abatement Cost Curve for 2030 (Cost below EUR 100/tonne)

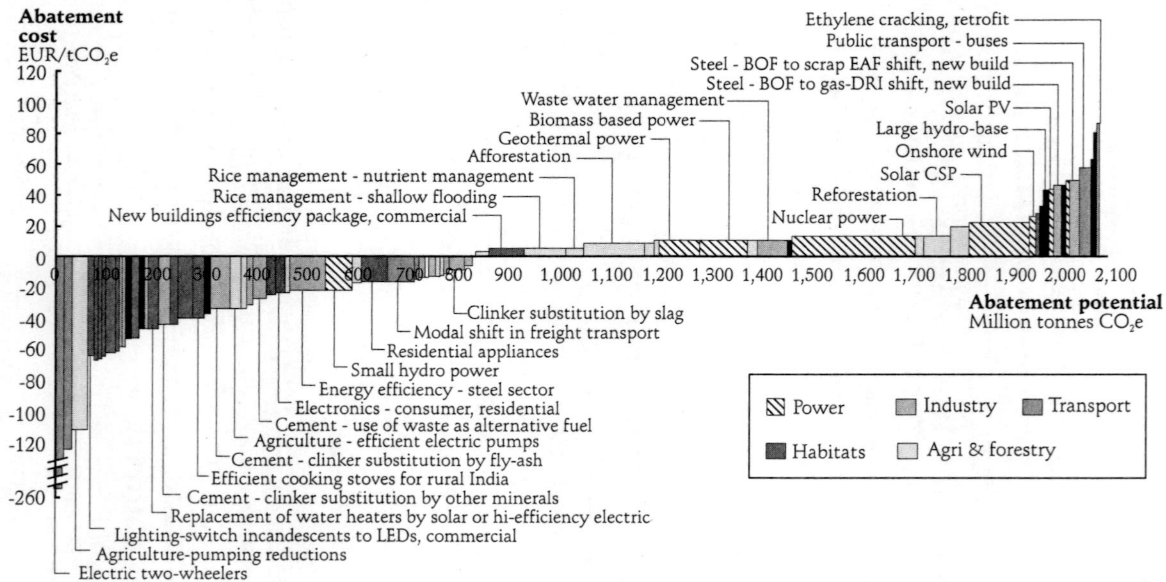

Note: 1. This curve highlights 2.1 billion tonnes CO_2e of potential. Additional potential below Euro 100/tonne includes reduction in technical T&D losses (190 million tonnes CO_2e (mt), auxiliary consumption (~50 mt), efficiency improvement in other sector (~200 mt), improved urban planning (~30 mt), and distributed generation using combined heat and power (CHP) (~15 mt).

2. Levers costing above EUR 100/tonne (not included in the cost curve) have a total abatement potential of 80 mt. Important levers are public transport infrastructure (metors) (7 mt), electric vehicles and full hybrids (6 mt).

3. 8 per cent discount rate assumed for the cost curve analysis, based on benchmark yield for long-term Indian government bonds.

Source: McKinsey India Cost Curve Model.

These differences in the starting point does not mean that the two sets of concerns have to remain separated in distinct programmes. Such an approach will merely extend the environment-development clash to the programmatic level. The real challenge is to get each set of actors to recognise the relevance for their agenda of the other's concerns. One could start from the categories that define environmental concerns like climate change, air and water quality, bio-diversity and so on and graft development imperatives into programmes designed for these purposes. Or one could start from development concerns and add an environmental dimension to these. The latter is the track chosen here on the ground that public policy in India will start always from development imperatives.

The primary developmental concern from the perspective of social justice is clearly poverty eradication which would cover income generation, access to basic services, improved health and education opportunities. From the perspective of sustainable development and environmental security, the main challenge is to connect these goals with better resource and environmental management. In what follows, this paper spells out what integrating these two sets of concerns means for programme design in four areas. The first is the link between anti-poverty and resource management in rural development plans and the second carries this story forward into decentralised environmental management. The third area involves the difficult and contentious issue of land acquisition and mega projects. The fourth shifts the emphasis to urban areas which will increasingly become the space where the challenge of social justice and environmental management will have to be faced.

(a) Linking anti-poverty and area development programmes

In rural areas the most important task is to recognise that poverty eradication and resource conservation can be mutually supportive. In fact sustained improvements in rural living standards and employment requires that the conservation of the natural resources, land, water, forests, fishing grounds, on which people depend for their livelihood. The reverse of this argument is also valid. A resource cannot be protected by denying access to it to people who need it for earning their livelihood. Hence, household-oriented anti-poverty programmes must include provisions for resource management and, in turn, area oriented resource management programmes must include differential support for poor households.

In India we have both types of programmes. Anti-poverty programmes are largely target group oriented and deliver subsidies in one form or another to BPL households. We also have area-oriented resource management programmes for instance for dryland and desert areas, for hill areas and for forests. These two types of programmes need to be brought together. Poverty stricken households may be the target group in both types of programmes, but the planning should be built around the concept of sustainable livelihoods, starting first with the existing activity base of these households. The NREGA is a little different in that it is an area-oriented programme that delivers work rather than a subsidy. It can help to link anti-poverty and area development programmes if it is used creatively to provide the local infrastructure needed for supporting sustainable livelihoods.

One dimension of this that is of particular importance both for development and for environmental management is rural energy supply, a matter which rarely receives attention in typical anti-poverty programmes. This acquires a special salience in the light of the concerns about climate change that are now so large a part of the environmental agenda. In fact, in India certain forms of renewable energy, like bio-gas and even off-grid solar, were promoted more to meet rural energy needs than for carbon reduction. This logic remains valid and climate change provides an additional reason for promoting these rural energy options.

Water is another important element in the link between anti-poverty programmes and environmental management. The key goal here is the fair management of emerging scarcities. With rising demands and wasteful use, freshwater shortages, seasonal or endemic, are evident in the lives of the Indians who live in the one-sixth of the country that is prone to chronic droughts. With rising population and increases in industrial and urban demands the experience of scarcity is now much more widespread. Water is becoming a marketable commodity subject to private appropriation and private profit. Efficiency is essential for managing scarcity; but so is equity. That is why water management has to look beyond market principles to social responsibility.

The role of water is also strategic in that in the process of managing water communities are forced to get many other things right as well. If we economise on water use and ensure safe drainage, the environment is protected. If the use of water for irrigation and industrial uses is optimised, economic advancement is promoted. Where water is scarce share it equitably and social justice is ensured. Maintain and improve water quality and good health follows. In this sense water is a strategic resource for development and one could argue that the key to the linkage between anti-poverty and resource management that we seek can be secured by getting water management right at the local level.

There is a broader issue of justice that is central to the role of water in development. The water that we use may come from or through our neighbour's property, so also what we dispose off as waste and this is true at the local, regional and national level. Hence, we have to cooperate at all levels in managing the use of water and its drainage.

The health dimension of poverty is closely connected to environmental issues like water availability and quality, indoor air quality (closely connected with the issue of rural energy supply mentioned above) and control of communicable diseases, many of which are vector borne and linked to local environmental conditions. Often it is the poorest households who are most vulnerable because of where they are forced to live or because they lack adequate access to safe water and sanitation. Hence, local environmental management has to be seen as part of the drive to improve the quality of life for poor people. Better health, besides being a necessary goal in its own right, also has beneficial effects on the ability to work and on productivity. Improvements in water supply, sanitation, energy availability have been shown to have a beneficial effect on school attendance, particularly by girls.

(b) Decentralisation of programmatic responsibilities

The management of an environmental resource or issue requires a certain coherence between national policies and local implementation. All resource management is ultimately local. But the capacities required for this and the authority necessary for effective action are seldom available at the local level.

Development administration has been decentralised for quite some time now. Local capacities for project and programme formulation, monitoring, coordination around critical development goals have been built up over the six decades of planned development. There could be some doubts about the quality of skills and effectiveness of institutions. But the basic structure is in place. This is not the case for environmental management. Forest and irrigation departments and other offices charged with resource management responsibilities do have a local presence; but the orientation of these is towards production enhancement and not necessarily towards environmental management. In other areas like air and water quality management the tasks are relatively new and much of the capacity available is at higher levels. But action is required at the local level and that is where public capacity needs to be strengthened.

The strengthening of public capacity to manage the environment at the local level can be done through the promotion of local capacity for primary environmental care. This local capacity has to be designed as the first point of a system for:

- monitoring the environment (air, water and land quality, local flora and fauna, eco-system integrity, etc.),
- ensuring observance by local enterprises of norms set by legislation (emission and waste management standards, chemical safety standards, etc.),
- providing referral services for environmentally sound technology to local enterprises,
- providing early warning of impending environmental problems, coordinating the relevant local activities of line departments (land and agriculture, forests, fisheries, transport, energy, industry, etc.),

- providing a space for public participation in environmental management and for addressing local environmental disputes.

The primary environmental care centre could perform these functions for the state and central departments that are charged with the responsibility for the implementation of the relevant laws or programmes. The *panchayati raj* system can provide the structure for this decentralisation. Environmental stress affects people's lives very directly. Natural resources loom large in local politics. Responsibilities for development programmes are already decentralised. Hence, the proposal here for local environmental care capacity will strengthen the pressure for a better integration of environment and development at the local level. Episodes like what happened in Nandigram and Niyamgiri, where local sentiments surfaced late in the approval process may well be avoided if the local level plays a role in decision-making at the first rather than at the last stage.

Some of the line departments and programmes at the state and central level may also need reorientation. An important instance of this is the injection of an eco-system management orientation in planning for land use, water resource development, forest management and support systems for agriculture and related activities. Line departments and programmes dealing with these are often organised around schemes for specific crops or products, or inputs, or functional specialisations. An eco-system orientation means that the organising principle should be to group functions, personnel and resources according to eco-systems like dryland, deserts, uplands, etc., and frame all interventions as integrated plans for these.

(c) Land acquisition, displacement and ecological protection[5]

The reconciliation of land rights and development is perhaps the greatest test for the idea of social democracy in India today. Many cases of large-scale land acquisition for mega-projects end up in agitations and court cases. These conflicts and differences

5. This section draws heavily on Desai (2006; 2007).

over land acquisition frequently involve both environmental and social concerns as the areas involved are often ecologically fragile and the people displaced, poor and powerless. The difficulties that have attended some recent projects in forest areas with a large tribal population illustrate how the two sets of concerns come together.

The issue is sometimes seen as the need to avoid the loss of cultivable lands. Cultivable and uncultivable lands coexist side-by-side wherever there is a settled population. Even so-called wastelands are used by local people for firewood or grazing or fodder. Large stretches of uncultivable land would be available only in reserved forests, which, in any case are out of bounds, or in remote desert and mountain areas quite unsuitable for mega projects.

From the perspective of social justice the central issue is not the encroachment on land for agriculture but the displacement of people.[6] Almost all of these people are involuntary displacees because we relied for far too long on the Land Acquisition Act of 1894. This allows the government to exercise the right of eminent domain for compulsorily acquiring private lands for a public purpose, which, it must be noted, is a major departure from market principles. The Act is silent on what constitutes public purpose and has been used to acquire land for commercial projects on the argument that there would be some collateral generation of public benefit like food security or employment or self reliance. The record of resettlement and rehabilitation of the persons displaced is abysmal.

This colonial procedure is now under review and a new approach is being established that relies more on negotiated purchase of land and substantial improvements in the resettlement and rehabilitation. From the point of view of social justice the important point is to recognise that large scale land acquisition for development will disrupt the life of some functioning community and of all who live in it, not just the land-owners. In fact the ones worst affected will be the share croppers and labourers, the petty

6. The numbers displaced by development projects in post independence India are not known because the government has not released any reliable figures on this. Informed estimates put the number at 40 to 50 million persons.

traders and service providers. These landless ones do not even have a juridical basis for compensation if the transaction is seen simply as a sale of land, voluntary or compulsory.

Large scale land acquisition, which affects a whole village or more, has to be treated as a transaction between the corporate or public buyer and the community and not just as a transaction with individual land owners. That is the only way we can take into account the interests of those who lose not land but livelihood. It will also allow the community to assert its interest in common properties and heritage which would be lost in a set of individualised transactions.

What we need is a procedure similar to what we have in collective bargaining in labour relations. One possibility is to have Land Purchase Act that would apply to any large scale purchase of land by a commercial entity. The Act would specify a process for negotiation between the buyer and the affected community including a procedure for determining who can speak for and negotiate on behalf of the affected community. It must strike a balance between community and individual land-rights for instance by specifying the minimum proportion of rights holders who have to assent to the terms negotiated. It must include an obligation to provide alternatives to those whose livelihoods are lost. The state will have a role, as it does in labour relations, as an arbiter of last resort.

The essential point is that we move beyond compensation to ensuring that the affected community shares in the gains from development. This can be done in many different ways. For mineral development, the answer may lie in providing a share in the royalty to the local community. In other cases, the corporate buyer could assign equity in the project or pay for the transfer of development rights. For infrastructure development, the public authorities can use land adjustment schemes that aggregate a large tract of land, say for transport development, use some part for the infrastructure and return the rest in agreed proportion to the original owners, who can then cash the capital gains in any way they wish.[7]

---

7. There is an example near Pune in the Magarpatta development where the land owners themselves got together and planned a development that is becoming a major township.

Mega-projects that involve the use of large tracts of land inevitably lead to large scale changes in land use. This may involve the loss of forest cover, threats to rare species, major disruptions of hydrological regimes and other ecological changes that may threaten livelihood and health and cultural values in the project area and elsewhere. When these broader environmental and social effects are taken into account, many who are not necessarily residents of the project area itself are also in effect stakeholders and their interests have to be taken on board in the procedures for environmental clearance.

These environmental and ecological concerns have usually been articulated by activist NGOs and academics who may not have any formal contractual rights but whose expression of public interest has been recognised as relevant by many courts. The challenge here is to specify an efficient procedure for public hearing and clear rules on the right to information so that there is a greater sensitivity to the ecosystem impact.

In theory the rights of the community to benefit from land use changes and the rights of a wider set of people to environmental protection may clash. It must be noted though that most of the recent cases of large scale land acquisition have involved not a clash but a congruence of interests between the local community and the environmental activists. The theoretical possibility of a clash between the desires of the local community and the compulsions of environmental protection can be handled by a fair system of compensation for denial of development rights.

A broader objection to the approach advocated here is that it would increase the costs of mineral exploitation and industrial and infrastructure development. This is a specious argument. If such developments are unable to bear the costs of compensating local communities fairly or protecting the environment to preserve options for future generations then it is best not to undertake them. In reality these plaints about high costs are arguments for a hidden subsidy from the displaced community and from those who will bear the consequences of environmental deterioration to corporations and other large investors or, to put it more starkly, from the poor and the powerless to the rich and the powerful.

(d) Urban development

According to the UN population projections the absolute size of the rural population will start declining by 2025-2030 and by 2050 it will be 125 million less than now. This reduction in the pressure of people on the habitat will make both development and environment management in rural India an easier task.

The urban population will grow continuously and be 525 million larger in 2050. The numbers would look even larger if we were to include many peri-urban villages that are classified as rural in the census. The counterpart of the declining rural population is the occupational shift from traditional activities which may involve some 200 million people. This will imply a massive change in the urban rural distribution and the pace of urbanisation may be even more rapid than the trend projections, particularly in the Northern states of UP, Bihar, Rajasthan, Madhya Pradesh and Jharkhand. It is in these urban areas that India will face the greatest challenges both for social justice and for environmental management.

The scale of effort required to cope with the projected growth in urban population is quite stupendous. Take for instance the provision of mass transit. Delhi is planning nearly 400 km. of metro and bus rapid transit corridors. The McKinsey projection[8] or the country as a whole calls for 7400 km. by 2030—a bit like putting up the equivalent of a Delhi Metro per year! We have not yet begun the effort required to cope with three key challenges—the functioning of urban land markets, the financing of massive infrastructure investments and the reform of municipal governance.

In some ways the land management challenge is the crucial one. Our present system is based on large scale public ownership of land and tight planning controls on the operation of private land markets. In practice this, pushes the poor into slums. Private developers are pushed to peri-urban villages on the edge of the controlled leading to an urban sprawl that taxes the infrastructure to breaking point. Urban development requires the assembly of large tracts of land by private or public entities. It also requires

8. McKinsey Global Institute (2010).

transport and infrastructure investments that lead rather than follow the geographical evolution of the city. The vexed issue of land acquisition can be tackled by a wider use of land adjustment schemes. Typically these involve the developer negotiating an agreement with land owners who part with their land for redevelopment and get back some agreed proportion which they can then cash in any way they wish.

The greatest challenge for social justice is for living space and some minimal standards of water supply and sanitation. In urban areas, where living space is commercialised, a poorly functioning land market and inadequate or poorly conceived public interventions in this market, pushes the poor into slums and unauthorised colonies.

The greater part of urban India lives in cities that people have made for themselves rather than in precincts nicely planned by urban authorities or developers. For most of them water supply is already privatised and they buy their requirements from tankers often run by local political bigwigs. Sanitation is what nature provides. This is where we will face the most challenging environmental problems and where we will see the worst of the inequities that bedevil our society. If there is one place the agenda for social democracy and for environment come together it is in the slums and unauthorised colonies of our cities.

We need a programme that guarantees every urban dweller with a package of basic minimum needs that would certainly include living space, water and sanitation. We will not be able to do this with master plans and bureaucratic controls to implement them, which frankly lead not to better cities but to corruption. Planners must learn to work with incoming migrants and other poor city dwellers and work with them to improve water, drainage, health, safety and housing quality.

We also need to look more closely at city form to see how we can reduce the environmental footprint of city transport in terms of carbon and other emissions and in terms of reduced congestion. Many of our cities are a mixture of densely packed old cities, surrounded by cantonment type low density areas and new higher density areas of organised and unorganised development. This generates a huge transport load, particularly for poor people who are pushed to the outer fringes of the city where land is less valuable.

We need to move towards compact cities with high densities and high rise where needed. This will reduce pressure on agricultural land, involve shorter travel distances and can be walking and cycling friendly. There are huge social benefits from proximity of work, residence and leisure, particularly for poor people. The greater localisation of services, work places and businesses reduces infrastructure cost. High and well distributed densities will also allow affordable public transport and help to contain high infrastructure costs.

Concluding words

The programmatic areas identified above do not exhaust the substance of either the social democratic or the environmental agenda, which will include many elements that are not covered by the activities envisaged as part of these programmes. Nor are the linkages entirely absent in these excluded activities. Thus, to take an example, environmental action on chemical hazards has an anti-poverty dimension since it is usually the poor who are most exposed because of where they are forced to live. Yet another example is the social democratic agenda on access to education which can be linked to environmental awareness. But inter-connection between the two agendas in these instances is perhaps less compelling than in the four programme areas elaborated above.

The social democratic and environmental agendas have one big thing in common—they challenge existing power structures. Each of them has a capacity to mobilise people around goals and related campaigns. They articulate voices that are not always heard in the corridors of power. A clearer and more explicit link between the two agendas would add strength to each group's political base. Hence, the greatest need is for a substantive agenda that can provide a basis for a stronger political coalition of environmental and social activists.

The four areas elaborated in this paper—integrating anti-poverty and area development schemes, decentralising environmental management, linking justice and environment effectively in land acquisition and displacement of people and a change in the pattern of urban development—can provide a basis for combining the political activism of environmentalists and social democrats. The four programme areas provide what could be described as a common minimum programme for social justice and sustainable development. This was implicitly what Mrs Indira Gandhi asked for in Stockholm and this is what we need if we are to meet that demand.

References

Gandhi, Indira (1984). "Man and Environment (Plenary Session of UNCHE, 14 June 1972)", in *Indira Gandhi on Environment*. New Delhi: Department of Environment, Government of India. p.23.

Desai, Nitin (2006). "Land for Infrastructure", *Business Standard*, April 20.

———. (2007). "Land Rights and Development", *Business Standard*, January 18.

McKinsey Global Institute (2010). *India's Urban Awakening: Building Inclusive Cities, Sustaining Economic Growth*. April.

Section III(a) contd...

The Political Economy of Social Democracy

PRESENTATIONS • DISCUSSIONS

This section presents the proceedings of the Third Session of the Tenth Indira Gandhi Conference, November 19-21, 2010, New Delhi.

Chair
- Nemat Shafik

Presentations
- Vijay Kelkar
- Kaushik Basu
- Nitin Desai

Discussants
- Nandan Nilekani
- Pranab Bardhan
- Sri Mulyani Indrawati
- Jamshyd N. Godrej
- Kumar Mangalam Birla
- Chanda Kochhar
- Joseph Stiglitz
- Erik Solheim
- Montek Singh Ahluwalia
- Jean Drèze
- Joakim Palme
- Sunita Narain
- Aruna Roy
- Vijay Kelkar
- Kaushik Basu
- Nitin Desai

24

NEMAT SHAFIK

Introductory Remarks

It is a real honour for me to chair this session. My name is Nemat Shafik, also known as Minouche. I have a special affinity for India because I have gone through my entire life assuming I was Indian. In fact, my parents and my family hailed from another ancient country—Egypt. But since I've been treated as an Indian all my life, I believe I have a special connection.

This session is on political economy. It's about who counts, who gets what and what gets counted. The three papers by Vijay Kelkar, Kaushik Basu and Nitin Desai look at the issue from different perspectives. They ask about the resources needed to fulfil social democratic ambitions, the trade-offs and compromises between growth, taxation, and basic service delivery and social protection. How does one reconcile social democracy with sustainability?

There are three themes that I want to draw out and which also come out quite clearly in these papers. One is compromise; the second is incentives and the third is living within one's means. The importance of compromise is obvious between different social groups as they negotiate social democratic projects. There is the issue of incentives and of managing them for citizens, taxpayers, entrepreneurs, government officials and especially for politicians. Living within our means pertains to both the fiscal means as well as natural resources.

I shall say something very briefly about each of those themes. First, on compromise; I thought I'd draw a little on the UK experience. As all of us know, the UK at the moment has its first coalition government in decades. This is a huge break from the winner-takes-all politics that has dominated the UK for much of its history. It has been fascinating to watch politicians learn the art of compromise within the government. They have had to make some difficult compromises in the context of the spending review and the fiscal adjustment the UK has had to make recently. One view of the situation the UK faces is that they wanted a Swedish-style welfare state paying US rates of taxation. One can't reconcile the social democratic ambitions of Sweden with US taxation rates. The implications of that is one of the largest fiscal deficits currently in the world—12 per cent of the GDP and cuts of 81 billion pounds, which means that every single organ of government will have to be cut by between 20 to 30 per cent over the next four years. Every part of society will be affected by those cuts. There are job losses in the pubic sector, pay freezes have been imposed, pensions and welfare payments are being cut, university fees are being raised and even the defence budget has been slashed. So there really are across-the-board cuts.

Now it is interesting to see what has been protected. There are two organs of government spending that have been protected—the National Health Service, spending on which has been kept flat in real terms, and the International Development Budget, which is what I manage. It is interesting to ask how this happened. The International Development Budget isn't merely being kept flat; it's actually increasing by 36 per cent, the only government budget that is increasing in these incredibly difficult fiscal times.

How has this happened? Isn't it remarkable that a Conservative government in a time of incredible fiscal difficulty protects only one thing—the International Development Budget? Of course, it is an interesting case of an alliance between civil society and NGOs, which, as mentioned earlier, is a very powerful force. An alliance between civil society and progressive politicians can work together to mobilise the public. That makes it interesting; it's not just an elite project, but increasingly, it has got much wider public support. I spoke to a Conservative MP recently, admittedly from North Oxford, who said that her mailbag was full of letters on global poverty and international development. This was the topic on which she got the maximum letters from her constituency.

What an extraordinary phenomenon! Of course, there has been controversy and criticism, with some newspapers, especially the right-wing tabloid press, saying that "charity begins at home", to which politicians counter that charity begins at home but doesn't end there. Progressive politicians are also saying that we won't balance our books on the backs of the poorest people in the world. We have a very interesting example of a set of compromises that ended up in a very progressive place in very unlikely circumstances.

We shall also say something about incentives. I wanted to draw on the example of Brazil, because I think it is particularly appropriate, given that President Lula has just been awarded the Indira Gandhi Prize, for the huge progress he has made in terms of equality in Brazil. As many of us may know, Brazil has been one of the most unequal societies in the world. The introduction of the cash transfer schemes has contributed to the reduction of at least a third of the poverty in Brazil in the recent period. The decline has been very dramatic. Twenty-eight (28) per cent of people in Brazil were below the poverty line in 2003, and only five years later, which is nothing in economic historical time, it had fallen to 17 per cent. So we have more than a 10 per cent rate of drop in the rate of poverty in just five years.

The question is: how did Lula create the incentives to make this social transfer happen in a society as divided as Brazil? He used some very clever incentives. He persuaded the elites, who were concerned about the undeserving poor, by making the transfers conditional, which made them politically more palatable. Families had to send their children to school and health clinics to make it acceptable. Also, they had incredibly rigorous evaluation of the impacts of their programmes, so they could persuade the public that these cash transfers had very direct consequences for reducing poverty and improving the lives of poor people. Therefore, this combination of incentives, packaging and measurement was significant enough to persuade the elite to contribute to this social democratic project.

The last point I wish to make is on living within one's means, which many of the papers also draw on. Many people feel that in the recent period, we've strained our financial and environmental means, and as always, the poor are the worst hit. The financial crisis has increased poverty across the world, and certainly, environmental degradation hits the poorest the most. Seventy-five (75) per cent of the poor depend on natural resources for their livelihood. In India, that number is very huge—352 million people depend directly on natural resources. The degradation of those resources has consequences on health; a fifth of all diseases in the developing world are because of environmental health risks. It also has consequences for people's livelihoods.

In that sense, it's quite exciting that India is going to be the first country to publish a new set of national accounts to track natural wealth alongside GDP. As we all know, what gets measured gets acted upon. That, I think, is quite an interesting example of trying to get people to live within their means by being much more creative about what gets measured and therefore, what are the political debates and compromises made around.

25

PRESENTATION BY VIJAY KELKAR

Indian Social Democracy

The Resource Perspective

I started my career under former Prime Minister Mrs Indira Gandhi and wish to utilise this opportunity to pay my tribute to one of India's great prime ministers.

We have had a fascinating discussion on the theory of social democracy. I wish to focus more on political economy, which Manish Sabharwal described as the plumbing of the problems and not their poetry.

Social democracy is one of the key constructs of political economy in the 20th century and I have little doubt that this is India's future. There are a number of defining characteristics of social democracy. For me personally, the Scandinavian social model is really what one could aspire for in this country and in my paper, I attempt modestly to map a possible powerful transition towards the future. I will focus on the resources issue. This is a joint paper with my younger colleague professor Ajay Shah, who is a professor at the National Institute of Public Finance. It is still a work in progress, and so you may treat this as tentative preliminary views. I will be grateful for your reactions to improve upon it.

The other limitation is that the title of the paper is 'Resource Perspective', which only focuses on fiscal resources. There are many other resources that are very important but we have taken only the fiscal part of it. This really has to do with the fiscal resources to transition towards the Scandinavian or Swedish model of social democracy. At the present stage, a large fraction of our people live a very different life and better functioning is of critical importance in improving the lives of the people, both through impact on everyday life through public goods and also through private GDP growth. In terms of the central task of the government, we feel that the most important things at the present are effective legal protection, defence and internal security, efficient supply of public goods, education, public health and environment. Policy towards reduction in maximum number of risks and income transfers to people below the poverty line and towards reduction in transaction costs also have to be considered. The key task faced by the new economic reforms today is that of a state apparatus which can deliver these functions efficiently, the required resources being obtained in a non-distortionary manner. Many in India aspire for two additional functions—namely, providing these instruments to the population at large and undertaking population-wise redistribution, which is one of the central features of the Scandinavian set-up. But we believe that this is a much more ambitious social objective; there has to be an evolutionary path towards these Swedish or Scandinavian models.

Why are resources important? In recent months, television screens worldwide have highlighted the contrasts between Greece and Sweden; both countries aspire towards constructing social democracy. While Sweden has been able to achieve stability, Greece has been living beyond its means. We believe that it is the gap between the resources commanded by the state and expenditure that makes a difference. In Sweden, if I am not mistaken, the collection of resources by the state is almost 50 per cent of GDP. The difference between your resources and expenditure aspiration is administrative borrowing either from foreigners or domestically. Now financial markets often accept such sovereign borrowings but at some point of time, the market abruptly gets extremely uncomfortable about the sovereignty of the government. This leads to a national crisis in the economy that sets us back by many years.

These non-linear *benami* financial markets suggest that the present relative conditions in India should not induce complacency. It is important to be in clearly safe territory. This is necessary so that we are fiscally healthy and rule out a scenario of a sudden fiscal crisis.

What is the danger zone? There is a lot of literature on this and the current consensus is that 60 per cent seems to be the safe territory. I am talking about the debt GDP ratio of 60 per cent as safe territory for most countries because there is a very interesting book by Prof Ryan identifying this kind of a level. Of course, India has some advantages on the outlay of debt because of high growth. Yet, if we want to ultimately become a high-income country, it is foolish to assume that markets will vary this for India. We will therefore, become uncomfortable if the ratio of our debt to GDP is very high.

We have then identified the transmission mechanism between debt and deficit growth and why this is important. The advantage of having a low GDP ratio is that in crisis, government has one more instrument to protect the people. It can take very aggressive anticipatory fiscal policy. As the chair pointed out, in a financial crisis, the poor suffer the most if you don't take contra-cyclical policies.

The reduction of debt/GDP ratio critically depends on upturning a surplus through budgets and high GDP growth. In our paper, we have given a table in which a number of countries achieved this massive debt reduction through appropriate policies. Today, India's debt GDP ratio, if one takes all the balance sheet items, would be roughly around 70 to 80 per cent which is the sort of level from where we want to come back to 60 per cent.

India has a large history of fiscal stress and so it is important that we focus on this part of fiscal policy. We must follow this fiscal policy to ensure that our debts steadily come down. Sixty (60) per cent looks like a reasonable level to aspire to. Recently, the Finance Commission has given a report to the government to follow this strategy and how this can be achieved over a 10-year period.

Once we have this general framework of government borrowing, then the critical question is how to obtain the resources for the kinds of objectives set out—public goods and transition towards what I called the Scandinavian model. Here come in the architectures of the tax system, to which I now turn.

In designing a tax system, the obvious simple channel one can tend to is higher taxes. But of course, it has two main problems; one is tax evasion and the second is that it leads to financial distortions. Thinking about tax policy, the ideal channel is the one where tax reforms are undertaken, which yield higher tax revenue by increasing efficiency, providing incentives, thus increasing the GDP and growth, and built-in mechanisms to obtain this tax revenue which are difficult to evade. Towards this, we have proposed, or are at least thinking about, three strategic perspectives. One is fiscal loans; in fiscal loans, the simple rule is the one which Chancellor Gordon Brown started in the UK namely, that government shall not borrow for consumption. It is now the golden rule. It meets all tax resources for covering tax and non-tax revenue, and limits expenditure aspirations.

The second is that the tax system should accept the critically central role that it must foster growth because it is only growth that will give us the fiscal space for what we want to do, which is to improve efficiency and growth.

The third is also a continuous awareness of the possibilities of collecting taxes, and at what level. We have quoted a study which was done in almost all developed market economies. It suggests that until our per capita income is $15,000 per head, a tax rate above 20 per cent is really very unlikely. That roughly tells us the tax level and tax revenue this country can aspire for. Currently, our tax GDP ratio is 17.2 per cent: I am taking all the taxes, central, state and local bodies into account. Our headcount is about 2 to 3 per cent at the present stage of our income. We have 20 per cent as a sort of benchmark towards which we should aspire, remembering that we should have a tax policy which uses resources most efficiently and maintains growth.

We have two or three simple elements of a possible tax policy. One is the implementation of a goods and services tax (GST) which has now been accepted by the central government; states have also accepted it in principle. But there is still no agreement as to how exactly we should roll it out. We have given what we consider a Future Model GST. Many of the colleagues, who have come from abroad, may not know that India is one country but still not a common market, with a number of internal tax distortions. GST will remove all the tax distortions within the states and simplify the tax structure. For the first time, we will see India as a common market with all the commensurate benefits of growth, development and higher tax earnings. There is another advantage in GST. We have proposed to bring real estate in GST. That, I think, will improve governance enormously in this country by loosening a very large amount of black money. In some ways, governance is emerging as a very strategic issue in this country to accelerate growth. The way we have structured our proposed tax policies also promotes better governance. GST has a very interesting feature of reducing transaction costs and improving governance.

The second feature we are proposing is to simplify direct taxes on income. The interesting question here is how to tax capital. The recent review of virtual optimal taxes and capital has appeared in a very interesting paper by Prof Mankiw, which gives the present mainstream view of economic theory and I quote: "the logic of low capital tax is powerful: the supply of capital is highly elastic, capital taxes yield large distortions to inter-temporal consumption plans and discourage savings and capital accumulation." We have argued that in the present stage of India's development, it is most critical to maintain growth and capital accumulation. If that is India's strategic problem, we have argued that taxes on capital income should be as low as possible. In fact, we have made the suggestion to completely eliminate taxes on corporations and shift all taxes entirely onto individuals in terms of fully taxing their incomes obtained as the owner of capital, but completely to remove tax on corporations: current taxes really imply double taxation on risk-taking, on capital accumulation and it leads to, in my view, creeping problems of crony capitalism. Once you have tax concessions they are a major source of creeping crony capitalism. I have proposed eliminating this problem of governance in the system. It will also create incentives for growth and maintain investment in the economy.

We have similar proposals for customs duty. We have suggested that we should opt for a zero for zero option. India could benefit greatly from integration in the world economy, perhaps we should become proponents of the zero for zero option because that will strengthen the multi-trading system in which India has a larger stake now. These are the perspectives for how to arrange resources.

And finally, we have also suggested bringing back high estate duty to improve inter-generational equity.

We then come to the second part of the equation. How do we spend our resources? People in this country have realised that our major problem is efficiency in our expenditure. We have suggested incentive-compatible mechanisms essentially around three aspects. One is using Nandan Nilekani's Aadhar programme, which has tremendous potential to improve allocation efficiency in the system. Second, completing the unfinished revolution of decentralisation of Rajiv Gandhi. The only way we can increase efficiency in expenditure is by genuinely following the path started by Rajiv Gandhi. The third is using the tremendous possibilities in private production for public provision. It reduces costs and improves incentives. Through these, we can improve utilisation. Other resource possibilities that we have pointed out are from reallocation of public assets. In the first stage is the suggestion that the Indian state disinvest in goods and services which are now efficiently produced by the private sector. We do believe that we can shift this ownership now and acquire a new public structure like urban infrastructure, better rivers, better water possibilities, and better cities and get out of steel producing and other trading products. These are very large resources. On a market-to-market basis, 50 per cent of Indian GDP or 500 billion dollars is really what is possible for engaging into a new mix of India's challenges, which is really what we should do.

We think that it is by using incentive-compatible expenditure programmes and raising resources more efficiently that India can make a major breakthrough towards increasing its growth rate and moving towards the Scandinavian model of social democracy.

We have presented in this paper two alternative scenarios. One is an inefficient scenario and the other an efficient scenario, based on these kinds of reforms and the dramatic difference they would cause. We have made very modest assumptions. In fact, in reality, it may turn out to be more dramatic. It really shows the importance of making the right choices at this point of time so that India can maintain its high growth rate. This may make it possibly to transit towards what we all aspire for, namely, the Scandinavian model of social democracy.

26

PRESENTATION BY KAUSHIK BASU

Social Democracy, Capital and Growth

Having meetings of this kind, with an open and progressive intellectual agenda, fairly raises the bar on what the country can do. I thank the organisers for giving me the opportunity to speak and participate. Over the last two days, as I have been hearing people, I have been making copious notes and my own paper has been changing very rapidly. The one which has been circulated, if you have read it, is not all loss; I have acquired some knowledge but not the knowledge that will be used and is relevant right now.

I keep saying that there are phases when you need nationalism for a nation to do well. But you would see in Indira Gandhi's and Nehru's pronouncements that we have to keep in mind that it is a smaller world and we have to really think in international terms. You see this very often in Nehru's writings even as Prime Minister. He was most uncomfortable when he was appealing to nationalism, almost reminding us that we must not be narrow-minded and forget that there are other countries in the world doing badly. They must be in our awareness and we must not forget them. We could see this in Tagore's writings repeatedly and this is very much a part of early Indian thinking. I am recalling this because it is easy to fall into small and narrower categories.

From 1990, for four years, I did repeat visits to a very poor village now in Jharkhand in Giridih district with different batches of students, collecting data and information. The idea was to do something important. I was actually planning to show off by living about 20 days in this village but with Aruna Roy here who lives in one and Sudha Murthy who has been doing big stretches of 20 days a year for 20 years, I decided that I'd better keep quiet. But my own idea was really research. I went in to find out what was going on. Those were the days when new concepts had been born. In fact, Joe Stiglitz, Pranab Bardhan were all in the forefront and we went with students to study inter-linkage and those ideas. I collected copious amounts of material, did a census of the village, spent a lot of time with the students, but nothing came of it. For me, the zeal was that of an anthropologist. I thought some day I should write a book out of this like M.N. Srinivas did. But of course, that never happened. But these things leave a mark and I have to say they have left a mark.

One thing is that you need direct action to reach these people. You can't just sit back on growth and say that it will reach the people. First of all, it is not clear that it will reach and even if it did, you can't wait that long because if you see the abysmal conditions in which these people were living, you just feel that you have to do something direct. That always comes away as an axiom. In addition to that, as Mrs Gandhi in her opening address pointed out, unless we attend to people living in these conditions, they will come to destabilise the whole economy and that is actually true. But I would go a step further. Even if it did not destabilise the society, we have to think of this as a moral commitment. Even if leaving these people in these conditions did nothing to us and they stayed exactly the way they are or there was no political instability, this has to be a moral commitment for a nation growing as rapidly as India is doing to reach out to this segment.

I want to go into some troublesome discussions regarding market forces. Market forces have a natural propensity to bolster growth and deliver on efficiency. There are a lot of writings from the time of Adam Smith about these powers of the market. But market forces do not have a natural propensity to reach out to the poor, those who have failed, and those who have not even come into the market arena. These groups are outside the market forces. That's why you need purposive and planned action to reach out to them. And you may have to violate certain things which are regarded as sacrosanct, like not taking from one person and giving to another. We might have to do that. Of course, we try to do that, our taxation system is meant to do that.

I am going to go the converse way and point out that rational thoughts make us open up to agendas and ideas. I want to talk about the converse mistake, which is leaving the market to itself. You will have these people being pulled in. But the converse mistake is, when we don't like the straits of the market, we often go into a denial of its existence, but the market nonetheless exists. It is almost like gravity. It will exist whether you like it or not, you may detest gravity because it keeps pulling you downwards but if you deny gravity and try to move, you will make mistakes. On the converse side, we make the mistake very often of denying that the laws of the market exist. You have to understand the laws of the market and weave in whatever programmes and agendas you are trying to develop in order to reach out to this segment by understanding the laws of the market as much as possible. This is a bit of a professional task. It is not a two-plus-two-equals-four, as in engineering, although there is an element of that. A lot of professions, especially the progressive end of our profession, have the same kinds of objectives but make a realistic assessment of the market, of what the market can do and what it cannot. Passion and commitment are extremely important; you can't get to these kinds of progressive objectives without them, but they are not sufficient.

For example, you are building a bridge. The decision to build the bridge can come collectively from populist opinion. But take the nitty-gritty of building the bridge. If it is just left to each decision being taken by majority vote, I would not step on that bridge that was built by this process. You need to bring in the best professional inputs. Keep the progressive targets that you have but bring in the best professional inputs in the construction of that bridge. Oligarchy and populism were talked about but what was not talked about is that there is also a line between populism and professionalism. Populism should ably set out the ultimate targets which are the things we want to design and do. But the design does need professional input. When I actually look at the Left Front government in West Bengal, 30 years of its regime, I believe that at least in their early years, they were genuinely concerned about some of the targets that they had of eradicating poverty. But the tragedy is that they did very poorly on that and this was because I think the design was flawed. I am not talking about industrial growth in Bengal, but if you look at various poverty indicators, the state did not do as well as it should have with the genuine commitment with which these people first came in. I think the flaw in their agenda was an intellectual flaw. It is just that the plans were not designed properly enough to be able to deliver.

Let me go into something very specific. Let me talk about the food security that has been discussed a lot. I am in favour of trying to reach out to a comprehensive population. In fact, we have a lot of very profligate, very badly handled subsidies which go waste. A lot of it ends up with corporations which ultimately does not reach the farmers and the poor. Instead, if we have a few comprehensive schemes, I think that is really worthwhile. But the details of that do not interest me as much as how you do it and how you deliver the package.

Regarding the Food Security Bill, there have been estimates of the amount of food grains that will have to be procured if we use the current system to deliver this. I have not gone through these carefully, but 70 million tonnes are being talked about that will need to be procured. If we try to reach 70 million tonnes to the poor through the present system, first of all, we will be procuring about one-third of the grains being produced. There is a risk of repeating the kind of mistakes that we have made in the past, which sort of over-reached in trying to use the state machinery to collect and deliver it.

What do we do? I would like the target to remain the same. We do want to reach the same population. How do we do that? There are two things that I just want us to think about. One is that the whole thing does not have to be steered through the state machinery. People can be empowered so that they buy and it is the private sector that remains the delivery mechanism but not for the entire thing. I believe I have been misquoted on this. I do believe that the PDS system has a role to play but the PDS ought to face competition, a bit like what we did with our airlines, with a vast improvement in our airline performance. The PDS should be opened up to competition from the private sector and I feel it is possible to design it so that the full 70 or 72 million tonnes which are supposed to reach this target population can be got there. We can broaden the target even further but we create incentives in the private sector so that the private sector delivers a part of this.

For that various ideas have been discussed, like the use of smart card and technologies like the UID to offload a part of this scheme and this target. I don't want to waver from this target, but I do want us to think in terms of mechanisms.

I have just one final word on this. Currently, we have very good studies to show that in wheat, massive amounts missed the target. In fact, the study that I like the most, which is actually a very academic study, shows that 67 per cent does not reach the poor. Rice is a bit better. But if we try to reach 70 million tonnes and say that half of it misses the target, by the present system, we will have to acquire 140 million tonnes, to get 70 million tones to reach the target. Unless we give great thought into the design of this, we will either continue with what we have done for a long time or we will begin to go fiscally bust.

I am going to just skim over the rest of my presentation. There will be a longer paper with things being written on governance, which troubles us all and of which many of us are a part. India moves too slowly when it comes to decisions being taken. Having been a professor who moved into government, I can see the contrast which you people who have been in government for too long, would not even remember because I really can get little and trivial things done very quickly now, like renewing a license and things like that, which I have memories of really wasting inordinate amounts of time trying to do in the past. For me, the memories of these things are fresh. Two years ago, I would do that. I would stand in queues which are meaningless. One just needs a little bit of reorganisation. Data is pouring in; India is 134th in the world in terms of doing business and efficiency; China is 79th. Here is one very interesting piece of information. In India, now we have regional studies; so we can learn how to do these things better from each other.

I will take one minute to speak of something very different. This is what we were talking about on the identity of poor people and how they perform. We are still catching the importance of this now in statistical studies. There is one done by, in fact, one of Joe Stiglitz's students, Carla Hoff and the co-author is my student, Priyanka Pande who went to a village in Uttar Pradesh. It is actually a very touching study. They took children of different caste groups, assembled them in a hall and made them take IQ tests. They performed very close to one another. There was no caste difference. This was done statistically in a very careful manner. They did it repeatedly. Then, when they read out the names of the students, they read out their caste as well and at one level, you feel these people have been living in a caste-based society and it should do nothing to them, but having a public announcement of their caste and then making them take the same test, the performance of the disadvantaged castes dropped dramatically. The withering effect of a load of discrimination for centuries being made public in this group at one level does something to your psychology of belonging, on what it can do for you to perform better.

I did some very simple experiments in some slum schools which my sisters run, I won't go into the details but it confirms this. There are other studies which show that identity and how you are treated and viewed actually influences and can change your very performance. I know I am saying this out of context. But there will be a paper where I will put all this in.

27

PRESENTATION BY NITIN DESAI

Social Democracy and Environmental Protection

The central point that I would wish to make is that the social democracy and environmental protection are entirely compatible. The question of a conflict between the two does not really arise because both are driven by the idea of injustice in one way or another. The environmental problem arises invariably when there is some injustice; when somebody can pull you into hot water and cause harm to somebody else without having to pay for it. Even when we talk of inter-generational equity, it is a way of passing on the damage caused to somebody else. In some ways, we will never get an environment problem unless there isn't some core of unfairness and injustice somewhere.

Social democracy is entirely about justice and fairness. It is not just about justice and fairness in the sense of income poverty and in terms of deprivation. It is also about justice and fairness in terms of vulnerability, discrimination and marginalisation. I would argue that in many ways even with these other dimensions of fairness that we are concerned with, there are links with environment. It is not just that lots of poor people live in ecologically fragile regions but it is also true that vulnerability is something that affects the poor more. They are more likely to live in flood plains of rivers; they are more likely to live in marshy low-lying coastal lines in cities like Bombay; they are more likely to live in places that are exposed to chemical risks as in Bhopal; it was an unauthorised colony of poor people who were exposed to the poison there. Even the other dimension of poverty and the deprivation that we are concerned with do connect a lot. Even on discrimination, you mentioned a touching example of where just a fact of recognition of caste has an effect on people. But let us also recognise the connection that if we go to any village in India, people of lower castes are usually exiled to the worst areas at the edge of the village. I would argue that in many ways, an agenda of social justice is frankly incomplete if we don't address environmental issues. Because so much of what we are concerned with as social democrats are issues which do not connect with the issues that environmental activists are ever connected with. The idea that the two can be in conflict sometimes comes up because of the issue of resources. In some ways, as Pierre Resanvallon reminded us, social democracy arises from the fear of revolution. Growth is our answer to the fear of revolution because growth generates resources, which allows us to take care of the poor. The argument is that if we start worrying about environmental protection, in some ways it erodes the possibilities of growth. Yes, it is true that there is a strand in the environmental movement which has been driven by some sort of anti-growth concern. But in countries like India, there is a widespread recognition amongst environmental activists that it is not possible to protect the environment by leaving people in poverty. We cannot conserve a bio-diversity reserve. We cannot protect the tiger if we do not worry about the livelihood of the people who live in and around those forests. We have discovered this again and again. Hence, in a poor society, growth and development are in fact, necessary for environmental protection. We will not be able to protect the environment unless we have more growth. In some ways, these things came together in the concept of sustainable development of the Brundtland Commission. I have had a lot to do with it in the past 25 years but there is a certain parallelism between the two concepts of social democracy and sustainable development.

I am not going into that but there is one parallelism which is very interesting. They are both rich concepts which try to bring together two different sets of activists. In the case of social democrats, we are trying to bring together the socialists, who want immediate action on poverty, while the democrats want to protect freedom. They are two different epistemic communities we are trying to bring together. It is the same thing with sustainable development; we are trying to bring together people whose primary concern is development and people whose primary concern is environmental protection. In some ways, what these concepts provide is a language that gets people who are otherwise not connected, talking with one another. That certainly was the motivation behind sustainable development when it was introduced in the Brundtland Commission. I believe it is also a motivation behind the idea of social democracy. The problem with bridges is that sometimes people are not sure and they don't treat it as their bridge.

There is also the problem of the political dimension. It is true that there is one strand in the environmental movement which is focused very strongly on conservation which at one time was associated with the old aristocracy, tiger protection and all that; old aristocracy and aspirants to the aristocracy. But that is a much more limited group now. If we look at India, I would say that the environmental agenda which really drives activism is very different. It is basically an agenda which focuses on the stress on livelihoods and helps on the resource rights of the poor, on marginalised people, on the importance of people's participation in resource management. That particular agenda is really an agenda which fits in fairly well with a Left agenda rather than with the classical Right agenda of the environmental movement. One should always keep that in mind. There are only two issues that I still see at the political level. One is the question of global dimension. In the very nature of things, a social democratic movement is national in character because it has two focuses. It is a political movement and in the case of environment, it is virtually impossible to address issues unless we take the global dimension into account. Climate change is an example. Therefore, there is a need for a global social democratic agenda as a way forward the point which Pascal Lamy raised earlier. The second is inter-generational equity. This is an issue, because the very nature of things in a social democracy is concern with what we are going to do here and now for people today, whereas environment really requires us to take a longer view; climate change requires us to take a view of what will happen 30 years from now.

What I have also tried to do is translate this into more programmatic terms. I would suggest four focus areas for their programmatic integration. The first is a much better linkage between anti-poverty programmes and area programmes. We have anti-poverty programmes which started subsidies. We have area development programmes for hill areas, drought-prone areas and watershed development, which do not have an anti-poverty component. The first thing I would urge is to bring these two things together in one framework and not put them in two separate frameworks. Within that, we focus very strongly on rural energy and water. Water is a strategic resource; get water resources right and you get many other things right. We cannot get water resources right unless we get a lot of other things right in agriculture, distribution of water, water conservation and many other issues.

The second thing that I have focused attention on is the need for decentralisation of environmental responsibility. Today, we have done that in development to some extent but our environmental development and control management systems are much more centralised at state level or central level. I think there is a case for looking at the possibility of primary environmental care centres linked with *panchayats* so that we start the process of getting local people engaged in resource management.

The third and more difficult area that I have emphasised in programmatic terms is the reconciliation of land rights and development, which perhaps is the greatest test of this integration that we face today, including obviously the displacement of people. Here I have suggested three things.

First, large-scale land acquisition must be treated as a transaction between the buyer and the community. You also have to include people who do not necessarily own land because they are also going to be displaced.

Secondly, give people a stake; the 26 per cent tax idea on mining is one example. The sale of development rights is another example. Land adjustment schemes are the third example. In this, the community effect is where social justice comes in. But when we bring the environment in, we have to interpret the community as a wider one. Because when I bring an environmental issue in terms of the impact of that mega project on a forest or water body, what I am really talking about is a much wider community of concern. This is where issues of consent through public hearings, the point which Sunita was raising earlier, come in. We need more efficient and better procedures for that. There are theoretical possibilities of clashes between the community that holds property and something which it wants to develop when environmentalists think it is a bad idea. I think this can be handled. There are countries that have a system of payment for denial of development rights to people. Britain has such a system. But I think the idea that it will raise the cost of industrial development is a specious one. What it basically says is that the industry will not bear the cost of the environmental deterioration; other people can. If there is a cost involved in terms of environmental deterioration, I don't see the cost argument as relevant.

The final programmatic area that I have suggested is urban development. Urban development, to me, is the greatest challenge. That is where the challenges of social justice and environment are really going to be seen in India because that is where the bulk of the growth is going to take place. In the two areas that I have focused on, I haven't touched on finance and governance because many people have talked about them. One is urban land management. We will never get our urban policy right unless we rethink urban land management. Our present procedure asking large public sector enterprises to control the bulk of the land, with tight controls on private management, is driving the poor into slums and private developers into semi-urban areas on the edge of the city, leading to urban sprawl and slums; the two things which are a total disaster from an environmental perspective. We need to rethink urban planning, which is much more compact, which does not treat unauthorised colonies as a scourge but works with them. Have a look at the Aaya Nagar project on the outskirts of Delhi on the way to Gurgaon where people are trying to do that. People are making their own cities; no poor person gets municipal water free, they all pay for it. It is privatised for them as in most urban areas in India. They are doing it themselves; it is not being done by the master planners. Let us learn to work with these people as they are trying to do in phases in Aaya Nagar.

Let me finally end with one comment on the political field. What we really have to do is to bring together the social democratic movement and the environmental movement, the activists on both sides, in a common minimum programme. I believe the programmatic areas that I am identifying provide the basis for that. Aruna Roy and Sunita Narain must come together.

My final plea is that it isn't enough to simply leave it to activists. This is a political matter and it would be very appropriate if Indira Gandhi's party were to pick this issue up and bring this idea of social democracy and environmental protection together at a political level and make it a part of its platform for the next elections.

28

SECTION III(a)

Discussion

Nandan Nilekani

Actually, I had planned to just learn and listen but there were many references to the UID project, mostly favourable. I thought I should set the record straight about what it is all about for our international delegates and set the context. Basically, the UID or Aadhar project is to give a number to every Indian resident, man, woman and child. It is to make sure that the number is unique so that a person does not have more than two numbers and to create an online infrastructure for identity verification which can be used in a variety of public services.

Now, why do we need this? We have a large number of Indians who do not have any form of acknowledged existence by the state. They don't have a birth certificate, a school certificate, a house address, and these people are completely being left out of the social democracy that we keep talking about. Because they are not accessible, they cannot come on to any kind of a list, they can't access public services, and we need to do something about that.

The second thing is that India is becoming a migratory country; we have more than a hundred million migrants. In the next 20 years, thanks to urbanisation, global warming and other issues, we will have even more migration happening and there is no mobile identity which people can take with them which is a big source of the problem.

The third thing is that, on the other hand, because of security concerns, our verification processes for people's identity have gone up, thanks to things like the Anti-Money Laundering Act and so on and so forth. It is becoming more and more difficult for the people who do not have an identity to access basic services like opening a bank account, getting a mobile connection or getting on to a BPL list. Therefore, we have to bridge this gap between higher concerns on security and the need for inclusion.

We have the whole issue of improving the efficiency of public service delivery as we increase our spending on public services. We have seen in a very small way, how technology can help in improving the income tax collection. One of the success stories in India has been the Tax Information Network (TIN), which essentially used technology and a permanent number for taxation and thanks to these reforms, India's tax collections went up from 16 billion dollars in 2001 to 84 billion dollars in 2010, a 500 per cent increase, essentially just by using technology in a very smart way. There is a huge value for technology in public governance.

We also have the challenge of re-engineering our public services so that we can deliver things much better. We are increasingly putting more and more onus on the state. We want the state to deal with globalisation, demographic dividend, rapid education, development *versus* environment, urbanisation, etc. We want more things from the state but we must also put in the appropriate capacity in the state to deliver on these extra commitments. There are thus very good reasons for doing this particular project.

I would also like to address the concerns about privacy and security. This is a very important concern. There are many aspects of what we are doing in our projects which address these concerns but we believe that the real way to address the issue is in a larger umbrella legislation which covers privacy and data protection. We ourselves wrote proactively to the government to start this process. The government set up a working group. They have come out with an approach paper on privacy and data security which addresses a lot of these things. Because it is not just about Aadhar; it is about mobile phone conversation, it is about how you use different databases, the whole host of things that we need to worry about. I think we need a larger thing which we have already initiated. Again, going back to the question of whether technology is dangerous for India, I think many of India's successes have been thanks to technology. I gave the example of the TIN which has generated so much resources that are paying for our welfare schemes, but we also have the example of the railway reservation system. Today, it books millions and millions of tickets. The common man is able to book tickets using a mobile phone because of technology. He is benefitting from that. Our elections are held on Electronic Voting Machines (EVMs); it is again a great example of how technology has been used. We have 700 million people using mobile phones today and they are benefitting from that. A common man is able to get a job or able to get information to his family. There is no shortage of examples of how technology can be used for social purpose. We shouldn't be particularly reticent or shunning about technology.

We must remember that opposition to technology has also been common in Indian history. In the 1980s, when Prime Minister Rajiv Gandhi took up IT, I don't know whether people know that March 1 was "Anti-Computer Day". Today, it looks a little quaint that there was something called "Anti-Computer Day" but it was there. There were agitations and people burnt effigies of computers. The Reserve Bank was so scared that when they came out with the report on bank computerisation, they called them "ledger posting machines" because they did not want the unions to get angry with them. And when they came out with their second report on more powerful computers, they called them "advanced ledger posting machines".

The point I am trying to make is that this technological opposition has been sort of a standard feature of the Indian scenario. When Sam Pitroda and Prime Minister Rajiv Gandhi promoted telecommunications, there was a huge objection saying that this was a luxury product and the common man did not need telecommunications but needed something else.

On consultation, we have had 150 consultations with NGOs, lawyers, civil activists, state governments and banks. This is one project where there has been so much of consultation. A law has gone through consultation. I don't think any of those claims are valid. I do believe that if we are serious about social democracy, if we really want a billion people to be included in our society and economy, the state must give them an acknowledged existence; and we must re-engineer our public services so that we can deliver services to them in a much more effective, efficient and equitable manner. I see no way we can do so without a fundamental identity infrastructure which is what we are building.

Finally, this is not my project. I am a nominee of the central government. I exist through a cabinet decision. My budget is approved by parliament. The project has been reviewed by the Standing Committee of Finance of Parliament. The Supreme Court has advocated the use of this in the PDS. So please, for God's sake, understand this is not my personal project.

Pranab Bardhan

I have just two comments. One arising out of something that Vijay Kelkar was going to talk about, but didn't. Just to induce him to talk more about it, in my judgement, on resource raising, one of the big changes in the last 10-15 years in terms of resources, quite often untapped by the state, is the huge rental income that is being generated by scarce resources like land, mining rights, things which were always there but now with economic growth, their values are rising, and the state is not getting a large enough share out of it. In fact, the mining mafia is getting much more of the rental income out of the increasing value of the mining rights. Why shouldn't the mining rights be auctioned? If the telecommunications spectrum is auctioned, mining rights too should be auctioned and used to fund the welfare of the tribals. Similarly, there are all kinds of natural resources, including land, around infrastructure projects. Why shouldn't there be a betterment levy on everybody whose land increases many times in value? It leads to political corruption but the state does not get much out of it and that is an increasing source of resource revenue that I think I would like Vijay to comment on. In fact, about the mining rights, it is not just the mining mafia. The so-called Maoist movement in parts is becoming an extortion racket. It is extorting from mining companies, some legal and some illegal, essentially for money to buy guns. These extortions are going on because the state is not doing much about raising this revenue.

The other comment relates to Nitin Desai. He brought up the issue of land. In a sense, it is related. I think land acquisition is an issue which has become politically quite explosive in different parts of India. I do not agree with some things mentioned here. There are politicians in India, one from my state in West Bengal, who have been saying that the market should decide about land. There should not be land acquisition by the government. I think it is completely wrong because if it is left to the market, it will result in two problems. One is that the small seller is at a disadvantage en masse against large corporate buyers. Secondly, in India, usually what will happen whenever a project is announced is not even thought about. The land mafia is going to preemptively buy or sometimes intimidate the land seller to give up land at a throwaway price. So again the rent will go to the land mafia or to the corporate buyer. This is where the state's involvement in land acquisition is absolutely essential.

Sri Mulyani Indrawati

Nemat, I would like to comment on your introduction on compromising incentive and living within means. I think this is also relevant with many of my own experiences when I was in Indonesia. Just for comparison, the debt to GDP ratio when I was first appointed as the Minister of Finance, was close to 60 per cent. The tax ratio is only 11 per cent. The tax payers are only 3 million out of a 220 million population and around a 100 million labour force in Indonesia. The growth is only 4 per cent. When we tried to push reforms, specifically because of the commitment of a government elected through the open democratic system, which throughout the campaign was always very populist, bringing this social democratic agenda as the main attraction for the voter, we had to work hard in terms of delivering on the promise within our means where the tax revenue is quite limited. The only choice is how to combine the package of this compromise incentive and make sure that the social democratic or even the populism of the political promise can be delivered prudently and sustainably. Reforms are actually a combination to get the support or compromise from the business sector. It is actually saying that the tariff rate can be reduced so that importing goods will be cheaper because the manufacturing sector in Indonesia is still dependent on importing intermediary goods. The tax rate is reduced but at the same time, we tell the business community and the people that we are going to reform the tax department and customs, which is very notorious as the most corrupt institution in Indonesia. I am very proud that within six years, it has become the most reformed institution. At the bottom are now the police and the parliament and the judicial system.

We are no longer at the bottom, which is good. But this is just to get the support from the business community and to reassure them that we are not going to harass them. One has to become more open and transparent and give them the promise of what one is going to deliver from this reform, combining it with reducing the tax rate from 35 per cent to 25 per cent. You get quite a lot of support from the media and NGOs because they like good governance and want corruption to be tackled. The business community loves it because the rate is reduced. Our own confidence and trust of the people make our bureaucracy work well because they have this pride now, of being associated with the reform movement.

What happened in the first four or five years? We had a growth of 6 per cent and the debt-GDP ratio was reduced to only 28 per cent; the number of tax payers went up from 3 million to 16 million and that created the connection. People in the middle class in Indonesia feel proud to be tax payers as there is a link between the tax payer status, democracy, openness and accountability. With the money that we can collect as revenue, which increased from 20 billion to reach 70 billion, our budget size has increased from 30 billion to more than 100 billion, you can actually transfer more of the money to the local government. Of course, in this case, you also have to create incentives for the local governments, given their weakness of capacity and vulnerability to corruption. One has to combine with a certain system of education to make sure that they can deliver. Half has been delegated to the local government. Now you can improve education making 12 years compulsory and reduce the illiteracy rate.

We launched a new programme for free health treatment for the poor, with the result that Indonesia has been very successful in family planning because of which the government's spending on health as well as on poor people has reduced. We can improve what we call the social spending even more by making sure that it can reach the poor.

We also have this food subsidy. Kaushik Basu mentioned food subsidy and food security. When your fiscal position is healthy, you can actually have a degree of manoeuvrability. When we had a food crisis in 2006 and 2009, the government could provide a one-time subsidy. You are not going to make it permanent because once it becomes permanent it becomes very difficult for you to actually move the goalpost within the budget. It protects the poor through a combination of subsidies through goods and not price because if it is through price, it distorts the whole economy. If you give subsidy in terms of commodities, the challenge is on delivery. Rice and cooking oil are going to be put in the subsidy basket targeted at the poor people and this is related to the ID number. As the finance minister, I know that in Indonesia, one doesn't have a single identity. A company has three different financial statements for the bank, for the tax office and for their own IPO. You have to really consolidate these and we are also launching the same identity number. We procure it within Indonesia because usually when you have a big country of the size of Indonesia, you have this tendency to use your own national capacity whether it is in technology, software and so on. But in terms of having a single identity number which is linked to tax as well as the social benefit, I think it is very important as the basis for action. It comes from the idea of populism, to try to protect our people, especially the poor. You have to administer and execute it in the right manner through a good administration. It will also be good in terms of their accountability. Therefore, politically too, it is going to be good because you can empower the people and tell them your achievement in reaching the poor, when you have all the foundations of information and administration. I fully agree with what Kaushik mentioned: translating the idea of social democracy or setting goals targeting the poor or creating equality does require quite a lot of work in reforming administration. The sequencing of reaching that goal is very important. How does one really make sure that institution-building is going to fit with that goal? When you also try to open up the institution, the most difficult part is usually government and parliament. Even though it makes our life complicated, it is necessary for us to be accountable. It puts constant pressure on us to be open and transparent. As Nemat mentioned, in Brazil you get a lot of support when you communicate with the people about the result, because you are using people's money in order to create public goods and reach public objectives. This is not my money but the government's money. It is not the minister's money but public money. When they know that the taxpayer will be happy, they become more compliant. They are proud to become taxpayers. They know where the money is going and so the revenue side should also be consolidated. There is minimum interaction between our officers and the money itself. It is all done through the banking system. As such, it will reduce corruption further. With openness, you can actually also detect a lot of wrong doings.

I just want to conclude that this has also happened in many other countries. It has been confirmed by my very short experience as the Managing Director in the Bank, meeting many finance ministers actually involved in dealing with this question of how they can provide proper resources in order to achieve the goal, which is usually set politically by the head of the state or the Prime Minister.

Jamshyd Godrej

I just want to draw attention to the link between social democracy and pro-poor policies and infrastructure. I think we have not put enough emphasis on understanding how infrastructure development really benefits the poor. One good example in India is mobile phones and Nandan referred to that. The pro-poor dimension of roads, power, urban infrastructure, both the hard infrastructure and soft infrastructure, never comes into the debate on infrastructure which is always about who is doing which project, where the financing is coming from and what the return is. We need to reorient the entire thinking on infrastructure to understand how it is really benefiting the poor. If we could do that, we would make a lot more decentralisation on infrastructure development and that way we would get to do it much faster.

The other thing I want to mention is on Nitin's point on environment and social development. The main point really is on health which needs to be emphasised. We need to see, especially in our large cities, the type of degradation of health. There are certain pockets in Bombay, like Chembur for instance, which is so heavily polluted that every single person who lives in that area has a lung disease. We don't seem to realise how these environment issues are creating this huge cost on the economy. If you can really focus on some of that, it will be a lot more useful.

Kumar Mangalam Birla

Let me begin by saying that for someone who is neither an economist nor a student of political science, this has been a great learning experience. I want to make a few comments on each of the speakers who spoke today.

A few points on Dr Kelkar's outstanding paper. He talked about protecting vulnerable individuals from fluctuations in health and income by reducing macroeconomic fluctuations. I think India has done particularly well on that front, something that the world recognises. He also talked about reducing duties on manufacturing to zero. The only point I really wish to make here is I think that manufacturing, given its importance in the Indian economy which we talked about earlier, needs to have some visibility into the future. Manufacturers need to be told that zero duty is something that they can expect by 2015 or 2020 and that timeline should be linked very closely with the development of infrastructure that we expect in that timeframe. There also needs to be a political consensus around that.

Mr Basu made a point about slow decision-making and how it impacts growth. I want to point out to the fertiliser sector in India for example. Whilst the government is spending huge subsidies in importing fertilisers, we are talking about cutting debt by reducing subsidies. On the other hand, the fertiliser industry has not added any capacity in the last 15 years because of the policies withering.

Whilst the intent is good, what we are looking for is perfect solutions. We need to have well thought through working solutions. Let us not get into this situation of analysis-paralysis. It is very important to get ahead with decision-making and implementing decisions.

There was a point Dr Desai made about trust. Today in India, there is still a trust deficit when it comes to the private sector. That is something we need to now overcome. There is lots of work that can be done in partnership between the private sector and the public sector. Let us not denigrate the private sector as someone who is stealing things away. Let us give the private sector its rightful due.

Chanda Kochhar

I have three points to make. The first is, as Mr Kaushik Basu said, that we have to realise that these people who are not included in growth could destabilise the economy. But even if they don't, we should look at it as a moral obligation. I would say that we should actually go the third step as well to say that it is not just a moral obligation. Let us actually believe in the fact that this is where India's next growth is going to come from. It is, in a way, an economic imperative as well, because we have almost 700 million people residing in these villages who have not so far been included in the growth. If India's growth which could go to 9 per cent, driven mainly by the urban areas, and a few hundred million people got added to the middle income group, imagine what can be done to the growth levels if a few hundred million would move up from the poverty line to the next stage and so on. This third dimension is saying that for all of us, this is the next India, maybe not two years from now, maybe five years or ten years, I don't know. It all depends on us how fast we accelerate it. But this is the next driver of growth for India. Another way of looking at it is how we will all be more and more inclined to work towards that.

My second comment is again on one of the points that Kaushik made. When you get people to move away from the constraints of either caste or creed that they have been associated with and they get freed from those, their performance really reaches the next level. I want to share an example of what we have been doing at ICICI. We realised that there was no real skill training in the banking sector per se. What we were always doing was to pick up the MBAs from the best MBA schools and then training them on the job, spending a lot of time training them and then finally using them in competition. We thought of doing some amount of skill development and training by creating a kind of our own MBA programme and ensured that we would do the admissions after the regular best MBA school admissions are over. We would go to those undergraduate schools where we did not compromise on education standards at all. We also went through the same selection process but we selected those people who did not apply to the best MBA schools. The reason they did not apply was because they could not afford it. We found that there are thousands of such people. Even thousands is probably a lesser number because we can only manage about a thousand but there were so many students who could not participate in doing an MBA whereas they were academically as good as the others. We took them as a part of our own MBA and then employed them in our organisation. These are people who have come from very different economic backgrounds but, in a way, this has given them an ability to participate in a different level of economic activity. This really works very well. We should look at how we could undertake more initiatives of this kind.

The third point I have is picking up from what Nandan said on technology. Of course, he was referring to the point that technology was not bad and that's the way we need to look at it. I want to add another dimension. This refers to the use of technology by Indians. Here again, when I say Indians, I really mean those 600-700 million more people whom we need to include in economic development, foster ability to use technology and change their lives. Again, we are undermining them. I would say the more we make technology available, the way these people would respond to the use of technology will really create a sea change in their own economic levels. Just to elaborate this a bit more, it was only about 10 to 12 years ago when India did not even have ATMs in a big way in the country. At that time, the understanding of the people of an ATM was simply not there. Even in the largest of cities, I remember as we began rolling out ATMs, when the display screen said 'enter PIN', most people in the urban areas would actually look for a safety pin because they just did not know how to use an ATM! From there, we have come a long way where just about 10 per cent of our banking transactions get done in the branches and all other transactions are being done on technology. It is not just in the urban areas but also in the remotest of the areas where our people move with suitcases with just a biometric card and card reading machine, and banking is delivered there. Along with the UID, I think it is incumbent upon us to take the other forms of banking to these people and make banking accessible to them. We would then see a huge difference that can happen to the economy. Nandan said that a lot depends on us and they were putting a lot of burden on our shoulders. I just want to say that there are many shoulders like ours which will work along with him. We have to work together to make the kind of difference that accessibility and technology can make to India. Let us not undermine the ability of these people to be responsive to technology. A whole lot of difference can be made to India on that basis.

Joseph Stiglitz

I want to go back to the issue of resources to begin with. I very strongly agree with Pranab that vast amounts of resources are basically public resources, for which the government does not get value. Land is one, mineral resources, spectrum, which has developed some sensitivity recently, are others, but these things are true in all countries. There is a strong political economy aspect. The US has designed the auction and the way they are sold can make a very big difference. And the mining and oil companies want designs that are a zero sum game. They want to pay as little as possible, while the government should want to get the most. Basically, these are rents and hundred per cent of them really should be going to the public sector.

There is a problem distinguishing rents from the capital in extracting the rents, but the principle should be very clear. The second point is there is a wide range of taxes, where taxes can actually improve economic efficiency by taxing bad things. I am talking about the problem of pollution and environment. An environment tax can be an important source of revenue, particularly with carbon emissions that can generate substantial amounts of revenues that can be used simultaneously for improving the efficiency of the economy and used for socio-democratic objectives. An example that is getting a lot of attention in Europe now is financial transaction taxes and a whole lot of taxes on the banking sector, because it is recognised that these short-term financial transactions contribute to economic de-stabilisation. If you design appropriate financial transaction taxes, you actually improve economic efficiency and generate revenue.

The third thing is the category of taxes that will improve efficiency; it is what was talked about earlier. Amongst various tax expenditures, expenditures through the tax system and through subsidies that go to upper income individuals represent, in almost all countries, a distortion of the economy. Again, eliminating those improves economic efficiency and provides revenues for helping achieve a social democratic agenda.

The fourth thing is that almost all tax systems have all kinds of special provisions and designing a pure tax system which will get social support of the kind that you were talking about, can generate more revenue. The particular category here—and this is where maybe Vijay and I disagree—is taxes on capital gains and capital. I think they can actually be an important part of the tax system. Let me put it in a couple of ways. First, the interest in elasticity of savings is sufficiently low at the end of the day. In the US, special provisions for exempting interest and capital gains actually led to lower national savings because while it may stimulate a little bit of private savings, the cost to the government was greater, so that the deficit that was increased actually offset the slight gain in the private savings. From the point of view of maximisation of savings, special provisions are not desirable. From the point of view of social inclusion, one might want to encourage savings by poor individuals and middle income individuals. That is why retirement accounts and even some kinds of matching savings programmes can be good as part of the social inclusion programme but exempting interest I think is a mistake.

Let me make an interesting proposal to eliminate the corporate income tax. Most economists think that is an interesting idea. It was a part of President Bush's agenda. He used the same rhetoric of double taxation but what happened is that, rather than going to single taxation, he went to zero taxation. That is what happens in many countries, it is done during midnight, when nobody is looking, they change it and simultaneously eliminate the taxes and dividends and at the same time create a whole set of exemptions so that the effective tax rate is actually lower.

With modern technology, you can't trace back who is the ultimate owner and the tax is concurrently back to the privileged and foreign owners. You have a lot of money coming in from Mauritius, which one suspects is because Mauritius is not really that active or interested. Withholding that tax at the corporate level and truly identifying who the new owner is will be taxing at a high rate until they control the right to know who the real owners are. That, I think, will be an important step for increasing transparency in the whole tax structure. You might be able to use this as a way of opening up.

Regarding the problems occurring when debt-GDP ratios get too high, obviously, it is fundamental; one cannot obviously have excessively high debt-GDP ratio. But this particular study should not influence thinking in India.

Erik Solheim

Let me continue on taxation, because some people tend to believe that Scandinavians are tax-lovers. On the contrary, our government was elected on the explicit promise that it would not increase the taxes round the corner. We stick to that and that is the way to be elected. Scandinavians can never be elected on the promise of collecting a lot more taxes. We can be elected on the promise that we will increase the support for elderly people and kindergarten schools. For that purpose, if people believe that we will really deliver on that, we need some taxes. We do not have high corporate taxes or progressive income tax, an essential element, as some people said. The progressive element basically hits the middle class. As the middle class is very small, it is not a major source of revenue gain for the government.

The main source for the region of Northern Europe is the IT, indirect taxes. We pay 23 per cent flat on more or less everything we buy. There is hardly any exemption from that. That is the big source of income for the government. I admit that it is much more difficult in a nation which has so many poor like India, unlike Northern Europe, where most people belong to the middle class. The second most important thing is we believe in a very severe high tax level on natural resources, because natural resources often yield super profits. One needs a normal tax on profit if one is into manufacturing like Birla, or into banking. But there is no reason for that to happen to foreign oil or foreign gold, or whatever it may be, that will have a super profit; not a normal profit like any other business. We have 79 per cent tax level on the oil and gas sector. I still recall explaining the system to President Lula of Brazil: you could see from his face how he started counting. Why should there be super profits in these sectors? There should be complete transparency and whatever is gained above the normal profit should be for the benefit of the average people through the state.

Another factor was to expand the tax base. When billing is into the labour market, if you have a very low unemployment rate, you have a much bigger tax base. More people are taxed which gets more money into the system.

These are the basic principles in which we believe. We can have not a very high, but relatively high, tax level. Of course, it is a social contract. People must believe that they will get something. It must be delivered as a wise scheme of taxation. I would very much underline what Joe Stiglitz says. We must fight all the illicit capital flows; the tax savings by way of avoidance are a shame to humanity. Why should we accept billions of dollars when we don't know who the owners are? We had a tragic accident in a ship at one of our harbours and people were killed; no one could establish the ownership of the ship even after 10 years. It was not possible to know who owned the ship. How can this be acceptable in the modern world? We need international cooperation to fight tax evasions.

Montek Singh Ahluwalia

I agree with Vijay. I can guess why Joe does not like 60 per cent. What comes out to me from the conference is a very strong support for social democracy notwithstanding perhaps the feeling that beyond South Calcutta, it cannot be extended.

What we have is an aspiration for social democracy and we need to convert that to architecture. A lot of the fiscal stuff is really what will build that architecture, without which the whole thing will collapse. I really wish that civil society and also political groups that support social democracy as architecture put their weight behind the GST. GST is viewed as some weird thing that finance people and economists worry about. It is very, very important.

Maybe Abhijit Sen and I need to sit with our colleagues to try and put this in the Twelfth Plan. If we do this, we will attribute it to this conference. There is a big difference between the architecture and a collection of schemes. We don't yet have architecture but we have long schemes. Some view them as very good while others have suspicions or doubts about them. To my mind, you cannot get architecture by adding up schemes. I think we need to go back and let the scheme continue and expand them. Let us be clear in our minds that we need the architecture to replace the schemes in five or ten years. They ought to have a self-destruct clause.

What is that architecture? Interestingly, some elements of it would be common to all countries and would be relevant for us when we have become a social democracy: there would be things like a health insurance system or health service delivery system. There will certainly be old-age pensions; there would certainly be unemployment benefits to cope with temporary dislocation. I will include one or two other things too.

Then there are certain things that are not really social security; they are basic services and even the rich want them. For example, having a proper health system which means a lot of public hospitals and clinics in addition to private; having water supply, sanitation. These are not part of social security; these are part of essential basic services, infrastructure which is also a permanent need. The difference between the social security architecture and these is that while social security architecture should be the responsibility of the central government. With Nandan's UID, we can deliver old-age pensions directly. We don't have to go through state governments to do it and many other things like that. But in the case of delivery of services, the central government has no role to play other than foot a part of the bill. Take the Right to Education, which has a terrific legislation. The actual responsibility rests with state governments. The architecture must take that into account; some things will be done by the centre and in my view, people should know that they are being done by the centre.

Then there is what I would call the livelihood support schemes; NREGA is a very successful scheme that I think will do much better than what it is currently doing. It is actually a livelihood support scheme, not a permanent part of the infrastructure. It may not be needed 20 years from now. I think we need to separate these things, though each one is important. But architecture means architecture; otherwise, you get the sort of houses that rich people in India build. If somebody likes the White House, you have a collonade in the front; if somebody likes Spanish architecture you have a Spanish balcony. These are places that are liveable but are not architecture. That is what I want. It will be nice if in the course of the rest of the conference one could get responses from people on what they think about it.

Jean Drèze

I wish to pose a couple of comments and questions. When economists get into advising on social policy, I get a little nervous, especially with economic theorists. It is not because I doubt their intelligence or their competence within their own domain and even their commitment. I am sure that Kaushik is as committed as anybody else to the objectives. It is a nervousness borne out of experience and particularly the whole experience and the debate on the National Rural Employment Guarantee Act (NREGA), to which economists have virtually contributed nothing till this day. In fact, they stay opposed very strongly, though not all of them, of course. But many were opposed and the rest kept quiet and individually did not make any constructive contribution whereas it was really an initiative that held huge promise, which has now been vindicated and recognised. If 50 million people today get employment every year under NREGA, it is to some extent because the negative advice has been ignored. It would be interesting if one had time to reflect about what the problem is. Economic analysis is one important thing. When you get into advising on social policy, you have to first get into real-world economic issues, which is sometimes not the same as the analytic models that we study. Then we also need to think about the politics, legal aspects and so on. These are not things that we are well trained to think about. To give a very simple example, you can go through an entire page in economics without ever having heard of the word 'rights', except in the term property rights. Therefore, we are not well placed in recognising the importance of putting social policy in our legal framework. But the entire experience in the last five years has been that it really can make a huge difference starting with the Supreme Court order on maintenance, which has led to some of the best programmes in India today. If we go to any remotest possible village in Bihar or Jharkand, we will find a functioning mid-day scheme meal there. Of course, in many states there is still scope for improvement but it is a useful programme. In many states, the quality of the meal is not bad at all and there can be further improvement. All this has been made possible because of the legal battle and the pressure of the Supreme Court. The consciousness that has developed is that this is something by way of a right and there is no question of it not being there. The fact is that if it is a law, nobody can say no. One can try to wriggle out but cannot say that one is not going to have a mid-day meal scheme in schools.

The same principle applies with respect to the Right to Information Act, NREGA, and the Right to Education Act. I think now with the Food Security Act, we have another really extraordinary opportunity to enable the poor to have a bit more of a share in this enormously growing national wealth, so little of which is reaching them. The idea that activists are people of passionate commitment but we professionals are economists who are going to, as you say, flesh it out, is quite a flawed and misleading view. I am always reminded of what Keynes said about economists that "if they could manage to get themselves thought of as humble, competent people on a level with private dentists, that would be splendid." We should remember that every day. That is not to deny that economists have important things to contribute. We would like to see them doing it. For example, thanks to the Employment Guarantee Act, there is a crisis now for wage policy and the government has tied itself into knots by putting itself in a position where the minimum wages will have to be paid. That requires some coherent wage policy. Is the wage going to be set by the states, some by the central government? If it is essential now, based on what principle is it going to be indexed?

These are things on which you would have expected economists to have quite a lot to say, including its potential impact on private employment. Till date, I have not seen one intelligent paper by an economist on the issue of wage policy in NREGA which was so obvious, so glaring right from the beginning of the design. In fact, this is a crisis that is born of the defect in the design of the law which could have been avoided if, five years ago, we had had an intelligent debate about wage policy for NREGA. I am saying this partly because I feel a bit of a repeat of that happening today. There is this massive Food Security Law coming up which is creating a lot of nervousness and anxiety. I think economists really have things to contribute.

Food stamps, to me, are not adequate. I can recognise analytically, as you told me on different occasions, that food stamps are better, I agree with that. We have done a model; food stamps will beat the present system anytime because you will create competition and all that. But to make it work on the ground is completely a different ball game and if you look at the Food Stamps Act in the US, which has a fraction of Food Stamps programme, it is extraordinarily detailed with huge amount of regulations, safeguards. You can't just put out the stamp and give it to people and then let them go and fight it out in the market. I am not opposed in principle to food stamps but I would like to see the idea fleshed out and see it work. All the pilot programmes that have been tried out in the last three years for the food stamps and smart cards have failed. That does not mean that they will always fail. Maybe, they can be improved and may work one day. But I would really like to see it work. Let us try it out, maybe, in urban areas and if it can work, I personally don't have any principled opposition.

The final point is an extension of that point, on technology. Again I have no principled opposition to technology at all. I have some anxieties about new IT projects for different dealings but I think we have to be conscious of the fact that technology can also cause havoc. I would just like to give an example. In the last two years, there was a very rushed transition to bank payments of NREGA wages which was not a bad idea. In the long-run, it is a very effective protection against corruption at least in the wage component of NREGA and it has really helped to contain corruption. But it was too rushed and was not appropriate, especially in the remote rural areas where people are far from the banks and don't know how to use a bank account. It should really have been done gradually starting with areas where the banking system reaches and then extending it. One of the things, I am sorry to say, about this project is that it is going to bring NREGA to a standstill because the Ministry of Rural Development is already putting in place regulations such that one will not get a job card unless one has a UID. I can already see the kind of jam that has happened in the last two years because of the transition to the banking system. It will be repeated because of the transition system to the UID and a huge amount of chaos being created if it is done to speed without adequate safeguards and without adequate technology being tested. I think we need to be very cautious in all these matters.

Joakim Palme

From the Scandinavian perspective, I feel that we have come to the core of social democracy, which in the Scandinavian perspective is about a personal identification number: this is number one. The second thing is to actually talk seriously about taxation. Gunnar Myrdal wrote a beautiful essay in 1932 where he said that on the spending side, there was no difference between the Liberals and the Social Democrats. The difference comes in taxation, because the Liberals don't have the guts to raise enough taxes to have resources for their spending ambitions, but the Social Democrats have. I think it is more than that. It is a very good starting point for actually thinking in more realistic terms on what is possible, starting to build the right kind of architecture, and also clarifying what is possible in terms of providing a more universalistic approach. I think that sounds very promising. I also think it is important to get a focus on the revenue side if we are serious about increasing our revenues. In Europe today, we see the reverse happening. Even 2020, which is the future agenda of Europe, has a focus on spending control and not on increasing revenues. I think that is not the way forward.

Sunita Narain

I wish to raise a few issues. Let me try and piece together some of the issues that were raised today. Firstly, I think we tend to polarise issues unnecessarily. I don't think any one of us is against technology or for technology. I don't think any one of us is against private sector or for private sector. I don't think any one of us is against development or for environment. I get a sense that we are almost having a sort of mock battle constantly putting everyone into little boxes and we like to make sure that we are in the biggest box. It is very important for us to understand that the debate is really about the nature of development that we are going to have. That is the issue which is not sufficiently understood or internalised, either in planning today and certainly not in implementation. Nitin has said very rightly, it is not about environment *versus* development. If I can just sharpen it, I think it is really about development *versus* development, because there is a nature of development which has been a dominant paradigm over the last 30-40 years with the growth of the industrial revolution, with the kind of intensification of growth that has happened, which in some ways is coming to be questioned across the world because of climate change. Also because of the fiscal breakdown and financial meltdown that happened. The fact is that it is so consumption-driven and growth-driven that in our part of the world, it is beginning to be questioned. It must be questioned for the fact that it is not inclusive. But the bottom line of all that development is that it is capital-intensive, resource-intensive and inherently iniquitous. It is both costing the earth and our ability to be able to reach people. I think that is what we need to debate more and more. That is why, Dr Ahluwalia, the house and the architecture of the house that we are going to build is going to be about the house. I don't think we even have a vision sitting in this room of what that house is going to look like.

I don't even want to repeat the fact that we have built an airport in Delhi which is more a shopping mall, not an airport. It illustrates why we really need to talk about what is development and our strategy for the future. That is where we need to learn from the lessons of the people we seem to want to emulate. That is what worries me. When I look at agricultural policies in India, we have a tremendous sense of hope that it is going to be a silver bullet in the name of GM crops or biotechnology. Again, I am not against biotechnology per se but there is an unaffordable agricultural model in the rest of the world today, which is based on very high input costs and high levels of subsidies, which is never recognised in both planning as well as policy. Yet today, we in India very much want to be able to talk about it. We have talked about the fascinating issue of health and Jonathan's health analysis from the US. Again, we don't seem to understand when there is an attack on our generic medicines and our affordable medicine business, what that really means in terms of health security for the future. It is not about private *versus* public per se, but certainly about public provisioning and the fact that across the world, the private sector has not been able to deliver affordable services to a large number of poor people, a problem that goes on. I can give you a whole list of issues. Regarding water and sanitation, the current sewage-based capital-intensive model cannot at all supply water for all, and certainly not clean our rivers. We can put in as much money as we want in the Ganga Action Programme but it is more money down the drain. That is what we are really talking about, the whole issue of resources and justice. We need to talk about them.

That really needs to get connected to fiscal issues which I don't think Dr Kelkar did sufficiently. For me today, it is the poor who are more taxed than the rich. If you really want to reform our fiscal system, tax the car and not the bus. It is as simple as that. There are many such examples. I can give you a whole list of things in which it is the rich who are actually subsidised in the name of the poor. It is not about GST per se, it is about really getting an idea of what should be our development strategy for the future. It is important to bring in that perspective here. What is that development strategy for the future? We cannot learn from the West because the West has really got its strategies wrong. How we reinvent growth without pollution, how we reinvent growth in an inclusive way, is important. That is what I hope the next Plan will reflect. It is not about schemes, or building a house; it is about knowing what the house is all about. If we don't know that in 60 years, it is time we started thinking about it.

Aruna Roy

There is one very important thing which India has to take into account. We have been talking of resources. I think India's biggest resource are its people. Manish asked me whether we should upgrade their skills. If only we were to try our hands at using the *phawda*, or pick-axe, or shovel for only one day, we would know how skilled they are. What they do in one day, we cannot do in a week. When we do resource management, we must recognise that India has resources and skills. We don't look at traditional knowledge and skills. For example, a weaver who produces a Putki or Sambalpuri saree is an extremely skilled person but we dub him as illiterate because he is not literate. We don't look at the extraordinary amount of skills that go into weaving that saree. One of our biggest mistakes in resource management is not recognising what exists in India today. One reason why the technology debate becomes important is that technology sometimes destroys these extraordinary skills.

Vijay Kelkar

I will just take two points and will deal with others bilaterally. Pranab is absolutely right in the point he raised about natural resources. I have been remiss not mentioning this. I will give one example. We have a structure in the hydrocarbon sector in which the marginal tax is about 80 per cent. The entire upside emerging is taken by the government. It depends how we design our contracts;

the same thing can be replicated in the mineral sector so that all the upside is taken by the government. We do about 80 per cent in the hydrocarbon sector but the same thing can be done in minerals too.

I also missed mentioning about eco taxes. In India, we subsidise petroleum products. We under-price kerosene and diesel, and essentially have to bring them back to par. You said that a carbon tax should be back in place. I agree with you. As for the third point which you mentioned, I have proposed fully taxed capital gains and dividends because the corporation is shown only as an intermediary. Therefore, nothing takes place there. In fact, our proposed system is also fully for tax interest purpose and would be more stable financially. The leverage will go down, which is today tax induced. Every profit and capital gains would be fully taxed at the rate of the receiver. It is more regulatory in the present system. The proposed system will reduce transaction costs, promote equality and by simplifying taxes, get better responses. We are, in fact, proposing full taxation of capital gains and profits at the hands of the receiver. Foreign flows from Mauritius would also be fully taxed in the proposed system.

Kaushik Basu

I think I should first talk about Jean's points. All I can say is I am totally surprised. After last session's discussions, I thought we were roughly on the same plane but I am totally surprised by this. It is not as if I insist on a particular mechanism. I feel we should have our eyes and ears open to new ideas. In fact, I got on to this when Jean called me up and suggested that NREGS doesn't let the government pay wages in grains because that has a big risk: the grain could be adulterated when it is being paid. It made me change my views on what had sounded like a very clever idea. It then put me in thought about other forms where the same kind of problems could arise. My mind was changed by what Jean said.

I feel you can't take a morally righteous attitude about an entire group. I have worked with economists enough to know that there is a huge chunk of the profession without common sense. That is true. But that is true also of engineers, doctors. You can't just shun the entire groups. It would be a dangerous moral attitude to take.

Let me take one or two concrete things that came up. Again, Jean, one thing that really opened my eyes is 3G, which was a good design. We in the Ministry of Finance sat and we did our calculations in February; we were expecting ₹ 35000 crore to come. Just having it well designed, you realise that it can transform certain things like auctions. This is a good example where there is a lot of very good analysis about auction. This does not have to be inimical to what civil society is doing. You can't take a moral stand against good design.

We have to debate and discuss. You can't distance yourself from every group you once worked with, like the economists that you once worked with. Kumar Mangalam Birla's point about the fertiliser expansion is a very good thought. I have not worked in that sector. But I have worked on petroleum. Here again, I have seen a very concrete thing. At times, the government makes the mistake of going in for cost-plus subsidy. You tell a firm that no matter what its cost is, you are going to cover the cost and it doesn't have to worry. Once you go into a cost-plus mode with a corporation, the corporation's incentive to cut down on costs and to expand everything goes. I have seen that mistake happen in various sectors. I don't know the fertiliser sector well enough but I feel again through careful design, the private sector's energy can be harnessed into greater expansion of the sector with greater cost efficiency as well.

I actually agree with decontrol and straight tax instruments. We have to draw some of the profit back. Sri Mulyani, you mentioned about price distorting subsidy, which is a very important point. I thought I would add one more thing to that: when you want to give subsidies to the poor, it is best to give them as directly as possible instead of distorting prices. I am glad you brought this up. I will give you one example of another kind of problem that arises. This relates to trying to reach out to a segment through subsidising a particular item and its different prices in other countries. Again, the petroleum sector comes to mind. We in India sell kerosene much cheaper than our neigbouring countries, Pakistan, Bangladesh, Sri Lanka and Nepal; about three times cheaper. When we distort this price to give subsidy, a lot of it just goes across the border. We are actually beginning to get hard evidence that a large chunk is going across, but we still want to reach this population by giving it a subsidy. We must try to get it as directly as possible to these people instead of through a distortion of price.

As a last comment, I feel that a world of free basic food grains is a possibility. It does not have to be a distant idealistic world. But it has to be a global contract. The world is today in a position where we can give basic food grains free to everybody. This will then have to run through state machinery. It cannot be done in a single country because the free food in that country will flow out to countries where there is high food price but there is a global contract possible on certain basic goods. These are again matters that we have to think and talk about.

Nitin Desai

I will make two quick remarks. One is on what Jamshyd said about infrastructure. My only request to Jamshyd is that we should really focus as much attention on the last man, the infrastructure which reaches the village and the slums, as we do on mega projects.

I am glad Sunita has sharpened my point but I think it is also necessary that when you define alternative development, you must also show how we get from here to there. That is equally important.

Finally, there is the no-trust issue in relation to the private sector. I don't think that is the point. The real question is of accepting responsibility for the consequences of your actions. That is all.

Index

J

K

T

X

Y

Z